The Psychology of Consciousness

G. William Farthing
University of Maine

Prentice Hall, Upper Saddle River, New Jersey 07458

Library of Congress Cataloging-in-Publication Data

FARTHING, G. WILLIAM.
 The psychology of consciousness / G. William Farthing.
  p. cm.
 Includes bibliographical references and index.
 ISBN 0-13-728668-6
 1. Consciousness. 2. Altered states of consciousness.
3. Neuropsychology. 1. Title.
BF311.F36 1992   91–7185
153—dc20   CIP

Acquisitions editor: Susan Finnemore
Editorial/production supervision
 and interior design: Mary Anne Shahidi
Cover design: Carol Ceraldi
Prepress buyers: Debra Kesar and Kelly Behr
Manufacturing buyer: Mary Ann Gloriande

Acknowledgments **Chapter opening quote, p. 1:** Reprinted by permission of the publishers from *Psychology: Briefer Course,* page 140 from THE WORKS OF WILLIAM JAMES, Frederick Burkhardt, General Editor; Fredson Bowers, Textual Editor, Cambridge, Mass.: Harvard University Press, Copyright © 1984 by the President and Fellows of Harvard College. **Chapter opening quote, p. 45:** Reprinted by permission of the publishers from *The Principles of Psychology, Vol. I,* page 185 from THE WORKS OF WILLIAM JAMES, Frederick Burkhardt, General Editor; Fredson Bowers, Textual Editor, Cambridge, Mass.: Harvard University Press, Copyright © 1981 by the President and Fellows of Harvard College. **Figure 11.1 p. 283:** For non-exclusive worldwide rights (outside of the United States) to reprint "The French Nurse's Dream," acknowledgment is made to Sigmund Freud Copyrights, The Institute of Psycho-Analyses, and The Hogarth Press Ltd. to reprint from *The Standard Edition of the Complete Psychological Works of Sigmund Freud,* translated and edited by James Strachey.

Printed in the United States of America
10 9 8 7 6 5 4 3 2

ISBN 0-13-728668-6

Prentice-Hall International (UK) Limited,London
Prentice-Hall of Australia Pty. Limited, Sydney
Prentice-Hall Canada Inc., Toronto
Prentice-Hall Hispanoamericana, S.A., Mexico
Prentice-Hall of India Private Limited, New Delhi
Prentice-Hall of Japan, Inc., Tokyo
Pearson Education Asia Pte. Ltd., Singapore
Editora Prentice-Hall do Brasil, Ltda., Rio de Janeiro

To Carol
with appreciation and love

Brief Contents

Contents

Preface

The concept of consciousness has returned to a central position in psychology following a long period of banishment during the behaviorist era (Hilgard 1980). When I was an undergraduate in the early 1960s, introductory psychology textbooks made little or no reference to mentalist concepts such as consciousness, introspection, attention, mental imagery, dreaming, and hypnosis. Today most introductory textbooks include a chapter on states of consciousness and many colleges and universities offer courses on consciousness.

The psychology of consciousness covers a wide range of topics related to normal waking consciousness and altered states of consciousness, including: characteristics of consciousness, factors that influence the stream of consciousness, the distinction between conscious and nonconscious mind, the relationship between the brain and consciousness, introspection, daydreaming, sleep, dreams, hypnosis, meditation, psychedelic drug states, and other topics listed in the first chapter.

I approach the psychology of consciousness from a natural science and cognitive psychology viewpoint. In this view, consciousness is a natural phenomenon—a product of the brain's functioning. I emphasize research on topics of interest to cognitive psychologists, cognitive neuropsychologists, and personality and social psychologists. I also discuss clinical applications for a number of topics, such as hypnosis and meditation. And although the emphasis is on research and theoretical interpretations, important conceptual and philosophical issues of consciousness are also discussed, particularly in the first four chapters.

The incentive to write this textbook developed over a period of years during which I have taught a course on the psychology of consciousness at the University of Maine. The reading assignments have come from a variety of short paperbacks and reprinted journal articles. The reading list has never been satisfactory because it has been hard to find materials with the right breadth and depth of coverage while also being up-to-date. It became apparent that a comprehensive textbook on the psychology of consciousness was needed. Thus, the major reason for writing this book is to provide, in a single volume, a review of research and theory on the psychology of consciousness at a level suitable for advanced college courses.

A second reason for the book is to introduce psychologists to the psychology of consciousness. Many of today's academic and clinical psychologists went through graduate school without having any systematic exposure to these topics. I hope that the book will stimulate interest in teaching and research on topics of consciousness.

In order to make it easier for teachers to adapt the book for their courses, I have broken the material for some topics into two or three chapters. In these cases the first chapter covers the most basic and essential material, while additional interesting material is covered in the second (and third) chapter(s).

I would like to hear about reactions to this book from teachers, students, and other readers. In particular, I would like to know which chapters teachers assign in their courses, and which topics they would like to have greater or lesser emphasis on in future editions. Please write to me at the address listed below.

Acknowledgments.   This book has been improved with the help of many people. I thank the following people for commenting on one or more chapters in their area of expertise: John Antrobus, David Foulkes, Michael Gazzaniga, Irving Kirsch, William McKim, Richard Nisbett, Alan Rosenwasser, Nicholas Spanos, Peter Suedfeld, Timothy Wilson, Michael West, and Lawrence Weiskrantz. Thanks to Ernest Hilgard for helpful and encouraging comments on early versions of three chapters. Also, thanks to the following people for correspondence regarding their work: David Holmes, Eric Klinger, Daniel Schacter, and Endel Tulving. Students in recent sections of my psychology of consciousness course have read most of the chapters and offered helpful comments. I would also like to thank the following reviewers for their helpful comments and suggestions: Daniel Kortenkamp, University of Wisconsin-Stevens Point; and Robert C. Webb, Suffolk University. Any remaining errors of fact or judgment are, of course, my own responsibility.

Thanks to Susan Finnemore, psychology editor at Prentice Hall, for her support for this project, and to Mary Anne Shahidi for guiding the book through the production stage.

Thanks to my friend Fred Pratt for introducing me to the topic of hypnosis about fourteen years ago. Our conversations were one of the important factors that swayed my interests in a direction that ultimately led me to write this book.

Thanks to my parents, Gene and Nancy Farthing, for their encouragement throughout my education and career.

And, last but not least, special thanks to my wife, Carol, for her patience and support over the five years that I spent working on this project. With appreciation and love, I dedicate this book to her.

G. WILLIAM FARTHING
Professor of Psychology
University of Maine
Orono, Maine 04469

chapter 1 ··

The Concept of Consciousness

> The first and foremost concrete fact which everyone will affirm to belong to his inner experience is the fact that *consciousness of some sort goes on*. *"States of mind" succeed each other in him*. If we could say in English "it thinks," as we say "it rains" or "it blows," we should be stating the fact most simply and with the minimum of assumption. As we cannot, we must simply say that *thought goes on* (William James 1892/1984, p. 140).

Consciousness is the fundamental fact of human existence, from the viewpoint of persons examining their own experience. Taking the viewpoint of outside observers, scientists have concentrated on studying the human brain and behavior objectively. In doing so they have largely ignored consciousness, since they cannot directly observe other people's conscious experience. Yet the fact of consciousness remains, and no account of human life can be complete if it ignores consciousness. It is psychology's particular responsibility, among all the sciences, to try to come to grips with the fact of consciousness. What is it? What are its forms? What does it do? What is its origin?

In their research and clinical practice, psychologists have learned a great deal about various *aspects* of consciousness, such as perception, mental imagery, thinking, memory, and emotion. But in most of the theoretical discussions of these topics, the concept of consciousness has been merely implicit, not explicit. Though psychology originated in the late nineteenth century as the science of consciousness, consciousness *per se* was largely ignored through most of the twentieth century, until recently. This avoidance of consciousness was particularly true of experimental psychology in North America, which was dominated until recently by behaviorism, a school maintaining that psychology is about behavior, not about the mind.

The reasons why most psychologists have avoided discussing consciousness are complex and historical. They boil down to the fact that consciousness is one of the most difficult of all scientific problems. The first difficulty is the conceptual problem: What do we mean by "consciousness"? What is it that we are trying to understand? A second difficulty is the methodological problem. Since we cannot objectively observe other people's conscious experience, how can we study it? A third problem is the enormous variety of conscious experiences, both within individual persons from one moment to another, and between different persons. The methodological problems are formidable, and there are no perfect solutions. Yet the methodological problems must be faced if we are to gain a scientific understanding of the causes, and effects, of the variety of conscious states.

In recent years more and more psychologists have been willing to face the problems of studying consciousness and theorizing about it. The change has come about for a variety of reasons, including recent developments within psychology and associated areas of cognitive science, brain science, and philosophy. One factor in the change is an increased realization that the subject matter of psychology—human behavior and experience—is unique. Psychology can no longer try to model itself after classical physics, but must devise its own methods of research and theorizing.

THE PSYCHOLOGY OF CONSCIOUSNESS

The *psychology of consciousness* is the branch of psychology that is concerned with problems of consciousness. Psychologists may not agree on a *definition* of "consciousness" or of "the psychology of consciousness," but they can, to a large degree, agree on which topics and problems are included within the *domain* of the psychology of consciousness (Natsoulas 1981). Among the problems are: What do we mean by the concepts of mind and consciousness? What methods can be used for studying consciousness, and what are the advantages and disadvantages of each? What are the different forms and aspects of consciousness? What factors influence the stream of consciousness—moment to moment changes in the content of consciousness? What is the relationship between conscious and nonconscious (unconscious) mind, and what are the varieties of nonconscious processes? What is the relationship between consciousness and the brain? Between consciousness and perception? Between consciousness and behavior? Between consciousness and language? How does consciousness develop in the individual? What is the role of consciousness in the human mind/brain system?

Among the most distinctive topics of the psychology of consciousness are the "altered states" of consciousness. Altered states of consciousness are temporary, reversible conditions in which one's pattern of subjective experience, and sometimes the ability to control one's own behavior, appear to be different than in one's normal waking state. Among the altered states are sleep and dreaming, hypnosis, meditative and mystical states, and states induced by psychoactive drugs and by restricted environmental stimulation. Besides being of interest in their own right, altered states are relevant to understanding the basic nature of consciousness. Also, altered states may have practical applications, as in clinical applications of hypnosis. Altered states will be a major topic in this book.

The psychology of consciousness is concerned mainly with consciousness in normal people, though it has connections with abnormal psychology and psychopathology. Also, research on brain-damaged patients by neuropsychologists has important implications for understanding normal consciousness. In fact, the psychology of consciousness has connections with most branches of psychology, though in this book the emphasis will be on topics that are central to understanding consciousness but that are not discussed extensively in textbooks for other psychology courses. The psychology of consciousness also has important connections with the philosophy of mind, and some topics of mutual interest to the different disciplines will be discussed in this book.

Overview of This Book

In this chapter I will discuss the meaning of consciousness and related concepts, such as mind and awareness. I will present a levels-of-consciousness model to describe the relationship between conscious and nonconscious mind. Chapter 2 describes several higher-order characteristics of consciousness—such as selectivity, change, and continuity—as well as some more specific features of conscious experience—such as mental imagery, verbal thought, and volition. In Chapter 3 I will discuss introspection, the method of studying consciousness by "looking within" and trying to describe one's own conscious experience. Several introspective methods will be discussed, along with their limitations. Chapter 4 is about the mind-body problem, an ancient philosophical problem concerning the relationship between the mind and the body or brain, which has implications for both religious beliefs and the psychology of consciousness. Chapter 4 also considers the other-minds problem: the question of how we can recognize consciousness in other beings, including animals and children that cannot speak to describe their conscious experiences.

Chapter 5 is about neuropsychological research on split-brain patients and its implications for understanding consciousness. Of special interest is the question whether split-brain patients have two minds in one body. Chapter 6 presents evidence for nonconscious information processing. It discusses dissociations between consciousness and behavior (such as "blindsight" and amnesia) in brain-damaged subjects, as well as several types of evidence from normal subjects (such as subliminal perception).

Chapter 7 ("Introspection II") discusses research on the question of whether we have introspective access to the causes of our own behavior. Chapter 8 is about daydreaming and the stream of consciousness, including research on personal and situational factors that influence daydream frequency and content. Chapter 8 also discusses the effects of sensory deprivation on consciousness and behavior. In Chapter 9, I present some general considerations about altered states of consciousness, such as dimensions of subjective change in altered states, before discussing specific altered states in later chapters.

Chapters 10 through 13 are about sleep and dreaming, topics that have fascinated people for centuries, and which are favorite topics of many students of the psychology of consciousness. Chapter 10 is about sleep, including the physiological correlates of different sleep stages, the effects of sleep deprivation, and sleep disorders. Chapter 11 discusses modern sleep-laboratory research on dreaming, including the characteristics of dreams and factors that influence dream contents, including nightmares as well as normal dreams. Chapter 12 discusses some of the major theories of dreaming—from the psychoanalytic, neurophysiological, and cognitive viewpoints—and related research, including research on dreaming in children. Chapter 13 considers two special topics: the problem of dream recall and forgetting, and lucid dreaming, in which you know you are dreaming as you sleep and dream.

Chapters 14 through 16 are about hypnosis, another favorite topic among students, and currently the most active area of research and theoretical debate among the altered-states-of-consciousness topics. Chapter 14 is a general overview of the basic principles of hypnosis and factors related to individual differences in hypnotizability. It also discusses clinical applications of hypnosis, and the question of whether hypnosis is dangerous. Chapter 15 goes into more detail on recent theories of hypnosis and related research on hypnotic analgesia (pain control) and amnesia, and the controversy whether hypnosis is really an altered state of consciousness. Chapter 16 is about two special topics, hypnotic age regression and hypermnesia—the use of hypnosis in attempts to improve memory recall, which has implications for psychotherapy and criminal investigations.

Chapter 17 describes basic meditation practices and their effects on consciousness, and practical applications such as reduction of stress and anxiety. Characteristics of mystical states—sometimes reached through meditation—are also described. Chapters 18 and 19 are about psychedelic drugs and their effects on consciousness and behavior. Chapter 18 is about marijuana, a widely used minor psychedelic; Chapter 19 discusses the major hallucinogens, with emphasis on the hallucination experience.

Now, let us turn to the question of the meaning of consciousness, mind, and related concepts. Over the years philosophers, psychologists, and brain scientists have devised dozens of definitions of these terms. I do not want to get too bogged down in arguments about definitions, so I will explain how I intend to use these terms in this book and contrast my definitions with a few of the most important alternative definitions. Then I will introduce the idea of levels of consciousness, which will help to relate several important concepts to each other.

MIND

Consciousness is not the same as mind. Mind is the broader concept: it includes both conscious and nonconscious mental processes. Donald Hebb defined mind as follows:

> *Mind* is the capacity for thought, and thought is the integrative activity of the brain—that activity up in the control tower that, during waking hours, overrides reflex response and frees behavior from sense dominance (Hebb 1974, p. 74).

Here is my definition: *Mind is the functioning of the brain to process information and control action in a flexible and adaptive manner*. Both my definition and Hebb's are *materialistic* in that they say that mind is a result of brain activity and cannot exist apart from the living brain, which is a material object.[1] Both definitions are *functional* in that they say what mind does: it processes information (including perception, memory, and thinking) and controls action. Further, they state that flexible behavior is an indicator of mind: an organism with mind does not behave in a purely reflexive manner, always reacting to the same stimulus in the same way. Rather, the creature with mind uses thought processes to adjust its behavior to suit the situation.

The concept of mind implies mental processes. A *mental process* is a more-or-less specialized program or procedure used in processing information (as in perception, memory, and thinking) and controlling speech and other actions. Mental processes use symbols or *representations* for objects, concepts, events, actions, and so on. Cognitive psychologists try to discover and describe the various types of mental processes (or cognitive processes), and the interactions between them, that are necessary to explain human perceptions, thoughts, and actions. At the psychological level, mental processes can be described in terms of their functions, including the type of information they take in, the types of transformations they effect, and the types of outputs or responses they make. Neuropsychologists and other brain scientists are concerned with discovering the specialized brain structures and processes that carry out the various mental functions. Sometimes I will use the term *mind/brain system* when I want to emphasize the point that mental processes are carried out by the brain—a biological entity.[2]

None of these definitions of mind or mental processes say anything about consciousness. Mind is a broader concept than consciousness. Mind includes both conscious and nonconscious mental processes.

CONCEPTS OF CONSCIOUSNESS

It is harder to define consciousness than it is to define mind. It is not possible to specify precise objective criteria for identifying consciousness. Nor can consciousness be given a clear functional definition, since its specific function within the mind system is still a matter of controversy.[3]

Consciousness is one of those concepts that we understand intuitively, but it is difficult or impossible to describe it adequately in words. We can describe many conscious *contents*, such as sensory perceptions or mental images, in a fairly straightforward way. And we can talk indirectly about other conscious experiences, such as love and pain, using metaphors to liken the experience to something else. ("My headache makes me feel like I have a tight metal band around my head.") The best we can do in trying to describe consciousness *per se* is to resort to metaphors. For example, to say that consciousness has contents is to make an analogy to a vessel or space. Julian Jaynes (1976, 1986) pointed out that much of our language for describing mind and consciousness is based on visual-spatial metaphors ("mind-space"), and mental acts are described by analogy to behavioral acts in the visual world.

> We "see" solutions to problems, the best of which may be "brilliant" or "clear" or possibly "dull," "fuzzy," "obscure." These words are all metaphors, and the mind-space to which they apply is generated by metaphors of actual space. In that space we can "approach" a problem and "grapple" with its difficulties. Every word we use to refer to mental events is a metaphor or analog of something in the behavioural world. And the adjectives that we use to describe physical behaviour in real space are analogically taken over to describe mental behaviour in mind-space. We speak of the conscious mind as being "quick" or "slow", or of somebody being "nimble-witted" or "strong-minded" or "weak-minded" or "broad-minded" or "deep" or "open" or "narrow-minded." And so like a real space, something can be at the "back" of our mind, or in the "inner recesses" or "beyond" our minds (Jaynes 1986, p. 132).[4]

But while metaphors are useful for enabling some conscious creatures to talk with each other about their conscious experiences, they are not sufficient for a good objective definition of consciousness. Consciousness isn't really quite like anything else. Consciousness is, in a sense, the fundamental fact of human existence, as William James pointed out in the quote at the beginning of this chapter. At the same time, the concept of consciousness is a very high level abstraction: it is what all of our conscious contents and experiences have in common. We come to know the meaning of consciousness intuitively, through experience, rather than through definition.

Psychologists are more likely to agree that thinking or consciousness of some sort goes on than they are to agree on a particular verbal definition of consciousness.[5] Nonetheless, I believe that to facilitate communication I should present a working definition of consciousness, and try to be consistent in the way I use the term in this book. In the next section I will define consciousness in terms of subjective awareness. Then I will describe two major alternative meanings of consciousness—as wakefulness and as an executive control system—and relate those meanings to my definition.

Consciousness as Awareness

As a working definition, *consciousness is the subjective state of being currently aware of something, either within oneself or outside of oneself.* In this case, being aware or having awareness refers to cognizance or knowing.

Consciousness is always about something. It concerns perceptions, thoughts, feelings, and actions. Consciousness has contents.[6] The variety of contents is enormous. Consciousness can include perceptual awareness of objects and events in our immediate environment, as well as body sensations such as joint pains and tummy rumblings. Consciousness can also include memories of personal past events or impersonal factual knowledge. Also imaginary scenes, as in our daydreams and night dreams, which may be either realistic or fantastic. Consciousness includes emotional feelings and inner speech, such as thoughts about personal problems and goals. But while consciousness can have an enormous variety of contents, it cannot have very many contents at one time. As we will see, the selectivity of consciousness is one of its main features.

Conscious knowledge is knowledge that is "currently present."[7] At any moment most of our knowledge is nonconscious; it is stored in long-term memory and we are not aware of it at that particular moment, though we could quickly recall much of it given the right retrieval cues. To remember something means to retrieve it into consciousness.

Consciousness involves *subjective* experience, which means that it is directly accessible only to the person having the experience. It cannot be directly observed by other people. In humans, at least, conscious experience typically involves some sort of self reference, either explicit or implicit.[8]

Normal adult humans can usually make some sort of verbal report about the contents of consciousness—their immediate, or past, subjective experience. The *introspective verbal report* is the primary criterion for detecting the existence of consciousness, and the main way to know about the contents of another person's consciousness. Of course, some things cannot be described very well in words, and sometimes we forget what we were thinking before we can report it. (In Chapters 3 and 7 I will discuss the uses and limitations of introspective reports in some detail.)

The definition of consciousness in terms of awareness of content links consciousness to the problem of representation of knowledge—how knowledge is coded in memory—which is a fundamental problem for cognitive psychology. Consciousness always involves some form of representation of objects, ideas, events, and so on. But consciousness is more than just awareness of individual objects and events. It also involves comprehension, relating various objects and events to each other and to prior knowledge and past experiences. Conscious experience is not just a passive response to stimuli. It is—or results from—an active process of interpretation and construction in which we use available data from sensory inputs and memory and search for new pertinent data to produce a comprehensible view of the world (that is, our social and physical environments) or to construct imaginary worlds in which to act. (We will encounter the theme of consciousness as a product of interpretive and constructive processes in later chapters.)

An important implication of the definition of consciousness as awareness of something is that—contrary to the teachings of certain meditation systems—it is meaningless to speak of "pure consciousness" or "pure awareness" (consciousness or awareness without content). We can discuss consciousness as an abstract concept without referring to any particular content. But in actual instances of consciousness in persons, consciousness always has contents. The meditator who thinks "Wow, my mind is empty! I have reached the state of pure consciousness!" does, in fact, have consciousness with contents. Consciousness without contents is conceivable only in an altogether different sense of the term consciousness—consciousness as wakefulness.

Consciousness as Wakefulness

One of the most common meanings of "consciousness" is in the sense of wakefulness. In this usage, a person who is awake is conscious, whereas one who is asleep, in a coma, or knocked out by a blow to the head, is unconscious.

Wakefulness, or being awake, is a region on a continuum of arousal ranging from hyper-aroused wakefulness, through normal wakefulness, to the hypnagogic state (between waking and sleep), sleep, and finally, coma. Wakefulness and sleep can be distinguished by a combination of behavioral (responsiveness to external stimuli) and physiological (brain wave) criteria, though there is a transition period in which one is neither clearly awake nor clearly asleep.

Consciousness in the sense of wakefulness is not the same thing as consciousness in the sense of awareness of something. Occurrences of consciousness in these two senses are correlated to a degree, in that when we are awake we usually are aware of something. On the other hand, being asleep does not necessarily imply an absence of awareness. The mind/brain system is intensely active during sleep. Dreaming involves awareness of something, namely visual and auditory mental images linked together in a story-like manner. Thus, consciousness as awareness of content can go with unconsciousness in the sense of being not-awake (asleep).

These two meanings of "consciousness"—as awareness and as wakefulness—can be so contradictory that I will avoid using "consciousness" in the sense of wakefulness. When I wish to distinguish the waking state from the sleeping state I will say "wakefulness" or "awake." I will reserve the term consciousness to refer to the state of being subjectively aware of something. Thus, it will be possible to ask without contradiction of terms whether there are instances in which an individual may be awake but without consciousness, that is, awake but with no subjective awareness of anything. Similarly we will be able to ask about consciousness during sleep.

Consciousness as an Executive Control System

Making decisions and initiating voluntary actions are important aspects of conscious experience. It is natural, therefore, to think of consciousness as the decision maker, the executive that chooses among various alternative goals and courses of action to reach those goals. Thus, one of the most common meanings of "consciousness" is an executive control system that supervises and coordinates the activities of the overall mind/brain system.

Consciousness as an executive control system fits well with the notion that consciousness is active. Consciousness is not merely a passive recipient of sensory input and memories, nor a passive commentator on experience. Rather, consciousness chooses goals, seeks out information relevant to those goals, and initiates actions.

The idea of consciousness as an executive control system has been particularly important in cognitive psychological theories that have developed under the influence of an analogy between the human mind and computer system. For example, Tim Shallice (1978) saw consciousness as the selector of the "dominant action system," from among a myriad of relatively independent, competing action production systems. Ernest Hilgard (1977) and John Kihlstrom (1984) emphasized two related functions of consciousness: "*Monitoring* ourselves and our environment, so that percepts, memories, and thoughts come to be accurately represented in phenomenal awareness; and *controlling* ourselves and our environment, so that we are able to voluntarily initiate and terminate behavioral and cognitive activities" (Kihlstrom 1984, p. 150). Hilgard (1977) suggested that hypnosis involves a dissociation or disconnection between monitoring and control aspects of consciousness. (His ideas will be discussed in the hypnosis chapters, particularly Chapter 15.)

Philip Johnson-Laird (1983, 1988) suggested that the mind/brain system operates as a hierarchically organized parallel-processing system whose highest level, the operating system, corresponds to consciousness. The conscious operating system controls behavior by interacting with various nonconscious, lower-level subsystems or modules. It receives processed inputs (such as percepts) from subsystems, and selects and coordinates actions (such as memory retrieval and overt responses) to be executed by subsystems, without knowing the details of the subsystems' operations. Subjective awareness corresponds to the contents of the operating system—more precisely, its working memory. Self-awareness corresponds to the systems' knowledge of its current situation, current operating status, and its capabilities, predilections, and preferences.

Whether "consciousness" is to refer to subjective awareness or to an executive control system is a matter of preference, but it is important to note that subjective awareness and control functions are not equivalent concepts. Johnson-Laird and others are probably correct in arguing that the human mind/brain system has some sort of executive control system, and that there is an important relationship between subjective awareness and the contents or activities of the executive system. The nature of that relationship is still a matter of theoretical controversy. In any case, I believe I am consistent with the most common usage of "consciousness" by restricting it to subjective awareness. For clarity, it would be best if the executive control system were given a separate, distinctive name.

I should warn you that many writers slip back and forth between two or more of the meanings of consciousness (such as awareness, wakefulness, control system), including some writers who will be cited in this book. Such oscillation can be confusing. In trying to limit the use of "consciousness" to awareness I do not mean to deny the importance of the ideas behind the other uses of the word.

Consciousness in Cognitive Psychology

Some cognitive psychologists try to avoid using the word "consciousness" due to the conceptual and methodological problems that it presents. However, the subjective fact of consciousness cannot be denied, and a satisfactory theory of the human mind/brain system must find a place for it. In considering the place of consciousness in the human information processing system (mind system), cognitive psychologists have linked consciousness with three closely related concepts: working memory, attention, and controlled (effortful) processing (Kihlstrom 1984; Klatzky 1980, 1984).

In the multistore theory of human information processing, working memory (also called short-term memory, STM) is distinguished from long-term memory (Atkinson & Shiffrin, 1968). *Long-term memory* (LTM) is the relatively permanent storehouse of knowledge about our past experiences, the meaning of words, miscellaneous facts, and procedures for doing things. *Working memory* is a system that carries out various cognitive (mental) control processes, such as processes for solving problems, making decisions, and initiating actions. Also, working memory temporarily stores recent perceptions and retrieved memories to be used in these processes. The capacity of working memory is severely limited, and its contents are lost within a few seconds once you stop rehearsing or thinking about them. For example, if you look up an unfamiliar telephone number you have to keep rehearsing it until you dial it; if something interrupts the rehearsal process (for example, someone asking you a question), then you will probably forget the number before you can dial it.

Consciousness can be related to working memory in two ways. In terms of the definition of consciousness as awareness, the current contents of consciousness are equivalent to the current contents of working memory. In terms of consciousness as an executive control system, consciousness is largely equivalent to working memory as a general-purpose, high-level, or final-stage information processing system that makes decisions and initiates actions.

Some psychologists have argued that it is misleading to link consciousness with working memory, if working memory is thought of as a *place* in the information processing system. George Mandler argued that a content is not conscious merely because it is *in* short-term (working) memory. Rather, "consciousness is a *mode* of processing." (1984, p. 89) Conscious contents are contents that are undergoing the conscious mode of processing. The capacity of consciousness is limited because of limitations on the conscious-processing mode.

The levels-of-processing model of memory (Craik & Lockhart 1972) does not distinguish between STM and LTM, but postulates a single storage system. In terms of the levels-of-processing model, consciousness can be largely identified with *primary memory*, the currently activated contents of the memory storage system.

In a related idea, Schneider and Shiffrin (1977) explained several aspects of human performance in terms of a distinction between *controlled* (or effortful) processes (limited capacity, flexible, slow) and *automatic* processes (practically unlimited capacity, relatively inflexible, fast). Consciousness is associated with controlled processes, such as flexible thinking for solving new problems, whereas automatic processes, such as those that execute habitual responses and highly learned skills, operate outside of conscious awareness.

In everyday speech, consciousness is related to "attention." To pay attention to something is to be consciously aware of it. In cognitive psychology there are two different but related meanings of attention. First, *attentional capacity* refers to a general-purpose, limited-capacity information processing resource that is critically important for carrying out many cognitive tasks, especially those that require flexibility for dealing with novel situations. If we try to do two tasks at the same time (such as listening to a lecture and writing a letter), then the tasks will interfere with each other if, together, they require more attentional capacity than is available. Kahneman (1973) identified limited attentional capacity with mental effort, whereas other cognitive processes are effortless, such as rapid pattern identification and rapid memory retrieval. Under most conditions, using attentional capacity for a task, such as reading, is associated with conscious awareness of the information being processed.

The older and more common meaning of "attention" concerns *selective attention*, which is a set of processes that determines which of the many competing stimuli get through to consciousness. The classic example of selective attention is the cocktail party situation, in which several people in the room are talking at once and you can selectively focus on one voice at a time while ignoring the others. In terms of the multistore theory, selective attention selects inputs to working memory. Because of the limited capacity of working memory, it is necessary to select inputs according to some sort of priority system.

The three cognitive psychology concepts of working memory (STM), controlled processing, and attentional capacity were developed in different theoretical and research contexts. However, for our purposes we may regard them as essentially equivalent. They have in common the characteristics of being general in purpose, limited in capacity, and necessary for tasks in which flexible information processing—thinking—is required. All three concepts are closely associated with conscious awareness, on the assumption that conscious contents (words and images, for example) refer to information currently being processed (that is, processed in working memory or with attentional capacity or controlled processing). Like its cognitive psychology counterparts, consciousness, too, is limited in capacity, general in purpose, and associated with higher-level thought processes. All three cognitive concepts allow for other types of cognitive processes—such as long-term memory and automatic processes—that occur nonconsciously, that is, outside of conscious awareness.

A LEVELS OF CONSCIOUSNESS MODEL

Figure 1.1 shows a levels-of-consciousness model that indicates the relationship between different levels of conscious and nonconscious mind. The model is based on a combination of introspection and psychological theory and research. The different levels of consciousness have to do with different degrees of *availability* or retrievability of contents from those levels to reflective consciousness and introspective reporting (Kihlstrom 1984). The levels model does not attempt to explain the different levels of consciousness. Rather, it is a descriptive model that shows what needs to be explained.

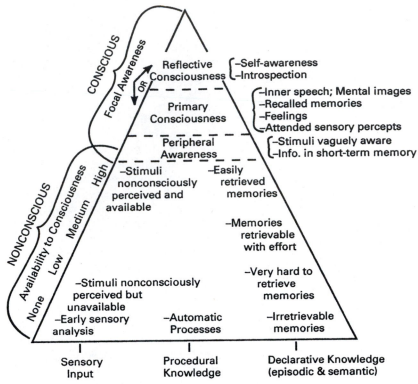

FIGURE 1.1. A descriptive model of levels of consciousness. Levels are defined in terms of the availability of contents to reflective consciousness and introspective reporting. The triangular shape of the diagram is intended to convey the idea that the total amount of content tends to decrease at successively higher levels.

As a particular content progresses from lower to higher levels it presumably undergoes different types of processing, and the content is transformed at different levels or stages of processing. However, all contents at the same level of availability are not necessarily at the same level for the same reason. For example, particular percepts (sensory perceptions of objects and events) and memories may be equally available to consciousness, but they are undergoing different types of processing. Now I will try to describe or characterize the different levels of consciousness.

Primary and Reflective Consciousness

We can distinguish two types of (adult) human consciousness: primary consciousness and reflective consciousness. *Primary consciousness* is the direct experience of percepts and feelings, and thoughts and memories arising in direct response to them. It also includes spontaneously arising memories, thoughts, and images, including dreams and daydreams. Within primary consciousness, sensory percepts and emotional feelings are the most primitive aspects in that they occur in animals and preverbal children. Other aspects develop later in childhood.

Reflective consciousness consists of thoughts about one's own conscious experiences *per se*. In primary consciousness you are the *subject* who does the thinking, feeling, and acting in regard, mainly, to external objects and events. But in reflective consciousness your own conscious experiences—percepts, thoughts, feelings, and actions—are the *objects* of your thoughts. Thus, in primary consciousness you might perceive an event (such as an automobile accident) and have thoughts about that event. But in reflective consciousness you might have thoughts not about the event itself, but about your thoughts concerning the event—asking yourself, "What did I think and feel, and why?" Reflective consciousness makes it possible to judge our knowledge, to interpret our feelings, to revise and improve our thoughts, to evaluate our actions, and to plan future actions.[9]

For example, recently I had the primary conscious experiences of seeing an acquaintance's face and hearing his voice ("I hear we're going to have freezing rain tonight."), my thoughts in direct response to his words ("It could be dangerous. I'd better go home early tonight, before it starts."), and my reply to him ("So what else is new? Freezing rain, this must be Maine!"). In the next moment I reflected on my preceding thoughts and words: "That was a dumb thing to say. Why did I say that? It cut the conversation short. I was in a hurry. How dangerous will it get? Am I really afraid? It's kind of scary. I don't want to have an accident like Julie's. But I can't leave early, I have too much work to do."

Reflective consciousness is necessary for an elaborated *self-awareness*. Self-awareness involves the realization that you are a unique individual, separate from others, with your own personal history and your own future. In reflective consciousness you relate your current experience to your *self concept*, which is your concept of your personal nature, including your desires, values, goals, interests, intellectual and physical abilities, and personality traits.

Reflective consciousness includes the process of *introspection*, which means looking into one's own mind. In basic descriptive (phenomenological) introspection, you attempt merely to observe or recall your primary conscious experiences without analyzing or interpreting them. Introspection can be a purely internal process, or you may try to communicate your introspections to others through *introspective verbal reports*. Thus, you must introspect to answer questions such as "How do you feel about that?" or "Why did you say that?" But reflective consciousness can go beyond mere observation or recall to include analysis and interpretation of your thoughts, feelings, and actions. Reflective consciousness operates at a higher level than primary consciousness in that contents in reflective consciousness are more immediately available for introspective verbal reporting. In the early days of psychology it was thought that all mental contents and processes are open to introspection, but now we understand that introspection can examine only what reaches primary consciousness. Reflective consciousness is sometimes called "introspective awareness."

The concept of reflective consciousness seems to imply at least a brief time gap between an event in primary consciousness and reflective thinking about it. Sometimes the gap is large, as when we recall the events of yesterday and try to evaluate and interpret them. But more commonly, primary consciousness and reflective consciousness are interwoven with each other so much that we cannot easily distinguish between them. We do not necessarily feel any difference between primary and reflective consciousness. The distinction is more abstract, and sometimes the boundary between them is fuzzy.

One reason why it is hard to distinguish introspectively between primary and reflective consciousness is that whenever you try to think about your percepts and thoughts objectively as they happen, you are necessarily engaged in reflective consciousness. The distinction may be clearer if we take a more long-term retrospective view. For example, in many sports activities—such as Alpine skiing, whitewater kayaking, racquetball, and basketball—there are periods of several seconds at a time when you are totally involved in what you are doing. You concentrate exclusively on changes in the situation—the ski slope, the rapids, the position of your opponent and the ball—and on making your next move. You operate in a state of relatively pure primary consciousness. You simply perceive and react, without asking yourself why. Only later, when there is a pause in the action, do you have the opportunity to recall what happened and reflect on it and ask what you did right or wrong, and why, and how to do better next time.

Neither primary nor reflective consciousness is a fixed, clearly defined capacity. Primary consciousness evolves in children as they mature and learn: perceptual awareness and emotional feelings come first, mental imagery and verbal thinking come later. Reflective consciousness develops out of primary consciousness. The complexity of reflective consciousness increases as the child's linguistic and other intellectual abilities develop.

Humanist psychologists have emphasized the importance of reflective consciousness as a uniquely human capacity. Marian Kinget described reflective consciousness (awareness) and its significance:

> Reflective awareness [is] the ability not only to know but to know that one knows—hence, the ability to engage in imagination, self-scrutiny, scientific hypothesizing, philosophical speculation, the evolution of a self-concept, and similar internal behaviors without which the existence of countless observable behaviors and products (e.g. literature, biography, ritual, and commemoration) could not be accounted for (Kinget 1975, p. 3).

Kinget quoted Rollo May on the relationship between primary and reflective awareness—the capacity to experience ourselves both as subject and object—and its significance:

> We are not simply describing two alternate ways of behaving. Nor is it quite accurate to speak of our being subject and object simultaneously. The important point is that our consciousness is a process of *oscillation* between the two. Indeed, is not this dialectical relationship between experiencing myself as subject and object just what consciousness consists of? The process of oscillation

gives me potentiality—I can choose between them, can throw my weight on one side or the other. . . . It is the gap between the two ways of responding that is important. My freedom, in any genuine sense, lies not in my capacity to live as "pure subject," but rather in my capacity to experience both modes, to live in the dialectical relationship (May 1967, p. 9).[10]

Thus, primary and reflective awareness are not like two minds in one brain; rather, they are different aspects of the consciousness of a single person.

Conscious experience in the normal adult human involves both primary and reflective consciousness. Some writers have defined consciousness strictly in terms of reflective consciousness, with the implication that animals and young children who are incapable of reflective consciousness are not conscious beings. But that view is too narrow. Mind exists at different levels of complexity. Some minds experience only perceptual awareness and emotional feelings, while others have a fuller primary consciousness that also includes mental images and verbal thoughts. At higher levels of complexity the capacity for reflective consciousness develops.

The entire levels-of-consciousness model (Figure 1.1) represents a still higher level of thought, meta-consciousness. *Meta-consciousness* is abstract thinking about consciousness itself, trying to understand its nature and its origin. Whereas reflective consciousness is strictly personal, meta-consciousness is an attempt to draw general conclusions about consciousness that would apply to all humans, or to all conscious beings. Meta-consciousness theorizing may draw upon one's personal introspections, philosophy, literature, and scientific research and theory about cognitive processes and the brain. Reflective consciousness is presumably a normal characteristic of adult humans, but meta-conscious thought is characteristic of only a minority of humans, namely psychologists, philosophers, scientists, writers, and others who are interested in mind and consciousness as topics of study.

Focal and Peripheral Awareness

The mental content—percept, thought, or feeling—that dominates your conscious awareness at the moment is in *focal awareness* (focal attention). Focal awareness can shift rapidly back and forth between different percepts, thoughts, and feelings in primary consciousness, or between primary consciousness and reflective consciousness. *Peripheral awareness* includes mental contents that are on the fringe of focal awareness. They can be brought into focal awareness almost instantaneously through either voluntary or involuntary (automatic) attention-switching processes. Peripheral awareness is at the border between conscious and nonconscious mind.

Two types of content may be in peripheral awareness: (1) Stimuli of which one is vaguely aware and which are being processed automatically while focal awareness is directed elsewhere. For example, when you are driving on a highway lost in thought, visual stimuli of the road, other cars, objects, and so on, are mostly in peripheral awareness; so are voices that you can hear but are not attending to, as in the cocktail party situation. (2) Events that have been in focal awareness very recently—within the last few seconds—so they are still in short-term memory and can be rapidly retrieved to focal awareness.

Nonconscious Mind

Nonconscious mind consists of knowledge and mental processes that are not currently in consciousness. That is, we are not subjectively aware of them at the moment—they are not "currently present".[11] In Mandler's (1984) terms, nonconscious contents are not currently being processed in the conscious mode, though they may be processed in various nonconscious modes. While we are awake our nonconscious mind is intensely active, doing preliminary processing of sensory inputs, retrieving information from memory, and carrying out automatic actions. Conscious mind is like the tip of the iceberg; most of our mental activity goes on nonconsciously. Yet nonconscious mind is not like an alternate, hidden consciousness, carrying out the same sort of mental activities that you do consciously. Nonconscious mental processes, to a large degree, serve different functions than do conscious ones.

Levels of nonconscious mind.   Nonconscious contents and processes may be arranged on a continuum, according to how easily retrievable they are into primary consciousness and, ultimately, into reflective consciousness. Though nonconsciousness is really a continuum, it is convenient to think in terms of levels to which we can attach labels or brief descriptions. The levels range from contents that can be quickly and easily retrieved (such as many long-term memories and recently registered but unnoticed sensory perceptions), through those that can be made available with some effort (such as memories hard to retrieve and motives that become apparent through careful self-analysis), to those that cannot reach consciousness with any amount of time or effort but can be known only through inference (such as highly practiced automatic mental processes or procedures, and lower-level "subroutines").

There is a continuous interaction between adjacent levels of conscious and nonconscious mind. It is not the case that one's mental activity as a whole shifts between different levels of consciousness. Rather, mental activity is going on at all levels simultaneously—or in oscillation, in the case of primary and reflective consciousness. Though information may "move" between different levels of consciousness-nonconsciousness, it does not stay the same as it moves. Rather it is transformed by different mental processes at different levels.

Types of nonconscious contents and processes.   Most nonconscious mental contents and processes fall into one of four major categories:

(1) *Sensory inputs registered but not attended.* The capacity of consciousness (or working memory) is limited. Selective attention processes select for consciousness the information that is most pertinent from the vast array of sensory inputs. Prior to selection these inputs are recognized nonconsciously, in the sense that they are matched to corresponding items, such as words, objects, and concepts, in long-term memory (Norman 1968). Nonconscious recognition of the meaning of a stimulus may be critically important in deter-

mining whether it is selected for consciousness. For example, you may be able to read while ignoring the voices of people who are talking nearby. But if one of them says your name you will probably notice it. Presumably all of the words were recognized nonconsciously, but only your name was important enough to your interests to be selected for consciousness. Nonconsciously registered events sometimes reach consciousness, and sometimes they don't. Sometimes nonconsciously recognized events influence our thinking and behavior even though they never reach consciousness (for example, subliminal [nonconscious] perception). (See Chapter 6 of this book and Dixon 1981.)

(2) *Declarative knowledge in long-term memory (LTM)*. Declarative (propositional) knowledge is of two types: (a) *semantic knowledge* (said to be in *semantic memory*), including the meanings of words, names of things, and miscellaneous impersonal facts and theories (including most of what you learn in college); and (b) *episodic knowledge* (in *episodic memory*), which consists of your memories of personal experiences in your life (Tulving 1983, 1985a). For example, remembering the facts and concepts that you learned in a course last semester would involve retrieval from semantic memory. But remembering your personal experiences in the course—such as how you reacted when the professor stood on the table to make a point—would involve retrieval from episodic memory.

At any moment, almost all of the thousands of things you know in semantic and episodic memory are nonconscious. You can easily retrieve much—perhaps most—of that information into consciousness (or working memory), given the right retrieval cues. But sometimes retrieval from LTM is difficult, and sometimes it temporarily fails. For example, you have probably had the experience of wanting to introduce two new friends to each other and not being able to recall one of their names. In such cases you may experience a "tip-of-the-tongue" effect, in which you know that you know the name, but you just can't retrieve it at the moment. The tip-of-the-tongue effect demonstrates the difference between not knowing something and knowing it but not being able to retrieve it from memory. In the case of *repressed memories*, people may be unable to remember the details of personally traumatic experiences, such as being the victim of a violent crime. According to Freudian theory, repressed memories are actively prevented from reaching consciousness, though they may influence our emotions and behavior even while they remain nonconscious.

In recent years psychologists have studied *implicit memory*, in which behavior is influenced by nonconscious knowledge—knowledge that is not, or cannot be, retrieved into consciousness. For example, social judgment processes—such as our judgments of people's friendliness, competence, and so forth—may be influenced by prior knowledge of which we are not currently aware. (See Chapter 7 in this book and Newman & Uleman 1989.) Also, people suffering from amnesia due to brain damage may be able to learn certain skills through practice, though they cannot remember the experience of practicing. Thus, there is a failure of recall from episodic memory, even though procedural memory (memory for skills) remains intact. (See Chapter 6 in this book; Schacter 1987; Tulving 1985a.)

(3) *Automatic cognitive and sensory-motor programs*. The knowledge of how

to perform various cognitive and sensory-motor skills is called *procedural knowledge*, and it is stored in *procedural memory* (Anderson 1983). The skill-control programs of procedural memory operate automatically and nonconsciously. Such automatic processes are at the lowest level of nonconscious mind in that we *cannot* be directly aware of the processes themselves, though we may be aware of their final results or outputs (and often of results at intermediate stages, too). For example, when you read you are consciously aware of the identity of familiar words. But you are not aware of the stages of the recognition process itself, wherein printed words are analyzed and compared against various patterns stored in long-term memory until a match is found. The pattern recognition process operates rapidly and automatically, and you are aware only of its results. Nonconscious processes that produce a conscious result are sometimes called *preattentive processes*. We know about preattentive processes only through inference, not through introspection (Kihlstrom 1987).

Besides cognitive skills (such as recognition of printed or aural words), sensory-motor skills can also operate largely outside of awareness. For example, when a skilled typist copies a sentence, each word is a stimulus that elicits a rapid sequence of directed finger movements. The sequence of finger movements is controlled by an automatic process, which has been established through extensive practice. In fact, if the typist tries to type with conscious awareness of each finger movement, typing will be severely slowed. Athletic skills are another example: extensive practice—such as shooting baskets in basketball—makes execution of the movements largely automatic.

What types of cognitive or sensory-motor programs can operate automatically? Tasks can be carried out automatically when there is a consistent relationship between input stimuli and output responses—in other words, when the response is habitual in that situation (Schneider, Dumais, & Shiffrin 1984). Automatic processes must be developed through extensive practice. In the early stages of practice you have to be consciously aware of almost everything that you do, for example, in learning typing or athletic skills. With practice, some parts of the skill become automatic. Most skills involve an interaction of controlled (conscious) and automatic (nonconscious) processing. Controlled processing sets the goals and plots the strategies or sequences of actions, and automatic processes execute the actions. Then, depending on the rate of information input, you may be able to alternate attention between the task and other thoughts (daydreams). For example, while driving a car, you consciously choose your destination and the route, but you can drive largely on "autopilot" while you are lost in daydreams—provided that you are an experienced driver and the driving conditions are easy. Periodically you switch attention between driving and daydreaming.

Automatic processes may be triggered by an external stimulus. For example, when someone speaks, your speech recognition process automatically recognizes the words. Or while driving along a highway you may automatically turn off at a particular exit, if you have driven that route to work many times. Then the next time you drive that highway, intending to go beyond the familiar exit to a different destination, you may automatically—but unintentionally—turn at that exit if you are daydreaming and driving on autopilot. In order to get past the familiar exit you have to attend to driving and override the autopilot.

(4) *Nonconscious motives*. Freud's psychoanalytic theory was built around the idea that our conscious thoughts and behavior are influenced by unconscious motives or desires, particularly sexual and aggressive desires. According to Freud, awareness may be prevented through an unconsciously controlled repression process; or we may deliberately suppress unwanted thoughts, perhaps by turning attention elsewhere (Wegner 1989). The conceptual status of this category—nonconscious motives—is somewhat problematic. What is a motive? One could define "motive" as a need, interest, or desire that activates an organism and directs its behavior toward a specific goal. Ordinarily, when we consciously seek a particular goal, we have a consciously felt need, interest, or desire. If a consciously felt need, interest, or desire were of the essence of motivation, then it would not be appropriate to speak of nonconscious motives. But it can be argued that consciously felt needs and so forth are *not* of the essence of motivation. Rather, the essence of motivation is whatever processes—conscious or nonconscious—activate the organism and direct its behavior toward particular goals. Thus, insofar as people are unaware of the causes or processes that control their goal-directed behaviors, we can say that they are influenced by nonconscious motives. We—or they—may be able to infer their motives from their behavior, even if they cannot introspectively report them.

In later chapters I will discuss some of the research that supports the claim that much of our mental processing occurs nonconsciously. Chapter 6 will cover nonconscious processing in brain-injured patients (such as the "blindsight" and amnesia syndromes) and nonconscious (subliminal) perception in normal people. In Chapter 7 I will explore the question of whether people ordinarily have introspective awareness of the causes of their own behavior.

Subconscious knowledge.   Ernest Hilgard, in his book *Divided Consciousness: Multiple Controls in Human Thought and Action* (1977), called attention to several puzzling psychological phenomena that have a family resemblance to each other, including multiple personality, fugue states, hypnotic analgesia, posthypnotic amnesia, and others. In all of these cases people have perceptual experiences or perform actions of a type that would normally occur with conscious awareness, but they are unaware of the events at the time that they occur and/or they cannot subsequently recall the events, which are of a type that ordinarily could be recalled. Kihlstrom (1984) uses the term *subconscious* to refer to the knowledge or perceptions that are unavailable to people in these situations. Subconscious knowledge can be distinguished from ordinary unperceived or unattended events because subconscious knowledge may later, under special circumstances, be retrieved to consciousness.

For example, individuals with the *multiple personality* syndrome sometimes spontaneously (nonvoluntarily) shift from their ordinary personality to an alternate personality. (In some cases there are several alternate personalities.) The alternate personality is distinctly different from the normal personality in some ways: it may, for example, have different interests and values, and be more socially extraverted than the normal personality. The alternate personality may do things that the ordinary personality would never do, such as go on a shopping spree or flirt with strangers. Hours or days later, when these individuals shift back to the ordinary personality, they will have no recollection of what they did during the time in the alternate personality. They will be amnesic for that period of time—though when they later shift back to the alternate personality, they will recall what they (the alternate personality) did earlier. A *fugue state* is a kind of functional amnesia (not involving brain damage), in which individuals, perhaps as a reaction to stress, are unable to recall their personal past (their jobs, their families, and so on), and wander away from home and start over somewhere else. Later— perhaps years later—they may again recall their earlier life, perhaps after being tracked down by their families and/or aided by psychotherapy.

Elaborating on ideas presented earlier by the French psychiatrist Pierre Janet (1889), Hilgard interpreted these phenomena in terms of a *dissociation* hypothesis, which says that there is a disconnection between certain mental subsystems—monitoring, action-control, and memory systems—that normally communicate with each other. He argued that hypnosis can produce temporary, reversible dissociations. For example, Hilgard's research suggested that during hypnotic analgesia (pain reduction) a sort of divided consciousness effect may occur, in which a "hidden observer" may be aware of pain of which the hypnotized self is not aware. Hypnosis apparently can also facilitate "automatic writing," in which subjects can write answers to questions without being aware of doing so.

In Chapter 15 (Hypnosis II) I will go into some detail on Hilgard's research on dissociation in hypnosis. We will see that—as least as far as hypnosis is concerned—the idea of dissociation processes and subconscious knowledge is controversial. Some theorists argue that "subconscious" knowledge is held out of awareness by diversion of attention, rather than by some special process such as dissociation (Spanos 1986a). But for now the main question is how subconscious knowledge fits into the levels of consciousness model.

Insofar as subconscious knowledge can, with difficulty, sometimes be retrieved into consciousness and reported, it seems that it is a variety of nonconscious knowledge. Subconscious knowledge is like many episodic long-term memories: it is hard, though not impossible, to retrieve. Bear in mind that the levels-of-consciousness model is descriptive, not explanatory, and it does not assume that contents at the same level of availability are at the same level for the same reasons. Thus, we can fit subconscious knowledge into the levels model as another type of nonconscious knowledge, and defer until later the question of whether any special processes are involved in situations—such as hypnotic analgesia—that produce subconscious knowledge.

Comparison to Freud's Levels of Consciousness

Sigmund Freud (1900/1965), distinguished between consciousness, the preconscious, and the unconscious. In his writing Freud used "consciousness" in the sense of awareness, as I do, though he defined consciousness as "a sense organ for the apprehension of psychical qualities" (p. 613), a metaphor that I find to be misleading. Freud's "unconscious" consists of repressed memories, desires, and motives that cannot be brought into conscious awareness, and thus cannot be the object of introspective verbal reports. Freud's "preconscious" consists of perceptual events and memories that are not currently in conscious awareness but which can easily be brought into awareness and reported. Thus, in comparison to my levels model (Figure 1.1.), Freud's preconscious includes both peripheral awareness and all of the nonconscious contents of long-term memory that can be retrieved into consciousness. Thus, my concept of nonconscious mind—all of those contents and processes that are not currently in consciousness—is broader than Freud's concept of unconscious mind. Nonconscious mind includes Freud's unconscious and most of his preconscious knowledge. In addition, it includes procedural knowledge. Kihlstrom (1987) said that procedural knowledge is "unconscious in the strict sense of that term" in that we *cannot* retrieve it to consciousness (p. 1450). Freud's concepts of preconscious and unconscious have not been used much in cognitive psychology, since it seems more useful to talk about different memory structures and different degrees of memory retrievability (Kihlstrom 1984).

SUMMARY

I define *mind* as the functioning of the brain to process information and control action in a flexible and adaptive manner. As a working definition, *consciousness* is the subjective state of being currently aware of something, either within oneself or outside of oneself. Consciousness is always about something: it has contents (percepts, thoughts, feelings). Nonconscious mind consists of various mental processes and contents of which we are not currently aware, though many of them, such as long-term memories, can be retrieved into awareness.

The concept of consciousness as awareness is contrasted with two other common uses of the term: consciousness as wakefulness, and consciousness as an executive control system. It is suggested that consciousness can be identified with or related to some basic concepts in cognitive psychology, including working memory (short-term memory), limited attentional capacity, and controlled processing.

A descriptive levels-of-consciousness model (Figure 1.1) gives some order to the distinctions between conscious and nonconscious mind and the different levels within them. The different levels of consciousness have to do with different degrees of *availability* or retrievability of contents from those levels to reflective consciousness and introspective reporting.

At the conscious level, we can distinguish between primary consciousness and reflective consciousness. *Primary consciousness* is the direct experience of percepts and feelings, and thoughts and memories arising in direct response to them. It also includes spontaneously arising memories, thoughts, and images, including dreams and daydreams. *Reflective consciousness* consists of thoughts about one's own conscious experiences *per se*. In primary consciousness you are the *subject* who does the thinking, feeling, and acting, mainly in regard to external objects and events. But in reflective consciousness your own conscious experiences—percepts, thoughts, feelings, and actions—are the *objects* of your thoughts. *Focal awareness* (focal attention) can shift rapidly between different contents in primary consciousness or between primary and reflective consciousness. *Peripheral awareness* includes contents on the fringe of focal awareness, that can be brought into focal awareness almost instantaneously.

Levels of nonconscious contents and processes can be distinguished in terms of their retrievability to consciousness. Four major types of nonconscious contents and processes are described: (1) sensory inputs registered but not attended; (2) declarative knowledge in long-term memory; (3) automatic cognitive and sensory-motor programs (procedural knowledge); and (4) nonconscious motives. Also classified as a type of nonconscious knowledge is subconscious (dissociated) knowledge, where—in cases such as multiple personality or hypnotic analgesia—subjects cannot perceive or recall certain events, though they are of a type that ordinarily could be perceived or recalled.

ENDNOTES

[1] It is a common convention of speech to say that "mind (or consciousness) is produced by the brain." However, such a statement does not mean that mind is separate from the brain, as a factory product is separate from the machine that produced it. The idea that mind and brain are separable is due at least partly to the fact that we use psychological terminology when talking about the mind and neurological terminology when talking about the brain.

[2] Some brain processes sense and respond to biological information, such as the homeostatic processes that maintain optimum levels of glucose, oxygen, and body temperature. These processes are not considered to be mental processes, since they are concerned only with body maintenance and operate automatically and internally. Mental processes uses symbolic representations of external objects and events, whereas biological information processing is nonsymbolic—it deals directly with chemicals, temperature, and so on. However, sometimes the distinction between mental processes and biological information processing is fuzzy, especially when conscious experience or action are directly affected by biological responses. For example, when we feel hunger due to stomach pangs or emotional excitement accompanied by a pounding heart, we make decisions and undertake actions instigated by our biological responses.

[3] I use the term *mind system* to emphasize the idea that mind is a constellation of specialized mental processes. Consciousness may be related to one or more of the mental processes, but not necessarily to all of them.

[4] As an interesting contrast to Jaynes (1986), Belenkey et al. (1986) made this observation in a study involving extensive interviews with women of various socioeconomic levels: "We found that women repeatedly used the metaphor of voice to depict their intellectual and ethical development; and that the development of a sense of voice, mind, and self were intricately intertwined. [This] is at odds with the visual metaphors (such as equating knowledge with illumination, knowing with seeing, and truth with light) that scientists and philosophers most often use to express their sense of mind" (p. 18).

[5] A recent dictionary of psychological terms characterized consciousness as follows: "Consciousness: The having of perceptions, thoughts and feelings; awareness. The term is impossible to define except in terms that are unintelligible without a grasp of what consciousness means" (Sutherland 1989, p. 90). Natsoulas (1978, 1983) discussed six different definitions of consciousness, taking the definitions in the *Oxford English Dictionary* as his starting point.

[6] In their technical jargon, philosophers use the term *intentionality* to refer to the directionality or "aboutness" of consciousness. Conscious states (or intentional states), such as perceptions, beliefs, and desires, are said to point to or be about something other than themselves; they have contents. For example, a state of desire is a desire for some particular object or activity. Likewise,

to say that mental processes use representations of objects, events, and so forth is to say that mental processes have intentionality.

I find the term "intentionality" to be confusing, so I will often avoid it in favor of terms like "content" or "aboutness." (See Natsoulas [1981] for a discussion of intentionality from a philosopher-psychologist's viewpoint.)

[7]I am using the word "knowledge" in the broadest sense as anything that might be expressed in a propositional statement, however vaguely—for example, "Jeff is tall." "I am hungry." "My skin feels 'pringly'." "I feel like I am inside of a black sponge." "I imagine myself flying." "I am floating in a green void." "The president's term of office is five years." A propositional statement need not be true to qualify as knowledge in this sense. The point is that any knowledge—conscious or nonconscious—can, in principle, be expressed in a propositional statement, or a set of such statements, if we can find the right words. (I am assuming that mental images can, in principle, be translated into sets of propositional statements.)

[8]Several terms are used virtually interchangeably by various writers who, I believe, would be sympathetic with my working definition of consciousness. A detailed analysis shows slightly different shades of meaning or emphasis. These terms include "subjective experience" and "subjective awareness," which emphasize the *subjective* aspect (accessible only to the person having the experience). "Conscious awareness" sounds redundant, but it emphasizes conscious as opposed to nonconscious knowledge. "Phenomenal experience" (Marcel 1988) or "phenomenal awareness" (Schacter 1989) emphasizes the "raw feels" or "qualia" of sensory experience, but also includes conscious thoughts and memory images. "Experience" in these contexts (conscious experience, subjective experience, phenomenal experience) refers to any contents or events—percepts, thoughts, images, feelings—occurring in consciousness. Thus, for example, conscious experience includes things that you imagine or dream, as well as things that you do physically with your body.

[9]Some writers use the term "*reflexive* consciousness" for what I and others call "*reflective* consciousness." "Reflexive" is a particularly inappropriate word here, because it carries the connotation that the consciousness it describes is some sort of simple, automatic reaction (analogous to an eyeblink or knee-jerk reflex), whereas in fact we are talking about a complex, high level thought process. "Reflection" may be a misleading metaphor too, since it suggests that conscious contents are directly copied in reflective consciousness, whereas in fact they are selectively recalled and reconstructed. I use "reflective" consciousness because it is the more widely used term for this idea, and because its incorrect connotations seem less harmful than those of "reflexive" consciousness.

[10]May's "dialectical relationship" is an interactive play of thoughts that can mutually change each other.

[11]Regarding "nonconscious" versus "unconscious": "Nonconscious" is coming to be the preferred term to refer to the broad category of mental contents and processes that are currently outside of awareness (e.g., Kihlstrom 1987; Marcel 1988). Some writers use the term "unconscious" with the same meaning. The advantage of "nonconscious" is that it avoids confusion with both (a) unconscious in the sense of coma or sleep, and (b) Freud's concept of the unconscious as repressed desires and memories that can *never* be retrieved into consciousness. I will use "nonconscious" as I defined it, though I will sometimes cite or quote writers who use "unconscious" with the same meaning. I'll make it clear if I mean unconscious in some other sense, such as the Freudian Unconscious.

chapter 2 ··

Characteristics of Consciousness

What can a scientific approach have to say about conscious experience? It would be asking too much to expect science to explain in detail the moment-to-moment changes in the contents of consciousness in one individual at a particular time and place. And it seems ludicrous even to attempt to *predict* such changes in any detail. The variety of experience and the complexity of the causal factors—both internal and external—is just too complex for a detailed account. A more reasonable goal for a scientific approach is to try to explain the processes that produce certain abstract characteristics of conscious experience, and the conditions under which these characteristics may vary. By abstract characteristics of consciousness I mean descriptive characteristics of conscious experience in general—characteristics that apply over a broad range of individual instances of conscious experience.

It will be useful, then, to list some of the abstract characteristics of human consciousness with which the psychology of consciousness is concerned. Any such list will be influenced by the goals and theoretical viewpoint of the list maker. Lists and categorization schemes are made by humans for human purposes, and it is not a matter of which list or categorization is correct, but rather, which one is most useful for a particular purpose. Thus, I do not pretend that this is a complete list of all of the characteristics of consciousness.

The following list covers some of the characteristics of conscious experience in normal adult humans which are of particular interest from a cognitive psychology viewpoint. The list involves relatively large categories that are not entirely independent of each other. The list is divided into two parts. First there are five higher-order characteristics of consciousness that apply across the whole range of specific contents: (1) subjectivity; (2) change; (3) continuity; (4) intentionality ("aboutness"); and (5) selectivity. Second, there are eight abstract features that are more closely related to particular types of conscious experience. At any one moment the contents of consciousness can be characterized by one or more of these features, though not necessarily by all of them at the same time: (1) sensory perception; (2) mental imagery; (3) inner speech; (4) conceptual thought; (5) remembering; (6) emotional feeling (7) volition; and (8) self-awareness. At the end of the chapter I will consider the question of conscious unity—how all of these characteristics seem to go together.

HIGHER-ORDER CHARACTERISTICS OF CONSCIOUSNESS

William James (1842–1910) has been called the greatest of the nineteenth-century introspectionist psychologists. In his monumental textbook, *The Principles of Psychology* (1890/1983), he described five higher-order characteristics of consciousness. These characteristics are higher order in that they apply across a wide range of specific conscious contents, which may vary from moment to moment. These characteristics apply mainly to consciousness as we know it through introspection. I will briefly describe and comment on each of them.

Subjectivity

Every thought is part of a personal consciousness. . . . The universal conscious fact is not "feelings and thoughts exist," but "I think" and "I feel" (James 1890/1983, pp. 220–21).

Each thought belongs to a single individual, a single personality or personal self. (James used the word "thought" broadly, to refer to the whole variety of conscious experiences and acts.) Even when two people are in the same place at the same time, seeing and thinking about the same things, their thoughts are separate and personal. Thoughts are subjective, in that they belong only to one individual and are directly known only by that person.

In our usual daily activities we have thoughts about objects and events (". . . red car approaching . . . horn honking . . . danger . . . jump back") where the "I" is implicit; this is primary consciousness. But when we introspect on our conscious experiences, the "I" becomes explicit: "I see." "I think." "I feel." This is reflective consciousness. In reflective consciousness we are most aware that our thoughts belong to us as a separate, unique personal self.

Change

Within each personal consciousness thought is always changing (James 1890/1983, p. 220).

There are two senses in which conscious experience is always changing. First, the contents of consciousness are continuously changing. Our perception jumps rapidly from one object to another and our daydream images change from moment to moment like scenes in a movie. Our inner speech drifts from one topic to another, like a rambling conversation. Even when we try to focus our attention on a particular topic, we are soon distracted by external stimuli or daydreams.

But to suggest that the contents of consciousness change in a passive way, merely in reaction to changing stimulation or to daydream images floating up from memory, is to overlook one of the fundamental properties of humans: people actively seek to change their conscious experience. We find unchanging situations to be boring and unpleasant, so we seek varied experience by exploring new environments and social situations, either in person or vicariously, through books and movies of fact and fiction.

The human mind/brain system is continuously active. Consciousness continues to change even when external stimulation is absent or held constant. Experiments on sensory deprivation have shown that when people are kept in a restricted environment for long periods of time, they often develop a "hunger" for varied sensory stimulation (see Chapter 8). And in the absence of sensory stimulation they provide their own mental stimulation by becoming absorbed in daydreams or reveries, which may be particularly vivid under such conditions. And when we are asleep at night, under conditions of nearly total sensory deprivation, our mind is continuously active in the form of vivid dreams or other types of sleep mentation.

It is normal for the waking mind to be continuously active. If we were to succeed in deliberately holding the contents of consciousness constant, then we would produce an altered state of consciousness; this is the goal of concentrative meditation.

The second sense in which consciousness is constantly changing, which was emphasized by James, is that "no state [of consciousness] once gone can recur and be identical with what it was before" (p. 224). James used the term "state of consciousness" (or "state of mind") to refer to the full momentary contents of consciousness, including the central percept or thought as well as any emotional background and contents in peripheral awareness.[1] He assumed that each conscious state corresponds to a brain state, and that the brain in its subtle details is continuously being changed as a result of the individual's experiences. Thus, when you perceive an object the second time, the brain that perceives it is different than before, so your conscious experience is different the second time, at least in subtle details. To be sure, you may see the same object again, or think about the same topic again, but it is only the object or topic that is the same. Your conscious experience is different, at least in a subtle way.

For example, when you see a movie for the second time, you experience it differently than you did the first time. There are two reasons why the experience is different the second time. First, the social and physical context of the event has probably changed in some details. But more important is the fact that *you* have changed since the first time, as a result of the original experience itself (for example, you remember certain things about the movie so there are fewer surprises the next time you see it), and as a result of other experiences since then (such as changes in knowledge, attitudes, motives, and mood that give you a new perspective).

Continuity

James used the famous metaphor the *stream of consciousness* to portray the idea that while the specific contents of consciousness change from moment to moment, consciousness itself seems to be continuous:

> Within each personal consciousness, thought is sensibly continuous. . . . Even where there is a time-gap [as in sleep] the consciousness after it feels as if it belonged together with the consciousness before it, as another part of the same self. . . .
> Consciousness, then, does not appear to itself chopped up in bits. Such words as "chain" or "train" do not describe it fitly. . . . It is nothing jointed; it flows. A "river" or "stream" are the metaphors by which it is most naturally described. *In talking of it hereafter, let us call it the stream of thought, of consciousness, or of subjective life* (James 1890/1983, pp. 231, 233).

The continuity of subjective consciousness is maintained in the short run by short-term memory of events within the last few seconds or minutes, and in the long run by recall of personal events from long-term memory (episodic memory). Thus, each day when you awaken you continue as the same person, with the same personal memories that you had before you fell asleep (plus perhaps a few more, if you can recall your dreams).

The feeling of continuity of consciousness is critical for maintaining one's sense of personal identity. Serious *depersonalization* would result if, each time you awoke, you could recall nothing of the events of the previous day. Exactly this sort of depersonalization occurs in cases of severe *anterograde amnesia*, in which brain-damaged patients are unable to transfer new information—including memories of personal experiences—from working memory to long-term memory.

Temporal gaps in waking consciousness are rare. We are always attending to either external events or to daydreams, and short-term memory bridges the gaps between them. On rare occasions we may be shocked by what appears to be a break in the continuity of consciousness. A typical case occurs in incidents of so-called "highway hypnosis" (Williams 1963). You may have had this experience while driving on a very familiar road or perhaps on a long straight highway, under easy driving conditions without much traffic, most likely at night. Suddenly you become aware that you have no recollection of having driven the last mile or so. You don't recall anything about the road or traffic or things along the way. You may wonder whether you blacked out. What happened is that the simplicity of the driving task, at which you are highly practiced, enabled you to switch to "autopilot," allowing automatic, nonconscious processes to do the driving. Meanwhile your conscious awareness turned inward, to daydreams. Then later, when your awareness suddenly switched back to the driving task, you were unable to recall recent events related to driving because they were not stored in memory during the period on autopilot. The illusion of a gap in consciousness will be magnified if you are also unable to recall the daydreams that you had while driving on autopilot. Such gaps in conscious experience are more likely to occur if you are stoned on marijuana, which interferes with short-term memory and transfer of information from STM to LTM. (I do not recommend this as an experiment. It could be dangerous. Marijuana can cause you to become so internally focused that you may miss external stimuli that are critical for driving safely. More on this in Chapter 18.)

Intentionality ("Aboutness")

Human thought appears to deal with objects independent of itself; that is, it is cognitive, or possesses the function of knowing (James 1890/1983, p. 262).

The fact that consciousness is about something—it has contents—is its most critical defining feature. Nowadays philosophers and psychologists say that consciousness has *intentionality* (Bechtel 1988; Churchland 1988). "Intentionality" is derived from one of the less common meanings of *intend*, to point to something. Various conscious attitudes have intentionality in the sense of pointing to something other than themselves: "I know WWW." "I believe that XXX." "I want YYY." "I intend to do ZZZ." Personally I find "intentionality" to be confusing, so I usually speak of the "aboutness" of consciousness: consciousness is about something, it has contents.

Psychologists may try to distinguish between consciousness in the abstract, and the particular contents of consciousness at a particular moment. But James pointed out that in personal conscious experience one does not necessarily distinguish between conscious content and the fact that one is conscious of it. Both primary and reflective consciousness have contents, but only in reflective consciousness do we distinguish between conscious contents (percepts, thoughts, images) and the fact that we are conscious of them.

Selectivity

[Consciousness] is always interested more in one part of its object than in another, and welcomes, rejects, or chooses, all the while it thinks. . . . We find it quite impossible to disperse our attention impartially over a number of impressions. . . . But we do far more than emphasize things, and unite some, and keep others apart. We actually *ignore* most of the things before us (James 1890/1983, p. 273).

Here James was referring to the fact of selective attention: at any moment we are consciously aware of only a limited part of all of the stimuli—external and internal—of which we might potentially be aware. A selection process is necessary because of the limited capacity of consciousness or working memory. The direction of attention is influenced by both voluntary and nonvoluntary factors. You may try to attend to the task at hand, such as listening to a lecture, selecting only those stimuli that are most relevant. But frequently you are distracted by irrelevant stimuli, such as nearby whispers, or by your daydreams. James emphasized the voluntary aspect of attention, but in fact the selection process itself for the most part operates automatically, nonconsciously, to determine what gets into consciousness.

The fact that attention is selective and habitual, and that perception is heavily influenced by our interests and expectations, led James and other psychologists (for example, Ornstein 1977) to conclude that our conscious experience is *constructed.* In a sense, reality is constructed in consciousness, rather than being merely reflected in consciousness. An implication is that there are alternative ways to construct reality in consciousness. James gave this colorful example:

> A man's empirical thought depends on the things he has experienced, but what these shall be is to a large extent determined by his habits of attention. . . . Let four men make a tour in Europe. One will bring home only picturesque impressions—costumes and colors, parks and views and works of architecture, pictures and statues. To another all this will be non-existent; and distances and prices, populations and drainage arrangements, door- and window-fastenings, and other useful statistics will take their place. A third will give a rich account of the theaters, restaurants, and public balls, and naught beside; whilst the fourth will perhaps have been so wrapped in his own subjective broodings as to tell little more than a few names of places through which he passed. Each has selected, out of the same mass of presented objects, those which suited his private interest and has made his experience thereby (James 1890/1983, pp. 275–76).

Psychotherapists know that people's problems often derive from the way they construct their personal reality, perhaps selecting and emphasizing the negative and ignoring the positive things in their lives.

The notion that consciousness is a personal construction has been carried to extremes by some writers (such as Carlos Casteneda 1971) who suggest that our ordinary everyday reality is quite arbitrary, and that equally valid alternate realities can be produced merely by a shift in our attitudes and attention. Yet, our ordinary reality, as constructed in consciousness, is *not* arbitrary. Consciousness is ultimately a biological phenomenon. Our functions of perception and selective attention evolved as they did because they enabled our species to survive on this particular planet. Thus, it continues to be meaningful to believe that our everyday reality—the world as we ordinarily perceive it—is more "real" than, say, the world of our nighttime dreams or the world of someone who is tripping on LSD. The world perceived in altered states of consciousness—in which processes of selective attention, perception, memory, and judgment are altered—is actually less real than the world of our ordinary waking consciousness.

ASPECTS OF CONSCIOUS EXPERIENCE

Endel Tulving pointed out that "one of the problems with the concept of consciousness has always been that it is too global, and hence in principle it cannot be expected to be particularly useful" (personal communication, 1990). He drew a parallel between the concept of consciousness and the concept of memory. Formerly, memory was thought of as an undifferentiated, unitary storage system. In recent decades, however, cognitive psychologists have advanced the understanding of memory by distinguishing between different types of memory. For example, Tulving (1985a) proposed a distinction between episodic, semantic, and procedural memory, and he suggested that each type of memory is associated with a different type of consciousness (more on this in the section on remembering, to follow).

Here I will differentiate conscious experience into several aspects or types, in hopes of helping to advance our understanding of consciousness. Some critics have argued that psychology has made little progress in understanding consciousness. But in fact psychology has already made a good deal of progress in understanding different *aspects* of consciousness (Flanagan, 1985). The greatest difficulties have been encountered in trying to deal with consciousness as a unified concept. It is hard to let go of the idea of conscious unity, insofar as introspection suggests that consciousness is unified. In the final section of this chapter I will have something to say about the unity of consciousness. But first I will briefly sketch the different aspects of consciousness that have been studied by various specialized branches of psychology. Each of these aspects relates to some but not necessarily to all of the ever-changing contents of consciousness. Each aspect has been advocated by one writer or another as *the* fundamental feature of human consciousness.

Sensory Perception

Sensory perception includes both exteroception and interoception. *Exteroception* refers to the perception of external objects and events by means of our senses of vision, hearing, touch, taste, and smell. *Interoception* refers to the perception of body states and events, such as kinesthesis (sense of movement), proprioception (sense of body and limb position), and feelings of pain, internal pressure, tummy rumblings, and other discomforts.

Sensory perception may be regarded as the fundamental aspect of consciousness for several reasons. (1) Sensory perception ordinarily has priority in waking consciousness, because it is critical for guiding our interactions with the environment. Inner speech often occurs concurrently with sensory perception, but perception is dominant in the interaction between them, insofar as perceptual inputs can disrupt the flow of inner speech, more than vice versa. (2) Sensory perception is the foundation, the starting place, of mental development. In the course of human development, sensory perception develops first and leads to higher levels of thinking, including mental imagery (such as visuo-spatial problem solving) and verbal-conceptual thinking and reflective awareness. (3) Sensory perception is an aspect of consciousness that occurs in animals, though the nature of perception varies among species. In an evolutionary sense, sensory perception is the first stage toward the development of higher-level cognitive aspects of consciousness.

Conscious perception—at least exteroception—involves objects and events, not raw sensations. For example, you perceive this thing on your desk as a book, not as a set of raw visual inputs (white quadrilaterals, etc.). Though the specific nature of the sensory inputs varies depending upon your perspective, you always see the object as a book regardless of the angle from which you look at it.[2] Thus, perception is a process of interpreting sensory inputs. The interpretive process occurs mainly at a nonconscious level, but it results in conscious perception of objects and events.

The *constructivist* theory of perception says that perception is an interpretation of sensory data, based on our prior knowledge, beliefs, and expectations (Best 1989; Neisser 1976). Perception is a not a passive response to sensory inputs. Rather, according to Neisser (1976), it is an active process involving a three-way interaction between sensory inputs, *schemata* (knowledge structures in LTM), and behavior. Neisser called this three-way interaction the *perceptual cycle* (Figure 2.1). Sensory inputs are analyzed and interpreted according to appropriate schemata. The schemata also guide acts of exploration in which we search for more information, thus producing new sensory inputs to further influence our interpretations. The schemata may be modified by experience, thus changing future interpretations and exploratory acts. Thus, perception depends not only on sensory inputs, but also on prior knowledge, beliefs, and expectations. Usually this process produces accurate, efficient perception of the external world, though sometimes it can produce errors or illusions. For example, in an experiment by Bruner (1957) subjects had to identify rapidly flashed visual stimuli. When the experimenter flashed a red ace of spades, the subjects thought they saw an ace of hearts. Their prior knowledge led them to expect red hearts, not red spades.

We will see that the constructivist view of perception has wide applications to consciousness that extend beyond sensory perception (Ornstein 1977, 1986). For example, our explanations of our own behavior may be based more on prior assumptions than on accurate assessments of the influ-

FIGURE 2.1. The perceptual cycle. Sensory inputs from objects or events are interpreted through schemata, which are organized knowledge structures. Schemata also direct exploratory behavior, which leads to new sensory inputs, which can modify the schemata. Thus perception is influenced by both sensory inputs and prior knowledge and expectations. [Adapted from Neisser, U. *Cognition and reality.* Copyright ©1976 by W. H. Freeman and Company. Reprinted with permission of W. H. Freeman and Company.

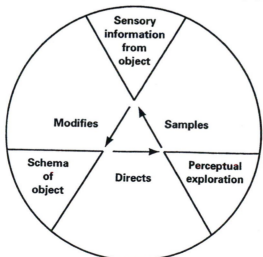

ence of causal stimuli (see Chapter 7). And waking fantasies and night dreams are fictions constructed from knowledge in memory (see Chapter 12).

Mental Imagery

Answer these three questions: (1) "How many years are there in the president's term of office?" (2) "What is the meaning of *justice?*" (3) "How many windows are there on the front side of the house that you lived in when you were a senior in high school?"

Now introspect on the processes by which you answered each of these questions. The answer to the first one probably occurred to you instantaneously and effortlessly, whereas the second and third took more time and effort. Assuming that you did not have ready-made answers to the "justice" and "window" questions, answering them was like solving a problem. Both required thinking, but the nature of the thinking was different. Defining an abstract concept like "justice" is mostly a matter of thinking in words. But thinking about concrete objects is done mostly in visual mental images. In answering the third question, you first constructed a conscious image of the house, and then you "looked" at the house image and counted the windows. Subjectively, thinking in visual mental images "feels" different than thinking in words.

A *mental image* is a quasi-perceptual experience that exists in the absence of the stimuli that are known to produce its genuine perceptual counterpart (Richardson 1969, p. 2). Mental images are constructed from information stored in long-term memory. Although humans can generate mental images in all sensory modalities, visual mental images are the most important type, along with internal speech, which is a special class of auditory images. *Mental imagery* is thinking in mental images.

The most distinctive characteristic of visual mental imagery is that it involves a representation of the shapes of objects and of their relative positions in space. Hence Julian Jaynes's term, *spatialization*, to refer to this important aspect of conscious experience (1976). Jaynes sees spatialization as of-the-essence of conscious experience.

Visual mental images serve several functions: (1) Memory of the appearance of physical objects, as in the window example. (2) Solving problems involving physical objects and their arrangement and movements in space. For example, planning how to construct a bookcase of bricks and boards. (3) Considering various personal actions, and imagining their consequences. For example, imagining taking the left turn, rather than the right turn, at a fork in the road. (4) Reverie—fantasy for the sake of wish fulfillment or entertainment. (5) Mental practice of skilled movements—such as movements in dart throwing, diving, or karate—using visual and kinesthetic imagery, may lead to improved performance (Ryan & Simons 1982; White, Ashton, & Lewis 1979).

From one instance to another, images can differ on two fundamental dimensions: vividness and spontaneity. *Vividness* refers to the clarity or lifelikeness of the image. For most people, night dreams are vivid in both color and visual detail. Waking visual hallucinations, such as those produced by psychedelic drugs, may also be quite vivid. Ordinary waking images, such as those used in memory or problem solving, are only slightly to moderately vivid for most people. When one is relaxed and engaging in waking reverie, the images can sometimes be strikingly vivid, though more commonly daydreams are only slightly to moderately vivid.

Spontaneity refers to the degree to which images occur and undergo changes in a seemingly automatic manner, without any conscious volition or control. Night dreams and psychedelic hallucinations are very spontaneous, waking reveries are moderately so. But when we use images for memory, planning, and problem solving, we generate and manipulate them voluntarily, and their changes occur with conscious control. Thus the opposite of spontaneity is *control.*

Psychologists have developed tests to measure individual differences in the ability to generate vivid mental images and the ability to control them— transforming their size, shape, and orientation at will (White, Sheehan, & Ashton 1977). Such measures are correlated to some extent with individual differences in the ability to use images for memory, mental practice, and problem solving. Interestingly, controlled images may be very helpful for solving visual-spatial problems even though the images are not particularly vivid (Richardson 1969).

Research by cognitive psychologists (e.g. Kosslyn 1980) has led to two general conclusions about imagery processes: (1) Thinking in mental images requires limited, general purpose processing resources (working memory). This conclusion is indicated by experiments that show that thinking in images can interfere with a variety of other types of thinking that require working memory. For example, you cannot very well visualize the construction of a house and do mental arithmetic at the same time. (2) Thinking in mental images uses certain modality-specific processing resources. This conclusion comes from experiments showing that interference between two concurrent tasks is greater when they are in the same modality than when they are in a different modality. For example, visual mental images interfere with detection of dim visual signals more than they interfere with detecting soft auditory signals; but auditory images interfere with auditory signal detection more than visual detection (Segal & Fusella 1971).

Inner Speech

Talking to yourself is normal—as long as you don't do it out loud. A large part of conscious thinking in adult humans involves thinking in words. A study focusing on college students found that 73 percent of thought samples contained some degree of interior monologue (inner speech), while 67 percent had some degree of visual-spatial mental imagery (Klinger & Cox 1987–88; more on this in Chapter 8 on daydreaming).

Communicating in language is the most distinctive aspect of human behavior. Language develops first to communicate about objects and about ourselves with other people. Later we learn to use language to talk to ourselves about ourselves. Language and consciousness are inextricably intertwined both in the mental evolution of the human species and in the mental growth of the individual human child (Kagan 1981; Luria 1978).

Inner speech—thinking in words—cuts across several other aspects of consciousness. Thinking in words is important for two distinctive characteristics of human consciousness: conceptual thought and reflective consciousness. Inner speech is involved in deciding upon and planning volitional acts. The processes that organize inner speech may occur nonconsciously, but inner speech itself is a conscious experience.

Perhaps most commonplace is the use of inner speech in *narratization*—our ongoing commentary on our personal experience (Jaynes 1976). Narratization includes interpreting our present experience and behavior in terms of its causes and expected effects, and fitting it into the story of our lives. Whenever you ask yourself "Why is this happening to me?" or "What am I going to do?", you are narratizing. Narratization also may involve mental imagery and spatialization. For example, you may think of a series of personal events in terms of an arrangement of events in space, representing the flow from past to present to future in a left-to-right pattern. Narratization is an important feature of self-awareness.

Conceptual Thought

Conceptual thought is thought involving abstraction and inference. Rather than thinking only about specific individual objects or events, in conceptual thought we can group objects into categories according to their similarities of appearance or function (such as birds, fruits, tools). Thus, we can discover generalizations that apply to all objects in a category, and, if we know their category, we can infer that objects probably have certain features that we have not yet observed. (For example: Do bats give milk? Yes, since bats are mammals and all mammals give milk.) Some types of conceptual thought are formalized in inductive and deductive logic, and at a more abstract level in mathematics and symbolic logic.

The capacity for conceptual thought is highly developed in humans because of our capacity for language, in which a category of objects, events, or experiences can be represented by a single word. Thus, most conceptual thought is a matter of inner speech—thinking in words—which has the advantage that it can be readily communicated to other people. In contrast, most thinking of specific objects and events—concrete thought—is done in mental images. However, just as concepts can be represented by nonverbal visual symbols, some types of conceptual thought employ nonverbal mental images; this is particularly true in mathematical thinking.

Even when concepts are labeled by words, we may use visual-spatial thinking to understand the relationship between them. For example, hierarchical categories may be thought of in terms of a spatial arrangement, with the larger, more encompassing categories located above the smaller, more specialized categories. (For example, superordinate categories—animal and musical instrument—are above basic-level categories—birds and fish, drums and pianos—which in turn are above subordinate-level categories—hawks and ducks, kettle and bongo.) In hierarchical categories, one level—*the basic level*—is learned first by children and is used most commonly in conceptual thought (Rosch 1973). Basic-level concepts can be represented by mental images as well as by words, and they contain enough descriptive information to be useful for most purposes, without going into too much detail.

Conceptual thought frees us from being bound to the immediate stimulus situation. We can think of high-level abstractions, such as peace, justice, freedom, and principles of morality—good and evil, right and wrong. We can think of objects not present, and we can conceive of objects that do not exist. We can think of events that happened in the past, or that might happen in the future. And if we can imagine objects or events that are desirable and possible, then we can begin planning actions to make them a reality (Kinget 1975).

Remembering

Remembering is a conscious experience. We can distinguish between *memory* as a flexible system in which information is stored, and *remembering* or recollection as the conscious experience that accompanies retrieval of information from the memory system. Memory is one of the two sources of information input to consciousness, the other source being the sensory systems. Remembering involves conscious mental images or inner speech that represents the knowledge or personal events that have been retrieved from memory.

Tulving (1985a, 1985b) described three separate but interrelated long-term memory (LTM) systems, and argued that each is associated with a different type of conscious experience. *Procedural memory* is concerned with how things are done. It deals with the acquisition, retention, and utilization of perceptual, cognitive, and motor skills. *Semantic memory* has to do with symbolically represented knowledge about the world. It includes knowledge of the meanings of words and of miscellaneous impersonal facts. *Episodic memory* concerns the personal events of our lives—knowledge that relates to ourselves as the actor and experiencer. For example, if you recall that the *Challenger* spaceship exploded in January 1986 it would be a case of semantic memory—an impersonal fact. But if you recall when and how and where you learned about the explosion, it would be a case of episodic memory—related to yourself as the experiencer. Dramatic episodic memories often include recollection of our emotional reaction at the time of the original event.

Tulving (1985b) argued that the three long-term memory systems are associated with different types of consciousness: procedural memory with *anoetic* (nonknowing) consciousness, semantic memory with *noetic* (knowing) consciousness, and episodic memory with *autonoetic* (self-knowing) consciousness. Tulving described autonoetic and noetic consciousness as follows:

> *Autonoetic (self-knowing) consciousness* is a necessary correlate of episodic memory. It allows an individual to become aware of his or her own identity and existence in subjective time that extends from the past through the present to the future . . . (1985a, p. 388). [It] confers the special phenomenal flavor to the remembering of [personally experienced] past events, the flavor that distinguishes remembering from other kinds of awareness, such as those characterizing perceiving, thinking, imagining, or dreaming (1985b, p. 3).

> The object of *noetic consciousness* is the organism's knowledge of its world. (1985a, p. 388). . . . Noetic consciousness allows an organism to be aware of, and to cognitively operate on, objects and events, and relations among objects and events, in the absence of these objects and events. The organism can flexibly act upon such symbolic knowledge of the world. Entering information into, and retrieval of information from, semantic memory is accompanied by noetic consciousness (1985b, p. 3).

Thus, autonoetic consciousness emphasizes the personal memory aspect of self awareness. Noetic consciousness emphasizes the memory aspect of concrete thought (dealing with specific objects and events) and conceptual thought (concerning categories of objects and events).

The concept of anoetic consciousness has not been developed as much as noetic and autonoetic consciousness. Apparently, *anoetic consciousness* is a sort of minimal awareness of external stimuli necessary for executing conditioned reflexes, automatic habits, and overlearned skills, with no concurrent awareness of the past or future or thoughts about any other objects or events outside of the present situation. The cognitive and motor control programs of procedural memory are themselves unavailable to introspection, and the programs are often executed nonconsciously (Kihlstrom 1984, 1987).

Tulving (1985a, 1985b) hypothesized that the three memory systems are arranged in a hierarchical relationship, in which episodic memory is a subsystem of semantic memory and semantic memory is a subsystem of procedural memory. The hierarchical arrangement was inferred from observations on brain-damaged patients suffering amnesia, in which episodic memory for new experiences was most severely disrupted, semantic memory was less severely disrupted, and procedural memory was least disrupted. Similar dissociations of memory systems sometimes occur in normal people. For example, people may recall information that they have learned, without recalling when and where they learned it—this *source amnesia* is a type of episodic recall failure. (I will go into more detail on amnesia and its implications for consciousness in Chapter 6.)

Tulving's three types of memory and consciousness can be related to the levels-of-consciousness model described in Chapter 1, though they do not correspond exactly to the different levels. Procedural memory operations (habits, skills) are carried out largely or entirely at a nonconscious level. Knowledge from semantic and episodic memory are used in primary conscious thinking to decide how to react to a situation, rather than reacting in a habitual or reflexive manner. Episodic memory knowledge (autonoetic consciousness) is a critical aspect of self-awareness, which is an aspect of reflective consciousness. Tulving's noetic consciousness also implies epistemic awareness—knowing what we know (Klatzky 1984)—which is an aspect of reflective awareness.

Tulving's ideas are important for showing the intimate relationship between remembering and consciousness. As he says, "there is no such thing as 'remembering without awareness'" (1985b, p. 5). Behavior can be influenced by stored information without conscious awareness, but "remembering" implies consciousness. Furthermore, Tulving's hierarchical model of memory interconnects the ideas of different memory systems with different levels of consciousness, with stages of development of consciousness in children (episodic memory and autonoetic consciousness develop after semantic memory and procedural memory), and with the localization of different memory systems in different parts of the brain.

Emotional Feeling

The subjective feeling of emotion is one of three major aspects of emotion, the other two being the pattern of physiological reactions and the overt expression, including facial expressions and other responses. Emotional feeling can vary on the dimensions of intensity and quality. Increasing subjective emotional intensity is correlated fairly well with stronger physiological reactions, such as increased heart rate, breathing rate, vasodilation (facial flushing), and release of adrenalin. The simplest qualitative classification of emotion is in terms of pleasant versus unpleasant. Pleasant or positive emotions increase our feeling of well-being and are associated with a tendency to approach objects or situations that produce them, whereas unpleasant or negative emotions have the opposite characteristics. However, human emotion is too complex to be described simply in terms of pleasant versus unpleasant affect. Most theorists propose six or more qualitative types of human emotions (Ortony & Turner 1990; Plutchik, 1980).

Different emotional reactions are produced by different types of stimuli or situations, and the different subjective feelings are accompanied by different facial expressions. Ekman, Friesen, and Tomkins (1971) analyzed photographs of the faces of people showing different emotions and devised a scoring scheme based on the muscles involved in the different expressions. Their analysis indicated that there are six clearly distinguishable primary human emotions, plus three less clearly distinguishable ones. The *six primary emotions* are happiness, sadness, anger, fear, surprise, and disgust. The three less well established ones are curiosity, guilt, and contempt. In studies using photographs of actors showing different emotions, Ekman and Friesen (1971) demonstrated that facial expressions of the six primary emotions can be recognized across widely different cultures. The processes underlying emotions are complex, and several competing theories have been proposed to explain the causes of different emotions and their subjective and expressive qualities (see Mook 1987, Chapter 12, for a brief review).

Caroll Izard (1980) suggested that emotion is "always present in ordinary consciousness, giving it a particular experiential quality and maintaining its purposeful flow." He assumed that there is a relatively limited set of primary human emotions. Though strong emotions may be relatively infrequent, weaker emotions are always present, in his view. He counted *interest* (or *curiosity*) as an emotion that occurs whenever it is not suppressed by stronger negative or positive emotions. Izard saw emotions as "motivational phenomena that give impetus and directedness to perceptual and cognitive processes and to motor acts" (p. 193).

Izard argued that emotional feeling, not sensory perception, is the first stage in the development of consciousness in infants. In neonates the dominant emotion is distress in response to uncomfortable internal stimuli. The crying response ultimately brings relief, since it calls the caretaker who attends to the baby's needs (food, warmth); this is the first occasion for learning about cause-and-effect relationships. Soon the emotion of interest in response to external stimuli appears. Infants follow objects with their eyes, focusing more on moderately complex patterns than on very simple ones. Thus interest motivates attention and exploration that lead to complex perceptual skills, including the ability to perceive the similarities and differences between objects, and their interactions in time and space. Next, the emotion of joy and the social smiling response promote positive social interactions and the beginning of a self concept, in which self is differentiated from other people, and people are differentiated from other objects. The initial emotions of distress, interest, and joy are followed by others, including anger, fear, and shame/shyness, by the end of the first year. The emotions motivate interactions with other people and the environment, which promotes learning (including language, social skills, and sensory-motor skills) and vastly expands the variety of conscious experiences.

Volition

Volition may be defined as "the act of deciding upon and initiating a course of action. Synonym: will" (English & English 1958). Volitional acts can be either overt behaviors or further cognitive acts. Volitional cognitive acts can include such things as deciding what to attend to (for example, the textbook rather than the TV), deciding what to imagine, deciding what to rehearse for memorization, and deciding what facts or experiences to retrieve from memory.

Volitional acts are accompanied by a *feeling of volition*, a conscious feeling or belief that our actions are the result of a personal choice between viable alternatives, in which we are consciously aware of those alternatives. The choice may involve *what* to do, *when* to do it, or both. Once the choice is made, there is the feeling that it could have been otherwise.

Reflexive responses, such as withdrawing your hand from a hot flame, do not involve any decision making. Thus, reflexive responses are not volitional acts, and they are not accompanied by a feeling of volition. However, volition is involved when you inhibit a reflexive response; for example, if you were to hold your hand in a flame and resist the impulse to withdraw it. Likewise, many automatic or habitual behaviors occur without a conscious decision. Volition is needed to counteract a habit. For example, volition (or willpower) is required for a nicotine addict to resist the impulse to smoke a cigarette.

The role of consciousness in volition.   Traditionally, it has been assumed that volition is equivalent to making a *conscious* decision, in which consciousness is the decision maker, the executive part of the mind/brain system. However, doubts have been raised about the traditional view. Logically it would seem that if consciousness makes a decision, then consciousness should know—and be able to report—why it made the decision. Yet research in recent years indicates that people often cannot introspectively report the causes or reasons for their behavior (Chapter 7). The implication is that consciousness *per se* is not the decision maker. Decisions may be made

largely, or entirely, by nonconscious computational processes. This is not to deny that consciousness plays an important role in decision making. However, the exact role of consciousness is still a matter of research and debate. If consciousness is more of a monitoring system than a decision-making system, then probably one role of consciousness has to do with perception, selection, and organization of some of the data relevant to decision making. Another role has to do with being aware of decisions in order to be able to communicate them, to evaluate the effectiveness of our actions in carrying them out, and to influence further decision-making processes.

Thus, in the monitoring-system view of consciousness, to make a conscious decision means, at a minimum, to be aware of the decision and able to report it. To act intentionally or volitionally means to be consciously aware of the decision to act before the action is initiated. The *feeling of volition* is an aspect of conscious experience. Volition—making decisions about actions—is not necessarily a direct function of consciousness *per se*. However, decision making is a function of the individual's personal mind/brain system. Therefore people are morally responsible for their volitional acts.

Consciousness and the motivational sequence.

Much of human behavior is *purposive*, that is, it is done in the pursuit of conscious goals. Purposive behavior involves anticipation of the future, selection of goals, and the planning and execution of actions intended to bring about the desired goals. Purposive behavior is part of a *motivational sequence*.

An idealized fully-conscious motivational sequence could be described as follows: (1) you consciously feel a need or desire (such as for food, companionship, sex, prestige); (2) you consciously choose a specific goal (object, person, situation) to satisfy the need or desire; (3) you consciously plan a course of action to reach the goal; (4) you consciously assign priorities to different goals, which in turn affects the priorities of different actions; (5) you consciously initiate the action at the appropriate time; and (6) you consciously control the action while it is in progress, using feedback information to modify the action as needed until the goal is reached.

In fact, most motivational sequences are not fully conscious. Conscious choice among goals and actions occurs mainly in novel or complex situations. In relatively simple or familiar situations much of our behavior is more a matter of automatic habit than conscious choice.

Conscious choice is more important for the selection of actions than for the actual initiation and control of them. We may select automatic programs that in turn trigger the actions when certain internal or external conditions are met (Heckhausen & Beckman 1990; Norman & Shallice 1986). For example, at a swimming race the racers must be prepared to dive immediately when they hear the "Bang!" of the starter's gun; they don't have time to think "There's the gun, now go!" Perhaps you have had the experience of lying in bed in the morning after having shut off the alarm, and thinking "I must get up!" But you don't move, you just lie there like a dead raccoon for several minutes. Then suddenly you spring out of bed, but you have no awareness of initiating the movement. It seems to happen by itself. Apparently some sort of nonconscious timer prompts you to spring out of bed when you have loafed too long after the alarm. Such odd happenings are not evidence against volition, but they show the complexity of the processes involved. Motivational sequences, from the emergence of needs and the selection of goals through the initiation and control of actions, typically involve a mixture of conscious and nonconscious processes.

Free will and determinism.   The concept of volition has often been equated with the idea of *free will,* insofar as people feel that they are able to choose any one of several conceivable courses of action. Free will has traditionally been contrasted with determinism. *Determinism* is the notion that whatever happens in the world—including people's actions—is due to certain antecedent (prior) causes. Free will has been taken to mean that people's voluntary actions follow from free choices that are not determined by antecedent causes, as if the mind could function independently of the physical world of cause-and-effect. But this contrast of free will and determinism is a misconception. Donald Hebb made the point:

> Free will is not a violation of scientific law; it doesn't mean indeterminism; it's not mystical. What it is, simply, is a control of behavior by the thought process (Hebb 1974, p. 75).

Free will is not opposed to determinism. In fact, free will or volition *requires* that we live in a world that operates to a large degree on deterministic—cause and effect—principles. This is not to say that volitional choices and behavior are produced in a rigid, mechanistic manner. Determinism is not absolute. Rather, determinism is probabilistic: a particular cause will produce a particular effect with some degree of probability. Understanding the relationships between causes and effects is complicated because of both their probabilistic nature and the multiplicity of causes that influence decision making and behavior. But if we could not count on a large degree of consistency in the way the world works—including natural and man-made objects, the behavior of other people, and the functioning of our own minds and bodies—then we would be incapable of carrying out our plans with voluntary actions.

The contrast between free will and determinism is a false dichotomy. The opposite of free will or volition is reflex behavior. The opposite of determinism is randomness. Volition involves decisions based on the integration of a variety of information from both the immediate situation and from our prior knowledge and experience, and influenced by our personal temperaments, desires, and interests. Our choices are necessarily limited by our knowledge, our powers of reason and imagination, and constraints of the current situation. We have freedom to make choices within those limits.

Self-Awareness

Self-awareness refers to having a *self-concept*—your sense of personal identity and your knowledge and beliefs about yourself—and to being aware that your actions and experiences *belong* to the person to whom the self-concept refers. Your self-concept influences—either implicitly or explicitly—your interpretation of your experiences and your choice of actions.

The self-concept appears at some point during development when you become aware that you are a unique person, separate from other persons, with your own unique personal history and your own desires, interests, values, knowledge, abilities and limitations. You come to think and speak of yourself as "I." Based on evidence from language and other behavior, Kagan (1981) concluded that self-awareness emerges in most children during the second half of the second year. For example, when a twenty-month-old child says "I can't do that," these words imply that the child has a self-concept, with knowledge of his or her own abilities and limitations. Your *body image*— knowledge of your personal appearance and of the shape and movement skills of your body—is another aspect of your self-concept. Though your self-concept is relatively fixed over the short run, it can change as a result of new experiences.

Your self-concept is based on selected information about yourself. The way you see yourself is not the same way that other people see you, since other people have different information about you than you do about yourself. You know your intentions, whereas other people know only your behavior. And as psychotherapists are well aware, people's self-images are sometimes based on delusory beliefs about themselves. For example, people suffering from major depression usually have undeservedly negative self-concepts.

Self-awareness depends critically upon episodic memory and the capacity for reflective consciousness. We oscillate between primary consciousness and reflective consciousness, between being the acting, experiencing subject and being the object whose actions and experiences are thought about. When you think "Why did I do that?" or "What do I want to do?", the "I" of reflective awareness is not just your physical body, but your self-concept. Reflective awareness relates and integrates your mind and body action here and now with your self-concept. A frightening feeling of *depersonalization* can occur under certain conditions (such as stress or drugs) when it seems that one's actions are not one's own. In amnesic patients the loss of episodic memory can alter or destroy the self-concept.

According to self theory, the self-concept is a major long-term guiding principle for our actions, since we tend to make our actions more-or-less consistent with our values and our beliefs about our abilities and the sort of person that we are. Albert Bandura (1986) has developed the concept of *perceived self-efficacy*—people's beliefs about their skills and abilities—and has shown that the actions that people attempt, and their success at those attempts, are related to their perceived self-efficacy. Furthermore, the self-concept or self-image is the basis for self-referential attitudes such as pride, guilt, conscience, and the sense of personal responsibility for our actions (Kinget 1975).

THE UNITY OF CONSCIOUSNESS

Despite the enormous variety of sensory percepts and thoughts and their ever-changing nature, we have an overall impression that our conscious experience is unified. At one moment, or in a rapid succession of moments, you may be looking out the window, listening to a lecture, writing notes, feeling a headache, recalling yesterday's picnic, and imagining what you hope to do next weekend. Subjectively, it does not seem that each of these experiences represents a different consciousness. Rather, they all seem to go together in a single unified, indivisible consciousness—your own.

It has traditionally been assumed that the feeling of conscious unity is an immediately given aspect of conscious experience. The feeling of conscious unity has been interpreted by some people (dualists) as evidence for a unified, indivisible soul that is the basis of conscious experience. Others (some materialists) have interpreted it as evidence that a single brain structure or system is responsible for conscious experience. An alternative view is that conscious unity is an illusion. Different aspects of conscious experience—different sensory modalities and modes of thought and memory—may be functions of different brain subsystems, each with its own separate and limited capacity for awareness.

If conscious unity is an illusion, the feeling of conscious unity may result from an interpretation of the variety of conscious experiences—an interpretation influenced by certain beliefs and constraints on our experience. O'Keefe (1985) suggested three influences on the feeling of conscious unity.

(1) There is usually a short-term stability in the background or context of experience. We can distinguish between the foreground or central object of consciousness and the background or physical and mental context of the experience. (William James, 1890/1983, referred to the "halo" or "fringe" of consciousness.) For example, in the last few minutes I have had a variety of sensory perceptions and thoughts. All of them have occurred in the physical context of my office (including some glances out the window) and the mental context of writing this chapter (plus some daydreams about an upcoming canoe trip). Though the momentary focus of awareness is constantly changing, the relatively constant context contributes to a feeling of conscious unity.

(2) Temporal gaps between experiences are bridged by memory. I have already discussed the role of episodic memory in maintaining the continuity of consciousness over time. Each experience is part of the story of our life, a personal narrative that is being continuously updated. Where memory is incomplete we can bridge the gaps by constructing plausible accounts, aided by our knowledge of *scripts* (descriptions of typical sequences of events for various occasions, such as a typical day at work, going to a restaurant, and so forth).

(3) We have a sense of ownership of our subjective experiences: *my* percepts, *my* thoughts, *my* actions. One source of this sense of ownership is that the experiences all relate to the same body: objects seen with my eyes, thoughts in my brain, actions by my hands. More important is the ability to relate personal episodes to an ongoing self-concept.

The bottom line is that the feeling of conscious unity derives from a variety of sources. Our overall conscious experience seems to be the result of a constructive process in which a variety of data are interpreted and related to each other to produce a coherent, unified experience. But if this is the case, what part of the mind/brain system is responsible for the processes of interpretation and construction? We'll consider a possible answer to this question in Chapter 5 on split-brain research and its implications for consciousness.

SUMMARY

It seems unlikely that a science of consciousness could ever explain, much less predict, the moment to moment changes in the contents of consciousness in one individual in any detail. A more reasonable goal is to try to describe certain abstract features of consciousness, and to try to explain the processes that produce them and the conditions under which they vary.

Following William James, I described five higher-order characteristics that apply regardless of the particular contents of consciousness. (1) *Subjectivity*: every thought is part of a personal and private consciousness. (2) *Change*: the contents of consciousness are continuously changing, and no momentary conscious state ever recurs in exactly the same way as before. (3) *Continuity*: James's famous metaphor, the *stream of consciousness*, portrays the idea that while the specific contents of consciousness change from moment to moment, consciousness itself seems to be continuous. Continuity is maintained in the short run by working memory and in the long run by long-term episodic memory. (4) *Intentionality ("aboutness")*: consciousness has contents; it is about something. (5) *Selectivity*: at any moment we are consciously aware of only a limited part of all of the stimuli—external and internal—of which we might potentially be aware. Selective attention is necessary because of the limited capacity of consciousness.

I also discussed eight specific aspects of conscious experience that relate to some, but not necessarily all, of the contents of consciousness. (1) *Sensory perception* of objects and events, both external (exteroception) and internal (interoception), is the most fundamental aspect of consciousness. (2) *Mental imagery*, or thinking in mental images, involves quasi-perceptual experiences that exist in the absence of the stimuli known to produce their genuine perceptual counterparts. The most distinctive aspect of visual mental images is *spatialization*, in which the shapes of objects and their positions and movements in space are represented. We can imagine alternative actions and their consequences. (3) *Inner speech*—thinking in words—constitutes a major part of adult conscious experience. Our ongoing commentary on our own experience is termed *narratization*. Inner speech is critically involved in two characteristically human traits, conceptual thought and reflective consciousness. (4) *Conceptual thought* involves thinking in terms of abstract categories (sets of objects or events based on certain shared features) and making inferences. (5) *Remembering* as a conscious experience can be distinguished from memory as a system for information storage. Tulving distinguished three interrelated long-term memory systems—procedural, semantic, and episodic—each of which is associated with a different type of conscious experience. (6) *Emotional feeling* is one of three aspects of emotion, along with a pattern of physiological reactions and overt expression (especially facial expression). Fundamental human emotions include: happiness, sadness, anger, fear, surprise, disgust, and possibly others. (7) *Volition* is the act of deciding upon and initiating a course of action. It is problematic whether consciousness *per se* is the decision maker or action initiator, since nonconscious processes are also involved. The *feeling of volition*—the belief that our actions are the result of personal choice—is an aspect of conscious experience. (8) *Self-awareness* refers to having a self-concept and being aware that one's actions and conscious experiences belong to the person to whom the self-concept refers. Self-awareness depends critically upon episodic memory and our capacity for reflective consciousness.

Despite the wide variety of ever-changing conscious contents, they all seem to be part of a unified consciousness. It has traditionally been assumed that the feeling of conscious unity is a directly given aspect of conscious experience. Alternatively, the apparent unity of consciousness may be an illusion. It appears that our conscious experience is the result of a constructive process in which a variety of data are interpreted and related to each other to produce a coherent, unified experience.

ENDNOTES

[1]Nowadays psychologists more commonly use "state of consciousness" in a different, broader sense having to do with an overall pattern of subjective experiences that is maintained over an extended period of time. When the pattern of experience is distinctly different than normal it is termed an "altered state of consciousness," as in sleep (Chapter 9). You can interpret the different senses of "conscious state"—momentary or extended—from the context in which it is used.

[2]To be sure, you could consciously analyze this (book) perception into its elements, which might be described in terms of white rectangular surfaces (the pages), or trapezoids or irregular quadrilaterals, depending upon your angle of view. This process of backward conscious analysis of perceptions, from objects and events to simple shapes and surfaces, is a case of *reflective perceptual awareness*. Gibson made the distinction between primary and reflective awareness this way: "The modern adult can adopt a naive attitude or a perspective attitude. He can attend to visible things or to visual sensations" (Gibson 1982, p. 279; discussed in Natsoulas, 1985).

chapter 3 ·····································

Introspection I: Methods and Limitations

> *Introspective Observation is what we have to rely on first and foremost and always.* The word "introspection" need hardly be defined—it means, of course, the looking into our own minds and reporting what we there discover. *Everyone agrees that we there discover states of consciousness* [i.e., thoughts and feelings] (William James 1890/1983, p. 185).

Introspection—or the introspective verbal report—is used in one form or another in virtually all research on consciousness or aspects of conscious experience, such as perception, mental imagery, and so forth. Introspective reports are also used in psychotherapy and in everyday communications between people who are trying to describe how they feel or explain their own behavior. Philosophers and novelists, as well as psychologists, have drawn profound conclusions about human nature from their personal introspections.

In William James's day, introspection was psychologists' primary means of studying consciousness and the mind. Indeed, James (an American) and most British psychologists did not distinguish between consciousness and the mind. They thought that introspection was a general method for studying mental processes (Danziger 1980). Now we know—as many German psychologists suspected even in James's day—that many mental processes are nonconscious, and are not available to introspection. Since 1890 a variety of more objective methods of studying psychological processes have been developed, and introspection has gone through a cycle of being distrusted and rarely used during the Behaviorist era (roughly 1913 to the early 1960s), to return to frequent but cautious use in the present day. As we will see, introspection has some severe limitations as a means of studying mental processes. But it is still the best method we have for learning about a person's stream of consciousness.

Because introspective reports are so important for the research discussed in this book, it is important to give, early on, an overview of the types and methods of introspection and their limitations. In addition I will consider the question of what is really going on during introspection. Is it really a matter of "looking within?"

INTROSPECTION AND INTROSPECTIVE VERBAL REPORTS

First we need to distinguish between introspection and introspective verbal reports. In the spirit of William James and common usage, let us tentatively define *introspection* as "looking into one's own mind and observing its contents." In other words, introspection is observing your conscious experience. An *introspective verbal report* (IVR) is a verbal description of your conscious experience. For example, suppose you were riding an elevator with an attractive stranger, and suddenly he or she grabbed you and kissed you. You would have certain physical sensations and emotional feelings—either pleasant or unpleasant—and certain thoughts, such as deciding whether to push the stranger away or kiss him or her back, and follow-up thoughts, such as "Could this get serious?" If you then think to yourself, "What am I sensing/feeling/thinking?" and look within to find the answer, you are introspecting. That is, you are observing your conscious experience. You may also ask yourself *why* you are sensing/feeling/thinking as you are. Such thoughts are *interpretive introspections*. If you subsequently try to describe your subjective experiences to someone in words, then you are making an introspective verbal report. (For brevity I will use the term introspection rather than introspective verbal report when it is obvious from the context that I am talking about introspective verbal reports.)

It is important to bear in mind that characterizing introspection as "looking within" is merely a metaphorical description of the introspective process. It is *as if* one is looking within. But as we will see, it would be incorrect to explain the process of introspection as literally a matter of looking within or of internal observation, as if it was closely analogous to visual observation of something outside of ourselves. In terms of the levels-of-consciousness model that I described earlier, introspection is a case of reflective consciousness. It is thinking about one's conscious experience. The initial "raw" experience is a matter of primary consciousness.

Introspection or inner observation is an everyday occurrence for most people.[1] Just as attention to external stimuli is selective, introspection is selective. You select what is relevant to your purpose at the moment. Most introspection and reporting is informal, with little attempt at precision. In psychological research, however, people may be asked to do formal introspection, in which they try to introspect in a systematic manner and report their inner observations as precisely as they can.

Introspective reports versus ordinary verbal responses. Introspective verbal reports (IVRs) are a type of verbal behavior. We should distinguish IVRs from ordinary verbal responses. Verbal responses are the primary data in a wide variety of psychology experiments. For example, people answer questions "yes" or "no"; they name what they see (such as "triangle" or "circle"); and they report lists of words recalled from memory.

It is not possible to draw a fine line between introspective verbal reports and ordinary verbal responses. In general, ordinary verbal responses are responses to the primary cognitive task of an experiment (for example, tasks requiring perception, memory, judgment, or decision making). Verbal responses may be simple behavioral outputs from mental processes. They could in most cases be replaced by simple mechanical responses, such as pushing one of two or more buttons labeled by appropriate words.

In their analysis and theoretical discussion of ordinary verbal responses, researchers usually disregard the question of whether the verbal responses indicate anything about conscious contents. If consciousness is considered at all, usually there is an assumption of *concordance* between behavior, mental processes, and conscious experience (Tulving 1989). Ordinarily, responses in visual discrimination tasks follow from consciously perceived differences between objects. And reports of remembered information ordinarily follow from memories recalled into consciousness. However, the assumption of concordance has rarely been tested. As we will see in Chapter 6, there are some cases, such as "blindsight" and subliminal perception, in which concordance breaks down and behavioral responses and conscious awareness become dissociated from each other.

When subjects perform cognitive tasks and make ordinary verbal responses, experimenters are mainly interested in the question of how accurately subjects process information, rather than in their conscious experience of the information. On the other hand, introspective verbal reports are intended to be reports on the subject's conscious experience *per se*, including reports on conscious contents and mental processes related to the task at hand, and on daydreams—thoughts unrelated to the task at hand.

Ordinary verbal responses have been accepted without question in psychological research. Introspective verbal reports, on the other hand, are highly controversial as a type of data. There are two reasons why introspective reports are controversial. First, some psychologists, especially radical behaviorists such as B. F. Skinner (1987), believe that consciousness is a mere epiphenomenon—that it plays no role in causing people to behave the way they do. Thus, in their view, introspective reports on conscious experience are unimportant. Second, even for psychologists who believe that conscious experience plays a role in controlling behavior, there is the problem that introspective reports are often inaccurate and unreliable. Errors may occur in both the recall and the reporting of conscious experiences.

In Chapter 7, "Introspection II," we will consider in some detail the question of whether introspective reports on conscious experience provide useful information about underlying mental processes and the causes of behavior. But aside from that issue, conscious experience is an important phenomenon in its own right, and introspective reports are critically important for finding out about people's conscious experiences. Introspective reports can be useful for some purposes, if we understand the various factors that affect their accuracy and reliability. Next I will describe three types of introspection, followed by a discussion of the limitations of introspective reports.

TYPES OF INTROSPECTION

We can distinguish three types of introspection—analytic, descriptive (phenomenological), and interpretive—in terms of what they attempt to describe or explain.

Analytic introspection. Analytic introspection—sometimes called "classical introspection" (Boring 1953)—involves attempting to describe one's conscious experiences in terms of their elementary constituents. Analytic introspection was advocated by Edward B. Titchener (1867–1927), a professor at Cornell University. Titchener developed an approach to psychology called *structuralism*, based on a model borrowed from chemistry. Titchener believed that conscious experience is constructed from a limited number of "elements" of sensory experience and simple feelings, and that these elements can be discovered through introspection. More complex percepts and ideas are the "molecules" of experience.

Titchener taught that it was important for introspecting subjects to avoid the *stimulus error* of ascribing meaning to their experience, that is, confusing the complex percept (the molecule) with its sensory elements. For example, while observing a table across the room an observer might describe his or her experience as a visual sensation of a quadrilateral form (not a rectangle, since the retinal image of a table viewed from the side is quadrilateral—a "rectangle" is a higher-order perception), shading from grey to white (according to how light reflects from its surface), with columnar appendages (the legs) hanging from three corners (only three legs are visible from the observer's position) at such-and-such angles, and so on. An observer who said "I see a table" would be committing a stimulus error, according to Titchener, though such a report would be perfectly acceptable for a researcher who was interested in phenomenological reports. In order to minimize the stimulus error, Titchener used rigorously trained introspective observers rather than experimentally naive subjects.

Analytic introspection is rarely used today, for four reasons. First, its theoretical foundation has been discredited. Max Wertheimer and other Gestalt psychologists in Germany argued convincingly that—contrary to Titchener's claims—objects are perceived as unified configurations rather than as sets of elementary sensations: "The whole is more than the sum of its parts." Also, Oswald Külpe and his colleagues at the University of Würzberg, Germany, discovered "imageless thought." When asked to introspect and report on the mental events that occurred while they solved a problem, subjects described a sequence of thoughts or images, each one leading closer to the goal. The subjects were not, however, consciously aware of any process that guided the sequence and accounted for the transformations between one thought and the next. Ach coined the term "determining tendency" for the nonconscious process that guides thinking. Determining tendencies can be established by prior instructions (Ach 1905, cited in Lieberman 1979). If thinking can occur without any accompanying conscious sensations, then elementary sensations cannot be the basis for all complex thoughts.

A second problem was that analytic introspection was unreliable, with different observers giving different reports under ostensibly the same conditions. Third, it was largely sterile, for it led to no understanding or practical applications regarding complex thinking, motives, emotions, and overt behaviors. Fourth, following John Watson's introduction of Behaviorism in 1913, young psychologists had an alternative to Structuralism and analytic introspection that promised much more in the way of practical understanding and applications. Thus, analytic introspection largely disappeared from the psychology laboratory after the death of Titchener in 1927 (Boring 1953; Danziger 1980).

Descriptive introspection.   Descriptive or phenomenological introspection is the simplest and most natural type of introspection. It is simply the description of one's conscious experience in natural language terms. It asks "*What* did I perceive/think/feel?" It concerns meaningful events, objects and people, and thoughts about them, rather than abstract generalizations or unnatural analyses of objects into their sensory elements. Descriptive introspection can be about dreams and daydreams as well as about real perceptions and actions.

Although descriptive introspection is concerned with immediate experience, it is not the immediate experience *per se.* Descriptive introspection is one step removed from the immediate experience. While immediate experience is primary consciousness, descriptive introspection is a matter of reflective consciousness. It asks "What am I experiencing?" or "What did I experience?", trying to consider the experience objectively, perhaps to prepare for verbally reporting it. Descriptive introspective reports describe conscious experiences in everyday language as closely as possible to the way we originally experienced them. Descriptive reports necessarily involve categorizing one's experiences (insofar as descriptive words are category labels), but they include no analysis or interpretation of their causes.

Interpretive introspection.   Interpretive introspection is introspection intended to discover the causes of our thoughts, feelings, and actions. While descriptive introspection asks "*What* do I feel?", interpretive introspection asks "*Why* do I feel this way?" Where descriptive introspection asks "*What* did I do?", interpretive introspection asks "*Why* did I do that?" In interpretive introspection we attempt to discover the *antecedents* of our thoughts, feelings, and actions, such as relevant prior events and thoughts. As we will see in Chapter 7, some psychologists dispute the validity of interpretive introspection (Nisbett & Wilson 1977). That is, they doubt that we can know the causes of our own thoughts, feelings, and actions through introspection alone.

The distinction between descriptive and interpretive introspection seems clear enough when we are dealing with perceptual or quasi-perceptual (mental-image) experiences. However, there are some cases in which the distinction between description and interpretation of conscious experiences is not so clear. Are reports of our mental states—such as attitudes, motives, hopes, desires, and intentions—to be accepted as simple descriptions of immediate conscious experiences? Or are such reports really inferences, based on our interpretation of the situation and what we have done? For example, is love a directly felt conscious experience, or is it an inference, based on how we behave when we are with the loved one, and how we think about this person when he or she is absent? This is a complex issue (Wilson 1985). My distinction between descriptive and interpretive introspection is based on people's intentions when they introspect—whether they are to describe their conscious experiences in a relatively straightforward, naive way, or to attempt to interpret the causes of these experiences. By this criterion, attempts to report mental states such as attitudes and intentions are classified as descriptive introspection, whereas attempts to explain those states are classified as interpretive introspection.

LIMITATIONS OF INTROSPECTIVE VERBAL REPORTS

Here we are concerned mainly with descriptive (phenomenological) introspective reports by normal adults. Suppose that you were asked to describe your conscious experiences—perceptions, thoughts, images, feelings—over, say, the last five minutes, without attempting to analyze or interpret them. There are several factors that could limit the accuracy of your report.

Forgetting. Forgetting is the most important factor that limits the accuracy of introspective verbal reports. Conscious experiences may be forgotten within a matter of seconds or minutes.

Ericsson and Simon (1980) described the verbal report process in terms of the multistore model of memory. In this model, only the contents of short-term memory (STM or working memory) can be verbally reported. STM holds information currently undergoing controlled (flexible, volitional) processing; one is consciously aware only of information that is undergoing such processing. STM has a very small capacity (about seven items), and its duration is only a few seconds except when its contents are maintained by rehearsal. Information is easily lost from STM through interference caused by distraction or by the surpassing of STM capacity by current thinking or memory demands. Some conscious STM contents may be transferred to long-term memory (LTM), depending on factors such as their salience (that is, their conspicuousness, due to such factors as loudness, novelty, surprise, or emotional impact), and the amount and type of rehearsal or thinking about them that you do while they are in STM. In order to report experiences that occurred more than a few seconds after you were last aware of them, you would have to recall them from LTM.

Thus, according to the multistore model, you can report conscious contents under one of two conditions: (1) the contents are still available in STM; or (2) they have been transferred to LTM and can be retrieved from LTM into STM.

Verbal reports of events will be inaccurate or incomplete under any of four conditions: (1) You never attended to the event, so it was not stored in STM and is not available for verbal reports. For example, if you are attending to a task, such as reading, you might not consciously notice a voice speaking softly nearby. (2) The information is in STM and potentially available for verbal reporting, but for some reason you do not report it. Failure of reporting, or incomplete reporting, might occur because you are too busy doing some other task, or because you are withholding the report to protect your personal privacy (for example, you might not report a potentially embarrassing daydream). (3) The information was at one time in STM but was not transferred to LTM. For example, you might briefly notice something—such as a dog on the curb as you drive by—but it is so trivial that you immediately switch your attention to something else, so the event (dog) is lost from STM and not transferred to LTM. (4) The information is in LTM but you cannot retrieve it into STM for verbal reporting.

Ericsson and Simon's analysis has several implications for research methodology: (1) Verbal reports on conscious experiences will be most accurate if they are collected within a few seconds of the original experience, while the information is still in STM. Retention in STM will be best under conditions that minimize interference. (2) Where longer delays in reporting are necessary, accuracy will be greatest under conditions that increase the likelihood that the experience will be transferred to LTM. These conditions include: (a) foreknowledge that the experience is important and that a report will be requested; (b) unique and inherently interesting experiences that would be spontaneously stored; (c) the experience occurs at a time when STM information-processing demands are low, so there is time for mnemonic storage processes to operate.

Reconstruction errors. Reports on episodic memories—long-term memories of personal life events—are not based on a detailed videotape-like replay of the original event. Rather, the report is a *reconstruction* of the original event, based partly on factual recall and partly on filling in the gaps with plausible details (Ashcraft 1989). The same principle applies to recall of conscious experiences, regardless of whether they concern overt actions or dreams, daydreams, or other thought processes. Two types of reconstruction errors can occur: (1) people may report more than they accurately recall, by filling in memory gaps with plausible fabrications; and (2) the memory report may be more orderly than what was really recalled. For example, you might describe a dream as if you are telling a connected, coherent story, when in fact the dream was quite disorderly and you recalled only part of it. Reconstruction errors can occur in reports on either STM or LTM contents, though they are likely to be greatest in LTM recall.

Verbal description difficulties. Some conscious experiences cannot be adequately described in words. For example, you probably cannot describe in any detail the feelings that go with strong emotions (love, fear), or novel sensations such as pains, tastes, and odors. Experiences that cannot be described in words are called *ineffable* experiences, though this term is applied most commonly to mystical religious experiences. Of course ineffability is a matter of degree; some experiences can be described better than others. Sometimes we have to resort to metaphors and similes. For example, in describing a headache you might say "It feels like my head is being crushed in a vise." People differ in their verbal descriptive skills, and poets will likely be better than engineers at describing their subjective experiences. The problem with metaphorical descriptions is that they do not communicate precisely. They may mean different things to different people. The problem of verbal description difficulties may be partially overcome by training subjects to use special vocabularies to describe their subjective experiences.

Distortion through observation.   In atomic physics, one cannot know both the velocity and the position of an electron at the same time, because the process of observing an electron's position with high-energy light waves changes its velocity. This discovery led to the formulation of the Heisenberg Uncertainty Principle, which says that the process of observation may alter the thing that is being observed. An analogous *Introspective Uncertainty Principle* applies in psychology: attempting to introspectively observe one's conscious contents may change the contents that are being observed. For example, if you introspect on your thoughts while you solve a difficult problem, you may try to attend and store in memory more details than usual, thus causing the thought process to go slower and perhaps take a different course than it otherwise would. If you try introspectively to judge the frequency of a certain type of thought—such as aggressive thoughts, or guilty thoughts— then the frequency of that type of thought might be altered by the introspective process. (A demonstration: For the next ten minutes, try to avoid thinking about pink elephants. But count the number of times that you think about pink elephants over the next ten minutes.) If research subjects know that they will be asked to report their thoughts, as in experiments on daydreaming, then they may try to inhibit thoughts that they would be embarrassed to report.[2] Thus, if researchers want to minimize distortion through observation, they must ask for *retrospective* reports, without giving subjects any advanced warning. (Retrospective reports, on the other hand, are plagued by the problem of forgetting. No method is perfect.)

Censorship.   Sometimes people choose to keep secrets. This is a minor problem in most cases. But in studies of daydreams, subjects may be reluctant to reveal embarrassing thoughts—for example, sexual or aggressive thoughts about the experimenter. Subjects may give false reports or claim that they do not recall anything. To reduce this problem, researchers can ask for reports on the general nature of the conscious experience without asking for details. For example, subjects can classify thoughts into labeled categories.

Experimental demands.   Introspective verbal reports are overt behaviors, and they may be influenced by a variety of factors that also affect other overt behaviors. Among the factors that can affect people's behavior in psychology experiments are the demand characteristics. The *demand characteristics* of an experiment are the situational cues from which subjects try to figure out what the experimenter expects them to do (Orne 1962). Subjects may try to be helpful and do what they think the experimenter expects them to do. Thus, their verbal reports may be altered directly through deliberate exaggeration or distortion, or indirectly by trying to produce subjective experiences of the expected type and then accurately reporting them. For example, suppose you were a subject in an experiment on dreams. Before you go to sleep you are asked to watch a movie about a soldier's frightening wartime experiences. You might assume that the experimenter expects that the movie will influence the content of your dreams. Then in your subsequent dream reports you might exaggerate the frightening nature of your dreams, or selectively report only the unpleasant dreams, in order to help the experimenter confirm his or her hypothesis. The problem is that the experimenter's hypothesis would be confirmed artifactually, as a result of the effects of experimental demands on your verbal-reporting behavior, rather than as a result of the true effects of the movie on your dreams.

Lack of independent verification.

In studies using introspective methods, we may say that subjects observe their conscious experiences, then report their observations to the researcher.[3] But researchers have no way to independently check on the accuracy of subjects' reports. For example, I could not check on the accuracy of your dream report, or of your description of the thoughts you had while trying to write a poem.

That observations can be independently verified by others is a fundamental principle of scientific research, and the fact that introspective observations cannot be independently verified is the major reason why introspection has been rejected as a research method by many psychologists. However, this problem is not as serious as is sometimes supposed. Researchers can make reasonable judgments about the accuracy of introspective reports by considering: (1) their consistency with other reports, by the same person or other persons, made under similar conditions; (2) their consistency with other behavioral evidence, such as facial expressions, eye movements, or physiological measures; and (3) their consistency with specific theories about the mental processes that occur in the situation under consideration.

Substitution of inferences for observations.

A special type of error sometimes occurs when people are asked to do interpretive introspection, to explain the causes of their behavior or feelings. When people do not have direct introspective access to the stimuli or mental processes that caused their feelings or behavior, they may make plausible inferences, using whatever information is available. Such inferences are heavily influenced by people's *a priori* theories about the causes of human actions (Nisbett & Wilson 1977). For example, if you were to eat very rapidly, devouring a hamburger in four bites, and someone asked you "Why did you eat so fast?", you might reply "I was very hungry." In fact, you might have a habit of eating rapidly all of the time, regardless of how hungry you are. You don't know why you eat so rapidly, but it seems reasonable to attribute it to great hunger. (I'll go into more detail on the problem of introspective access to the causes of our actions, and the problem of substituting inferences for observations, in Chapter 7.)

Conclusion.   Psychologists have to keep in mind two aspects of introspective verbal reports. First, they are behavioral data, and all behaviors are influenced by a variety of causal factors. Second, they are attempts to accurately describe subjective experience. Numerous factors may prevent verbal reports from accurately or completely describing conscious experience. However, the topic of conscious experience is too interesting and important for it to be ignored merely because of difficulties in studying it.

METHODS OF OBTAINING INTROSPECTIVE REPORTS

Several methods of obtaining reports on conscious contents have been used in psychology research (Ericsson & Simon 1980; Klinger 1978). Each method has its good and bad points. Which method is best depends on the specific question under investigation. You will encounter research based on these methods throughout this book.

Thinking out loud.   In the thinking-out-loud method, subjects make a continuous verbal report on conscious contents while they are in a particular situation, for example, solving a chess problem, or relaxing with their eyes closed. The advantage is that the researcher can obtain a lot of detailed information about the stream of consciousness, with relatively little loss due to forgetting. The disadvantage is that both the introspection process and the verbal reporting may alter the flow of conscious experience. For example, the flow of your daydreams would be less spontaneous than normal if you had to describe them as they occurred (Pope 1978). The thinking-out-loud method has, however, been popular in research on thought processes that occur during problem solving. Ericsson and Simon (1980) argued that thinking out loud does not affect ongoing thought processes during which subjects can make a direct report of ongoing verbal thoughts. Thought processes may be slowed if people have to use words to describe nonverbal experiences, such as visual-mental images. Thought processes may be altered if people have to attend to information to which they would not ordinarily attend—for example, in trying to describe their thoughts step-by-step while solving a problem. In some cases thinking out loud actually improves performance on cognitive tasks, perhaps because it gets people to attend to relevant information that they might otherwise overlook.

Thought sampling.   In thought sampling, subjects are instructed that whenever a designated signal (such as a brief tone) occurs, they are to report what they were thinking at the moment that the signal occurred. Then they go about their activities in a (presumably) normal way until the signal occurs again at some unpredictable time. While thought sampling does not yield as much detailed information about the stream of consciousness as thinking out loud does, thought sampling causes less distortion of the normal progression of thoughts. Since the sampled thoughts are reported immediately after they occur, the reports come directly from short-term memory. Depending upon the purposes of the experiment, thought samples may be either brief verbal narrative descriptions, responses to brief questionnaires, or nonverbal responses (such as pushing a button to classify the thought into one of several prearranged categories). Thought sampling is used in laboratory research on dreaming, when experimenters periodically awaken subjects to obtain dream reports.

Retrospective reports.   Whereas the thinking-out-loud method and the thought-sampling method are used for studying the ongoing stream of consciousness, retrospective reports are used to collect data about thoughts that occurred on a specified previous occasion in reference to a specified previous event. For example, subjects might solve a problem that requires creative thinking, then afterward try to recall and report their thoughts that led to the solution. Or they might respond to particular stimuli (words, pictures), then later try to recall the thoughts that preceded their responses. Retrospective reports may be either verbal narratives or responses to prepared questionnaires.

The advantage of retrospective reporting is that it does not interfere with ongoing thought processes during the main task, particularly if subjects do not know in advance that they will be asked to make an introspective report. But forgetting may be a serious problem with the retrospective reporting method. This problem will be greater the more time that elapses before the report. Retrospective reporting may be especially susceptible to the problems of reconstruction errors and of substituting inferences for observations. In dream research, the retrospective reporting method is used when subjects record their dreams upon awakening in the morning.

Event recording.   Researchers and psychotherapists use event recording when they need to know how often a subject (or client) has a particular type of thought, but they do not need to know the full range of thought contents. In event recording, the subject notes each occurrence of the designated type of thought (such as anxiety or aggression thoughts). The thought events can be recorded in a notebook or on a tape recorder. Usually a brief notation of the time and place is sufficient; detailed reports are not usually required. In the laboratory subjects can report simple thought events by pushing buttons, with precise time records being kept automatically. Event recording is useful for tracing changes in the frequency of a particular type of thought. For example, a therapist might collect data about the frequency of anxiety thoughts before, during, and after a treatment program. Event recording has the advantage of reports being made from short-term memory rather than long-term memory, though subjects may sometimes forget to record pertinent thoughts. Knowing that one is supposed to report a certain type of thought may initially affect the frequency of such thoughts, though this problem will decrease after an adaptation period.

Diaries.   Diaries are written narrative reports on one's activities and thoughts, in which entries are made periodically over a period of several days, months, or years. Diaries can provide abundant useful information about individuals over a long period of time, for example, about the thought processes of creative thinkers. Diaries are necessarily very selective in what they report. Ordinary diaries may be quite unsystematic, especially when entries are made at irregular time intervals and express different types of thoughts and experiences on different occasions, depending on the individual's shifting interests and current concerns. Besides being selective and unsystematic, diaries are subject to the problems of forgetting and reconstruction errors. Because diaries consist of unsystematic reports made under uncontrolled conditions, they are not useful for rigorous testing of research hypotheses. However, a good feature of diaries is that they are open-ended; people are not constrained by a particular questionnaire format, so they can report anything that happens. Thus, for researchers, diaries can be valuable for showing the range of possibilities for human conscious experience, and they may be a rich source of ideas that can be tested with systematic research. The usefulness of diaries for systematic research, such as dream research, can be increased by teaching subjects to keep systematic diaries.

Group questionnaires.   With group questionnaires the purpose is to get a lot of data from a lot of people as quickly and cheaply as possible. Group questionnaires have been used, for example, to find out about the frequency of different types of contents in night dreams or daydreams. The questions are usually of the multiple-choice, true-false, or percentage-estimation types, that yield quantitative data that can be scored and analyzed by computers. (For example, about what percent of your daydreams are about sex? About financial problems? About acts of violence?) Questions are chosen on the basis of prior research and/or theoretical hypotheses. Group questionnaires are useful for comparing groups of people, based, for example, on gender or age or socioeconomic status. However, they have serious disadvantages, particularly the problem of forgetting. Also, they are closed rather than open, in the sense that people can give only responses that fit the question-and-response formats on the questionnaire. When they use questionnaires, researchers cannot discover anything that is totally different from the possibilities that they had anticipated.

THE PROCESS OF INTROSPECTION

Earlier I provisionally defined introspection as "looking within one's own mind and observing its contents." I pointed out that this is simply a metaphoric description of introspection. What is really going on during introspection?

What Introspection Is Not

It will be easier to explain what introspection is if we first consider what introspection is not (Lyons 1986). First, though introspection concerns conscious contents or experiences, *introspection is not equivalent merely to hav-*

ing conscious experiences. Recall the distinction between primary consciousness and reflective consciousness (Chapter 1). Introspection is an act of reflective consciousness. It attempts objectively to describe, identify, and interpret our primary conscious experiences. But *introspection does not deal with all conscious experiences*. Most primary conscious events are so fleeting that they are immediately forgotten and are not available for introspection. Introspection is not like a videotape replay of our conscious experiences. Introspection is selective, and it is limited by gaps and distortions of attention and memory.

Second, *introspection is not a sensory process*. There is no introspective organ that stands apart from consciousness and observes it. Unlike the sensory modes of vision, hearing, and so forth, introspection does not have any unique sensory qualities. Rather, though it can deal with the senses, it is mainly a matter of verbal thinking. Furthermore, to conceptualize introspection as a sensory-perceptual process is similar to the *homunculus fallacy*, that there is someone (a homunculus or little person) inside of your brain who observes your conscious experience and then reports it. The problem with the homunculus is that you then have to explain how the homunculus could observe your consciousness—so you end up with an infinite regression (a homunculus inside the homunculus, and so forth).

Third, *introspection is not a brain scanner*. A strict materialist- or identity-theory view of the mind/brain relationship says that mind and brain are one. Thus, it might be inferred that introspecting consciousness is really introspecting brain processes. Introspection has been equated with a specialized "brain scanner" that scans the parts of the brain that produce conscious experience (Armstrong 1968). But subjective conscious experience and objective neurophysiological observations are two different perspectives on the brain, and you cannot see one type of phenomenon from the opposite perspective. Introspective reports describe conscious experiences, not brain processes (Lyons 1986).

Fourth, *introspection is not simply the making of inferences about our mental states, based on our overt behavior*. From a behaviorist viewpoint, it has been claimed that an introspective report of a felt desire for something is really just an inference. A "desire" is nothing more than a tendency to do things that lead to certain goals (food, sex, achievement, and so on). We infer that there is a mental state—a "desire"—that produces our goal-oriented behavior. Though I do not deny that introspective reports are influenced by inferences, I argue that some conscious contents or experiences are immediately given and available to descriptive introspection, without inference. For example, desire has components of thoughts, images, and feelings, as well as behavior.

Fifth, *introspection is not direct inner observation*. This point is rather subtle, but important. Direct inner observation of ongoing thinking is impossible, according to the nineteenth-century French philosopher Auguste Comte. By analogy to the fact that you cannot directly see your own eye, Comte argued: "The thinker cannot divide himself into two, of whom one reasons whilst the other observes him reason. The organ observed and the organ observing being identical, how could observation take place?" (1830, pp. 34–37 cited in James 1890/1983, p. 188).

Franz Brentano (1874), an Italian-German psychologist, had a similar opinion. He distinguished between the ideas of *Selbstbeobachtung* (active self-observation) and *innere Wahrnehmung* (passive inner perception). (James characterized *Wahrnehmung* as "the immediate feltness of a feeling," [1890/1983, p. 189]. It apparently is the same as what I call primary consciousness.) Brentano argued against the possibility of active self-observation (*Selbstbeobachtung*). He said that we cannot directly observe our ongoing conscious experiences "because in doing so we would thereby draw away the attention necessary for the existence of the first-order mental life of thoughts, feelings, and volitions. To attempt direct inner observation therefore was *ipso facto* to diminish or destroy what one was attempting to observe" (Lyons 1986, p. 4).[4]

Now that we know what introspection is not, we are closer to understanding what it is.

What Introspection Is

Two principles are relevant to all types of introspection. First, introspection is a thought process—or a set of thought processes. It is an act of reflective consciousness. Introspection is, essentially, thinking about one's primary conscious experiences (including verbal thoughts, images, perceptions, feelings, intentions, and actions) for the purpose of describing and interpreting them. Introspection is not fundamentally different from other cases of descriptive and interpretive thought, except that the topic of introspection is one's own (primary) conscious experiences.[5] Second, the data of introspection come from memory. Strictly speaking, introspection is retrospection.

Descriptive (phenomenological) introspection is the most natural, straightforward type of introspection: the attempt to describe (to ourselves or to others) the contents of our stream of consciousness—our thoughts, feelings, and perceptions—without attempting to explain them or analyze them in any detail. Descriptive introspection is not a passive process—it is not the mere having of conscious experiences. Descriptive introspection is an active thought process, involving discriminating, classifying, and naming of experiences, and describing them, often with the help of metaphor or analogy.

The first problem for understanding descriptive introspection is to explain the nature and source of the data of introspection. In ordinary (non-introspective) thought, the data come from both ongoing perceptions and memory of past experiences and conceptual knowledge. The situation is more complicated for introspection. Introspection is about our own (primary) conscious experience, but as Comte and Brentano explained, we cannot directly observe our ongoing conscious experience because the attempt to observe it directly would modify or destroy it.

So where do the data of introspection come from, in order that we may introspect without interfering with the thoughts that are introspected? As James (1890/1983) argued, the data of introspection come from memory. *Introspection is really retrospection:* observing (that is, thinking about) our remembered past conscious experiences. Introspection deals with either immediately past experiences retrieved from short-term memory, or more distant past experiences retrieved from long-term (episodic) memory.

Questions about introspection as retrospection.   In cases where we are introspecting—thinking about—conscious experiences that were clearly in the past, there does not seem to be any problem in interpreting introspection as retrospection. But you may ask, "If introspection is really retrospection, why does it seem that I can introspect and report on my *current* conscious experiences, such as my current thoughts, feelings, and perceptions?" Three comments are pertinent here.

First, the act of introspection is not the same as the experience that is introspected. For example, thinking in order to solve a problem is not the same as introspectively thinking about the problem-solving thought process. Nor is feeling an emotion the same as introspecting it, trying to classify and describe it. Introspection involves a temporary change in attitude toward conscious events, one in which we attempt to think about them objectively (reflective consciousness), rather than experiencing them in a simple, direct, natural manner (primary consciousness).[6]

Second, the illusion that introspection occurs concurrently with the introspected primary conscious experience arises because in many cases primary experience remains more-or-less constant over a period of time. This can occur because the conditions that produce the primary experience remain relatively constant. Thus, we can alternate attention back and forth between introspection and primary experience. Finding that the primary experience remains unchanged each time we return to it, we have the impression that we are introspecting concurrently with the primary experience. For example, a feeling of pain or anxiety might remain unchanged as we alternate between the primary experience and introspective thoughts about it.[7] Each period of introspection is a retrospection of the immediately preceding moment of primary experience.[8]

Third, current perception—at least visual perception—seems to be an exception to the claim that introspection is retrospection. If you want to make a descriptive introspective report on your current conscious perceptions, you don't have to rely on memory; you can just keep your eyes open and describe what you see. Lyons (1986) argued that it is not appropriate to speak of introspection of ongoing perceptions. Nor are verbal descriptions of perceptions equivalent to introspective reports. For example, you might report "I see a train," but it would be redundant to say "I am experiencing the sight of a train."

We can try, however, to distinguish between perceptions and introspection of perceptions. Conscious sensory perceptions are about things in the world: recognized objects, sounds, and so forth. Introspection is about conscious experiences. According to the constructivist theory of perception, when we are describing something that we currently perceive in the world we are, strictly speaking, describing our conscious experience and not the object or scene itself. (The constructivist theory says that our perceptions are interpretations of sensory inputs, based on our past experiences, assumptions, and expectations [Best 1989; Neisser 1975].) But for most practical purposes we can take a naive realist view and accept descriptions of perceived objects as descriptions of the objects themselves. Probably nothing is to be gained by thinking of such descriptions as introspective reports.

It is appropriate, however, to speak of introspection of perceptions in certain cases: (1) Thoughts about ongoing perceptual experiences *as perceptual experiences* (in contrast to thoughts about the perceived objects) are introspective thoughts, for example, the attempts of the classical introspectionists to analyze perceptions into their sensory elements. Similarly, a painter analyzes a scene in terms of forms, colors, and light values. Of course, when you are in an analytic introspective attitude, you are not perceiving in a natural, naive way. [See Chapter 2, Endnote 2, on Gibson.] (2) Attempts to describe past perceptions, retrieved from memory, are cases of retrospective introspection. Describing what we saw and heard in the past involves more than simple memory retrieval: it also involves a large component of thinking, in which we must reconstruct our past experience based on the limited available data (Best 1989). More often than not, introspection of perceptions is concerned with past perceptual experiences—either immediately past (from STM) or in the more distant past (from episodic LTM)—not with ongoing perceptions.

Reconstruction and inference in introspection.   Conceiving of introspection as retrospection explains how we can describe our stream of consciousness without destroying it through the process of observing it. But accepting introspection as retrospection acknowledges that we can never give a completely detailed and perfectly accurate description of our conscious experiences. The data available for introspection are limited by: (1) incomplete storage, where selective processes determine which experiences are stored in short-term or long-term memory; (2) incomplete retrieval of stored information from memory; and (3) distortions when we try to reconstruct our experiences.

Memory research indicates that when people try to describe a past event (such as a story or personal experience) and their recall is incomplete, they will attempt to reconstruct the prior experience, making plausible inferences about what must have happened to fill in the gaps in memory and create a more orderly description. The same reconstruction processes occur when we try to describe our prior thoughts, feelings, and so forth. For example, in trying to describe our feelings in a situation involving personal failure, we might describe how we think we should feel, or how we have felt in typical, similar situations in the past, without necessarily recalling how we felt during the specific situation in question.

Likewise, interpretive introspection—in which we try to explain the causes of our thoughts, feelings and actions—is limited by our limited recall of pertinent antecedent events and thoughts. Interpretive introspection is often based more on inference than on memory, and it is heavily influenced by our prior beliefs about the causes of people's thoughts, feelings, and actions (Nisbett & Wilson 1977; Wilson & Stone 1985). (In Chapter 7, I will go into more detail on the role of inference processes in introspection.)

The bottom line is that introspection as a source of information about conscious experience is inherently restricted by limitations of memory storage and retrieval processes.[9] These problems can be reduced, but not necessarily eliminated, when introspective reports follow the primary experience very quickly, so that pertinent experiences can be retrieved from short-term rather than long-term memory. Descriptive and interpretive introspection are not fundamentally different from other cases of descriptive and interpretive thought. The main difficulty of introspection is the problem of obtaining accurate data about our conscious experiences from memory, and the problem of distinguishing accurate memories from plausible but possibly erroneous reconstructions.

CONCLUSION

Contrary to the beliefs of some earlier introspectionist philosophers and psychologists, introspection does not give us direct access to all mental events. At best, it gives us limited access to a limited aspect of mental life, namely, conscious experience. Fortunately, psychology is not limited to the introspective method for studying how the mind works. Psychologists have made considerable progress in understanding mental processes by making inferences from nonverbal behavior as well as nonintrospective verbal responses. Physiological responses, such as brain waves and evoked potentials, have also been useful. However, if we want to study conscious experience *per se*, then we must rely on introspective reports as one of our methods. Other measures, such as physiological responses and various nonverbal behaviors, are useful insofar as they have been validated by showing their correlation with introspective reports on conscious experience. For example, in Chapter 11 we will see that brain wave recordings are useful for studying consciousness in different sleep states, insofar as different brain wave patterns are correlated with different patterns of subjective experience as revealed in introspective reports (such as dream reports). Thus, if we are to study consciousness we must use introspection and introspective reports, and we must understand their potentials and their limitations.

We will encounter instances of introspection and introspective reporting throughout this book. In the next chapter we will see how Descartes used introspection to try to understand the relationship between the mind and the body, and drew conclusions with profound implications for psychology, philosophy, and religion. In Chapters 5 and 6 we will see how introspective reports have been used in research on the brain processes that underlie conscious experience, and we will discuss some of the evidence for the claim that many mental processes occur nonconsciously. Then in Chapter 7 we will discuss the question of whether we have introspective access to our higher mental processes and the causes of our actions. In later chapters, introspective reports will be critical for studying conscious experience during daydreaming, dreaming, hypnosis, meditation, and states induced by psychedelic drugs.

SUMMARY

Introspection was tentatively defined as looking into one's own mind and observing its contents, in other words, observing one's conscious experience. An introspective verbal report (IVR) is a description of one's conscious experience in words. Three types of introspection were distinguished: analytic, descriptive (phenomenological), and interpretive. Eight limitations on the accuracy of introspective verbal reports on conscious contents were discussed: (1) forgetting; (2) reconstruction errors; (3) verbal description difficulties; (4) distortion through observation; (5) censorship; (6) experimental demands (7) lack of independent verification; and (8) substitution of inferences for observations.

Six methods of obtaining introspective reports, and their particular limitations, were described: (1) thinking out loud; (2) thought sampling; (3) retrospective reports; (4) event recording; (5) diaries; and (6) group questionnaires. None of the methods is perfect; researchers must select the method that is best suited for the specific problem being investigated.

The question of what is really going on during introspection was discussed. Introspection is not literally "looking within" in a perceptual sense, nor can one directly observe one's ongoing thought processes. Rather, it was argued, introspection is a thought process—thinking about our (primary) conscious experiences—and the data of introspection come from memory. Thus, introspection is retrospection. Due to limitations of memory and errors of reconstruction and inference, introspection is inherently an imperfect method for studying conscious experience. Nonetheless, it is a critical method, so researchers need to learn about its potentials and its limitations.

ENDNOTES

[1]Does everyone introspect? To people who are in the habit of introspecting it may seem obvious that introspection is natural and that everyone does it. But this is not necessarily the case. Introspection is a sophisticated kind of thinking. We know little or nothing about the prevalence or nature of introspection in simple-minded people or in primitive people who have good practical intelligence but little interest in psychological questions. In a study involving extensive interviewing of subjects, Belenkey et al. (1986) found poorly developed capacities for introspection, reflective thought, and self-concept among some people from lower socioeconomic and educational levels. The authors attributed these underdeveloped capacities to negative social experiences in childhood and adulthood (such as being abused or ignored), and suggested that reflective thought could be enhanced through more positive social encounters.

[2]Attempts to suppress unwanted thoughts are only partly successful, and there may be a rebound of increased frequency of such thoughts after we stop trying to suppress them (Wegner et al. 1987). See Wegner (1989) for an interesting discussion of the psychological consequences of attempting to suppress unwanted thoughts.

[3]It should be clear that in talking about introspective observation, I do not mean observation in the sense of looking at something. Rather, I mean observation in the sense of "an act of recognizing and noting a fact or occurrence" (*Webster's Ninth New Collegiate Dictionary*).

[4]For more on the nineteenth-century psychologists' ideas about introspection, see Danziger (1980) or Leahey (1987); or see Fancher (1990) for a brief and entertaining account. See Lyons (1986) for a contemporary analysis.

[5]In Chapter 1 I said that introspection is an aspect of reflective consciousness. In fact, there is no clear distinction between the concepts of introspection and reflective consciousness. Both refer to thoughts about our own thoughts. The term "introspection" is used more commonly when reflective thought is intended to lead to an introspective verbal report for the purpose of psychological research or philosophical writing. "Reflection" (or "reflective thought" or "reflective consciousness") is used more commonly in regard to more private, informal ruminations. The processes of evaluating our thoughts and actions, and comparing them to a self concept, are aspects of reflective consciousness.

[6]Here and elsewhere, conscious "experience" is a somewhat problematic term, because the

word "experience" may seem to imply passiveness (like something that happens to us), whereas the term "conscious experience" is intended to cover active thinking and perceptual searching as well as more passive perceptions, feelings, and images. No entirely suitable English-language generic term exists to cover the full range of conscious contents, but it seems preferable to settle arbitrarily on a single term such as "experiences" rather than repeating each time a list of what is intended (perceptions, thoughts, feelings, and so forth). (William James struggled with this terminology problem, and settled on "thoughts" as a generic term, though "thoughts" has its own unintended connotations—it seems to stress intellectual activity over perception and feeling.)

[7]To say that the primary conscious experience continues more- or-less unchanged is not to say that the primary experience is not affected by the act of introspection. A primary conscious experience might well have been somewhat different if it had been allowed to flow without interruption by periods of introspection. For example, a spontaneous sensuous experience might be less spontaneous and sensuous if you introspect on what you are doing and feeling. But the point is that, given that the primary experience is being introspected, the experience-as-introspected may remain relatively unchanged through several cycles of alternation of introspection and primary experience.

[8]Peripheral awareness of current sensory perceptions (discussed in Chapter 1) can continue during introspection. For example, you might introspect on a recent emotional experience while you are driving a car with visual guidance. My argument is that focal attention alternates between primary consciousness and introspection; we cannot focally attend to both at the same time. But highly practiced actions such as driving a car can be carried out in a largely automatic manner; they require little focal attention, so there is little interference with introspection. Only under unfamiliar and difficult conditions (such as heavy traffic) when driving requires almost continuous focal attention is it likely to interfere with introspection—or vice versa.

[9]Natsoulas (1985) argued for a concept of "direct (reflective) consciousness," which involves direct observation or recall of conscious experiences, without reconstruction or inference. My argument is that reconstruction and inference processes are common in descriptive introspection (as well as interpretive introspection), and we have to be cautious about assuming that introspective reports are direct reports of directly observed or recalled conscious experience. Natsoulas's term, "direct (reflective) consciousness," can be confusing because "direct" sounds like what I call primary consciousness, but Natsoulas is really referring to pure (noninferential) reflective consciousness.

chapter 4 ••••••••••••••••••••••••••••

The Mind-Body Problem

Some of the most important questions concerning mind, brain, and consciousness had their origin in philosophy, but they are no longer the exclusive property of philosophy. Empirical and theoretical developments in psychology, the neurosciences, and artificial intelligence have a direct bearing on them.

What are the mind and body, and what is the relationship between them? Is mind a product of brain activity, able to exist only within a living brain? Or is mind some immaterial thing, perhaps spiritual and eternal? The *mind-body problem* has implications for one's fundamental beliefs about human nature and selfhood, as well as for the psychology of consciousness. A related issue, *reductionism,* concerns the question whether it is possible to explain mental phenomena in terms of neurophysiological events.

How can we determine whether another being is conscious? After all, we cannot directly see or feel another person's conscious experience. What if the other being is a child too young to talk, or an animal, or an intelligent robot? The problem of finding an objective criterion by which to recognize the presence of mind or consciousness is known as the *other-minds problem.* Its solution is tied to our understanding of the concept of consciousness, and the question of its place in science.

In this chapter I will review some of the major viewpoints on these controversial issues: the mind-body problem, reductionism, and the other-minds problem. Besides being interesting in their own right, these issues are directly related to some of the topics in the following chapters, particularly Chapters 5 and 6 on the brain and consciousness.

APPROACHES TO THE MIND-BODY PROBLEM

To attempt to solve the mind-body problem in detail, in all of its philosophical, psychological, and neurobiological aspects, is the most difficult and complex intellectual adventure of all. The problem may be unsolvable. The philosopher Schopenhauer called it the "world knot."

What are the essential natures of the mind and the body, and how do they relate to each other? In philosophers' terms, the mind-body problem is an *ontological problem*, that is, a question about what things really exist, and what their essential nature is. Some writers call it the "mind/brain" problem, since we now know that the brain is the part of the body that is most critical for mind, though there once was a time when people believed that the mind or soul was in the heart.

To begin with, let us grant that the body, including the brain, is made of material (physical) substance, complexly organized, and operating largely according to principles of cause and effect. I will dismiss as too mystical the notion that the world, including my body, is merely an idea in someone's (God's?) mind (*idealism*, or mentalistic monism).

The critical issue, then, is whether mind is produced by the material brain. Or is mind a product of some immaterial substance, capable of existing independently of the brain? And exactly how do mind and brain relate to each other, for example, do they operate in parallel, or are they identical, or do they interact—and if they interact, how do they do it? There are many specific theories on the mind-body problem, but they can all be classified into two broad categories: dualism and materialism.

Dualism is the belief that the mind and brain/body are made of different substances.[1] The brain is made of material substance, whereas the mind is made of some sort of immaterial or nonphysical substance. Dualism implies that the mind can exist independently of the brain. Dualism is consistent with most religions, in which mind is identified with the soul. If you believe in some sort of continuation of your mental life after the death of your body, then you are a dualist.

Materialism (materialist monism) is the belief that there is only one type of substance, namely material substance. Thus, mind and consciousness are functions of complexly organized matter, probably (but not necessarily) limited to organic brains. If your brain dies, your mind dies. Materialism is the viewpoint adopted by most scientists, although there are some noteworthy exceptions.

It could be argued that there are at least two mind-body problems, one concerning mind in the sense of the control of behavior by thought processes, and another concerning consciousness in the sense of subjective experience (Weimer 1976). This distinction was not made in most of the older philosophical discussions of the mind-body problem, since it was thought that mind and consciousness are synonymous. However, as Nagel (1979) suggested, "Without consciousness the mind-body problem would be much less

interesting. With consciousness it seems hopeless" (p. 166). I am more optimistic than Nagel, but I agree that consciousness makes the mind-body problem especially difficult.

There are at least five varieties of dualism, and a comparable number
of varieties of materialism (P. M. Churchland 1988). I will describe only a few
of the most influential viewpoints on the mind-body problem. But first I
must say a bit more about the importance of the problem.

Why the Mind-Body Problem Is Important

Science is concerned with discovering the principles of organization
and cause-and-effect relationships that govern natural phenomena. Only if
you adopt a materialist viewpoint can you be confident that a science of
mind is possible. If mind is dependent upon the physical brain, then it is
reasonable to assume that both behavior and mental phenomena, including
consciousness, operate according to some reasonably consistent general
principles that can be discovered by scientific methods. But if you adopt a
dualist viewpoint then there is no reason to believe that there are any general principles, or if there are, then you cannot assume that they will be dis-
coverable by scientific methods. If you adopt a compromise position, saying
that behavior is a function of the material brain but that consciousness is not,
then you have to settle for a limited psychology that does not even attempt to
answer questions about consciousness with scientific methods.

The materialist viewpoint is also valuable for clinicians—such as neu-
rologists, neuropsychologists, psychiatrists, and clinical psychologists—who
deal with abnormal mental functioning. The materialist view tells us that it is
reasonable to search for the causes of such abnormalities in the physical
world. The ancient theory of demonic possession has been replaced by concepts such as brain damage or dysfunction, inadequate learning experiences,
and psychologically stressful environments.

Finally, your stand on the mind-body problem is fundamental to your
view of what it means to be human. Are we entirely the creation of our biology and our culture, with intimate ties to the natural world because of our
origin in it? Or are we somehow fundamentally different and separate from
the natural world, due to the presence of some immaterial mind-soul? Will
our self-awareness die when our brain dies, or will it continue, immortal, in
some nonphysical realm?

DUALISM

The most important variety of dualism is *interactionist dualism*. Its best statement was made by the seventeenth-century French philosopher René
Descartes (1596–1650), and so it is often called *Cartesian dualism*.

Descartes asserted that the behavior of animals can be explained by assuming that they are merely complex reflex machines. If their behavior can
be explained in this way, then there is no reason to believe that animals have
mind or consciousness. However, Descartes believed that human behavior is
governed by rational thoughts, not reflexes. Rational thinking is a product of

mind, or soul, which is something entirely different from the material body. (Note that Descartes lived over two hundred years before Darwin published the theory of evolution and Freud published his psychoanalytic observations. Thus, Descartes was unaware of the evolutionary continuity between animal and human minds/brains, and he was unaware of the role of nonconscious and nonrational mental processes that influence human behavior.)

There were two reasons why Descartes believed in mind for humans but not for animals (P. M. Churchland 1988). First, there was the *argument from religion*. It was consistent with Descartes' Catholic religious beliefs to hold that humans have an immortal soul, and that the soul is responsible for our thoughts. Second, there was the *argument from introspection*. Descartes introspected on his conscious experience and came up with his famous dictum, *"Cogito, ergo sum"* ("I think, therefore I am"). What he meant was that he observed that he thinks, and therefore somebody must be doing the thinking. Thoughts seem to be immaterial phenomena. He could not conceive how his physical brain/body could be responsible for his thoughts. Therefore, he concluded that mental phenomena *cannot* be caused by mind/brain processes (*argument from irreducibility*), and so he attributed his thoughts to an immaterial entity, the soul. Furthermore, introspection led him to conclude that the actions of his physical body depended upon his mind's rational thoughts, and that the body's senses kept the mind informed of the body's actions. Mind and body are of different substance, but the different substances interact: hence, Cartesian dualism is *interactionist* dualism.

The German philosopher Leibniz (1646–1716) proposed *parallelist dualism* (also called psychophysical parallelism), the theory that an immaterial mind/soul has perceptions and ideas that are correlated in time with the body's actions, but that the mind/soul does not actually control the body. The parallelist dualism idea has never had many supporters, however, compared to interactionist dualism.

Critique of Cartesian dualism. Paul M. Churchland (1988) summarized several of the materialist arguments against dualism. First, there is the *principle of parsimony*, a fundamental principle of scientific theorizing which says that if two competing hypotheses are equally good at explaining a phenomenon, then we should choose the simpler one. Another version of the same principle is known as "Ockham's Razor," after the medieval philosopher who first stated it. Ockham said "Do not multiply entities beyond what is strictly necessary to explain the phenomena." By this rule, materialism is to be preferred because it postulates only one kind of substance (material), whereas dualism postulates two types (material and spiritual).

Dualism can be rejected prior to the application of Ockham's Razor because of its *explanatory impotence*. Dualism makes no attempt at a detailed explanation of how mind accomplishes things such as perception, memory, thinking, emotion, and control of the body's movements. Materialistic neuroscience, on the other hand, has made considerable progress toward an explanation. Though a detailed explanation of how the brain produces mental phenomena is not yet available, there is evidence that firmly supports the materialist viewpoint, namely, the fact that thinking and consciousness can be severely altered by brain damage and by drugs that affect the transmission of neural impulses in the brain. (I will be reviewing some of this evidence in later chapters.)

A major problem with interactionist dualism is that it cannot explain how an interaction between a nonphysical mind substance and material brain substance could occur. Something nonphysical could not produce a physical effect without violating the laws of conservation of mass, energy and momentum. For example, how could something nonphysical push or pull a physical object to make it move?

Dualism's strongest card is the *argument from introspection* combined with the *irreducibility argument*. Introspectively, the subjective qualities of our sensations (sensory "qualia"), emotional feelings, mental images, and the meaningful contents of our thoughts seem to be entirely different in kind from physical substance. Hence, dualists argue that it will forever be impossible reductively to explain mental phenomena in terms of physical, neurophysiological events. Churchland refuted the argument from introspection:

> The argument is deeply suspect, in that it assumes that our faculty of inner observation or introspection reveals things as they really are in their innermost nature. This assumption is suspect because we already know that our other forms of observation—sight, hearing, touch, and so on—do no such thing. The red surface of an apple does not *look* like a matrix of molecules reflecting photons at certain critical wavelengths, but that is what it is. The sound of a flute does not *sound* like a sinusoidal compression wave train in the atmosphere, but that is what it is. The warmth of the summer air does not *feel* like the mean kinetic energy of millions of tiny molecules, but that is what it is. If one's pains and hopes and beliefs do not *introspectively* seem like electrochemical states in a neural network, that may be only because our faculty of introspection, like our other senses, is not sufficiently penetrating to reveal such hidden details. Which is just what one would expect anyway. The argument from introspection is therefore entirely without force, unless we can somehow argue that the faculty of introspection is quite different from all other forms of observation (1988, p. 15).

To continue this argument by analogy, just as the eye cannot directly see what it itself is made of or how it works, the mind cannot directly perceive what it is made of or how it works. For the eye to see itself, it needs a mirror. For the mind to perceive itself it needs tools more complex than mirrors, such as the tools of brain science, neuropsychology, and experimental psychology. Introspection alone is not sufficient. With the argument from introspection defeated, the irreducibility argument loses most of its force. Whether mental phenomena are reducible to neurophysiological events is a matter to be decided by scientific research and clinical observations, not by *a priori* arguments.

Parapsychological Experiences: Evidence for Dualism?

Aside from the arguments from religion and introspection, is there any independent evidence to support a dualist viewpoint on the mind-body problem? The answer depends largely on your prior beliefs. Over the centuries, many people have claimed to have had *parapsychological experiences*—experiences that *seem* to be contrary to the laws of nature as understood by orthodox scientists (Irwin 1989). People have reported seeing apparitions (ghosts), having houses haunted by poltergeists (noisy ghosts), and communicating with dead loved ones through mediums (people supposedly able to make contact with the spiritual world). Some have claimed that they themselves are reincarnated souls and that they have memories of a prior life. Also, *psi experiences* (clairvoyance [extrasensory perception, ESP], telepathy, precognition, psychokinesis) have been reported by many people. For example, many people have reported that they somehow "knew" that a loved one had died at the moment of death, even though the loved one was far away and the death was unexpected. More mundane types of psi experience, such as remote perception (clairvoyance) of events such as the cards turned up in a randomly shuffled deck, have been studied experimentally by parapsychologists.

In the absence of ready explanations of parapsychological experiences by materialist scientists, some dualists have claimed such experiences as evidence in proof of some sort of *paranormal* processes or things, such as immaterial mind-stuff or souls, that have characteristics that are contrary to the physical world as we know it. In fact most scientists ignore claims for parapsychological experiences, dismissing them as either without adequate proof or, at worst, downright fraudulent (Moss & Butler 1978; Randi 1982). Admittedly, parapsychological experiences are so contrary to current materialist scientific beliefs about how the world works that most scientists do not want to spend time examining the evidence. The evidence that is available is highly controversial, at best. Whether people accept the available evidence as proof of the reality of paranormal phenomena depends largely on what they want to believe. If psi experiences represent genuine psi phenomena, then they cannot be explained by current materialist, scientific theories. On the other hand, dualist theory cannot explain psi phenomena, either. There is merely the assertion that, since these strange events cannot be explained by materialist theory, therefore by default they support dualism (Irwin 1989).

In recent years there has been increased attention to two types of parapsychological experiences, the out-of-body experience (OBE) and the near-death experience (NDE), that have been offered as evidence for a dualist viewpoint. Compared to psi and other parapsychological experiences, the OBE and NDE have been taken more seriously by scientists. Rather than disputing the reality of the subjective experiences, scientists have attempted to explain them in materialist terms.

In the *out-of-body experience* (OBE), the center of awareness appears to the individual to occupy temporarily a position that is spatially separate from his or her body (Irwin 1985, 1989). For example, while lying in bed you might have the experience of floating out of your body and then looking down on it from a place near the ceiling. It has been estimated that OBEs have occurred in about 8 to 15 percent of the general population. Estimates among college students are greater (20 percent or more), perhaps because college students are more willing to report such experiences. According to introspective verbal reports by OBEers, in about 80 percent of OBEs the things seen by the (allegedly) out-of-body consciousness appear to be naturalistic. Fantastic or transcendental experiences occur mainly in cases where the

OBE is a component of a near-death experience. In typical cases, OBEers say that their mental state during the OBE was one of relaxed alertness, mental clarity, effortless concentration, peacefulness, and emotional detachment. Some people claim to be able to control the content of their OBE experience by shifting their attention. If the OBE is truly what it subjectively seems to be—a separation of consciousness from the body—then it would support a dualist position on the mind-body problem. However, scientific explanations have been offered.

About 90 percent of OBEs occur while the individual is physically inactive, usually while lying down. Also, most OBEs occur under conditions of reduced sensory stimulation. This suggests that reduced attention to body senses (kinesthetic [movement] and proprioceptive [position]) may be an important condition for OBEs. Supporting this inference are reports that shifting attention to bodily processes brings the OBE to an end (Irwin 1989). It has been suggested that OBEs occur in the hypnagogic (drowsy, presleep) state, or in REM sleep, when vivid dreams occur. LaBerge (1985) found OBEs to be associated with lucid dreams—REM dreams where the dreamer is aware that he or she is dreaming. However, while some OBEs may occur in hypnagogic or sleep states, there are many exceptions. H. J. Irwin (1985) argued that the OBE depends on a combination of physical factors (relaxation, sensory deprivation) and cognitive factors (absorbed imagination, inattention to body processes). However, other factors may be involved when an OBE occurs in the context of a near-death experience.

The *near-death experience* (NDE) is a special sort of mystical experience that has been reported by many people who have narrowly escaped death. For example, NDEs have occurred in cases of people nearly killed by drowning, automobile accidents, or heart attacks, or during or after major surgery. Though not all NDEs are the same, Raymond Moody (1975) reported that most NDEs have some of the following characteristic features (cited in Irwin, 1989): (1) *Positive affect*, with feelings of peacefulness or joy; or simply emotional detachment, with freedom from fear or pain. This is the most common feature of NDEs, occurring in almost all cases (Ring 1980; Sabom 1982). (2) *Out-of-body experience*. For example, some people have reported that they could see their body, and the activities of people trying to revive them, from an objective viewpoint. Unfortunately there have been few attempts to verify the accuracy of these descriptions. OBE is one of the most common features of NDE; estimates of OBE in NDE range from 37 percent to 99 percent. (3) *Floating through a dark and empty space*, sometimes described as a tunnel. (4) *Emerging from the darkness into a realm of brilliant light*, which seems to signal entry into a nonphysical realm. The light has a reassuring quality. Sometimes it is experienced without first passing through darkness. (5) *Encountering some sort of "presence,"* described by Moody (1975) as a "being of light." The being's presence may be known intuitively, rather than sensed directly. Sometimes there is a discussion with the being over whether the individual is to die or return to the physical body. Encounters with a "presence" occur in about 40 percent of NDEs. Some studies (such as Ring 1980; Sabom 1982) have found that there is no relationship between experiencing the "presence" and the individual's prior religious beliefs. On the other hand, "it is feasible that even the most avowed atheist becomes an instant 'believer' when confronted with imminent death, if only for the duration of the threat to life" (Irwin 1989, p. 189). (6) *Panoramic life review,* involving a sequence of vivid visual images of events from the individual's life. The panoramic review occurs spontaneously, without any effort of recall by the individual. It occurs in about 25 percent or less of NDEs. (7) *Entering a transcendental (unearthly) realm,* usually described as a pastoral paradise with lush green grass, trees, beautiful flowers, and vivid colors. Some individuals report encountering the spirits of deceased loved ones, who reassure them. Interestingly, the transcendental realm in NDEs is rarely described as being like Biblical descriptions of heaven. In rare cases it is described as more like hell. The transcendental realm is estimated to occur in 20 to 54 percent of NDEs.

NDEs often have profound aftereffects on peoples' attitudes. Ring (1984) found that the NDE can serve as a "spiritual catalyst": core NDEers (people who had had profound NDEs) reported that afterward they felt closer to God, less materialistic, more appreciative of life and other people, more self-confident and secure, and that they had a greater belief in the underlying unity of all religions. NDEers reported a reduced fear of death, and an increased belief in some sort of afterlife. Furthermore, these attitude changes were not due merely to the close brush with death *per se.* Among people who had nearly died, the attitude changes were greater for those who had had an NDE than for those who had not had an NDE.

Near-death experiences would seem, on the surface, to provide strong support for the dualist view that consciousness can exist independently of the body and can survive the death of the body. However, alternative interpretations of NDEs have been offered by scientists who take a materialist viewpoint on the mind-body problem (Irwin 1989; Shaver 1986). NDEs may be hallucinations produced by physiological and/or psychological states that occur in near-death situations (Siegel 1980). *Hallucinations* are mental images, usually vivid, that occur spontaneously, without voluntary control by the individual, and that the individual interprets as real sensory perceptions. Hallucinations may be produced by oxygen deprivation (or equivalently, by an increase in carbon dioxide) in the brain, or by high fever. A sudden massive release of endorphins—morphine-like neurotransmitters that reduce pain and produce a sense of psychological well-being—could account for some aspects of NDEs. Some NDEs can be explained as hallucinations produced by surgical anesthetics or other drugs. NDE hallucinations might result from a general disinhibition of cerebral activity, or more specifically, from seizure-like discharges in the temporal-parietal region, which is involved in mental imagery and in the body image. None of these physical hypotheses accounts for all aspects of NDEs, though each is probably relevant to some cases of near-death experience. Psychological factors, such as fear of death and strong desire to survive, probably interact with physical factors to produce the NDE in many cases. Some aspects of hallucinations, such as a dark tunnel or a bright light, may be produced by physical factors, but the individual's interpretation of the experience depends on psychological factors. In general, NDEs can be explained as vivid hallucinations resulting from brain state changes that produce vivid mental images combined with a decreased ability to distinguish imagination from reality, where the specific nature of the imagery and/or its interpretation is influenced by psychological factors such as fears, desires, and memories associated with the near-death situation.

Logically, the availability of a naturalistic interpretation of NDEs does not disprove the dualistic interpretation, but it makes the dualistic interpretation unnecessary. It is worth noting that persons who reported the near-death experience *did not really die*. Thus, we have no first-hand reports of life after death. Some of the questions raised by the NDE may never be answered because it is impossible to do experimental research on this topic. Research ethics committees at universities and hospitals will not allow psychologists to cause research subjects to nearly die, so the NDE cannot be studied under controlled laboratory conditions. Meanwhile, acceptance of the naturalistic interpretation of NDEs does not prevent us from agreeing with Ring's idea (1984) that the NDE may be a critical, age-old source of spiritualistic religious beliefs.

VARIETIES OF MATERIALISM

The many varieties of materialism are united only by their assumption that mental phenomena are produced by organized physical substance. I will briefly summarize some of the most influential of the materialist viewpoints on the mind-body problem.

Epiphenomenalism

Epiphenomenalism is the view that consciousness exists, and that it is produced by the brain, but that it plays no role in controlling the actions of the body. (The notion that consciousness has no causal efficacy brings to mind Leibniz's parallelist dualism.)[2] The epiphenomenalist viewpoint was adopted by radical behaviorists in the 1920s. The behaviorists wanted to establish psychology as an empirical science that studies only objectively observable behavior, and not subjective mental states. "Behaviorism claims that consciousness is neither a definable nor a usable concept" (Watson 1924, p. 3). Since they did not know how to study mental events objectively, the behaviorists justified their ignoring of mental events by denying that mental events are important for controlling behavior. More recently B. F. Skinner (1971, 1974) restated the behaviorist viewpoint on mental events:

> We do not need to try to discover what personalities, states of mind, feelings, traits of character, plans, purposes, or other perquisites of autonomous man really are in order to get on with a scientific analysis of behavior.... We do feel certain states of our bodies associated with behavior. . . ; they are by-products and not to be mistaken for causes (Skinner 1971, pp. 13–14).

We will see that there are reasons to believe that conscious states are something more than mere useless by-products of brain processes.

Identity Theory

Identity theory says that *mind and brain are one*. Or to be more precise, for each unique mental state there is a corresponding brain state.[3] From this viewpoint *all* mental phenomena can, in principle, be reduced to specific brain phenomena. Hence, identity theory is sometimes called *reductive materialism* (P. M. Churchland 1988).

To identify mind with brain is to say that they are inseparable. They exist in the same time and space. We have the impression that they are different, and we describe them with different vocabularies, because we have two different perspectives—subjective and objective—on the same thing.

From the objective perspective, when we examine another person's brain (or our own brain, with our skull opened up, using a mirror) we see only a mass of tissue, and we do not see any mental processes. Even if we slice up a brain and look at it under a microscope, or measure its electrical activity with implanted electrodes, or measure its bloodflow with a PET scanner, we see only physical structures and events, not mental processes. We describe what we see in the language of neuroscience, using words like "neuron" and "synapse" and "neurotransmitter."

Subjectively, as intact living and functioning people, we know our brain from a different perspective. We perceive objects and we have mental images and verbal thoughts. These mental events are brain events perceived from the subjective viewpoint, and from that viewpoint they appear to be very different from neural events. Because mental events are phenomenally so different from objective neural events, we use a different vocabulary to describe mental events.

The identity theory is particularly popular among neuroscientists. The promise of identity theory is that ultimately it will be possible to translate all statements about mental states or processes into statements about brain states or processes. Insofar as this has not yet been accomplished, it must be admitted that the identity theory rests on a reductive materialist faith. This faith is sustained by the progress that neuroscience is making in understanding how the brain works.

What is the difference between identity theory and epiphenomenalism? If consciousness is identical to brain events, can it have any role in controlling behavior? D. L. Wilson (1978) gave an identity theorist's reply to epiphenomenalism:

> According to the identity theory, consciousness is both a brain process and an active force in the behavior of higher organisms. That active force can be viewed from the personal side, as the experiencing self does, or it can be viewed, in principle, by the neurophysiologist with implanted electrodes and so forth. This is not a dual-aspect position, but is merely two perspectives on the same brain events. Those who question why consciousness should have evolved and what survival value it has apart from brain events are assuming a dualistic view in order to attack a monistic position. Within an identity theory paradigm, to ask about the Darwinian survival value of consciousness is to ask about the survival value of the brain processes that *are* conscious events. Since these are likely the processes involved in situation-analysis and decision-making in the brain, their survival value is obvious. Furthermore, as the identification of mind with brain allows for a causal role of mental functions in human behavior, it allows for personal dignity, freedom of choice, and other humanistic attributes, despite opinion to the contrary (p. 13).

The main complaint against identity theory is the dualist argument from introspection and the irreducibility argument, which says that subjective experience is so different from brain processes that they could not be two aspects of the same thing. I have already presented Churchland's (1988, p. 15) refutation of the dualist argument.

Irving Kirsch (1985; Kirsch & Hyland 1987) proposed the principle of *causal isomorphism* to account for the relationships between mental events, neurophysiological events, and behavior. The main idea is that the causal relationships between two mental events are *functionally equivalent* to the causal relationships between the corresponding physiological events. The principle of causal isomorphism, according to Kirsch, rests on three related assumptions:

> (a) There is (in principle) a physiological counterpart to any instance of a mental event; (b) the relation between a mental event and its physiological substrate is better described as an identity relation than as a relation of cause and effect ... ; and (c) then for any causal sequence of mental events, there must be a corresponding sequence of physical events (Kirsch & Hyland 1987, pp. 421–22).

Point (b) deserves emphasis. According to identity theory it is not strictly correct to say that mental states are *produced by* physiological states; rather, mental states *are* physiological states, as they are subjectively experienced. Likewise, it is not strictly correct to say that mind and body *interact*, since such phrases suggest a dualist view that mind and body are separate and different things. Rather, physiological states interact with each other, and some of them correspond to mental states.

Figure 4.1 shows some diagrams that Kirsch and Hyland (1987) used to illustrate the principle of causal isomorphism. Figure 4.1A illustrates causal relationships in psychosomatic illness, in which mental states such as "feeling inadequate" are said to cause illness. But "feeling inadequate" corresponds to Brain State 1, which is part of the sequence of physiological events that leads to illness. Figure 4.1B illustrates an example of a drug placebo effect, in which a person is given an inert substance (a placebo) and told that it is a stimulant, with the result that he feels more tense. Strictly speaking, the placebo and instructions produce a brain state corresponding to expected arousal, and that brain state produces physiological responses (increased pulse rate, etc.) and a brain state that corresponds to a subjective feeling of tension. Figure 4.1C shows the events in an emotional reaction, in which perceived danger (such as the presence of a lion) is followed by feelings of fear. Strictly speaking, a brain state corresponding to "perceived danger" is part of a sequence of physiological events leading to increased pulse rate and other body and brain responses that corresponds to the feeling of fear. This sequence illustrates the important point that causal sequences of physiological events often include some nonconscious physiological events that do not correspond to any conscious mental state.

In conclusion, to reiterate Wilson's point (1978), to deny the adaptive significance of mental events is to deny the importance of the brain events to which they correspond. It *is* appropriate to develop theories about the causal

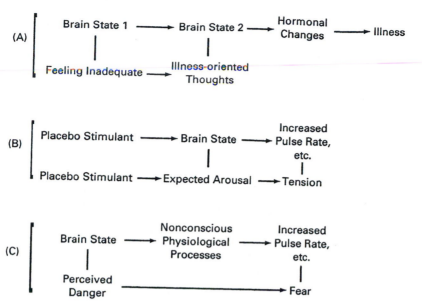

FIGURE 4.1   Examples of causal isomorphism between mental states and physical states. Functionally isomorphic mental and physical states are linked by vertical bars. Causal sequences are shown by horizontal arrows. (A) Psychosomatic illness. (B) Placebo effect. (C) Emotional reaction. [From Kirsch, I. & Hyland, M. E. (1987). How thoughts affect the body: A metatheoretical framework. *Journal of Mind and Behavior, 8,* 417–34. By permission of the publisher.]

efficacy of mental states, since mental states correspond to physiological states that have causal efficacy.

Emergent Interactionism

Roger Sperry (1969) argued that consciousness cannot be understood merely by analyzing the physiological and molecular processes of the brain. Rather, consciousness is an *emergent* phenomenon. An emergent phenomenon is one that appears as a result of a unique relationship among the parts of an organized system, and which cannot be predicted from a knowledge of the parts alone. Life itself is an emergent phenomenon: its characteristics cannot be predicted from a knowledge of the properties of organic molecules. Nor can the characteristics of complex organisms be predicted from a knowledge of their individual cells.

Sperry's emergent interactionism emphasizes the causal efficacy of consciousness as an emergent phenomenon:

Consciousness awareness, in the present view, is interpreted to be a dynamic emergent property of cerebral excitation. As such, conscious experience becomes inseparably tied to the material brain process with all its structural and physiological constraints. At the same time the conscious properties of brain excitation are conceived to be something distinct and special in their own right. They are 'different from and more than' the collected sum of the neurophysico-chemical events out of which they are built.

Compared to the elemental physiological and molecular properties, the conscious properties of the brain process are more molar and holistic in nature. They encompass and transcend the details of nerve impulse traffic in the cerebral networks. . . . It is the emergent dynamic properties of certain of these higher specialized cerebral processes that are interpreted to be the substance of consciousness. . . . The subjective mental phenomena are conceived to influence and to govern the flow of nerve impulse traffic by virtue of their encompassing emergent properties. . . . (Sperry 1969, pp. 533–34).

Some critics (such as Bindra 1970) have accused Sperry of being a dualist, since they interpret Sperry's hypothesis as implying that once consciousness emerges from cerebral excitation it has an autonomous existence and can act independently of the underlying neural organizations. In reply, Sperry (1970, 1980) argued that his position is both mentalist and materialist, but not dualist. Sperry's position is materialist in asserting that mental forces are identical with the holistic properties of cerebral excitation, and "in denying that these mental forces can exist apart from the brain process of which they are a direct property." It is mentalist "in accepting the existence of potent mental forces that transcend the material elements in cerebral function" (Sperry 1969, p. 534). Recently, Sperry (1987) reemphasized the importance of "downward control" of more elementary physiological brain processes by higher-level conscious mental processes, and suggested that downward control is a revolutionary scientific concept and a major reason for the renewed interest in consciousness in psychology and neuroscience.

There are three major differences between Sperry's emergent interactionism and identity theory (Sperry, 1976). First, identity theory argues that a reductive explanation of all mental processes in terms of brain processes is possible in principle. Sperry denies that reduction is possible, even in principle, in regard to higher-order, conscious mental processes. He was specific on this point:

The process of reducing an entity to its material components, physically or conceptually, inevitably destroys the space-time components at the affected level. . . . The spacing and timing of the parts with reference to one another largely determine the qualities and causal relations of the whole but the laws for the material components fail to include these space-time factors (1980, p. 203).

Second, Sperry draws a sharper distinction between conscious and nonconscious processes than identity theory does. There is more of a continuity between conscious and nonconscious processes in identity theory. Third, the concepts of interaction and emergent downward control are not used in identity theory, insofar as they imply that consciousness is something different than physiological brain processes. Of course, neuroscientist identity theorists acknowledge that the complex organization of the brain is critical for mental processes, including consciousness, and that hierarchically-organized control systems are important. But rather than saying that consciousness interacts with elementary brain processes, identity theory says that various brain processes interact with each other, and some of those processes are identical to conscious experiences. (See Natsoulas 1987 for a discussion of criticisms of Sperry's interactionism.)

Sperry has been heavily criticized by neurophysiologists for denying that a reductive explanation of mind in terms of brain is possible, in principle. But this very point has made Sperry's hypothesis popular among many psychologists. Most psychologists take a materialist viewpoint, in view of the obvious effects of drugs and brain damage on thinking and consciousness. But many psychologists do not believe that it is fruitful to try to develop detailed explanations of mental phenomena in terms of brain processes. Psychologists have proceeded to develop theories that try to explain learning, memory, thinking, emotion, consciousness, and behavior in terms of higher-level, psychological constructs, without paying much attention to neuroscientific evidence on how the brain works.

I must admit that I am torn between the identity theory and emergent interactionism. I lean toward the identity theory, since it seems to be more consistent with the notion that consciousness can exist in a variety of forms, and it is clear that some degree of mind-brain reductionism is possible, particularly in regards to the "lower-level" processes of sensation and motor control and some aspects of emotion. On the other hand, while I am in principle a materialist regarding the entire mind-body problem, I admit that the higher-level aspects of thinking, consciousness, and personality are so complex that it seems unlikely, as a practical matter, that they will be explained reductively in very much detail. There is still a very practical role for psychological theories, since they can explain mental processes in ways that are useful for education, psychotherapy, interpersonal relationships, self-understanding, and self-control.

Functionalism

According to modern functionalist theory, mental states have meaning only in a particular context. They are not independent entities. In this view, a mental state (a belief or feeling, for example) can be defined according to its *functional role* in a cause-and-effect network involving (a) stimulus inputs to the organism, (b) other mental states, and (c) the organism's actions (P. M. Churchland 1988). For example, the mental state of fear is elicited by certain objects (such as grizzly bears), and it serves the functional role of producing certain actions (such as running away or preparing to defend yourself).

Though functionalism is materialist, it is not particularly concerned with the microscopic details of the physical bases of mental processes. If the important thing about mental states is their functional role, then it does not make much difference what their physical basis is. Mind might be produced by either a brain or a computer, in the modern functionalist view. Thus, modern functionalism disagrees with the identity theory argument for *type physicalism*, in which all mental states correspond to specific neurophysiological brain states. Instead, functionalism supports a *token physicalism*, in which all functional mental states correspond to specific physical states in *some* physical system—but the physical system does not have to be an organic brain of the type that has evolved on Earth over the last 500 million years (Fodor 1981).

The token physicalism principle has made functionalism particularly popular among cognitive psychologists and artificial intelligence research-ers. Cognitive psychologists feel justified in developing theories about cogni-tive processes described in abstract terms, without worrying about their neu-rophysiological basis. Artificial intelligence (AI) researchers write computer programs to carry out the functional equivalent of mental processes—that is, to make the same kinds of decisions that a human mind could make. From the functionalist viewpoint, it is conceivable that computers (perhaps a fu-ture generation of parallel-processing computers) could have mental states, including consciousness. Mental states and processes must be produced by physical matter, but the important thing about them is what they do, not the type of physical substance that does it.

Fodor (1981) sees functionalism as a combination of the best ideas of identity theory and logical behaviorism. *Logical behaviorism* says that mental-ist terms have *implicit operational definitions*, that is, they can in principle be defined in terms of people's *dispositions* to behave in particular ways in par-ticular situations. For example, the mental state of pain can be defined in terms of people's dispositions to behave in certain ways in response to cer-tain types of stimuli, such as when they smash their toes against chair legs while walking barefoot across a room in the dark. But identity theory, unlike logical behaviorism, says that mental states (being identical to neurophysio-logical states) have causal efficacy in themselves. Functionalism combines the idea of implicit operational definitions of mental states with the idea that they have causal efficacy.

The main criticism of functionalism is that it does not account for sub-jective consciousness experience (such as sensory qualia and feelings). Func-tionalists argue that the exact nature of subjective experience is not impor-tant; what is important is the functional role that it plays in regulating the person's behavior. For example, consider the *inverted spectrum thought-experiment* (P. M. Churchland 1988). If we both see a light of 700 nm wave-length, and I have a subjective experience of "red" and you have a subjective experience equivalent to what I would call "blue," it does not make any prac-tical difference so long as you call it "red" and react to it in the same way that I react to a red light (hit the brakes!). And maybe Martians do not feel exactly the same way that we do when they stub their toes, but they still hop around on one foot and say bad words.

So far, OK. But functionalism's problem with conscious experience is more serious. There is the *absent qualia problem*. Modern functionalist theo-ries can get by with no subjective qualia all. In principle, twenty-second-century androids might have mental processes that would be functionally equivalent to those of humans, from an objective viewpoint, but the an-droids would not subjectively feel anything at all. They would be noncon-scious automatons. But humans are not nonconscious automatons. Con-sciousness is an intensely real aspect of our existence.

Another complaint against modern functionalism, with its emphasis on computer modeling of mental processes, is its assumption that all mental processes are computational processes (P. S. Churchland 1986). There is growing evidence that the computational model is inadequate to account for mental processes, including consciousness. Minds are like computers only in a very loose analogy, and the analogy cannot be carried very far toward understanding the mind/brain system. The "new wave" in cognitive theory is to design "connectionist" models of mental processes based on complex multiple and parallel connections between simple elements—models more like a brain than like a computer (Bechtel & Abrahamsen, 1991; Martindale 1991). If connectionist models succeed better than computer models of mental processes, the implication is that the token physicalism principle is wrong. The physical basis of mental processes is not arbitrary (Thagard 1986). Brains, or brain-like structures, are necessary to produce mind and consciousness.

REDUCTIONISM

The mind-body problem is intimately interwoven with the question of reductionism. Is it possible, in principle, to explain mind and consciousness in terms of neurophysiological processes in the brain? Dualism says no. Identity theory says yes. Emergent interactionism takes an intermediate position.

Dualism insists that the subjective "qualia" of experience are so totally different that it is inconceivable that they can be explained in neurophysiological terms. If we cut open a brain and examine it microscopically we cannot see anything that resembles subjective experience. Nor do chemical processes at neuron synapses resemble subjective experience.

Methodologically, the best that we can hope for is to find detailed *correlations* between specific subjective experiences and specific patterns of neural activity in the brain. Much progress has already been made in this direction. But we will not be able to observe anything that looks like a direct cause-and-effect relation. We will not be able actually to *see* that a specific neural action causes a specific subjective experience in a manner analogous, for example, to the way we can see that if we push a book over the edge of a desk then the book will fall to the floor. The problem is that we cannot see or feel another person's subjective experience. Thus, methodologically, it would seem to be impossible for empirical science to prove that conscious experience is caused by brain processes. Reductionism is not possible, in principle, by this argument. But the modern view of reductionism escapes from this methodological problem.

In the modern view, what is required is *intertheoretical reduction*. It must be possible to make a direct statement-by-statement translation between a psychological theory of mind and a neurophysiological theory of brain processes. If a psychological theory could explain everything about thinking and behavior in psychological terms, and a neurophysiological theory could explain everything in neurophysiological terms, and all statements in the psychological theory could be shown to correspond to statements in the neurophysiological theory, then the psychological theory would be successfully *reduced* to the neurophysiological theory. In principle, the neurophysiological theory would make the same predictions about behavior that the psychological theory would make.

An extreme modern view on the mind-body problem, *eliminative materialism*, says that intertheoretical reduction will not, and cannot, succeed (P. M. Churchland 1988; P. S. Churchland 1986). In particular, elminative materialism argues that folk psychology—popular conceptions of mind based on introspection and mentalist concepts (desire, belief, intention)—is inaccurate, misleading, and unsuitable for intertheoretical reduction. Nor are current formal psychological theories suitable candidates for reduction. Not only do they fail to provide a full account of thinking and behavior, but they are not expressed in terms that are suitable for translation into neurophysiological theory terms. Therefore, in the eliminative materialist view, psychological, and especially mentalist, concepts should be—and will be—eliminated as scientists learn more about the brain and develop better neurophysiological explanations of human behavior.

In reply, there are two points: First, eliminative materialism concentrates on neurophysiological explanations of behavior but it ignores conscious experience as something worthy of being explained. Thus, like behaviorism, eliminative materialism would eliminate a major aspect of human nature from scientific study. Second, it could be argued that intertheoretical reduction *might* be possible at some time in the future, if brain scientists and psychologists were more mutually aware of each other's work, and if neurophysiological and psychological theories were to evolve together (P. S. Churchland 1986; Hatfield 1988). However, intertheoretical reduction is more likely to succeed for relatively simple functions (such as early visual processing, motor control, classical conditioning) than for more complex ones (such as complex perception and learning, language, creative problem solving). In any case, it seems likely that psychological theories could be improved by taking neuroscientific findings into account. To that end, in the next two chapters I will discuss the brain and some neuropsychological research that has implications for understanding consciousness.

Thought Experiment:

Imagine that this is the twenty-third century and that you are a scientist doing field work on a distant planet. You have contracted to spend three years there studying the life cycles of the primitive life forms. You have been entirely without human companionship for a year. Then one day a supply spaceship arrives from Earth. The ship has a crew of one person, an exceptionally beautiful, witty, charming person of your preferred sex. You are immediately attracted to each other. You walk, you talk, you hold hands, you become lovers, and so forth. He/she agrees to stay with you for the next two years, and sends the supply ship back to Earth on autopilot. Your spirits soar, you have a renewed enthusiasm for work and for life, since you have a new companion and lover. Then one day, while exploring your beautiful lover's sleeping body, you find something that you hadn't noticed before. Lining the inside of his/her navel there is a silver ring, and imprinted on it are the words, "Made in Japan." Your lover is an android, a synthetic human! The question is, would you still accept this "person" as a conscious, feeling being, as you did before you discovered the ring? Why did you accept him/her as a conscious being in the first place? And would you still love him/her, after you discovered the ring?

THE OTHER-MINDS PROBLEM

The only conscious experience that we can ever directly know is our own. We cannot directly know the conscious experience of other adult humans, much less preverbal children or animals. How, then, can we know whether another being is conscious at all? This is the *other-minds problem*. It is one of the two main *epistemological* problems (having to do with the nature of knowledge) regarding mind, the other being the problem of how—and what—we can know about our own minds through introspection (P. M. Churchland 1988).

To clarify the problem we must ask what we mean by consciousness in regard to other minds. We can distinguish three aspects of conscious experience that are particularly relevant to the problem at hand: perceptual awareness, intelligent thought (particularly conceptual thought and volition—the flexible control of behavior by thought processes), and self-awareness. We can consider the other-minds problem in regard to each of these three aspects of consciousness. There are three main approaches to the other-minds problem: (1) the argument from analogy; (2) the argument from behavioral criteria; and (3) the argument from hypothetico-deductive theory.

The Argument from Analogy

We can never directly know another being's conscious experience. The best we can do is to *infer* that another being probably is conscious, and to infer the nature of its conscious experience, based on some sort of objective evidence. The practical problem is, on what basis can we make plausible inferences about consciousness in other beings?

The simplest solution is the argument from analogy: If one creature is known to be like another creature in *some* characteristics, then the first creature may be assumed to be like the second one in *other* closely related characteristics. (A corollary of the argument is that the more similar the creatures are in some characteristics, the more similar we would expect them to be in other characteristics, too.) For example, you know that you are a human being and that most of your behavior is accompanied by conscious experiences, such as perceptions, emotional reactions, and thinking in words or images. You observe that your friend has a human body, and that his or her behavior suggests emotional reactions of anger, fear, surprise, and joy in the same situations in which you would feel these reactions. Your friend also shows complex behaviors, such as speech, learning, and problem-solving abilities, that you know to be accompanied by conscious thought in your own case. Noting that your friend's appearance and behavior are in many ways similar to your own, you infer—by analogy—that your friend has conscious experiences similar to your own.

The argument from analogy seems reasonable if we limit it to cases in which there is a high degree of similarity between ourselves and another creature in both body and behavior. In a looser application it could be extended to children or animals. For example, I could argue that my cat, Farfel, is a conscious being as follows: Disregarding the form of the body and concentrating on the brain, and taking an identity theory approach that identifies mental processes with brain processes, I say that to the degree that there is a similarity of brain and behavior, there is likely to be a similarity of consciousness. Differences in brain and behavior imply not the absence of consciousness, but differences in consciousness. Thus, from my knowledge of cat brains and my observations of Farfel's behavior I infer that she is a conscious being, though a stupid one.

There are, however, some arguments against the argument from analogy (P. M. Churchland 1988). First, in inferring by analogy that another creature is conscious, I am trying to make an inductive generalization based on only a single case. I believe that there are certain relationships between my brain, behavior, and consciousness, and I assume that such relationships are true of all other creatures, too. Thus, I am ready to attribute consciousness to other beings whose brain and behavior are similar to mine. The problem is that I know only one consciousness, my own, and I might be wrong in assuming that my case of brain-behavior-consciousness relationships is typical. Conceivably, another creature might have a similar brain and behavior, but not be a conscious being. Perhaps it is a nonconscious automaton. Thus, it could be a mistake to infer consciousness in other beings based on their apparent similarity to myself. But what is the alternative? Perhaps *solipsism*, the belief that only one consciousness exists, namely my own. But solipsism is too arrogant a notion to be acceptable. It seems to me to be more reasonable and plausible to argue by analogy that some other beings are conscious.

Going beyond the inference *that* another being is conscious, the greater problem is to infer in any detail the *nature* of that being's conscious experience. The problem is greater, the greater the difference between that being and ourselves. Thus, a second argument against the argument from analogy is that we can reasonably infer in other minds only what we find in our own conscious experience. Presumably a color-blind person could not infer color perception in other people. In an essay titled "What Is It Like to Be a Bat?," Nagel (1979) argued that we *cannot* know, we cannot even imagine it, because bats are too different from us. However, inferences about consciousness in other beings need not be based entirely on direct analogies to our own experience. Using special instruments and behavioral tests, scientists have determined that bats can navigate by sonar, and that snakes can see infra-red wavelengths and bees can see ultra-violet, even though humans do not have those abilities. The analogy to our experience is looser here—at least we can hear echoes and see wavelengths in between infra-red and ultra- violet. This is not to deny that there are severe limits on our inferences about the nature of consciousness in other beings, but the limits may not be quite as severe as is sometimes supposed. In any case, an argument from analogy is still useful for inferring *that* another being is conscious.

The main problem with the argument from analogy is that it is too vague. It is generally applied informally to make plausible guesses about consciousness in other beings. Sometimes one sort of similarity to ourselves is emphasized, and sometimes another, depending on the situation and the creature at hand. Perhaps this is excusable, insofar as consciousness in other beings may bear only a loose family resemblance to our own. Just as children of the same parents may be similar to each other in some respects but not others—one pair having similar eyes and hair, another pair having similar -face shape—different creatures in the family of conscious beings may be similar to each other in some features of behavior and consciousness but not in others. However, in order to develop scientific theories of consciousness, it would be desirable to develop specific objective criteria for inferring consciousness that could be applied in every case.

The Argument from Behavioral Criteria

There is no general agreement among scientists about specific objective criteria for inferring consciousness in other beings, but two general approaches can be outlined: (1) introspective verbal reports, and (2) intelligent behavior. Both of these approaches involve inference by analogy, but they attempt to be more specific than the usual "argument from analogy."

Here, the distinction of three aspects of consciousness becomes more important. There is little problem in developing criteria to infer sensory-perceptual awareness. For example, operant conditioning procedures can be used to train animals like pigeons and cats and monkeys to make different responses in the presence of different stimuli. This implies basic sensory awareness. Further, operant methods have been used to train laboratory animals to recognize simple perceptual concepts, in which they have to distinguish the similarities between pictures that differ in their details (for example, recognizing pictures of humans, as distinct from pictures of various other animal species). When the animals respond correctly to new examples of a concept (such as a picture that they haven't seen before), it implies that they have learned the perceptual concept (see review in Roitblat 1987).

The problem of developing objective criteria is more acute for intelligent thought and self-awareness. Here I will be especially concerned with the problem of intelligent thought and self-awareness in intact humans and animals. (In the next chapter I will discuss the problem of intelligent consciousness and self-awareness in the nonspeaking disconnected right hemisphere in human split-brain patients.)

Introspective verbal reports.   The most widely accepted behavioral evidence for intelligent thought and self-awareness is the introspective verbal report (IVR): a verbal description of one's conscious experience. The IVR criterion comes from certain introspective observations, some assumptions, and an argument from analogy. First, I note (introspectively) that most of my conscious thoughts are verbal. Verbal thinking is a fundamental feature of consciousness as I know it. Therefore, I assume that *all* conscious creatures have verbal conscious thoughts. Second, I can make introspective verbal reports describing my conscious experiences. Not only can I describe my verbal thoughts, I can also describe—with varying degrees of accuracy—my nonverbal conscious experiences, such as things that I see and feel. I assume that all conscious creatures can make introspective verbal reports on their conscious experience. Therefore, a creature that cannot make an introspective verbal report is not conscious. Third, I assume that *only* a conscious being could make a verbal description of conscious experience. Therefore, if another being makes a verbal report that sounds like an introspective verbal report of conscious experience, I will accept that being as a conscious one.

Setting aside the problem of the limited accuracy of introspective verbal reports, by the IVR criterion we can accept adult humans, and also children with good verbal skills, as conscious beings.

Nonetheless, there are three problems with the IVR criterion of consciousness. First, it assumes that *only* conscious beings can make verbal reports that sound like reports of conscious experience. What if a cleverly programmed computer or android made such reports? Conceivably, a computer might someday answer even your trickiest questions about its conscious experience in a manner indistinguishable from the way a human would answer such questions. Logically, by the IVR criterion we would have to accept such a computer as a conscious being. This view is consistent with the functionalist approach to the mind-body problem, though anthropocentric (human-centered) bias will make it tough for computers to gain general acceptance as conscious beings.

A second and more serious problem for the IVR criterion is the assumption that *all* conscious beings can make introspective verbal reports. If we grant, temporarily, the assumption that verbal thinking is fundamental to consciousness, there is still the possibility that some beings might have verbal thoughts but be unable to make IVRs. For example, adults who have suffered strokes on the left side of their brain, making them *aphasic* (unable to speak), could not make IVRs. Nor could young children who have learned to talk but who cannot yet understand a request to describe their conscious experience, or who don't have a rich enough vocabulary and an understanding of metaphor to describe their thoughts. Both adult stroke victims and young children may do many things that make us suspect that they are conscious beings, but by the IVR criterion we could not accept them as conscious. An IVR advocate might try to solve this problem by saying that having the *potential* for someday making IVRs, or having had the ability to make them in the past, could be accepted as tentative evidence for consciousness, but such a solution is merely an escape from the problem of specifying a clear behavioral criterion for consciousness.

The third and most serious problem with the IVR criterion is its assumption that verbal thinking is a fundamental characteristic of consciousness in all conscious creatures. This anthropocentric view would deny, *a priori*, the possibility of consciousness in nonhuman animals and preverbal children. But there are other important aspects of consciousness besides verbal thought, and there is abundant evidence that thinking without words occurs in both humans and animals (Weiskrantz 1988b).

Intelligent behavior.   What behavioral criteria can we use as evidence for conscious thinking in beings that cannot make introspective verbal reports? Donald Griffin (1984) suggested as a general criterion "versatile adaptability of behavior to changing circumstances and challenges" (p. 37). To expand on Griffin's definition, intelligent behavior—behavior influenced by conscious thought—would be expected to show the following characteristics: (1) *Adaptiveness:* the behavior is suited to adaptive goals. It is appropriate to the organism's needs. (2) *Spontaneity:* actions are initiated autonomously by the organism, rather than being mere reflexive or conditioned responses to stimuli. (3) *Flexibility:* responses to stimuli change according to changing circumstances, rather than being mere inflexible habits. The organism can initiate appropriate actions in novel situations. (4) *Conceptual learning*: behavior is influenced by acquired knowledge (not necessarily verbal) that can be utilized in a variety of situations. Conscious thought is more than perceptual awareness; it can represent objects and events not currently present and use knowledge gained in past experience to deal with the present situation. (5) *Anticipation*: adaptive intelligent behavior suggests that the organism anticipates at least the short-term future. The ability of conscious thought to represent things not currently present can be extended to anticipation of future needs, actions, and events.

I am suggesting that an organism that is capable of conscious thinking will show these features in some of its behavior—not necessarily in all of its behavior. The fact that the flexible behavior of animals is sometimes maladaptive or stupid is not evidence against conscious thinking (Griffin 1984). We don't deny consciousness to humans who sometimes do stupid things. Also, the fact that some adaptive behaviors of animals can be explained as simple nonconscious instincts, reflexes, or conditioned responses is not evidence against the possibility that some animal behaviors are influenced by conscious thinking.

Griffin (1981, 1984) gave numerous examples of flexible, adaptive animal behaviors that suggest conscious thinking. It is beyond the scope of this book to go into any detail on this evidence, and I refer the interested reader to Griffin's books. But to list briefly just a few of his examples: optimal nesting-territory selection by marsh-dwelling redwing blackbirds; learning to open aluminum-foil milk bottle tops in England in the 1930s by two species of birds; cooperative group hunting by lions and hyenas; dam-building by beavers; tool-using, such as chimpanzees using sticks to extract termites from a mound, and sea otters using rocks to dislodge and crack open shellfish; and imitative learning in apes and porpoises and others. Most important of all is the abundant evidence for communication among many animals by gestures and cries; for example, they can signal threat, appeasement, invitation to mating, the location of food, and warnings about predators. "Because communicative behavior, especially among social animals, often seems to convey thoughts and feelings from one animal to another, it can tell us something about animal thinking" (Griffin 1984, p. 38).

Besides the naturalistic observations by ethologists, we can add the studies by psychologists who have taught apes to communicate by sign language (such as Gardner & Gardner 1969; Miles 1983; Terrace 1979). Chimpanzees, gorillas, and an orangutan have learned to make simple requests and answer simple questions by signs, and they have shown some degree of inventiveness in making new combinations of signs. Whether the communication accomplishments of apes really deserve to be called a language in the human sense—with novel ideas expressed in grammatically correct sentences—is a matter of controversy (see Terrace, Petitto, & Bever 1979). Nonetheless, the evidence from these studies strongly suggests that the apes are consciously thinking when they use sign language.

Griffin (1984) suggested that there would probably be a lot more evidence for conscious thinking in animals if ethologists had been looking for it in their field studies. But such evidence has often been ignored because most ethologists do not believe that animals are capable of conscious thinking. Ethologists and behavioral ecologists have tried to explain most natural animal behaviors in terms of blind instincts—behaviors programmed mainly through heredity rather than through specific learning experiences. Behaviorist comparative psychologists have tried to explain complex animal behaviors in terms of conditioned reflexes and chains of conditioned operant responses. Both groups of researchers have denied that animals do any conscious thinking.

Historically, the denial of animal consciousness derives from two ideas. The first is *anthropocentrism*, the belief that humans are the most significant beings in the universe, which carries with it the attitude that humans must be absolutely unique in some important way. The denial of the possibility of animal consciousness reflects the same sort of anthropocentric thinking that led to Descartes' dualist philosophy. The second is the principle of parsimony and the denial of anthropomorphism. In the early 1900s there was a reaction by scientists against some writers' over-indulgence in *anthropomorphism*, the attribution of human-like mental processes to animals. Attributing mental processes to animals was thought to be against the principle of parsimony (using the simplest explanation) when animal behavior could be explained in mechanistic terms. But as Griffin (1984) suggested, our increased knowledge of the complexity and flexibility of animal behaviors now makes it seem more parsimonious to suggest that at least some behaviors of some animals are controlled with the help of conscious thinking. The alternative—that animals are nonconscious automatons whose flexible behavior in changing circumstances is due entirely to genetic-preprogramming of behavior and/or complex conditioned-response chains—is becoming harder and harder to believe. Griffin went so far as to suggest that not only behaviors based on learning, but also those with a large hereditary or instinctive component may be accompanied by conscious awareness and thinking. He proposed a "cognitive ethology," a science of mental processes in animals. His proposal is highly controversial among animal behavior researchers, but it is consistent with the liberal attitude toward consciousness that I am advocating in this book (see Griffin 1978 and accompanying commentaries).

Self-awareness.   Earlier I defined self-awareness in terms of an awareness of one's individuality and having a self-concept, including knowledge of one's appearance, one's abilities, and one's personal history. It would seem that a conscious animal must be aware that most of its actions are undertaken to serve its own needs. However, it is hard to conceive what sort of specific evidence might indicate that an animal had self-awareness. Griffin (1984) cited some evidence for a rudimentary self-awareness in some animals, limited to awareness of its own physical appearance, and knowledge of how it appears to others. For example, it has been suggested that a predator's attempt to conceal its body behind bushes as it sneaks up on prey suggests some degree of self-awareness, as does the prey's attempt at self-concealment. Gallup (1977) showed that chimpanzees can learn to recognize themselves in mirrors. He first let the chimpanzees become familiar with their own mirror image, then he marked their faces with rouge while they were under anesthesia. The chimps subsequently showed startled reactions when they recognized their altered appearance in the mirror. Other attempts to show mirror self-recognition in animals have been unsuccessful more often than not, though it is not clear whether the failures were due to methodological problems or the animals' limitations. In any case, mirror self-recognition is an unnatural task, and it is conceivable that some animals might have a rudimentary self-awareness without necessarily being capable of mirror self-recognition. On the other hand, it seems likely that a well-developed self-concept depends critically on reflective-awareness and linguistic thinking—capacities well-developed in humans, but little or none in even the most intelligent of nonhuman animals. In any case, the problem of finding a satisfactory objective criterion for self-awareness in the absence of introspective verbal reports remains unsolved.

The Argument from Hypothetico-Deductive Theory

A third approach to the other-minds problem is to use conscious mental states (beliefs, feelings, volition, and so forth) as hypothetical explanatory constructs in a theory about how the mind works. From theoretical assumptions about how the hypothetical mental states work, deductions can be made to predict the organism's behavior. To the extent that the predictions about the organism's behavior are successful, it suggests that the organism has the mental states specified by the theory.

P. M. Churchland (1988) argued that this is exactly what we do in "folk psychology" theories, that is, our everyday assumptions that we use to explain why people do what they do, and to predict what they will do next. For example, I believe that when people are insulted they feel angry, and they are likely to retaliate if they think they can get away with it. Folk psychological theory is useful. For example, it leads me to predict that if I insult my boss, then he will retaliate against me. Bandura (1986) developed a formal social-cognitive theory that uses mental states as constructs to explain human behavior. Formal psychological theories are more successful than folk psychology theories at predicting human behavior.

In principle, one could develop mentalist theories to explain the behavior of nonhuman animals, such as dogs, horses, and chimpanzees. The rules of the game are the same as for mentalist theories of human behavior. You would describe certain mental states and processes and explain how they interact with each other and with the immediate situation to produce the animal's behavior. The animal's hypothetical mental states might be quite different from those of humans. To the extent that the theory succeeded in predicting the animal's behavior, the argument for the existence of the hypothetical mental states would be supported. The argument from hypothetico-deductive theory does not depend upon introspection or an argument from analogy. Though people sometimes apply informal, folk psychology theories to familiar animals, psychologists have not developed elaborate mentalist theories for animals because they are not convinced that such theories would be any better than the mechanistic theories of behaviorism. It remains to be seen whether this attitude will change, in view of the renewed interest in cognitive processes in animals (Burghardt 1985).

Concluding Comment

The other-minds problem is difficult, but it will not disappear. People who live or work closely with animals recognize that apes and horses, dogs and cats, are conscious beings, though their consciousness is very different from our own. I would argue that our recognition of consciousness in other beings is not a mere projection of human-like attributes onto unconscious automatons. Rather we, as conscious beings, can *intuitively* infer consciousness in other conscious beings. Future theoretical and methodological developments will lead to the development of more objective, scientifically acceptable means of recognizing consciousness in other beings. Progress on this topic might be aided by a better understanding of intuitive inference processes.

In the next chapter we will encounter a special case of the other-minds problem, the question of dual consciousness in split-brain patients. How can we determine whether the nonspeaking, disconnected right hemisphere is conscious in its own right, independently of the speaking left hemisphere?

SUMMARY

The *mind-body problem* asks what is the relationship between the mind (or consciousness) and the body (or brain). The two major positions are dualism and materialism. *Interactionist dualism* (Cartesian dualism) holds that mind and body are made of different substances: the body is material but the mind is some immaterial soul stuff, and the mind interacts with the body to control human behavior. Parapsychological phenomena (clairvoyance, telepathy, precognition) have been offered in support for dualism, but their reality status is a matter of controversy. Out-of-body and near-death experiences have also been offered in support of dualism, but alternative, naturalistic explanations of these experiences are available. Dualism's strongest card is the argument from introspection combined with the irreducibility argument: introspectively it seems that conscious experience is quite different from brain processes, and therefore consciousness cannot be a product of brain processes. But introspection is limited; it cannot reveal the true nature of things.

Materialism is the view that mind and body are inseparable: mental events are produced by brain events. Four varieties of materialism were discussed. *Epiphenomenalism* is the view that consciousness is a side-effect of brain activity but it has no role in controlling behavior. *Identity theory* says that mental events are identical with brain events; they are different viewpoints on the same events. For each mental event there is a corresponding brain event. The principle of causal isomorphism says that the causal relationships between successive mental events are functionally equivalent to the causal relationships between corresponding physical (brain) events. Mental events have causal efficacy in that they are identical with brain events that have causal efficacy. *Emergent interactionism* is the hypothesis that consciousness is an emergent phenomenon: it is produced by brain processes, but it has holistic properties of its own and it exerts downward control on brain processes. Emergent interactionism differs from identity theory by claiming that consciousness cannot be fully understood by reductionist analysis of brain processes; its holistic or field properties must be considered. *Functionalism* is the view that the functional characteristics of mental processes (what they do) is their critical feature, and it doesn't make any difference whether the physical substrate is a brain or a computer.

The *other-minds problem* is the question of how we can recognize consciousness in other beings. Three approaches were discussed. The *argument from analogy* says that we infer consciousness from similarities of structure and function between other beings and ourselves. The closely related *argument from behavioral criteria* requires that specific behavioral criteria for consciousness be developed. Introspective verbal reports on conscious experience are widely accepted as evidence of consciousness, but they are limited to adult humans and verbally skilled children. Several signs of intelligent behavior were suggested as a criterion for recognizing consciousness in animals. These criteria are controversial because some scientists argue that "intelligent" behaviors might be produced without consciousness. Finally, the *argument from hypothetico-deductive theory* suggests that we develop mentalist theories to explain behavior. When a theory successfully predicts behavior then the argument for the actual existence of the mental processes specified by the theory is supported.

ENDNOTES

[1]To be more precise, I am talking here about *substance* dualism. Another type of dualism is *property* dualism, the view that while there is only one type of substance (physical substance), the brain has special properties (mental properties) that are possessed by no other type of physical object. In property dualism it is assumed that mental properties, such as conscious sensations, thoughts, and feelings, cannot be reduced to or explained solely in terms of the physical properties of the brain (P. M. Churchland 1988).

[2]Epiphenomenalism is sometimes classified as a type of *property* dualism (see endnote 1) because of its claim that while consciousness is produced by the brain, it has the special property—unlike other brain events—of playing no further role in the cause-and-effect processes of the brain. However, I classify epiphenomenalism as a variety of materialism because of my emphasis on the source (or substance) of consciousness, where epiphenomenalism acknowledges that consciousness is a product of brain activity and cannot exist without the brain. Epiphenomenalism has a closer kinship with the materialist identity theory than it does with Cartesian dualism.

[3]By "mental state" or "conscious state" I mean here the relevant set of conscious contents at a particular moment, including percepts, feelings, inner speech, and so on.

chapter 5 ·····································

Brain and Consciousness I: Split-Brain Research

Today, no one, psychologist, philosopher, neurologist, or humanist, is entitled
to an opinion on the mind-body question if he is unfamiliar with the split-brain
procedure and its results in human patients (Hebb 1974, p. 76).

The fundamental assumption of the materialist viewpoint on the mind-body
problem is that mind and consciousness are functions of the brain. The ultimate promise of neuroscience is to explain how the brain produces the
whole range of human mental processes: perception, memory, language,
thinking, emotion, control of action, and last but not least, subjective consciousness. Cognitive neuroscience is still a long way from explaining mental
processes in detail, but dramatic progress has been made in the last twenty
years (see Ellis & Young 1988; Gazzaniga 1984). It is beyond the scope of this
book to go into any detail on neuroscience research. However, in this chapter and the next I will discuss some neuropsychology research that is particularly relevant to the mind-body problem and questions of the nature of
consciousness, including the question of conscious unity.

No neuropsychological research has caught the attention of psychologists, philosophers, and the general public so much as the "split-brain"
research. It has stimulated hundreds of studies of hemispheric specialization
in normal people as well as in split-brain patients (Springer & Deutsch 1985).
It has led to speculations about the bimodal nature of consciousness (Ornstein 1977) and the possibility of dual-consciousness: two separate, independent centers of consciousness, one in each cerebral hemisphere. In 1981

Roger Sperry won the Nobel Prize for his pioneering research on the psychological effects of split-brain surgery.

As background to the discussion of neuropsychological research in this chapter and the next, I will begin this chapter with a brief description of the organization of the brain, for the benefit of readers who need a review of this topic. Then I will selectively review some of the split-brain research, beginning with a discussion of the rationale for split-brain surgery, and its typical effects on psychological test performance. Next I will take up the question of dual-consciousness. Then I will discuss split-brain evidence for specialized cognitive modules in the brain, which has implications for the nature of consciousness and the question of conscious unity. Finally, I will comment on the exaggerations and unjustified conclusions that some people have derived from split-brain research.

A BRIEF OVERVIEW OF BRAIN ORGANIZATION

In this section I will briefly describe the organization of the human nervous system and brain, emphasizing the cerebral cortex because it is particularly important for higher cognitive functions and consciousness in humans.

The nervous system is divided into two main parts: (1) The *central nervous system* (CNS), which includes the brain and the spinal cord. (2) The *peripheral nervous system*, which carries messages to and from the CNS. The peripheral nervous system includes: (a) The *somatic system*, which controls skeletal muscles and relays sensory messages about touch, pressure, pain, temperature, and muscle movement to the CNS. Also, the *cranial nerves* relay sensory messages (such as vision and hearing) and control muscle movements (such as speech) in the head and neck region. (b) The *autonomic system*, which controls the glands and energy organs such as the heart, blood vessels, lungs, and intestines. The autonomic system is divided into the *sympathetic* branch, which expends energy (as in emotional arousal), and the *parasympathetic* branch, which accumulates and conserves energy (as in relaxation and digestion).

The brain consists of three major divisions: the central core, the limbic system, and the cerebrum. The *central core* is the oldest part of the brain in evolutionary terms, being basically similar in humans, other mammals, and reptiles. Its parts include the brain stem (medulla and pons), cerebellum, thalamus, and hypothalamus. Figure 5.1 shows the location of these structures and their functions. In general, the central core controls basic body functions (such as heartbeat [medulla] and metabolism [hypothalamus]) and coordinated movements (such as walking [cerebellum]). The central core also includes the reticular system, which is a network of neurons that extends through the brainstem and thalamus, and is responsible for regulating the brain's level of arousal (as in the sleep-wakefulness cycle, and alertness to incoming stimuli).

The *limbic system* wraps around the central core and lies between it and the cerebrum. ("Limbic" means border.) Its main structures include the hippocampus, which is critical for memory storage and retrieval processes, and

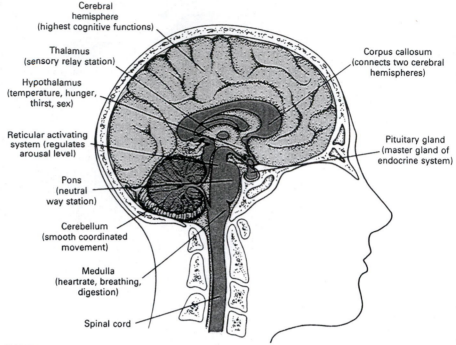

FIGURE 5.1. Cross section of the human brain, showing the locations of subcortical structures. [From Darley, J. M., Glucksberg, S., & Kinchla, R. A. (1991). *Psychology* (5th ed.). Englewood Cliffs, NJ: Prentice Hall. Adapted by permission of the publisher.]

the amygdala, which is important for both memory and emotional behavior (such as aggression).

The *cerebrum* is divided into two *cerebral hemispheres*, left and right, which are connected to each other via a bundle of neurons called the *corpus callosum*. The cerebrum's surface, the *cerebral cortex*, is responsible for higher mental functions. The cortex is about three millimeters thick, and consists of four to six layers of *neurons* (nerve cells) that interconnect both vertically and horizontally.[1]

The cerebral cortex.   Figure 5.2 shows a left-side view of the cerebral cortex, including the four cortical lobes: frontal, temporal, occipital, and parietal. The cortex covers the brain somewhat like a football helmet covers a head. But the surface area of the cortex is much greater than that of a football helmet, because of the way the cortex is wrinkled and folded in on itself. The ridges of the cortex are called *gyri* (singular, gyrus), while the valleys in between the ridges are called *sulci* (singular, sulcus), and the deeper valleys that mark off the cortical lobes are called *fissures*.

Areas of the cortex are classified as primary sensory-motor areas or as association areas. *Primary sensory areas* do the first stages of analysis of incoming stimuli in the various sensory modalities. The primary sensory areas include the primary visual cortex (at the back of the occipital lobes), the primary auditory cortex (in the temporal lobes, mostly hidden from view inside

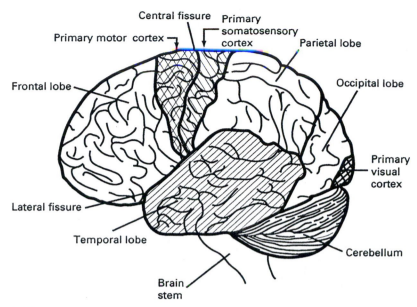

FIGURE 5.2.   Side view of the cerebral cortex, showing the four lobes. Primary motor cortex is at the back of the frontal lobe; somatosensory cortex is at the front of the parietal lobe. The cerebellum is part of the central core.

the lateral fissure), and the primary somatosensory cortex, which feels the skin senses (touch, pressure, pain, temperature), and is located in the parietal lobes, just behind the central fissure. Damage to primary sensory areas can cause sensory losses. For example, damage to the primary visual cortex (striate cortex) can cause cortical blindness, even though the patient's eyes function normally. (In the next chapter I will discuss "blindsight," in which some cortically-blind patients can respond correctly to visual stimuli that they do not consciously see.) *Primary motor cortex* (in the frontal lobes, just in front of the central fissure) is responsible for controlling movements of the skeletal muscles to carry out actions programmed in the frontal lobes.

Cortical areas outside the primary sensory-motor areas are called *association cortex* because they associate stimuli from various modalities with each other, associate stimuli with memories and memories with each other, and generally carry out higher-level cognitive functions such as complex perception, thinking, memory, and control of actions.

Though the cerebral hemispheres look symmetrical, the left and right sides have different functions, particularly in the temporal and parietal lobes. Both *temporal lobes* are important for memory storage—particularly, episodic and semantic memory storage—working in conjunction with limbic system structures (hippocampus and amygdala). Bilateral (both sides) damage of the temporal lobes can cause *amnesia*, disruption of memory functions. The left temporal lobe is responsible for language understanding and production and it is slightly thicker than the right temporal lobe in humans. Damage to the left temporal lobe can cause various types of *aphasia*, disruptions of language functions. Because of the importance of language for thinking and communication, the left hemisphere is often called the *dominant hemisphere*.[2]

The *occipital lobes* process visual information, starting with elementary visual analysis in the primary visual cortex, and proceeding to more complex analysis and object perception in more anterior (forward) areas of the occipital lobes and adjacent areas of the parietal lobes. Damage to the occipital-parietal lobe area can cause *visual agnosia*, in which patients cannot recognize objects that they see.[3]

The *parietal lobes* are important for recognition of objects and for integration of information from different sensory modalities (for example, to compare what you are seeing with what you are touching). The left parietal lobe is especially important for naming objects, whereas the right is important for spatial perception functions, including the spatial relationships between objects, navigating in space, recognizing objects seen from unusual angles (such as a bucket seen from the top), and aiming movements. (Don't ever play darts with someone who has parietal lobe damage!) The left parietal lobe is important for short-term memory of verbal information, whereas the right is involved in short-term memory for nonverbal information (such as the locations of objects; see Kolb & Whishaw 1990).

The *frontal lobes* are critical for formulating plans for reaching goals, regulating the sequence of actions, inhibiting inappropriate responses, and programming specific sequences of coordinated movements. Damage to the frontal lobes can disrupt the ability to plan and carry out voluntary actions, and produce inflexible and perseverative behavior that fails to meet the requirements of the situation at hand. The frontal lobes, through their connections with the limbic system, are also important for regulating emotional behavior and aspects of personality organization (Kolb & Whishaw 1990; Luria 1973).

Contralateral organization.   The cortex is organized according to the principle of contralateral organization, in which the left hemisphere analyzes stimuli and controls actions of the right side of the body, and the right hemisphere does the same for the left side of the body (see Figure 5.3). The left *somatosensory cortex* receives and analyzes skin sense and kinesthetic (muscle sense) information from the right side of the body; and vice versa. The left *motor cortex* controls voluntary movements of the right side of the body, such as the right hand and foot; and vice versa. A stroke, in which breaking or blocking of an artery on one side of the brain causes brain cells to die, usually causes partial paralysis on the contralateral side of the body.

Contralateral organization also applies to the senses of hearing and vision. The left primary auditory cortex has better neural connections with the right ear than with the left ear. Thus, the left hemisphere hears better from the right ear than the left ear; and vice versa. Contralateral organization for vision is more complex. The general principle is that the left occipital cortex sees the *right visual field* (RVF)—the area to the right of the *fixation point*—and the right occipital cortex sees the LVF. Figure 5.3 explains how this happens.

Normally sensory information and thoughts are shared between the

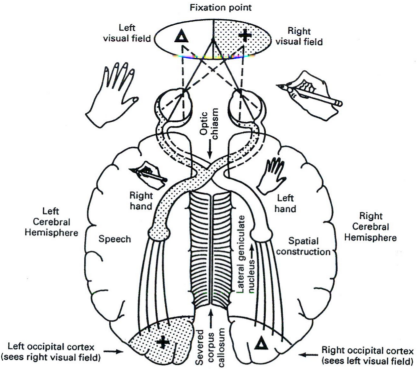

FIGURE 5.3. Sensory inputs to the two cerebral hemispheres in the split-brain patient. In accordance with the principle of *contralateral organization*, the left hemisphere controls movements and receives skin sensations from the right side of the body; and vice versa. The left hemisphere sees the right visual field (RVF) because light from the RVF falls on the left side of the retina of each eye, which connects to the primary visual area of the left occipital cortex via the optic nerves and the left lateral geniculate nucleus (a sensory relay station in the thalamus); and vice versa for the right hemisphere. [Adapted from Sperry, R. W. (1968). Hemisphere deconnection and unity in conscious awareness. *American Psychologist, 23,* 723–33. Copyright 1968 by the American Psychological Association. Adapted by permission.]

two hemispheres via the *corpus callosum,* the "great cerebral commissure." The corpus callosum is the largest fiber tract in the human brain, with over 200 million neurons. For the most part, the callosum connects *homotopic* or corresponding points between left and right frontal, parietal, and occipital lobes, and part of the temporal lobes, though there are also many instances where a point in one hemisphere connects to a point that is not exactly homotopic in the opposite hemisphere. A smaller left-right commissure, called the *anterior commissure* (not shown in Figure 5.3) connects portions of the anterior temporal lobes and also the *amygdala,* a limbic-system structure that plays roles in memory and emotional behavior. Any direct sensory input to one hemisphere can be transmitted almost immediately to the opposite hemisphere when both the corpus callosum and the anterior commissure are intact. But as we will see, when the commissures are cut, as in split-brain surgery, then sensory inputs and thoughts cannot be transmitted directly from one hemisphere to the other.

SPLIT-BRAIN RESEARCH

The effects of *commissurotomy*—surgical transection (cutting) of the corpus callosum—have been studied in both animal and human subjects. In the 1950s Roger Sperry and Ronald Myers did experimental research with cats and monkeys that proved that the corpus callosum is critical for communicating information between the left and right cerebral hemispheres (Sperry 1964). They showed, for example, that if a "split-brain" (commissurotomized) monkey's left hemisphere was trained on a visual discrimination task (choosing a triangle instead of a circle in order to get a food reward), then the right hemisphere did not know what the left hemisphere had learned.[4] Commissurotomy did not, however, have any harmful effects on the animal's functioning outside of the experimental testing situation.

The purpose of commissurotomy in human patients is to try to control severe epilepsy. In an epileptic seizure the normal complex patterning of brain activity is disrupted, and abnormal synchronous firing of neurons occurs over large areas of the cortex. Major seizures can be dangerous, since the victim can lose consciousness and motor control for several minutes. (Imagine what would happen if you had a major seizure while driving a car.) Seizures typically start in one hemisphere, and major seizures can spread rapidly to the opposite hemisphere. Thus, it was reasoned that if seizures could be confined to one hemisphere by cutting the corpus callosum, then their effects would not be so dangerous to the patient.

The first commissurotomies on human patients were done in the 1940s. Unfortunately, in most patients the procedure was not as effective in controlling epilepsy as had been hoped, so the procedure was temporarily abandoned. About twenty years later, two California neurosurgeons, Philip Vogel and Joseph Bogen, reconsidered the question of commissurotomy and epilepsy. They examined earlier surgical records and more recent animal and human research, and concluded that commissurotomy had failed to help control epilepsy in most of the 1940s patients because in most cases only a partial commissurotomy had been done. Vogel and Bogen hypothesized that a complete transection of both the corpus callosum and the anterior commissure would prevent the conduction of epileptic seizures between the two hemispheres. Their first full commissurotomies were a complete success. The patients' seizures were controlled as predicted. And commissurotomy produced no harmful effects as far as the patients' daily lives were concerned. They could go about their work and play and interact with family and friends as well as before—or better, because of the reduced epilepsy problem.

However, extensive testing by neuropsychologists Roger Sperry and Michael Gazzaniga subsequently showed a number of subtle but profoundly important psychological effects of the split-brain procedure in human subjects. I will describe some of the prototypical results from the "California series" of some two dozen split-brain patients. However, before I describe the split-brain research some preliminary comments and cautions are in order.

Preliminary comments.   The advantage of testing split-brain subjects is that it enables researchers to study a hemisphere's functioning directly, by seeing what the intact hemisphere *can* do, rather than relying on studies of dysfunctions resulting from damage to the hemisphere. Yet split-brain test results must be interpreted with caution for several reasons: (1) The brains of the split-brain patients are not entirely normal, since these patients were afflicted with severe epilepsy. Thus, results from split-brain research cannot always be generalized to normal brains. (2) The number of split-brain subjects is relatively small, and it is risky to draw big conclusions from a small sample. (3) To make matters worse, the split-brain subjects show considerable variability among themselves. The prototypical results that I am summarizing here do not necessarily apply to all of the split-brain subjects. The differences between subjects are due mainly to differences in the amount and location of damage to one or the other hemisphere prior to the split-brain surgery. For example, in some patients the right hemisphere is relatively unresponsive. The results that I describe come from patients with responsive right hemispheres. (4) When one hemisphere is damaged, the other hemisphere may be able to acquire some of its functions. Thus a certain amount of functional reorganization of the brains of some patients may have occurred prior to surgery. For example, the surprising degree of right-hemisphere speech-recognition ability in some split-brain patients may reflect an abnormal acquisition of language by the right hemisphere as a result of left-hemisphere damage from epilepsy. (5) Also, if each hemisphere can learn independently, then after the surgery each hemisphere might acquire some functions that it did not have prior to surgery. Thus, some of the split-brain research may show what the separated right and left hemispheres are capable of learning to do, rather than what the connected hemispheres normally do in normal brains. This presents a problem in interpreting some studies that were done months or years after the surgery. With these caveats in mind, let us consider some of the research with split-brain patients. The results are fascinating and they have raised some important new questions.

Neuropsychological Testing

To understand the rationale behind the test procedures it is important to bear in mind the principle of *contralateral organization* of the sensory and motor systems (Figure 5.3). In the fully commissurotomized patient the left hemisphere sees only the right visual field, and vice versa. However, under ordinary viewing conditions the patient, by moving his or her eyes, can see an entire scene with each of the two hemispheres. Thus, in order to test each of the two hemispheres independently (unilateral testing) it was necessary to limit stimulus inputs to a single hemisphere. Several methods were devised for doing this. (In what follows I will simplify things by describing the procedure and results for typical right-handed patients, in whom language production mechanisms are in the left hemisphere.)

The simplest method of unilateral testing involved asking subjects to identify objects (such as spoon, key, pencil) by touch alone. The objects were out of sight, inside of a box. Subjects stuck a hand through a hole in the side of the box to feel the objects. When the right hand was used, the subjects could name the object, just like normal people. But when the left hand was used, they could not name it. Thus, the left hemisphere knew what object the right hand had felt, and named it accurately. But the right hemisphere could not name what the left hand had felt. However, the fact that the right hemisphere *knew* what the left hand had felt was shown by the fact that it could show how to use it: for example, while blindfolded, subjects could use the left hand to show how to use a spoon or a paintbrush, using appropriate motions.

You might wonder how the experimenter explained to a subject's non-speaking right hemisphere what it was supposed to do in the left-hand tests. Verbal instructions were sufficient for some patients, since their right hemisphere had some degree of speech recognition ability, though it could not produce speech. In other cases it was necessary to demonstrate the testing procedure, and the right hemisphere learned by observing.

In order to test the left and right hemispheres separately for recognition of visual stimuli, a projection tachistoscope ("T-scope") was used to *lateralize* the visual stimuli (Figure 5.4). Subjects focused on a dot at the center of the screen, then a visual stimulus—a picture or a word—was flashed on either the right or left side of the screen. The flash was so brief—about 150 milliseconds—that the subjects did not have time to move their eyes during the flash. Thus, for example, if a picture was flashed on the left side of the screen (in the left visual field, LVF), only the right hemisphere could see it, since the subjects could not move their eyes leftward quickly enough to see the picture on the left side of the screen in the right visual field (RVF), with the left hemisphere.

In a typical T-scope test, the subjects were told to name whatever object was shown in a picture flashed on the screen. If the picture was flashed in the RVF, subjects correctly named it. But if the picture was flashed in the LVF, they could not name it. In fact, they usually said that they saw "nothing." Yet, if they were asked to reach through an opening under the screen and feel several objects (such as a spoon, pencil, key, cigarette, and clothespin) with their left hand (without being able to see the objects) then they could select the object that *matched* the one seen in the LVF (*cross-modal matching procedure*). Again, the left hemisphere can name what it sees; the right hemisphere knows what it sees, but cannot name it (Gazzaniga 1970). Interestingly, the same results were obtained in some subjects when the stimulus was the printed name of the object ("SPOON"), rather than a picture of it. The right hemisphere could read common nouns, and select the corresponding object by touch, but it could not speak to read the words aloud.

Another test showed that the right hemisphere could understand concrete concepts. An object was flashed in the LVF, and the subject's task was to use the left hand to select by feel the object that "goes with" the object that he saw (while the identical matching object itself was not available). For example, if the subject saw a cigarette, his or her left hand selected a cigarette lighter. Thus, the right hemisphere understood concrete concepts having to do with functional or category relations between the objects.

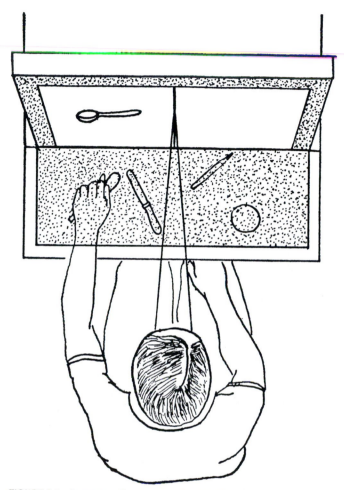

FIGURE 5.4. Apparatus for testing visual-tactile association in split-brain patients. Here the right hemisphere sees the picture projected in the left visual field; the left hand picks the matching object from among several objects that are out of sight on a shelf under the table. [From Gazzaniga, M. S. (1970). *The Bisected Brain*. New York: Appleton-Century-Crofts. By permission of Appleton & Lange.]

A more complex sort of recognition was demonstrated when, in the middle of a routine visual-recognition and naming test, a picture of a nude female was flashed to the LVF of a female subject. She giggled and blushed, as if embarrassed. When asked what she had seen, she said "Nothing, just a flash of light." When asked why she had laughed, she replied "Oh Dr. Sperry, that's some machine you have!" This example shows that the right hemisphere not only recognized the picture, but initiated an automatic emotional reaction to it—one based on the patient's social learning experience. The speaking left hemisphere did not know what had been seen, but it tried to interpret the emotional reaction, as shown by the remark about "some machine." (Later, I will have more to say about the significance of the left hemisphere's attempt to interpret the right hemisphere's actions.)

Visuospatial superiority of the right hemisphere.   Numerous studies of split-brain patients have indicated that the left hemisphere is superior to the right for verbal and conceptual tasks, whereas the right hemisphere is superior for many nonverbal tasks, particularly visuo-spatial tasks involving drawing and construction (Gazzaniga & LeDoux 1978). For example, in the *block-design test* the subject is required to use a set of colored blocks (cubes with a different color of paint on each side) to construct a pattern that matches a sample pattern shown in a picture. The sample pattern remains in full view during the construction test. Split-brain subjects can construct the correct block pattern quickly and easily using their left hand (right hemisphere), but they find the task difficult or impossible with their right hand (left hemisphere).

Figure 5.5 illustrates the right hemisphere's (left hand) superiority in drawing, in right-handed split-brain patients. Gazzaniga and LeDoux (1978; Gazzaniga 1985) argued that the right hemisphere's superiority in spatial tasks is limited to tasks that require some sort of manipulation of objects in space, construction of figures, or tactile recognition of shapes. On tests involving mere matching of figures and pictures, in which a simple pointing response is used, the left hemisphere usually performs as well as the right hemisphere. Thus, Gazzaniga and Ledoux argued for *manipulo-spatial* superiority of the right hemisphere, rather than a general visuo-spatial superiority.

Face recognition.   The right hemisphere is better than the left at recognizing faces. This was demonstrated in a study by Levy, Trevarthen, and Sperry (1972) that used composite pictures, with the left half from one face and the right half from a different face (see Figure 5.6). Such composite figures are called *chimeric figures* (after Chimera, an ancient mythical monster whose various parts [head, body, forelegs, and so forth] came from different animals). The chimeric face was flashed briefly on the T-scope screen, then the subject had to choose the face that she had seen from among a set of four faces. If subjects responded by pointing, the responses were controlled by the right hemisphere, and they were nearly always correct. The fact that the responses were controlled by the right hemisphere was known by the fact that subjects chose faces that matched the left half of the chimeric face stimuli.[5]

When subjects were required to respond verbally rather than by pointing, they usually chose faces that matched the right half of the chimeric face, indicating control by the left hemisphere. Face-matching performance was better for right-hemisphere control than for left-hemisphere control, though the left hemisphere still matched at better than a chance level. (Another experiment showed similar results with chimeric stimuli made of common objects, such as a rose, eye, or bee.) Gazzaniga and LeDoux (1978; Gazzaniga 1985) found that the right hemisphere's superiority at face recognition was limited to tests involving similar faces, in which it was hard to discriminate

EXAMPLE   LEFT HAND   RIGHT HAND

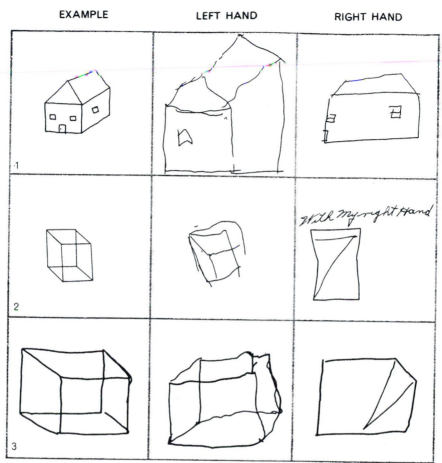

FIGURE 5.5. Drawings by three split-brain patients. After commissurotomy, these right-handed patients could copy designs better with their left hand (right hemisphere) than with their right hand. Conversely, only their right hand (left hemisphere) could write words spontaneously (without copying). [From Gazzaniga, M. S. (August, 1967). The split brain in man. *Scientific American, 217,* 24–29. By permission of the author.]

between the different faces. The left hemisphere did a good job when the faces were distinctively different. This latter finding illustrates an example of a general principle that, in many cases, differences between left hemisphere and right hemisphere abilities are relative, not absolute.

One rather striking finding in the studies using chimeric stimuli was the phenomenon of *visual completion,* in which patients subjectively perceived figures as complete when in fact they had seen only half of the figure (in either the LVF or RVF). For example, in the chimeric face study, the patients perceived unified whole faces, not half faces or chimeric faces. This phenomenon is not understood, but it seems to be a complex case of the Gestalt perception principles of good continuation and closure. (Visual

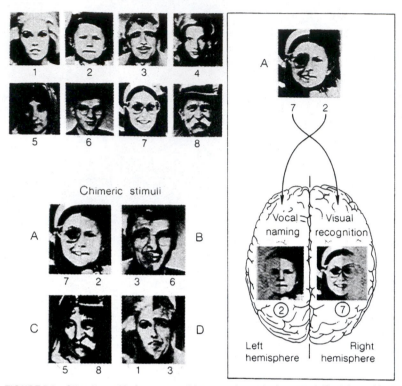

FIGURE 5.6. Stimuli used in face recognition experiment by Levy et al. First the subject saw a chimeric stimulus (A, B, C, or D) flashed on the screen, then he was asked to point to the face that he had seen, choosing from pictures 1–8. When they responded by pointing, subjects typically chose the whole face that matched the left side of the chimeric face (seen in the right hemisphere); for example, chimeric face A was matched to picture 7. But when they responded verbally, they chose a whole face that matched the right side of the chimeric face (seen in the left hemisphere); for example, chimeric face A was matched to picture 2. [From Levy, J., Trevarthen, C., & Sperry, R. W. (1972). Perception of bilateral chimeric figures following hemispheric disconnection. *Brain, 95,* 61–78. By permission of Oxford University Press.]

completion is greatest soon after surgery; over a period of time it may decrease, and the patient will notice that his or her visual field is incomplete.)

Other left-right differences. Besides visuo-spatial or manipulo-spatial superiority, other superiorities of the right hemisphere on nonverbal tasks have been claimed, with varying degrees of evidence. For example, it has been suggested that the right hemisphere is superior to the left in recognizing musical melodies. Special techniques have been devised to study hemispheric differences in normal subjects, with normal brains. This research is beyond the scope and purpose of this book, but see Springer and Deutsch (1985) for a good review of the research on hemispheric differences in normal and abnormal brains in adults, children, and animals.

Hemispheric dominance and specialized abilities. The left hemisphere has traditionally been called the *dominant* hemisphere since it controls speech and since verbal thought seems to be so important for the control of voluntary action. However, the split-brain research shows that under appropriate conditions the right hemisphere can take charge and perform tasks that suit its talents (such as the face-recognition and block-designs tasks). Levy and Trevarthen (1976) used chimeric object pictures to show that the left hemisphere usually controls responding in a function-matching task (matching objects that are used together, such as a fork and a birthday cake), but the right hemisphere usually controls responding when the task requires matching of objects according to their visual similarity.

It appears that each hemisphere is capable of thinking independently, insofar as thinking is required for correct performance on the various tasks used by neuropsychologists to test the split-brain patients. This raises the question, do split-brain patients have two minds? And especially important, do they have two separate centers of consciousness, one in each hemisphere? We will consider this fascinating question in the next section.

THE QUESTION OF DUAL CONSCIOUSNESS

The question of interest here is whether the split-brain operation, involving complete commissurotomy, produces two centers of consciousness within one body. That is, can it be said that the separated left and right hemispheres are independently conscious just as one would say that two different brains in two different bodies are independently conscious? The main controversy has been over whether the separated right hemisphere is conscious. The speaking left hemisphere seems to function in a normal manner, making introspective verbal reports in casual conversation, so there has not been any serious doubt that the separated left hemisphere is conscious.

The question of dual consciousness is highly controversial among psychologists, philosophers, and brain scientists (Beaumont 1981; Globus, Maxwell, & Savodnik 1976). The two most important reasons for disagreement on this issue are: (1) failure to agree on an objective criterion for consciousness, and (2) limitations of the empirical evidence. The conclusions that different writers have drawn from the available evidence seem to depend heavily on their prior philosophical or theoretical beliefs about consciousness and the brain.

The Problem

The question of whether a split-brain patient's mute right hemisphere is a conscious being is a special case of the *other-minds problem*, which I discussed in the previous chapter. The speaking left hemisphere has no direct knowledge of the right hemisphere's experience. It can only make inferences based on emotional reactions and behavior initiated by the right hemisphere. Thus, to the split-brain patient's left hemisphere, the right hemisphere is an "other mind." However, in ordinary day-to-day life the patients are not concerned with this other mind. They do not say "I feel like my consciousness is split" or "I think that I have two minds." Except for occasional "alien hand" episodes, in which the left hand does something suggesting independent volition, the right hemisphere is so unobtrusive that the possibility of a second center of consciousness does not occur to the split-brain patients. It is mainly psychologists and philosophers and brain scientists who are interested in the question.

Taking the objective viewpoint, we must approach the question of right hemisphere consciousness in the same way that we would approach the other-minds problems in regard to animals or pre-verbal children. We must develop some objective criterion with which to infer consciousness. The criterion that we choose will be influenced by our ideas about what consciousness is, and the level of consciousness with which we are concerned.

In the most conservative view, linguistic thought is an essential feature of consciousness, and the introspective verbal report (IVR) is a necessary criterion for consciousness (or at least for self-awareness; Beaumont 1981). The IVR criterion was advocated by John Eccles (1977), an interactionist dualist who claimed that the left hemisphere (particularly the prefrontal lobe and the linguistic circuits of the temporal lobe) is a "liaison cortex" that transmits knowledge from an immaterial entity, the "self-conscious mind," which has subjective conscious experiences. Thus, in Eccles's view, language centers do not produce consciousness, rather, they receive knowledge from an immaterial consciousness, and can make introspective verbal reports about it. Though Eccles himself is an eminent brain scientist, his theory of "liaison cortex" has not been accepted by very many other brain scientists. Brain scientists taking a strictly materialist view (such as Gazzaniga 1985, 1988), have argued that higher-level conscious processes (above mere sensory perception) are highly correlated with the presence of linguistic circuits normally found only in the left hemisphere, and IVR is the most useful indicator of consciousness, though not necessarily the only one.

Roger Sperry (1968, 1976) took a more liberal attitude toward the possibility of consciousness occurring in the right hemisphere, independent of language circuits and introspective verbal reports:

> Everything we have seen so far indicates that the surgery has left these people with two separate minds, that is, two separate spheres of consciousness. What is experienced in the right hemisphere seems to be entirely outside the realm of awareness of the left hemisphere. This mental division has been demonstrated in regard to perception, cognition, volition, learning, and memory. One of the hemispheres, the left, dominant or major hemisphere, has speech and is normally talkative and conversant. The other, the minor hemisphere, however, is mute or dumb, being able to express itself only through nonverbal reactions. (Hence: "mental duplicity" from this surgery but no "double talk.") (1966, p. 299).

Sperry conceived of subjective consciousness broadly, covering the whole range from perceptual awareness to self-awareness. He did not see linguistic thinking as an essential feature of consciousness, nor did he require introspective verbal reports as an objective criterion for subjective consciousness. Rather, he took *intelligent behavior*—behavior adaptive to the current situation and controlled by flexible thought processes rather than reflexes—as sufficient evidence from which to infer consciousness. Sperry's attitude on a criterion for consciousness is consistent with his emergent interactionism theory (discussed in Chapter 4), in which consciousness is identified with the holistic properties of neural activity and plays a causal role in controlling behavior. While consciousness is unified via the corpus callosum in the normal brain, the split-brain operation creates separate centers of consciousness in the two hemispheres, since their holistic neural activities are now separate.

The notion of intelligent action as a criterion for consciousness also makes sense from an identity-theory viewpoint on the mind-body problem. In any case, recall that both solutions to the other-minds problem—the IVR and the intelligent action criteria—depend ultimately on an argument from analogy. We attribute consciousness to creatures that we see as being similar to ourselves. The argument is over which criterion of similarity to use.

The Evidence

Here I will describe several lines of evidence for conscious thinking in the right hemisphere, according to the criterion of intelligent behavior.

Cognitive tasks.   We have already seen that both the left and right hemispheres of split-brain patients are capable of intelligent action, though they have different talents. In normal adult humans, conscious thinking is highly correlated with intelligent behavior and presumably plays some role in producing it. Though intelligent action is usually related to conscious verbal thinking—a function of the left hemisphere—it can also follow from thinking in visual-spatial mental images, which is a special talent of the right hemisphere.

To give another example (Gazzaniga 1985): A picture of a horse was flashed to patient JW's right hemisphere (LVF). The left hemisphere said it did not see anything. But in response to the experimenter's request to "draw what goes on it," JW's left hand drew a picture of an English saddle. The drawing was ambiguous, and JW (left hemisphere) said he did not know what he had drawn. Then in response to the experimenter's request to "draw what you saw," the left hand drew a horse. JW then grinned and, pointing to the first drawing, said "That must be a saddle." Again, the right hemisphere followed instructions and carried out the task, operating independently of the left hemisphere. Thus, it appears that intelligent behavior of the disconnected right hemisphere is influenced by conscious, though nonverbal, thinking in that hemisphere.[6] The alternative interpretation would be that the right hemisphere is an automaton that conducts intelligent behavior in a non-conscious, computer-like manner. Those who claim that verbal thinking is of the essence of consciousness would classify the right hemisphere as a non-conscious entity as a matter of a prior definition.

To argue that the right hemisphere controls intelligent behavior is not to say that the right hemisphere is as smart as the left hemisphere. LeDoux

(1985) suggested that, "In the absence of extensive linguistic representation, the cognitive capacities of the right hemisphere are more like those of a chimpanzee than like those of a fully developed human" (p. 208). LeDoux, like Gazzaniga, argued that only the left hemisphere is conscious in the typical split-brain patient. However, I would argue that chimpanzees are conscious beings (Griffin 1984), so equating the human right hemisphere with a chimpanzee does not support the argument that the right hemisphere is not conscious.

Volition and the alien hand.   Most of the time split-brain patients go about their daily lives without any apparent conflict between their two brain hemispheres. The right hemisphere either cooperates with the dominant left hemisphere, helping where it can, or else it remains passive and does not interfere. Laboratory studies show that the right hemisphere can follow instructions, making responses that suit the demands of the task at hand, within the limits of its talents. But can the right hemisphere initiate voluntary actions on its own initiative, independently of instructions from an experimenter or from its left-hemisphere companion? Evidence for spontaneous, presumably voluntary action by the left hand would support the hypothesis of independent consciousness in the right hemisphere of split-brain patients. Unfortunately, there is no systematic research evidence on this point. However, a few compelling incidents have been reported.

Gazzaniga (1970) described conflicts between the left and right hemispheres of his "Case I," a forty-eight-year-old war veteran:

> [He] would sometimes find himself pulling his pants down with one hand and pulling them up with the other. Once, he grabbed his wife with his left hand and shook her violently, while with the right trying to come to his wife's aid in bringing the belligerent hand under control (p. 107).

In another incident a patient's left hand slammed a drawer on his right hand, when his right hand reached into the drawer to get a pair of socks.

A French neurologist labeled such independent actions of the left hand as "la main étrangère," the *alien hand*. Some of the alien hand incidents seem to show conflict between the left and right hemispheres.

A dramatic instance of independent action by the left hand was caught on film (Gazzaniga 1970, p. 100; 1975 [film]). Case I was being tested on the blocks-design task, which involves arranging a set of colored blocks to match a printed pattern. The left hand (right hemisphere) constructed the pattern easily. The right hand (left hemisphere) was incompetent at the task, repeatedly making false starts. Then suddenly, while the right hand was fumbling with the blocks, the left hand reached out for the blocks and started to construct the pattern. This happened several times. It was necessary to ask the subject to sit on his left hand, to keep it out of the way so the right hand could be tested. Even while being sat upon, the left hand sometimes seemed to be trying to get loose. (It should be pointed out that Case I was unusual in that he never acquired ipsilateral control of the hands. Most split-brain patients develop ipsilateral control within a few months after surgery, so that the right hemisphere can control the right hand in doing the blocks design test.)

Cross-cueing.   Several cases of cross-cueing between the hemispheres have been reported, in which, for example, the left hemisphere is able to guess what the right hemisphere has seen or felt by noticing the right hemisphere's overt responses to the situation (Gazzaniga 1970). I have already mentioned the case of the woman who blushed and giggled when her right hemisphere saw a slide of a nude. The left hemisphere did not know what the right hemisphere had seen, but correctly guessed that it was something unusual or funny. This is a case of inadvertent cross-cueing, with the left hemisphere interpreting responses that were made spontaneously but unintentionally by the right hemisphere.

Another example: A subject was being tested for his ability to name color patches that were flashed to either the left or right visual field. When the right hemisphere saw the flash (in the LVF), the left hemisphere could not name the color. But performance improved when the subject (that is, the speaking left hemisphere) was allowed to make a second guess. For example, after a red flash he guessed "green," then changed his answer to "red." The experimenter noticed that after the incorrect first guess the subject frowned and shook his head, then changed his answer. Apparently the right hemisphere heard the first response and realized that it was wrong. Its response (frown and head shake) was noticed by the left hemisphere, which then changed its answer. In this example it is not clear whether the right hemisphere's reaction to the error was a spontaneous emotional reaction or a deliberate cue to the left hemisphere; maybe it was spontaneous at first, and later became a deliberate cue.

Some cases of cross-cueing look strongly like deliberate attempts of the right hemisphere to send information to the left hemisphere via overt responses. For example, in a test in which only the right hemisphere could see pictures of familiar people, and the left hemisphere tried to guess who was in the pictures, one subject's left hand traced letters on the back of the right hand. When the right hemisphere saw the subject's aunt Elizabeth, the left hand traced an "E" on the back of the right hand, then the patient (left hemisphere) said "Elizabeth!" (Sperry, Zaidel, & Zaidel 1979).

It must be pointed out that incidents suggesting independent action by the right hemisphere/left hand are relatively rare. Furthermore, there is no evidence that the right hemisphere independently sets long-term goals and plans a series of actions to meet those goals. The available evidence suggests, at best, independent right-hemisphere action that is either impulsive or in pursuit of short-term goals in response to the demands of the immediate situation. Ordinarily the patients' voluntary actions seem to be controlled by the speaking left hemisphere, and the right hemisphere either actively cooperates or quietly acquiesces with the left hemisphere's dominance. It is not clear how one could detect long-term goal setting and planning by the right hemisphere, independent of the left. But there is no reason to expect the right hemisphere to have goals that conflict with those of the left hemisphere—after all, the two hemispheres have "lived together" for many years, and they are parts of the same person, in the same body. Nonetheless, the evidence for at least short-term voluntary action by the right hemisphere is strong enough to suggest that the right hemisphere is conscious, independently of the left hemisphere.

Self-recognition and social values.   The evidence from cognitive tests suggests that the right hemisphere of split-brain patients has perceptual consciousness and conscious thinking. But what about self-awareness? It is difficult to test the mute right hemisphere for the full range of self-knowledge and self concept that is implied by the concept of self-awareness, and little research has been done on this topic. However, Sperry, Zaidel, and Zaidel (1979) devised an ingenious way for testing self-recognition, the most elementary aspect of self-awareness. They also studied the right hemisphere's sense of values or social awareness, to determine whether it was similar to what one would expect in a normal conscious, socialized human being.

Sperry et al. used a special contact lens, the "Z lens," that was designed to limit the subject's vision to the left visual field (right hemisphere). Subjects could examine photographs for an unlimited amount of time and shift their focus from one part of the picture to another. Thus, the experimental procedure could be much more flexible than it was with the T-scope apparatus used in earlier studies, in which stimuli were briefly flashed to one visual field or the other.

The subjects were two split-brain patients who had been operated on eight to ten years previously. They viewed a series of fifty stimulus cards, each of which had an array of four to nine drawings or photographs. Ten of the cards contained pictures of personal significance to the subject, such as pictures of the subject himself/herself, friends, relatives, or personal belongings. Other cards included famous people. For each card the subjects were instructed to point to one of the items that they recognized, or would like to have, or would use in a specified situation. They were asked to evaluate the chosen item with a "thumbs-up" or "thumbs-down" signal.

The results are so interesting that it is worth quoting some of the test protocols for the right hemisphere in detail. Here is one for subject NG, a married woman with two children. Keep in mind the fact that the experimenter is conversing with the subject's *left* hemisphere, which does not know what the right hemisphere is seeing in the pictures.

> *Protocol NG.*   The subject had just completed six trials on comparatively neutral stimuli including foods, flowers, animals, children, and people with questions centered around her special preferences, likes and dislikes, the responses to which had been relatively casual and routine. On the seventh trial we presented four portrait head and bust photos in black and white, all of the subject herself in different poses along with the impersonal instruction: "Here are four people; again, point out the one you like best."
>
> NG: "OK," and she paused silently for about seven seconds while she examined the test array. She then burst forth with an abrupt loud exclamation: "Oh no! . . . Where'd you g . . . What *are* they?" This was followed by a very loud laugh, another exclamation, "Oh God!", and a three-second pause. She then asked hesitantly, "Dr. Sperry . . . You sure there's people there?"
>
> Ex: "Which one do you like . . . that one?" (referring to the one where the subject was pointing).
>
> NG: "Uh-huh."
>
> Ex: On removal of the choice array the examiner asked, "What was in the picture?"

NG: Still in an extra loud, emphatic voice, "Something nice whatever it was . . . Something I wouldn't mind having probably." This was followed closely by another loud laugh. (Sperry et al. 1979, p. 158. Copyright 1979 by Pergamon Press, Inc. Reprinted by permission.)

The experimenters interpreted the subject's loud emotional outburst at the unexpected sight of a picture of herself as strong evidence of self-recognition in the right hemisphere. They suggested that "the emotional components of the reaction triggered in the right hemisphere crossed rapidly to the left hemisphere through brain stem mechanisms and colored the tone of speech in the vocal hemisphere," though the left hemisphere did not know what the right hemisphere had seen that had triggered the emotional response. The subject's initial exclamation "Oh no! Where'd you g . . ." and "Oh God!" may have come from the right hemisphere, which may be capable of emotional vocal reactions, though it does not control conversational speech.

On a later test with a similar array of four pictures of herself, NG made a correct verbal identification. First she guessed "Probably me . . . ," then she said in a more definite tone, "Yeah, that's a picture of me." Apparently the right hemisphere heard and affirmed the left hemisphere's guess; the left hemisphere detected the affirmation and then made a positive identification of the picture.

Here are two protocols from a male subject, LB. His right hemisphere made blatant, overt attempts to cue the left hemisphere by using the left hand to trace letters on the back of the right hand.

Protocol LB.1.   The subject was shown an array of four pictures of people, singly and in groups. Three of the pictures contained unknowns and one in the upper left included a picture of Hitler in uniform standing with four other men. LB was asked to point to "any of these that you recognize."

LB: examined the card for about fourteen seconds and then pointed to the face of Hitler.

Ex: "Do you recognize that one? Is that the only one?"

LB: again inspected the full array but did not point to any others.

Ex: "Well, on this: is this one a 'thumbs-up' or a 'thumbs-down' item for you?"

LB: signaled "thumbs down."

Ex: "That's another 'thumbs-down'?"

LB: "Guess I'm antisocial." (Because this was his third consecutive "thumbs-down.")

Ex: "Who is it?"

LB: "GI came to mind. I mean . . ." (Subject at this point was seen to be tracing letters with the first finger of the left hand on the back of his right hand.)

Ex: "You're writing with your left hand; let's keep the cues out."

LB: "Sorry about that."

Ex: "Is it someone you know personally, . . . or from entertainment, . . . or historical, or . . . ?"

LB: interrupted and said "Historical."

Ex: "Recent or . . . ?"

LB: "Past."

Ex: "This country or another country?"

LB: "Uh-huh—okay."

Ex: "You're not sure?"

LB: "Another country, I think."

Ex: "Prime Minister, king, president, . . . , any of them?"

LB: "Gee," and pondered with accompanying lip movements for several seconds.

Ex: Giving further cues: "Great Britain? . . . Germany . . . ?"

LB: interrupted and said definitely "Germany" and then after a slight pause added "Hitler" (Sperry et al. 1979, pp. 159–60).

Here LB's right hemisphere promptly recognized Hitler, and a negative emotional reaction prompted the "thumbs down" signal. The right hemisphere's subtle reactions to the experimenter's prompts cued the left hemisphere to guess "governmental" and "historical," while rejecting other alternatives. The right hemisphere, which could spell but not speak, tried to signal "Germany" to the left hemisphere by tracing letters with the left hand. Finally, recognizing the right hemisphere's affirmative reaction to the experimenter's "Germany" prompt, the left hemisphere confidently and correctly guessed that the picture was Hitler. Only Hitler could have produced such a strong negative reaction consistent with "governmental," "historical," and "Germany."

> *Protocol LB.2.* In the preceding trials with the left visual field LB had responded with "thumbs-down" evaluations for Castro, Hitler, overweight women in swim suits, and a war scene. Intermixed with these and other responses, "thumbs-up" signals were obtained for Churchill, Johnny Carson, pretty girls, scenes from ballet and modern dance, and a horizontal neutral thumb signal for [then President] Nixon. Toward the end of this testing session, LB was presented with a choice array containing four portrait photos of adult males, three strangers, and one of himself in the lower left position. Asked for a thumb sign evaluation, he gave a decisive "thumbs-down" response but unlike other "thumbs-down" signals, this one was accompanied by a wide, sheepish and (to all appearances) a self-conscious grin. When we then asked if he knew who it was, LB after only a short hesitation guessed correctly "myself" (Sperry et al. 1979, p. 163).

Here LB's right hemisphere readily recognized his own portrait. The "thumbs down" signal combined with the wide grin "indicates not only self-recognition in the minor hemisphere but also a subtle sense of humor and self-conscious perspective befitting the total situation." The distinctive emotional reaction and other cues enabled the left hemisphere to identify the picture correctly as the subject himself.

Sperry et al.'s (1979) study indicates self-recognition in the right hemisphere of patients NG and LB, and self-recognition is the minimum criterion for self-awareness and a self-concept. The emotional reactions and thumb signals indicate an appropriate sense of social values in the right hemisphere, which suggests a self that holds those values. Independent volition by

LB's right hemisphere was shown by its attempts to signal the left hemisphere by tracing letters with the left hand.

Conclusions.   Research by Sperry and his colleagues supports the notion of dual consciousness in split-brain patients (at least in those whose right hemisphere is not badly damaged). The right hemisphere shows perceptual awareness and conscious thinking by the criterion of a pattern of intelligent behavior (adaptive, purposive [at least in the short-term], flexible and spontaneous). Only by the narrow criterion of introspective verbal report could right-hemisphere consciousness be denied. The evidence also indicates right-hemisphere self-awareness, though the evidence does not necessarily indicate that right-hemisphere self-awareness is fully equivalent to that of the left hemisphere. Insofar as the self-concept depends on reflective consciousness, which is largely verbal, one would not expect a highly developed self-concept in a nonverbal (or minimally verbal) right hemisphere.[7]

In the next section I will describe research by Gazzaniga, who argues that right-hemisphere consciousness is rare in split-brain patients, and that when it occurs it is highly correlated with the presence of language abilities in the right hemisphere.

CONSCIOUSNESS, LANGUAGE, AND BRAIN MODULARITY

Michael Gazzaniga (1983; Gazzaniga and LeDoux 1978) argued that the right hemispheres of most split-brain patients are not conscious. A few split-brain patients have a conscious right hemisphere, and right-hemisphere consciousness is highly correlated with the presence of at least a moderately high degree of right-hemisphere language ability. Furthermore, in his assessment of split-brain patients, those without right-hemisphere language have shown no ability to carry out complex cognitive tasks—beyond basic perceptual recognition—with their right hemispheres.

Evidence for Consciousness in P.S.'s Right Hemisphere

Gazzaniga and LeDoux (1978) first found evidence for right-hemisphere consciousness, associated with right-hemisphere language, in patient P.S., a right-handed, left-hemisphere dominant fifteen-year-old boy. Though P.S.'s right hemisphere could not speak at the time of initial testing, it could spell words by arranging Scrabble letters (letters printed on little plastic squares) with the left hand.

Values and self-concept.   Questions were directed to P.S.'s right hemisphere in the following manner: The experimenter spoke aloud the first few words of the question, but the critical final word was flashed to P.S.'s right hemisphere (left visual field) on a tachistoscope screen. Then P.S.'s right hemisphere spelled out the answer by arranging Scrabble letters with the left hand.

The first question was "Who *are you?*" (Italicized words were flashed to the right hemisphere only.) P.S. spelled "PAUL." The right hemisphere knows its name. "Would you spell your favorite *girl?* Response: "LIZ." (P.S.'s girlfriend at the time.)

"Would you spell your favorite *person?*" "HENEY WI FOZI" (Referring to Henry Winkler, who played the TV character Fonzie, P.S.'s idol.)

"Would you spell your favorite *hobby?*" "CAR"

"What is *tomorrow?*" "SUNDAY" (Correct.)

"What would you like for *a job?*" "AUTOMOBILE RACE." (This is interesting, because in conversation P.S.'s left hemisphere says that he wants to be a draftsman.)

"What is your *mood?*" "GOOD." (Gazzaniga & LeDoux 1978, p. 143.)

Questions of this sort indicated that P.S.'s right hemisphere is conscious and has a self-concept, including a sense of personal values. To a large degree the left and right hemisphere agree on their likes and dislikes. But the experimenters noticed that on days when P.S.'s left and right hemisphere disagreed very much, P.S. seemed to be in a worse mood than on days when his two hemispheres were in close agreement. P.S.'s right hemisphere's ability to spell out an answer (rather than merely pointing to one of a few limited choice stimuli, as in most split-brain tests) indicates self-generated, voluntary behavior.

On the question of dual consciousness in P.S., Gazzaniga and LeDoux (1978) concluded:

Thus, it would appear that the right hemisphere, along with but independent of the left, *can* possess conscious properties following brain bisection. In other words, the mechanisms of human consciousness *can* be split and doubled by split brain surgery.

Because P.S. is the first split-brain patient to clearly possess double consciousness, it seems that if we could identify the factor that distinguishes his right hemisphere from the right hemisphere of other split-brain patients, we would have a major clue to the underlying nature of conscious processes. That factor is undoubtedly the extensive linguistic representation in P.S.'s right hemisphere. As we have seen, his right hemisphere can spell, and in addition, it can comprehend verbal commands, as well as process other parts of speech and make conceptual judgments involving verbal information. While it is possible that the conscious properties observed in his right hemisphere are spuriously associated with these linguistic skills, the fact remains that in all other [split-brain] patients, where linguistic sophistication is lacking in the right hemisphere, so too is the evidence for consciousness (1978, p. 145).

Understanding action verbs.   Though the right hemispheres of some earlier split-brain patients could recognize spoken or printed nouns (object names), the right hemispheres of Gazzaniga's P.S. and a newer patient, V.P., have the unusual ability to show their understanding of action verbs by performing the actions indicated by them. They can make appropriate responses to verbs such as "laugh" or "rub," or to nouns that imply actions, such as "boxer," when the words are flashed to the right hemisphere (LVF). When asked to name the word that had been flashed, the left hemisphere (which had not seen the word) makes a guess based on the action that was being carried out (see Figure 5.7). Sometimes the guesses are wrong, though they are reasonable interpretations from the evidence available to the left hemisphere. For example, when the word "walk" was flashed to the right hemisphere, the patient started to leave the testing area (a trailer parked in front of his house). When asked what he was doing, he said "Going to my house to get a Coke."

Emotional reactions. When P.S.'s mute right hemisphere saw the word *kiss*, the left hemisphere blurted out "Hey, no way, no way. You've got to be kidding." When he was asked what it was that he would not do, he could not say. Later, when *kiss* was flashed to the left hemisphere, he replied "No way, I'm not going to kiss you guys!" The interesting thing about the kiss episode is that it suggests that the right hemisphere could recognize a word, have an appropriate emotional reaction to it, and communicate the specific emotional reaction to the left hemisphere without communicating the word itself. There seems to be a direct communication of emotion between hemispheres. (The explanation of this in P.S.'s case probably lies in the fact that, though his corpus callosum was completely severed, his anterior commissure was left intact. The anterior commissure connects the bilateral halves of

FIGURE 5.7. Split-brain subject's responses to commands flashed to the left visual field (right hemisphere). The right hemisphere made a vocal or manual response to the word, then the left hemisphere tried to interpret the response and guess what the word was. The responses to "laugh" and "rub" were ambiguous, and the left hemisphere made a reasonable but incorrect guess. The response to "boxer" was less equivocal, and the left hemisphere guessed correctly. [From Gazzaniga, M. S. & LeDoux, J. E. (1978). *The Integrated Mind.* New York: Plenum Press. By permission of the publisher.]

the [subcortical] limbic system, whose structures [hippocampus, amygdala] are critically involved in emotional reactions.)

In other research with P.S. it was shown that his right and left hemispheres could independently evaluate words, such as "Dad," "Liz," "school," on a five-point like-dislike scale. The two hemispheres usually agreed on their evaluations. Furthermore, the left hemisphere could accurately evaluate words flashed only to the right hemisphere. This indicates a direct communication of an emotional reaction between right and left hemispheres, even though the left hemisphere did not know what the right hemisphere had seen.

A dramatic implication of the observations on P.S. is that even in normal people the speaking, conscious left hemisphere may sometimes detect emotional reactions without knowing their cause. This happens because emotions may be elicited by stimuli not attended to by the verbal system, for example, odors that were associated with emotional reactions in past experience. In such cases the left hemisphere may try to interpret the feelings, making use of whatever information is available. For example, a pleasurable emotion might be attributed to the person we are with, or the scene we are looking at, when unknown to the left hemisphere the pleasurable reaction is really elicited by an odor associated with past pleasures. The left hemisphere's interpretations of our emotional reactions and behaviors may be a fundamental source of our values and beliefs (Gazzaniga 1985; Gazzaniga and LeDoux 1978).

The Interpretive Cortex and the Illusion of Mental Unity

In more recent work, Gazzaniga (1985, 1988a) has identified consciousness with a left-hemisphere interpreter system. In his view, the mind/brain system is made up of a number of modules. *Modules* are relatively independent functional units that can receive information, compute, store and retrieve memories, trigger emotional reactions, and produce behavior. Ordinarily, they cannot make verbal responses (they have no access to the verbal response system), though they can produce other types of overt responses. The modules are nonconscious in that we do not have direct introspective access them, so we cannot make introspective verbal reports on their computational activities, though we may be aware of their outputs or responses.[8] A special module, the *interpreter system*, tries to interpret the diverse actions of the various modules, to explain why they occurred, and to fit them into the narrative sequence of events of our lives and conscious experience. The interpreter system ordinarily occurs only in the left hemisphere, and it probably occurs only in humans. *Consciousness* is associated with the activity of the interpreter system:

> Consciousness in my scheme of brain events becomes the output of the left brain's interpreter and those products are reported and refined by the human language system. The interpreter calls upon an untold number of separate and relatively independent modules for its information (Gazzaniga 1985, p. 135).

Though the interpreter normally occurs only in the left hemisphere, in close association with the language system, it is not the language system itself. "The 'interpreter' idea is not bound by language. . . . Language and speech systems merely report out the activities of the interpreter" (Gazzaniga 1989, personal communication). The separability of the interpreter and the language system is indicated by recent evidence that, under some conditions, a module may produce a correct verbal response to a stimulus even though the conscious interpreter system cannot identify the stimulus (Gazzaniga 1988a).

We have already seen several examples of the left hemisphere's interpretations of the right hemisphere's responses. For example, recall Sperry et al.'s (1979) subjects' verbal responses to photographs seen only by the right hemisphere. Also, P.S. and V.P.'s interpretations of the right hemisphere's responses to action verbs (Figure 5.7). Additional observations on P.S. provide more evidence for a conscious interpreter in the left hemisphere. The two experiments to be described here were done during two different postoperative phases. The first, in Phase I, was during the time when P.S. could understand spoken and written words and spell with the right hemisphere, but could not speak with the right hemisphere. The second experiment was done in Phase II, when P.S.'s right hemisphere had started speaking, which occurred three years after his surgery.

Experiment I.   P.S. was seated before a projection screen and a row of eight choice pictures (Figure 5.8). His task was to point to the choice picture that best went with a picture flashed on the screen. When two pictures were flashed on the screen simultaneously, one to each hemisphere, the right hand pointed to a choice picture related to the picture flashed to the left hemisphere (RVF), and the left hand pointed to a choice picture that went with the picture flashed to the right hemisphere (LVF). Both hemispheres performed at a high level.

The most interesting point, however, was the left hemisphere's verbal interpretations of the left hand's behavior. For example, in Figure 5.8, when asked "What did you see?", P.S. responded "I saw a claw and I picked the chicken, and you have to clean out the chicken shed with a shovel" (Gazzaniga and LeDoux 1978, p. 148). The left hemisphere knew only what it had seen, namely, the chicken claw flashed in the RVF, and the choice stimuli selected by each of the two hands. It did not know that the right hemisphere had seen the snow scene. So it interpreted the left hand's selection of the shovel in terms of the chicken theme. Similar results were obtained in other tests with P.S.

Experiment II.   After P.S.'s right hemisphere started talking, it was possible to test him with a new procedure (Gazzaniga 1983, 1985). P.S. was shown a series of slides with words, flashed one after another, as in Figure 5.9. If a normal person were to read the words, he or she would tell a simple story: "Mary Ann may come visit into the township today." But P.S. could not read the words left to right. He could read them only sequentially, for each

FIGURE 5.8. Method of presenting two matching tasks simultaneously to the split-brain patient, P.S. Different pictures were flashed simultaneously in the left and right visual fields. The subject's right hemisphere (left hand) chose a picture that went with the one it had seen in the left visual field, while the left hemisphere (right hand) chose a picture that matched what it had seen in the right visual field. Then the left hemisphere tried verbally to explain the responses. [From Gazzaniga, M. S., & LeDoux, J. E. (1978). *The Integrated Mind.* New York: Plenum Press. By permission of the publisher.]

hemisphere separately. Thus, P.S.'s left hemisphere read (silently, from the RVF) "Ann come into town today," while the right hemisphere read (silently, from the LVF) "Mary may visit the ship."

After the whole story was presented, P.S. was asked to say what he had read. The left hemisphere (which was still dominant for conversational speech) immediately responded, "Ann come into town today," reporting what it had seen. Then P.S. was asked if that was the full story. He paused briefly and blurted out, "on a ship . . . to visit . . . to visit Ma." This addition must have come from the right hemisphere, since the left hemisphere did not know what the right hemisphere had seen. Finally, when he was asked to repeat the whole story, he replied, "Ann came into town today to visit Ma on the ship." The final report from the left hemisphere told the whole story, making use of what it saw and what it heard the right hemisphere say. Gazzaniga concluded:

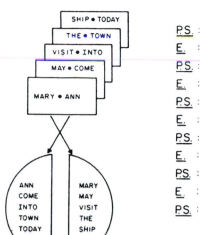

RESPONSE

P.S. : Ann come into town today.

E. : Anything else ?

P.S. : On a ship.

E. : Who ?

P.S. : Ma.

E. : What else ?

P.S. : To visit.

E. : What else ?

P.S. : To see Mary Ann.

E. : Now repeat the whole story.

P.S. : Ma ought to come into town today to visit Mary Ann on the boat.

FIGURE 5.9. Method of presenting two stories simultaneously, one to each hemisphere of split-brain subject P.S. A series of word pairs was flashed on the screen sequentially, with one word in each visual field. The left hemisphere quickly reported its whole story, then the right hemisphere reported its story in fragments. Finally the left hemisphere combined the responses into a single coherent story. [From Gazzaniga, M. S. (1983). Right hemisphere language following brain bisection: A 20-year perspective. *American Psychologist, 38,* 525–37. Copyright © 1983 by the American Psychological Association. Reprinted by permission.]

Once again we see the integration of disparate behaviors into a coherent framework. With the development of bilateral access to speech, behaviors generated by the right hemisphere, which now initiates the spoken word, are incorporated into the conscious stream of the left hemisphere (1983, p. 535).

Modules and mental unity.   Based on the test results of P.S. and other patients, Gazzaniga (1985) suggested that many human behaviors and emotional reactions are initiated by nonconscious modules. Such behaviors are automatic or unwilled, in the sense that they are not voluntary acts of the conscious interpreter system. The interpreter system then explains or rationalizes to itself the unwilled actions—such as impulsive violent or lustful behaviors—making a plausible story based on what it knows. The interpreter can also make introspective verbal reports on its interpretations. But the interpreter's accounts cannot be entirely accurate because it does not have direct access to all of the inputs and computational activities of the nonconscious modules—it only knows their responses.

The implication of Gazzaniga's account is that mental unity is an illusion. Our actions are not all controlled by a conscious executive system. Most of them, including many complex cognitive acts, are the products of nonconscious modules. Yet our culturally instilled, folk-psychological belief in conscious control of our actions is so strong that when the left hemisphere interprets the behaviors elicited by nonconscious modules, it typically interprets them as if they had been consciously controlled. Thus, the interpreter system gives us an illusion of conscious mental unity.

Gazzaniga has extrapolated the idea of the interpreter system to account for a wide variety of conscious experiences. The interpreter generates conscious emotional reactions, such as love, anxiety, or depression, through its interpretation of physiological responses produced by nonconscious modules (1988b). The interpreter also is responsible for constructing systems of values and beliefs, including personal, religious, and scientific beliefs (Gazzaniga 1985, 1988a).

Discussion of Gazzaniga's Ideas

You may have noticed a shift in emphasis over the course of this section on Gazzaniga's research, from the early discussion of consciousness in P.S.'s right hemisphere to the later discussion of the conscious interpreter system of the left hemisphere. It seems that Gazzaniga's ideas on consciousness have changed as new research results have become available. Let me try to summarize and interpret this change.

In 1978 Gazzaniga and LeDoux interpreted P.S.'s Scrabble-letter responses to personal questions, and other data, as evidence for consciousness in the right hemisphere. They (and Gazzaniga 1983) argued that right-hemisphere language is rare among split-brain patients, and that without language the isolated right hemisphere is passive and simple-minded. Only when the right hemisphere has "extensive linguistic representation" can it carry out complex cognitive tasks and show evidence of consciousness. Gazzaniga's ideas have had several critics: (1) Myers (1984) argued that Gazzaniga underestimated the frequency of right-hemisphere language ability, by counting split-brain patients whose right hemispheres were damaged (by epilepsy) prior to surgery. Among undamaged right-hemispheres, word recognition (though not speech production) is fairly common (Levy 1983; Zaidel 1983). (2) Levy (1983) argued that a right hemisphere without language can be active and spontaneous and perform complex tasks involving space perception and spatial construction. Only badly damaged right hemispheres are passive and simple-minded.

The extent of right-hemisphere language ability and its relation to intelligent action and consciousness is still a matter of controversy among specialists, and it is difficult for the nonspecialist to sort out the conflicting claims. In any case, more recently Gazzaniga (1985, 1988a) seems to have backed off on associating consciousness with the linguistic system. Consciousness is now associated with the "output of the left-brain interpreter system." The interpreter occurs in close association with the linguistic system, but is not identical to it. The linguistic system merely reports the activities of the interpreter system.

The separability of the conscious interpreter from the linguistic system has been shown in several experiments (Gazzaniga 1988a). For example, the right hemispheres of subjects with right hemisphere word recognition (JW), or with both word recognition and speech production (PS and VP), did poorly at inference tasks that presumably require the interpreter system. In one demonstration, two words were flashed successively to the right hemisphere (such as "pin" and "finger"). In a multiple-choice test, pointing with the left hand, the right hemisphere could not reliably choose a word showing the causal implication of the two words ("bleed"), even though it could choose simple associates of each word (pin, needle, finger, thumb). The implication of this research is that right hemisphere language ability does not necessarily indicate the presence of an interpreter system in the right hemisphere.

Where does this leave right-hemisphere consciousness? If consciousness is identified with the activity of the interpreter system, the implication is that the right hemisphere is not conscious, even in split-brain patients who have some degree of right-hemisphere language ability. Responses previously interpreted as indicating right-hemisphere consciousness are now interpreted by Gazzaniga (1985, 1988a) as the product of nonconscious right-hemisphere modules that can perform some cognitive tasks, generate emotional reactions, and initiate actions. Only the left-hemisphere interpreter is truly conscious, and it interprets some of the right-hemisphere responses to create an illusion of conscious unity. The right hemisphere can carry out relatively simple cognitive tasks, but there is no clear evidence for a complex interpreter system in the right hemisphere. A further implication is that animals are not conscious, insofar as they do not have an interpreter system.

In reply to Gazzaniga, let us grant that humans have some sort of system—call it the "interpreter system"—that carries out complex cognitive functions of interpretation and inference, and that this system ordinarily occurs only in the left hemisphere in split-brain patients. The point of argument is whether consciousness is to be identified only with the interpreter system. I suggest that to limit consciousness to the interpreter system is to set too high a criterion for consciousness. Recall from Chapter 1 the idea of levels of consciousness, in which I distinguished between primary consciousness and reflective consciousness. In some important respects, Gazzaniga's interpreter system idea is similar to the idea of reflective consciousness. Reflective consciousness tries to interpret our actions and experiences, relates them to our past experiences and self-concept, and makes introspective verbal reports on its observations and interpretations. Reflective consciousness deals with some (though not all) of our primary conscious experiences. Having language ability does not necessarily imply having reflective consciousness or an interpreter system, though linguistic thought is involved in the more complex aspects of human reflective consciousness, interpretation, and inference.

The research by Sperry (subjects NG and LB; Sperry et al. 1979) and Gazzaniga (subjects PS, VP, and JW) suggests primary consciousness in the right hemispheres of their split-brain subjects.[9] Both primary and reflective consciousness can vary in complexity and comprehensiveness, both between subjects and between hemispheres. These subjects' right hemispheres have perceptual experiences, emotional reactions, and the ability to recognize and evaluate words or pictures, carry out simple cognitive tasks, and initiate spontaneous responses. Higher-level cognitive functions of reflective consciousness, complex linguistic thought, and interpretation and inference processes appear to be restricted mainly, or entirely, to the left hemisphere.

But the right-hemisphere appears to be conscious in itself, in its own right. It is nonconscious only from the viewpoint of the left hemisphere, which cannot directly introspect and verbally report the right hemisphere's experiences. If my interpretation is correct—that primary consciousness can occur independently of language or the interpreter system—then the possibility remains for primary consciousness in simpler organisms, such as animals and young children, who do not have those abilities.[10]

The research by Gazzaniga and his colleagues has made important contributions to our understanding of mind, brain, and consciousness. We can anticipate that future work will clarify the answers to questions about the nature of the nonverbal modules and what they do, and the relationships between consciousness, language, and the interpreter system.

LEFT-BRAIN, RIGHT-BRAIN MANIA

The empirical findings from the split-brain research have been interpreted, misinterpreted, overgeneralized, and extrapolated to reach conclusions far removed from the actual data. Of course it is customary for researchers to form speculative hypotheses based on limited data. But some of the generalizations and speculations have gone so far from the data, especially in the popular press, that a word of caution is in order.

Numerous articles in the popular press have contrasted the intuitive, creative right hemisphere with the rational left hemisphere. Critics of the schools bemoan the overemphasis on teaching the verbal left hemisphere, and call for programs to educate the right hemisphere and draw on its talents. Under the label of "hemisphericity," some people are thought to be more left-brained while others are more right-brained, according to their preferred styles of thinking. Some teachers try to classify children as left-brain learners or right-brain learners, and design teaching programs accordingly. Eastern meditative practices are advocated as a way to free the right hemisphere, which is presumably repressed in Western culture. The public's fascination with and ready acceptance of left-right dichotomies has gone so far that it has been called "left-brain, right-brain mania" (Gazzaniga 1985, p. 47).

The fascination with simple left-right dichotomies has roots in antiquity, in various cultures. The right and left hands have been associated, respectively, with male and female, good and evil, day and night, rational and intuitive (Corballis 1980). (The English word "sinister" is derived from a Latin word meaning "on the left side." Left-handers are "sinistral.") Some modern writers reverse the traditional left-right associations (associating left with rational, for example), since we now know that the left hemisphere controls language and the right hand.

For centuries philosophers—and more recently, psychologists—have advocated various dichotomies to summarize what they see as fundamental distinctions in human ways of thinking. Some of these dichotomies are summarized in Table 5.1. Note that there is a family resemblance between the concepts within each column.

TABLE 5.1   Dichotomies of Mind

Convergent	Divergent
Intellectual	Intuitive
Deductive	Imaginative
Rational	Metaphorical
Vertical	Horizontal
Discrete	Continuous
Abstract	Concrete
Realistic	Impulsive
Directed	Free
Differential	Existential
Sequential	Multiple
Historical	Timeless
Analytical	Holistic
Explicit	Tacit
Objective	Subjective
Successive	Simultaneous

From Springer, S. P., & Deutsch, G. (1985). *Left Brain, Right Brain* (Rev. ed.). New York: W. H. Freeman. Copyright © 1981, 1985 by Sally P. Springer and Georg Deutsch. Reprinted with permission of W. H. Freeman and Company.

Much of the modern fascination with left and right hemispheres can be traced to Robert Ornstein's book, *The Psychology of Consciousness*, first published in 1972. In the "bimodal consciousness" model, Ornstein (also Bogen 1969) argued that various mental dichotomies such as those shown in Table 5.1 represent two different modes of consciousness, and that the two modes are due to the different cognitive styles of the left (verbal, rational) and right (spatial, intuitive) hemispheres, respectively. The dual modes of consciousness are said to exist simultaneously within the normal (unsplit) human brain. However, such extrapolations from split-brain data to statements about modes of consciousness do not stand up to close scrutiny (Corballis 1980; Gazzaniga 1985). They involve a series of generalizations and analogies that go beyond the data.

Since the first split-brain operations there has been a progression of labels used to describe left and right hemisphere functions (Springer & Deutsch 1985). Table 5.2 shows the most widely used labels, which form a hierarchical five-step series. At each level the labels usually include and go beyond the characteristics in the preceding levels. The labels at the top of the list are based on experimental evidence, the second level labels are based on controversial interpretations of available evidence, while the next three levels involve analogy and metaphor that go progressively further from the evidence. The general public, not knowing the nature and limitations of the actual data, has accepted the interpretation "rational left brain, intuitive, creative right brain" as if it is based firmly on the facts, which it is not.

It is easy to understand why Ornstein's reasoning has been so popular.

TABLE 5.2   Progression of Labels

LEFT HEMISPHERE	RIGHT HEMISPHERE
Verbal	Nonverbal, visuo-spatial
Sequential, temporal, digital	Simultaneous, spatial, analog
Logical, analytical	Gestalt, holistic, synthetic
Rational	Intuitive, creative
Western thought	Eastern thought

Source: Modified from Springer, S. P. & Deutsch, G. (1985). *Left Brain, Right Brain* (Rev. ed.). New York: W. H. Freeman.

It has seemed to provide a respectable scientific foundation for certain popular philosophical, religious, and psychological ideas. If materialist scientists do not take those ideas very seriously, they surely take the brain seriously, and linking philosophical and psychological dichotomies with particular parts of the brain makes them seem more respectable, more like "hard" science rather than mere "soft" philosophy and social science.

Distinctions between different styles of thinking and related philosophical, religious, and psychological theories may have great merit in their own right. But it is an inaccurate oversimplification to link them with one hemisphere or the other. A more accurate view is that in the normal brain different styles of thinking (rational, intuitive, imaginative) are complex processes that involve the interaction of different subsystems (or modules) within each hemisphere as well as interactions between the right and left hemispheres. Creative writing, for example, requires the special abilities of both hemispheres. Furthermore, recent evidence indicates that even relatively simple tasks (such as the blocks-design test) previously thought to be the specialty of a single hemisphere are often performed better by the intact brain than by the single (right) hemisphere (Gazzaniga 1988a, 1989).

SUMMARY

As background to the discussion of neuropsychological research in this chapter and the next, this chapter opened with a brief overview of the organization of the brain and nervous system, with an emphasis on four lobes of the cerebral cortex: occipital, temporal, parietal, and frontal. The "split-brain" operation involves severing the corpus callosum, a large tract of neurons that connects the left and right cerebral hemispheres. Testing the cognitive abilities of a single hemisphere requires that stimulus inputs and response outputs be limited to that hemisphere. This is done by taking advantage of the principle of contralateral organization, whereby each hemisphere receives sensory inputs only from the opposite side of the body, and controls movements of the opposite side. Test results show that in typical right-handed patients only the left hemisphere can speak. The right hemi-

sphere can make pointing responses (with the left hand) to show that it recognizes objects, as well as common words in some cases. The right hemisphere is superior to the left in visual-spatial tasks, such as discriminating
between similar-looking faces; the superiority is most apparent in tasks that
require drawing or construction of patterns (such as the blocks-design test).

The question of dual consciousness—whether split-brain patients have
a separate, independent consciousness in each hemisphere—boils down to
the question of whether the right hemisphere is conscious, since there is no
doubt about consciousness in the speaking left hemisphere. The difficulty in
deciding the issue is that the right hemisphere cannot make introspective
verbal reports. Sperry argued that consciousness can occur without language, and that a pattern of intelligent behavior (adaptive, spontaneous,
flexible) is a suitable criterion for consciousness. Several types of evidence
suggest right-hemisphere consciousness, including cognitive task performance, "alien hand" incidents, behavioral cross-cueing between hemispheres, and self-recognition and a sense of personal values.

Gazzaniga argued that the brain is composed of a number of relatively
independent, nonverbal, modules that can process information, make decisions, and produce emotional reactions and overt behaviors. Consciousness
is the output of a special interpreter module, which creates a sense of conscious unity by interpreting the outputs of various nonverbal, nonconscious
modules, which makes cause-and-effect inferences, and which can make verbal reports on its activities. The interpreter system normally occurs only in
the left hemisphere, in close association with the linguistic system, but it is
not identical to the linguistic system. Right-hemisphere cognitive activity is
carried out by nonconscious modules, in Gazzaniga's view. I suggested that
Gazzaniga's interpreter system is similar to the idea of reflective consciousness, and the evidence suggests that both the left and right hemispheres have
primary consciousness, but reflective consciousness may be limited to the
left hemisphere.

Finally, some popular extrapolations from the split-brain research
were discussed, whereby the two hemispheres have been identified with alternative "modes of consciousness" (left: analytical, rational; right: holistic,
intuitive, creative). Though these modes of thought are important in their
own right, the attempt to enhance their scientific validity by linking them
with the individual hemispheres goes beyond the research evidence. In normal
brains, complex cognitive activities use the abilities of both hemispheres.

ENDNOTES

[1]It is unnecessary for our present purposes to go into detail on the structure of neurons and
neural networks, the chemical processes of neurotransmission, or other aspects of fine brain
structure such as the columnar organization of neurons. Nor will we be concerned here with
more detailed aspects of gross neuroanatomy, such as the peripheral nervous system. For readers wanting to review these elements, most general psychology textbooks provide an adequate
introduction (for example, Atkinson et al. 1987; Darley et al. 1991). For more advanced discus-

sions see textbooks in physiological psychology (such as Carlson 1986; Rosenzweig & Leiman 1989) or neuropsychology (Kolb & Whishaw 1990).

[2]Left-hemisphere language is true of virtually all right-handed people, and about 70 percent of left-handed people. Roughly 15 percent of left-handed people have reverse dominance, with language functions in the right temporal lobe. Another 15 percent have mixed dominance, with language functions divided between the two temporal lobes. It has been speculated that mixed dominance is not the best way to organize language functions, and this may be related to the fact that left-handed people are statistically somewhat more likely than right-handed people to have speech and reading difficulties.

[3]For a striking case study of visual agnosia, see the title story of *The Man Who Mistook His Wife for a Hat*, by neurologist Oliver Sacks (1987). Sacks' book contains some twenty-four very interesting and readable case studies of patients with different types of brain damage and defects. For example, the chapter titled "The Lost Mariner" describes a Korsakoff's syndrome patient with severe amnesia. In *The Man with a Shattered World*, Alexander Luria (1987) described the case of a brain-injured war veteran whose speech and verbal thinking were severely impaired, but whose will-power led him to devise a strategy for writing his own autobiography. Both Luria (1973, 1978, 1987) and Sacks (1987) stressed the point that in most cases brain-injured people strive actively to compensate for their injuries. It is an oversimplification to talk about the deficits caused by injuries. Brain-injured individuals are still people with lives to live and goals to fulfill. They use the sensory, motor, and intellectual abilities that are still intact to compensate and navigate through life as well as possible. However, successful adaptation depends on having relatively intact frontal lobes to make plans and control voluntary actions.

[4]In their animal research, Myers and Sperry cut both the corpus callosum and the optic chiasm. This operation created a subject in which the left hemisphere could see only with the left eye, and the right hemisphere could see only with the right eye. (To be precise, the left hemisphere could see only the right visual field, through the left half of the retina of the left eye [and vice versa for the right hemisphere], as explained in Figure 5.3.) Thus, the monkey's left hemisphere could be trained on a visual discrimination by covering the right eye, so only the left-eye/left-hemisphere could see. With the left hemisphere in control, the monkey used its right hand to respond to the test stimuli (recall the principle of contralateral organization); the left hand was restrained. Subsequently, to test what the right hemisphere knew, the monkey was tested with its right eye open (left eye covered) and left hand free (right hand restrained).

[5]Subjects chose faces matching the left side of the chimera regardless of whether they pointed with their left hand or their right hand. This result can be explained by the fact that each hemisphere has some degree of movement control over its *ipsilateral* (same side) hand, even though the dominant control is contralateral. Thus, the right hemisphere can control gross pointing movements of the right hand, though it cannot control fine-skilled right-hand movements.

[6]It is worth noting here that Howard Gardner (1985) has presented evidence that there are several specialized "intelligences" that can solve problems in different spheres of activity, using different sorts of mental codes, mostly nonverbal. The six intelligences discussed by Gardner are: linguistic, musical, logical-mathematical, spatial, bodily-kinesthetic (movement, as in dance and athletics), and personal (including social relationships and self-understanding). Conscious thinking is implied in the flexible, adaptive control of various specialized activities by these specialized intelligences or mind-brain subsystems. Gardner's theory of specialized intelligences contrasts with the older theory of a single, general-purpose intelligence.

[7]Extrapolating from the evidence for dual consciousness in split-brain patients, some writers (Puccetti 1981) have suggested that dual consciousness—independent consciousness in each hemisphere—also occurs in normal brains. The dominant hemisphere normally suppresses the nondominant one, and the split-brain operation merely reveals a double consciousness that was always there. However, few researchers support this idea. Those who accept the evidence for dual consciousness in split-brain patients argue that dual consciousness was created by the commissurotomy (see commentaries following Puccetti 1981).

[8]Gazzaniga's conception of modules as "functional units that can produce behaviors and trigger emotional responses" is broader than the conception of modules proposed by other theorists (such as Fodor 1983; Schacter 1989), who see modules as more narrowly specialized computational subsystems that contribute to broader functional systems, such as language and men-

tal imagery systems (Gazzaniga 1988a). Gazzaniga mentioned modules for visual perception, visual mental imagery, and face perception. But like most writers, he declined to provide a detailed list of modules and their functions. That is a challenge for future research.

[9]Gazzaniga (1985) hinted at the possibility of right- hemisphere primary consciousness in a passage where he said that nonverbal modules should not be characterized as nonconscious merely because they "cannot internally communicate with the dominant hemisphere's language and cognitive system." A nonverbal module "is very conscious, very capable of [making decisions and] effecting action" (p. 117). He used the term "coconscious but nonverbal mental modules," but he did not expand on this conception. Instead he continued to emphasize the association of consciousness with the interpreter module, which has direct access to the verbal system.

[10]As we will see in later chapters, others besides Gazzaniga have proposed an intimate link between consciousness and interpretation processes. Either consciousness is an interpreter system, or conscious experience results from, or is influenced by, an interpreter system or interpretation processes. Just as there are different levels of consciousness, there are different levels or types of interpretation procesess. Thus, it is not strictly correct to say that reflective consciousness involves an interpreter system but primary consciousness does not. Rather, primary conscious experiences (such as sensory perception and dreaming) involve lower levels or different types of interpretation processes than those involved in reflective consciousness. Similarly, the disconnected right hemisphere might be better characterized as using lower level interpretation processes, rather than by the complete absence of a right-hemisphere interpreter system.

chapter 6 ··

Brain and Consciousness II: Dissociations between Consciousness and Behavior

One of the main concerns of the psychology of consciousness is the distinction between conscious and nonconscious mental processes. In order to understand the nature of consciousness and its functions, we need to know when conscious awareness does, or does not, accompany mental processes. Endel Tulving (1989) noted that until recently the relationship between consciousness and the cognitive processes of memory and perception was largely ignored by cognitive psychologists. He attributed this neglect to an implicit assumption, which he termed the *doctrine of concordance* of cognition, behavior, and experience:

> It holds that there exists a close and general, even if not perfect, agreement between what people know, how they behave, and what they experience. Thus, conscious awareness is [assumed to be] required for, and therefore accompanies, the acquisition of knowledge, or its retrieval from the memory store; retrieved knowledge guides behavior, and when this happens, people are aware of the relation between the knowledge and the behaviour; future behaviour is planned and ongoing behaviour is executed under the watchful eye of consciousness (p. 8).

Because of the doctrine of concordance, researchers assumed that human performance necessarily involves conscious awareness of the relevant stimuli or information stored in memory, and they did not look for exceptions to the rule. When evidence against concordance was found, such as evidence for subliminal perception, it was either ignored, regarded as a curiosity but not taken seriously, or vehemently attacked.[1]

Conscious versus nonconscious processing. Nowadays, however, most cognitive psychologists agree that much—perhaps most—of our mental processing occurs nonconsciously (Kihlstrom, 1987). Here, I distinguish between conscious and nonconscious processing as follows: *Conscious processing* is processing that occurs with awareness of the contents being processed. Awareness of contents might occur either at the end of the process, at intermediate stages along the way, or both. For example, conscious processing occurs when you see a word ("apple") and you consciously recognize the word and its meaning (an edible fruit) or you have an image associated with the word (such as a visual mental image of an apple). *Nonconscious processing* is processing that occurs without awareness of the contents being processed, that is, there is no awareness of either the outcome of the process or of intermediate stages along the way. Nonconscious processing is important because its outcome may affect peoples' behavior, their emotional reactions, or other mental processes that produce conscious outcomes. The prototype example of nonconscious processing is subliminal perception, where peoples' behavior is influenced by stimuli that are too brief to be consciously recognized.

It is important to note that conscious processing, by the definition given above, does not mean that people are introspectively aware of the mental processes themselves; it means only that they are aware of the contents or outcomes of the processes. For example, when you read a word ("apple"), you are not aware of the processes that analyze the visual pattern and match it against the thousands of word shapes stored in long-term memory until the correct word and its meaning are located. You are only aware of the result or outcome of the process, in which a particular word ("apple") and its meaning are consciously recognized. As I explained in Chapter 1, basic cognitive and sensory-motor skills or procedures—such as pattern recognition, memory retrieval, and selective attention—are stored in procedural memory and they operate automatically or by habit; we have no introspective access to their operational details. Thus, the distinction between conscious and unconscious processes depends on whether we are aware of their contents or outcomes, not whether we are aware of the processes themselves.

The purpose of this chapter is to describe some of the evidence for nonconscious information processing. The occurrence of nonconscious processing is demanded by a number of cognitive psychological theories (Kihlstrom 1987) as well as by the absence of introspective access to certain cognitive processes, such as pattern recognition. However, it has taken extraordinary ingenuity for researchers to provide explicit experimental demonstrations of nonconscious processing. The criterion for experimentally demonstrating nonconscious processing is to show behavioral evidence of information processing in the absence of conscious awareness of that information. In other words, we need to demonstrate a *dissociation* or disconnection between task performance and consciousness. A stimulus input or information stored in memory must affect subjects' responses, without them being aware of the stimulus or stored information. Ordinarily, when subjects perform experimental tasks, such as perception and memory tasks, they are consciously aware of the input stimuli or remembered information that they use to perform the task. Thus, it has been necessary to develop special procedures to demonstrate nonconscious processing. This chapter will emphasize research on nonconscious processing in brain-damaged subjects. I will also describe some evidence for nonconscious processing in normal subjects (such as subliminal perception).

Neuropsychological syndromes.   Neuropsychologists have discovered several syndromes in which brain-damaged patients show a dissociation or disconnection between consciousness and performance on certain types of tasks (Schacter, McAndrews & Moscovitch 1988; Weiskrantz 1988a). That is, the brain-damaged patients/subjects can perform the tasks without being consciously aware of the external stimuli or memory information that affects their responses—though the test procedure is one in which normal people would be aware of the relevant stimuli or memory information. The last chapter discussed research on split-brain patients, a dissociation syndrome in which the mute right hemisphere can perform a variety of cognitive tasks without the speaking left hemisphere knowing what the right hemisphere is seeing, thinking, or doing. This chapter considers dissociations in patients that have suffered injuries to specific parts of the brain, resulting in impairment or loss of certain cognitive functions; for example, patients with cortical blindness or amnesia. In "blindsight," cortically blind patients are able to respond to visual stimuli that they do not consciously see. And amnesic patients can use information stored in memory, without consciously recalling that information or the occasion when they learned it. Such cases can help us understand what sorts of cognitive processing can occur without awareness, and it gives important clues about the relationships between brain processes and consciousness.

Schacter et al. (1988) described dissociations between awareness and performance as dissociations between explicit and implicit knowledge. *Explicit knowledge* is knowledge that subjects can use to perform a task while also being consciously aware that they possess the knowledge. *Implicit knowledge* is knowledge that is used to perform a task without subjects being consciously aware that they possess it. Implicit knowledge is nonconscious; it does not have access to consciousness.

BLINDSIGHT

In normal visual perception you are consciously aware of objects. You can point to them, identify them, and verbally describe them. You respond to objects with a high degree of confidence in your perception: you know *that* you are seeing and you know *what* you are seeing. Under special circumstances, however, people can respond to objects without knowing what they are seeing, or even knowing that they are seeing. In *blindsight*, patients with damage to the brain's primary visual area can respond discriminatively to different stimuli, even though they deny seeing the stimuli.

Visual stimuli are analyzed primarily in the *occipital lobe* of the cerebral cortex. The first stage of visual analysis for object recognition occurs in the *striate cortex* (also known as the primary visual area), which is located at the very back of the occipital lobes (see Figure 5.2, Chapter 5). When someone has a lesion (wound) in the striate cortex, some degree of cortical blindness will occur. The person will be totally blind if the striate cortex is totally destroyed, even though the eyes and optic nerves are undamaged. More commonly, however, only part of the striate cortex is destroyed, and the person is blind in only part of their visual field. The visual field is mapped precisely on the occipital cortex, so that damage in a particular part of the cortex will cause blindness in a particular part of the visual field. The visual fields are mapped on the occipital cortex *contralaterally,* such that the right visual field (RVF, the part to the right of the visual fixation point) is mapped on the left striate cortex, whereas the left visual field (LVF) is mapped on the right striate cortex (Figure 5.3). A blind spot in part of the visual field, caused by a striate lesion, is called a *scotoma.* Thus, a lesion in part of the left striate area would cause a scotoma in the RVF. Complete, or nearly complete, loss of vision in one visual field caused by extensive damage to the contralateral striate area is termed *hemianopia.*

A puzzling difference between the performance of monkeys and humans with striate damage has been known for over one hundred years (Weiskrantz, 1980). Like humans with accidental striate lesions, monkeys with extensive experimental striate lesions appear to be blind, according to observations of their behavior under ordinary conditions. But with special training, cortically blind monkeys were able to learn to perform conditioned responses to visual stimuli, and to discriminate the location and orientation of visual stimuli. Yet, when humans with similar (accidental) lesions were asked to make the same visual discriminations, they said that they couldn't see anything. Two questions arise: First, how could cortically blind monkeys perform visual discriminations? Second, why couldn't cortically blind humans do this?

Neuroanatomical research has shown that monkeys have not one, but ten different visual pathways from the optic nerves to various parts of the cortex (Weiskrantz, 1990). The primary visual pathway, with a large majority of the one million neurons in each optic nerve, goes through the dorsal-lateral geniculate nucleus in the thalamus (a sensory relay station in the central core) to the striate cortex in the occipital lobes. But some 150,000 of the neurons go via other relay stations to secondary visual areas in other parts of the occipital lobes and temporal lobes. Thus, when the monkey's primary (striate) visual area is destroyed, some degree of visual capacity remains due to the secondary visual areas. But since visual-system neuroanatomy is quite similar for humans and monkeys, it was puzzling that secondary visual areas did not seem to be able to support simple visual discriminations in humans as they do in monkeys. The solution to this puzzle came when neuropsychologists developed special testing procedures for cortically blind humans, to demonstrate their residual visual capacities.

Lawrence Weiskrantz and his colleagues (Weiskrantz, Warrington, et al. 1974; Weiskrantz 1980, 1986) tested a man who had had a tumor removed from his right visual cortex. The result was that the patient—known as D.B.—had a left hemianopia, in which he was blind in the lower half of the left visual field, as well as most of the upper half. D.B. could not name or describe objects presented in his blind field, and he reported no awareness of them. Weiskrantz et al. devised ways of testing D.B.'s visual sensitivity, using forced-choice procedures. In *forced-choice procedures*, subjects are required to choose among a limited number of alternative responses (such as "yes" or "no"), even if it is just a guess; they are not allowed to say "I don't know." In the first test, the patient focused on a fixation point in the middle of a projection screen, then a small spot of light was flashed very briefly in the blind LVF area. The spot was flashed in different positions to the left of the fixation point on different trials. D.B. was required to point to the position where he thought the spot was flashed. It took some coaxing to get him to respond at first, since he said he did not see anything, and he felt silly trying to point to something that he didn't see. Yet, his pointing performance was remarkably accurate (see Figure 6.1). Thus, D.B. showed a dissociation between conscious visual experience and pointing performance on the spot-location task. In Schacter et al.'s (1988) terms, D.B. had implicit knowledge of the spot's location.

D.B. has also shown dissociations between conscious visual experience and performance on several other visual tasks. For example, he can distinguish between vertical, horizontal, and diagonal lines, and also between simple patterns (X versus O; straight-sided versus curved-sided triangles), provided that the stimuli are larger than a critical size. D.B.'s visual acuity was measured by asking him to discriminate the presence versus absence of gratings (patterns of crossed vertical and horizontal lines). In a random sequence, sometimes the stimulus was a grating, and sometimes it was a blank white screen of equal brightness. Visual acuity was measured by varying the grating's spatial frequency (number of lines per centimeter), where gratings of higher spatial frequency required finer visual acuity to distinguish them from the blank screen. In some regions of the "blind" field, acuity was actually higher than in some off-center regions of the sighted visual field.

In all of these visual tasks, successful performance depended on using a forced-choice response, such as requiring D.B. to say "yes" or "no," or point, or choose from a limited set of alternatives. In all cases in which stimuli were presented in the blind field, he insisted that he did not see anything. Performance on particular tasks tended to improve with practice, even though D.B. was not given any feedback on the correctness of his responses. In some cases, after extensive practice, D.B. reported a vague awareness that "something was there" (referring to a stimulus), but the subjective experience was not a visual experience. The distinction between visual experience and its absence was shown in some tests in which stimuli were presented in a small *amblyopic* area (area of spared vision) in the damaged LVF. D.B. reported that he could "see" patterns in the amblyopic area; he had a subjective visual experience, even though his vision was fuzzy in that area. In contrast, he said he could not see anything when the pattern was presented in a nearby scotomic (blind) area. Yet the grating test showed that visual acuity was actually better in some parts of the scotomic area than in the amblyopic area.

Blindsight is not found in all patients with cortical blindness. But by using forced-choice procedures various investigators have shown that some patients can discriminate one or more of the following visual stimulus dimensions: presence, position, orientation, flicker, wavelength (color), move-
-ment, and simple forms (results are somewhat ambiguous for forms; Weiskrantz 1986, 1990). The different patterns of residual visual abilities are

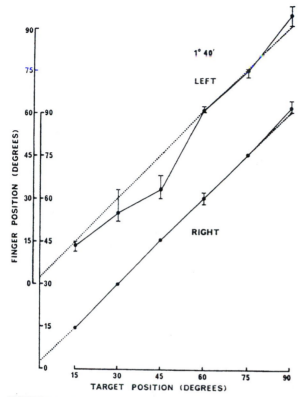

FIGURE 6.1. Average finger-reaching responses for blindsight subject, for targets in the left (blind) and right (normal) visual fields. The horizontal axis shows the position where the target (a spot of light, 1°40′ in diameter) was flashed, in degrees to the left or right of the central fixation point. The vertical axis shows the average position of the subject's reaching (pointing) response; vertical bars show the ranges. Perfect performance is indicated by the dotted line. The graph for the right visual field is displaced downward by 30 degrees. [From Weiskrantz, L., Warrington, E. K., Sanders, M. D., & Marshall, J. (1974). Visual capacity in the hemianopic field following a restricted occipital ablation. *Brain, 97,* 709–28. By permission of Oxford University Press.]

bly related to the different location and extent of the lesions in different patients. What the patients have in common is that with forced-choice procedures they can successfully perform certain visual tasks even though they insist that they cannot see the stimuli. But they cannot perform tasks requiring explicit, conscious recognition, such as naming different objects shown in their blind field.

A problem in using forced-choice procedures is getting the subjects' cooperation: "Sometimes the subjects are so adamant that they cannot see that the forced-choice guessing requirement is dismissed as nonsense. Some stubbornly refuse to play such a game, and even accuse the experimenter of forcing them to lie" (Weiskrantz 1990, p. 257). After D.B. had had several years of practice on forced-choice tasks, during which his performance improved, Weiskrantz asked him whether he could see the stimuli any better than before. D.B. replied "No, but I now feel free to make this kind of [forced-choice] judgment. I have confidence. At first I was always afraid that I was somehow cheating or doing something silly" (p. 257).

Forced-choice procedures may be called *direct methods*, in that they require subjects to respond directly to a test stimulus in their blind field (as in pointing to it). In order to bypass the difficulties of direct methods, researchers have developed *indirect methods* of testing that do not require subjects to respond to stimuli that they deny seeing (Weiskrantz 1990). Some indirect methods take advantage of bilateral interaction effects, in which the response to a stimulus in the sighted field is affected by a stimulus in the blind field. For example, in the *visual completion effect*, when a circle is flashed—centered on the fixation point, such that the left half falls in the sighted field and the right half in the blind field—subjects report that they saw a whole circle. But if only the left half-circle is flashed to the sighted field, they report that they saw a left half-circle, whereas if the right half-circle is flashed to the blind field, they report that they saw nothing (Torjussen 1978). Thus, a figure in the blind field can complete a figure in the sighted field, though the figure in the blind field cannot be consciously seen by itself. Other indirect testing methods use unconditioned reflexes to stimuli projected to the blind field. For example, Zihl et al. (1980) measured the galvanic skin response, and Weiskrantz (1990) measured pupil-contraction responses.

In all cases of blindsight, regardless of the behavioral measurement technique, subjects with striate damage respond to visual stimuli that they cannot consciously see. The implication is that only the primary visual pathway, via the striate cortex, connects to brain circuits that generate conscious visual experience. The primary pathway is necessary for the full range of visual perception, including object recognition and complex visually guided locomotion. But secondary visual areas are sufficient for some types of visual discriminative responding, without awareness. Thus, contrary to a behaviorist analysis that equates seeing with discriminative responding to visual stimuli, blindsight studies show that discriminative visual responding is not equivalent to conscious seeing.

AMNESIA

In the amnesic syndrome, the dissociation between consciousness and performance is a matter of explicit versus implicit memory. Patients may be able to perform certain tasks that require them to use remembered information or skills, but they have no conscious recollection of the information or of having learned the skill (Schacter 1987; Schacter et al. 1988; Weiskrantz 1988a).

Amnesia is a partial or total loss of memory due to brain injury or disease. There are two varieties of amnesia: (1) *anterograde amnesia*, the inability to learn new information or to recall events that have occurred since the injury; and (2) *retrograde amnesia*, the inability to recall information learned or events that occurred prior to the injury. In most cases amnesia is not com plete, but patchy, with some events being recalled and others not. Antero-grade amnesia is the most characteristic feature of the *amnesic syndrome*; retro-grade amnesia may or may not be present, depending on the nature and extent of the injury (Kolb & Whishaw 1990). This discussion concerns anterograde amnesia.

The full-blown amnesic syndrome is most likely to occur in patients with lesions of the medial temporal lobes, including the hippocampus, which is a part of the limbic system that intrudes into the inner region of the temporal lobes (Weiskrantz 1985, 1988a). Amnesic syndrome can also be caused in several other ways, including closed head injury, disrupted blood supply to part of the brain (due to plugged arteries [stroke] or broken arteries [ruptured aneurysms]). Amnesia is probably most common in cases of Alzheimer's disease and Korsakoff's disease. Alzheimer's is a mysterious, progressive, irreversible disease involving plaques and tangles of nerve fibers, which affects a significant minority of persons over sixty-five years old. Korsakoff's disease is characteristic of long-term alcoholics who suffer from malnutrition; specifically, it involves a deficiency in thiamine (vitamin B_1), which is critical for proper brain functioning.

Amnesia can occur despite preservation of perceptual, linguistic, and most intellectual skills. Short-term memory is usually intact, as is shown by the ability to repeat immediately a random string of digits or words. However, severe amnesics have no ability to recall information to which they were exposed only a minute or two earlier, or to recognize names or faces of people that they met a minute or so earlier. One of the classic amnesia cases is H.M., who had both of his medial temporal lobes surgically removed in order to eliminate severe, incapacitating epilepsy. Afterward, he could still carry on routine conversations, though he was unlikely to initiate them. He would sometimes read the same magazine over and over again, because he couldn't recall having read it the previous day, or earlier that same day. Neuropsychologists who studied H.M. described his experience:

> During three of the nights at the Clinical Research Center, the patient rang for the night nurse, asking her, with many apologies, if she would tell him where he was and how he came to be there. He clearly realized that he was in a hospital but seemed unable to reconstruct any of the events of the previous day. On another occasion he remarked "Every day is alone in itself, whatever enjoyment I've had, and whatever sorrow I've had." Our own impression is that many events fade for him long before the day is over. He often volunteers stereotyped descriptions of his own state by saying it is "like waking from a dream." His experience seems to be that of a person who is just becoming aware of his surroundings without fully comprehending the situation, because he does not remember what went before (Milner, Corkin, & Teuber 1968, pp. 216–17).

H.M. and other severe amnesics cannot perform tests of explicit memory, such as recalling and reporting lists of words or phrases to which they have been exposed. Nor can they perform tests of recognition memory for words or faces to which they have recently been exposed. Forgetting is most severe if there is a delay of a minute or more between exposure and test, and an opportunity for interference to occur. The amnesic syndrome, involving an intact short-term memory (STM) and an inability to transfer new information from STM to long-term memory (LTM) while still being able to retrieve old (pre-accident) information from LTM, is one of the main pieces of evidence supporting multistore theories of memory (Warrington 1982).

In contrast to their inability to learn semantic information and recall personal experiences, global amnesic patients are often able to learn new motor skills through practice, though they cannot consciously recall having practiced that skill. For example, H.M. improved with practice on the pursuit rotor task, which involves trying to track manually a dime-sized spot as it rotates around-and-around on a turntable. H.M.'s percent of time-on-target increased with practice. His ability to perform mirror drawing, accurately tracing patterns (such as a star) in a situation where he could see the pattern and pencil only in a mirror, also improved with practice. Thus, H.M. showed a dissociation between performance and consciousness. He had implicit memory of the prior practice sessions, insofar as his performance improved with practice, but he had no explicit, conscious memory of having practiced the tasks previously.

The implicit-explicit memory dissociation in amnesics has also been shown in cognitive tasks. For example, Warrington and Weiskrantz (1974) showed amnesics lists of words to study. Just a few minutes later the amnesics could not perform tests of explicit memory: that is, they could not consciously recall the words that they had studied or reliably recognize them in a list of old (previously exposed) words mixed with new words. However, they showed enhanced performance in an implicit memory test, the word-stem completion test. In the *stem completion test*, word stems are shown and subjects are required to fill in the blanks to complete the words. (Try it: tur__ __ __; spa __ __ __ __ .) Normal people do stem completion tests more accurately for words to which they have recently been exposed than for words to which they have not recently been exposed; this is a type of *repetition priming effect* (Schacter 1987). Like normal people, amnesics show a repetition priming effect on word stem completion tests (as well as on word completion tests with blank spaces in the middle of the word, instead of the end; for example, s __ __ d __ r). Yet, amnesics do not consciously recall that they previously saw the words on a list; they treat the completion test as a sort of "guessing game." Table 6.1 shows data for amnesics and normal control subjects on stem completion and yes/no recognition tests involving words on lists seen ten to fifteen minutes before testing. Amnesics did much worse than normals on explicit recognition tests, but they did not differ significantly from normals on stem completion (implicit memory) tests. In a later

TABLE 6.1   Probabilities of Recognition and Stem Completion for Previously Exposed Words in Amnesic and Normal Subjects

	MEASURE OF MEMORY RETENTION	
Subjects	RECOGNITION	STEM COMPLETION
Amnesic patients	0.25	0.34
Control subjects	0.73	0.28

Data from Warrington, E. K., & Weiskrantz, L. (1974). The effect of prior learning on subsequent retention in amnesic patients. *Neuropsychologia, 12,* 419–28. (Exp. 1).

study (Graf, Squire, & Mandler 1984), when amnesics were instructed to use the word stems deliberately to help them recall the previously studied words, they did worse than controls on the stem completion test. Apparently the instructions had the effect of changing the completion test from an implicit memory test to an explicit one, at which amnesics do poorly.

In another implicit memory test involving a repetition priming effect, Schacter (1985) showed amnesics a series of word pairs to study; the pairs were from common idioms (such as SOUR-GRAPES). Later, the subjects did well in an implicit memory test, in which the experimenter showed them the first word of each pair, and asked them to simply write down the next word that came to mind. Like normal subjects, amnesic subjects responded with the correct word to complete the idiom pair more often for pairs that they had previously studied than for control idiom pairs that they had not seen in the experiment. But the subjects did poorly in an explicit memory test, in which the experimenter showed them the first word of each pair and asked them to recall the second word. Again, it appears that the experimenter's instructions can change the task from a test of implicit memory, at which amnesics can do well, into a test of explicit memory, at which amnesics do poorly. Repetition priming effects indicate that amnesics can store and use information about words to which they have recently been exposed, though they cannot explicitly recall the words or the occasion when they saw them.

In describing the memory deficits and abilities of amnesics, we can sort out most of the effects in terms of different types of long-term memory: episodic, semantic, and procedural memory (Tulving 1983, 1985a). Amnesia affects episodic and semantic memory, but not procedural memory. The most consistent memory deficits involve episodic memory, the recall of personal experiences. For example, severe amnesics cannot remember reading a particular magazine or meeting a particular person earlier in the day. Recalling or recognizing lists of words learned in an experiment is a special case of episodic memory, and amnesics fail at explicit recall and recognition attempts. However, amnesics may have normal semantic memory of prior knowledge about the words, that is, they can still read and understand words that they knew prior to their injury.

Explicit memory for newly presented semantic information, such as impersonal facts and the meanings of new vocabulary words, is ordinarily poor in amnesics. However, some ability to acquire new semantic information often remains. When amnesics are able to recall newly presented factual (or fictitious) information (such as "Bob Hope's father was a fireman") they are usually unable to recall when and where they learned the information (Schacter, Harbluk, & McLachlan 1984; Shimamura & Squire 1987). This dissociation between semantic and episodic memory is termed *source amnesia*.

Amnesics also show a dissociation between episodic and procedural memory. They can learn new sensory-motor skills (such as pursuit rotor) that involves procedural memory, but they do not recall the experience of practicing the skill on previous occasions. Skills in procedural memory can be executed without direct conscious control. Procedural memory apparently involves different brain mechanisms than episodic memory.

The pattern of deficits and abilities in amnesics is complex, and no theory accounts for all of the findings (Schacter 1987). In particular, repetition priming effects cannot be readily explained in terms of the episodic-semantic-procedural memory types. It is noteworthy that repetition priming occurs in normal subjects as well as amnesics, and it has been demonstrated in normals using faces and drawings of objects and abstract geometric figures, as well as words. The effect can last for several days or more, though it decreases with time. In normals, repetition priming occurs regardless of whether subjects can explicitly recall or recognize the stimuli seen previously in the experimental context. Thus, in normals as in amnesics, priming can occur even when subjects do not consciously recognize the stimuli as familiar (Schacter 1987; Tulving & Schacter 1990). Also, normal subjects tested during posthypnotic amnesia show repetition priming effects for words previously memorized during hypnosis, though they cannot explicitly recall the words previously seen (Kihlstrom 1980).

The ubiquity of repetition priming and its independence from explicit (recognition) memory have led Schacter and Tulving (Schacter 1990a; Tulving & Schacter 1990) to suggest that repetition priming—which they now call *perceptual priming*—indicates a newly discovered type of memory, the *perceptual representation system* (PRS). The PRS is "hyperspecific," in that it concerns the exact appearance of objects (or printed words) rather than their abstract characteristics or meaning. The PRS involves specialized brain modules, probably in the anterior occipital lobes (forward of the striate area) for visual stimuli. The PRS is normally connected with episodic-semantic memory systems, but it can become disconnected from them and continue to function on its own, as in amnesia. The PRS can operate nonconsciously. Thus, the PRS can produce repetition (perceptual) priming effects, without subjects being aware that they were previously exposed to the stimuli in the experimental context.

In conclusion, amnesics are able to perform certain tasks involving implicit memory, despite a lack of conscious knowledge of the information used in performing those tasks, and without being able to recall when and where they learned the relevant information or skill. The parallel to blindsight is that whereas blindsight patients show an effect of current stimuli on performance, without conscious awareness of the stimuli, amnesics show an effect of past stimuli on performance, without conscious recall of the stimuli. In a later section I will describe Schacter's DICE model that attempts to account for both blindsight and implicit memory effects, but first I will briefly describe some related neuropsychological phenomena.

OTHER NEUROPSYCHOLOGICAL DISSOCIATION SYNDROMES

Several other syndromes have been discovered where, as in blindsight, brain-damaged patients can perform certain perceptual tasks even though they are not consciously aware of the stimuli or cannot consciously discriminate between them (reviews by Schacter et al. 1988; Weiskrantz, 1988a).

Blind-touch. "Blind-touch" is a tactile analogy to blindsight (Paillard et al. 1983). A patient with damage to the somatosensory cortex had no conscious awareness of being touched on her hand, yet in a forced-choice procedure she could discriminate between different touch locations.

Prosopagnosia.   Prosopagnosia is a deficit in the ability to identify familiar faces. It is usually caused by bilateral (both sides) lesions to the occipital-temporal cortical regions, though it occurs in some cases with only right-side damage. Prosopagnosics are unable to identify familiar people, such as family members and famous people, by their faces alone. In most cases they are still able to identify other familiar visual objects, and they can distinguish between faces and objects that are not faces, but they cannot consciously discriminate between familiar and unfamiliar faces. They continue to recognize familiar names, and know who the names represent, but they cannot name familiar faces. Special procedures have shown that some prosopagnosics have nonconscious, implicit knowledge of familiar faces. For example, Bauer (1984) showed a prosopagnosic patient pictures of famous faces, such as actors and politicians. The patient could not name the faces, and on multiple-choice tests in which the experimenter read five names aloud (all from the same category, such as actors), the patient selected the correct name at only a chance level (20 percent correct). Yet on a physiological measure, the skin conductance response (SCR), the subject responded maximally to the correct name on 60 percent of the trials. (Normal control subjects could name almost all of the faces, and made correct SCRs on 90 percent of the multiple-choice trials.) The well-above-chance SCR performance of the prosopagnosic patient showed that he had implicit knowledge of the face names.

Dyslexia.   Dyslexia refers to disruptions of the ability to read, due to some sort of brain damage or developmental abnormality. Dyslexias usually involve damage or abnormalities in the left posterior (rear) temporal lobe and adjacent areas of the occipital cortex. There are several varieties of dyslexia, of greater or lesser severity, associated with different brain conditions. In the syndrome of *alexia without agraphia*, patients can identify individual letters but they cannot read whole word patterns. They can identify words by the slow process of decoding them letter-by-letter. Landis et al. (1980) tested such a patient's implicit word recognition ability by flashing words (object names) very briefly on a screen, making the flash much too brief for the patient to decode the word letter-by-letter. The patient could not consciously identify the word. Yet on a forced-choice test he was able "intuitively" to choose the correct object (such as a pencil) from among a large array of objects on a table. The choice could not be based on the word's first letter alone, since there were always at least two objects whose name started with the same critical letter (pencil and paper). When the patient was asked to deliberately base his choice on the first letter (instead of choosing intuitively), his performance deteriorated. Landis et al. (1980) concluded that the patient was capable of pure "iconic reading"—in which visual word stimuli automatically access semantic information about the words, which is sufficient for correct "intuitive" object choices—though the words were not translated to verbal-acoustic codes with conscious recognition. Apparently, attempts to explicitly translate the visual word to a verbal-acoustic code interfered with the rapid iconic reading process.

Aphasia.   In general, aphasia is a disruption of language processes, including either production or comprehension processes, as a result of brain damage. It occurs as a result of damage to the left temporal lobe and/or nearby areas of the frontal, parietal, or occipital lobes. There are several types of aphasia, associated with damage to different brain areas. Of particular interest here is *Wernicke's aphasia*, characterized by problems in both speech comprehension and speech production. Though their speech may be quite fluent and often grammatically correct, sentences produced by Wernicke's aphasics are largely meaningless. They include mispronounced words, substitution of inappropriate words, and sometimes neologisms (invented words). Aphasics' speech has been characterized as a "word salad." It appears that connections between consciousness and semantic memory are disrupted in Wernicke's aphasics, insofar as they are unable to retrieve suitable words to express their conscious intentions. In a test of explicit semantic knowledge, Wernicke's aphasics performed at a chance level when asked to make yes/no judgments of the semantic relatedness of various word pairs (such as sport, football; fruit, rose; see Milberg & Blumstein 1981). However, their semantic memory seemed to be functioning normally in a test of implicit semantic knowledge: In the *lexical decision task*, they were required to judge, as quickly as possible, whether a string of letters was a word (such as "monkey" or "murdey"). Like normals, Wernicke's aphasics responded faster to words ("bank") when they followed semantically related words ("money-bank") than when they followed unrelated words ("monkey-bank") or nonwords ("murdey-bank"). It appears that though Wernicke's aphasics could not judge the semantic relatedness of words at a conscious level, they had implicit, nonconscious knowledge of semantic relatedness.

Hemineglect.   Hemineglect (unilateral neglect) is one of the strangest of the neuropsychological syndromes. Patients with parietal lobe damage may neglect the side of space contralateral to the lesion. Most commonly this occurs in patients with damage to the right parietal lobe. Subsequently, if asked to draw a scene, they will draw only the right side of it. If asked to bisect a horizontal line, they will place their bisecting mark to the right of center, as if they did not see all of the left side of the line. Some patients fail to groom the left side of their body. This left-side neglect occurs even though the patients are free to move their head and eyes to see the whole scene in either the left or right visual field. Hemineglect is a disorder of space perception, rather than of vision. Patients sometimes report objects from the left side of space, but mistakenly locate them in the right side.

Nonconscious perception of the neglected side of space has been shown in hemineglect patients in a study of the phenomenon of extinction to double simultaneous stimulation (Volpe, LeDoux, & Gazzaniga 1979). Some patients can accurately describe single stimuli (pictures, words) placed in either their left or right visual field, but if stimuli are presented simultaneously in both fields, only the right-side stimulus can be accurately described; they are either unaware of the left-side stimulus, or vaguely aware of it but unable to describe it. Yet, if required to judge whether the two stimuli are the same or different in a forced-choice procedure, their performance is well above chance (88 to 100 percent).

Marshall and Halligan (1988) reported a novel case of implicit knowledge in a hemineglect patient. The patient was presented simultaneously with two line drawings of a house, aligned centrally, one above the other. The drawings were identical except that one of them had flames coming out the left side. On repeated trials, the patient reported that the two drawings were identical; she did not notice the flames. When asked which house she would prefer to live in, she thought it was a silly question "because they're the same," but nonetheless she reliably chose the house that was not burning. In another series of trials, one of the houses had flames coming out the right side, and she immediately noticed the flames. Finally, during another series of trials with flames on the left side, she suddenly exclaimed "Oh my God, this one's on fire!"

Schacter et al. (1988) pointed out that the interpretation of hemineglect is still a matter of debate. One view is that it is analogous to other neuropsychological dissociation phenomena, such as blindsight: in hemineglect, spatially coded information cannot gain access to consciousness. An alternative view is that hemineglect is a disorder of attention, in which left-side spatial information is potentially available to consciousness, but attention is systematically directed away from it. At this point, it is uncertain whether the explanations applied to syndromes such as blindsight can also be applied to hemineglect.

EXPLAINING DISSOCIATION SYNDROMES

In blindsight, amnesia, and other neuropsychological syndromes involving dissociations between performance and consciousness, the claim that the patients are not consciously aware of the stimuli that control their performance is based mainly on their introspective verbal reports. For example, blindsight subjects *say* that they cannot see the test stimuli, even though their forced-choice performance is good and indicates that at some level the stimuli are perceived. Thus, in trying to explain the dissociation syndromes, we should first consider the alternative that the patients really are aware of the critical stimuli, but that there is a defect in their subjective verbal reports. How might the introspective verbal reporting process be defective in these patients?

One possibility is that in blindsight, for example, there is a dissociation between consciousness (that is, the conscious brain structures or circuits) and the verbal reporting mechanisms of the brain. Such an explanation is appropriate for split-brain patients, whose mute right hemisphere cannot verbally report what it consciously sees; only the left hemisphere can verbally describe its visual experiences. However, there are reasons to doubt that this explanation applies to blindsight, amnesia, and so forth (Schacter et al. 1988). First, the patients can verbally report aspects of conscious experience that are not affected by brain damage. For example, blindsight patients can verbally report visual perceptions from their sighted field. And amnesics can verbally describe memories of experiences that occurred prior to the onset of amnesia. Second, claims of lack of explicit, conscious knowledge of stimuli do not depend entirely on introspective verbal reports. The lack of explicit knowledge has also been shown with tests involving forced-choice procedures, for example, prosopagnosics failing to select the correct names for familiar faces in multiple-choice tests. Third, the patients' subjective experiences in the dissociation syndromes are quite different from those in certain syndromes that specifically involve disruption of language processes. For example, *anomia* is a type of aphasia in which patients cannot name familiar objects. Yet, anomic patients can consciously recall and use knowledge about such objects: what they do, where they are found, how to use them. There is a big difference between consciously knowing something while being unable to verbally describe it (as in anomic patients), versus not consciously knowing something and saying that you do not know it (as in the dissociation syndromes). Thus, the idea that subjects with blindsight and other dissociation syndromes cannot make introspective reports of their conscious experience can be rejected.

A second possible explanation of dissociation effects in terms of subjective report failures is that dissociation patients have a *conservative response bias*. For example, Campion et al. (1983) suggested that blindsight patients might actually have *degraded* subjective visual experiences of stimuli in their blind fields (rather than *absence* of subjective visual experiences), but they are reluctant to say that they see something when they really do not see it very well. However, this explanation fails to capture the essence of blindsight patients' actual subjective experiences. The subjective reports of blindsight patients clearly distinguish between stimuli presented in their blind area, where they say that they cannot consciously see the stimuli at all, versus stimuli presented in amblyopic areas, where they say that they see the stimuli but that the stimuli are very fuzzy. Yet, forced-choice tests with line gratings show that visual acuity may be as sharp, or sharper, in parts of the blind area as in the amblyopic area (Weiskrantz 1986).

The evidence indicates that dissociation syndromes cannot be explained simply as a disconnection between consciousness and verbal reporting mechanisms. Rather, there is a disconnection between consciousness and mechanisms that perform the tasks that reveal implicit knowledge. It is important to note that the dissociation syndromes are *domain specific*, that is, the failure of awareness is limited to specific types of information (Schacter et al. 1988). For example, blindsight patients are not amnesic; prosopagnosics cannot consciously recognize faces but they can still read and identify other objects. An important implication of domain specificity is that different types of cognitive tasks may be carried out by different specialized *cognitive modules* of the brain. The dissociation syndromes apparently involve disconnection of specific modules from consciousness.

DICE: A model to explain dissociation syndromes.

Daniel Schacter (1989) developed a theoretical model to explain dissociation syndromes. The model is nicknamed DICE, for Dissociable Interactions and Conscious Experience. The model, shown in Figure 6.2, includes several subsystems (boxes) and arrows to indicate the direction of information flow or control

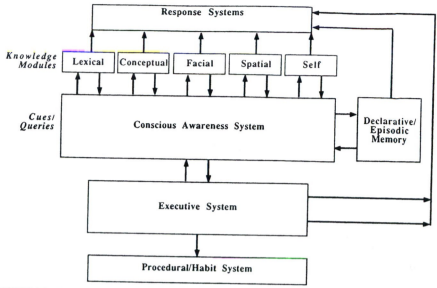

FIGURE 6.2. A schematic depiction of Schacter's DICE model. Conscious awareness of specific types of information depends on intact connections between the Conscious Awareness System (CAS) and individual knowledge modules or declarative/episodic memory. [From Schacter, D. L. (1989). On the relation between memory and consciousness: Dissociable interactions and conscious experience. In H. L. Roediger & F. I. M. Craik (Eds.), *Varieties of Memory and Consciousness* (pp. 355–389). Hillsdale, NJ: Lawrence Erlbaum. By permission of the publisher.]

between subsystems. The subsystems include: (1) The *Conscious Awareness System* (CAS), which enables subjective awareness of many types of information coming from various knowledge modules. (2) *Knowledge modules*, each one specialized for different types of tasks. Knowledge modules store thoroughly learned information (semantic memory knowledge) relevant to their type of processing, control responses (such as verbal, manual) to carry out their tasks, and produce outputs to the conscious awareness system about the information contents being processed. (3) The *executive system*, which makes decisions and initiates voluntary actions; it is especially important for flexible responding in novel situations. Note that the conscious awareness system does not control actions, though it provides information to the executive system to use in making its decisions about voluntary actions, and to the specialized modules to use for controlling their responses. The executive system produces outputs to CAS, so CAS knows about the executive decisions. (4) The *procedural/habit system*, which is used by the executive system to carry out learned, automatic cognitive and motor skills. The procedural/habit system produces no inputs to CAS; thus its activities occur nonconsciously. (5) The *declarative/episodic memory system*, which stores knowledge of recent events, indexed according to their context in time and space. It provides CAS with recently learned information, as well as knowledge of the context in which that information was learned or in which the person had a particular personal experience.

According to the DICE model, all conscious experiences of perceiving, remembering, and knowing depend on the Conscious Awareness System (CAS). The specific nature of a conscious experience depends on an interaction between CAS and a specific knowledge module or declarative/episodic memory. In dissociation syndromes there is a disconnection between CAS and a specific knowledge module or declarative/episodic memory. Implicit knowledge can still be used because of the connections between the specialized modules and the response systems, but the individual has no awareness of the knowledge being processed. For example, blindsight subjects are not consciously aware of the location of a spot because the spatial-perception module is disconnected from CAS, but the spatial module can still control pointing responses. Also, amnesics can show repetition priming effects because the declarative/episodic memory system can control responses, such as filling in the blanks on word-completion tests—though as a result of the declarative/episodic system being disconnected from CAS, the subject is unaware that the words were previously presented in the experimental context.[2]

Schacter (1989) pointed out that one risk of a theory that attempts to identify conscious experience with a particular mechanism (such as CAS) is that that mechanism will come to be endowed with homunculus-like properties, and used to explain all sorts of activities that are associated with consciousness. To avoid the homunculus fallacy, it is important to try to specify what the consciousness mechanism does and does not do. Schacter explicitly separated CAS from the executive control system, so CAS is not a decision-maker or response-implementer. Rather, CAS is a monitoring system that can integrate and relate information from several specialized knowledge modules. CAS constructs a "global database" (Baars 1983) that can share information between modules and which provides inputs to the executive system to use in making its decisions. The idea that consciousness—phenomenal awareness—is the function of a monitoring system, not of an executive system, has also been advocated by other researchers (Weiskrantz 1988a).

What is the neuroanatomical basis for CAS and the executive system? Schacter cited Dimond (1976), who described evidence for a "consciousness circuit" in the posterior cerebrum, critically involving the inferior (lower) parietal lobes and the cingulate area in posterior corpus callosum. The inferior parietal lobes receive inputs of highly processed information from various perceptual modules, and thus are a plausible candidate for a global database. The cingulate area is part of the bridge that links the left and right parietal lobes. Lesions of the cingulate area have been associated with confusional states, "which are characterized by disordered thought, severe disorientation, and a breakdown of selective attention—in short, a global disorder of conscious awareness" (Schacter 1989, p. 371). Unilateral damage to the parietal lobes can also produce attentional disorders. On the other hand, executive functions appear to be localized mainly in the frontal lobes, especially the prefrontal area. Damage to the frontal lobes can disrupt the ability to make appropriate new voluntary responses, though the ability to make habitual responses to stimuli is maintained. Habitual responses may persist even when they become inappropriate.

The DICE model is not intended as a general theory of mind and consciousness. It was designed specifically to explain dissociations between performance and consciousness. Schacter (1989) acknowledged that the DICE model is speculative, and that it will undoubtedly have to be modified or abandoned when researchers learn more about the relations between brain, behavior, and consciousness. We do not yet know how many specialized modules there are, or exactly what their functions are. Alternative interpretations of some dissociation effects have been offered that do not assume a central conscious system (CAS), but which assume that each module has its own conscious mechanism that can become disconnected from other parts of the module (Schacter 1990b). However, at this stage of understanding, DICE is useful as a heuristic model, to help us organize our knowledge about dissociation effects, and to suggest new lines of research.

NONCONSCIOUS PROCESSING IN NORMAL SUBJECTS

Several different types of evidence support the claim that nonconscious processing occurs in normal people (that is, non-brain-damaged people). Some of this evidence has been controversial, though there is no doubt about the overall conclusion to which it leads: that peoples' behavior and task performance can be influenced by stimuli and memories of which they are not consciously aware. It is beyond the scope of this book to go into detail on most of these types of evidence, but I will briefly describe them here.

Nonconscious processing in psychopathology.   Pierre Janet (1889) described dissociations between consciousness and perception or memory in hysterical patients, for example, hysterical blindness, functional amnesia, and multiple personality (discussed in Chapter 1). Freud described the influence of repressed motives and memories on neurotic symptoms, and generalized his ideas to the "psychopathology of everyday life"—for example, in slips of the tongue and forgetting of unpleasant appointments. (For more on nonconscious processing in psychopathology, see Nemiah [1984] and Perry and Laurence [1984].)

Hypnotic dissociations.   Hilgard (1977) argued that hypnotic analgesia (pain reduction) and posthypnotic amnesia are cases of dissociation between consciousness and perceptual or memory systems. I will discuss his theory and research on the "hidden observer" effect in Chapter 15.

Subliminal perception.   In general terms, subliminal perception refers to nonconscious recognition of stimuli that cannot be consciously recognized. Operationally, subliminal perception may be defined as a change in behavior or performance caused by the identity or meaning of a stimulus, where the stimulus is presented in such a way that the subjects cannot consciously detect or recognize it. In most tests, subliminal stimuli are too brief or too weak to be consciously recognized.

Public interest in subliminal perception was first stimulated in 1957 by a book by Vance Packard called *The Hidden Persuaders*. The author claimed that advertisers could use subliminal messages—messages below the detection threshold—to induce people to buy specific products. For example, it was claimed that the subliminal message "DRINK COKE," flashed very briefly on a movie screen, could induce people to go out and buy Coca Cola, even though they had not consciously perceived the message. The general public reacted to Packard's book with alarm, while psychologists reacted with skepticism. The main reason for skepticism was their implicit "doctrine of concordance" (described at the beginning of this chapter). Another reason was the lack of convincing research evidence.

There have been numerous attempts to demonstrate subliminal perception in controlled experiments, some successful, some not (see reviews in Dixon 1971, 1981). Critics have argued that many of the apparently successful experiments have methodological flaws and/or that the results can be interpreted in terms of other processes besides subliminal perception (Eriksen 1960; Holender 1986). Nonetheless, the best experiments show that subliminal perception can occur under some conditions.

Nowadays many experimental psychologists accept the idea of subliminal perception. The main reason for the shift in attitude is that subliminal perception is consistent with some modern cognitive psychological theories of perception, pattern recognition, and attention (such as "preattentive processing," discussed in Neisser 1967; Kihlstrom 1987). If anything, theoretical acceptance may be ahead of the research evidence, though there is some good research evidence. It is important to note, however, that neither the theories nor the research support the notion that subliminal stimuli can be used effectively in advertising to induce people to go out and buy products that they do not need (Bowers 1984; Kihlstrom 1987). The effects are more subtle.

The best evidence for subliminal perception comes from research with masked visual stimuli. In the *pattern masking procedure*, a stimulus word is briefly flashed on a screen, followed after a short delay by a masking stimulus (a jumbled mixture of broken letters). The interval between the onset of the stimulus word and the onset of the pattern mask is called the *stimulus onset asynchrony* (SOA). If the SOA is too long the stimulus word can always be consciously detected, but if the SOA is short enough the stimulus cannot be consciously detected; the key is to find an SOA that is short enough to prevent conscious recognition, but long enough to allow nonconscious recognition. In most subliminal perception studies the SOA has been set at the *objective detection threshold*. The objective detection threshold is measured by a forced-choice procedure: stimulus trials are mixed randomly with blank trials (no word presented), and subjects are required to respond "yes" or "no" on each trial to indicate whether a stimulus word occurred. The objective detection threshold is the longest SOA at which detection is at a chance level (50 percent correct yes/no detection). Presumably, stimuli at this level cannot be consciously recognized.

Anthony Marcel (1983a, 1983b) demonstrated subliminal perception of masked words in a lexical decision task. In a *lexical decision task*, subjects are presented with a series of letter strings that are either words (such as "doctor") or nonwords ("tordoc"), and they have to push one of two buttons as quickly as possible to indicate whether or not the letter string was a real English-language word. The critical finding concerns the *associative priming effect*, in which the reaction time to a word (such as "nurse") is shorter if it is
–immediately preceded by a semantically related "priming" word ("doctor-

nurse") than if it is preceded by an unrelated prime ("butter-nurse"). Marcel (1983a, Exp. 4) showed equal associative priming effects for words preceded by unmasked primes and those preceded by masked primes. The prime-to-mask SOA was at the detection threshold, so subjects could not consciously recognize the masked primes, though they could consciously recognize the unmasked primes.[3] Thus, performance (RTs to critical words) was affected by masked prime words that were subliminally perceived. Apparently, pattern masking allows the pattern recognition process to proceed up to the point of nonconscious recognition, but blocks it from proceeding to the point of conscious recognition (Marcel 1983b).

Holender (1986) criticized Marcel's experiments and similar ones by other researchers, mostly in regard to the question of whether the objective detection thresholds were accurately measured. But Jim Cheesman and Philip Merikle (1986; Merikle & Cheesman 1986) argued that Holender's point is moot, because the objective detection threshold is not the correct threshold to use for subliminal detection research, anyway.

"Subliminal perception" has always implied perception without awareness, which is not the same thing as perception without discriminative responding. In fact, discriminative responding—as in forced-choice measures of stimulus detection—can sometimes be done successfully even though subjects do not consciously see the stimuli; for example, in blindsight. Cheesman and Merikle (1984, 1986) found discriminative responding without awareness in masking experiments with normal subjects, where at short prime-mask SOAs the subjects could detect the presence of masked words at better-than-chance levels, while at the same time they insisted that they did not really "see" the words and that their responses were just guesses. They argued that the correct SOA for masking experiments on subliminal perception is not the objective detection threshold, but the *subjective threshold*. The subjective threshold is the longest SOA at which subjects say that they cannot consciously detect or recognize the stimuli at a better-than-chance level.

Cheesman and Merikle (1984, Exp. 2) carefully measured both objective and subjective threshold SOAs for prime words. As expected, objective detection threshold SOAs were consistently shorter (mean 30 msec) than subjective threshold SOAs (mean 56 msec). At the subjective threshold SOA, when subjects thought that their detections were just guesses (25 percent correct), their detection performance was actually well above chance (mean 66 percent correct). Subsequently, Cheesman and Merikle found significant priming effects for masked words at subjective threshold SOAs, but not for words at objective threshold SOAs. The authors suggested that previous experiments that claimed to show subliminal perception of masked stimuli at objective detection threshold SOAs probably used SOAs that were really closer to the subjective threshold. This appears to have been the case in Marcel's (1983a, Exp. 4) lexical decision experiment (see Footnote 3). (There were several procedural differences between Cheesman and Merikle's experiment and Marcel's experiment; see the original articles for details.)

One problem with subjective thresholds is that they depend on subjects' subjective judgments about what they saw, and they can be affected by response biases (such as saying "I saw it" when they aren't certain). As an additional, more strict criterion for subliminal perception, Cheesman and

Merikle (1986) recommended that *qualitative* differences between conscious and nonconscious perception should be demonstrated. (Dixon [1971] and Marcel [1983b] made similar suggestions.) For example, a qualitative difference between conscious and nonconscious perception would be shown if an independent variable (such as subjects' expectancies) had different effects for consciously perceived (unmasked) stimuli versus nonconsciously perceived stimuli (masked at subjective threshold SOAs). Such qualitative differences have been demonstrated by Cheesman and Merikle (1986) and Marcel (1980), though the experiments are too complex to describe here.

Nonconscious perception of unattended stimuli.

Some stimuli are nonconsciously perceived, though they are not consciously noticed (Bowers 1984). The difference between this category and subliminal perception is that subliminal stimuli *cannot* be consciously perceived, because they are too brief or too weak, whereas unnoticed (unattended) stimuli are potentially capable of being consciously perceived (in that they are strong enough, and long enough in duration), but they are not consciously perceived because attention is directed elsewhere.

Selective attention is often illustrated by the "cocktail party effect," in which, while standing in the middle of a room where several people are talking, you can selectively attend to one of the voices at a time while ignoring the others. You hear the other voices as a background rumble, but you do not consciously recognize what they are saying. In the "lunch line effect" you are engaged in conversation with someone while ignoring other conversations, when suddenly you notice that someone has mentioned your name in a nearby conversation, even though you had not been attending to that conversation and you cannot recall anything that was said before your name was mentioned, and it was mentioned in a normal tone of voice. The lunch line effect is evidence for a nonconscious monitoring process that automatically recognizes all incoming stimuli, and automatically shifts your attention to personally significant stimuli. Besides your own name, significant stimuli might include other personally significant names (such as that of a girlfriend or boyfriend), certain emotionally charged words ("sex," "blood," and so forth), and conditioned emotional stimuli.

Norman's Pertinence Model of attention (1968) provided for nonconscious recognition of all incoming stimuli, with the selective attention process selecting for consciousness only those nonconsciously recognized stimuli that are most pertinent to the task at hand. For example, in listening to a conversation, certain words are most pertinent according to how their meaning fits expectations generated by the context: the topic, the preceding statements, and the current sentence (syntax effects).[4]

Most research on nonconscious perception of unattended stimuli has used the dichotic listening procedure, a laboratory analog of the cocktail party situation (review in Best 1989). Subjects are presented with two simultaneous verbal messages, one in each ear through stereo headphones. They are instructed to focus attention on the designated *target message* (in either the left or right ear). To force them to focus attention closely, subjects are required to *shadow* the target message, that is, to repeat it word for word as it is spoken. A number of dichotic-listening experiments have shown that subjects usually recall nothing of the content of the nontarget message. Even when the same word or digit is spoken several times in succession in the nontarget message, subjects usually do not notice it and cannot later recall it. On rare occasions when they do recall words from the nontarget message, it is because they briefly shifted attention from the target to the nontarget message.

Several dichotic-listening experiments have claimed to show that even though words in the nontarget message cannot later be recalled, they are recognized nonconsciously when they occur. For example, MacKay (1973) showed that words in the nontarget message can affect the interpretation of ambiguous statements in the target message. Other studies (Corteen & Wood 1972; Von Wright, Anderson, & Stenman 1975) showed that critical words in the nontarget message can elicit a physiological response (the GSR, galvanic skin response), when those words have previously been established as conditioned emotional stimuli through a classical conditioning procedure.

Holender (1986) argued that dichotic-listening experiments have not convincingly demonstrated nonconscious perception of unattended stimuli because they have not ruled out the possibility that subjects briefly shifted their attention to the nontarget message, so that the critical words were perceived consciously rather than nonconsciously. However, Michael Venturino (1983) carefully assessed attention-shifting to the nontarget message, in an experiment that measured skin responses to critical words in the nontarget message.

In Venturino's (1983) experiment, in a preliminary classical conditioning procedure, subjects heard a list of random nouns (one every 10 seconds), with CS+ words (three different bird names) being paired with electric shock on several occasions. After this training, the CS+ words reliably elicited a SCR (skin conductance response, similar to GSR), but CS− words (not previously paired with shock) did not elicit SCRs. Next, subjects were tested in a dichotic-listening procedure, in which different random word lists were presented at a rapid pace (one word every 0.8 seconds) in each ear (read by different voices), and subjects had to shadow the words in the target message. From time to time, test words were presented in either the target or nontarget message. Test words included the original CS+ words, semantically related words (other bird names), acoustically related (rhyming) words, and control words unrelated to the CS+ words. SCRs to the test words were measured, but shocks were not presented during dichotic listening testing.

In order to identify occasions in which subjects might have momentarily shifted attention to the nontarget message, Venturino carefully analyzed tape recordings of their shadowing performances for errors. Errors included omissions (the most common type), mispronunciations, hesitations, fusions, and intrusions. On the conservative assumption that all shadowing errors indicated attention shifts, all test-word trials with shadowing errors were eliminated from the main data analysis. (About half of the trials with CS+ words in the nontarget message, and fewer of the other test trials, were eliminated by this restriction.)

Figure 6.3 shows the probability of a SCR response (greater than a cri-

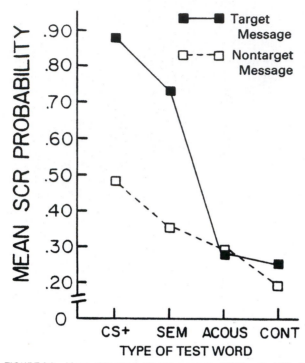

FIGURE 6.3. Mean skin-conductance-response (SCR) probability for four types of test words presented during dichotic listening: CS+ words (paired with electric shock in preceding classical conditioning procedure); SEM (semantically similar to CS+ words); ACOUS (acoustically similar to CS+ words); and CONT (control words, unrelated to CS+ words). The words were presented at unpredictable times in either the target (shadowed) message (filled squares) or the nontarget (nonshadowed) message (open squares). [From Venturino, M. (1983). *Perceptual Monitoring and Allocation of Attention.* Doctoral dissertation, University of Maine, Orono. By permission of the author.]

terion amplitude) for the four types of test words, for words presented in either the target message or the nontarget message. These data come only from trials in which there were no errors in shadowing the target message. Several aspects of the results are noteworthy: (1) When CS+ words occurred in the nontarget message, conditioned SCRs were elicited on almost half of the trials. SCR probability was reliably greater for CS+ words than for control (CONT) words in the nontarget message. (2) SCR probability was reliably greater for words semantically similar (SEM) to the CS+ words than to control words, in both the target and nontarget messages (semantic generalization effect). But SCR probability for words acoustically similar (ACOUS) to CS+ words was not reliably greater than for control words, for either the target or nontarget messages. These results show that words in the nontarget message were nonconsciously perceived. Further, the finding of semantic generalization but not acoustic generalization shows that SCRs to CS+ words occurred due to their meaning, not merely due to their sound. (3) SCR probability was greater for CS+ words in the target message than in the nontarget message. Thus, words that are consciously perceived elicit conditioned responses more reliably than words that are nonconsciously perceived.

An additional interesting finding of Venturino's experiment was that shadowing errors were more likely to occur during (or immediately after) CS+ words in the nontarget message (50 percent) than during unrelated non-test words in that message (14 percent). This result indicates that shadowing errors during CS+ words were rarely a result of spontaneous switching of attention from the target to the nontarget message. Rather, in most cases in which shadowing errors occurred during CS+ words in the nontarget message, they resulted from the CS+ word *drawing* attention to the nontarget message. As a consequence, shadowing of words in the target message was disrupted.

The fact that CS+ words in the nontarget message caused shadowing errors is further evidence that unattended words are nonconsciously perceived. If the CS+ words in the nontarget message had not been nonconsciously perceived, then they would not have drawn attention away from the target message. Finally, it is noteworthy that while all of the subjects sometimes had shadowing errors during CS+ words in the nontarget message, only 45 percent of them recalled after the experiment that they had sometimes noticed a CS+ word in the nontarget message. Apparently, briefly attending to a word that is irrelevant to the task-at-hand (shadowing) is not sufficient to guarantee that it will subsequently be recalled.

Venturino's (1983) experiment provides evidence for a nonconscious monitoring process that nonconsciously recognizes unattended stimuli. Most nonconsciously recognized stimuli are ignored and produce no further effects, since they are unimportant. But in some cases, when the stimuli are significant the monitoring process will automatically shift attention to them, so that previously unattended stimuli are consciously noticed. In other cases, though attention shifting does not occur, significant nonconsciously recognized stimuli produce measurable physiological responses. They may produce other subtle effects, too, such as effects on our interpretations of consciously perceived events (MacKay 1973) and our emotional responses to them.

Stimuli noticed but not appreciated.   In some cases, events are consciously noticed when they occur, and they influence our moods or behavior but we do not consciously appreciate the fact that they affected us (Bowers 1984). Events may influence our moods or behavior without us being introspectively aware *that* they influenced us, and/or without us being aware *how* they influenced us. For example, while watching a TV advertisement you surely notice the sexy bodies of the models, but subsequently when you buy the advertised product you may not be aware that your decision was influenced by your association of the product with sex symbols. In such cases, consciously noticed stimuli subsequently affect our behavior through non-conscious processes, so we do not know why we do what we do. The idea that people do not have introspective access to the causes of their own behavior has been controversial, as it challenges the idea of people having full, conscious, volitional control of their behavior. I will discuss this issue in the next chapter.

SUMMARY

Tulving argued that, until recently, cognitive psychologists largely ignored the question of the relationship between consciousness and cognitive processes of perception and memory, due to an implicit *doctrine of concordance*. The doctrine assumes that consciousness accompanies and is necessary for perception, memory, and the control of behavior. This chapter presented evidence for nonconscious perception and memory processes that is contrary to the doctrine of concordance.

Neuropsychologists have studied several types of dissociations between consciousness and performance in brain-damaged people. Schacter discussed such cases as dissociations between *explicit knowledge*, in which people are consciously aware of the knowledge that they use to perform a task, and *implicit knowledge*, which can be used to perform a task without the person being consciously aware that they possess the knowledge. For example, damage to the striate cortex of the occipital lobe produces scotomas, blind areas in the visual field. Weiskrantz showed that some people with cortical blindness have *blindsight*, a condition in which they are able to respond accurately to certain visual stimuli presented in their blind areas—for example, pointing to the position of a spot of light—even though they insist that they cannot *see* the stimuli. Patients with *amnesia*, caused by damage to the temporal lobes, have little or no ability to learn new vocabulary words or impersonal facts (semantic memory) or to recall recent personal experiences (episodic memory). However, they can learn new sensory-motor skills (procedural memory), even though they do not recall practicing the skill. Also, implicit knowledge is shown by *repetition priming effects*, in which amnesics show improved performance on certain verbal tasks (such as completion of word fragments) if they have previously been exposed to the words in the experimental context, even though they do not consciously recall that they were previously exposed to the words. Other neuropsychological dissociation syndromes include blind-touch, prosopagnosia, some types of dyslexia (alexia without agraphia), Wernicke's aphasia, and hemineglect.

Schacter proposed the DICE model to account for neuropsychological dissociation syndromes. In the DICE model, the performance of cognitive tasks involves various specialized brain modules that normally connect with a conscious awareness system (CAS). When the modules are disconnected from CAS they can continue to perform simple or overlearned tasks nonconsciously. CAS is a monitoring system that provides a global data base for the specialized modules and for the executive system, which makes decisions and controls voluntary actions.

Several types of evidence for nonconscious processing in normal (non-brain-damaged) subjects was described, including: (1) nonconscious process-ing in psychopathology (e.g. dissociation states such as hysterical blindness, multiple personality); (2) hypnotic dissociations, as in hypnotic analgesia; (3) subliminal perception, in which stimuli are nonconsciously recognized even though they cannot be consciously perceived because they are too brief or too weak; (4) nonconscious perception of unattended stimuli that could po-tentially be consciously perceived (long enough, strong enough), but are not noticed because attention is directed elsewhere; and (5) stimuli noticed but not appreciated, where events may influence our moods or behavior without us being introspectively aware *that* they influenced us, and/or without us being aware *how* they influenced us. All of these types of evidence, from brain damaged and normal patients, support the claim that behavior is influ-enced by nonconscious information processing.

ENDNOTES

[1]Tulving's (1989) remarks may be compared with a comment made by Marcel in replying to a critical, largely negative review of subliminal perception research: "A peculiar state of affairs seems to exist in cognitive psychology. Most current accounts of perception, cognition, and task execution have no place for consciousness. Phenomenal experience and subjectivity are appar-ently unnecessary for models of cognition, and there is certainly no evidence of them in the behaviour of artificial intelligence programs and automata, from which information processing [theory] is derived. Yet information-processing theorists react with skepticism when models and data are offered that explore the idea that phenomenal experience is dissociable from or not a prerequisite for the processing of sensory data" (Marcel 1986, p. 40, in commentary on Holen-der 1986).

[2]Schacter's (1989) DICE model was published before he and Tulving proposed the percep-tual representation system (PRS), a "hyperspecific" memory system that stores the exact appear-ance of objects (Schacter 1990a; Tulving & Schacter 1990). Thus, Schacter (1989) did not say how PRS fits into the DICE model. However, Tulving and Schacter said, "We view PRS as a complex system that comprises several subsystems, including word form, structural description, and other subsystems" (Footnote 10, p. 305). Thus, in a revised DICE model, PRS might be a set of special modules interconnected with each other and with the declarative/episodic memory system.

[3]Strictly speaking, the prime-to-mask SOAs used by Marcel (1983a, Exp. 4) were very slightly longer than the 50 percent chance detection threshold. He used SOAs (measured individually for each subject) that produced between 50 and 60 percent correct detections of word stimuli. This was done so the critical SOAs could be measured reasonably quickly, while avoiding acci-dentally making the SOAs so short that subliminal perception could not occur. Even with the 50 to 60 percent detection criterion, Marcel's subjects reported that their detection responses were mostly guesses, and they were not sure that they had actually seen the primes (Cheesman & Merikle 1986). The SOAs ranged from about 30 to 80 msec for different subjects.

[4]The *orienting response* (OR) to novel or unexpected stimuli is a special case in which unrecog-nized stimuli may attract attention. When a novel or unexpected (markedly out of context) stim-ulus occurs—such as an odd noise—you are likely to shift attention to it long enough to deter-mine whether it is significant. Besides a shift of conscious attention, the orienting response has physiological correlates, such as the GSR, brief changes in heart rate, and blocking of alpha brain waves (Rohrbaugh 1984). The orienting response is further evidence for the claim that all incoming stimuli are nonconsciously processed, though in this case it is nonrecognition or sur-prise that elicits attention shifting. Norman's (1968) pertinence model of attention would have to be modified to account for the orienting reaction.

chapter 7 ···

Introspection II: Access to the Causes of Behavior

Why did you major in psychology? Why do you think Dr. Smith is a good teacher? Why do you like Bill better than Ben? Why did you go to movie X, instead of movie Y? When you are asked to explain why you made a particular judgment, decision, or behavior, you can usually give some plausible explanation. On the surface, it would seem that people use introspection—looking within their own minds—to determine why they like what they like, and do what they do. However, some psychologists have come to doubt that people really have introspective access to the causes of their thoughts and actions.

Most of the empirical evidence for nonconscious information processing has come from research on *lower-order* mental processes, including perception, memory retrieval, and control of habitual actions. (I reviewed some of the evidence in the last chapter.) In a famous article titled "Telling More than We Can Know," Richard Nisbett and Timothy Wilson (1977) supported the radical proposal that *higher-order* mental processes—processes involved in judgments and decisions leading to voluntary actions—are also nonconscious. The belief in conscious awareness of higher-order thought processes is an illusion, in their view.

The research discussed by Nisbett and Wilson is related to an important topic in social psychology, the *attribution problem*, which concerns people's attempts to explain the causes of human behavior. Attribution research is concerned with factors that influence people's tendencies to attribute other people's behavior (such as unusually friendly or hostile behavior) to internal causes (such as personality traits) versus external (situational) causes. Nisbett and Wilson were interested in the *self-attribution* problem, concerning people's attempts to explain their own behavior, attitudes, and emotional reactions. They concluded that, when people attempt to explain their own behavior, they do not have introspective access to the causes or thought processes that produce their behavior. Rather, they said, when people try to give introspective reports on the causes of their behavior, what they are really doing is making reasonable *inferences* about what the causes must have been.

Nisbett and Wilson's conclusion is contrary to the common-sense belief that we can look into our own minds to find the causes or reasons for our actions. Of course, Nisbett and Wilson were not the first to make such a proposal. Around 1900 Sigmund Freud, the father of psychoanalysis, argued that people's decisions and actions are influenced by desires and memories that are unconscious—in the sense that we cannot retrieve them to consciousness even if we try. In the psychoanalytic view, unconscious desires and memories are unconscious because they are repressed; that is, they are actively blocked from consciousness because to make them conscious would cause great anxiety. Nisbett and Wilson's proposal was broader than Freud's, since they suggested that a lack of introspective access to the causes of our behavior is commonplace, and is not limited to cases of repression of knowledge that might produce personal anxiety.

Nisbett and Wilson's arguments deserve to be considered carefully because, if their conclusions are correct, they are profoundly important, for two reasons. First, their conclusions imply that introspection is worthless as a psychological method for studying higher-order thought processes. In particular, the validity of interpretive introspection—attempts to look into our own minds to find the causes and reasons for our thoughts, feelings, and actions—is in question. Second, their conclusions have implications for our views of human nature and the limits of self control and moral responsibility. If we cannot truly know the causes of our decisions and actions as they happen, then how can we be expected to control them and take moral responsibility for them?

I will describe the main points of Nisbett and Wilson's (1977) arguments against introspective access to higher-level mental processes and the causes of behavior, and I will describe some of the supporting research. Then I will present some of the counter-arguments offered by other psychologists, and some newer research that suggests a more moderate conclusion.

NISBETT AND WILSON'S ANTI-INTROSPECTIONIST THEORY

Behavior controlled by higher-order thought processes may be distinguished from mere reflexive or habitual responses to stimuli. Control of behavior by thought processes implies the ability to respond flexibly and adaptively to changing situations. To do this, a variety of pertinent stimulus information from the immediate environment must be combined with information from memory, through a series of flexible judgment and decision processes. The external stimuli that enter into thought processes are among the causal determinants of behavior. Nisbett and Wilson (1977) assumed that if people have introspective access to the thought processes that control their behavior, then they should be able to report the external stimuli that entered into those thought processes, and also to report how the stimuli affected their behavior.

Research and Conclusions

Nisbett and Wilson described a series of experiments designed to determine whether people can report the causes of their behavior. The general plan involved these steps: (1) Subjects were tested under two or more different stimulus conditions that were known to produce measurable differences in behavior, in a controlled situation where they had to make inference-based responses (that is, nonhabitual responses based on higher-order thought processes). (2) Afterward, the subjects were asked to report why they responded the way they did. (3) The reports were analyzed to determine whether the subjects reported the stimuli that the experimenters manipulated and that the experimenters knew to be true causal influences on the subjects' responses.

Nisbett and Wilson argued that the research supported these three major conclusions: (1) People do not have introspective access to the causal relationship between stimuli and their responses. That is, they cannot accurately report from introspection *which* stimuli affected their responses, and/or they cannot report *how* the stimuli affected their responses. (2) Reports of effects of stimuli on responses are based not on introspection, but on *a priori theories* (prior beliefs) about the causal connections between the stimuli and responses. (3) When people's reports on stimulus-response relationships are correct, it is because their a priori theories happen to be correct, not because of correct introspection. I will explain the rationale for these conclusions in more detail.

No introspective access to stimulus-response relationships. People often cannot report accurately on the effects of stimuli that influenced their responses. Sometimes they cannot report that the critical stimuli occurred. Sometimes they cannot report that the critical *response* occurred. Sometimes they are aware of the stimuli and the responses but they cannot report how the stimuli affected the responses. Sometimes people report incorrectly that certain stimuli affected their responses. Sometimes when people are informed which stimuli really affected their responses, they deny that this was the case.

For example, consider the "bystander apathy effect." Latane and Darley (1970) showed in several experiments that subjects were less likely to help a stranger in distress—such as someone who was apparently sick or injured—when there were several other people around than when they (the subject) were the only person available to help. When the subjects were asked why they had failed to lend assistance they said nothing about being influenced by the fact that other people were present. Furthermore, when the experimenter suggested that their behavior had been influenced by the pres--ence of other people, the subjects denied that this was the case. Thus, the subjects were unaware of the influence of a critical factor (presence of others) that had, in fact, affected their behavior according to the experimenter's objective analysis.

In a study of the relation between symptom attribution and pain tolerance, Nisbett and Schacter (1966) asked subjects to take a series of electric shocks that would increase steadily in intensity until the subjects said that they had reached the limit of their pain tolerance. Prior to the shocks series, half of the subjects were given a placebo pill (a substance with no physiological effects), and they were told that the pill would produce symptoms such as increased heartbeat rate, breathing irregularities, hand tremor, and butterflies in the stomach. These are the symptoms of anxiety that are normally produced by electric shock. As it turned out, the placebo group tolerated four times as much shock intensity as the control group. The experimenter's interpretation was that the placebo group attributed their anxiety symptoms to the pill, whereas the control group attributed their symptoms to the shock. Thus, when the anxiety symptoms became unpleasant the control group wanted to quit taking shocks, whereas the placebo group was willing to continue the shocks because they thought the anxiety symptoms were caused mainly be the pill. But when the placebo subjects were asked why they were willing to endure so much electric shock, they did not report that the pill had anything to do with it. Even when the experimenter explained that the pill was a placebo and that they had probably attributed their anxiety symptoms to the pill, the subjects denied that the pill had affected their responses to the shock.

A priori theories about the causes of behavior.
Nisbett and Wilson argued that when people are asked to explain the causes of their own behavior, they do not do so by directly introspecting on the stimuli and thought processes that produced their responses. Instead, they make *post hoc* (after-the-fact) inferences about the causes of their responses. An inference is a conclusion based on some combination of reasoning, observations, and prior knowledge or beliefs, rather than on observations alone. Nisbett and Wilson emphasized the role of a priori theories, that is, the subjects' beliefs about causal connections between stimuli and responses—beliefs that existed prior to, and independently of, a particular attempt to introspect on the thought processes that led to a particular response.

Nisbett and Wilson suggested several possible origins for the a priori theories: (1) There are socially learned rules that govern much of our behavior. For example, one rule is "Stop at red lights." Thus, in explaining your behavior of stopping at an intersection, you could refer to the rule, without actually introspecting on the effect of the stimulus (red light) on your response. (2) The culture or subculture provides theories about causes of behavior and feelings—what some writers call "folk psychology" theories. For example, one folk-psychology theory is "Personal failures make people feel depressed." In explaining your feeling of depression, you might make use of the theory and say "I feel depressed today because I got a 'D' on a history exam." Your explanation would not be based on introspection, and you might entirely miss the fact that your depression was caused by physical factors. (3) A causal theory may be based on personal observation of *covariation* between types of stimuli and types of responses. For example, you might have noticed in the past that you are usually grouchy after you play golf if you fail to break 100. If you are asked why you feel grouchy today, you might attribute it to your failure to break 100. In fact, other factors—either physical or psychological—might well be more important causes of your grouchiness. (Perhaps excessive fatigue caused both your poor play and your grouchiness.) (4) People may generate causal hypotheses based on judgments of connotative similarity between the stimuli and responses. That is, the stimuli and responses seem to go together, such that one seems to imply the other. For example, "I feel happy today. It must be because I was with Jane, who is always in a happy mood."

In general, the methods that people use to make inferences about causality are analogous to the *availability* and *representativeness* heuristics in category judgments (Kahneman & Tversky 1973). Availability means simply that people base their judgments or inferences more on highly salient or readily available information than on less obvious information that might really be more relevant to the problem at hand. For example, you might attribute your headache to loud rock music coming from the next room, whereas you might overlook less obvious factors that are really the cause of your headache (such as tension from worrying about a personal problem; or caffeine withdrawal, if you are a coffee or cola addict and you haven't had a "fix" recently).

In judgment research, according to the representativeness heuristic, people estimate the probability that a particular object is in category X by comparing the object with known objects that they believe to be typical or representative of category X. For example, if you believe that librarians are typically female, quiet, orderly, and love books, and you observe that Ruth is quiet, orderly, and loves books, then you might conclude that it is likely that Ruth is a librarian. You would be ignoring the more important fact that most quiet, orderly, book-loving females are *not* librarians.

Similarly, according to Nisbett and Wilson, we infer that a particular stimulus caused our behavior, not through introspection of our actual mental processes, but by judging whether the stimulus is representative of the category of stimuli that usually cause that sort of behavior. For example, anger is an emotional response to certain stimuli. According to (a priori) folk-psychology theory, frustrations and insults are representative of the type of stimuli that produce anger. If you feel irritable or angry, you might search your environment and memory for a recent case of frustration or insult. Failing to find an obvious case, you might interpret someone's ambiguous remark as an insult. (Professor to student: "You seem to be having a lot of trouble with this course." Student's thought: "That turkey! He thinks I'm stupid.") You might entirely overlook the influence of other factors on your feelings of irritability or anger (such as fatigue, sickness, hangover, food allergy, sexual frustration, or physiological cycles).

Implications.   Nisbett and Wilson took the strong position that people have little or no introspective access to mental processes, and that their verbal reports on the causes of their behavior are based entirely on a priori theories. This position carries two important implications: (1) People may sometimes report accurately on the causes of their behavior. But since their reports are based on a priori theories, their reports will be correct only if their a priori theories are correct. (2) People's reports on the causes of their own behavior will be no more accurate than the reports of observers who use the same a priori theories.

The second point needs elaboration because it provides the rationale behind several experiments—some of them to be described here—on introspective access to the causes of behavior. The basic idea is that if your explanations of the causes of your behavior are based not on introspection but on a priori theories, then another person—an "observer"—who obviously does not have introspective access to your mental processes, should be able to provide the same explanations of your behavior. This assumes that the observer is the same gender as you, about the same age, and a member of the same culture as you, so that they would have the opportunity to learn the same a priori theories about the causes of human behavior, and also that they know the important details of the situation in which you made the responses in question. Since—according to Nisbett and Wilson—your explanation of your behavior did not benefit from introspective access to your own mental processes, it should not make any difference that the observer has no direct knowledge of your mental processes. The important point is that you would share the same a priori theories, so this person would explain your behavior in the same way that you would, and equally accurately or inaccurately. It should be noted that Nisbett and Wilson did not deny that people have introspective access to some of their conscious experiences or contents. But they denied that people use this introspective knowledge to explain their own behavior.

Though Nisbett and Wilson's argument may seem to go against your intuition and your everyday experience, there is some compelling experimental evidence to show that they are at least partly right, if not entirely so.

Criterion for introspective access. From the argument described above, Nisbett and Wilson (1977) derived a criterion for introspective access to the causes of behavior. They said that introspective access would be demonstrated if it were shown that real subjects who respond in a particular experimental situation can subsequently make verbal reports on the causes of their responses that are more accurate than the reports obtained from observers. The observers' task is to report the causes of the real subjects' responses, in cases where the observers are provided with a general description of the experimental situation, including the stimuli and responses in question, but where the observers do not make their own responses to the experimental situation.

Nisbett and Wilson (1977; Wilson & Nisbett 1978) described several experiments intended to test for introspective access to the causes of behavior, according to the criterion described above. None of the studies found clear evidence for introspective access. For example, Nisbett and Bellows (1977) compared the reports of observers with those of real subjects in a study of stimulus factors that influence judgments of people. (Henceforth, I will follow the jargon of this research literature and call the real subjects "actors," in the sense of one who takes action or responds to a situation.) Different actors read different descriptions of a job applicant that varied on several stimulus factors (such as the applicant's attractiveness, academic credentials, and so forth). Then they judged the applicant on several person dimensions (likability, sympathy, flexibility, intelligence). Finally, the actors tried to report the causes of their responses by estimating how much each of the stimulus factors had influenced each of their person judgments. For comparison, observer subjects were given only a brief description of each of the stimulus factors, and were asked to estimate how much each of them would affect the actors' judgments of job applicants on the person dimensions. Two aspects of the results were important: (1) The actors and observers agreed closely in their estimates of how much each stimulus factor would affect each of the person judgments. (2) These estimates were not accurate, according to the researcher's data analysis that showed how the person judgments had actually varied in relation to the stimulus factors. Thus, Nisbett and Wilson concluded that the actors and observers had used the same a priori theories to explain the actors' responses. Furthermore, both groups were wrong, with one exception. Actors and observers were both correct in saying that the description of the job applicant's academic credentials influenced the actors' judgments of the applicant's intelligence. In this case, the a priori theory happened to be correct.

In another example, in research on the bystander apathy effect (described earlier), observers have sometimes been asked to explain why actors failed to lend assistance to a person in distress. Like the actors, observers almost always failed to mention the fact that other people were present, even though the research has objectively shown the presence or absence of other people is a critical factor influencing the likelihood of helping behavior. Thus, from these and other studies, Nisbett and Wilson concluded that people do not have introspective access to the causes of their behavior. Rather, they base their reports on a priori theories, that may or may not be correct.

Reasons for belief in introspective access.   If we do not truly have introspective access to the causes of our own behavior, why do we continue to believe that we usually are aware of the causes of our behavior? Nisbett and Wilson suggested that people have an illusion of introspective access because they confuse awareness of mental *contents* with awareness of mental *processes*. Mental processes make various computations and judgments on pertinent information to produce particular decisions, which in turn guide behavior. Nisbett and Wilson argued that we do not have introspective access to these mental processes. Rather, we have introspective access to the *results* of those processes, which are mental contents, such as decision outcomes (not the decision process itself). We also may have access to intermediate results at various stages of the mental processes that lead to decisions. (This is analogous to intermediate results that you get during computation of a long mathematical formula.) Thus, we may think we are introspecting mental processes when we are really introspecting mental contents.

Critique of Nisbett and Wilson's Theory

Nisbett and Wilson's anti-introspectionist theory may seem contrary to our personal intuitions and everyday experiences, but that in itself is not sufficient proof against it. Arguments based on logic and evidence from controlled research are more pertinent to establishing the validity of a scientific theory.

Problems of logic.   Several critics (Smith & Miller 1978; P. White 1980) have argued that Nisbett and Wilson did not clearly distinguish mental processes from mental contents. They did not provide definitions that were clear enough to enable one reliably to judge whether subjects were describing mental processes or mental contents. Nisbett and Wilson themselves were prepared to accept actors' reports of pertinent stimuli as evidence for introspective access to mental processes (if their reports were more accurate than those of the observers), though it could be argued that the remembered stimuli are mental contents and not mental processes.

Also, Smith and Miller (1978) suggested that any mental process can be described at several different levels, ranging from high-level strategies or rules for problem solving and social behavior, through intermediate-level computation and judgment stages, to the lowest level of activities in various brain circuits that actually perform the computations and control the behavior. People may be able to make introspective reports on the higher-level mental processes, but not on the intermediate or lower-level processes.

In more recent work it has been acknowledged that it is difficult to make a clear distinction between mental processes and mental contents, and perhaps this distinction should be deemphasized (Wilson and Stone 1985). What is more important is the question of whether people can report which stimuli influenced their behavior, and how.

On this point, Kenneth Bowers (1984) argued that while people may sometimes have introspective access to the stimuli that cause their behavior, it is logically impossible to have introspective access to the causal connection between the stimuli and their behavioral effects. Rather, understanding of the causal connections between events is always and necessarily a theoretical inference. Psychologists devise formal theories to explain people's behavior, based on controlled research, and ordinary people devise informal theories based on informal observations. But in no case can the causal connection between events be directly observed; it has to be inferred. For example, you might observe that almost every time that you feel tired you also are irritable, and so you infer that tiredness causes irritability. But you do not directly observe the process that links tiredness with irritability. (And in fact, tiredness might not cause irritability; they might both be caused by another factor that happens sometimes to be correlated with both of them.)

Thus, regarding the illusion of introspective access to mental processes, what is more important than the confusion between mental processes and mental contents is people's failure to distinguish between their introspective observations and their inferences. People may introspectively (or retrospectively) observe certain stimuli and responses, then infer a causal connection between them, and subsequently report (wrongly) that they introspectively observed that a particular stimulus caused a particular response. What they really did was to infer that the stimulus caused the response.

The implication is that we can still ask whether people have introspective access to the stimuli that influence their behavior, but we should understand that their reports on *how* the stimuli affects their behavior are based on inferences, not introspective observations. People's inferences about causal connections may be based on a priori theories that are shared by observers from the same culture, as Nisbett and Wilson argued. Or alternatively, some of their inferences may be based on privileged knowledge that is not available to observers.

Finally, you should note that Nisbett and Wilson's criterion for introspective access—more accurate reports on causal stimuli by actors than observers—does not work in reverse. That is, failure of actors' reports to be more accurate than those of observers does not in itself prove lack of introspective access. In some cases, actors might have introspective access to pertinent stimuli, but make inaccurate reports because they made incorrect inferences about the relationships between the stimuli and their responses. In other cases, actors and observers might both be very accurate, with the actors having introspective access to information similar to that assumed by observers on the basis of a priori theories. In such cases, actors are actually using introspective information, but it is hard to prove it by objective criteria.

Problems of research method.   Several psychologists have criticized some of the research that Nisbett and Wilson used to support their arguments. One problem was that actors' reports on causal influences on their behavior were all made retrospectively, several minutes or hours after the critical behavior occurred. Thus, they may have forgotten pertinent information that they would have known if they had been questioned sooner.

Another problem frequently mentioned (Smith & Miller 1978) was that most of the experiments involved *between-subjects designs*, in which different subjects (or groups of subjects) received different stimuli or experimental treatments, and made different responses. In order to understand how a stimulus influences one's behavior, it is important to have an opportunity to experience *covariation* between the stimulus and the response. That is, you need to have a chance to notice that your response is different when the stimulus is different. In the between-subjects experiments, it might be unrealistic to expect actors to know that a stimulus influenced their behavior, when they experienced only one stimulus condition and made only one response. For example, in the bystander apathy effect, if you experienced only one condition—an apparently injured person, with a crowd of people standing around—and you failed to help the injured person, it might not occur to you that the crowd had an important influence on your decision not to help, and that you would have helped if you had been the only person on the scene.

In reply to the criticism of between-subjects experimental designs, Nisbett and Ross (1980) argued that such experiments are most realistic in comparison to people's everyday life judgments. Often we try to judge the _effect of a stimulus on our behavior in situations where we have only experienced that stimulus once, and we have not had a chance to observe covaria-tion between the stimulus and our response. Other researchers have argued, however, that if we want to find out whether people *can* have introspective access to the causes of their behavior, then we should test people under con ditions that maximize the opportunity for introspective access and accurate reporting. Thus, it has been recommended that experiments on introspec-tive access should involve *within-subjects* designs, in which all subjects experi-ence each of the different stimulus conditions on several occasions, so they have the opportunity to notice how their responses covary with the stimulus conditions. Another advantage of within-subjects designs is that it enables experimenters to evaluate the accuracy of individual subject's reports of stimulus-response relationships, rather than trying to draw conclusions from average group accuracy computed in between-subjects designs. In the next section I will describe some newer research, using within-subjects designs, and the conclusions that have followed from that research.

EVIDENCE FOR INTROSPECTIVE ACCESS

Since the original review by Nisbett and Wilson (1977), several studies have used the recommended within-subjects experimental designs to test for in-trospective access to the causes of behavior. In each of these studies, real sub-jects (actors) made judgments of each of several different stimuli (such as different people), in situations where the stimuli varied on several factors or attributes. Most of the studies found evidence for introspective access—or at least some sort of privileged information access—by showing that the actors' reports of the effects of different stimulus factors on their judgments were more accurate than the estimates made by observers. I will briefly describe some of these studies, going into more detail on the first one so you can bet-ter understand the rationale and method and results.

Experiments Using Within-Subjects Designs

Kraut and Lewis (1982) had some ninety-six subjects (actors) watch a film showing a series of short interviews of fifty international airline passen-gers conducted by U.S. Customs inspectors. The inspectors asked the passen-gers questions about things such as their age, home residence, length and purpose of trip, occupation, and purchases. The passengers varied widely in age, social class, and behavior. The subjects judged each of the passengers (target stimuli) for three person characteristics: intelligence, friendliness, and deceptiveness. The person judgments were made on six-point rating scales, ranging from "1, below-average" to "6, above average," compared to the other passengers.

After the subjects had made person judgments for all fifty passengers, the subjects were asked to estimate the impact of each of eighteen stimulus factors on their judgments. The stimulus factors—characteristics of the pas-sengers—included things such as age, sex, occupation prestige, attractive-ness, frequency of smiles, eye contact, formality of dress, formality of speech, response latency, and volunteering of information. The subjective impact estimates were made on thirteen-point scales, ranging from negative influence through no influence to positive influence. (For example, a subject might estimate that passengers who smiled more frequently had been judged as more friendly or that smiles had had no influence on judgments of intelligence.) Also, observer subjects—who did not see the film and did not make person judgments—used the same thirteen-point scales to estimate how they thought each of the eighteen stimulus factors would influence each of their person judgments (friendliness, intelligence, deceptiveness) if they were actually to make such judgments. The ratings of stimulus-factor impacts by the actor subjects are termed *actor estimates*, whereas those made by the observers are termed *observer estimates*. Finally, for each actor subject, the *actual impact* of each of the eighteen stimulus factors on each person judgment was determined by computing the correlation of each stimulus-factor level with each judgment rating. (For example, the passengers' actual frequencies of eye contact with the inspector were correlated with the subjects' ratings of their deceptiveness, across all fifty passengers.)

Four results of the data analysis are important in regard to the question of introspective access to the causes of behavior: (1) The accuracy of actors' estimates of the influence of the various stimulus factors on their person judgments was determined by correlating the actor estimates with the actual impacts. Averaged across all subjects, judgments, and stimulus factors, the *actor-actual correlation* was $+0.42$, which indicates a moderate degree of accuracy.[1] (2) The accuracy of observers' estimates of the influence of the stimulus factors was determined by randomly pairing each observer with an actor subject, and computing the correlation of the observers' estimate with the paired actors' actual impacts for each stimulus factor and each judgment. Overall, the average *observer-actual correlation* was $+0.35$. By the rationale suggested by Nisbett and Wilson (1977), the fact that the actor-actual correlation was higher than the observer-actual correlation (0.42 versus 0.35) suggests that the actors had some additional information, not known to the observers, that enabled the actors to be more accurate. This additional information might come from introspective access to the effect of stimulus factors during the actual judgment process. (3) To find out how much observer estimates were similar to actors' estimates, these two variables were correlated with each other. The *actor-observer correlation* of $+0.48$ indicates that actors' and observers' estimates were moderately similar, perhaps due to both of them using the same a priori theories about the relationship between stimulus factors (such as smiling, eye contact) on person judgments (such as friendliness). However, the correlation is far from perfect, which suggests that to a moderately large degree the actors and observers used different information in estimating the influence of the various stimulus factors on person judgments. (4) The most direct test of introspective access involved measuring the degree to which the actors' stimulus-factor impact estimates were accurate due to information not known to observers. This was done by computing a partial correlation between actors' estimates and actual impacts, while statistically controlling for observers' estimates. (In other words, the observers' accuracy was subtracted from the actors' accuracy, to determine how much residual actor accuracy remained.) The *actor-actual partial correlation* was $+0.31$, which indicates that actors' estimates of the impact of various stimulus factors on their person judgments was based on a significant amount of information not known to the observers. Presumably, this additional information involved introspective access to their judgment process, though as we will see, other sorts of privileged information may also have been involved.

Similar results have been found in other studies that employed different judgment tasks but similar within-subject experimental designs. Wright and Rip (1981) had high-school juniors read descriptions of thirty-two colleges that varied on five stimulus factors (tuition cost, size, distance from home, living patterns, [percent of students living on campus], and median SAT scores). Then the subjects judged the colleges in terms of how much they wanted to apply to them for admission. Finally, they estimated the impact of each stimulus factor on their judgments. The correlation of actors' estimates with actual effects of the stimulus factors was higher ($+0.38$) than the observer-actual correlation ($+0.32$).

Gavanski and Hoffman (1987) had subjects read brief profiles of sixty-four male university students, which varied on six stimulus factors (such as whether they smoked, how hard they worked, whether they often swear when annoyed). Subjects judged how much they thought they would like each of the students (on a thirteen-point scale), then estimated the impacts of the different stimulus factors on their judgments. Actor-actual correlations were much higher ($+0.81$) than observer-actual correlations ($+0.24$), for observers who had not seen the student profiles or the actors' judgments.

On the other hand, a study by Wilson, Laser, and Stone (1982) did not find evidence for introspective access. Every day for five weeks, subjects filled out questionnaires in which they rated their mood (on a seven-point scale from "very bad" to "very good") and several predictor factors, such as their health, personal relationships, workload, amount of exercise, and amount of sleep the previous night. Finally, they estimated what impact each of the predictor factors had on their mood over the five weeks. The correlation of actors' estimates with actual impacts was slightly lower ($+0.42$) than the observer-actual correlation ($+0.45$).

Overall, then, most of the published studies using within-subjects designs—where each subject judges numerous stimuli that vary on several stimulus factors—have found actors' estimates of the impacts of stimulus factors on their judgments to be somewhat more accurate than observers' estimates. To the extent that actors' and observers' judgments are similar, the results suggest that they are using the same a priori theories to explain their judgments, as Nisbett and Wilson (1977) claimed. However, to the extent that actors' estimates are more accurate than observers, the results suggest that actors are using privileged information—perhaps from introspection—that is not available to the observers to explain the actors' judgments.

Types of Information People Use to Explain Their Own Behavior

What type of information might people use to explain the causes of their own behavior—such as their judgments of people? Wilson and Stone (1985) distinguished between several types of information: (1) *Shared theories* are those theories that are known by both actors and observers in the same culture. Shared theories include a priori theories—folk-psychology theories—that are learned by virtually all members of the culture, and also theories that can be derived by all members from their similar experiences. Actors and observers would be expected to have the same shared theories. (2) *Privileged information* is known only to actors—the people whose behavior is in question—and not by observers. There are three types of privileged information. (a) *Introspective data* on the "workings of one's own mind," such as remembered instances of particular stimuli and responses, and the sequence of decisions and affective reactions (feelings) that lead one to make particular responses to particular stimuli. (b) *Covariation data*, the accumulated knowledge of one's different responses to different stimuli, that can be used to infer a cause-and-effect relationship. (For example, you might notice that you rather consistently judge giggly people to be nervous, and so you infer that giggling causes you to judge people as nervous. Such an after-the-fact inference from covariation data is not the same thing as introspecting thoughts on specific occasions where someone's giggling caused you to conclude that they were nervous.) (c) *Idiosyncratic theories*, unique to the individual (such as "Coffee makes me sleepy."), that may be wrong due to faulty data analysis or faulty inference.

Wilson and Stone (1985) acknowledged that recent research shows that actors often use privileged information—information not available to observers—in trying to explain their own behavior. This conclusion departs significantly from the original Nisbett and Wilson (1977) argument that causal explanations are based only on shared a priori theories. However, Wilson and Stone concluded that *the use of privileged information does not necessarily make actors more accurate than observers* in explaining their (the actors') behavior. Sometimes actors analyze covariation data incorrectly, or use idiosyncratic theories that are wrong. Furthermore, in most cases in which actors' reports are more accurate than observers' reports, the differences are not large, and observers' and actors' reports are moderately highly correlated. The implication is that shared theories still account for a significant portion of actors' reports, though actors also use privileged information.

Covariation assessment.   In cases in which actors use privileged information and their reports are more accurate than those of observers, it is difficult to determine whether the privileged information used by actors is based on actual introspection of ongoing decision processes or on after-the-fact inferences based on accumulated covariation data. The evidence suggests that covariation data can be used under some circumstances, though it does not account for all privileged information reports. Research on human inference processes has indicated that, in a variety of situations, people are usually poor at making accurate inferences based on covariation data (Nisbett & Ross 1980). The larger the number of stimulus factors that can vary, the harder it is to determine their relationship to people's responses. Also, the greater the time interval between different stimulus-response instances, the harder it is to accumulate useful covariation data, since some instances will be forgotten or remembered incorrectly.

Wilson and Stone (1985) ranked several self-attribution studies in terms of how hard it would be for actors to assess stimulus-response covariation, and they concluded that the easier it was for actors to assess covariation, the greater the advantage of actors over observers in accurately explaining the actors' judgments (regarding persons, colleges, and so forth). This conclusion has been substantiated in a more recent study. Gavanski and Hoffman's (1987) procedure—in which subjects judged how much they would like students, based on brief profiles—made it relatively easy for subjects to detect covariation. They judged a large number of profiles in a relatively short time period, and the profiles varied on only six "yes-no" stimulus dimensions (such as "Does the student smoke?"). Subjects (actors) were unusually accurate in judging the impact of stimulus factors (actor-actual correlation +0.81), whereas observers with no covariation information were very inaccurate (observer-actual correlation +0.24). Furthermore, an observer group that was given covariation information—they read the student profiles and examined an actors' judgments of the profiles—were almost as accurate as the actors themselves in estimating the impact of the different stimulus factors on the actors' judgments (covariation observer-actual correlation +0.71). The superior accuracy of observers with covariation data over observers without covariation data shows that people can use covariation data in situations of this type, and suggests that the actors also used covariation data. However, other data analyses indicated that the accuracy of actors' reports could not be attributed entirely to covariation information. The actors used additional, privileged information, not known to the covariation observers, and in fact they used covariation information somewhat less than covariation observers did. Apparently, actors' reports were based partly on their introspections of individual judgments, in addition to their after-the-fact covariation analysis of the relationships between stimulus factors and their responses.

Wilson and Stone argued that although people might be able successfully to assess stimulus-response covariation in relatively simple, controlled laboratory situations, it might be difficult or impossible to do so in the real world. In real-life situations, the number of varying stimulus factors would often be so great, and/or the time intervals between relevant stimulus-response instances would be so great, that it would be hard to notice any consistent stimulus-response covariation. (For example, you might not notice that a particular food causes you to feel lethargic, because that particular food is consumed along with a variety of other foods that do not affect your mood.) Thus, in real-life situations, actors might have little or no advantage over observers that could be attributed to privileged access to covariation data by actors. On the other hand, as Gavanski and Hoffman's (1987) analysis suggests, the superior accuracy of actors' causal attributions is not due only to the use of covariation data. Actors have additional private information—presumably from introspection of stimuli, responses, feelings, and ongoing thought processes. Thus, we would expect that actors' explanations of their own behaviors should be more accurate than those of observers, even in real-life, real-world situations in which covariation assessment is difficult or impossible.

In evaluating these and other conclusions based on comparisons of actors' and observers' explanations of actors' responses, recall that it was assumed that the observers were of the same age, gender, and culture, and had educational backgrounds similar to the actors. Under these conditions, observers' explanations have been either less accurate, or at best, equally as accurate as actors' explanations. But observers may be more accurate than actors in explaining the actors' behavior, in cases where the observers are experienced psychologists armed with accumulated knowledge based on clinical experience, research results, and formal psychological theories that are more valid than the folk-psychology theories used by ordinary observers.

Finally, it should be noted that the process of assessing stimulus-response covariations for one's own behavior is, in a sense, an introspective process. Regardless of whether covariation analysis is done as a continuing process throughout the series of behavioral events, or done afterward, it is a private mental process involving the attempt to interpret one's own experience and behavior. In that sense it is interpretive introspection, which I linked earlier with reflective consciousness.

CONCLUSIONS

Wilson and Nisbett (1977) argued that people do not have direct introspective access to the causes of their behavior, and that their attempts to explain their own behavior are based on a priori theories about why people do what they do and feel what they feel. More recent research leads to a less extreme conclusion. The research indicates that in some cases actors' explanations of their own behavior are more accurate than observers' explanations, due to privileged information access by actors. This privileged information access includes some degree of introspective access to pertinent causal stimuli and thought processes by actors. Also, actors usually have better access to stimulus-response covariation data about their own behavior. Thus, people's attempts to explain their own responses are not based entirely on their a priori theories. A priori theories are, nonetheless, an important component of people's causal explanations, as is shown by the similarity of explanations by actors and observers. In some cases, privileged information access by actors does not improve the accuracy of their explanations, if they misinterpret the information and make incorrect inferences. Introspective access to the causes of behavior is limited.[2]

Two mental systems.   To the extent that people are unable to introspectively report the causes of their behavior, the results of these experiments are consistent with theories that distinguish between a global-database conscious awareness system (CAS; Schacter 1989) or conscious interpreter system (Gazzaniga 1985) versus nonconscious modules and/or an executive system that actually controls behavior. In a similar vein, Wilson (1985) suggested that there are two mental systems. One, the *behavior production system*, is responsible for producing behavior, especially unregulated (nonvolitional) behavior. It operates largely at a nonconscious level, so its processes are not directly available to introspection. The other, the *verbal explanatory system*, -attempts to assess and interpret our feelings and behavior, using whatever information is available to it. This system operates at a conscious level, so its conclusions are available for introspection and verbal reporting.

Although the behavior production system's processes are not directly introspectible, some of its inputs (stimuli) and outputs (such as intermediate results in thought sequences, and consequent affective reactions) have conscious consequences and are introspectible. Thus, people would be expected to have some degree of introspective access to stimuli and thoughts related to the causes of their behavior.

Conditions that Promote Introspective Access

Under what conditions would we expect people to be more accurate in making introspective verbal reports on the causes of their own behavior and emotional reactions? Introspective (or retrospective) access to pertinent information should be better under conditions that promote attention to pertinent stimuli and thoughts as they occur, and that increase the likelihood that such information will be stored in memory. The distinction between controlled (effortful) processes and automatic processes is useful here. We would expect better introspective access for novel tasks that require flexible, controlled processing that has a large conscious component. Introspective access would be less likely for habitual tasks that are performed largely through automatic, nonconscious processes. Smith and Miller (1978) made a similar point:

> A dimension that can distinguish situations in which correct self-reports will be possible from those in which they will not . . . is the degree to which the subject is asked to report on tasks that are novel and of interest. Tasks that are novel and engaging for subjects, such as choosing a college or solving challenging problems, often seem to evoke accurate introspective awareness of process. Tasks that are, on the other hand, overlearned, routine, or of minimal interest may well be "run off" in such a way that subjects cannot report on intervening processes (pp. 360–61).

Given that the task is a nonautomatic one that engages one's attention, awareness of causal factors should be increased by conditions that make covariation between responses and pertinent stimuli or thoughts easier to detect. Covariation detection should be easier when there are relatively few pertinent stimulus dimensions and they are highly salient (conspicuous, novel, interesting), and when one has an opportunity to experience several variations on the stimuli, with consequent variations in responses, over a relatively short time interval.

We would expect people to be able to report the causes of their behavior more accurately if they introspect on their thought processes while the task is in progress, rather than waiting until the task is finished and relying entirely on retrospection. In the self-attribution studies that I described, subjects did not know that they would be asked to report on the influence of stimulus factors until after the judgment tasks were finished. Thus, their reports were based on retrospection. Some studies have examined the effects of concurrent introspection by comparing the accuracy of subsequent causal explanations for subjects who are given advance instructions to attend to pertinent stimuli and thoughts while they make their judgments (such as person judgments) versus subjects without prior attention instructions.

Surprisingly, advance attention instructions do not necessarily increase the accuracy of causal explanations (such as stimulus-factor impact estimates). In some cases, advance attention instructions reduced the accuracy of causal explanations (Gavanski & Hoffman 1987). An interpretation of this outcome is that introspection during the judgment process can interfere with the judgment process, making the judgments less reliable, so that the relationship between causal stimuli and judgments is less consistent and harder for subjects to detect. Thus, introspection on our thought processes during a task can change the natural flow of thoughts and make introspective reports less accurate. This mutual interference between concurrent introspection and task-related thought processes would be expected to be greater the more complex the task at hand. Thus, reports of concurrent introspections of task-related thoughts should be more accurate for simpler tasks—provided that the task is novel and interesting enough to engage our attention.

SUMMARY

Nisbett and Wilson (1977) were concerned with the self-attribution problem, concerning the processes by which people attempt to explain the causes of their own behavior. As a criterion for *introspective access* to the causes of one's own behavior, they proposed that access would be shown if subjects ("actors") who respond in a particular experimental situation can subsequently make verbal reports on the causes of their responses that are more accurate than reports made by observers who have only general information about the situation. They reviewed numerous experiments that, they argued, supported three major conclusions: (1) People do not have introspective access to the causal relationships between stimuli and their responses. That is, they cannot accurately report, from introspection, *which* stimuli affected their responses, and/or they cannot report *how* the stimuli affected their responses. (2) Reports of effects of stimuli on responses are based not on introspection, but on *a priori theories* (prior beliefs) about the causal connections between the stimuli and responses. (3) When people's reports on stimulus-response relationships are correct, it is because their a priori theories happen to be correct, not because of correct introspection.

Critics of the Nisbett-Wilson position argued that their supporting research used between-subjects designs, in which each subject experienced only one stimulus condition. Thus it would be hard for subjects to judge causal effects of stimuli because they had no chance to observe that different stimuli were associated with different responses (stimulus-response covariation). Several more recent experiments have used within-subjects designs, in which each subject responds on several occasions to different stimuli (such as judgments of the person characteristics—friendliness, etc.—of different people). Most within-subjects experiments have found actors' reports on the causes of their behavior to be somewhat more accurate than observers' reports. More recent research suggests that—contrary to Nisbett and Wilson's argument—people's reports on the causes of their behavior are not based entirely on a priori theories. Observations of stimulus-response covariation, and introspective access to pertinent events, are also important. Introspective access is expected to be more accurate for behavior in novel, interesting tasks, as contrasted with habitual, automatic task performances.

ENDNOTES

[1]For readers who are unfamiliar with correlation coefficients: A correlation coefficient (r) is a mathematical index of the degree to which two different variables (such as measures of behavior or experience) covary, or change together, such that high scores on one variable (variable A) tend to go with high scores on the second variable (variable B), and low scores on the first variable go with low scores on the second one. To compute the correlation it is necessary to have a set of scores (both A and B) for each member of a group of subjects. A perfect correlation, $r = +1.0$, means that the higher the value (or magnitude) of variable A, then the higher the value of variable B, so you could predict B if you knew A. (Or, a perfect -1.0 correlations means that high scores on A go with low scores on B.) At the other extreme, if $r = 0.0$, then the two variables are unrelated, so knowing the value of variable A would be useless for predicting B. Usually a correlation of about 0.7 to 1.0 is considered to be high, 0.5 to 0.69 is moderately high, 0.3 to 0.49 is moderate, 0.2 to 0.29 is low, and below 0.2 is very low to negligible.

[2]Wilson (1985) raised the question whether people have introspective access to *mental states*, such as attitudes, desires, and feelings that influence their behavior. He argued that inconsistencies between verbally reported attitudes and certain unregulated behaviors—behaviors not under voluntary control, such as spontaneous facial expressions and physiological responses—indicate that people sometimes do not have accurate introspective access to mental states. Furthermore, attempts to increase the accuracy of attitude reports through close introspective attention to the reasons for one's attitudes, can actually reduce the accuracy of attitude reports, under some conditions (Wilson, Dunn, et al. 1989). Space limitations prevent me from describing this research, but you should read the articles cited here if you want to learn more about the limitations of introspection.

chapter 8 ••••••••••••••••••••••••••••••

Daydreaming and the Stream of Consciousness

William James coined the metaphor "stream of thought" (1890/1983) or "stream of consciousness" (1892) to convey two of the fundamental facts of consciousness: that within each personal consciousness the contents are always changing, and yet personal consciousness is continuous.

You know from your own experience how the contents of consciousness—perceptions, thoughts, images, feelings—are constantly changing.[1] Thoughts change in response to changing external stimuli and the changing demands of the "task at hand" (such as reading, driving, conversation). Daydream thoughts can roam widely from one topic to another, often being set off by something we have seen or heard, and then continuing in their own autonomous string of associations until we end up thinking about something quite different from what we started out with, as in the following example:

> O.K. I'm looking at that piece of wood down there in the corner. I'm thinking that this is a really, very interesting stream of consciousness. I'm looking at my coat now. I got it from uhm Hadassah. And there's this great Jewish lady there that was uh, oh, I'm thinking about this tie that I had. Oh, now I'm thinking of a tie of my grandfather's. I'm thinking about the day that my grandfather died. I was at junior high school and [name] walked into the office. I was in the office and I was crying and I didn't really care if he, if he cared that I was crying, uhm. I walked outside. I remember walking down by the football field. It was a long, curvy driveway sort of and I remember looking over through my tears at them playing football. Now I'm thinking about my coach in uh junior high school. He was [name] and he used to beat up all of, all of these, these kids uhm, but he

liked me. I'm thinking of his big nose and bald head. . . . I'm looking at this piece of cellophane from a cigarette package . . . and I'm thinking that I'm smoking too many cigarettes. I should quit because I'm worried that I'm going to wind up just like my father . . . (Excerpt from tape recorded stream of consciousness report by participant in thinking-out-loud study; Pope 1978, p. 288).

The stream of consciousness is much like the flow of conversation at a party, with successive topics being connected by associations having to do with factors such as similarity of relationship (child, spouse, parent), location (school, city, country), activity (work, sports, travel), emotional reaction (joy, anger, depression), life events (birth, marriage, divorce, death), or news events (politics, economy, war). An ever-changing stream of consciousness is a fundamental human characteristic, and it is normal to engage frequently in daydream thoughts—thoughts, either fantastic or mundane, that have nothing to do with the task at hand. A realistic representation of human conscious experience has been attempted by a number of writers using the "stream of consciousness" style, most notably James Joyce's *Ulysses*. Of course, one limitation of this literary technique is that it cannot show the visual mental images that are an important part of the waking thoughts of many people.

Psychologists are interested in trying to understand the factors that influence the stream of thought, that is, the factors that determine the selection of topics and their sequence. Cognitive psychologists are beginning to realize that a complete understanding of the human mind cannot be developed by studying only thinking during rational decision-making, memory, and problem-solving tasks. It is necessary also to study the spontaneous flow of thoughts that occurs in daydreaming (and also night dreaming). In studying the stream of consciousness the psychologist faces serious practical difficulties due to the limitations of verbal introspective reports, as I discussed in Chapter 3. But the topic is so interesting and important that, rather than abandon it, we must face the difficulties. Clinical psychologists want to know about the stream of thoughts so that they can understand their clients and help them with their personal problems. One of the tenets of cognitive approaches to psychotherapy is that our feelings and actions are influenced by our conscious thoughts, and we can change our maladaptive feelings and actions if we adopt strategies to change our conscious thoughts.

In this chapter I will first discuss a system for classifying the ever-changing thoughts in the stream of consciousness. Then I will discuss research on daydreaming, including personality correlates of daydreaming, experiments on task variables that influence daydreaming frequency, and physiological correlates of daydreaming. Next I will discuss the effects of sensory deprivation on conscious experience. Finally, I will present some conclusions and hypotheses about factors that influence daydreaming and the stream of consciousness.

DIMENSIONS OF THOUGHT IN NORMAL WAKING STATES

The first stage of studying a natural phenomenon is to develop a system to describe and classify various instances of the topic under study. In order to study the stream of consciousness, we need a descriptive system that classifies moment-to-moment changes in conscious experiences according to abstract categories that cut across the variety of specific contents and that are likely to be meaningfully related to various personal and environmental variables (including experimental independent variables). In Chapter 2, I described various aspects of conscious experience—percepts, verbal thoughts, mental images, feelings, and so forth—that can vary in the stream of consciousness. But for a more detailed analysis we need to describe dimensions on which these aspects of experience can vary.

Several writers have tried to describe conscious thoughts in terms of two broad categories. For example, Freud (1900/1965) distinguished between secondary and primary process thinking: *secondary process thinking* is more controlled, verbal, rational, and oriented to reality, whereas *primary process thinking* is more spontaneous, imaginative, visual, and oriented to gratification of instinctive needs. Both night dreams and vivid wish-fulfilling daydreams and reveries involve primary process thinking.[2] Berlyne (1965) made a similar distinction between directed versus autistic thinking, whereas Hilgard (1962) distinguished realistic versus impulsive thinking.

All of these dichotomies are intended to capture the distinction between the more realistic, task-oriented type of waking thought (such as making a practical decision, solving a problem, reading a technical book) and the more imaginative, spontaneous type of thinking that occurs commonly in daydreaming and reverie. For purposes of experimental research on daydreaming, Singer (1975a, 1978) defined daydreaming in terms of *stimulus independent mentation* (SIM), on the assumption that thinking about a task at hand (such as driving a car or listening to a lecture) involves attention to external stimuli, whereas daydreams are thoughts that are unrelated to the task at hand and hence independent of current environmental stimuli.

Eric Klinger (1978, 1978–79) argued, however, that simple dichotomies do not capture the richness and variety of waking thoughts and images. For example, some thoughts classified as daydreams because they are not about the current task at hand are nonetheless quite realistic and rational thoughts about solving practical problems in one's life, rather than with wish-fulfilling fantasies. In other cases a train of spontaneous thoughts, either realistic or fantastic, may be elicited by current environmental stimuli, though the thoughts are not directly related to the task at hand. (For example, something you read in a textbook might remind you of a personal event in your life, and so you would start reminiscing.)

In order to describe more fully the variety of waking thoughts, Klinger proposed that they can be classified on each of several different dimensions. Each dimension is a continuum, ranging from high to low, or from one pole to another. The dimensions are independent (or semi-independent) of each other, so two thoughts on two different topics might be rated as similar on some dimensions but different on other dimensions. Though the dimensions are continua, I will describe them as if they are dichotomies, since the continua are best understood by describing their extreme ends.

Operant versus respondent thoughts.   Klinger (1971) distinguished between operant and respondent thoughts, by analogy to Skinner's (1953) distinction between operant (emitted) and respondent (elicited) responses. Operant thoughts are thoughts directed toward accomplishing a task that requires controlled attention, rather than mere automatic, habitual performance.

> In very general terms, operant thinking [differs] from respondent thinking in that it is accompanied by a sense of volition, is checked against feedback concerning its effects, is evaluated according to its effectiveness in advancing [toward] particular goals, and is protected from drift and distraction by the thinker's deliberately controlling his or her attention (Klinger 1978, p. 235).

Conversely, respondent thoughts are elicited either by stimuli or by other thoughts, and they flow without any voluntary control over their direction. Respondent thinking is not concerned with accomplishing any task at hand, and so it is not evaluated according to its effectiveness in accomplishing particular goals, nor is it deliberately protected from attentional drift. Working on a calculus problem would involve operant thought, whereas daydreaming about a sexual fantasy or about winning a million-dollar lottery would involve respondent thought.

In general, operant thought is voluntarily directed, whereas respondent thought is undirected. This is not to say that respondent thought is necessarily "directionless." An elaborate but spontaneous fantasy may lead to some conclusion, but it does so in an automatic fashion, without foreknowledge of the conclusion or voluntarily leading it to the conclusion. The direction of the fantasy is apparent only in retrospect. Fantasies that involve some degree of voluntary control fall somewhere nearer the middle of the operant-respondent continuum. Aimless mindwandering is respondent thought.

Stimulus-bound versus stimulus-independent thoughts. Stimulus-bound thoughts are related to the current setting or task at hand, whereas stimulus-independent thoughts are unrelated to the current setting or task at hand. Stimulus-independence is the criterion that Singer (1978) and Antrobus (1968) used to identify daydreams in their experimental studies (to be described in a later section), in which they defined stimulus-independent mentation (SIM) as any thought that was not related to the task at hand. Klinger (1978) argued that stimulus-independence alone is too crude a criterion for classifying daydreams, since some stimulus-independent thoughts are rational and related to practical concerns (other than the task at hand), rather than being pure fantasy or recollection. Though most task-related thoughts may be operant thoughts, the two dimensions (operant/respondent and stimulus-bound/independent thoughts) are defined as independent dimensions. Table 8.1 shows examples of how thoughts can be either related or unrelated to the stimulus setting or task, and either operant or respondent.

Fanciful versus realistic thoughts. Realistic thoughts are thoughts about things that have happened or are currently happening, or things that might plausibly happen given the thinker's current life situation or the world situation. Fanciful thoughts are imaginative thoughts about things that are either impossible or extremely unlikely to happen given the

TABLE 8.1   Examples of Thoughts to Illustrate Different Combinations of Stimulus Relatedness and Operant/Respondent Dimensions

TYPE OF THOUGHT	SETTING AND ACTIVITY	THOUGHT CONTENT
Stimulus-bound (related to task or setting):		
Operant	1. Driving home from work	Thinking about best route to avoid road repair work on way home.
	2. Reading *Abnormal Psychology* text book in library	Trying to recall and paraphrase the main points of the chapter section that I just finished reading.
Respondent	1. Driving home	Thoughts/images of traffic accident that I saw on this stretch of road last month.
	2. Reading textbook (chapter on depression)	Recalling a friend's suicide attempt, and how I felt about it.
Stimulus-independent (unrelated to task or setting):		
Operant	1. Driving home	Thinking about gathering the information I need to compute my income tax.
	2. Reading textbook	Trying to estimate the best time to leave the library in order to run two errands and get home in time for supper.
Respondent	1. Driving home	Images of kayaking last weekend, and the feel of cold water on my face.
	2. Reading textbook	Wondering whether Xxx was really flirting with me, or whether it was my imagination.

thinker's current life situation or the world situation. Note that realistic and fanciful are relative terms. For example, my fantasies about sailing an expensive sailboat might be similar to my dentist's realistic memories of last weekend's adventures. Many people daydream about what they would do if they were president, but such thoughts are realistic for only a few people. Fanciful thoughts are usually respondent and unrelated to the task at hand, but they can be operant and related to the task at hand, such as when you think of a very imaginative but impossible solution to a practical problem. (For example, I could end the threat of nuclear war if I were Superman and I could gather up all of the nuclear weapons and hurl them into the Sun.)

Well-integrated versus degenerated thoughts. This dimension distinguishes relatively orderly, connected, coherent trains of thought from those that are relatively disorderly, disconnected, and incoherent.

> Ordinary waking thought more often than not has about it a certain quality of intactness that sets it off from dreamlike thought: Particular thoughts tend to have a coherent quality, things that are separate topics retain their separateness, and images of different things retain their individual character; whereas dream images often flow without respect to beginnings or endings, shift gears drastically in the middle, interweave different concerns with one another, and offer images that seem to be the fused representatives of different basic ideas or forms (Klinger 1978, p. 241).

Klinger argued that the degenerateness dimension is functionally independent of the other dimensions, though not necessarily statistically independent. For example, most operant thought is well-integrated, but it may become degenerated if we are especially drowsy or in a drugged state. Most degenerate thoughts are respondent and fanciful, for example, the bizarre hypnagogic images that occur when you are drowsy and falling asleep. But some fanciful thoughts are well-integrated, with consistent characters and images, as in a good fantasy novel.

Vivid versus nonvivid mental images. Mental images are quasi-perceptual experiences of people, objects, and so forth, that occur in the absence of their real perceptual counterparts. Mental images can vary on a dimension of vividness, from high to low. Most people's night dreams involve vivid or life-like visual mental images. People differ widely in the vividness of their waking mental images. Mental images (visual, tactile, auditory) are common in fanciful, respondent daydreams, and they tend to be more vivid under relaxed or drowsy conditions. But images can occur in operant thought, too, such as when you visualize how you want to arrange your furniture, or how to build a brick-and-board bookcase. Auditory images often occur (musical melodies, animal sounds), but purely verbal thoughts are counted as a separate category, even though we may "hear" our own voice in our verbal thoughts.

Evidence for Klinger's Dimensions of Thought

Klinger's analysis of the abstract dimensions of thought makes sense in relation to his own introspections—and mine, too. But the dimensions of thought that you discover through introspection depend to some extent on your prior theoretical notions and the aspects of thought that you attend to during introspection. In order to find out whether his dimensions of thought were applicable to the thoughts of other people, Klinger (1978, 1978–79) analyzed the introspective reports of a dozen college students. The reports were collected in a systematic manner, but under uncontrolled, real-life circumstances. As they went about their daily activities the subjects carried an electronic gadget that beeped at random intervals averaging forty minutes between beeps. Whenever the gadget beeped, the subjects stopped what they were doing and answered questions about their most recent thought segment (thoughts on one topic) on a thought-sampling questionnaire. First, they wrote a brief narrative description of the thought and the situation in which it occurred. Then they answered a series of fifteen questions about the thought segment, concerning its duration, directedness, specificity, visualness of imagery, detail in imagery, controllability of imagery, attentiveness to environmental events, and familiarity or strangeness of the thought. Afterward, Klinger had independent judges rate each thought segment according to its degree of relationship to the setting or task at hand.

Some 285 analyzable thought samples were collected in a wide variety of situations, ranging from resting or doing homework to driving or feeding cows, and they covered a wide range of topics, ranging from homework and death to travel and sexual seduction. The median duration of the thought segments was only five seconds; most thoughts were very brief, though some lasted nearly a minute. Correlational analysis of the data supported the notion that the first two dimensions, operant/respondent thought and stimulus dependent/independent thought, are largely independent of each other ($r = 0.20$); they are not simply two different ways of measuring the same thing. Of the 285 analyzable thought samples, 69% were judged to be clearly setting-related; of these, 65% were rated as wholly or mainly operant, and 27% as wholly or mainly respondent. Some 21% of the thought samples were judged to be clearly independent of the setting; of these, 37% were rated as wholly or mainly operant, whereas 25% were rated as wholly or mainly respondent. Thus, the correspondence between operantness and setting-relatedness is far from perfect ($r = 0.18$); the two dimensions are largely independent of each other. A factor analysis of the data (Klinger 1978–79) revealed three relatively independent factors corresponding to the dimensions of operant versus respondent thought, external versus internal attention, and fanciful versus realistic thought.[3] Also, thought samples varied on a vividness of imagery dimension.

The main results of the earlier study were replicated in a follow-up study using a larger sample size (n = 29; 1425 thought samples; Klinger & Cox 1987–88). In addition, the more recent study showed that most thought samples (73%) contained some degree of *interior monologue* (talking to oneself) and also most (67%) had some degree of *visual-spatial mental imagery*. As for the integrated versus degenerated thought dimension, in most thought samples (78%) the thoughts/images were well connected or organized, though 22% of the samples showed disconnected or disorganized thoughts. Only 3% of the thoughts/images were highly distorted, but another 22% contained some degree of dream-like distortion. In most cases (76%) the subjects had good confidence in their memory for their most recent thought. (Bear in mind that these are average results for twenty-nine subjects; there was considerable variability between subjects.)

Klinger's thought-sampling research is noteworthy for showing that waking thoughts can be reliably classified on several relatively independent dimensions, having to do with operantness, setting-relatedness, fancifulness, integration, and imagery vividness. His work shows that whereas the prototype daydream (stimulus-independent) thought might be respondent, fanciful, and vivid, some daydreams may be operant, realistic, and nonvivid, or any other combination of the different dimensions. Klinger's studies (1978; Klinger & Cox 1987–88) can be criticized for their failure to include questions about affective dimensions of the stream of consciousness. In informal reports of their stream of consciousness, people often refer to the pleasant or unpleasant nature of their experiences, or to more specific emotions such as anxiety and joy. The task that remains is to discover the personal and situational variables that affect the characteristics of thoughts and feelings in the stream of consciousness—what Singer (1984) called the "private personality."[4]

RESEARCH ON DAYDREAMING

If you take a moment for retrospection of your thoughts over the last several minutes you will probably find that you have not focused your attention continuously on this textbook. Rather, from time to time your thoughts have shifted briefly to other things, including external stimuli, such as music or voices from the next room, and daydreams, such as thoughts about someone you hope to see later tonight. Perhaps your thoughts about that person produce emotional feelings, such as joy or anger. And perhaps these reactions have gotten you off on a train of associations that leads to still other daydreams, keeping your attention away from this text for minutes at a time. [SNAP OUT OF IT! This stuff is important! Study now, daydream later!]

Singer (1975a, 1975b) argued that daydreams differ so widely that they cannot be defined simply in terms of their content or quality. Rather, daydreams are defined as thoughts that are not directly related to the task at hand or to the setting (social or physical environment):

> Probably the single most common connotation is that daydreaming represents a shift of attention *away* from some primary physical or mental task we have set for ourselves, or *away* from directly looking at or listening to something in the external environment, *toward* an unfolding sequence of private responses made to some internal stimulus. The inner processes usually considered are "pictures in the mind's eye," the unrolling of a sequence of events, memories or creatively constructed images of future events which have varying degrees of probability of taking place. Also included as objects of daydreaming are our awareness of our bodily sensations, our emotions and our [interior monologues], those little inner voices we hear talking to us somewhere in our heads (Singer 1975b, pp. 3–4).

Daydream thoughts may arise directly from memory, or they may be elicited by distracting physical stimuli or even by stimuli from the task at hand. Whatever their initial stimulus, once irrelevant thoughts get started they often continue for several seconds or minutes, one thought leading to another in what could be termed a stream of thoughts or associations, or a stream of consciousness.

Here I will describe research on several factors related to daydreaming, including personality differences, ongoing tasks, and physiological correlates of daydreaming.

Individual Differences in Daydreaming

Jerome Singer and John Antrobus (1972; Singer 1975a, 1975b, 1978) developed an elaborate questionnaire, The Imaginal Processes Inventory (IPI), for studying individual differences in daydreaming. The IPI consists of twenty-nine scales (of twelve items each), covering topics such as frequency of daydreaming, positive reactions in daydreams, acceptance of one's daydreams, fear of failure in daydreams, sexual daydreams, heroic daydreams, hostile-aggressive daydreams, guilty daydreams, visual imagery in daydreams, problem solving in daydreams, and mindwandering. Singer and Antrobus (1972) did a factor analysis the IPI answers of some 579 college freshmen from two universities. Three factors emerged, suggesting three different daydreaming styles: a positive-vivid daydreaming style (PV), a guilty-dysphoric style (GD), and an anxious-distractible style (AD). Table 8.2 shows some examples of IPI items.[5]

TABLE 8.2   Examples of Items from the Imaginal Processes Inventory

Subjects check each item on a 1 to 5 scale according to how much they think it applies to themselves. The label before each item shows the IPI scale to which it belongs. The initials after each item (PV, GD, AD) show the IPI daydreaming style factor to which the scale relates most strongly.

Positive reactions: "My daydreams often leave me with a warm, happy feeling."   PV
Frightened reactions: "My daydreams have such an emotional effect on me that I often react with fear."   GD
Visual imagery: "The pictures in my mind seem as clear as photographs."   PV
Auditory imagery: "In a daydream I can hear a tune almost as clearly as if I were actually listening to it."   PV
Problem-solving: "Sometimes an answer to a very difficult problem comes to me during a daydream."   PV
Future-oriented: "I picture myself as I will be several years from now."   PV
Bizarre-improbable content: "I daydream about utterly impossible situations."   GD
Fear of failure: "I imagine myself failing those I love."   GD
Hostile-aggressive: "I imagine myself getting even with those I dislike."   GD
Sexual: "While reading I often slip into daydreams about sex or making love to someone."   PV
Heroic: "I picture myself risking my life to save someone I love."   GD
Guilt: "In my daydreams I am always afraid of being caught doing something wrong."   GD
Absorption in daydreams: "Some of my daydreams are so powerful that I just can't take my attention away from them."   AD, PV
Hallucinatory vividness: "Voices in my daydreams are so distinct and clear that I'm tempted to answer them."   GD
Mindwandering: "No matter how much I try to concentrate, thoughts unrelated to my work always creep in."   AD
Distractibility: "I find it hard to read when someone is on the telephone in another room."   AD

Source: Singer, J. L., & Antrobus, J. S. (1972). Daydreaming, imaginal processes, and personality: A normative study. In P. Sheehan (Ed.), *The Function and Nature of Imagery* (pp. 175–202). New York: Academic Press .

Daydreaming styles.   People with a *positive-vivid* daydreaming style could be called "happy daydreamers." Positive-vivid daydreamers tend to daydream frequently, have positive reactions to their daydreams, have vivid visual and auditory images in their daydreams, and use daydreams to help solve personal problems. Such people may develop fairly elaborate fantasies and show a lot of interest in their inner experience.

The *guilty-dysphoric* daydreaming style is characterized by daydreams showing guilt, hostility, fear of failure, heroism, achievement-orientation, hallucinatory vividness, and frightened reactions. Guilty-dysphoric day-dreamers "seem to be people who are given to a great deal of tortured self-examination, driven toward achievement and heroic accomplishment, and characterized by a generally negatively toned fantasy life" (Singer 1975a).

The *anxious-distractible* style (also termed "mindwandering-distractible style") is associated with mindwandering through daydreaming, worrying, boredom, and distractibility. Paradoxically, such people may become very absorbed in daydreams without being able to maintain concentration on a single daydream topic; their daydreams jump around a lot, so they rarely develop extended fantasies. Such people tend to be extremely anxious, self-doubting, and fearful, with relatively low achievement motivation.

In extreme cases of people who score high on one factor and low on other factors, we could say that positive-vivid daydreamers are generally well-adjusted; guilty-dysphoric daydreamers are obsessive-compulsive neurotics; and anxious- distractible daydreamers are anxiety neurotics (Singer & Antrobus 1972). However, it is important to note that most people fall in between the extremes, perhaps being mostly of one daydreaming-personality type but also having some elements of the other types. For example, you might commonly have visually vivid, pleasurable fantasies characteristic of the positive-vivid daydreamer, but also sometimes have heroic or aggressive daydreams that are more characteristic of the guilty-dysphoric type.

Research using the IPI with college students and other people of various ages shows that nearly everyone daydreams fairly often, though some people daydream more than others. A high frequency of daydreaming is not, in itself, a sign of psychopathology. Older people show the same daydream-ing styles as college students, though with advancing age there tends to be a decrease in daydreams about the future, sexual daydreams, and daydreams showing guilt or anxiety (Giambra 1974).

Correlates of daydreaming styles.   Several studies have shown rela-tionships between IPI daydreaming types and other measures of fantasy, thought, or behavior. Starker (1974, 1978) found a correspondence between IPI daydreaming styles and night dreaming styles. He administered the IPI to college students and also asked them to keep dream diaries for two weeks. For each IPI daydreaming type, three subjects were selected who were the most clear-cut examples of that type, and their dreams were analyzed in de-tail. Judges who were "blind" to the subjects' IPI daydreaming style scored the dream reports on several dimensions. The night dreams of positive-vivid daydreamers showed more positive emotionality, and less bizarreness, than did either guilty-dysphoric or anxious-distractible daydreamer types. Of the three groups, night dreams of the anxious-distractible types showed the most emotionality, the most bizarreness, and the greatest number of different idea units per dream. (The latter result suggests that the anxious-distractible types tended to have dreams that were more fragmented—jumping around from one scene to another—than did the other types.) Nightmares—defined as anxious dreams that awakened the subject—never occurred among the positive-vivid daydreamers; they were most frequent among the anxious-distractible types. In another study, Starker (1978, 1982) asked college students to make up dreams, describing their "best possible" and their "worst possible" fantasies. Interestingly, guilty-dysphoric types tended to include negative affect even in their best possible fantasies, whereas positive-vivid types minimized negative affect in their worst fantasies. Starker's research shows a continuity between waking fantasy and dream fantasy: your positive or negative temperament shows up in both your daydreams and your night dreams.

Antrobus, Coleman, and Singer (1967) studied daydreaming during a *vigilance task*, in which brief auditory signals occurred at irregular intervals, and subjects were supposed to press buttons whenever they detected the signals. The subjects who scored highest on the positive-vivid daydreaming factor reported the most daydreams during the vigilance task; as the boring task wore on, their daydream frequency increased, while their signal-detection performance deteriorated more rapidly than did the performance of low-frequency daydreamers.

Isaacs (1975) examined the language used to describe daydreams that occurred during a vigilance task. Positive-vivid daydreamer types described more elaborate daydreams, and used more metaphoric ("this is like that") language in describing them, compared to other subjects. Fusella (1973) found that positive-vivid daydreamers can generate visual mental images that are so vivid that they can interfere with the detection of dim visual signals, more so than people who score low on the PV factor.

Daydreams may reveal your desires or fears more than they reveal what you actually do in your life. For example, people of all three daydreaming styles, both male and female, daydream fairly often about sex, though the specific nature of sexual daydreams tends to differ for the different daydreaming-personality types, showing themes characterized more by either pleasure, guilt, or anxiety. But elaborate and exciting sexual daydreams, for most of us, reveal what we would like to do rather than what we have actually done. Males tend to have heroic daydreams more often than females, though people with heroic daydreams may never have done anything heroic in their lives. And some people have highly aggressive daydreams in which they may brutally destroy real or imagined enemies, though their actual behavior toward other people may not be particularly aggressive. Only when someone is obsessed with aggressive fantasies, and has little realization of the consequences of aggression, is there likely to be a relationship between aggressive daydreams and actual behavior (Singer 1978).

To say that your daydreams do not necessarily reveal your actual behavior is not to say that your daydreams are unrelated to your life experiences. Our life experiences give us a variety of desires, successes, failures, and personal concerns that can become the source of daydream fantasies involving either pleasurable recollection, imaginative compensation, or practical planning for the future.

Experimental Studies of Factors that Affect Daydreaming

As you know from your own experience, you are most likely to day-dream at times when you do not have to respond to information from the environment—that is, when there is no external "task at hand"—or when the environmental input is so redundant or boring that you stop attending to it. Antrobus and Singer did several experiments on the influence of various task variables (such as task difficulty, and payoffs for good performance) on daydreaming frequency.

Daydreaming and information load.   Antrobus (1968) examined the re-lationship between daydreaming frequency and the rate of information presentation, or *information load*, in a vigilance task. Vigilance tasks were orig-inally devised by psychologists after World War II to study factors that affect human performance in monitoring radar screens, an activity in which ob-servers must spend long periods of time looking for new blips—possibly in-dicating enemy warplanes—to appear on the screen. In Antrobus's study a series of brief tone signals was presented to the subjects, and they were re-quired to press a telegraph key each time they heard a tone. Under some conditions tones of two or three different pitches (high, medium, or low) were used, and subjects had to press one of two or three different keys, de-pending on which pitch they heard. The difficulty of the vigilance task was manipulated by varying both the signal presentation rate (from 2.0 tones per second to 0.2 per second [that is, one every five seconds]) and the number of different tones that might occur (1, 2, or 3). When two or three different tones were used, tones of different pitches were presented in a random se-quence. Table 8.3 shows how the different signal presentation rates and number of possible tones were systematically combined, on different trials, to produce nine different information presentation rates (information load) measured in *bits per second*.[6] Over the course of a 2-hour session each subject

TABLE 8.3   **Information Load in Bits per Second under Nine Test Conditions in Antrobus's (1968) Experiment: Three Signal Presentation Rates Crossed with Three Tone Conditions (Multiplicative Rule)**

NUMBER OF DIFFERENT TONES	SIGNAL PRESENTATION RATE: SIGNALS PER SECOND		
	2/sec.	1/sec.	0.2/sec.
1	2	1	0.2
2	4	2	0.4
3	6	3	0.6

From Antrobus, J. S. (1968). Information theory and stimulus-independent thought. *British Journal of Psychology, 59,* 423–30.

was tested with each of the nine different information loads on 20 different trials, in a randomized sequence. As an incentive for good performance the subjects were paid a small monetary bonus based on the number of correct keypress responses (correct signal detections). In order to minimize extraneous distracting stimuli, the subjects were tested in a soundproof chamber, with a masking noise and with the lights turned off (partial sensory deprivation conditions).

The frequency of daydreaming was measured by a thought-sampling method. Daydreaming was strictly defined as *stimulus-independent mentation* (SIM), that is, a thought or image that was not directly concerned with performing the vigilance task. Prior to the experiment, subjects were given extensive training in classifying their thoughts as either task-relevant thoughts or "outside thoughts." During the vigilance task, at the end of each fifteen-second trial the subjects reported whether they had had any outside thoughts during the trial. They merely reported whether they had had any outside thoughts (daydreams); they did not have to report the content of the daydream. (This simple yes-no reporting procedure was designed to minimize interference with the natural flow of the stream of consciousness.) The next trial started immediately after the thought report.

Figure 8.1A shows the proportion of trials with daydreams ("stimulus-independent responses") as a function of the information-presentation rate. The frequency of stimulus-independent thoughts decreased as a direct linear function of the information-presentation rate, from about 60% at the lowest information rate to about 35% at the highest rate. Figure 8.1B shows the bits/second encoded by the subjects (correct responses) as a function of the bits/second presented (information load). The fact that the bits encoded are less than the bits presented indicates that vigilance performance was far from perfect, especially at higher information presentation rates. Figure 8.1C shows the relationship between frequency of stimulus-independent thoughts and actual task performance in bits/second encoded. Daydreaming occurs less frequently, the greater the amount of external information that is being encoded.

Besides showing, as expected, that daydreaming decreases as an information-processing task becomes more difficult, Antrobus's (1968) study revealed a rather surprising result: Even under the most difficult vigilance task conditions, in which signal detection performance was only about 50% correct (about 3 bits encoded out of 6 bits presented), the subjects still daydreamed on 35% of the trials. You might think that people could resist daydreaming in order to perform well on a difficult task. But it appears as if there is a strong internal need or pressure to daydream, and so daydreaming will occur even during a difficult task, particularly when the task is as boring as a laboratory vigilance task.

Incentives for task performance.   One day I was discussing Antrobus's (1968) experiment in an undergraduate course when a student spoke up and suggested that Antrobus's subjects daydreamed so much because they were not sufficiently motivated to do well on the task. At best they could only earn a few dollars by good performance. The student then described one of his own experiences. He said that he was a Viet Nam war veteran, and that dur-

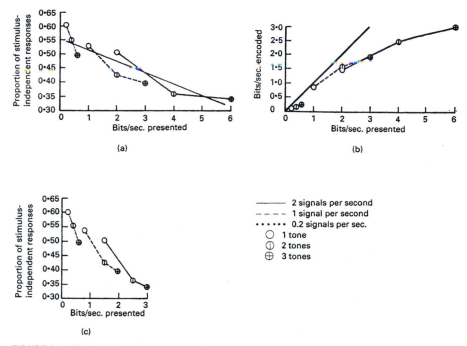

FIGURE 8.1. Relationship between stimulus-independent thought (daydreaming) and information load in a signal detection task. (A) Relative frequency of stimulus-independent thought reports as a function of information-presentation rate. (B) Rate of information encoding as a function of the rate of information presentation. If task performance was perfect then the data points would fall on the diagonal line (for example, 3 bits presented would correspond to 3 bits encoded). (C) Relative frequency of stimulus-independent thought reports as a function of the rate of information encoding. [From Antrobus, J. S. (1968). Information theory and stimulus-independent thought. *British Journal of Psychology,* 59, 423–30. By permission of the British Psychological Society.]

ing the war he had been the radar man on a bomber that flew bombing missions over Hanoi and other targets. It was his job to operate equipment designed to jam the enemy's radar so they couldn't shoot down the bomber. It was a real-life vigilance task, requiring rapid processing and responding to a variety of external stimuli. His life, and the lives of the other crew members, depended upon his doing his job correctly. He said: "Under those conditions, when we were being fired upon, I did not daydream. It was like I was part of the machine."

Of course, nobody asked the radar man about his daydreams *during* the bombing runs, before he had had a chance to forget any daydreams that he might have had. But the radar man's report is consistent with other real-world observations. Perhaps you have had similar experiences in which your daydreaming was reduced to zero or near-zero for several seconds or minutes while you were engaged in some dangerous task that required your full attention, such as skiing down the expert slope or kayaking through treach-erous rapids.

Undoubtedly motivation to perform the task at hand is an important factor influencing daydream frequency. Antrobus, Singer, and Greenberg (1966) manipulated incentives in a signal detection task (2 bits/second presented) by varying the size of a monetary penalty for errors. The error penalty amounts were to be subtracted from the subjects' earnings for participating in the experiment. The frequency of stimulus-independent thoughts decreased from 65% with no penalty to about 32% with the highest penalty. Thus, daydreaming frequency was affected by incentives, but even under the best conditions daydreaming frequency remained relatively high. Of course, the total amount of money to be earned for perfect performance was only a few dollars.[7] But even under the best of laboratory conditions, with a diffi-cult task and a monetary incentive for good performance, it is doubtful whether daydreaming could be reduced to a really low level. The vigilance task is probably a good laboratory analogy to a real-world task such as listen-ing to a boring lecture, but it may not be a very good analogy to real-world tasks in which life or limbs are at stake.

Incentives for daydreaming.   Daydreaming is influenced not only by the task at hand, but also by recent events that are personally significant to you. For example, if you were to receive bad news, such as news that a close friend had been in a serious automobile accident, just before you entered a classroom, then you would probably be less attentive to the lecture than usual because you would be thinking about your friend. Antrobus et al. (1966) modeled this situation after the vigilance signal detection task. Sub-jects had to wait for fifteen minutes in a waiting room before doing the vigi-lance task. During that time a music radio program was played through a loudspeaker. For subjects in the experimental group, the music program was interrupted by a special (phony) news bulletin that said that China had en-tered the Viet Nam war and had sunk two U.S. aircraft carriers, and that local draft boards should "call in for physical examinations, as soon as possible, all unemployed youths over 18 and all eligible college graduates" (p. 411). (This experiment was done in mid-1965, during the first major escalation of the Viet Nam war, when college-age people were especially concerned about being drafted into the army.) During the vigilance task the experimental sub-jects reported daydreams (SIMs) twice as often as control subjects, and their signal detection performance was three times as variable as that of the con-trols. On a follow-up questionnaire most of the subjects reported that the "news bulletin" had caused them to feel anxiety and to have thoughts about the implications of the news for their future. They reported that, during the signal-detection task, they had had thoughts about things such as the possi-bility of themselves or friends being drafted, the effect of the draft on school plans, moving to Canada to escape the draft, "being tied to a tree in Vietnam and being tortured by Chinese," and so forth. Also there were some general thoughts about such topics as war, people being killed, and atomic explo-sions. This study shows how personally significant news can increase the incentive (payoff) value of pertinent daydream thoughts, so that daydreaming increases, even though daydreaming interferes with performing the task at hand.

The processing requirements of daydreams.

In the multistore model of the human information processing system, working (short-term) memory is a limited capacity, general-purpose information processing system. Researchers have shown an inverse relationship between daydream frequency and external task difficulty or task performance (Antrobus 1968; Antrobus et al. 1970). That is, daydreaming and performing an external task mutually interfere with each other. The implication is that both sorts of mental activity—daydreaming and doing tasks with external stimuli—require working memory.

While people are doing external tasks, some daydreaming occurs concurrently with responding to task stimuli (parallel processing). But most daydreaming occurs during the time gaps between responses to task stimuli. In a vigilance signal-detection task with signals presented at regular time intervals, the greater the interval between signals, the more subjects daydreamed (Antrobus et al. 1970). When the signals occurred at variable intervals, daydreaming occurred less often than when signals occurred at regular intervals (where the regular interval was the same [e.g. 5 seconds] as the mean interval under the variable interval condition). Thus, when we do not know exactly when to expect critical external events (variable intervals), we must be vigilant and prepared to respond at any moment, so we daydream less often. But when the critical events are predictable, we can relax and daydream during the intervals between them. In other words, we alternate attention between internal events (daydreams) and external events. Alternating between two external tasks, or between an external task and internal processing, is called *multiplexing*. Concurrent (parallel) daydreaming and task performance should be more common when you are doing a relatively simple or highly practiced, automated task, such as driving under easy conditions, whereas multiplexing should be more common with a more difficult or less automated task.

When daydreaming involves vivid visual or auditory mental images, specialized visual or auditory information-processing mechanisms are required, in addition to general-purpose working memory. This conclusion was suggested by an experiment in which one group of subjects did a signal-detection task with visual signals, whereas another group detected auditory signals. Within each group, half of the subjects were asked to make thought-sampling reports of daydreams involving visual mental images, whereas the other subjects reported daydreams involving auditory mental images. The critical finding was that, as the information load increased in the visual signal-detection task, the frequency of visual daydream images decreased more than the frequency of auditory images. And vice versa for auditory signals: auditory imagery decreased more than visual imagery. In other words, looking/listening for signals interferes with daydream images more for images in the same modality as the signal than for images in the other modality

(Antrobus et al. 1970). A complementary result was obtained in an experiment in which subjects were required to generate visual or auditory mental images while doing visual and auditory signal-detection tasks: visual images interfered with visual signal detection more than with auditory signal detection, and vice versa for auditory images (Segal & Fusella 1970).

Based on the rationale that when two tasks interfere with each other they must be competing for the same information processing mechanism, these studies suggest that visual and auditory mental images use some of the same mechanisms that are involved in later stages of visual and auditory perception, respectively. As a practical example, since driving a car is a visual task, we would expect more mutual interference between driving and visual mental imagery than between driving and auditory imagery. Thus, in principle, while you drive it should be safer to imagine singing or carrying on an imaginary conversation than it would be to visualize the action in a complicated ballet or baseball game.

Figure 8.2 shows how interference between daydreaming and task performance can be explained in terms of the multistore theory (Antrobus et al. 1970). Visual and auditory stimuli from external tasks (such as driving a car) are processed first through a series of modality-specific visual and auditory

FIGURE 8.2. Multistore theory explanation of interference between external tasks and daydreaming. Task performance and daydream imagery may interfere with each other at either (a) the working memory stage, or (b) the later stages of modality-specific processing, or both. Under some conditions (such as a difficult task with large task incentives) daydream images can be blocked (gate) from interfering with task performance. The return arrows (dashed lines) indicate the interaction between working memory and earlier processing stages. [Adapted from Antrobus, J. S., Singer, J. L., Goldstein, S., & Fortgang, M. (1970). Mindwandering and cognitive structure. *Transactions of the New York Academy of Sciences, 32*, 242–52. By permission of the N.Y.A.S.]

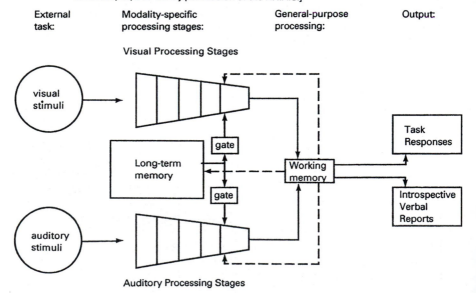

processing stages, then through a general-purpose processor (working memory) that makes the task decisions and initiates the task responses. Daydream imagery and task performance may interfere with each other at either (a) the working memory stage, or (b) the later stages of modality specific processing, both of which are limited in information-processing capacity. Visual and auditory daydream images come initially from long-term memory. They are actively transformed through interactions between their respective modality-specific processing stages and working memory. Interference is greatest when external stimuli and daydream images are in the same modality (both visual or both auditory), since interference occurs in both the modality-specific stages and in working memory. When task stimuli and daydream images are in different modalities (such as visual stimuli and auditory daydream images) then interference occurs only in working memory. The more complex the task or the daydream, the more of the limited working memory processing resources they require, so the more they interfere with each other.

Physiological Correlates of Daydreaming and Imagery

In laboratory studies of night dreaming, sleeping subjects are awakened periodically and asked to report what was going through their mind just before they were awakened. Visually vivid, story-like dreams are reported more often when subjects are awakened during REM sleep (rapid eye movements, fast low-amplitude brain waves) than when they are awakened during non-REM sleep (slow eye movements, slow high-amplitude brain waves).

Antrobus, Antrobus, and Singer (1964) examined physiological correlates of daydreaming under conditions similar to those used in laboratory studies of night dreaming. Subjects lay awake, with their eyes open, on a bed in a dimly illuminated room while their eye movements and brain waves were recorded by psychophysiological devices. Thought reports were collected via a thought-sampling procedure, where subjects were told that whenever they heard a signal they were to report what was going through their mind just before the signal. Signals were presented ten times, at irregular intervals, during a two-hour session. Half of the signals occurred immediately after four-second intervals of ocular quiescence (no eye movements or eye blinks), and half after intervals of ocular movement, in a mixed sequence. Blind judges rated the thought reports on dimensions of external visual perception and internal mental imagery. As one might expect, ratings of external perception were higher during periods of ocular movement than during ocular quiescence. But ratings of internal imagery were higher during periods of ocular quiescence. Also, alpha brain waves were more abundant during ocular quiescence than during ocular movement. (Alpha waves, 8–13 Hz [cycles per second], are an indicator of relaxed wakefulness. They are the slowest brain waves that commonly occur during wakefulness. Faster brain waves occur during alert wakefulness and REM sleep; slower waves occur during non-REM sleep.)

The results are opposite what one would expect if daydreaming were physiologically analogous to night dreaming: that is, night-dream imagery is greatest during fast eye movements and fast brain waves, but daydream imagery is greatest during ocular quiescence and relatively slow brain waves.

Why is vivid daydreaming associated with reduced eye movements? Antrobus et al. (1964; Singer & Antrobus 1965) found that the frequency of eye movements is related to the frequency of *changes* in thought contents. For example, in one experiment subjects were asked to engage in either relaxed thinking ("let your thoughts drift lazily") or active thinking ("make your thoughts race"), for one-minute intervals. Both eye movements and eye blinks were greater during active thinking than during relaxed thinking. The implication is that a low frequency of eye movements during spontaneous, vivid daydreaming may be related to a low frequency of thought content changes at such times.

During instructed mental imagery, when subjects generate images specified by the experimenter, both eye movements and eye blinks occur more often when subjects generate images involving movement (such as a tennis match) than when they generate static images (an orange on a table). The responses are the same with eyes open or closed (Antrobus et al. 1964). Also, subjects rate instructed mental images involving movement as more vivid than static images (eyes closed; Farthing et al. 1983). Undoubtedly a number of factors affect the frequency of eye movements during spontaneous daydreaming, night dreaming, and instructed mental imagery, and the factors may not be the same in all three situations. A correlation between eye movements and thought or imagery dimensions may not be a cause-and-effect relationship; the relationship may be mediated by other factors, such as the person's physiological state.

A temporal cycle in waking fantasy.   When people are asleep, the REM sleep stage and vivid, story-like dreams tend to occur on a regular cycle averaging about 90 minutes (80–100 minutes). The REM sleep cycle is regulated by a biological clock (see Chapter 10). Kripke and Sonnenschein (1978) asked whether there is a cyclic pattern to waking fantasy. In two studies using a thought-sampling method, subjects reported their thoughts whenever a tone sounded, at five- to ten-minute intervals over a ten- to twelve-hour period. In one study the subjects were isolated in laboratory room; in the other they went about their daily business, carrying an electronic beeper and portable tape recorder for making their thought reports. The thought samples were later rated on a five-point scale that ranged from (1) "present-time perceptual scanning" to (5) "vivid dreamlike fantasy."

Dreamlike waking fantasies occurred less often during ordinary daily activities than they did in the laboratory. But in both studies, a computerized "autocorrelation" analysis showed that the best fit for the fantasy ratings was a cycle averaging about 90 minutes (range: 72–120 minutes per cycle). In other words, thoughts tended to become more dreamlike, and less oriented to the immediate environment, about every 90 minutes. Also, in the laboratory study, eye movements and brain waves changed in a 90-minute cycle, with periods of slowest eye movements and maximum alpha waves tending to occur at the same time as periods with the most fantastic thoughts.

If waking fantasies tend to occur on about a 90-minute cycle, why don't we notice it? One reason is that the cycle length is variable; it averages about 90 minutes, but ranges from 72 to 120 minutes. Sometimes we might skip a cycle, when we are intensely involved in a demanding task. Also important is the fact that our daydream fantasies are so common and repetitive that we usually do not remember specific instances of fantasy, or when they occurred, so we cannot compare them and notice their cyclic nature. Unfortunately, a later study failed to replicate the earlier findings of a 90-minute waking fantasy cycle (Kripke, Mullaney, & Fleck 1985). Thus, at this time it is uncertain whether waking fantasy cycles are a common but subtle phenomenon, or one limited to some people under some conditions, or, perhaps, an artifact of certain experimental procedures.

You have probably noticed that there are moments during the day when it is exceptionally hard to resist letting your thoughts wander away from your work to vivid fantasy daydreams. Perhaps these times correspond to peaks in a daydream cycle. In any case, since it is so hard to resist daydreaming at such times, and since the daydreams interfere with your work anyway, perhaps it is just as well to indulge yourself, if possible, and spend a few minutes enjoying your daydream fantasy. Then hopefully you can get back to work with renewed vigor.

THE FUNCTIONS OF DAYDREAMING

Daydreaming may sometimes interfere with doing an important task, but often daydreaming serves valuable functions and it is far from being a waste of time. Insofar as daydreams are about current concerns they can have practical value, particularly if the emphasis is on planning rather than on worrying. Through daydreams we plan how to achieve our intermediate and long-term goals, and assess our progress toward our goals. Daydreams refresh our memory of what our goals are, and they can give us the opportunity to reevaluate and make changes in them. Imagining personal actions and their outcome can help us evaluate the likelihood of our actions being successful. It can also generate emotional states that either reinforce our goal strivings or suggest that we should change our goals (as when the anticipated outcome is unpleasant).

But daydreams that involve fantasies, rather than practical planning, also have their value. Daydreams that are pure wish-fulfilling fantasies may express our needs and desires without making any progress toward satisfying them. Such fantasy daydreams may be mere entertainment. They break the monotony of routine tasks, and so they make routine tasks more endurable. For the artist or writer, daydream fantasies may be a source of creative inspiration. Also, daydream fantasies may be important for mental health. As Freud hypothesized, when wish-fulfilling daydreams (or night dreams) are the only way to express our emotional needs and wishes, such imaginary expression may be better than no emotional expression at all. Finally, guided daydreams have been incorporated in cognitive psychotherapy to aid in the modification of goals, attitudes, self-concept, anxiety, and behavior (Singer 1975b; Singer & Pope 1978; Starker 1982). For practical suggestions, see Eric Klinger's book *Daydreaming: Using Waking Fantasy and Imagery for Self-knowledge and Creativity* (1990).

SENSORY DEPRIVATION AND CONSCIOUSNESS

We have seen that the frequency of daydreaming increases as the information presentation rate decreases in vigilance signal-detection tasks (Antrobus 1968). Normally, though we daydream frequently, the necessity of responding to external stimuli tends to direct our thoughts and put some restrictions on the flow of conscious experience. What would happen to the waking stream of consciousness if external stimulation was minimized or eliminated, and there was no external task to perform? This question was asked in research on *sensory deprivation*, which began at McGill University in the 1950s.

The McGill studies used a *monotonous stimulation technique*, in which subjects spent several days lying in bed in a lighted isolation chamber. Patterned sensory input was eliminated by translucent goggles, white noise, and cardboard-tube cuffs over the subjects' hands. Early sensory deprivation studies made several dramatic findings, including hallucinations, reduced cognitive efficiency, increased susceptibility to persuasive messages heard during isolation, and stress reactions (many subjects quit after only one or two days in sessions planned for six days or more) (Heron 1957; P. Solomon et al. 1961). These findings produced concern that sensory deprivation procedures might be dangerous and that they could be misused for political "brainwashing." However, more recent research, with different procedures and better controls, has generally failed to replicate the undesirable effects of sensory deprivation and has led to useful applications in psychotherapy (Suedfeld 1980; Suedfeld & Coren 1989; Zubec 1969, 1973).

Nowadays researchers use the term *Restricted Environmental Stimulation Technique* (REST), since such research does not really involve total sensory deprivation, and because researchers want to avoid the negative connotations associated with the older "sensory deprivation" research. Two different procedures are used in modern REST research (Suedfeld 1980). In *isolation chamber REST*, subjects lie in a bed in a dark, soundproof room. They are instructed to avoid unnecessary movement (no calisthenics), though no restraints or touch-preventing cuffs are used. Sessions typically last twenty-four hours, though some subjects have gone for six days without adverse effects. In *flotation REST*, subjects float on their back in a shallow water tank. The water is approximately body temperature and it is saturated with Epsom salt, which makes the body float high, so with the help of a floating pillow subjects can easily keep their face above water. The tank is in a dark, soundproof enclosure, with internal sounds masked by a fan. Sessions typically last forty to sixty minutes, rarely more than two hours. Now let us review some of the findings of REST research.

Research on Effects of Restricted Environmental Stimulation

Hallucinations and visual anomalies.   One of the most dramatic findings of the McGill studies was reports of hallucinations—usually visual, though sometimes auditory or tactile. Some subjects reported visual hallucinations similar to those reported following ingestion of hallucinogenic drugs, including simple geometric patterns and, at later stages, complex meaningful scenes (see Chapter 19). However, later systematic research showed that true hallucinations—where subjects have vivid mental images that they confuse with external reality—are in fact rare during REST (Zubek 1973; Zuckerman 1969b). In a large majority of cases subjects realized that their reported visual experiences were merely their imagination; only 2 percent were true hallucinations, in a three-day isolation-chamber REST study (Schulman, Richlin, & Weinstein 1967). Thus, vivid daydreams, but not true hallucinations, are common in REST.

Reports of hallucinations and visual anomalies (unusual visual percepts or images) during REST are influenced by subjects' expectations and experimental demands (Suedfeld 1980). Hunt and Chefurka (1976) suggested that some REST effects are cases of *introspective sensitization*—reports of unusual subjective experiences that occur simply as a result of sitting quietly and paying close attention to the bare features of one's immediate subjective experience. For example, Hunt and Chefurka instructed one group of subjects to attend closely to their immediate subjective experiences; a control group was told to just relax. After only ten minutes in an isolation chamber, attention group subjects reported visual anomalies and other altered-state-like experiences—such as uncanny emotion, cognitive disorientation, and feelings of interpersonal detachment and loneliness—more often than control subjects. Hunt and Chefurka and suggested that some apparent differences between REST and control procedures may result from the heightened set to attend to subjective experiences during REST. Introspective sensitization may also influence subjective reports in other situations, such as meditation, hypnosis, and biofeedback, and in experiments on effects of psychedelic drugs.

Daydreaming. Suedfeld et al. (1986) administered the Imaginal Processes Inventory (IPI) to 15 healthy college students both before REST, and immediately after 24 hours of isolation-chamber REST. Somewhat surprisingly, IPI scale scores did not change across this interval. The subjects reported fairly high daydreaming levels (with visual, auditory, and kinesthetic imagery) before REST, and these levels were not increased by 24 hours of sensory reduction. There were no reports of hallucinations or particularly bizarre ideation. The most frequently reported activities during REST included trying to determine the time, thinking about the future, sleeping, planning ahead, identifying sounds, recalling books, starring into space, and mental exercises. Thought sampling reports indicated that subjects daydreamed mostly about real personal events, usually involving their friends. During REST the subjects were usually wide awake, calm, and alert, and had no feelings of anxiety or stress.

Stress. The benign nature of REST subjects' experiences in recent research contrasts with the dramatic reports of hallucinations and stress in the McGill studies. In fact, the frequency and severity of stress reactions in the early research was exaggerated by popular reports. In fact, only 5 to 10 percent of subjects quit early due to discomfort, and almost all of the quitters were in research with the monotonous stimulation technique (Suedfeld 1980). Negative expectations about sensory deprivation's effects appears to have been a major factor in producing stress reactions in some subjects (Orne & Scheibe 1964). With current methods involving reduced stimulation (rather than monotonous stimulation) and instructions to eliminate negative expectations, stress reactions are rare even after six days of isolation chamber REST, and when they occur, stress reactions are mild (Suedfeld 1975, 1980). Flotation REST, pioneered by John Lilly (1977), is becoming increasingly accepted as a means of relaxation and inner exploration, and is being used therapeutically for stress reduction (Fine & Turner 1985; Suedfeld, Turner, & Fine, 1990; Turner et al. 1989). Commercial flotation tanks are available in some cities.

Reduced cognitive efficiency.   Reductions in cognitive efficiency have been found in some tests administered during prolonged REST. Peter Suedfeld (1980) reviewed over eighty published studies on cognitive effects, and classified the tasks used according to their complexity. He found that when subjects were tested during REST, impaired performance was more likely on relatively complex tasks ("open-ended" tasks such as story telling and creative problem solving) than on relatively simple tasks (such as rote memorization or mental arithmetic). Cognitive efficiency quickly returns to normal after the REST session is terminated.

Stimulus hunger.   In early REST research it was noted that subjects often had a craving for sensory stimulation. For example, they would attend closely to extraneous sounds or body stimuli. This need for stimulation was termed *stimulus hunger*. Several studies demonstrated *stimulus seeking behavior*, in which subjects would perform an operant response (pushing a button) in order to produce visual or auditory stimuli (A. Jones 1969). They would respond repeatedly to hear messages normally considered boring, such as out-of-date stock market reports or soap commercials. Responding increased with time during REST, and was greater for stimuli that varied each time than for stimuli that were repeated unchanged.

It is noteworthy that stimulus hunger rarely occurs during flotation REST. "This may have to do with the relatively short duration of such studies [usually forty to sixty minutes], but . . . almost all participants are quite happy in exploring the inner world during that period rather than seeking external stimuli. In fact, many are quite annoyed when their stimulus reduction is violated through external inputs required by the experimenter" (Suedfeld, 1989, personal communication).

Attitude change and suggestibility.   Early REST research showed that subjects are more likely to change their attitudes in response to persuasive messages heard during REST (Suedfeld 1969). For example, Bexton (reported in Scott et al. 1959) presented students who were mildly skeptical about psychic phenomena (ghosts, poltergeists, ESP) with a series of messages designed to convince them of the reality of such phenomena. Subjects who heard the messages during several days of monotonous-stimulation

REST showed greater increases in belief in and interest in psychic phenomena, compared to control subjects who heard the same messages under non-deprivation conditions. Similar results have been found with sensory-reduction isolation-chamber REST.

Suedfeld (1980) explained enhanced attitude change during REST in terms of two factors. First, stimulus hunger during REST increases attention to persuasive messages. Second, reduced cognitive efficiency during REST interferes with the usual process of carefully evaluating an argument and formulating counterarguments. Thus, REST can help "unfreeze" prior belief/opinion systems and allow restructuring of beliefs in response to persuasive messages.

Barabasz (1982) found that responsiveness to hypnotic suggestions was markedly increased following six hours of isolation-chamber REST. REST also increased pain tolerance. He speculated that increased imaginative involvement during REST could account for its effects on responsiveness to suggestions and pain tolerance.

Applications in psychotherapy. The effects of REST on attitude change, imagination, and suggestibility suggests that REST might be a useful adjunct to psychotherapy. This is indeed the case. Isolation-chamber REST has been found to enhance the effectiveness of therapeutic messages concerning smoking cessation (Suedfeld 1990; Suedfeld & Ikard 1974), weight reduction (Borrie & Suedfeld 1980), alcohol addiction, and phobias (Suedfeld 1980; Suedfeld & Kristeller 1982). Suedfeld pointed out that several psychotherapeutic techniques have a sensory restriction component, such as hypnosis, meditation, and progressive relaxation training.

Implications of Restricted Stimulation Effects for Consciousness

Sensory deprivation or REST has sometimes been characterized as a technique for producing an altered state of consciousness. Although conscious experience may be altered during REST, the variety of experiences varies so widely—depending upon the specific deprivation technique and its duration, experimental instructions and implicit demands, and subjects' personal characteristics and expectations—that it is not possible to describe a typical altered conscious state during REST (Zuckerman 1969a). With modern procedures, REST typically produces a pleasant, restful experience with plenty of daydreaming, rather than a dramatically altered state of consciousness.

Research on restricted environmental stimulation has some general implications for consciousness. The mind/brain system is continuously active, whether the brain is awake or asleep. The system is motivated to maintain varied conscious experience. During prolonged periods of sensory restriction, the occurrence of stimulus hunger and operant responding for varied sensory input shows that people are motivated to maintain varied conscious experience. The most satisfying input is that which is difficult or impossible to predict, since such input presents an intellectual challenge and combats boredom (Suedfeld 1980). When varied external input is not available, people vary their conscious experience through daydreaming. During the most extreme condition of sensory deprivation—when people are asleep—the mind/brain system maintains varied conscious experience through dreaming. Thus, varied mental activity does not depend upon external stimulation; it is self-generated. The mind/brain system both interprets the stimulation that it receives and seeks out or generates varied stimulation to interpret.

TOWARD A THEORY OF THE STREAM OF CONSCIOUSNESS

A comprehensive theory explaining and predicting moment-to-moment changes in the content of consciousness has not been developed. However, we can list several factors that affect the stream of consciousness and which are pertinent to developing such a theory (Pope & Singer 1978, 1980; Klinger 1978, 1987).

General Considerations

The mind/brain system is continuously active.   The mind/brain system is not a mere passive reactor to external stimuli, nor is it a mere storehouse of memories. Rather, the mind/brain system is continuously active. The system is motivated to maintain varied conscious experience. When people are awake they seek varied sensory inputs to process, and they experience stimulus hunger during prolonged periods of restricted stimulation. During periods of restricted or boring stimulation, people maintain varied conscious experience by daydreaming.

However, people do not daydream merely by default because there is nothing better to do. There is a positive motivation to daydream, such that people often daydream even during difficult tasks when it interferes with their performance. The implication is that the human mind/brain system is motivated to maintain a degree of *balance* between two types of conscious activity: outer-directed consciousness, which involves seeking out and responding to varied and challenging sensory inputs, and inner-directed consciousness, which involves recollection, daydreaming, and fantasizing.

A continuum of awareness.   The contents of consciousness can be described as falling on a continuum of awareness that ranges from the public to the private (Pope & Singer 1978). We can identify several points on the continuum: (1) *public events*, those external physical stimuli (objects and events) that can also be perceived by other people; (2) *interoceptive stimuli*, such as pains and tummy rumbles, that are directly sensed only by the individual (although electrophysiological instruments may be able to objectively measure the physiological events that produce these internal sensations); (3) *private conscious mental events*, such as verbal thoughts, mental images, and feelings, that cannot be known by other people except indirectly, through our introspective reports; and (4) *nonconscious mental events*, those mental processes, stimuli, memories, and desires of which we are not directly aware but which nonetheless may have an influence on the ongoing stream of thought.

Overview of factors that affect the contents of the stream of consciousness. Given that the mind/brain system is continuously active and that there is a continuum of awareness, the contents of the waking stream of consciousness are influenced by four types of factors: (1) factors that influence the direction of attention, particularly, whether attention is directed to external stimuli or internally to thoughts and images (daydreams); (2) factors that influence which external stimuli are selected for attention; (3) factors that influence the contents of daydreams; and (4) factors that influence the specific sequences of thoughts and images, and their transformations and combinations.

For each of these types of factors we can consider both general principles (psychological processes that operate in everyone and that determine the most general characteristics of the stream of consciousness) and individual difference factors (aspects of personality and personal past experiences that give each individual's stream of consciousness its unique features). Whereas cognitive psychologists tend to be more interested in general principles, personality and clinical psychologists are especially interested in the uniqueness of individuals.

Factors Affecting Attention to External Events versus Daydreams

Priority of external stimuli. External stimuli compete with daydream thoughts for the brain's limited information-processing resources. External events are likely to be critically important for our safety, nourishment, and well-being. Therefore, there is adaptive value in having the selective attention process give preference to external stimuli, particularly those that are novel, loud, or meaningful. Also, strong internal sensory stimuli, such as pain, have priority in selective attention. The bias favoring sensory stimuli is particularly strong when we must make some overt response to them.

Shift to daydreaming in predictable, dull, or barren environments. Both personal experience and laboratory studies show that daydreaming occurs virtually continuously when external stimuli are eliminated or held constant, and we do not have to respond to them. Also, during an ongoing task there is a shift to daydreaming when the rate of information input or responding is low, when the task is boring or our motivation to perform is low, or when the task is well practiced and our response to it is semi-automatic (Pope & Singer 1978). However, daydreaming is not limited to dull or barren environments. It may occur during performance of difficult tasks, particularly when the individual has pressing personal concerns that generate emotional reactions.

Level of arousal. Level of arousal refers to the degree to which you are feeling alert and energetic. Level of arousal is a continuum ranging from hyper-aroused emotional or activity states, through normal wakefulness, to drowsiness, sleep, and coma. In the waking state, in general, at higher levels of arousal you are more ready to respond to external stimuli whereas at lower levels of arousal your attention is more likely to be directed inwardly to daydreams. However, there is a reciprocal relationship between arousal and external task demands, such that more difficult tasks tend to increase arousal, whereas arousal decreases in the absence of demanding tasks (Eysenck 1982; Kahneman 1973). There are exceptions to these generalizations; for example, high arousal in the absence of a demanding task may produce inner-directed attention and anxiety.

Individual differences.   Individual differences in preferences for external attention versus daydreaming have been characterized in terms of personality measures of extraversion versus introversion, or Field-dependence versus Field-independence (Singer 1984). A bias for daydreaming may stem from positive temperamental factors such as acceptance of and taking pleasure in inner fantasies (positive-vivid daydreaming style), or from negative factors such as a tendency to worry and ruminate about personal concerns or imagined problems (guilty-dysphoric daydreaming style).

Factors Affecting the Direction of External Attention

We can attend to only a limited number of the objects and events in our environment. Which ones we select depends upon a combination of factors: (1) *Voluntary attention.* We voluntarily search for and attend to stimuli that are relevant to the task at hand (such as learning from a lecture or locating a friend on a crowded dance floor). (2) *Automatic (nonvoluntary) attention switching.* (a) Attention is automatically shifted to external stimuli that are novel (such as a peculiar noise from the car engine) or intense, or which have enduring personal meaning (such as your own name, or conditioned emotional stimuli). (b) Attention is also shifted automatically to certain stimuli that are related to personal current concerns and interests, even though the stimuli are not relevant to the task at hand. For example, at the moment my main task is writing this chapter, but I find my attention being distracted by birds singing outside my office window, since I am interested in birdwatching and learning to identify birds by their songs.

Factors Affecting the Contents of Daydreams

Daydreams may arise directly from memory or they may occur as an associative response to some external stimulus. In either case, there is a bias toward daydreaming about current concerns, such as unfinished business or unresolved stress.

Current concerns.   Klinger (1975, 1978, 1987) has developed the concept of current concerns in some detail. He defines *current concern* as "the state of an organism between the time it becomes committed to pursuing a goal and the time it either gains the goal or abandons the pursuit" (1978, p. 249). At any moment each individual has a wide variety of personal concerns, relating to short, intermediate, and long-term goals. For example, you might have long-term goals of graduating from college, finding a good job, and marrying a desirable mate, while at the same time having intermediate goals of finishing a term paper and planning a vacation, and short-term goals of buying a pizza and meeting your lover later tonight. A current concern need not be present in consciousness. At this moment you are not thinking about most of your current concerns. But as long as a concern is current it has the potential to affect your actions, your daydreams, your attention to external events, and your memory of your experiences.

Klinger (1978) demonstrated that current concerns can affect automatic attention switching. He first questioned subjects to determine their most pressing current concerns. Then he had them listen to dichotic tapes, where different fictional stories were presented concurrently to each ear through stereo headphones. The subjects did not have to listen to either story, but they indicated which message (left or right) they were listening to, if any, by pushing a toggle switch left or right. Brief segments related to the subject's personal current concerns (health, love, money, and so on) occurred periodically in either the left or right message. The data showed that subjects were more likely to shift attention to a passage that was relevant to a personal concern than to an irrelevant passage, and also that they spent more time attending to relevant passages, and subsequently recalled relevant passages better than irrelevant passages.

Klinger, Barta, and Maxeiner (1980) validated a *Concerns Dimensions Questionnaire* by showing a good correspondence between current concerns reported on the questionnaire and thoughts reported in a thought-sampling procedure as the subjects went about their usual daily activities during the next twenty-four hours. Thought-sampling data showed that subjects spent more time thinking about (a) goals that were particularly important to them (those that generated more pleasant emotional reaction by their achievement, or unpleasant reaction by their abandonment), (b) goals that were more likely to be attained, and (c) goals that were most likely to be attained very soon. Also (d) they thought more about goals in the pursuit of which they were meeting special challenges or unexpected difficulties (such as threatened personal relationships). Subjects spent relatively little time thinking about routine things in their lives, except for the minimal thinking that is necessary to accomplish routine tasks, even though the tasks may be important (such as grocery shopping, routine tasks at work).

Stress.   Unresolved personal stresses produce a particularly compelling tendency to daydream. For example, impending divorce, the death of a loved one, or being fired from a job, create stresses that make it hard to concentrate on attention-demanding external tasks and increase our tendency to daydream. In such cases goals formerly met have been wrenched from us, so that new goals, and hence new current concerns, are created.

Emotions.   Klinger (1975, 1987) argued that the success or failure of our goal strivings—our personal concerns—is a particularly important determinant of our emotional state: success brings joy, failure brings feelings of anger or depression. During daydreaming, we can imagine the emotional reactions that we will feel upon the future success or failure of our goal strivings. Such imagined emotional reactions—and actual emotional reactions induced by daydreams—are responsible for giving current concerns the power to motivate our behavior and influence the contents of our daydreams.

Individual differences.   Individual differences in daydream content are related not only to individual personal concerns, but also to long-term personality/temperamental differences. Research with the Imaginal Processes Inventory (Singer 1978; Starker 1982) revealed three daydreaming personality types: the positive-vivid type, with an emphasis on pleasant fantasies and daydreaming to solve personal problems; the guilty-dysphoric type, with an emphasis on themes related to achievement, guilt, and anger; and the anxious-distractible type, characterized by anxiety themes and easy distractibility from ongoing fantasies.

The Sequencing of Thoughts

Studies using the thinking-out-loud method indicate that when people are engaged in a complex problem-solving task, the sequence of task-related thoughts is related to the stage of progress in the task and the decision that has to be made in order to complete the next step. It is more complicated to explain the sequence of thoughts in situations where there is no task at hand, or where the task is so easy that people can daydream a lot. Klinger's observations led him to formulate the *induction principle* as a first step toward understanding the sequencing of thoughts in relatively nonstructured situations:

> At any given moment, the next thematic content of thought is induced by the combination of a current concern and a cue related to that concern. The "cue" is either a cognitively meaningful stimulus in the external environment or a symbolic event in the stream of the individual's own consciousness. This "induction principle" is still very general, in that it says nothing about the properties of current concerns that make them more or less influential in sensitizing people to cues, about the specific properties of a cue that make a person see it as concern-related, or about the properties of concern-related cues that affect their potency in influencing thought. Nevertheless, this principle is a starting point . . . (Klinger 1978, p. 250).

The induction principle implies that the sequence of daydream thoughts is not entirely random; there are causal or associative connections, at least of a probabilistic nature, between successive thoughts. But the task of explaining and predicting specific thought sequences in detail is enormously complex. The difficulty in developing a comprehensive theory of the stream of consciousness is that, while we have a pretty good idea about the different factors that influence the stream of thought, we do not know much about how the various factors interact with each other.

Subjective experiences in the normal waking stream of consciousness are highly varied, ranging, for example, from alert attention to external tasks to relaxed daydream fantasies. However, under some conditions our subjective experiences seem to go beyond the normal range of waking consciousness. If the overall pattern of subjective experiences seems to differ markedly from normal, we may conclude that we are in an altered state of consciousness, where our mind seems to be functioning differently from normal. The following chapters will be concerned with altered states of consciousness.

SUMMARY

Individual thoughts in the stream of consciousness may be classified on several abstract dimensions. Several thought dimensions proposed by Klinger were described: (1) operant versus respondent; (2) stimulus-bound versus stimulus-independent; (3) fanciful versus realistic; (4) well-integrated versus degenerated; and (5) vivid versus nonvivid mental images. Klinger's thought-sampling research showed the first two dimensions to be relatively independent of each other, and he found that most thought samples had either inner verbal monologue, visual-spatial mental imagery, or both.

Singer and Antrobus defined daydreaming in terms of stimulus-independent thought, that is, thoughts that are unrelated to the task at hand. Their research with the Imaginal Processes Inventory revealed three daydreaming styles, which are related to other aspects of personality and behavior: (1) positive-vivid daydream style (the well-adjusted, happy daydreamer); (2) guilty-dysphoric style (the obsessive-compulsive neurotic, plagued by hostility, fear of failure, and guilt); and (3) anxious-distractible style (anxiety neurotics, characterized by worrying and mindwandering). Most people are a blend of two or three types, rather than being purely one type.

In laboratory experiments Antrobus and Singer studied the conditions that affect the frequency of daydreaming. While subjects did a vigilance signal-detection task they were interrupted periodically for thought-sampling reports. Daydreaming frequency decreased, the greater the information load in the signal detection task. Daydreaming decreased with increased incentives for good task performance; daydreaming increased with increased incentives for daydreaming (as with increased need to think about important personal concerns). There is an inverse relationship between daydream frequency and task performance. Two factors determine the degree of mutual interference between daydreaming and performing external tasks: (1) the complexity of the task and the daydream thoughts (competition for limited-capacity working memory); and (2) whether the task stimuli and daydream images are in the same or different sensory modalities (competition for limited modality-specific processing resources). Studies of physiological correlates of daydreaming show that during periods when daydream imagery is most vivid, eye movements decrease and alpha brain waves increase, compared to periods without vivid daydream images.

Research on sensory deprivation, or the restricted environmental stimulation technique (REST), shows that it can produce vivid daydreams, though true hallucinations are rare. Prolonged REST results in stimulus hunger, in which subjects seek varied sensory inputs. Susceptibility to persuasive messages and hypnotic suggestions increase during REST; these effects have applications in psychotherapy.

Several factors that must be considered in developing a theory of the stream of consciousness were discussed, including factors that influence (1) the bias toward either external attention or daydreaming, (2) the direction of external attention, (3) the content of daydreams, and (4) the sequencing of thoughts. Klinger's research shows that personal current concerns (goals being pursued) and stresses are major factors affecting daydream contents. Daydreaming serves important functions including choice of goals, planning to achieve goals, entertainment, and wish-fulfilling fantasy.

ENDNOTES

[1]In *The Principles of Psychology* James discussed the nomenclature problem, to find a single generic class word to cover the various types of contents of consciousness, including thoughts, feelings, sensations, images, and ideas. Though he sometimes used "state of consciousness," he felt that it was cumbersome, and he wanted a noun that had a corresponding verb. He finally settled on "thought" as the generic noun for conscious contents (1890/1983, pp. 185–86). (At that time he did not have to worry about the confusion that might be caused when some modern psychologists talk about the possibility of nonconscious thinking, hence nonconscious thoughts.) Here I will follow James in using "thought" as the generic term (as did Klinger 1978), and I will use other words when I need to refer more specifically to sensations, images, feelings, and so forth.

[2]Freud called it "primary" process thinking because he thought that it was characteristic of infants and occurred before the development of secondary process thinking. Primary process thinking is sometimes called "regressive" thinking, because it is presumably more primitive or childlike than rational thought.

[3]Factor analysis is a statistical procedure for discovering underlying factors (such as personality or cognitive factors) that can account for the pattern of responses in a set of questionnaire data. In simplified terms, the method of factor analysis is as follows: After the questionnaire has been filled out by a large number of people, the numerical values (such as ratings on 1–5 scales) of the responses to each of the questions are correlated with each other, for all possible pairs of questions. Questions that correlate highly with each other are grouped together as one factor; other questions that correlate highly with each other, but not with those in the first group, are grouped together to form a second factor, and so on. Then the researcher examines the content of the questions in each factor and gives the factor a name that suits his/her interpretation of the factor. The types of factors that can be discovered is limited by, but not strictly dictated by, the nature of the questions in the questionnaire.

[4]In response to my comment about his omission of affective dimensions, Klinger replied: "The reason I have not included affect in my thought-sampling work is that I initially focused on properties of ideation, rather than of consciousness as a whole, and I labored under the impress of the Wundtian distinction between cognition and affect. . . . You are no doubt right that in omitting affect from my factor-analytic studies I have excluded perhaps the most prominent feature of consciousness. The next investigation, a dissertation just getting underway, will remedy that lapse" (Klinger, personal communication, December 1988).

[5]Note that in Table 8.2 the first twelve items include six each for the positive-vivid (PV) and the guilty-dysphoric (GD) factors. As a rough measure of how you rate on those two factors, you may answer each of the questions on a five-point scale (1 = applies to me not at all; 5 = applies to me very much). If you do not have normative data from your own class, compare your total scores (six items) on each dimension to these data from two of my classes (n = 57): PV mean = 20.2 (standard deviation 3.5); GD mean = 13.3 (sd = 2.9). If your score is more than one standard deviation above or below the mean on either factor, then you are notably different from average (approximately the top or bottom 16 percent of the range of scores). Bear in mind that this is a crude measure; the full IPI, with many more items, is needed for a more reliable measure.

[6]A *bit* is a technical measure of information quantity, where one bit is the information contained in a single yes/no response. Thus, when only one tone pitch could occur, and it was presented at a rate of one per second, the information presentation rate was one bit per second.

With three possible tones presented at the rate of two tones per second the information presentation rate was six bits per second (3 tones × 2 per second).

[7]When Antrobus tried to decrease daydreaming still further by offering subjects $50 (in today's dollars) for good signal-detection performance, the manipulation backfired. "No one believed we'd actually pay them!" (Antrobus, personal communication, December 1989).

chapter 9 ••••••••••••••••••••••••••••••

Altered States of Consciousness

Your normal waking consciousness involves a wide range of subjective experiences, depending upon factors such as the physical and social setting, your mood and level of arousal, and whether you are concerned more with the external environment or with your inner mental life of thoughts, images, and memories. Under some conditions your overall pattern of subjective experiences may change so drastically from the normal range that you may recognize that you are in an *altered state of consciousness* (ASC). In addition to changes in your subjective experiences, ASCs also may involve changes in cognitive functioning (such as attention and memory), overt behavior (things you do and say), and physiological responses (such as brain waves).

In the following chapters I will be discussing some of the major altered states of consciousness, including sleep and dreaming, hypnosis, meditation, and states induced by psychedelic drugs. In this chapter I will discuss several general considerations concerning ASCs, including the variety and importance of ASCs, the concept of ASCs, dimensions of altered experience in ASCs, and means of producing and identifying ASCs.

THE VARIETY OF ASCs

Major altered states of consciousness include: sleep, the hypnagogic (drowsy presleep) state, hypnosis, various types of meditation, mystical or transcendental experiences (including satori, samadhi, nirvana, cosmic-consciousness), experimental sensory-deprivation experiences, and states produced by psychoactive drugs such as alcohol, marijuana, LSD, and others. These are often considered to be the major ASCs not because they are necessarily more extreme than other states (though this is true in some cases, such as dream sleep and LSD states), but because they are relatively common and/or they have been studied most intensively. Daydreaming is different from active, externally oriented consciousness, but because it is within the normal range of conscious experience it is usually not considered to be an ASC.

Ludwig (1966) listed a number of less common or less studied conditions that may be classified as minor ASCs, for example, natural sensory-deprivation experiences (as in the arctic or desert), highway hypnosis, profound body immobilization (as in a body cast), brainwashing states, healing trances, religious conversion, spirit possession, fire walker's trance, orgiastic trance, shamanistic and prophetic trance states during tribal ceremonies, mental aberrations during certain *rites de passage* (primitive initiation ceremonies), ecstatic trance (as in the "howling" or "whirling" dervishes), prolonged vigilance (as in serving sentry duty or watching a radar screen), total mental involvement in listening to a charismatic speaker, the mystical, transcendental, or revelatory states occurring spontaneously (usually under ascetic conditions), reading trance (especially with poetry), profound aesthetic experiences, music trance, profound cognitive and muscular relaxation. The inspirational phase of creativity deserves special mention (Martindale 1981).

THE IMPORTANCE OF ASCs

The variety and frequency of occurrence of ASCs in both primitive and civilized cultures gives us every reason to believe that ASCs have been a common human experience since the origin of our species. The capacity to experience ASCs reflects something fundamental in the nature of our mind/brain system, and we cannot hope to understand this system fully until we gain a better understanding of ASCs.

How did the capacity for ASCs come about? Aside from sleep, which is a special case, ASCs may merely represent the malfunctioning of our mind/brain system in response to an abnormal situation. If the normal waking state evolved to serve the function of survival in a changing and potentially hostile environment, then ASCs might be seen as contrary to this survival function. For example, psychoactive drugs might be used to escape from unpleasant reality, to shirk responsibility, and to provide an excuse for uninhibited and irresponsible or aggressive behavior. But a number of positive functions may be served by ASCs.

Functions of ASCs

The adaptive functions of ASCs can be classified in three categories (Ludwig 1966): (1) promoting healing and feelings of well-being; (2) avenues to new knowledge or experience; and (3) social functions.

Promoting healing and feelings of well-being. ASCs have been used to maintain and improve mental health and feelings of well-being, and to relieve or cure physical symptoms that have a psychological basis (psychosomatic illness). For example, hypnosis is used in psychotherapy for a variety of psychological problems (such as trauma, phobias, bad habits) and for the control of pain. States akin to hypnosis have been used in a variety of cultures throughout history—these states include the trances that shamans or medicine men produce in themselves and their patients, and the practices of modern faith healers. Meditation techniques are an aid to relaxation and the reduction of anxiety. The true functions of sleep are not known with certainty, but it is speculated that it serves for maintaining psychological balance as well as for physical rest and restoration. And of course psychoactive drugs, such as tranquilizers, can be helpful when used appropriately.

Avenues to new knowledge or experience.   ASCs have served as avenues to mystical or religious experience and for reaching deeper insight into oneself and one's social relationships. ASCs have been sources of creative inspirations for artists, writers, and scientists. And ASCs can enhance aesthetic appreciation of art, music, and poetry, and nature. ASCs are sometimes pursued merely for entertainment, though in some cases (as in drug use) we should ask whether the benefits are really worth the risks.

Social functions.   ASCs have been incorporated into religious rituals that serve to promote group cohesiveness, for example, the peyote cult of the American southwest. Seeking of visions through ASCs has been part of tribal initiation rituals and a source of inspiration for religious leaders and their followers. Spirit-possession states serve to reaffirm religious beliefs and promote group cohesiveness. ASCs' social functions are not limited to primitive societies. Both alcohol and marijuana serve as social lubricants and group identifiers for certain segments of society in industrialized countries. Meditation practice has its own subcultures in the West as well as the East.

Why Study ASCs?

ASCs are a natural phenomenon of the human species. They are an interesting and important topic in their own right, and studying them helps to satisfy our curiosity about human nature and human potentialities. Gaining a better understanding of ASCs may help us to understand how they serve their adaptive functions, and perhaps it will enable us to improve the practical uses of ASCs. Also, increased understanding may help us to reduce or avoid possible harmful effects of certain ASCs, such as drug dependency.

The systematic study of ASCs may also help us better to understand the normal waking state of consciousness. Just as the study of psychopathology has helped us understand normal mind and behavior, and the study of people with abnormal or damaged brains has helped us understand normal brain structure and functioning, so also may the study of temporary alterations in consciousness help us to understand normal waking consciousness and cognitive processes.

THE CONCEPT OF ALTERED STATES OF CONSCIOUSNESS

Charles Tart, who coined the term "altered state of consciousness" (ASC) in its modern usage, likes to begin his lectures on ASCs by asking the audience this question:

> Is there anyone here right now who *seriously* believes that what you are experiencing, in this room, at this moment, may be something you are just dreaming? I don't mean picky, philosophical doubts about the ultimate nature of experience or anything like that. I'm asking whether anyone in any serious *practical* way thinks this might be a dream you're experiencing now, rather than your ordinary state of consciousness? (Tart 1975, p. 10).

Except for an occasional troublemaker, everyone generally agrees that they know that they are awake and not dreaming. The point of this demonstration is that we have ways of subjectively checking out our cognitive functioning, and comparing it against a remembered idea of our personal, normal functioning. We may not usually carry out this cognitive check-up in a deliberate, conscious manner. However, we will tend to notice automatically any marked change from normal functioning, such as an instability in our visual perception of the world, a feeling that we are floating, a feeling that time has speeded up or slowed down, or an inability to remember anything about a conversation that we have just finished.

Definition of Altered State of Consciousness

Following from the above considerations, an *altered state of consciousness* (ASC) may be defined as a temporary change in the overall pattern of subjective experience, such that the individual believes that his or her mental functioning is distinctly different from certain general norms for his or her normal waking state of consciousness (Ludwig 1966; Tart 1972b). Several comments on this definition are in order:

(1) *ASCs are not merely changes in the contents of consciousness.* After all, the contents of consciousness can change just because the external situation changes. It would be silly to talk about, for example, a "waterfall state of consciousness" or an "automobile state of consciousness." *Rather, ASCs involve a subjectively experienced change in mental functioning,* for example, the impression that your perception, thinking, memory, or behavior control processes, or some combination thereof, are markedly different from normal.

(2) *ASCs involve a changed pattern of subjective experiences, not merely a change in one aspect or dimension of consciousness.* Dimensions of changed subjective experience in ASCs include changes in attention, perception, imagery, inner-speech memory, emotion, and others to be discussed in more detail in the next section. The changed pattern of subjective experiences leads people to infer that their mental functioning has changed, indicating that they are in an altered state of consciousness.

(3) *ASCs are not necessarily recognized by the individual at the time that they are happening; they may be inferred afterward.* For example, if you are dreaming, or

under the influence of LSD, it may seem to you that reality itself has changed. Only later—when you return to your normal waking state—do you realize that it was your state of consciousness, not reality, that was changed.

(4) *ASCs are relatively short-term, reversible conditions* that may last from a few minutes to several hours. Changes in conscious experience, cognitive functions, and behavior can also occur in psychopathological conditions, such as major depression and schizophrenia, or as a result of brain injury. Major psychopathologies and brain injuries cause long-term or permanent changes in psychological functioning, so they do not fit the concept of altered states of consciousness as the term is used here.

(5) *ASCs are identified by comparison to the individual's normal waking state of consciousness.* But the concept of a "normal" waking state of consciousness is, in a sense, a convenient fiction. Your waking state can vary widely during the course of a day, from an alert, active, externally oriented state to a relaxed or drowsy, inner-oriented, daydreamy state. Also, the typical pattern of waking conscious experiences varies widely from one person to another. Thus, the concept of a normal waking state is a rather loose one. By the *normal waking state* I mean periods when you are awake, not asleep, and you have not done anything to produce an altered state in the usual sense. (For example, you are not in a drug state, hypnotic or meditative state, or under conditions of unusual sensory restriction.) A more detailed analysis might consider different *substates* of the normal waking state. For example, a condition of high arousal and externally oriented attention is a different waking substate than one of low arousal and internally oriented attention.

(6) *The essence of a state of consciousness is the individual's pattern of subjective experiences, not his or her overt behavior or physiological responses.* But researchers who try to study other people's ASCs must make inferences about their experiences from their verbal reports, other overt behaviors, and measurable physiological responses.

Some writers (such as Shapiro 1977) have argued that a state of consciousness must be defined in terms of both a changed pattern of subjective experience and a changed pattern of physiological responses. It is certainly an advantage to the researcher to know that a particular pattern of physiological responses is correlated with a particular pattern of subjective experiences. For example, in dream research the researcher knows that when the sleeping subject's pattern of physiological responses (brain waves, eye movements, muscle tension) indicates that he or she is in the REM sleep state, then it is highly probable that the subject will report a vivid dream if awakened. However, the problem with requiring a physiological pattern to identify an ASC is that for most subjectively altered states of consciousness no distinctive and unique physiological pattern has been identified. Furthermore, physiological patterns have meaning in regard to consciousness only insofar as they have been shown to be highly correlated with variations of conscious experience. Altered conscious experience is the essence of ASCs. Working from the identity theory perspective on the mind-body problem, I do not doubt that, at some level, each variation in subjective conscious state involves some change in brain state. Meanwhile, it would be a mistake to exclude interesting variations of conscious state from the study of ASCs merely because current research technology cannot identify a unique change in brain state correlated with the changed conscious state.

The subjective criteria by which individuals recognize their ASCs, such as apparent changes in perception or memory, are sometimes verifiable by objective research methods. However, in other cases attempts to obtain objective verification may lead to results that appear to contradict the subjective experience. For example, people who are stoned (intoxicated) on marijuana sometimes feel that their hearing is improved, since they are hearing things in music that they had not previously heard. But objective measures show that, in fact, their hearing sensitivity is no better in the stoned state than in their normal waking state. Nonetheless, it is the subjective experience, not the objective measure, that marks the essence of the ASC. (In this example, it seems that when people are stoned they often attend to notes and patterns in the music to which they do not normally attend, leading them to infer incorrectly that their hearing sensitivity has changed.) Discrepancies between the subjective experience (as revealed in introspective verbal reports) and independent objective measures present a problem for research and theory, but such discrepancies do not invalidate the concept of altered states of consciousness. The altered experience is the thing to be explained. To take another example, the fact that someone's dream of being chased by giant rats does not correspond to objective reality does not make the dream invalid or uninteresting; rather, the dream is the thing to be explained.

Though changed subjective experience is the essence of ASCs—that is why we call them altered states of *consciousness*—in many cases there are in fact objectively identifiable changes in mental functioning. The objectively identifiable changes may correspond to subjectively experienced changes. For example, people stoned on marijuana have noticed that, when they try to say a sentence that is too long, they sometimes forget the beginning of the sentence before they get to the end of it. The stoned individuals infer that their memory is not functioning normally. Laboratory research has confirmed the fact that short-term memory is impaired by marijuana. There are also some situations in which people in ASCs are unaware of certain changes in mental functioning, yet objective methods can show that a change has occurred. For example, a stoned or drunk driver might not know that his or her reaction time has slowed, but objective studies show that marijuana and alcohol both slow braking reaction time.

DIMENSIONS OF CHANGED SUBJECTIVE EXPERIENCE IN ASCs

People recognize that they are in an altered state of consciousness when their overall pattern of subjective experience is markedly different from that of normal waking consciousness (Tart 1975). There are several features or dimensions of conscious experience that can change, leading people to conclude that they are in an ASC. Here is a list of dimensions of conscious experience that can change in ASCs, which I will discuss in more detail momentarily: (1) attention; (2) perception; (3) imagery and fantasy; (4) inner speech; (5) memory; (6) higher-level thought processes; (7) meaning or significance of experience; (8) time experience; (9) emotional feeling and expression; (10) arousal; (11) self-control; (12) suggestibility; (13) body image; and (14) sense of personal identity. (This list was influenced by similar lists presented by Ludwig [1966] and Tart [1975].)

Several similarities between this list of ASC dimensions and the list of aspects of normal consciousness, presented in Chapter 2, will be apparent. However, it is useful to present a new list for our present purpose. Some aspects of consciousness become most conspicuous when they are changed from their normal character.

When I say that an ASC involves a changed *pattern* of subjective experience, I mean that there are changes on several of the listed dimensions. A change on only one dimension probably would not lead you to conclude that you are in an ASC. Nor is it necessary to change on all of the dimensions to be in an ASC. Different ASCs involve changes on different dimensions, and the specific nature of the change on a dimension may differ from one ASC to another. The listed dimensions of change are relatively broad. Some ASC experiences cut across two or more dimensions. Now I will describe the dimensions of subjective experience that can change in ASCs, and give some examples.

(1) *Changes in attention.* In the normal waking state the internal versus external direction of attention can range widely, from primarily external (as in sports) to primarily internal (as in daydreaming), or it can be mixed internal-external (as when you drive a car and daydream at the same time). The direction of attention can also alternate between internal and external in most ASCs. However, in some ASCs the normal flexibility is reduced and attention is directed inwardly to an extreme degree (as in dreaming or concentrative meditation). Also, ASCs may involve a heightened tendency to focus attention narrowly on either an internal or external object or event (as found in increased attentional absorption in concentrative attention and hypnosis). As a consequence of narrowly focused attention, people may notice aspects of their attentional object (such as music) that they would not normally notice, but they are less responsive than normal to other events.

(2) *Changes in perception.* Perception involves the recognition and interpretation of environmental objects and events. Some ASCs, such as drug states, may involve changes in the appearance of objects or changes in the way we hear sounds. Changes in what we perceive may occur due to changes in the direction of attention rather than changes in sensory-perceptual processes *per se*. Perceptual *illusions*, in which objects or events are misidentified, may increase in ASCs. In some drug states *synesthesia* may occur, a condition where input in one sensory modality (such as auditory) may be experienced in a different modality (visual). For example, one observer, stoned on marijuana, reported that when he listened (through stereo headphones) to J. S. Bach's *Goldberg Variations* (played on a harpsichord), it was an intense visual and tactile, as well as auditory, experience.

(3) *Changes in imagery and fantasy.* Visual mental images may be espe-

cially vivid in some ASCs. Increased image vividness may occur during relaxed daydreaming, but visual images are especially vivid in night dreams. Increased image vividness often goes with increased fantasy thought in which people imagine purely fictional stories, often of a fantastic nature, and usually with themselves as the main character. Dreams are the best example, but vivid fantasies also occur in other states, such as relaxed daydreaming or psychedelic drug states. Alternatively, people may experience *reverie*, a sequence of thoughts or images occurring in a free-association manner, without a coherent theme. *Hallucinations* are particularly vivid mental images that are believed to be real. For example, in an ASC you might have a vivid image of a deceased relative, and believe that the person is really there in front of you. Dreams are hallucinations during sleep, but hallucinations can also occur in other states, such as psychedelic drug states or following hypnotic suggestions. An interesting intermediate case between hallucination and illusion occurs when meaningless stimuli are grossly misperceived with the aid of imagination. For example, under conditions of need or anxiety you might hear voices in the wind, imposing structure on a more-or-less random mixture of sounds.

(4) *Changes in inner speech.* Inner speech and narratization may decrease, for example, during meditation and sleep. Also people's inner speech, such as volitional thoughts, may become less connected to their actions or current environment. Overt speech may become less coherent than normal, perhaps due to disruption of short-term memory (as in marijuana intoxication). Changes in verbal thought content are related to other changes in subjective experience, such as increased fantasy.

(5) *Changes in memory.* In ASCs people may notice a decreased ability to recall information from memory. For example, during marijuana intoxication the ability to recall recent events from short-term memory is impaired. The ability to recall events from long-term memory can be disrupted by hypnotic suggestions (hypnotic amnesia). Sometimes, as in hypnosis, people may have the impression that their memory recall is improved during an ASC, though it is often difficult to distinguish between a delusion (false belief) of enhanced recall and true hypermnesia (better than normal memory). A more subtle sort of memory change involves changes in the associations between words or images, such that the flow of ideas in the stream of consciousness is notably different from normal. Some such changes are mere nonsense, but in other cases truly creative combinations of ideas may occur in ASCs.

(6) *Changes in higher-level thought processes.* In ASCs people may have difficulty making decisions or solving problems, perhaps due to the disruption of short-term (working) memory. Also the specific decisions that they make may be different from normal, due to either disruptions of thought processes or changes in values or emotions. In an ASC, such as marijuana intoxication, people sometimes come up with truly creative solutions to practical or artistic problems. More often their solutions are no better, and perhaps worse, than normal, but in the ASC they have a delusion that they are more creative than usual.

(7) *Changes in the meaning or significance of experiences.* A fairly common

ASC experience involves the feeling that certain thoughts or events are pro-foundly important, perhaps of great creative or mystical significance. This sort of experience may be one of the main reasons why many people enjoy experiencing certain ASCs.

A good illustration of this is a scene from the movie, *Animal House*, in which some college students get stoned on marijuana with their English pro-fessor. One of the students becomes fascinated by the thought that an object is made of atoms, and each atom is a little solar system, the electrons being little planets swirling around the nucleus sun. And there must be little peo-ple on those little worlds! And Earth must be a planet in an atom on some object on a bigger world, with still bigger people! And so on and on and on. Wow!

Some people have filled pocket notebooks with the profound thoughts that they have had while stoned, lest they be forgotten and lost before they can benefit humankind. Yet, upon returning to the ordinary state these thoughts usually seem utterly boring or mildly amusing, at best.

Arnold Ludwig gave an example from one of his personal experiences when he took LSD for experimental purposes:

> Sometimes during the height of the reaction, I remember experiencing an in-tense desire to urinate. Standing by the urinal, I noticed a sign above it which read "Please Flush After Using!" As I weighed these words in my mind, I sud-denly realized their profound meaning. Thrilled by this startling revelation, I rushed back to my colleague to share this universal truth with him. Unfortu-nately, being a mere mortal, he could not appreciate the world-shaking import of my communication and responded by laughing! (Ludwig 1966, p. 229).

The *sense of the ineffable* (Ludwig 1966) is a special case of change in the meaning or significance of experience. An *ineffable experience* is, literally, one that cannot be communicated in words. Strictly speaking, many conscious experiences cannot be communicated very well in words, both in the normal state and in various ASCs. However, the term "ineffable experience" is usu-ally applied to a particular class of experiences that might better be charac-terized as mystical or religious. One of the main features of mystical experi-ence is a profound feeling of "oneness" with all people, with all life, or even with the universe as a whole (Deikman 1966). The true nature of such an experience cannot be communicated in words, yet a mystic experience can have a profound, lasting influence on a person's life. (Mystic experiences will be discussed in more detail in Chapter 17 on meditation.)

In contrast to the feelings of profundity that arise in some ASC experi-ences, the other side of the coin is that some ASC experiences seem to be exceptionally humorous. This is another case of changed meaning or signif-icance of experience. A group of stoned people may be rolling in fits of laughter at some shared joke, but the joke may be totally unfunny to some-one in a normal state of consciousness. Also, the feeling (perhaps delusional) that one's ideas become more creative is another case of changed meaning or significance experienced during ASCs.

(8) *Changed time experience.* The experience of temporal duration may change. For example, to someone who is stoned on marijuana, if their friend

leaves the room for five minutes to get some snacks, it might seem that he or she has been gone for fifteen minutes. Thus, external time seems to have slowed down. Apparent slowing of external time implies that some internal time-judgement process has speeded up. (For example, if an internal clock that normally "ticks" ten times in ten seconds were to tick thirty times in ten seconds during an ASC, then it would seem, subjectively, that the ten-second interval was really thirty seconds long.) Ornstein (1977) distinguished between our ordinary linear time-experience and a nonlinear experience of timelessness or eternal present that sometimes occurs in such ASCs as hallucinogenic drug states or in meditative or mystical states.

(9) *Changes in emotional feeling and expression.* Wide changes in emotional feeling are common in ASCs. These can range from negative emotions of fear, anger, and depression to positive emotions of humor, love, and joy. People may become highly emotionally reactive, responding to events to which they would not normally react. Alternatively, people may become emotionally unresponsive, as in a drugged stupor. The overt expression of emotions, such as affectionate touching, crying, or violent actions, may be uninhibited in ASCs.

(10) *Changes in level of arousal.* In the waking state people's subjective level of arousal may range widely, from low to high. In ASCs extremes of arousal may be reached: for example, extremely low in deep sleep; very low in the hypnagogic presleep state; extremely high in some drug states (as with amphetamines) and in mystical rapture. Fischer (1978; also Martindale 1981) systematically characterized and related a variety of normal and altered states in terms of a dimension of arousal, though of course states of consciousness differ on a variety of dimensions besides arousal.

(11) *Changes in self-control.* There are several aspects to changes in self control. People may become more impulsive, doing things that go against their usual social inhibitions. Or they may become lethargic, failing to initiate ordinary actions. The ability to carry out complex motor actions may be disrupted. All of these changes can occur, for example, during alcohol intoxication.

In some ASCs people's normally voluntary responses may seem to happen automatically, without a sense of volition (as in response to hypnotic suggestions). In some extreme cases (as in certain drug states), where the loss of self control is unintended and people's own actions seem to be happening to them without a feeling of volition, the result may be a frightening experience termed *depersonalization.* (Depersonalization, which can occur in schizophrenia as well as in ASCs, often involves changes in body image [perceived body proportions] as well as changes in self control.) On the other hand, in some extreme cases involving mystical, revelatory, or spirit possession states, people may voluntarily relinquish conscious control "in the hope of experiencing divine truths, clairvoyance, 'cosmic consciousness,' communion with the spirits or supernatural powers, or serving as a temporary abode or mouthpiece for the gods" (Ludwig 1966).

(12) *Changes in suggestibility.* Suggestibility has to do with responsiveness to suggestions. In general terms, a *suggestion* is a communication from one person to another that induces the second person to change his/her behavior or beliefs, without any argument or coercion being involved. Of particular

interest are hypnotic-type suggestions, which involve asking a person to viv-idly imagine some state of affairs such that, if the imagination is accepted as reality, the person's behavior will change in a manner consistent with the suggestion. For example, a hypnotized subject might be told that flies are swarming around his face and crawling on his skin. In response to the sug-gestion he might hallucinate the buzzing and the feeling of flies on the skin, and make overt responses of grimacing and brushing the flies away. An in-crease in this type of suggestibility (hypersuggestibility) occurs during hyp-nosis and also some other states, such as marijuana intoxication and shaman-istic ritual.

(13) *Changed body image.* Changes in perceived body proportions or weight, or inner sensory events, are fairly common in ASCs. For example, you might feel that your head, or whole body, has become very small or very large. Your body might feel very heavy, or so light that you feel that you are floating in the air (subjective experience of levitation). Sensitivity to pain might decrease, perhaps along with the feeling that part of the body has be-come numb, disconnected, or turned to wood or rubber (as in hypnotic anal-gesia).

Changes in body image contribute to changes in the sense of personal identity. When such changes occur in toxic or delirious states, they may be frightening. On the other hand, when they appear in a mystical or religious setting, "they may be interpreted as transcendental or mystical experiences of 'oneness,' 'expansion of consciousness,' 'oceanic feelings,' or 'oblivion' " (Ludwig 1966).

(14) *Changed sense of personal identity.* As a result of profound changes in a variety of experiential dimensions—thinking, memory, self-control, body image, and so forth—the sense of personal identity may change. People may feel that they are no longer themselves, since their perception of themselves no longer matches their remembered self-concept. Sometimes a change in perceived personal identity is a positive experience, as when people feel re-juvenated or reborn. At other times the change is unpleasant or frightening, particularly when people feel that they can no longer control their thoughts or actions, as in some drug states. Mystical experiences, in which people lose their sense of self as a separate person and have a sense "unity" with all peo-ple, or with all life, or with God, are usually felt to be pleasant experiences.

PRODUCING ALTERED STATES OF CONSCIOUSNESS

How can ASCs be produced? Some ASCs, such as sleep and "highway hypno-sis," occur spontaneously under the right conditions. In other cases ASCs are produced deliberately, as in hypnosis, meditation, and drug states. A tech-nique for deliberately producing an ASC is called an *induction technique* or procedure. The conditions that produce spontaneous or unintentional ASCs may be called *induction conditions.* I will not try to make a hard and fast distinc-tion between deliberate induction techniques and spontaneous induction conditions, since the psychological processes are similar in both types of sit-uations. But before I go into detail on the induction methods let us consider what, in more general terms, is required to produce an ASC.

Tart (1975) argued that our normal, alert waking state of consciousness is maintained by certain *stabilizing conditions*, including a sufficient level of physiological arousal, a changing array of external stimuli, and an attitude of maintaining attention to them so that we can make appropriate decisions and responses consistent with our motives. In order to produce an ASC we must first disrupt or *destabilize* the normal state. Destabilization of the normal state is accomplished by the induction technique or conditions. After normal consciousness is destabilized, certain *patterning conditions* produce a new pattern of subjective experience through which we recognize that we are in an ASC. Usually the same conditions that destabilized ordinary consciousness participate in patterning the ASC, though other factors may also be involved, such as the physical and social setting. The ASC will be maintained in a more-or-less stable manner as long as the ASC patterning forces are maintained.

Now I will describe four different types of events that may induce ASCs: (1) change in external stimulation; (2) change in physical activity; (3) change in physiological state; and (4) change in focus of attention (Ludwig 1966). In practice, ASCs are often induced by a combination of two or more of these procedures.

Change in external stimulation.   External stimulation may change along several dimensions. (1) The *amount* of sensory input might change, either in its intensity or its frequency. The amount of sensory input might be increased drastically above normal (sensory bombardment, as you might experience at a disco), or it might be decreased severely (as in an arctic white-out, or in sensory-deprivation experiments). The amount of input may change independently for the different modalities, as when you close your eyes but you can still hear. (2) The *variety* of sensory input might change, without necessarily changing the amount of input. For example, the same stimuli might recur over and over again (as in the incessant beating of drums to a constant rhythm), producing monotony and withdrawal of attention from the environment. (3) The *meaning* of external stimulation might change. The most important cases involve social situations in which we are influenced by what people say (as in a hypnotic induction). Other people's words or actions may influence our expectations or the direction of our attention.

Change in physical activity.   Physical activity might change in either amount or variety, or both. For example, you might continue the same circular dance for hours, or you might lie very still. Physical activity has two important features that can affect the state of consciousness: (1) Greater amounts of physical activity produce higher levels of physiological arousal, and conversely, restricted activity lowers arousal level. (2) Physical activity produces feedback in the form of internal, kinesthetic stimulation. In addition, the ability to move about freely enables you to increase the variety of external stimuli that you experience, thus reducing monotony.

Change in physiological state.   Each day we experience wide changes in level of physiological arousal. Arousal varies during wakefulness, and when arousal is low enough we fall asleep. The concept of induction is used loosely in the case of sleep. We can facilitate sleep by lying down in a dark, quiet room, but sometimes sleep eludes us even when we want and need to sleep (insomnia; Chapter 10). Under the right conditions the brain induces sleep in itself. Our voluntary control of sleep is mostly a matter of permission, allowing it to happen.

We can deliberately (or accidentally) induce ASCs by changing our brain's physiological state with psychoactive drugs, such as marijuana, LSD, alcohol, and so forth. Drugs change brain activity by changing the amount of certain *neurotransmitters* (complex biochemicals that transmit nerve impulses from one neuron to another), or by blocking normal neurotransmitter activity or by mimicking neurotransmitters. Particular drugs produce particular effects depending on which of several neurotransmitters they affect and the parts of the brain in which the affected neurotransmitters are located.

Brain functioning can also be altered by the absence of certain chemicals. "You are what you eat," somebody said. Your brain needs adequate levels of oxygen, energy (carbohydrates), protein (to build and maintain its structure), and various nutrients (vitamins, minerals) to produce the various neurotransmitters that keep the flow of neuronal activity going. ASCs might be produced by hypoxia (oxygen starvation), dehydration, starvation (or deliberate fasting), and malnutrition. In addition, some individuals are sensitive to specific foods, such as milk, that can produce symptoms such as sluggish thinking and irritability (Philpott & Kalita 1980).

Change in focus of attention. Here I am referring mainly to voluntary changes in thinking and attention, though sometimes these changes occur accidentally. In concentrative meditation, people deliberately restrict their focus of attention to a particular object (such as a candle), or repeat a particular word or phrase (mantram) over and over (either vocally or subvocally), or concentrate on a particular mental image (such as a waterfall). Trance states sometimes occur accidentally, as when people sit passively and stare absentmindedly at an object. Entry into an ASC (such as hypnosis) may involve a voluntary *suspension of reality testing*, in which we stop critically attending to events and comparing them with our past experience, so that the distinction between imagination and reality, between illusion and fact, becomes blurred (Shor 1959). Thus, in an ASC we may enter a world of hallucination and fantasy.

IDENTIFYING SPECIFIC ASCs

The essence of an altered state of consciousness is the individual's own pattern of subjective experiences. However, researchers need to be able to identify objectively states of consciousness in other people, so they will know when a research subject is in a particular ASC. Ideally, researchers like to have *operational definitions* of psychological concepts by which they specify the exact operation or procedure that is necessary to produce a specific psychological response. For example, it would be ideal if the marijuana intoxication state could be operationally defined as a specific response or set of responses (subjective and/or behavioral) that is reliably produced by the induction technique of smoking marijuana.

However, Tart (1975) argued that it would be a mistake to define operationally specific ASCs in terms of their induction techniques, since induction techniques do not reliably produce specific ASCs. In some cases an induction technique that works reliably for some people will not work for other people. For example, a substantial minority of subjects fail to enter an ASC in response to a hypnotic induction, and some people do not get stoned when they smoke marijuana (particularly if it is their first experience with marijuana). Also, among those who respond to an induction technique, the pattern of subjective and behavioral responses may vary from one person to another. Furthermore, a particular pattern of responses might be produced by more than one induction procedure. For example, among people who have experienced marijuana intoxication, hypnotic suggestions for "feeling stoned" may be sufficient to produce subjective experiences very similar to those experienced during marijuana intoxication.

Thus, it would be erroneous to say that a specific induction technique *causes* a specific ASC. It would be more accurate to say that the induction procedure *sets the occasion* in which one may enter an ASC. But, as Tart (1975) explained, the specific nature of the ASC, or whether one enters an ASC at all, depends upon the *interaction* of the induction procedure with other conditions, such as the individual's personality, mood, expectations (Kirsch 1985), physiological state, and the social and physical setting.

Tart (1975) argued that ASCs should be identified by the particular pattern of changes in subjective experience and psychological functioning, independently of the induction procedure. He suggested that states might be *mapped* on a multidimensional scale of psychological functions (such as degree of rationality, image vividness, STM duration). While the idea of state mapping is a good one in principle, in practice it presents formidable difficulties, since it would be impossible to measure quantitatively some psychological functions in some ASCs. For example, rational decision making might be measured in the normal waking state and in hypnosis or marijuana intoxication, but not during sleep or meditation. One approach to the problem of state mapping is to have subjects rate their subjective experience on several dimensions immediately after experiencing a particular stimulus condition or state of consciousness (see Pekala & Wenger 1983), though this procedure suffers from the usual memory retrieval problems associated with introspective reporting. Experiences might be recalled more reliably after some ASCs than others, making it difficult to compare different states.

Quasi-operational definitions of ASCs.   Since ASCs cannot be given strict operational definitions or reliably mapped in terms of subjective experiences alone, researchers usually define specific ASCs *quasi-operationally*, in terms of a *set* of psychological responses that follow from a particular induction procedure or that occur in a particular physiological state. The set of psychological responses that identify an ASC may include changes in subjective experience as revealed by introspective verbal reports, changes in cognitive task performance, and other behaviors that are believed to be characteristic of that ASC. In the quasi-operational approach, researchers may specify certain minimal defining features of the ASC, and/or variable characteristics of the ASC, or both.

The quasi-operational approach is less rigid than the traditional operational approach to defining psychological terms. The quasi-operational approach acknowledges that the details of psychological response to an induction technique may vary somewhat from one individual to another. Subjects are considered to be in a particular ASC if they show some, though not necessarily all, of the psychological responses that are characteristic of that ASC. Or if minimal defining features of an ASC are specified, subjects must show the defining features, and perhaps also some of the characteristic features. But subjects who do not meet some specified criteria of psychological response to the induction procedure are not considered to be in that ASC. For example, subjects may be considered to be hypnotized if they respond to several different suggestions for altered experience (such as response inhibitions, hallucinations, posthypnotic amnesia, and so forth; see Chapter 14), but no one specific response (such as hallucination) is required for subjects to be considered to be hypnotized. Or subjects may be considered to be intoxicated on marijuana if they report several of the characteristic subjective responses to marijuana (see Chapter 18). The quasi-operational approach allows that there can be varying degrees (greater or lesser) as well as varied patterns of psychological response in ASCs. For example, the hypnotic state can be experienced at varying degrees of subjective depth, and greater subjective depth is associated with responses to a greater number and variety of hypnotic suggestions.

Physiological responses may be used as indicators of states of consciousness, along with subjective and behavioral responses, in the quasi-operational approach. However, physiological indicators are valid only insofar as they correlate reliably with psychological indicators. For example, REM sleep is an *altered physiological state* that can be identified by certain defining physiological responses (fast brain waves, rapid eye movements, low muscle tension). But REM sleep is classed as an altered state of consciousness not because of its unique *physiological* response pattern, but because of its characteristic *psychological* response pattern, including vivid dreams, reduced rationality and reflective thought, reduced sensitivity to external stimuli, and lack of voluntary movement. REM sleep's physiological responses are so reliably correlated with its psychological responses that the physiological responses have become the main criterion for identifying the REM (dream) sleep ASC (Chapter 10). But REM sleep is a unique ASC. Most ASCs do not have unique identifying patterns of physiological responses, so physiological responses are neither necessary nor sufficient for identifying most ASCs by the quasi-operational approach. For example, though an increase in alpha brain waves is a characteristic response during concentrative meditation, alpha waves also occur in other relaxed wakeful conditions, so alpha waves are not considered to be a sufficient indicator of a meditative state of consciousness (see Chapter 17).

States as natural concepts.   States of consciousness are natural concepts. *Natural concepts* are categories of natural objects and events that have some things in common, though they may differ in some ways (Rosch 1973).

A natural category has a *prototype* that is the most typical or representative member of the category (for example, a robin is a prototypical bird). Other members of the category are more-or-less similar to the prototype, but things that are too different from the prototype are not members of the category. Similarly, a state of consciousness (such as marijuana intoxication or a meditative state) can be exemplified by a prototypical case in which certain characteristic responses (subjective, behavioral, physiological) occur. Cases that are similar enough to the prototype state on critical dimensions are considered to be examples of the same state of consciousness, whereas dissimilar cases are not. The point is that no two instances of an ASC are likely to be identical, but we include them in the same category because their similarities are more important than their differences.[1] The boundaries between different states are somewhat arbitrary; states are defined by experiencers and observers for human purposes of thinking and communication, research and theorizing.[2]

As a natural concept, a state of consciousness is a *descriptive category* of human experience. To say that someone is in an altered state of consciousness does not *explain* anything. Rather, the altered subjective experiences and behaviors *identify* the ASC. For example, it would be incorrect to say that a hypnotic subject experienced a temporary paralysis of the arm (in response to a hypnotic suggestion) because he or she was in a hypnotic state. Rather, the response to the suggestion is evidence that the subject is in a hypnotic state. Similarly, a hallucination is not to be explained by a psychedelic drug intoxication state; it is evidence that the person is intoxicated by the drug.

A state of consciousness does not explain anything. Rather, the state—that is, its characteristic subjective and behavioral responses—is what psychological scientists want to explain. There are three levels of analysis for explanations of ASCs: (1) discovering empirical relationships between various induction techniques (and interacting personal, social, physiological, and environmental variables) and the various psychological responses that are characteristic of an ASC; (2) developing psychological theories to explain the observed empirical relationships in terms of inferred mental (cognitive) structures and processes; and (3) developing neurophysiological theories to explain the empirical relationships in terms of brain structures and processes.

STUDYING ASCs: SUBJECTIVE AND OBJECTIVE KNOWLEDGE

As in the normal waking state, there are two types of knowledge about ASCs: direct personal experience and secondary or vicarious experience. Both are valid and important forms of knowledge, but they serve different purposes. People in ASCs may have experiences ranging from terror to entertainment to profound personal insight or religious revelation; the result may be to change the individual in some way, either positively or negatively. Psychological scientists, on the other hand, are interested in understanding how the human mind/brain system works in both normal and altered states of consciousness. It is the nature of science to try to develop theories based on objective evidence, that is, evidence that can be verified by other observers. Thus, while scientists cannot directly know other people's conscious experiences, they can make inferences about them from objective data including introspective verbal reports, performance on cognitive tasks, and physiological measures. Researchers having personal ASC experiences may develop, from their experiences, hypotheses about how the mind works in that ASC. But fair tests of hypotheses require research on other individuals—people who do not know about the hypothesis being tested. Since this book is concerned with the scientific study of consciousness, the emphasis in the following chapters will be on systematic experimental and correlational studies of ASCs.[3]

In the following chapters I will be discussing major altered states of consciousness, including sleep and dreaming, hypnosis, meditative states, and psychedelic drug states. Since it is impossible to discuss everything that is known about ASCs in a single volume, it is necessary to be selective in the coverage. For each state I will briefly describe the characteristic changes in subjective experience and related behavioral and physiological responses. I will go into more detail on selected topics that seem to be particularly important, either for their inherent interest, for their practical applications, or for their relevance to understanding how the mind/brain system works. For theoretical interpretations of the various states I will emphasize theories that are comprehendible from a cognitive psychological viewpoint, in which subjective experience and behavior are produced by processes in the mind/brain system.

SUMMARY

An altered state of consciousness (ASC) is a temporary change in the overall pattern of subjective experience, such that the individual believes that his/her mental functioning is distinctly different from certain general norms for his/her normal waking state of consciousness. The normal waking state refers to periods when one is awake and has not done anything to produce an altered state in the usual sense (that it, one has not used an ASC induction procedure).

For people who experience them, ASCs may be important for three reasons: (1) to promote healing and psychological well-being; (2) as avenues of new knowledge and experience, such as personal insight and artistic inspiration; and (3) to serve social functions, such as religious rituals and promoting group cohesion. Psychological scientists study ASCs as important natural human experiences, and to help understand how the mind/brain system works.

Some fourteen different dimensions of changed subjective experience that can occur in ASCs were described: (1) attention; (2) perception; (3) imagery and fantasy; (4) inner speech; (5) memory; (6) higher-level thought processes; (7) meaning or significance of experience; (8) time experience; (9) emotional feeling and expression; (10) arousal; (11) self-control; (12) suggestibility; (13) body image; and (14) sense of personal identity. Four means of inducing ASCs were described, including changes in: (1) external stimulation; (2) physical activity; (3) physiological state; and (4) focus of attention. Specific ASCs cannot be defined in terms of the induction procedure alone.

Though the essence of ASCs is the individual's pattern of subjective experiences, scientists need to be able to identify objectively a subject's state of consciousness. In research practice, specific ASCs are usually identified according to a quasi-operational procedure, whereby a specific induction procedure is followed by a characteristic set of psychological responses, including subjective experiences revealed through introspective reports, cognitive task performance changes, and other behaviors. Physiological indicators may also be used, insofar as they correlate reliably with psychological responses. In the quasi-operational approach, subjects must experience some, though not necessarily all, of the characteristic responses to be considered to be in a particular ASC. ASCs are natural concepts in that each ASC has its prototype or typical cases, and other cases are included if they are sufficiently similar to the prototype.

ENDNOTES

[1] A similar approach is used by psychiatrists and clinical psychologists for diagnosing psychopathological conditions. According to the guidelines in *DSM-III* (American Psychiatric Association 1980), each condition (major depression, paranoid schizophrenia, etc.) is diagnosed in terms of a set of behavioral symptoms, where to be diagnosed in a particular category, patients must have a specified number—but not necessarily all—of the listed symptoms. In some cases one or more specific symptoms are required, along with some (but not necessarily all) of the additional symptoms.

[2] Tart (1975) argued that each state of consciousness is unique and stable, and he coined the term *discrete state of consciousness* (dSoC) to emphasize these characteristics. According to Tart's theory, only a limited number of discrete states is possible, since the mind/brain system can stabilize itself in only a limited number of ways. (In physics, a "state" of matter is a relatively unique and stable condition [such as ice, water, or steam]. The word "state" is a loose metaphor when we talk about states of consciousness.) I would argue that, in fact, there is no compelling reason to believe that states of consciousness are necessarily discretely different from each other. Some states are very different from each other, but others may be similar, and it is uncertain whether any state is absolutely unique. Stability is a matter of degree: some states last for a few minutes, others for a few hours. Transition states may last for a few seconds. The longer a state lasts, the more conscious experience will change, and it is somewhat arbitrary whether we call a changed pattern of experience a new state or a variation of the original state. In any case, the question of the uniqueness and stability of states of consciousness is a matter for research; it cannot be settled by a priori theory.

[3] Creative writers' descriptions of their own ASC experiences can be a valuable source of information about ASCs, for both students and researchers. Though self-report case studies do not come from controlled research conditions, writers' descriptions may be of particular interest because they can communicate their subjective ASC experiences better than the typical research subject. For example, Aldous Huxley (author of *Brave New World*) described his mescaline trip in *The Doors of Perception* (Huxley 1954/1970). And Milton Erickson did a detailed case study of Huxley in a hypnotic state (Erickson 1965). Such reports can be a valuable source of ideas for systematic research. Yet we must acknowledge that the ASC experience can never be fully captured by writers' reports, case studies, or controlled research. All such productions are only selective samples of the ASC experience, at best.

chapter 10 ··································

Sleep

Sleep may be defined as a recurring state characterized by (1) reduced aware-ness of and interaction with the external environment, (2) reduced motility and muscular activity, and (3) partial or complete cessation of voluntary be-havior and self-consciousness (Anch, Browman, Mitler, & Walsh 1988). Sev-eral stages of sleep can be distinguished by their patterns of physiological correlates, though it is not possible to identify an exact moment of sleep onset in terms of physiological correlates (Dement 1976).

Sleep is the most important and unique of the altered states of con-sciousness, for several reasons. It involves dramatic changes in behavior and subjective experience, which are correlated with changes in physiological re-sponse patterns. Disruptions of the sleep-wake cycle are related to fatigue, performance problems, and physical and psychological disorders. And last but not least, dreams during sleep are some of the most dramatic, emotional, and bizarre experiences of our lives. Some psychologists believe that dream-ing serves important psychological functions. Understanding the dreaming process is important for understanding how the human mind/brain system works.

This chapter will concentrate on sleep, with an emphasis on the differ-ent stages of sleep and their physiological correlates, the question of the function of sleep in general and its different stages in particular, and sleep disorders. Dreaming will be discussed in detail in the next three chapters.

SLEEP-WAKE CYCLES

Under normal conditions, sleep occurs in a cyclic manner, termed a *circadian rhythm* (*circa-*, about; *-dies*, day). Diurnal animals sleep at night and are awake and active during daylight hours, whereas the opposite is true of nocturnal animals. For both diurnal and nocturnal animals, the sleep-wake cycle is synchronized with the day-night cycle. As the day-night cycle changes with the seasons, the animals' sleep-wake cycles change also. In ancient times and in primitive societies, human sleep-wake cycles were synchronized with day-night cycles. In modern urban societies, however, the cycle is more likely to be synchronized with clock time, such that people stay up well past nightfall, and tend to wake up at about the same time each morning throughout the year, regardless of how light it is outside.

Synchronization with an external timer—either the day-night cycle or a clock—is not the only reason for sleep-wakefulness cycles. A biological clock, located in the brain, is also involved. The biological clock is *entrained* to an external timer (usually the day-night cycle), such that the internal clock tends to maintain the sleep-wakefulness cycle even when external time cues have been removed. Laboratory experiments with animals have shown that when they are kept in constant light or darkness they continue to have regular sleep-wake cycles, though the cycles tend to drift gradually out of phase with the outside day-night cycle. In natural settings, animals' internal clocks reset daily as the day-night cycle changes with the seasons, thus maintaining their clocks' entrainment to the day-night cycle.

Biological clocks have been demonstrated in humans, too, in experiments in which people lived alone for several months in caves or laboratory apartments where all cues to the day-night cycle and clock time were eliminated. The subjects could control the electric lights in their isolation apartment. They were instructed to sleep whenever they felt like doing so, but to try to avoid naps and limit themselves to one sleep period per day (based on their own estimate of a "day"). The result was that most subjects soon fell into a consistent sleep-waking cycle of about twenty-five hours. That is, they went to bed an hour later each day, so that if they had gone to bed at 11 p.m. on the first night, ten days later they were going to bed at 9 a.m. Also, average sleep time increased from eight hours to eight and a half hours (Coleman 1986). Under such conditions, various physiological cycles (including temperature and blood levels of various biochemicals) that are normally synchronized with each other and with the sleep-wake cycle become desynchronized (see Anch et al. 1988).

The internal clock is the reason for *jet lag*, the feelings of fatigue and malaise that occur when people travel across several time zones in a relatively short period of time. It takes a few days (up to two weeks) for the internal clock to become entrained to the day-night cycle or local clock time in the new time zone. A similar problem occurs when people have to work on night shifts, such as at a factory or hospital. Some researchers have speculated that it should be possible for people to make a good adjustment to night-shift work if they would stay on the same sleep-wake cycle (awake at night, sleep in the daytime) consistently for several weeks. But in fact, most data show that night-shift workers rarely make a complete adjustment to night work. They sleep poorly in the daytime and are sleepy and fatigued at night. Their physiological cycles do not adjust to the night-work cycle. Probably one reason it is hard to make a complete adjustment to night work is that night workers usually revert to the normal day-wake, night-sleep cycle on weekends, so they can participate in normal social activities with friends and family. Also, work shifts are usually rotated every week or so. Thus, night workers never have a chance for their internal sleep-wake clocks to become entrained to the night-work cycle. This is a serious problem, since night-shift workers not only feel stressed and fatigued at night, but also have higher rates of accidents and health problems than day-shift workers (see Anch et al. 1988; Coleman 1986).

STAGES OF SLEEP

Sleep is not a uniform state. There are several different types or stages of sleep that occur in a cyclic pattern during a sleep period.

The most important discovery in the history of sleep and dream research—the discovery of REM sleep—came about by accident (Aserinsky & Kleitman 1953).[1] In 1952 Dr. Nathaniel Kleitman at the University of Chicago became interested in the slow rolling eye movements that accompany sleep onset. Kleitman and his research assistant, physiology graduate student Eugene Aserinsky, decided to study these eye movements in a subject throughout a full night of sleep. Aserinsky's task was to monitor the eye movements as they were recorded on a polygraph. To his surprise, after the subject had been sleeping for awhile he started making relatively large, rapid, binocularly coordinated eye movements. These movements occurred periodically through the night, separated by intervals with slow rolling movements. This discovery was unexpected because it had been thought that sleep was a time of general depression or inhibition of the central nervous system—not the sort of state likely to produce rapid, coordinated eye movements. Meanwhile, medical student William C. Dement joined the research team, and started measuring brain waves and other physiological variables during sleep. It was soon noticed that during periods of rapid eye movements the brain waves showed a distinctive pattern, and there was a change in breathing (Dement 1976).

The rapid eye movements were particularly interesting and puzzling. What could be their cause? The researchers speculated that they might be related to dreaming. For example, perhaps they occurred as a result of sleepers "watching" movements in their dreams. They tested the hypothesis of a relationship to dreaming by systematically awakening ten subjects and interrogating them about their thoughts, sometimes during rapid eye movement (REM sleep) periods, and sometimes during periods of ocular quiescence (non-REM, or NREM sleep). The subjects reported dreams after almost all of the REM awakenings, but rarely after NREM awakenings. The relationship between REM sleep and dreaming was so strong that the authors concluded: "This method furnishes the means of determining the incidence and duration of periods of dreaming" (Aserinsky & Kleitman 1953, p. 274).

The discovery of REM sleep had several important results. It demonstrated that sleep is not a uniform state, and further, that the distinctive sub-jective experience of dreaming occurs in conjunction with a distinctive phys-iological state. And most important, this discovery opened new worlds of possibilities for the experimental study of dreaming. It became possible to know when a sleeper is likely to be dreaming, and thus to collect dream re-ports immediately after awakening the subject, when dream recall is at its best. The discovery of REM inspired a surge of interest in laboratory re-search on the psychology and physiology of sleep and dreaming.

Physiological Criteria for REM and NREM Sleep

For most of our purposes it will be sufficient to distinguish between REM sleep versus NREM sleep though, as we will see in a later section, NREM sleep can be subdivided into four different stages. REM and NREM sleep are defined in terms of a systematic pattern of three physiological responses.

The three defining criteria include brain waves measured by the elec-troencephalogram (EEG), conjugate eye movements measured by the elec-trooculogram (EOG), and chin muscle tension measured by the electromyo-gram (EMG). These physiological responses involve small changes in the electrical potential of brain tissue and muscles. They are detected by means of small silver electrodes (less than 1 cm in diameter) that are taped to the subject's skin. (The electrodes are shaped like a shallow cup, and the cup is filled with an electrode jelly to ensure good contact with the skin.)

Figure 10.1 shows standard locations for EEG, EOG, and EMG elec-trodes in sleep research. The earlobe electrode is a reference point for the EEG and EOG voltage measurements. In some experiments additional phys-iological measurements are taken, such as measures of breathing, heartbeat, body temperature, or penile tumescence (erection). Also, EEG measures may be taken from several different scalp locations, and additional EOG elec-trodes may be used to record vertical eye movements (the standard arrange-ment distinguishes only lateral eye movements). Wires from the electrodes are collected in a "pony tail" and attached to a jackbox on the wall. On the other side of the wall, in an adjacent room, wires from the jackbox are con-nected to a machine called a *polygraph* or *polysomnograph*. The polygraph amplifies the voltage fluctuations and records them on moving chart paper (and also in computer data files, in modern research).

Figure 10.1 also shows polygraph recordings of a transition from NREM to REM sleep. During NREM sleep the eyes are not completely still, but they tend to drift slowly back and forth. At the transition from NREM to REM sleep, the EOG lines show a change from relatively quiescent eyes to frequent, relatively large conjugate lateral eye movements (REMs). ("Conju-gate" means that the eyes move together.) The fact that the EOG tracings move in opposite directions has to do with the fact that the electrical polarity of the electrode depends upon whether the eyes are moving toward it or away from it. Thus, if the eyes move to the right, then the right electrode becomes more positive and the left more negative, and vice versa.

REM sleep gets its name from the rapid eye movements that are charac-teristic of this stage of sleep, and which do not occur in other stages of sleep. However, while rapid eye movements are the distinctive behavioral charac-

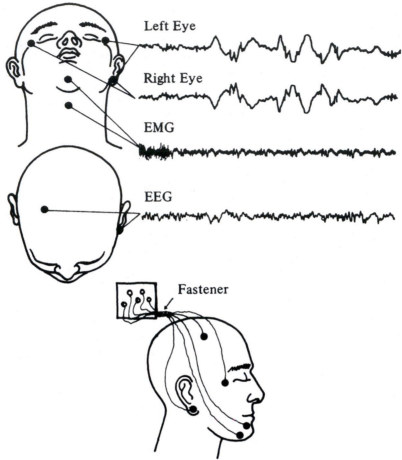

FIGURE 10.1. Standard electrode placements for sleep recordings. This is the minimum setup required for identifying different stages of sleep. The polygraph tracings show the transition from NREM to REM sleep. The tracings move horizontally over time; thus, they are read from left (earlier time) to right (later time). Greater response amplitudes (in microvolts) are shown by greater ranges of vertical movement of the tracings. The transition from NREM to REM sleep is indicated by three physiological events: (1) EEG, an increase in brain wave activity; (2) EOG, an increase in eye movements; and (3) EMG, a decrease in chin muscle tension. The standard chart speed is 10 mm per second, so a full 8 hours of sleep requires 288 meters (944 feet) of chart paper. [From Dement, W. C. (1976). *Some Must Watch While Some Must Sleep.* New York: Norton. Copyright by William C. Dement and the Stanford Alumni Association.]

teristic of REM period sleep, the eyes do not necessarily move continuously throughout a REM period. There are often intervals of several seconds (and occasionally up to a minute or more) without eye movements during a REM period.

The EMG tracing shows that in the transition from NREM to REM sleep the chin muscles relax further, that is, there is a decreased magnitude and rate of voltage oscillations in the EMG.

The EEG is a rather crude measure, since it is the average electrical voltage of thousands of neurons located on the surface of the cortex several millimeters below the scalp electrode. Nonetheless, the EEG is sensitive enough to distinguish different brain wave patterns in wakefulness and sleep. In the transition from NREM to REM the EEG shows an increase in brain wave activity, that is, an increased frequency of voltage oscillations, along with a decrease in mean brain wave amplitude. (The difference may be seen more clearly in Figure 10.2.) In general, EEG frequency and amplitude are inversely correlated, such that slower frequency goes with increased amplitude (especially in deep NREM sleep stages, Figure 10.2). Slower-frequency/higher-amplitude tracings are associated with an increase in the synchronization of firings of cortical neurons under the scalp electrode.

It should be emphasized that REM sleep is defined by the *pattern* of three physiological correlates, rather than by only one of them. Table 10.1 summarizes the patterns of psychophysiological correlates for waking and for REM and NREM sleep. (In the table the + and − symbols indicate relatively more or relatively less, respectively.) You can see that no single indicator is sufficient to distinguish between all three of these major states of consciousness.[2]

The Structure of Sleep

Sleep stages.   For a more complete description of sleep stages we need to distinguish between four NREM stages. Figure 10.2 shows typical EEG tracings for relaxed wakefulness, NREM stages 1, 2, 3, and 4, and REM sleep. In relaxed wakefulness, with the eyes closed, the EEG tracing shows a predominance of *alpha waves*, fairly synchronous brain waves occurring at a rate of about ten cycles per second (8–13 Hz). The transition from wakefulness to sleep is shown in Figure 10.6.

When we fall asleep we first enter NREM Stage 1, and then progress successively through NREM stages 2, 3, and 4, then back up through stages 3 and 2 to REM sleep. NREM Stage 1 is characterized by relatively low-amplitude, fast waves of mixed frequencies. In Stage 2 the mean brain wave frequency is somewhat slower, and mean amplitude somewhat greater, than in Stage 1. Also, in Stage 2 distinctive sleep spindles and K-complexes appear in the EEG (see Figure 10.2). The characteristic feature of Stage 3 is the emergence of rhythmic but very slow (0.5 to 2 Hz), high-voltage delta waves. Stage 4 is defined as the occurrence of delta waves that exceed 75 microvolts in amplitude in over 50 percent of the EEG tracing. Thus, Stages 2 and 4 are distinctive, while Stage 3 (about 20–50 percent delta waves) is a transition stage between Stages 2 and 4.

The EEG pattern during REM sleep is superficially similar to that during Stage 1 NREM in that both involve predominantly low-voltage, high-frequency, desynchronized waves of mixed frequencies (including occasional alpha). However, a more fine-grained analysis shows that REM EEG also includes distinctive "saw-tooth" waves of moderate amplitude and

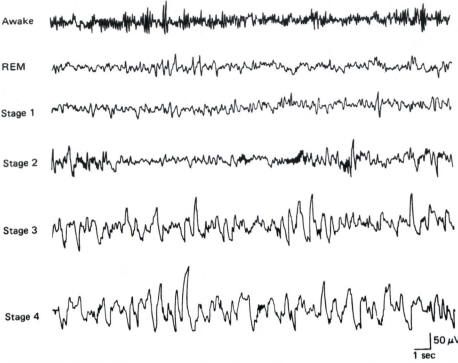

FIGURE 10.2. EEG in different stages of sleep. The recordings were made at the standard chart speed of 10 mm per second, with a 10 mm vertical deflection of the pen representing a 50 microvolt change in electrical potential. The first line was recorded during relaxed wakefulness, and shows mostly alpha waves of about 10 cycles per second (Hz). Going from NREM Stage 1 to NREM Stage 4, the general trend is toward slower and higher amplitude waves. The Stage 1 NREM tracing shows low amplitude, fast waves of mixed frequencies. The Stage 2 NREM tracing shows two features characteristic of that stage: several *sleep spindles*, which are the bursts of 12–14 Hz waves lasting about a second and appearing against a background of generally slower waves; and a *K complex*, which is the isolated high voltage spike in the right half of the recording. In Stage 3 NREM very slow (½ to 2 Hz), high-amplitude delta waves begin to appear. The stage is identified as Stage 4 NREM when over 50 percent of the tracing consists of delta waves exceeding 75 microvolts in amplitude. The REM tracing is largely similar to NREM stage 1, except for the occurrence of bursts of fairly uniform "saw-tooth" waves in REM stage (Anch et al. 1988; Dement 1976.) [From Rechtschaffen, A. & Kales, A. (1968). *A Manual of Standardized Terminology, Techniques and Scoring System for Sleep Stages of Human Sleep Subjects.* Washington, DC: U.S. Government Printing Office.]

about 2–3 Hz. Saw-tooth waves typically occur in bursts of two or three at a time, and often precede or coincide with rapid eye movements.

REM cycles.   During the course of a night's sleep of seven or eight hours, normal adults go through several cycles of NREM and REM sleep. Figure 10.3 shows a typical sequence of stages. This figure illustrates several points about a night's sleep for young adults: (1) The first REM period does

TABLE 10.1   Physiological Correlates of Waking, REM Sleep, and Non-REM Sleep States*

	DEFINING FEATURES			OTHER FEATURES		
	EEG	EOG	EMG			
	Brain Waves	Eye Move-ments	Chin Muscle Tension	Extero-ception	Vestibular System Activation	Autonomic Arousal
State						
Waking	Fast, low amplitude	+	+	+	+	+
REM Sleep	Fast, low amplitude	+	−	−	+	+
NREM Sleep	Slow, high amplitude	−	+	−	−	−

*Within each response system the "+" and "−" symbols indicate the relative amounts of activity in the different states. The pattern of EEG, EOG, and EMG responses taken together are the defining physiological features by which the relaxed waking state, REM sleep, and non-REM (NREM) sleep are identified. Exteroception, vestibular activation, and autonomic arousal are other state correlates, thought they are not used as defining features.

not occur until over an hour after sleep onset. (2) The duration of the first REM period is typically rather brief (5 to 10 minutes), but REM duration tends to increase in later cycles, averaging about 22 minutes in later cycles (though with considerable variability about the mean). (3) The first sleep cycle is defined as the time from sleep onset until the end of the first REM period. Subsequent cycles are defined as the time from the end of one REM period until the end of the next REM period. After the first cycle, subsequent cycles average about 90 to 100 minutes in length. (4) NREM Stages 3 and 4 are confined almost entirely to the first four hours of sleep; after that NREM time is almost entirely devoted to Stage 2. (5) Toward the end of the night it is common to awaken briefly from either NREM or REM sleep (Anch et al. 1988; Dement 1976).

Infants and animals.   Newborn human infants sleep about 16 to 18 hours per day, and spend at least 50 percent of this time in REM sleep. (Premature infants may spend as much as 75 percent of their sleep time in REM.) Figure 10.4 shows that as people mature the percent of sleep-time spent in REM decreases gradually to about 25% at age 3, to 20% in adolescents and adults (Roffwarg, Muzio, & Dement 1966). Nor is REM sleep unique to humans. It occurs in all mammals (except the echidna), but not in reptiles, and probably not in birds (Hartmann 1967). Much of what we know about the brain mechanisms involved in sleep comes from research on cats, whose sleep stages are quite similar to those of humans except that the mean cycle

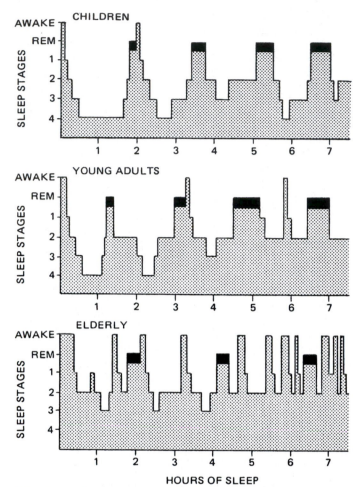

FIGURE 10.3. Cycles of sleep stages in a typical night of sleep for three age groups. In the young adult the first REM period does not begin until about an hour after sleep onset. After that, REM periods begin about every 90 to 100 minutes, on the average. Going from child to young adult to elderly, the amount of NREM Stage 4 decreases, while the frequency of brief awakenings increases. [From Kales, A. & Kales, J. D. (1974). Sleep disorders: Recent findings in the diagnosis and treatment of disturbed sleep. *New England Journal of Medicine, 290,* 487–99. By permission of the publisher.]

length for cats is only about 40 minutes, with REM periods of 5 to 10 minutes duration (Hobson & McCarley 1977). Adult cats spend about 17 percent of their sleep in REM state, but in newborn kittens nearly 100 percent of sleep is REM sleep. Whether nonhuman mammals dream is unknown, since they have no way of telling us.

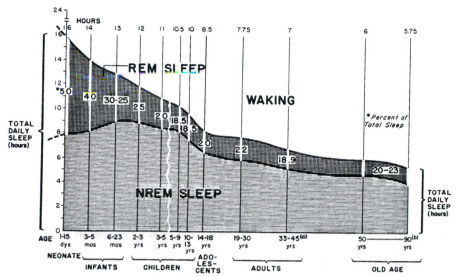

FIGURE 10.4. Changes in amounts of REM and NREM sleep with increasing age. Total sleep time decreases from infancy to old age. From infancy to about 10–13 years the decrease is in the amount of REM sleep. From 10–13 years onward the amount of REM stays fairly constant (about 1½ hours), whereas the amount of NREM continues to decrease. The percent of sleep time spent in REM stage is also indicated; it decreases from about 50 percent for infants to about 20 percent for adolescents and adults. [From Roffwarg, H. P., Muzio, J. N., & Dement, W. C. (1966). Ontogenetic development of the human sleep-dream cycle. *Science, 152,* 604–19. Copyright 1966 by the AAAS. Revised by the authors since original publication.]

Other Physiological and Behavioral Correlates of Sleep Stages

Besides the three defining criteria of REM versus NREM sleep—EEG, EOG, and EMG—there are several other physiological and behavioral correlates of sleep stages (Anch et al. 1988; Rechtschaffen 1973).

Exteroception. It is impossible to determine the exact instant of sleep onset solely by means of an EEG recording. According to Dement, "The essential difference between wakefulness and sleep is the loss of awareness. Sleep onset occurs at the exact instant when a meaningful stimulus fails to elicit its accustomed response" (1976, p. 27). For example, if you speak a person's name softly, then he or she would normally respond when awake, but not when asleep. Of course, if you shout the name, the sleeper will awaken. *Auditory arousal thresholds* are higher during sleep than during waking, and they are higher during Stages 3 and 4 than during other stages of sleep (Zimmerman 1970). (A higher arousal threshold means that it takes a louder noise to awaken the sleeper.)

Other sensory thresholds, such as smell and touch, are also higher during sleep than waking. Dement (1976) described a dramatic example of the sudden loss of visual responsiveness during sleep onset:

A sleepy subject lies in bed with his eyes taped open (which can be achieved, believe it or not, with relatively little discomfort). A very bright strobe light is placed about six inches in front of his face and is flashed into his eyes at the rate of about once every second or two. A microswitch is taped to his finger, which he is instructed to press every time he sees a flash. A simple task. How can he possibly avoid seeing the flash? The subject will press and press. Suddenly he stops. If we immediately ask why, he will be surprised. The light exploded right into his widely open eyes, yet he was totally unaware. In one second, he was awake, seeing, hearing, responding—in the very next second, he was functionally blind and asleep (pp. 27–28).

Though sensory thresholds are reduced during sleep, the sleeping brain can still detect stimuli, as is shown by the fact that stimuli during sleep can elicit physiological responses, such as evoked potentials in brain waves and heart rate changes. Meaningful stimuli (such as emotionally significant names) elicit different physiological reactions than meaningless stimuli (see McDonald et al. 1975). The arousal threshold is lower for a meaningful stimulus, such as a baby's cry, than it is for meaningless stimuli. Also meaningful stimuli during sleep are more likely than meaningless stimuli to affect the contents of dreams (see Chapter 11). All of these findings show that the sleeping brain is capable of discriminating between different external stimuli, even though the sleeping person is not consciously aware of the stimuli. Sensory discrimination ability is typically better in REM than Stage 2 NREM, and worst in Stage 4. (See reviews in Anch et al. 1988; Arkin and Antrobus 1978.) However, carefully controlled studies have generally failed to show that people can learn verbal materials, such as foreign language vocabularies, during either REM or other sleep stages. (See review by Aarons 1976.)

Muscle tension and movement.   In general, the muscles become more relaxed, and spinal reflexes (such as knee jerk) are reduced, in the transition from waking to NREM sleep. Muscle tension throughout the body is usually lower during REM than NREM sleep, and reduced chin EMG is one of the defining features of REM sleep. Paradoxically, aperiodic twitches of face and finger muscles occur more often during REM than in deeper sleep. Also the frequency of body movements is higher during REM than NREM sleep, with the rate of body movements progressively decreasing from waking to NREM Stage 1, REM, and NREM Stages 2, 3, and 4, respectively (Wilde-Frenz & Schulz 1983).[3] Thus, while reduced muscle tension is a *tonic* (long term, sustained) characteristic of REM sleep, muscle twitches and body movements can occur as *phasic* (brief, sporadic) events (Pivik 1978). The EEG often suggests a brief awakening during the body movements, although the individual is typically unresponsive at that time and does not remember the movement (Dement 1976). Sleepwalking (somnambulism)—which occurs during Stage 4—is considered to be a sleep disorder. (I will discuss sleepwalking further in the section on sleep disorders.)

Vestibular system activation.   The vestibular system is responsible for our *equilibratory sense*, which includes sensing the orientation of our head and maintaining our balance, and sensing the acceleration of our body through space. This is accomplished by the vestibular apparatus, which is located in the inner ear, next to the cochlea, on each side of the head. The motion of fluid in the apparatus bends hair cells, which send a unique pattern of neural activity to the brain to indicate head position and movement. During REM sleep, neural activity in the vestibular system increases, even though the sleeper is perfectly still. As we will see in Chapter 12 on theories of dreaming, Hobson and McCarley (1977) have speculated that this spontaneous vestibular activity during REM sleep can account for the sensation of movement during dreams.

Autonomic responses.   Heart rate, respiration rate, and systolic blood pressure decrease during the transition from waking to NREM sleep. However, these responses increase somewhat—about 6 percent—in REM compared to NREM sleep (Snyder et al. 1964). More dramatic is the increase in *variability* of these measures, about 55 percent. In other words, there are more momentary, phasic changes in autonomic responses during REM than during NREM sleep.

Heart rate, respiration rate, and blood pressure are controlled by the autonomic nervous system, and increases in these responses—such as during emotional arousal—indicate increased activation of the sympathetic part of the autonomic nervous system. It has been speculated that there is an association between autonomic arousal in REM and the emotionality of dreams. However, the situation is made more complicated when we consider the Galvanic skin response (GSR). The GSR (measured from the palm or fingers) indicates decreased electrical resistance in the skin (or conversely, increased electrical conductivity), related to increased neural activity in the sweat glands. The GSR is a component of the orienting reaction to novel or emotionally significant stimuli, and it is a standard measure on "lie-detector" tests. If REM is a more autonomically aroused state than NREM, then we would expect more GSRs in REM than NREM. In fact, the opposite is the case. Spontaneous GSRs occur so often during NREM Stages 3 and 4, and with such vigor, that they have been called "GSR storms" (Rechtschaffen 1973).

The reasons for the variability in heart rate and respiratory rate during REM, and for the paradoxical prevalence of GSRs in Stages 3 and 4 rather than REM, are not clearly understood. However, the data suggest that, contrary to an earlier hypothesis, it would be incorrect to characterize REM sleep as a state of tonically increased sympathetic arousal (Rechtschaffen 1973). Furthermore, autonomic responses, such as GSR and heart rate, are not necessarily reliable correlates of emotional dream events (Pivik 1978).

Penile erections.   Throbbing penile erections occur during REM sleep in normal males, including infants and children as well as adults (see Figure 10.5). Fisher, Gross, and Zuch (1965) measured erections during uninterrupted sleep in seventeen normal adult males, using several methods including a strain gauge (which measures changes in diameter), phalloplethysmograph (which measures surface blood flow), and direct observation. Other studies have used a sort of pneumatic donut to measure erections. Fisher et al. found that 60 percent of the REM periods were accompanied by full erections, 35 percent by partial or fluctuating erections, and only 5 percent by no

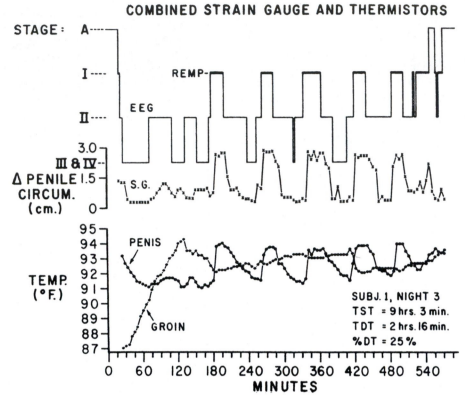

FIGURE 10.5. Penile erection cycle during sleep, for a representative subject. The upper graph shows changes in EEG sleep stages; REM (REMP) stage is indicated by the darker horizontal lines. The middle graph shows penis circumference as measured by a strain gauge; increases of 2.5 cm or more indicate full erection. Note that erections occur during REM periods. The bottom graph shows groin and penis temperatures. [From Fisher, C., Gross, J. & Zuch, J. (1965). Cycle of penile erections synchronous with dreaming (REM) sleep: Preliminary report. *Archives of General Psychiatry, 12*, 29–45. Copyright 1965, American Medical Association.]

erection. Erections tended to begin about the same time as REM, though sometimes they began a few minutes before REM onset. Maximum erection was usually attained about 5 minutes after REM onset, and once the maximum was attained it tended to be maintained throughout the REM period. The erections were maintained for a while after the end of the REM period, with full detumescence not occurring until 12 minutes after the end of REM, on the average. Thus, the common experience among males of waking up with an erection is due to the persistence of the erection from the last REM period before awakening. Ejaculation of seminal fluid ("wet dreams") sometimes occurs during REM erections.

Fisher et al. (1965) found no evidence of erections during NREM sleep, except for erections sometimes beginning in Stage 2 shortly before REM onset. Also, they found that REM erections occurred independently of the subject's recency of sexual gratification. Other studies have shown that REM erections are not necessarily associated with sexy REM dreams (Karacan et al. 1966). Thus, REM erections are elicited by the physiological events of REM sleep, rather than by REM dream images. REM erections are so commonplace for normal males that they can be used to aid in diagnosing the cause of chronic impotency (the persistent failure to get an erection when it is desired for sexual intercourse). Absence of REM erections would indicate that the impotency problem has some organic basis. On the other hand, if the patient gets erections during REM, then his failure to get them during sexual play probably has a psychological basis.

Genital arousal occurs during REM sleep in women, too, though not in such an obvious way as in men. Research with electrophysiological recording devices has shown that during REM women have increased vaginal blood flow, and erections of the clitoris, both responses being typical of sexual arousal.

Other measures.   Cortical blood flow and temperature increase during REM, as one might expect from the increased cortical activation during REM. And while the cortex may, in a sense, be more quiet during NREM than REM, the sleeper may be noisier during NREM: most snoring occurs during NREM sleep (Dement 1976). (See Anch et al. 1988, for more details and reference citations on all varieties of physiological responses during sleep.)

The Physiological Basis of Sleep Cycles

Two types of sleep cycles are of interest: the cycle of sleep versus wakefulness, and the REM-NREM cycle within sleep periods. Both types of cycles are produced by biological clocks in the brain. Neurophysiologists have used a variety of experimental procedures with animals (such as rats, cats, and monkeys) to discover the location of the biological clock or clocks. The procedures include ablation (destroying a localized part of the brain), disconnection (cutting the connecting neurons between two parts of the brain), electrical stimulation of neurons, and measurement of spontaneous electrical activity in localized cell groups during sleep. More recently, identification of specific neurotransmitter chemicals in different brain circuits, and stimulation of synapses by different chemicals, have also been employed. For obvious reasons, it has not been possible to do most of these experimental procedures with humans. However, the similarity of sleep in other mammals is sufficiently similar to that of humans to make it seem likely that the findings from animal research are also applicable to humans.

Sleep-wakefulness cycle.   Recent research suggests that the sleep-wakefulness cycle is controlled primarily by a biological clock located in the *suprachiasmatic nucleus* (SCN) of the hypothalamus (located just above the optic chiasm, where the optic nerves divide; see Figure 5.1). The SCN clock is normally entrained to the day-night cycle, though the clock continues to operate in constant light or darkness, with a tendency to drift toward a somewhat shorter or longer cycle (depending on the species). The SCN gets its own visual input from the eyes, as is shown by the fact that brain lesions or disconnections posterior to the chiasm, which produce blindness, do not prevent entrainment to light-dark cycles (Anch et al. 1988).

REM-NREM cycle.   Neural circuits in the *pontine reticular formation*, located in the pons section of the brain stem, are particularly important for controlling the REM-NREM cycle within sleep periods. Earlier it was proposed that the clock is located in the pontine reticular formation (Hobson & McCarley 1977). More recent evidence suggests that the clock is a widely distributed network of cells with reciprocal excitatory and inhibitory interactions, though the pontine reticular system is an important part of this network (Hobson 1988; Hobson, Lydic, & Baghdoyan 1986).

Hobson and McCarley (1977) concluded that the reticular system is responsible for directly eliciting several of the physiological features of REM sleep, including: (1) Tonic activation of the cortex, which produces the high level of brain-wave activity characteristic of REM sleep. (2) Inhibition of spinal cord motoneurons, which blocks muscle movements despite high levels of activity in the motor cortex. (Phasic muscle movements seem to involve occasional "breakthrough" of excitation against the inhibitory processes.) (3) Phasic activation of the oculomotor system to produce eye movements. (4) Phasic activation of the vestibular system. (In addition to possibly producing spurious sensations of movement, the vestibular activation also causes some of the eye movements. This occurs because one of the normal functions of the vestibular system is to coordinate eye movements with head movements.) (5) Blockade of exteroceptive sensory inputs to the cortex.

An implication of the evidence that the physiological correlates of REM sleep are directly elicited by a brain-stem mechanism is that there is no need to try to explain them as responses to dream images. (In Chapter 12 on theories of dreaming I will discuss Hobson and McCarley's provocative idea that the opposite is the case: their Activation-Synthesis Hypothesis proposes that dreams are the brain's response to the physiological events of REM sleep.)

THE FUNCTION OF SLEEP

It seems obvious that the sleep-wake cycle must have evolved because sleep has some sort of adaptive function. Presumably, we need to spend a certain amount of time sleeping each day. But why? A negative answer—that we feel crummy if we don't sleep—is not sufficient. We need a positive answer to the question: What is the function—or the adaptive value—of sleep? Surprisingly, despite decades of research on sleep, scientists cannot give a definite answer to this fundamental question.

The most obvious explanation of the need for sleep is that it serves some *restorative function*. Presumably, the body needs to rest each day in order to allow a period of time for physiological growth and repair functions to operate. But if rest for restoration were the only reason for sleep, then it should be sufficient to spend eight hours per day in physical relaxation, without actually sleeping. Yet, it is almost impossible for people to remain awake overnight while physically resting. It is easier to stay awake if we are engaged in some sort of physical activity. Clearly, physical rest is no substitute for sleep. Yet there is no clear evidence that sleep is essential for any particular physiological restorative function.

But sleep is more than a physiological state. It is also a kind of behavior. Taking a behavioral viewpoint, and looking at humans and other animals in the wild state, we could define sleep as the behavior of lying relatively still and temporarily suspending reactivity to the environment.

According to the *adaptive behavior hypothesis*, sleep has a clear adaptive value. For primates and other diurnal (active in daytime) animals, nighttime sleep ensures that they are quiet and inconspicuous at night, when nocturnal predators are out hunting for them. Presumably, prey animals with a tendency to sleep at night (in a safe place, such as a burrow, tree, or cave) are more likely to survive and leave offspring than those that are awake and active at night. Also, sleep is an *instinctive behavior*, according to these criteria: (1) it has a basis in heredity; (2) it is developmental in nature; (3) there is a positive motivation to do it; and (4) it shows regularities in response to the environment while maintaining some degree of flexibility. From the viewpoint of the adaptive behavior hypothesis, behavior is primary, and physiology is secondary, in the evolution of sleep. That is, the physiological sleep state evolved because it controls the behavior of sleep (Webb 1975).

Several comments on the adaptive behavior hypothesis are in order. First, while it seems appropriate to primates and other diurnal animals that tend to sleep through the night, it may not be applicable to animals with other sleep patterns (Allison & Cicchetti 1976; Zepelin & Rechtschaffen 1974). For example, cats tend to sleep at two- or three-hour intervals through the day and night, with a circadian rhythm that is much weaker than that of primates. Second, the adaptive behavior hypothesis does not explain the fact that we have several physiologically distinct types of sleep, including REM and the several NREM stages. The adaptive behavior function of sleep would be adequately served by a single physiological sleep state. Third, it cannot explain the devastating stressful effects of chronic sleep deprivation. For examples, rats totally deprived of sleep invariably die within ten to thirty days (Rechtschaffen et al. 1983). Thus, the adaptive behavior hypothesis is not a complete explanation of sleep-wake cycles and the need for sleep.

Possibly, sleep originally evolved as an adaptive behavior. Subsequently, REM and NREM sleep were differentiated out of an original unified sleep state, in order to serve different functions (Cohen 1979a). In a later section I will turn to the question of whether REM sleep has any unique function, distinct from that of NREM sleep. But first, let us consider the question of what happens when humans are deprived of sleep.

SLEEP DEPRIVATION AND HUMAN PERFORMANCE

In view of the fatigue and relatively high accident rates experienced by night workers, ranging from factory workers to truck drivers and airline pilots, it is important to ask what effects sleep deprivation has on human performance. There have been several studies on this question, but it is impossible to make generalizations that apply to all cases because the effects of sleep deprivation on task performance depend on several factors (Webb 1975): (1) The nature of the task: harmful effects of sleep deprivation are generally greater for intellectual tasks than for sensory-motor tasks, for complex tasks than for simple tasks, and for tasks requiring flexible thinking and variable responses than for routine, habitual tasks. (2) The individual worker's ability to do the task efficiently under stress; typically, this ability will be greater the more the worker has practiced the task. (3) The worker's motivation or desire to continue trying to perform well when fatigued: by exerting extra effort the worker may be able to compensate for reductions in performance capacity, at least temporarily.

The great paradox of sleep deprivation research is that while everyone "knows" that sleep deprivation hurts performance, in practice it has been difficult to demonstrate dramatic effects in controlled studies with objective measurements. With only a single night of total sleep deprivation, behavioral and performance effects are usually negligible. The only clear effect is persistent daytime sleepiness, which is objectively demonstrated by reduced sleep latency (Coleman 1986).

Total sleep deprivation.   Total sleep deprivation for four or five days causes modest physiological effects: hand tremor, occasional double vision, droopy eyelids, a lower pain threshold, and a reduction in EEG alpha. Performance on short-term tasks (a few seconds to a minute or so) is usually not affected, as long as the tasks are relatively simple or well-learned and emphasize visual-motor response coordination. Performance on complex reaction-time tasks (involving multiple stimuli and responses) and short-term memory tasks are more likely to be affected. Most affected is performance on tasks that must be sustained over a relatively long period of time, say thirty minutes or so. This is particularly true for boring tasks for which subjects are relatively unmotivated, such as vigilance tasks (signal-detection tasks requiring subjects to react to sensory signals presented at irregular intervals). Behaviorally, there are occasional and transient instances of confusion, disorientation, and irritability, but the personality is generally intact. Surprisingly, both appetite and sexual drive may increase. Truly bizarre behaviors are quite rare, though hallucinations and paranoia may occur with extended sleep deprivation (Webb 1975).

Laboratory studies may reveal the limits of human performance capabilities under sleep deprivation, but they do not necessarily predict what will happen in particular cases outside of the laboratory, such as at work. In the laboratory, when sleepy subjects are being watched, they may be motivated to muster their reserves and perform to the best of their abilities, and so they can perform successfully on short-term tasks. But outside of the laboratory, when people are fatigued and concentration requires great effort, they may choose to postpone a task or avoid it altogether. Thus, the total work output could suffer, even though what is done will usually be done satisfactorily. For example, sleepy power-plant operators may be perfectly capable of checking pressure gauges correctly, but if they are sleepy they may omit one or more of the scheduled checks. On the other hand, the capacity of sleepy people to do intellectual tasks, such as reading or listening to lectures, may be strongly disrupted, due at least partly to the difficulty of maintaining attention to the task at hand.

It is not necessary to make up for all of the lost sleep after a period of total sleep deprivation. After only a single night of total sleep deprivation, though mean sleep onset latency is reduced from ten minutes to about one minute, there is complete recovery to normal functioning after two successive nights of normal eight-hour sleep periods. Thus, while a night of prolonged sleep leads to faster recovery, it is not strictly necessary for recovery (Coleman 1986). Peter Tripp, a disk jockey, stayed awake for two hundred hours in a booth in Times Square, New York. Though he suffered hallucinations and paranoia, he returned to normal functioning after only thirteen hours of sleep, with no long-term effects. (EEG monitoring showed that Tripp experienced numerous "microsleeps" of two or three seconds during his ordeal. Microsleeps make it impossible to totally deprive someone of sleep for a prolonged period, though it is not clear to what degree microsleeps can substitute for normal sleep.)

Alertness and performance during sleep deprivation are affected by the circadian phase. In subjects sleep-deprived for several days, sleepiness and performance decrements are worst during the hours when the subjects would normally be sleeping. The low point is between 3 and 4 a.m. (Coleman 1986). (I can personally attest to this from two all-night vigils at the hospital maternity ward, keeping my wife company during labor. I felt particularly sleepy between 3 and 4 a.m., but by 6 a.m.—near my normal waking-up time—I felt much more alert.) The time of maximum sleepiness, 3 to 4 a.m., is also the time when body temperature is lowest during a normal 24-hour period with daytime wakefulness and nighttime sleep. Body temperature, sleepiness, and performance cycles are part of the same endogenously controlled circadian rhythm.

Partial sleep deprivation.   The effects of short-term *partial* sleep deprivation—for example, going with four or five hours of sleep per night for one night, or a few nights—are relatively minor (Coleman 1986; Anch et al. 1988). The main effect is sleepiness. Performance on short-term tasks is unaffected, though people may do worse on boring, routine tasks. People can adapt to partial sleep deprivation. In one study sleep was reduced from 8 hours to 5½ hours per night for 60 days (Webb and Agnew 1974). On a signal-detection task requiring the subjects to maintain vigilance, they responded less frequently, indicating that they were less motivated to maintain attention to the task. Other cognitive tasks were unaffected. Most subjects reported daytime drowsiness during the first week, but by the eighth week they had adapted and no longer suffered from drowsiness. Yet, when the study was over, virtually all of the subjects returned to their customary 8 hours of sleep, because they just "felt better" with more sleep.

Conclusion.   We can adapt—in task performance and feeling of alertness—to chronic (long-term) *partial* sleep deprivation. As for *total* sleep deprivation, all of the studies have used acute (short-term) deprivation, limited to four or five days (with one volunteer going ten days without sleep). The effects of acute total deprivation are relatively small, other than the overwhelming sleepiness, and complete recovery occurs quickly, with only one or two nights of extended sleep.

But what about the effects of chronic total sleep deprivation in humans? The question seems too dangerous to ask. In some experiments done in Italy in the 1890s, dogs were kept awake as long as twenty-one days. Some of them died before they got that far. In more recent experiments with rats, the animals died after ten to thirty days of sleep deprivation (Rechtschaffen et al. 1983). Prolonged total sleep deprivation is very stressful, too stressful to test in humans.

THE FUNCTION OF REM SLEEP

The discovery of different physiological sleep stages led to the question of whether the different stages have special functions. REM sleep is of particular interest, because of its association with dreaming and the paradoxical pattern of physiological responses that are similar to the waking state while the person is behaviorally asleep. Researchers have attempted to discover the function of REM sleep by selectively depriving subjects of REM sleep, while allowing them to sleep undisturbed in NREM stages.

The dreaming hypothesis.   One hypothesis about the function of REM sleep is that its main purpose is to enable people to dream. This idea followed from the early observation of a strong correlation between REM sleep and dreaming, and from Freud's idea that dreaming serves a valuable psychological function of allowing harmless expression of powerful instinctive drives. Thus, some of the earliest research on REM deprivation was conceived as a study of the effects of dream deprivation (Dement 1960). However, we now know that it is misleading to assume that REM deprivation is equivalent to dream deprivation, for two reasons: (1) Dreaming occurs during NREM sleep, as well as during REM sleep (more on this in the next chapter). Thus, selectively depriving people of REM sleep does not necessarily deprive them of all dreaming. (2) REM sleep is a complex physiological state, and it is unparsimonious to assume that effects of REM sleep deprivation are a result of dream deprivation. Physiological or psychological effects of REM deprivation are more likely to be due to disruption of physiological processes that are unique to REM sleep. With these caveats in mind, let us consider the effects of REM sleep deprivation.

Effects of REM Sleep Deprivation in Humans

The REM sleep drive.   Though the function of REM sleep is still a matter of controversy, REM deprivation studies indicate that there is a physiologically based motive, or drive, for REM-state sleep. In Dement's (1960) pioneering study of REM deprivation, the experimental procedure involved three phases: baseline, REM deprivation, and recovery. The baseline phase involved several nights of sleeping in the laboratory undisturbed, but with the usual physiological monitoring hookups. In the REM deprivation phase the sleepers were awakened each time the polygraph record showed that they had entered the REM sleep state. They were forced to stay awake for a few minutes before returning to sleep. Further, subjects were told not to sleep during the daytime, in order to be sure that they did not catch up on REM sleep during the daytime. Then, after four or five nights of REM deprivation, the subjects were allowed to sleep undisturbed for several recovery nights. Finally, as a control procedure the subjects were awakened during NREM sleep for several nights (with the number of awakenings matching the number that had occurred during REM deprivation), followed by more recovery nights.

Two aspects of Dement's results indicated a motive for REM sleep. (1) *REM pressure*: The number of REM onsets increased, as if the sleeper was trying to get into REM sleep. Whereas REM onsets occur four or five times per night in undisturbed sleep, they occurred an average of eleven times on the first REM deprivation night, and increased to twenty-three times by the last deprivation night. Sometimes the experimenters had to awaken a subject every five or ten minutes to prevent REM sleep. (2) *REM rebound*: On the first recovery night, with undisturbed sleep, the amount of REM sleep was greater than on baseline nights (30 percent versus 19 percent REM, respectively). Other researchers have confirmed Dement's results, and it has also been found that the amount of time from sleep onset to the first REM period decreases on successive nights of REM deprivation.

Behavioral effects of REM deprivation.   Dement's study supported the Freudian prediction, insofar as his results suggested that short-term REM deprivation caused some short-term psychological disturbances, including "anxiety, irritability, and difficulty in concentrating." One of the eight subjects quit the study "in an apparent panic" in the middle of the REM deprivation procedure, while two other subjects insisted on stopping REM deprivation one night short of the goal of five nights. Also, five subjects developed a marked increase in appetite during the REM deprivation period. However, all of these psychological disturbances disappeared as soon as the REM deprivation phase was over and the subjects were allowed to sleep undisturbed. And none of these disturbances occurred during the control phase, in which awakenings occurred during NREM instead of REM. Although none of the psychological effects of short-term REM deprivation were catastrophic, Dement speculated "It is possible that if the dream suppression were carried on long enough, a serious disruption of the personality would result" (1960, p. 1707).

Psychoanalysts were thrilled by Dement's findings, since they seemed to confirm the Freudian theory that dreaming is critical to maintaining mental health. Dement's findings were discussed in popular magazine articles and introductory psychology textbooks, often with exaggerations. However, subsequent research has usually failed to replicate Dement's findings of psychological disturbances. In most cases, assuming that the subjects do not experience any significant loss of total sleep time, selective REM deprivation does not have any clear-cut negative psychological effects. Some of the studies can be criticized on methodological grounds, such as failure to use NREM control awakenings, failure to used double-blind control procedures, failure

to use an adequate number of subjects, and the use of anecdotal report
rather than systematic psychological measurements (Ellman et al. 1978
However, the failure of REM deprivation to produce consistent psychologi
cal disruptions seems to go beyond methodological problems. One wonder
whether Dement's original results might have been affected by negative ex
pectancies on the part of the subjects. It has been shown that negative expec
tancies can produce unpleasant results in sensory deprivation experiment
(Orne & Scheibe 1964), and the same problem might occur in REM depriva
tion experiments if the possibility of unpleasant experiences was somehov
to be subtly communicated to the research subjects.

If there is a motivation for dreaming, then one might predict that REM
deprivation would produce an overflow of dreamlike thinking into the wak
ing state, producing an excess of vivid, fantastic daydreaming, and perhap
even waking hallucinations. However, this prediction has not generally beer
supported by research. As Hoyt and Singer (1978) pointed out, waking life i
characterized by frequent daydreaming in most people, and in some peopl
daydreams may be quite vivid and fantastic, even without prior REM depri
vation. There is an increasing realization that the psychological effects o
REM deprivation are likely to depend importantly on the personality charac
teristics of the individual, though unraveling the relationships is an enor
mously complex process (Cohen 1979a).

If REM deprivation has any consistent psychological effect at all, on
might expect to find it within sleep itself. For example, perhaps the "dream
iness" of NREM mentation would increase during REM deprivation. Or per
haps some qualitative aspects of REM dreaming would be intensified or
REM recovery nights. However, neither of these predictions was supportec
by the results of a careful experiment by Arkin et al. (1978).

In conclusion, researchers have looked for a variety of emotional anc
cognitive effects of REM deprivation, with inconsistent and largely negative
results (see reviews by Arkin et al. 1978; Cohen 1979a; Ellman et al. 1978
Hoyt & Singer 1978; Vogel 1975). Thus, there is no clear evidence that REM
dreaming (or REM sleep) is specifically necessary for the mental health o
adults. (This is not to deny that some form of sleep is important for physica
and mental health.) The idea that the function of REM sleep is to enable
people to dream appears to be discredited. Dreaming may be a by-product o
REM sleep, rather than a specific adaptive function of REM sleep (Hobson &
McCarley 1977).

Ideas About the Function of REM Sleep

Aside from the hypothesis that the function of REM sleep is to enable
people to dream, most speculations about the function of REM sleep have
had a neurophysiological orientation (Cohen 1979a).

The CNS development hypothesis.   Observing that both the percent of
sleep time spent in REM state and the total daily amount of REM drop pro
gressively and substantially during the first four years of life, Roffwarg et al
(1966) suggested that REM sleep may be critical for the maturation of the
central nervous system (CNS). A related, but narrower, idea is that REM sleep

is critical for the maturation of the oculomotor (eye movement) system. It seems impossible to test these ideas experimentally, even in animals, since it would be impossible to separate effects of the stress of repeated REM awakenings from effects of REM deprivation *per se*. Recent research indicates that protein synthesis in the brain increases during REM sleep, a finding that is consistent with the CNS development hypothesis. However, the functional significance of this finding is uncertain, since in the absence of information about the rate of protein breakdown during REM we do not know whether there is any net gain in brain protein during REM sleep (Horne & McGrath 1984). Of course, changes in protein "turnover" might be important, even without any net gain in protein.

The memory consolidation hypothesis.

Currently the most influential idea about the function of REM sleep is that it promotes the physiological processes involved in consolidating long-term memories. Several experiments with animals have suggested that REM sleep deprivation interferes with memory of recent learning experiences. The research on humans is less clear, though largely negative. Perhaps REM is unnecessary for simple learning in humans, but it may be more important for memory of more complicated material; there is not enough evidence for firm conclusions on this point. Changes in protein synthesis, RNA turnover, and neurotransmitter production during REM are potentially relevant, though their functional significance cannot yet be determined. Two major reviews of the literature have concluded that the evidence offers some support for the consolidation hypothesis, without being sufficient to prove it (Horne & McGrath 1984; McGrath & Cohen 1978). REM sleep may facilitate memory consolidation, but REM is not strictly necessary for all consolidation.

Crick and Mitchison (1983, 1986) proposed that the function of REM sleep is to promote forgetting, not memory. They noted that when computer models of neural networks are overloaded with too much information they can "freeze up" and become dysfunctional. Random inputs can unfreeze the network, making it functional again. By analogy, they suggested that the brain's information processing efficiency may be reduced due to "parasitic modes" of useless memories. Random neurophysiological events during REM sleep may serve to remove the parasitic modes, thus restoring the brain's efficiency. Thus, REM sleep supports a "reverse learning mechanism. . . . We dream in order to forget" (1983, p. 112). In particular, "unconscious dreams"—dreams that we can never recall—are side effects of the reverse learning (information-dumping) process. Also, this process may account for some of the bizarre features of dreams that we do recall, such as condensation, in which dreams seem incoherent because parts of the story have been left out. Crick and Mitchison admit that there is no obvious way to test their hypothesis, aside from computer models of the brain's neural network. However, it should be noted that the reverse learning hypothesis is not entirely incompatible with the memory consolidation hypothesis, since the elimination of trivial memories may allow more important memory traces to be strengthened (Anch et al. 1988).

Individual differences.   David Cohen (1979a) reviewed these and other ideas about the function of REM and NREM sleep in considerable detail. He argued that the mysteries of REM sleep will be unraveled only when researchers start to pay more attention to the interaction between sleep variables and individual difference variables, such as age, gender, temperament, and cognitive style. The issue of individual differences raises the problem to a level of complexity that is beyond the scope of this book, but it points out one reason why there are no easy answers to the question of the function of REM sleep.

Differential functions of REM versus NREM sleep.   REM sleep is common in mammals, but rare or absent in reptiles. The evidence from living animal species suggests that NREM sleep evolved earlier than REM sleep (Cohen 1979a). This conclusion is admittedly speculative, since it is not possible to measure brain waves in fossils. In any case, given that we have two major sleep states, what might be their different functions?

Ernest Hartmann (1973) proposed that the primary function of REM sleep is brain restoration and growth, whereas NREM sleep is more concerned with vegetative processes and somatic (body) restoration and growth. A corollary of Hartmann's theory is that a need for REM sleep is experienced as mental fatigue, whereas a need for NREM sleep is experienced as physical fatigue. Mental fatigue is associated with dysphoria, strain, tension, and "regressive" behavior, whereas physical fatigue is a more pleasant condition, without the neurotic-like features of mental fatigue. There is some evidence that is consistent with Hartmann's hypothesis, though not conclusive (see Cohen 1979a).

Studies of selective NREM Stage-4 deprivation indicate a drive for Stage 4, with Stage 4 pressure and rebound effects even greater than those following REM deprivation (Webb 1969). Some evidence tentatively supports the notion of a relationship between NREM and somatic restoration (Cohen 1979a). Circumcision and short-term starvation are associated with increased delta sleep. Also, some studies have suggested that physical exercise is followed by increased Stage-4 sleep, though the evidence is inconsistent. Following total sleep deprivation, Stage-4 rebound takes precedence over REM rebound. However, research on the effects of both selective and total sleep deprivation leads to the conclusion that neither sleep state is absolutely necessary for any important physiological process. Rather, certain physiological processes may be facilitated in certain sleep states. We are left with a great unsolved scientific mystery: although partial sleep deprivation produces discomfort and fatigue in humans, and total sleep deprivation produces death in animals, no specific, vitally necessary function of either REM or Stage-4 sleep has yet been identified.

SLEEP DISORDERS

In recent years the health and safety implications of sleep disorders have been increasingly recognized, and centers for diagnosing and treating sleep disorders have opened up across the country. A manual of criteria for diagnosing sleep disorders has been published by the Association of Sleep Disorders Centers (ASDC 1979).

Sleep disorders are classified in three major categories (Webb 1975): (1) *primary sleep disorders*, in which sleep intrudes on the waking state (termed DOES, disorders of excessive somnolence, in the ASDC manual); (2) *parasomnias*, in which waking-like behaviors intrude on sleep (termed DSWS, disorders of the sleep-wake schedule, in the ASDC manual); and (3) *insomnias*, in which the onset or maintenance of sleep is disrupted (termed DIMS, disorders of initiating and maintaining sleep, in the ASDC manual; Anch et al. 1988).

Primary Sleep Disorders

Narcolepsy. Narcolepsy is a chronic, lifelong condition characterized by excessive daytime sleepiness and the occurrence of REM at sleep onset (see Figure 10.6). "Sleep attacks," brief uncontrollable periods of sleep, may occur several times each day. The attacks, which usually last from about two to fifteen minutes, may occur at any time when the narcoleptic is going about his or her usual daily business. Sometimes they are brought on by strong emotional arousal; narcoleptics sometimes fall asleep while making love. Approximately five people in a thousand suffer from narcolepsy, which is known to have a genetic basis. In the large majority of cases the narcoleptic syndrome first appears between the ages of fifteen and twenty-five years.

There are four characteristic clinical symptoms of narcolepsy, called the "narcoleptic tetrad" (Anch et al. 1988; Webb 1975). (1) *Excessive daytime sleepiness.* The narcoleptic is chronically sleepy, even after a normal night of sleep. Narcoleptics tend to have recurrent "microsleep" episodes during the daytime. During these episodes, which last from five to fifteen seconds, the EEG pattern indicates bursts of theta waves or Stage 1 NREM. Without overtly napping, the individual has a glassy-eyed look, and perceptual processing and thinking decrease. The frequency of microsleep episodes tends to increase unless the narcoleptic takes a nap. When allowed to nap during the day the narcoleptic typically falls asleep in less than five minutes, compared to ten to fifteen minutes for the normal adult. However, chronic daytime sleepiness by itself is not an indicator of narcolepsy. Other symptoms must also be present, especially the occurrence of REM state at sleep onset during daytime naps; in normal adults brief daytime naps involve NREM sleep stages. When they go to sleep at night, narcoleptics usually go directly into REM stage, whereas the first REM period is delayed at least sixty minutes in normal adults. (2) *Cataplexy*, which involves muscular weakness, and may range from a feeling of tiredness to complete inability to move. It occurs in about 70 percent of the daytime sleep episodes. Cataplexy often occurs without the person actually falling asleep. It may be brought on by high emotional arousal. For example, a narcoleptic hunter, presented with an exciting opportunity to shoot a deer, may drop his gun and fall to the ground without necessarily losing consciousness. Cataplexy and extreme daytime sleepiness are the most frequent symptoms of narcolepsy. (3) *Sleep paralysis*, which involves a total paralysis during the time that the narcoleptic is falling asleep, and sometimes upon awakening from sleep. The muscular paralysis charac-

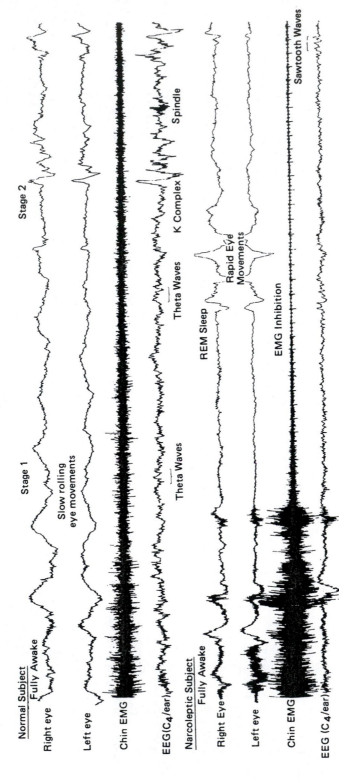

FIGURE 10.6. Polygraph recordings showing the transition from wakefulness to sleep in a normal subject and a narcoleptic subject. The normal subject moves from the waking state to Stage 1 NREM to Stage 2 NREM. Note the EEG K-complex and spindle in Stage 2. The narcoleptic subject moves from waking directly to REM stage sleep. Note that in REM stage the right and left eye movements are better synchronized (conjugate) with each other than in NREM sleep. Also note the deep muscle relaxation (EMG) in REM stage. [From Hauri, P. (1982). *The Sleep Disorders*. Kalamazoo, MI: The Upjohn Company. Reprinted with permission of the publisher.]

teristic of REM stage can occur before entering full REM sleep and continue after awakening. (4) *Hypnagogic hallucinations*, which involve vivid visual or auditory images—sometimes frightening—that occur at the beginning of the sleep attack, before the narcoleptic is fully asleep. Hypnagogic hallucinations also occur in normal people, but in narcoleptics they seem to be particularly frequent and frightening, perhaps due to their appearance along with sleep paralysis.

Narcolepsy has been characterized as a disorder of REM sleep, in which REM intrudes into the waking state. Sleep attacks can be dangerous, as when a person is driving a car, and they disrupt intellectual and social functioning. There is no cure for narcolepsy. The symptoms can be managed by careful planning of one's social and work schedule to allow for frequent planned daytime naps, and by stimulant drugs (Anch et al. 1988).

Hypersomnia. Hypersomnia involves excessive sleep, beyond twelve hours per day. A variety of different conditions may be related to hypersomnia in different patients. Often there is a brain disorder. Some cases are related to insomnia due to *sleep apnea*, which is disrupted sleep caused by a breathing disorder. Cases of "functional" hypersomnia (without a clear organic basis) are relatively rare. Such cases have distinctly different EEG profiles, compared to narcoleptics. Hypersomniacs spend a relatively large amount of time in Stages 3 and 4 NREM, and relatively little in REM. They may spend a lot of time napping, but their naps are not refreshing, and they have difficulty waking up afterward (Webb 1975).

Parasomnias

Parasomnias involve intrusions of certain wake-like behaviors into the sleeping state. These include sleepwalking, sleeptalking, enuresis (bed-wetting), and night terrors. The parasomnias often occur together in various combinations in the same patient. They all seem to involve episodic disturbances of NREM sleep. The parasomnias occur more often in males than in females, and there appears to be a genetic basis, in that they tend to run in families (Anders et al. 1980).

Night terrors.   Night terrors (*pavor nocturnus*, or sleep terrors) are panic reactions associated with sudden, spontaneous arousal from sleep, usually during NREM Stage 3 or 4. Night terrors rarely occur in adults. They occur most commonly in children three to five years old (affecting about 2 to 5 percent of this age group; Anders et al. 1980), and they may continue into early adolescence. The sleeping child sits up suddenly and screams. There are signs of intense emotional arousal suggesting panic: exceptionally rapid heartbeat, rapid breathing, perspiration, and a wide-eyed stare. Full waking consciousness may not occur until several minutes after the initial arousal. Parental efforts to comfort the child have no effect. The child usually has no recollection of any dream. When imagery is recalled, it is more likely to be a single frightening image, rather than a story-like dream. The whole episode usually lasts only a minute or two, after which the child goes back to sleep. The episode usually will not be recalled by the child in the morning.

Sleep laboratory studies have shown that night terrors occur during the first third of the night, usually about forty to sixty minutes after falling asleep. The large majority of cases involve sudden arousal from NREM Stage 3 or 4, usually from the first ones of the night. It is not uncommon for the night terror to be accompanied by sleepwalking or sleeptalking or enuresis, though these events can also occur independently of night terror.

Night terrors are more likely to occur during periods of daytime stress or fatigue. For example, the stress of moving to a new city, or starting school, may bring on night terrors in susceptible children. Sleep loss also aggravates night terrors (Anch et al. 1988). They may have an organic basis, such as neurological immaturity (Anders et al. 1980) or illness with a high fever (Kales, Kales et al. 1980).

Night terrors differ from nightmares in several ways (Hartmann 1984). *Nightmares* are emotionally disturbing dreams that typically occur in REM sleep, rather than NREM. People usually recall their nightmares vividly, whereas night terrors usually have no associated dream imagery (at least in children). Nightmares usually occur in the latter part of a typical night of sleep (six to eight hours), when REM sleep is most intense, whereas night terrors usually occur before the first REM period of the night. Nightmares may be accompanied by physiological signs of emotional arousal, though arousal is not as intense, nor is its onset so rapid, as in night terrors. Nightmares are more likely to emerge during ages seven to ten, whereas three to five is the age for most night terrors. Occasional nightmares are not unusual, but recurrent nightmares may reflect stress or anxiety that has a basis in daytime experience. Night terrors, on the other hand, are more distinctly an abnormality of sleep.

Broughton (1966) suggested that night terrors are disorders of arousal. That is, they stem from a rapid transition from Stage 4 NREM to waking. He suggested that in those relatively rare cases (in children) in which dreamlike images are associated with the terror, the images are in response to the terror, rather than the cause of the terror. Fisher et al. (1974), on the other hand, finding rather frequent frightening dream images associated with night terrors in adults, suggested that night terrors may be caused by frightening NREM dream images. The suddenness of the physiological arousal in night terrors (as contrasted with its more gradual buildup in REM nightmares) suggests that a sudden, unexpected and frightening dream image might elicit the terror reaction. (Fisher et al. observed that night terrors could sometimes be elicited also by a sudden, loud buzzer. External stimuli might account for some cases of night terrors in children.)

Fisher et al. (1974) found night terrors in adults to be associated with daytime stress and psychopathology, which is not necessarily the case in children. As present, we know only that frightening dream images are sometimes associated with night terrors in adults, though rarely in children. The direction of causality is uncertain. It may be that the causal factors in night terrors are different for children and adults.

Sleepwalking. Sleepwalking (*somnambulism*) occurs in Stage 4 sleep. Episodes may last from a few seconds to a few minutes. Sleepwalking is not the acting out of a dream. If you awaken a sleepwalker he or she will probably be confused, with no dream recall. Unless fully awakened during the episode, the sleepwalker will be amnesic for the event in the morning. The sleepwalker is relatively nonreactive to the environment. Behaviors during sleepwalking are typically habitual or "automatic" ones. Simple actions are most common, such as briefly standing up, then going back to bed. Somewhat more complex actions such as getting partially dressed, or going to the bathroom (perhaps mistaking the closet for the bathroom) also occur. Rarely, complex episodes occur, such as going downstairs and rearranging objects (Anch et al. 1988).

Sleepwalking is most common in children and adolescents, and is relatively rare in adults. Many people may know of one or two instances in which they have sleepwalked, without it being a common occurrence for them. Sleepwalking is sometimes, but not always, associated with night terrors. Sleepwalking in adults is associated with severe life stress and psychopathology (Kales, Soldatos, et al. 1980). Contrary to a popular myth, sleepwalking is potentially dangerous. To protect sleepwalking children, parents should lock doors and use stair gates. There is no danger in awakening a sleepwalker, though he or she is likely to be confused, and may need reassurance.

Sleeptalking.   Sleeptalking (*somniloquy*) may not be an every-night occurrence for most people, but it is not rare (Arkin 1978). Most people know of at least one instance when they have talked in their sleep, but the actual frequencies can never be known with much confidence, since people do not recall their own sleeptalking episodes; rather, their knowledge of their own sleeptalking depends on what other people have observed and reported to them.

Sleeptalking is not strongly associated with any particular sleep stage; it can occur in either REM or NREM, and it occurs more often in NREM because NREM takes up about 80 percent of a normal night's sleep. Sleep utterances are often associated with body movements. Some cases of sleeptalking occur at times when the EEG shows alpha waves suggesting wakefulness, though the person is behaviorally asleep in the sense of being nonreactive to the environment. Though sleeptalking sometimes is associated with psychopathology, it occurs so often in normal people that it is not, in itself, considered to be a sign of psychopathology. Sleeptalking sometimes occurs during night terrors (Kahn et al. 1978), but most cases have nothing to do with night terrors.

What is sleeptalking like? Arthur Arkin (1978), who has observed many sleeptalkers in the laboratory, said that it is not possible to give a brief description of sleep utterances because they show almost as much variability as those of wakefulness.

Although the majority of sleep speeches contain at least a few words, some consist of only one, such as "good," "no," "okay," "yes," or "Mm-hm." Others are of paragraph length, occasionally in excess of one hundred words. Most speeches last a few seconds or less, but longer ones may continue for a minute or more. The range of clarity extends from unintelligible mumbles to crystal-clear words. . . . Often, speeches contain silent pauses, in which case the context suggests sleep dialogues with hallucinated partners, sometimes resembling one side of a telephone conversation. Another frequent occurrence is sudden interruption of a speech in the middle, followed by sustained silence or an apparently meaningless mumbled petering out. The hearer is left with a feeling that a thought has been fragmented or left incomplete (Arkin 1978, p. 521).

What about the structural features of sleep speech? Sleep utterances are somewhat more likely to have correct syntax (word sequencing) and inflection when they occur during REM. When markedly abnormal utterances occur, they typically occur during NREM. Such abnormal speech can range from mildly distorted to sheer gibberish, in which clang (rhyme) associations and recurrent utterances are prominent, with occasional neologisms (novel, nonsense words; see Arkin 1978).

As for the content of sleep speech, Arkin (1978) was struck by the rarity of secrets. Though the telling of secrets during somniloqy is a popular device in literature (for example, in Shakespeare's *Othello*), in actuality it hardly ever happens. Nor do obscene utterances occur very commonly in sleep speech. Arkin reported that:

> the majority of intelligible, clear utterances sound like fragments of overheard, unremarkable daily conversations. . . . [Also, some cases] resemble words and sounds one utters in solitude while awake. Exclamatory words, phrases, sounds of surprise, curiosity, pleasure, agreement, and so on are common. In addition, one encounters utterances resembling wakeful vocal self-priming or stimulation as if someone were following a recipe or other stepwise task, and wondering aloud what to do next (Arkin 1978, p. 522).

Sleep utterances can suggest a wide range of emotions, from positive to negative. When sleeptalking occurs during night terrors or nightmares, the utterances may show strong emotion, such as anxiety or panic. But in most cases sleep utterances are unemotional.

One of the most interesting questions about sleeptalking concerns the degree of *concordance* between the content of sleep speech and the content of dream or thought reports obtained by waking the subject shortly after the speech episode. Arkin (1978) examined content concordance in 166 sleep speech episodes, obtained from 28 adult chronic sleeptalkers in the laboratory. When sleep utterances occurred, they were more likely to be followed by mentation reports for REM (96%) than for NREM Stage 2 (79%) or Stages 3–4 (62%). In cases in which mentation was recalled, high levels of content concordance were more common for REM periods (54% concordance) than for NREM Stage 2 (26%) or Stages 3–4 (17%). Only 15 percent of all sleep utterances occurred in REM.

Though concordances occurred fairly often, especially in REM, the sleep speech was not a detailed description of the dream events. Early hopes by researchers that sleeptalking would be a way to obtain "play-by-play" commentary on dream action have met with disappointment. In commenting on his sleeptalking data, Arkin (1978) suggested that failures of concordance may indicate "multiple dissociated concurrent streams of mentation." That is, the speech control mechanism may sometimes be under the control of a stream of thought that is dissociated (disconnected) from dream consciousness. Dream consciousness and another stream of consciousness may sometimes occur independently, in parallel, with only the latter controlling sleep utterances, and only the former controlling dream reports upon awakening.

Insomnia

People may complain of insomnia when they believe that they are having problems with any of four different aspects of sleep: (1) trouble falling asleep, or technically, long sleep onset latency; (2) frequent awakenings during the night, after initially falling asleep; (3) early awakening from sleep, without being able to get back to sleep; and (4) light sleep. Surveys have shown that approximately 15 percent of adults are often troubled by insomnia, and another 30 percent say they sometimes have insomnia (Webb 1975).

Insomnia presents an important practical problem. Sleep difficulties may be a symptom of other psychological problems, such as depression. And sleep difficulties may themselves be a source of anxiety. Insomnia produces daytime sleepiness. People often feel that their work or study performance, or their interpersonal relationships, would be better if only they could sleep better. Even though occasional or mild insomnia may not cause any serious decrement in performance, people believe that it does, and the belief increases anxiety over insomnia (and the anxiety may, in turn, exacerbate the insomnia problem).

Diagnosing insomnia is not as clear-cut as you might think. There are wide individual variations in sleep parameters (such as sleep onset latency and frequency of nighttime awakenings) within the normal range. So clinicians have to use some arbitrary criteria in classifying patients' insomnia problems. Wisle B. Webb (1975) used the following criteria, based on EEG recordings during sleep: (1) sleep onset latency: over 30 minutes; (2) nighttime awakenings: five or more, or totaling over 30 minutes; (3) early termination: spontaneous termination before six hours have elapsed; (4) light sleep: an EEG record showing over 12 percent of Stage 1 NREM, or less than 3 to 5 percent Stage 4 NREM. About 95 percent of healthy adults from twenty to forty years of age would be defined as normal according to these criteria, whereas about 5 percent would be classified as having at least transient (short-term, temporary) insomnia.

Transient insomnia.   Transient insomnia, lasting one or a few nights, is common. Virtually everyone experiences it at one time or another. Transient insomnia is a reaction to a temporary situation, such as anxiety over an upcoming exam or job interview, or sleeping in a strange place. (Transient insomnia is fairly common the first night subjects sleep in a sleep laboratory or clinic.) Transient insomnia does not require treatment—it clears up spontaneously when the source of anxiety is resolved, or when you adapt to the new situation.

Chronic insomnia.   Chronic insomnia—insomnia that persists for several months—can have a variety of causes, and it requires different treatments depending on the cause. Most cases of chronic insomnia fall into one of five categories (Coleman 1986).

(1) *Psychiatric insomnia* is the most common category (35 percent). In

these patients insomnia is a symptom of some more comprehensive psychological disorder, the most common being depression and anxiety. Thus, the main concern is treating the psychological disorder.

(2) In *stress-conditioned insomnia* (about 15 percent of cases) the patient's main problem is anxiety over whether he or she will sleep well and be able to function well the next day. Such a condition begins with what would ordinarily have been a transient insomnia in reaction to a stressful life event, but the insomnia becomes chronic because the patient worries that poor sleep will lead to poor performance the next day. Treatment requires a program of counterconditioning to establish better knowledge, attitudes, and habits regarding sleep.

(3) *Physiological insomnia* (30 percent) is a broad category that encompasses several types of physiological causes of insomnia. The most dramatic is *sleep apnea*, in which people stop breathing when they fall asleep. Loud snoring is a major preliminary diagnostic symptom of apnea. Snoring is caused by a progressive narrowing of the airway as throat muscles relax during sleep, or by an anatomical abnormality. When the airway is completely closed breathing stops. Subsequent buildup of carbon dioxide in the bloodstream triggers a brief awakening, when breathing starts again, until sleep resumes. Thus, such patients go though repeated cycles of brief sleep periods (about 30–60 seconds) and brief waking periods (5–10 seconds). In the morning they typically do not recall the brief nighttime awakenings. Since apneics sleep poorly, they often suffer from severe daytime sleepiness. Some clinicians believe that apnea is a cause of Sudden Infant Death Syndrome (SIDS), and death during sleep in the elderly. The standard treatment is tracheotomy, a surgical procedure that involves making a small hole in the trachea. At night the patient puts a tube in the hole, through which he or she can breathe while asleep.

Another group of patients who experience nighttime awakenings are those who make periodic reflexive leg jerks during sleep, which may occur as often as every 30 seconds in some patients. Various medical disorders, such as arthritis and biological rhythm disorders, also cause frequent nighttime awakenings.

(4) *Poor sleep habits* are characteristic of 10 to 15 percent of chronic insomniacs. They can be a part of other disorders, and also a problem in their own right. Excessive or inappropriate use of drugs, such as alcohol, caffeine, and sleeping pills, can seriously disrupt sleep cycles. For example, coffee after 6 p.m. may cause delayed sleep onset at 11 p.m. Alcohol does not interfere with sleep onset, but it may cause frequent awakenings or early termination of sleep. Irregular sleep schedules are another poor sleep habit associated with insomnia; a regular bedtime and awakening time are the solution. Insomnia is really a twenty-four-hour problem. Your habits during the day will affect how you sleep at night.

(5) *Pseudo-insomnia.* In this category (about 10 percent of sleep patients) are those puzzling cases in which the patient's complaint of chronic insomnia is not supported by the objective EEG records obtained in the laboratory or sleep clinic. When confronted with the objective evidence, some patients are relieved to find that they do not really have insomnia. Others are incredulous and insist that they had little or no sleep and that the EEG records are

in error; some patients have a paranoid reaction. Coleman (1986) suggested that "In some cases, our measuring techniques may not be sufficiently sensitive to detect small physiological arousals or active thinking, either or both of which may cause the perception of no sleep at all." Perhaps in some cases the subjects dreamed that they were awake. These patients had presleep anxiety about being able to sleep successfully, and these presleep thoughts may have affected their subsequent sleep mentation.

Drugs and Sleep

When people suffer from insomnia, doctors sometimes prescribe sleep-inducing drugs, termed *sedatives* or *hypnotics* ("sleeping pills," such as barbiturates). Hypnotics have disadvantages in that they may be addictive, they tend to reduce subsequent daytime alertness, and they suppress REM sleep. Withdrawal from hypnotics leads to REM rebound, sometimes with nightmares, and irregular sleep patterns characterized by frequent awakenings (Anch et al. 1988; Webb 1975). Drugs taken for other reasons may reduce alertness as a side effect (for example, antihistamines [used in allergy and decongestant medicines], tranquilizers, alcohol).

Stimulants (such as caffeine and amphetamine) are intended to counteract sleep and maintain alertness. Caffeine is the most widely used stimulant in the world (Schlaadt & Shannon 1986). It is found in coffee, tea, cola soft drinks (and also some noncola soft drinks—read the label), chocolate, and in some nonprescription drugs (such as *No-Doz*). As a method of maintaining alertness, caffeine is certainly safer than amphetamines. But caffeine has its drawbacks. People develop a tolerance to caffeine. As a general rule, the more often you drink coffee on a habitual, daily basis, the less effective a single cup will be in keeping you awake and alert. Thus, in order to produce the same stimulating effect, the dosage must be steadily increased. High doses cause "jitters" and a need for frequent urination. And caffeine is physiologically addicting. Coffee and cola drink addicts crave the drug, and when they try to quit they suffer withdrawal symptoms, such as headaches, nervousness, and irritability. The optimal way to use caffeine is to use it occasionally, when you really need it. Do not use it on a daily basis. That way you will get the maximum benefit from a single dose, but you will not suffer the disadvantages of addiction.

It is best to avoid using drugs to regulate the sleep-wake cycle. Some people get into a vicious circle when they use sleeping pills to help them sleep at night, then they feel sleepy the next day so they use stimulants to stay awake, and consequently they have trouble falling asleep that night so they take more sleeping pills, and so on and on until they develop serious drug dependencies.

SUMMARY

Sleep is characterized by reduced awareness of the external environment, reduced muscle activity and voluntary action, and reduced self awareness, as well as changes in brain waves and other physiological measures. Human sleep is not a uniform state. Rather, it involves several physiologically dis-tinctive stages that recur in a cyclic manner. The waking state, REM (rapid eye movement) sleep state, and non-REM (NREM) sleep state are distin-guished by their unique patterns of three physiological indicators: (1) brain waves (faster and lower amplitude in waking and REM than in NREM); (2) eye movements (more frequent in waking and REM than NREM); and (3) chin muscle tension (lower in REM than in waking and NREM). NREM may be subdivided into Stages 1, 2, 3, and 4, characterized by increasingly slower and higher amplitude brain waves. REM periods of several minutes' dura-tion recur on a cycle of about 90 minutes; successive REM periods are in-creasingly longer in duration. Vivid dreaming occurs during REM sleep.

The function of sleep is generally assumed to be physiological restora-tion. Animals totally deprived of sleep for several days or weeks have died. Yet specific, vitally necessary physiological processes that occur only in sleep have not yet been identified. In humans, sleep deprivation, either partial or total, is characterized by feelings of fatigue and irritability, and by decreased performance on tasks that require sustained attention. However, there is lit-tle or no effect on performance of brief tasks when their timing is under the subject's control and performance motivation is high. There have been sev-eral hypotheses about the functions of REM and slow-wave sleep, but none has been clearly confirmed. Selective REM deprivation in humans results in REM persistence (increased frequency of REM onset) and REM rebound (in-creased total REM duration on recovery nights), which suggest that there is some need or motive for REM sleep. However, no changes in personality or performance have been identified that can be attributed to REM deprivation per se.

Sleep disorders can be classified in three categories: (1) primary sleep disorders, in which sleep intrudes on the waking state; (2) parasomnias, in which waking-like behaviors intrude on sleep; and (3) insomnias, in which the onset or maintenance of sleep is disrupted. The major primary sleep dis-order is narcolepsy, characterized by excessive daytime sleepiness and microsleeps, REM at sleep onset during daytime naps, cataplexy (muscular weakness), sleep paralysis, and hypnagogic hallucinations. Parasomnias in-clude sleepwalking, night terrors, and enuresis, all of which tend to occur during Stages 3 and 4. Sleeptalking can occur in any sleep stage; its content is sometimes related to dream images, though it does not provide a detailed description of ongoing dream action. Insomnia may be associated with psy-chological stress, psychopathology (especially depression and anxiety), phys-iological disorders (such as sleep apnea, in which breathing stops during sleep), poor sleep habits (irregular sleep-wake patterns), and misuse of drugs that affect the sleep cycle.

ENDNOTES

[1]See Hobson (1988), *The Dreaming Brain*, for an interesting description of the history of re-search on sleep, dreaming, and the brain processes involved in them.

[2]A note on terminology: Alternate names for REM sleep, used by some writers, are: "Stage 1 REM", "ascending Stage 1" (Stage 1 NREM is "descending Stage 1"), and "paradoxical" sleep

(PS). REM is paradoxical because the brain waves, eye movements, and autonomic arousal response-measures give the appearance that the subject is awake, whereas in fact he or she is sound asleep. REM has also been called "D-state," referring to both desynchronized brain waves and dreaming, in contrast to "S-state" sleep for NREM sleep, referring to the more synchronized brain waves (Hobson & McCarley 1977). Stages 3 and 4 are sometimes called "slow wave" sleep (SWS). The transition period from waking to sleeping is called the "hypnagogic state" (to be discussed in Chapter 11).

[3]Some studies have found body movements to be more frequent in Stage 4 than in REM. The discrepancies in results between different studies probably have to do with different methods of measuring body movements (Anch et al. 1988).

chapter 11 ··

Dreaming I: Phenomenology and Influences on Contents

For thousands of years, probably well before recorded history, people have been fascinated by dreams. The emotional impact of dreams can be so powerful that it seems unlikely that they are a completely accidental or trivial phenomenon. The attribution of meaning to dreams has taken different forms in different times and different cultures. People in some cultures have believed that dreams are messages from the gods, and/or that they predict the future (Jaynes 1976; Van de Castle 1971). There are numerous dreams in the Bible, most of them of this type.[1] Some cultures have believed that the dream world is an alternative reality (Stewart 1972). In the modern Western world, psychoanalysts believe that dreams reveal profoundly important aspects of the dreamer's personality, and that dream analysis is a valuable psychotherapeutic technique.

Currently popular views about the meaning of dreams derive directly or indirectly from the psychoanalytic theory of Sigmund Freud, who published his fascinating book *The Interpretation of Dreams* in 1900. Freud characterized dreams as "the royal road to the unconscious." That is, he believed that the dynamic processes of the unconscious mind could be discovered through dream analysis. He distinguished between the *manifest* or *surface content* of a dream, which refers to the dream objects and events as directly experienced by the dreamer, and the *latent* or *hidden content*, which refers to the underlying ideas or wishes that are expressed symbolically in the surface content. He believed that *day residues*—perceptions and memories of waking life that appear in dreams—serve a symbolic function. In recent years some researchers with a cognitive-psychology orientation have become interested in dreams as a source of information about how the mind works, though their conclusions are quite different from those of Freud, as we will see in the next chapter (Foulkes 1985).

In the study of dreams it is important to bear in mind the distinction between the psychology of dreaming versus the psychology of dream interpretation (Jones 1970). The *psychology of dreaming* is concerned with the scientific investigation of issues such as the physiological correlates of dreaming, factors that influence the content and structure of dreams, dream recall, and the function of dreaming. *Dream interpretation*, on the other hand, is an attempt to discover the hidden meaning of dreams through the analysis of dream symbols.

Psychoanalysts believe that dream interpretation is a useful psychotherapy technique for revealing a patient's unconscious desires and conflicts. Whether dreams do, in fact, have any hidden meaning is a controversial issue. The major problem for theories of dream interpretation is that there is no way to determine empirically whether a particular dream interpretation is correct. Different psychoanalysts with different theoretical views will interpret the same dream in different ways. Thus, while dream interpretation may under some conditions be useful for psychotherapeutic purposes, it appears that dream interpretation is more an art than a science. In the chapters on dreaming I will be going into some detail on the psychology of dreaming, but I will have relatively little to say about dream interpretation.

In this chapter I will discuss research on the characteristics of typical REM dreams, NREM mental activity, and sleep-onset (hypnagogic) images. You will find that what you think of as "typical" dreams may not be so typical after all. I will compare home dreams versus laboratory dreams, and consider the question of why home dreams often seem to be more dramatic than those reported in sleep laboratory research. Then I will go into some detail on factors that influence the manifest contents of dreams, emphasizing the dreamer's personality (as in chronic nightmare sufferers), current personal concerns (such as health problems and divorce), and recent waking events. We will see that there is reason to believe that dreams often have some sort of associative or symbolic connection with current concerns and waking experiences, which can be discovered without going through psychoanalysis of deep hidden meanings. In the next chapter I will discuss theories of dream production and dream recall, and research that is particularly pertinent to the theories.

DEFINITION OF DREAM

All conscious mental events that occur during sleep are instances of *sleep mentation*. But not all instances of sleep mentation are dreams. The answers to a number of questions about dreams and the dreaming process depend upon how "dream" is defined. This definition is descriptive and consistent with popular usage, while avoiding heavily theoretical assumptions about the characteristics of dreams: A *dream* is a subjective experience, occurring during sleep, that involves (a) complex, organized mental images that (b) show temporal progression or change (Snyder 1970).

Several comments on this definition are in order. (1) By *mental image* I mean a quasi-perceptual conscious experience of an object or event that exists in the absence of its genuine perceptual counterpart. Although most dreams involve vivid visual images, I do not specify that dream images must be either visual or vivid, since there are individuals whose dreams are nonvisual, or visual but not vivid. Sleep mentation that does not involve any sort of images may be classified as *sleep thoughts*, not dreams. (2) The stipulation that dream images show temporal progression conveys the idea that dreams tell stories, or at least they are like scenes from a story. Dream images change over time. A report of an image that was static, like a snapshot, or that showed simple repetitive movement without true temporal progression or story development, would not qualify as a dream. Such static images are rare during sleep, though they often occur in the *hypnagogic* (presleep) state (to be discussed later in this chapter). (3) The definition says nothing about dreams being dramatic, bizarre, or emotional. As we will see, though some dreams have these characteristics, most do not; so these characteristics are not included in the definition of dream. (4) The definition says nothing about the delusional quality of dreams, the fact that our "dream world" usually seems to be real, while we are dreaming. As we will see, people sometimes know that they are dreaming while they are dreaming—an experience termed *lucid dreaming* (to be discussed in Chapter 13).

PHENOMENOLOGICAL CHARACTERISTICS OF REM DREAMS

What are the *phenomenological characteristics* of typical dreams, that is, the characteristics of dreams—their manifest contents—as they are experienced by dreamers? Are most dreams dramatic, emotional, and bizarre? How often do dreams tell plausible stories? Here we are concerned with *normative data*, the statistics from a large representative sample of the population.

Methods of Studying Dreams

The only way researchers can know about peoples' dreams is through their verbal introspective reports, and dream reports are subject to all of the limitations of introspective reports described earlier, such as forgetting, reconstruction errors, and verbal description difficulties (see Chapter 3). Occasionally dream diaries are supplemented by the individual's drawings (as in Hobson 1988), which can provide additional information but are nonetheless subject to the limitations of introspective reports.

There have been several attempts to collect normative data on dream contents using the *group questionnaire method* (Hall and Van de Castle 1966). Questionnaires are an efficient way to collect data from large numbers of people and to compare different groups, such as male versus female, or different cultural or socioeconomic or age groups. But questionnaire data are plagued by serious problems of forgetting and selective recall and reporting.

YOUR DREAM DIARY

You will get the most out of the chapters on dreaming if you can relate the information to your own dreams. In order to do this most effectively, you need to take a systematic approach to observing your dreams. I recommend that you keep a personal dream diary for at least three or four weeks.

The greatest problem in keeping a dream diary is that we often forget our dreams. *Interference* is probably the most important factor in dream forgetting. When we awaken from a dream, the dream is held in short-term memory. Short-term memory (STM) is particularly susceptible to interference from other thoughts and activities—this is true of all sorts of information in STM, not just dreams. The problem, then, is to transfer the dream information to long-term memory (LTM) before it is wiped out of STM by interference. The way to do it is by *rehearsal*.

When you awaken from a dream, the first thing you should do (after shutting off the alarm clock, if you used one) is to lie still and try to recall the dream in as much detail as possible. Do this before you try to write a description of the dream. Retell the dream events to yourself, trying to picture them in your mind as vividly as you can. Rehearse the full dream at least two times, and until you think that you have recalled all of the details that you can. Then write down a complete description of the dream. If, sometime later in the day, you recall additional details of the dream, record them as an "addendum" to the dream report; don't revise the original report, as it is uncertain whether the later-recalled details are as accurate as the original report. If you awaken during the night and recall a dream, you should rehearse and record it at that time, before going back to sleep; otherwise you probably will recall little or nothing about it in the morning.

When you write the dream description, try to be accurate. Do not try to make the dream report more orderly or logical or complete than what you really remember. You need to distinguish between what you really remember versus what you inferred, or what you assumed to have happened. (For example, you need to distinguish whether you clearly heard somebody say such and such in the dream, or whether in the dream you just knew what they were saying without really hearing it, or whether you inferred what was said after awakening.) In the initial report, just record what you are confident that you remember, and note where there are gaps in your memory—that is, points at which you believe that something happened in the dream, but you cannot recall what it was. Also, distinguish personal reflections on the dream that occurred during the dream itself from those that occurred after the awakening. (For example, during a dream you might talk to yourself about somebody's motives in doing something; keep this separate from speculations about motives made after you awaken.)

The third phase, after rehearsing the dream and then recording it, is to record your associations to the dream contents. The associations are critical if you are to attempt to interpret the dream. Are there any day residues in the dream? That is, do experiences of the preceding day appear in the dream, either directly or in some modified form? Do your current concerns, such as personal plans or problems, appear in the dream? Do you find any evidence for wish fulfillment in the dream? If you do not see any evidence of current concerns or wish fulfillment in the manifest content of the dream, could they be represented by some fairly straightforward dream symbolism? Keep in mind the fact that there are no

> hard and fast rules for dream interpretation. Most dreams are probably mean-
> ingless, though some may be meaningful. If there is any validity to an interpre-
> tation of supposed symbolic content in a dream, then the main way you will
> know it is if it "rings true" to you.

Clinical *case studies* may present dreams and the psychoanalyst's interpretation in great detail, but neither the dreamers nor their dreams are likely to
be typical. The *dream diary* method, when it is done systematically, may be an
improvement over the questionnaire and clinical case-study methods in
terms of better and less selective recall, more complete reporting, and better
representation of typical dreams and normal dreamers. However, the best
method is to collect dream reports under controlled conditions in a sleep
laboratory.

The problem with "home dream" reports using the diary method is
that they give us a biased sample of dreams. Modern sleep laboratory research tells us that we have several dreams each night, in several REM periods. Yet if we remember any dream at all in the morning, it is likely to be
from the last REM period of the night—the one from which we awakened.
Dreams from later REM periods tend to differ somewhat from those of earlier REM periods. As the night progresses and REM periods become longer,
dreams tend to become more vivid and intense, show more verbal activity
and better ego function, and be better recalled (Cohen 1979a; Schwartz et al.
1978). Furthermore, if dreams sometimes stir up emotional reactions sufficient to awaken us, then in home-dream diary-studies we will be likely to recall and report a disproportionately high number of dramatic and emotional dreams.

In order to get good normative data on typical dreams, we need to collect dream or sleep mentation reports throughout the night under controlled conditions. In the *laboratory arousal method*, EEG and other physiological measures are monitored while subjects sleep, and subjects are awakened
periodically from known sleep stages (either REM or NREM) and asked for
immediate reports of whatever was going through their mind just before
they were awakened. Subjects' oral reports are tape recorded and later tran-
scribed on paper for such purposes as the scoring of contents. Problems of
forgetting and selective reporting are minimized—though not eliminated—
with this method.

Normative Study of REM Dreams

The most thorough normative study of dreams using the laboratory
arousal method was done by Snyder (1970). Over the course of several years
Snyder and his colleagues collected 635 REM dream reports from about fifty
subjects that spent a total of 250 nights in the laboratory. Thus, the average
subject spent five nights in the laboratory, and provided about thirteen REM
dream reports. Snyder's subjects were normal young adult middle-class college and medical students, both males and females. This is the population on
which most laboratory dream research has been done. Thus, while the sample is relevant to most of the readers of this book, its data may not apply to
less educated people or elderly people.

Of all of the sleep mentation reports collected after REM awakenings, some three-fourths (635) met the criterion for a dream (complex images with temporal progression). The dream reports were analyzed for their descriptive characteristics. They were sorted into three classes according to their lengths—the number of words used by the subject to describe the dream (short, less than 150 words; medium, 150 to 300 words; long, over 300 words). In summarizing Snyder's dream data, I will, to simplify matters, give only the total percentages for medium and long dream reports combined. (Thus I will be presenting data for 285 dreams, some 45 percent of the dream reports analyzed by Snyder.) It should be noted that several of the descriptive characteristics were more frequent the longer the dream report. The length effect could be an artifact, to the extent that longer reports are simply more complete descriptions of dreams. Or it could be that longer reports come from longer dreams, and that longer dreams tend to have different characteristics than shorter dreams.

TABLE 11.1   Descriptive Characteristics of REM Dreams in Snyder's (1970) Normative Study*

Sensory Qualities

Visual images: 100%.
Color images: explicitly mentioned, 68% (actual % probably higher).
Non-verbal auditory images: 13%
Touch, taste, or smell: 1%.
Speech or conversation: 94%.

Setting and Events

Setting: familiar, 38%;
   unfamiliar but ordinary, 43%;
   exotic, 5%;
   fantastic, 1%.
Laboratory: 7% (mostly first night).
Automobiles: 15%.
Eating or drinking: 15%.

People

Dreamer was central actor: 95%.
Other people present: large majority.
Friends or relatives: 35%.

"Dream-like" Qualities

Bizarreness: nil, 60%; low, 27%;
   medium to high, 13%.

Credibility: medium to high, 90%.
Dramatic quality: medium to high, 27%.
Physical activity: medium to high, 48%.

Emotionality

Emotions mentioned: 30% (of these, ⅔rds were unpleasant).
Sexual content: 1%.

Cognition

Volition: 30%.
Reflection: 50%.
Inferential reasoning: 22%.
Memory experience: 4%.

Formal Characteristics

Temporal progression: all, by definition.
Coherence as a story: medium to high, 97%.
Complexity of plot and characterization: medium to high, 65%.
Clarity: medium to high, 80%.

*Percent of dreams with various characteristics, in a sample of some 285 REM dream reports over 150 words in length, collected from 50 subjects.

Source: Data from Snyder, F. (1970). The phenomenology of dreaming. In L. Madlow and L. H. Snow (Eds.), *The Psychodynamic Implications of the Physiological Studies on Dreams* (pp. 124–51). Springfield, IL: Charles C Thomas.

The characteristics of REM dreams in Snyder's (1970) sample are summarized in Table 11.1. It will help to make sense of Snyder's data if I first quote his conclusions:

> The broadest generalization I can make about our observations of dreaming consciousness is that it is a remarkably faithful replica of waking life, and many aspects of that statement are almost independent of length or detail of reports. . . . In almost every instance the progression of complex visual imagery described was a realistic facsimile of the visual perception of external reality; that is, it was "representational" (Snyder 1970, p. 133).

Now, to describe and comment further on selected aspects of Snyder's dream data:

Sensory qualities.   Less than 10 percent of the reports spontaneously mentioned color, but when the dreamer was questioned about the visual details of the dreams, color was mentioned in about 68 percent of the cases. Apparently most people dream in color most of the time, so they tend to take color for granted and usually fail to mention it spontaneously in their dream report. Speech or conversation was mentioned in 94 percent of the dreams, but it is not clear what proportion of these involved actual auditory imagery versus merely understanding the meaning of what was said, without actual auditory imagery.

Setting, events, and people.   Most of the reports described a setting for the dream action, with the setting being either a familiar place (such as the dreamer's house) or an unfamiliar but ordinary place (such as an office building) in a large majority of cases (total 81 percent). Settings that were exotic (such as a jungle) or fantastic (such as a strange planet) were rare (total 6 percent). The dreamer was the central actor in a large majority of the dreams, and the first person pronoun ("I") was used in 95 percent of the reports. The dreamer's self as a child appeared in only one dream, and the self flying or falling occurred in only one dream each. Explicit references to the laboratory situation occurred in 7 percent of the dreams; references to the laboratory were most common on the sleeper's first night in the laboratory (called the "first night effect").

"Dream-like" qualities.   Snyder defined *bizarreness* as "the extent to which the described events were outside the conceivable expectations of waking life; to put it bluntly: the craziness of the dream" (p. 146). He tried to distinguish between bizarreness and *credibility*: an event is credible if it is conceivable that it could happen in the real world. For example, a cat turning into a rabbit is bizarre. Daddy taking an airplane to work is unlikely, but moderately credible. If he flew a broomstick to work it would be highly bizarre. Interestingly, and contrary to popular beliefs about dreams, only 13 percent the dream reports were rated as medium or high in bizarreness.

Emotionality.   Some writers have included emotionality as a defining characteristic of dreams. Snyder had some difficulty in scoring the dream reports for emotionality, since he had to guard against the tendency to infer what would have been the appropriate emotion in the situation described in the report. There were some cases in which one might infer a particular emotion, yet the subject explicitly denied that emotion. Emotions were explicitly mentioned in only about 30 percent of the reports. Over two-thirds of the emotions were unpleasant, fear or anxiety being most common, and anger the next most common. Friendliness was the most common pleasant emotion. Clearly defined sexual content occurred in only 1 percent of the dream reports. Snyder concluded "The feelings expressed in dreams are usually bland and rather nebulous, attracting attention only when they become unpleasant; and perhaps that's the way life is" (1970, p. 142).

Cognition.   Volition was present in 30 percent of the dreams, *volition* being defined as the dreamed self deciding to do something or not do something, or engaging in sustained activity directed toward some specific goal. *Reflection*, defined as the subject silently commenting on something to himself or herself, occurred in 50 percent of the dream reports. For example: "We were at home in Pennsylvania and someone had just been fishing because there were dead fish lying around to be cleaned. I know I was interested in seeing what they caught, but at the same time I was thinking 'Look at those fish we're going to have to eat.' I don't like fish." *Inferential reasoning*, such as judging someone's motives from their behavior, occurred in 22 percent of the reports. A *memory experience*, defined as the dreamed self remembering something, occurred in only 4 percent of the reports. For example: "While I was sitting there on the subway I suddenly remembered that I had forgotten to bring my sister's dress" (Snyder 1970, p. 139). All of the cognitive characteristics occurred more frequently, the longer the dream report.

Formal characteristics.   Several global judgments of the formal characteristics of the dream reports were made. By definition, the dreams had to have some degree of temporal progression, and 50 percent had a medium to high degree of temporal progression. Some 97 percent had a medium to high degree of coherence as a story. "Extremely few were really disjointed or mixed up, and by far the largest number were about as coherent as we might expect from descriptions of real life events, especially so if they had been obtained after abrupt awakenings in the middle of the night" (Snyder 1970, p. 142). *Complexity*, having to do with the intricacies of plot and characterization, was medium to high in 65 percent of the dreams. The *clarity* of the dream report—the degree to which the reader of the transcript could recreate the dream in his or her own mind—was medium to high in 80 percent of the cases. Note that all of the formal characteristics of dream reports, particularly their clarity, would depend partly on the verbal-descriptive ability of the subject, as well as the characteristics of the dream itself.

Conclusions.   The exact percentages in the various descriptive categories are less important than the general conclusion to which they lead: the overwhelming majority of dreams are remarkably representative of everyday life in the real world. Most dreams are perceptually vivid, with vision being the dominant sense. Emotional tone is usually not noticed, though negative emotions are more likely to make an impression than positive ones. Most action occurs in familiar or realistic settings, with other people present, and conversation with other people is frequent. We have some degree of self-awareness in our dreams, we often reflect on our experiences, and we sometimes engage in inferential reasoning. In dreams we frequently act with a sense of volition, though much of our action occurs rather automatically, without conscious choice.

The fact that dreams are rarely bizarre, and only sometimes emotional or dramatic, seems surprising at first. It conflicts with our usual impression. But bear in mind the fact that you forget most of your dreams before you awaken. You are only likely to remember the last dream of the night, and you will not even remember that one unless you pause and think about it for a moment immediately after awakening. You are not likely to replay or "rehearse" the dream unless it had some bizarre or dramatic or emotional quality to it. Thus, the dreams that you ordinarily recall at home are not typical. Dream reports from the sleep laboratory, collected from REM awakenings throughout the night, give us a more accurate picture of typical dreams.

The experience of time in dreams.

Dreams are experienced as extending in time, like a story told in a movie. Phenomenologically, dream actions usually seem to take about the same amount of time that the same action would take in real life.

Yet, a retrospective interpretation has led some people to believe that dreams occur instantaneously. Schwartz et al. (1978) traced this belief to the guillotine dream reported by Maury (1861; cited in Freud 1900/1965) to have occurred during his youth in France, shortly after the French revolution. In his dream, Maury was watching condemned people being decapitated by a guillotine. He himself was one of the condemned. He dreamed that he mounted the scaffold, placed his neck across the block, and at the moment that he felt the blade fall on his neck he awoke in terror, only to discover that the top of his bed had fallen and struck him on the neck exactly as the blade had struck his neck in the dream. Maury inferred that the entire dream had occurred during the fraction of a second between the time the bed top struck him and the time that he awakened.

Other people have had experiences similar to Maury's, in which an external event was incorporated into a dream at virtually the same moment that it awakened the dreamer. For example, as I was returning with my family from a trip to Prince Edward Island, my wife was driving while I dozed in the front passenger seat. I dreamed that I was driving, and that I saw another car pull dangerously into my lane. I quickly pressed the horn button with my right thumb, and I actually felt my thumb move and heard the horn sound. At that moment I awoke, and realized that my wife had actually honked the horn. This unusual dream experience most likely occurred in the hypnagogic (sleep onset) state rather than during REM. We have no way of knowing whether Maury's experience occurred during REM sleep. In any case, such experiences seem to support the notion that dreams can be elicited by external events, and that a lot of dream imagery can occur in a very short period of time.

Nonetheless, there is good evidence that REM dreams ordinarily are extended in time, and that the sleeper has reasonably accurate time discrimination ability even while dreaming. Dement and Kleitman (1957) awakened subjects after either five or fifteen minutes of REM sleep, and asked them whether they had been dreaming for five minutes or fifteen minutes. Four of five subjects were able to discriminate reliably between the short and long intervals. Furthermore, in all subjects the length of the dream reports (in number of words) was longer for the fifteen-minute interval than for the five-minute interval.

Koulack (1968) found evidence for time discrimination in an experiment on the incorporation of external events into dreams. During REM, subjects were given electrical stimulation, and then they were awakened either thirty seconds or three minutes after the stimulus. In eleven of twelve cases in which the stimulus was incorporated into the dream, the subjects were able to report correctly whether the stimulus had occurred thirty seconds or three minutes prior to their being awakened. Thus, the evidence indicates that REM dreams ordinarily do not occur instantaneously, and that people usually can discriminate shorter dreams from longer dreams.

DREAMING IN NREM SLEEP

The Controversy over NREM Dreaming

One of the most controversial issues of the first two decades of laboratory dream research was the question of whether dreaming is limited to the REM sleep stage. In the first study of the association between rapid eye movements and dreaming, Aserinsky and Kleitman (1953) reported that dreams occurred in 74 percent of the REM periods, but in only 11 percent of the NREM periods. Other early studies also found dreaming to be prevalent in REM, but rare in NREM (Dement 1955; Dement & Kleitman 1957), with the combined percentages from several studies being remarkably close to the percentages reported by Aserinsky and Kleitman (Dement 1976). It seemed to make a lot of sense that dreams would occur only in REM stage, since the sleeper's eye movements could be interpreted as scanning of the visual dream images. Dement and Kleitman (1957) suggested that on those infrequent occasions when dreams were reported in NREM awakenings, the subjects were probably recalling a dream from a previous REM period. The association between REM and dreaming seemed to be so strong that some researchers used the terms "REM sleep" and "dream sleep" interchangeably, as if they meant the same thing.

However, things are not so simple. Since Dement and Kleitman's (1957) report, several studies have found strikingly high percentages of dream recall in NREM sleep awakenings. There is no doubt that dreaming is reported more often after awakenings from REM sleep than after awakenings from NREM sleep, but the question arises as to why some experimenters have found NREM dreaming to be common, while others have found it to be rare. Something more than random variation between samples seems to be involved. Another question is whether there are qualitative differences between REM and NREM dreams.

Herman, Ellman, and Roffwarg (1978) suggested several factors that could account for the different NREM dream-recall frequencies found in different studies: (1) how dreaming was defined; (2) how the subjects were interrogated (3) expectancy effects; (4) different subject samples; and (5) different schedules of awakenings. I will discuss the first point.

Different definitions of "dream."   Probably the most important factor in the issue of NREM dreaming is the experimenter's criterion for classifying sleep-mentation reports as dream reports. At one extreme, any report of any mental experience occurring during sleep, no matter how vague, could be classified as a dream. By this lenient criterion, dreaming occurs in 99 percent of REM reports, and 87 percent of NREM reports (Foulkes 1962). At the other extreme, one could use a very narrow criterion including not only vivid perceptual imagery but also factors such as complexity, plot continuity, bizarreness, and emotionality. Such a narrow criterion would reduce the apparent frequency of both REM and NREM dreaming, since strong emotionality and bizarreness are not characteristic of most REM dreams (Snyder 1970).

In published reports, experimenters have often failed to describe their criterion for classifying sleep-mentation reports as dreams. Apparently they thought it was obvious when a report represented a dream. Vivid perceptual imagery has usually been part of the stated or unstated definition, along with other factors that might differ from one study to the next, such as coherence, temporal progression, and complexity or detail.

A useful solution to the dream-criterion problem is to classify sleep-mentation reports into different categories, according to their characteristics. Orlinsky (reported by Kamiya 1961) developed an eight-point scale for classifying mentation reports. The points on Orlinsky's scale, and the percentage of some 400 NREM reports (from twenty-five subjects) that he classified at each point, are shown in Table 11.2.

Orlinsky seems to have taken it for granted that his subjects' sleep mentations involved perceptual images—he did not use the presence or absence of images as a factor in his scale classifications. By my (and Snyder's 1970) definition of a dream (images with temporal progression), reports in Orlinsky's categories 4 through 7 can be classified as dreams. By this criterion, 27 percent of Orlinsky's subjects' NREM reports were dreams. By the same criterion, 85 percent of their REM reports were dreams.

Using a laxer dream-criterion of identifiable content accompanied by perceptual images (though not necessarily with temporal progression), Foulkes (1962) classified 54 percent of NREM reports, and 82 percent of REM reports as dreams. He classified 20 percent of NREM reports as thoughts, that is, identifiable contents without perceptual imagery. (Foulkes also showed that dreams reported in NREM awakenings were not merely being recalled from prior REM periods—they were reported from early NREM periods that occurred before the first REM period as often as from later NREM periods that followed a REM period.) It is clear that the criterion for classifying sleep-mentation reports as dream reports is a critical factor influencing different experimenters' conclusions about the relative frequency of dreaming in NREM versus REM periods.[2]

TABLE 11.2   Orlinsky's Sleep-Mentation Scale and Percent of NREM Reports in Each Category*

(0) Subject cannot remember dreaming; no dream is reported on awakening. [43%]

(1) Subject remembers having dreamed, or thinks he may have been dreaming, but cannot remember any specific content. [11%]

(2) Subject remembers a specific topic, but in isolation: for example, a fragmentary action, scene, object, word, or idea unrelated to anything else. [14%]

(3) Subject remembers several such disconnected thoughts, scenes or actions. [5%]

(4) Subject remembers a short but coherent dream, the parts of which seem related to each other: for example, a conversation rather than a word, a problem worked through rather than an idea, or a purposeful rather than a fragmentary action. [14%]

(5) Subject remembers a detailed dream sequence, in which something happens, followed by some consequence, or in which one scene, mood, or main interacting character is replaced by another (different from category 3 either in coherence of change or in the development of the several parts of the sequence). [6%]

(6) Subject remembers a long, detailed dream sequence involving three or four discernible stages of development. [7%, for categories 6 and 7 combined]

(7) Subject remembers an extremely long and detailed dream sequence of five or more stages; or more than one dream (at least one of which is rated 5) for a single awakening.

---

*Based on 400 NREM sleep reports from 25 subjects.

From Kamiya, J. (1961). Behavioral, subjective, and physiological aspects of drowsiness and sleep. In D. W. Fiske & S. R. Maddi (Eds.), Functions of Varied Experience (pp. 145–74). Homewood, IL: Dorsey Press.

Conclusion.   It is now clear that the mind is active in NREM sleep as well as in REM sleep. Some NREM mentation consists of imageless thoughts, but a certain proportion consists of true dreams with perceptual images and temporal progression. Though dreams do occur in NREM sleep, their typical characteristics tend to differ from those of REM dreams. The nature of those differences will be discussed in the next section.[3]

Comparison of REM and NREM Sleep Mentation

REM mentation has been characterized as more "dreamy" than NREM mentation. That is, REM mentation is more visually vivid, dramatic, emotional, and bizarre, whereas NREM mentation tends to be more like daydreaming or imageless conceptual thinking. But however convenient it might be, this generalization is an oversimplification. The differences between REM and NREM mentation are relative, not absolute, and most REM dreams are not particularly dramatic, emotional, or bizarre. REM mentation usually is better recalled than NREM mentation, and we cannot be sure how much of the apparent differences in mentation quality are due to differences in recall of REM versus NREM mentation.

Deep sleepers versus light sleepers.   Zimmerman (1970) found that the differences between REM and NREM mentation are greater for deep sleepers than for light sleepers. He selected groups of light or deep sleepers according to their auditory awakening thresholds: the tone intensity required to awaken them was about 15 db louder for deep sleepers than for light sleepers. Sleep-mentation reports were collected from REM and NREM periods in the latter half of the night. Subsequently the reports were scored on several dimensions derived from a factor-analytic study of dream reports (Hauri, Sawyer, & Rechtschaffen 1967).

REM mentation reports did not differ for light and deep sleepers, but NREM reports of the two groups differed in some important ways. Light sleepers described their NREM experiences as dreaming (rather than thinking) 71 percent of the time, compared to only 21 percent for deep sleepers. It appears that NREM mentation is more dreamlike for light sleepers than for deep sleepers. In fact, light sleepers' NREM reports were virtually identical to their REM reports for several dimensions, including: (1) dreaming rather than thinking, (2) more perceptual than conceptual, (3) lack of volitional control, (4) belief in the reality of what is being experienced, and (5) distortion of content. But deep sleepers' REM reports scored higher than their NREM reports on those dimensions.

Equally important was the finding that REM and NREM mentation differed significantly on several dimensions for *both* light and deep sleepers. Compared to REM, NREM mentation involved: (1) less active participation by the subject, (2) less thematic continuity, (3) less emotion, (4) less clarity and vividness, (5) less dramaticity, (6) more contemporary content, (7) less physical activity, and (8) poorer recall. These are the *core dimensions* of distinction between REM and NREM mentation.

Though the differences between REM and NREM mentation are not absolute, they are great enough that "blind" judges—judges who do not know which sleep stage the reports came from—can classify reports as REM or NREM with about 75 to 85 percent accuracy (Monroe et al. 1965).

Continuity of content between REM and NREM periods.   Though it does not always happen, it is not unusual for the same topic to be continued across two or more successive sleep stages. Rechtschaffen, Vogel, and Shaikun (1963) compared successive REM and NREM reports within a single night and found that the same general topic may be represented in either type of report, though the REM reports typically are more perceptually vivid. The following example comes from five successive awakenings of the same subject on the same night:

1. REM period (time 62 minutes since initial sleep onset): I was dreaming. I remember the feeling that the dream contained a few people other than myself—contemporaries of mine. We were all in a *boat*. I remember worrying about the boat overturning and what we would do. And I remember the thought that we would just have to swim to save our souls.
2. NREM Stage 3 (time 95 minutes): I have the feeling that I was in a *boat* again, a small boat, like a rowboat. It being rather *sunny* out. . . . I don't remember think-

ing of what would happen if the boat overturned, as I did before. I was preoccupied with a thought. I really can't remember what it was.

3. NREM Stage 4 (time 187 minutes): I had been dreaming about getting ready to take some type of an *exam*. It had been a very short dream. . . . I don't think I was worried about them.

4. REM period (time 223 minutes): I was dreaming about *exams*. In the early part of the dream I was dreaming I had just finished an exam, and it was a very *sunny* day outside. I was walking with a boy who's in some of my classes with me. There was sort of a . . . break, and someone mentioned a grade they had gotten in a social science exam. And I asked them if the social science marks had come in. They said yes. I didn't get it, because I had been away for a day.

5. NREM Stage 2 (time 274 minutes): . . . dreaming about *exams*, and about having taken different exams . . . (Rechtschaffen et al. 1963, p. 544).

LABORATORY DREAMS COMPARED WITH HOME DREAMS

I have concentrated on laboratory dream research, rather than dream-diary research, because I believe that we are likely to get the most accurate information about dreaming from controlled laboratory research in which physiological responses are measured during sleep and mentation reports are collected immediately after awakening from known sleep states. However, some researchers have argued that dream reports collected in the laboratory setting do not accurately reflect the normal dreaming experience.

Two studies found significant differences between home dream-diary reports and laboratory dream-reports from the same subjects. Domhoff and Kamiya (1964) found a greater frequency of sexual and aggression/misfortune elements in home dreams, while laboratory dreams contained more bizarre elements. Hall and Van de Castle (1966) concluded that home dreams tend to be more dramatic than laboratory dreams. It could be argued from these results that laboratory dreams or dream reports are affected by the subjects' being in the novel laboratory setting, and/or the novel social interaction involved in reporting their dreams to strangers. Alternatively, or in addition, the differences might be due to the fact that the laboratory reports were always collected from REM awakenings, whereas subjects made their home dream reports after awakening spontaneously (or by alarm clock) from unknown sleep stages that might have been sometimes REM and sometimes NREM.

Weisz and Foulkes (1970) compared home and laboratory dream reports collected under conditions that were as similar as possible for the two different settings. Dream reports were collected from twelve subjects for two nights in the laboratory and two nights at home (in a counterbalanced sequence). For the home dream reports, subjects slept alone in their own bedrooms. When they slept in the laboratory they were wired for polygraph recordings in the usual manner, but, unlike most laboratory dream studies, they were never awakened by the experimenter. Both at home and in the laboratory the subjects slept undisturbed until they either awoke spontaneously or were awakened by an alarm clock at 6:30 a.m. When the alarm rang they privately recorded their sleep mentation recollections, if any, on a portable tape recorder.

Out of twenty-four subject-mornings in the laboratory, when the alarm rang the subjects were in REM sleep 29 percent of the time, in NREM 46 percent, and awake 25 percent. Presumably the proportions were about the same for the mornings at home (though there is no way of knowing for sure since polygraph recordings were not made at home). Independent blind judges—who did not know which mentation reports came from the laboratory and which from home—rated the reports on six scales (derived from Hauri et al. 1967). The percent of awakenings yielding scorable mentation reports was about the same (80 percent) for the laboratory and home, and the median report length was about the same (130 words) in both cases.

Home dream reports showed more verbal and physical aggression than laboratory reports, a finding that replicates the results of the earlier studies. However, home and laboratory dreams did not differ significantly in overt sexuality, and they were virtually identical on the dimensions of vivid fantasy, hedonic tone (pleasantness or unpleasantness), and active participation. The *vivid fantasy dimension* is particularly important, since it reflects the most distinctive dream processes: "feelings of *unreality* (imagination, distortion) coupled with *intensity* of experience (dramatization, clarity, emotion)" (Hauri et al. 1967, p. 18). Weisz and Foulkes (1970) concluded that the similarities between home and laboratory dreams are really more important than the differences. Particularly, their identity on the vivid fantasy dimension refutes the hypothesis that basic dream processes are somehow altered in the laboratory setting.

In specific dream contents, the home and laboratory dreams differed in that elements related to the experimental situation appeared in 50 percent of the laboratory dreams, but in only 6 percent of the home dreams. It is hardly surprising that the novel laboratory setting would appear as a "day residue" in the laboratory dreams. As for the greater frequency of aggression in the home dream-reports compared to the laboratory reports, it is not yet clear whether this difference represents an actual inhibition of aggressive content in laboratory dreams or a social inhibition on the *reporting* of aggression in the laboratory. Also, it is not known whether this difference is transient or permanent.

Selective recall.   All in all, Weisz and Foulkes's study shows that the similarities between home and laboratory dreams are more important than their differences, when they are collected under comparable conditions. Why is it, then, that the dreams that we remember at home are so often dramatic and emotional, whereas the dreams reported from REM awakenings in the laboratory are usually mundane (Snyder 1970)? Weisz and Foulkes (1970) argued that the most important factor is *selective recall* of home dreams. Only those home dreams that are particularly *salient*, due to their high degree of drama, emotion, or bizarreness, are likely to be spontaneously recalled at home. This is particularly true for the average person who has no particular interest in dreams, but it applies also to people who are especially interested in their dreams and attempt to recall them each morning. In Chapter 13 I will discuss salience and other factors influencing dream recall in more detail.

BETWEEN WAKEFULNESS AND SLEEP: THE HYPNAGOGIC STATE

As you fall asleep you go through a transition period in which you feel increasingly drowsy, not fully awake but not yet asleep. The drowsy transition period between wakefulness and sleep is called the *hypnagogic state* (derived from the Greek words, *hypno*, sleep, and *agogos*, to induce).[4] The hypnagogic state can be identified by brain wave patterns, and it involves mental phenomena termed *hypnagogic hallucinations* or images that are in some ways similar to REM sleep dreams, and in some ways different. You usually recall nothing of the contents of the hypnagogic period, since you usually pass through it into full sleep. However, if you are somehow aroused from this drowsy state, you may recall a brief dreamlike experience. Or you may have the impression that you were thinking or dreaming, and be able to recall some vague impression of it, like an aftertaste, without being able to recall any details. Brief daytime naps (about ten to fifteen minutes) may be spent largely in the hypnagogic state (Evans et al. 1977).

Schacter (1976) summarized some conclusions about hypnagogic imagery derived from dream-diary studies done before the advent of EEG technology.[5] Most hypnagogic images are in the visual mode, while auditory images are not unusual and tactile-kinesthetic images occasionally occur. Sometimes the visual images include flashes of light and geometric patterns that cannot be identified as objects. But more often the images portray people, objects, or scenes that are quite vivid, as vivid as night dreams. So far there have been no systematic, large-scale normative studies of the relative frequencies of different types of hypnagogic images. As with night dreams, hypnagogic images are quite variable, and they are strongly influenced by the individual's personality, personal concerns, and recent experiences.

EEG research on the hypnagogic state.   Sleep onset occurs at the beginning of descending NREM Stage 2. The transition to sleep may be described in terms of four stages: (1) Relaxed wakefulness, characterized by nearly continuous alpha EEG brain waves (8–13 Hz). (2) Alpha SEM, involving discontinuous alpha EEG with slow eye movements. (3) Descending NREM Stage 1, with EEG of mixed frequencies (mostly fast but including slow theta waves [4–7 Hz] and slow eye movements). (4) Descending NREM Stage 2, sleep onset. The hypnagogic state consists of alpha SEM and, especially, descending NREM Stage 1 (Foulkes & Vogel 1965; Foulkes, Spear, & Symonds 1966.)[6]

In a laboratory study, Foulkes and Vogel (1965) awakened subjects from the hypnagogic state to obtain mentation reports. Almost all reports contained some sort of mental content, and about 50 to 75 percent of them included dreamlike content. Foulkes and Vogel noted a particularly interesting difference between hypnagogic dreams and REM dreams: the hypnagogic period is distinctive in that its visual images are often rather static, in contrast to the dynamic, movie-like images of REM dreams. Hypnagogic dreams may show a sequence of events as a sequence of still frames. For example, one subject reported a hypnagogic dream that involved "driving from California to Tijuana, Mexico, of entering a bar there which featured a dancing girl, and of leaving the bar in the company of this girl." The dream report indicated that the subject had seen only three brief dream images: "an image of himself driving at one particular place in California, an image of the inside of the bar, and an image of the girl walking with him in the street" (Foulkes & Vogel 1965, p. 240). The apparent continuity of the dream report seems to have depended upon secondary revision or filling in the gaps between the images, either while in the hypnagogic state or afterward, while the dream was being reported. The snapshot character of some hypnagogic dreams suggests that the actual duration of hypnagogic dreams is briefer, on the average, than the duration of REM dreams, even when the verbal reports are of the same length.

While there are some differences between hypnagogic and REM dreams, the similarities are as striking as the differences. Both involve vivid visual images of hallucinatory (believed-in) quality, and both are usually storylike, though hypnagogic dreams tend to be briefer and are more likely to involve static scenes. Both types may involve distortions of reality and apparently symbolic transformations of reality. In both types the subject himself/herself is usually an active participant. Hypnagogic and REM dreams do not differ in ratings of aggression, sexuality, or hedonic tone. Mean scores on a dreamlike fantasy scale are about equal (though top-of-the scale scores occur more often in REM). Both types of dreams include personal material with possibly psychodynamic significance. The most dramatic difference between hypnagogic and REM reports is the subjects' depth-of-sleep ratings: they reported that they had been deeply asleep just before REM awakenings, but that they had been merely drowsy and just drifting off to sleep prior to hypnagogic awakenings (Foulkes et al. 1966).

The EEG research suggests the interesting conclusion that vivid dreamlike images are by no means limited to REM sleep—they also occur in the hypnagogic period. In fact, the similarity between REM and hypnagogic dreams is in many ways greater than the similarity between REM and NREM (Stages 2, 3, and 4) dreams.[7]

FACTORS THAT INFLUENCE DREAM CONTENTS

Dreams are constructed from knowledge stored in the individual's long-term memory. This knowledge includes: (a) the characteristics of people, animals, and objects, including how they look and what they can do; (b) personal past experiences (episodic memory); (c) types of story themes and scripts (such as typical sequences of events at a restaurant or dentist's office); and (d) the spatial organization of typical scenes, and how people and objects can move in them. But of course your dreams are not mere replays of remembered experiences or stories. Rather, they are creative stories constructed from your personal knowledge.

The question here is, what factors influence the manifest contents of dreams? That is, what variables affect the selection of particular memory contents—such as people, places, and story themes—to appear, perhaps in odd combinations, in dreams? I will be concerned here with empirical research on factors that influence the manifest or surface dream contents, not with theories about latent or hidden dream contents. This research is important for developing and evaluating theories about how dreams are produced. Most theories of dreaming endorse the *continuity hypothesis*, which says that peoples' dreams directly reflect their personalities, current concerns, and daytime experiences. Conversely, Jung's (1933) *compensation hypothesis* said that dreams may express virtually the opposite of the individual's waking personality, emotional reactions, and concerns. As we will see, the research evidence strongly supports the continuity hypothesis, though some evidence is consistent with the compensation hypothesis.

The factors that affect dream contents can be divided into several categories: (1) demographic and cultural factors; (2) personality and psychopathology; (3) current personal concerns and mood; (4) recent waking experiences; and (5) stimuli during sleep.

Demographic and Cultural Factors

The dreams of different groups of people—such as groups differentiated by gender, age, socioeconomic status, or culture—may show statistical differences in the relative frequencies of different types of contents. This type of research is typically done with relatively large samples, using questionnaires about dreams recalled at home. For example Winget, Kramer, and Whitman (1972) collected dreams reports from 300 people in four age groups, ranging from 21 to 65+ years. Some of their findings: (1) *Gender differences*: Women reported dreams more often than men (65 versus 53 percent). Compared to men, women were more likely to report dreams with characters, emotions, friendly interactions, and home and family. Men were more likely than women to report dreams with aggression and achievement-striving themes. (2) *Age differences*: Subjects 65 and older had more dreams with death anxiety and overt death themes, compared to younger subjects. (3) *Socioeconomic status*: Lower-class subjects had more dreams with people and more misfortunes; upper-middle-class had less death anxiety, compared to lower and lower-middle-class subjects.

Gender differences have often been the most potent demographic factor in questionnaire studies. However, in a laboratory study involving eleven males and eleven females awakened during REM sleep, no gender differences were found regarding aggression, misfortune, or social-interaction dream themes (Kramer, Kinney, & Scharf 1983a). One interpretation is that the typical dreams of males and females are similar, but males and females recall different aspects of their dreams in home dream-diary or questionnaire studies. An alternative interpretation is that large samples are needed to detect group differences, whereas laboratory studies usually have a relatively small number of subjects, perhaps too small to detect group differences.

Some studies have attempted cross-cultural comparisons. For example, Van de Castle (1971) compared dreams of Cuna Indians of Central America and age-matched Nicaraguans, and found less aggression in the dreams of the Cuna, which is consistent with differences in waking behavior between the two groups.

Findings regarding demographic and cultural factors may vary widely from one study to another depending on sample size, sampling method, and method of data collection. Demographic and cultural groups are heterogeneous—that is, they contain a wide variety of individuals, with different personalities, waking experiences, and personal concerns. Insofar as groups differ, it is because of differences in commonly shared experiences and concerns. Progress in understanding the variables that affect dream contents is more likely to be made by studying more homogeneous samples, in which known characteristics of the individuals and their experiences and concerns can be related to dream contents.

Personality and Psychopathology

Here the emphasis is on dream characteristics as related to personality types and traits, and psychopathology diagnostic categories. In general, the evidence indicates a continuity between waking personality and sleeping personality. For example, Starker (1978) compared dream-diary reports in subjects of three different daydreaming personality types (as classified by the Imaginal Processes Inventory, Chapter 8). Positive-vivid daydreamers, the mentally well-adjusted group, showed more positive emotionality and less bizarreness in their night dreams than did either guilty-dysphoric or anxious-distractible daydreamer types. Of the three groups, night dreams of the anxious-distractibles (anxiety neurotics) showed the most emotionality, the most bizarreness, and the greatest number of idea units per dream. (The latter result suggests that anxious-distractible types tended to have dreams that were more fragmented, jumping around from one scene to another, compared to other types.) Nightmares were most common among the anxious-distractibles; they never occurred among positive-vivid daydreamer types.

In a dream-diary study, Cann and Donderi (1986) found that introverts recalled dreams more often than did extraverts. In particular, introverts recalled more ordinary, plausible dreams than extraverts whereas introverts and extraverts were equally likely to recall unrealistic or bizarre dreams. Subjects rated high on the Jungian personality dimension of "intuitiveness" recalled more dreams of a highly emotional, irrational, and bizarre nature, which the authors interpreted as Jungian archetypical dreams. (In Jung's [1933] theory, archetypical dreams are [symbolically] about universal themes of human existence.) Subjects high in neuroticism recalled fewer archetypical dreams than those low in neuroticism. (See Cann and Donderi [1986] for references to other studies on dreaming and personality types.)

Methodological problems have made it hard to draw conclusions about the dreams of schizophrenic subjects (review by Schwartz, Weinstein & Arkin

1978). For example, schizophrenic patients are usually maintained on anti-psychotic drugs that might affect their dreams, and it is hard to determine how their reports are affected by their waking cognitive state. There is some support for the notion that schizophrenics' dreams are relatively impover-ished, which supports the compensation-hypothesis insofar as the waking ex-perience of some schizophrenics seems to be a blooming-buzzing confusion; but even this finding is tentative. Depressed patients tend to report relatively brief dreams, with more depression and masochism themes compared to normal people. There is a large literature of clinical case studies with dream reports, but it is beyond the scope of this book.

Chronic nightmare sufferers.

Nightmares are vivid dreams that cause enough fear or anxiety to awaken the dreamer. Nightmares occur almost ex-clusively during REM sleep, usually during relatively long REM periods in the latter half of the night. Nightmares are distinguished from *night terrors*, which are a sleep disorder involving suddenly awakening in a panic state. Night terrors occur during NREM sleep Stages 3 and 4 during the first half of the night, with either no dream report or a single frightening image. (See the section on sleep disorders in Chapter 10.)

Ernest Hartmann (1984; Hartmann et al. 1987) compared personality characteristics in a group of fifty chronic nightmare suffers (20 to 35 years old) to those of subjects in two control groups: vivid dreamers and nonvivid dreamers. The chronic-nightmare subjects reported a lifelong history of nightmares (since early childhood), and were currently experiencing night-mares at least once a week (average 3.5 per week); the controls rarely or never experienced nightmares. Typical nightmares were long, vivid, fright-ening dreams that seemed "real" at the time. The nightmares were not repet-itive; every dream was different, though the themes were often similar. The most common theme was being chased—by a monster in childhood, and in adulthood usually by a large man or a group of people. Sometimes the dreamer awakened in response to a frightening threat, before an actual at-tack occurred, though often the dreamer was attacked and beaten, shot, or stabbed. For example, one woman reported:

> I was swimming along in cool blue water. A strange man swam after me and started slicing me with a knife. It was all in brilliant color and I could feel every-thing. I felt the cool water and the hot pain of the knife slashing into my arm; I saw my blood spreading out in the water and I could see slices of my flesh drift-ing off away from me. It was very real. I could definitely feel the knife and feel the pain in this dream (Hartmann 1984, p. 60).

The subjects reported that nightmares occurred more often at times of per-sonal life stresses (such as moving, or breakup of a personal relationship), and that highly stressful events (such as being mugged) affected their night-mares for several weeks afterward.

Hartmann compared the three groups' responses to structured inter-views and several diagnostic personality tests, including the Minnesota Mul-tiphasic Personality Inventory (MMPI) and the Thematic Apperception Test (TAT). The vivid and nonvivid dreamer control groups did not differ from each other. Compared to the controls, the nightmare group scored more on the "psychotic" side of the MMPI profile, suggesting oddities of perception and thinking. Several had *DSM-III* diagnoses, such as schizotypical or border-line personality disorders.[8] However, none were diagnosed as psychotic, nor were they diagnosed as being highly anxious, phobic, dissociative, or having conversion-state or obsessive-compulsive disorder. Nor were the chronic nightmare sufferers unusually hostile or aggressive or fearful. Typically they reported that as children they were especially sensitive and introspective and felt "different" from other children, though there was no pattern of childhood abuse or traumatic experience. The nightmare sufferers, com-pared to controls, reported less stable personal relationships, and were more likely to be unemployed or underemployed; many had jobs or hobbies relat-ing to the arts (musicians, painters, poets, craftspersons).

Hartmann (1984) summarized his findings by characterizing chronic nightmare sufferers as having "thin boundaries" in a number of senses. They tend to be open, vulnerable, defenseless, and artistic. Their boundaries be-tween fantasy and reality, between self and others, between male and female identities, between adulthood and childhood, and between present and past, are less rigid than normal. Hartmann concluded:

> The nightmares themselves may be considered an aspect of thin boundaries. The TATs indicate that these nightmare sufferers are not persons with power-ful hostilities, and our impression from the interviews is that they are not per-sons with an unusual number of fears. It rather appears that the ordinary fear, feelings of helplessness, and rage of childhood, which we probably all experi-ence, 'get through' in these persons and enter into their dreams more than they do in most of us" (Hartmann et al. 1987, p. 56).

Hartmann's lifelong chronic nightmare sufferers were compared with a group of fifteen Vietnam combat veterans suffering from *posttraumatic nightmares* as part of a *posttraumatic stress disorder* (PTSD) (Hartmann 1984; Van der Kolk et al. 1984). The veterans typically had started having night-mares after the loss of a close buddy in combat, and several years later they were still having nightmares at least once a month. The unique thing about the PTSD veterans was that, unlike ordinary chronic nightmare sufferers, their nightmares represented events that had actually happened, and they were repetitive, replaying the same traumatic scene on each occasion. The PTSD veterans were abnormally anxious, particularly in regard to events that might remind them of their combat trauma, but they were not character-ized by the "thin boundaries" and semi-psychotic features of the chronic nightmare group. (A comparison group of ten veterans with lifelong night-mares was more like the original chronic nightmare group.) Unlike ordinary nightmares, posttraumatic nightmares apparently can occur in any sleep stage. Hartmann (1984) tentatively concluded that posttraumatic nightmares represent a third diagnostic category, separate from ordinary nightmares and night terrors. Of course, posttraumatic nightmares are not limited to combat veterans. They can occur in people who have experienced traumas such as violent crimes, near-fatal accidents, or the death of a loved one. Chil-dren are more prone to them than adults. Posttraumatic nightmares usually decrease over a period of a few weeks, though they may continue longer depending on the individual's personality and the seriousness of the trauma.

Current Personal Concerns and Mood

We know that current personal concerns are a major topic of daydreams, and it is not surprising that they also influence night dreams. In both cases, the current concerns are most likely to have an impact if they are tied to strong mood states. For example, hospitalized patients who are awaiting surgery often have dreams with elevated anxiety levels and themes that are symbolically associated with the impending surgery. In one case, a railroad worker who was awaiting surgery to remove a vascular blockage in his leg dreamed of trying to unclog a railroad switch that was jammed with sand and rust (Breger, Hunter, & Lane 1971). Pregnant women are more likely than other women to dream about babies, motherhood, and anxieties relating to childbirth (Van de Castle 1971). A female student's dream diary included several dreams, over a month's time, showing her anxiety and feelings of losing control of her body, related to her concerns over an abnormal pap smear and anticipation of surgery. For example:

> I dreamed that I was strapped to an examining table. My feet were in stirrups and I was sedated. I couldn't move or cry out. There were bright lights and a sensation of panic. I heard voices of people, but I couldn't see them because of the lights (RM, Sept. 1988).

At the end of the diary she commented:

> I have learned a lot about myself through keeping a dream diary. I see how the problems and concerns of each day "creep" into my consciousness through dreams. Many of the painful, hurt-filled or scary thoughts that I had "pushed away" during the day came out (often with a vengeance) in my sleep.

These examples show that dreams may be affected by current concerns including anticipated events as well as ongoing problems.[9]

Divorce and depression.   Rosalind Cartwright (1986; Cartwright et al. 1984) showed that the themes and emotions of people's dreams may be affected by their emotional reactions to major life events and current concerns. Her subjects were twenty-nine women who had recently been divorced (or were in the process of getting divorced). Divorce is usually associated with negative affect, and nineteen of the women were diagnosed as depressed according to the Beck Depression Inventory (BDI), while ten were not depressed. A control group of nine nondepressed, happily married women was also used. Dream reports were collected after REM sleep awakenings over a period of six nights. Among the most depressed subjects, the latency of the first REM period was reduced below sixty minutes—a result consistent with prior research on clinically depressed patients. Depression (BDI) scores were significantly correlated with scores on a questionnaire measure of traditionality of sex role orientation. In other words, more traditional women, for whom the social role of wife was an integral part of their self-identity, had the greatest emotional difficulty in dealing with their divorces.

The dreams of the depressed divorcées differed from those of non-depressed divorcées and happily married women in several ways. For example, in time orientation, depressed subjects favored the past, married subjects favored the present, whereas nondepressed divorcées used the full time-range of past, present, and future. Anxiety dreams were frequent in all of the groups, but in the depressed group it was attributed to the self-character significantly more often (82%) than in the nondepressed (60%) and control (55%) subjects. Nondepressed divorcées were more likely to dream of themselves in the role of wife, compared to depressed subjects. The dominant dream motives for nondepressed divorcées were esteem and control, whereas belongingness and safety were the most common motives among depressed and control subjects. Dream reports were about twice as long, on the average, in nondepressed divorcées than in depressed and control subjects. Here is a dream report by a depressed divorcée that shows her distrust of men and includes an association to her husband, who physically abused her, as well as associations to the sleep laboratory setting:

> I was ready to get up and two men who were with me in this sleep program were ready to go, and this other man was letting two policemen that were trying to steal my place rush ahead to get out first, get their electrodes off. We were rushing to a little booth to get electrodes off. We were sitting in cars in front of the hospital. One car was a convertible like my ex-husband had (Cartwright 1986, p. 423).

Here is a dream report by a nondepressed divorcée who was adapting successfully, ready to take risks to reach a better future:

> I was trying to get to where I live, an apartment on the second story with El [commuter train] tracks going by. I had to climb on the train tracks and lie down on a trampoline and jump from it into a window. It was only three feet but it was shaky, risky, and awkward to stand up. There were two other women wanting to do the same thing. One did it. It looked easy so I got up to do it. I felt scared. It felt like flying in the future, being jet-propelled (Cartwright 1986, p. 424).

In discussing her findings, Cartwright concluded:

> In general, the study supports the proposition that dreams are more adaptive during a period of life change [nondepressed divorcées] than during a period of relative stability [happily married], providing the change is not accompanied by a major mood disturbance [depressed divorcées]. When there is significant depression, dreams appear to be slowed down in the process of working through or accommodating to changes in reality. The self is seen as helpless, damaged, needing to be cared for, not motivated to affiliate but to engage in abasement in order to be nurtured. Dreams for the depressed are not employed as rehearsal for future wish fulfillment in which the self acts decisively in some desired new roles (1986, p. 425).

Cartwright's study shows that peoples' manifest dreams reflect their emotional reactions to major life events and current concerns. Both awake and asleep, different people's emotional reactions to similar experiences (such as divorce or death of a loved one) differ, depending upon their personal interpretations of the experience and their abilities to cope with the it. Breger (1969) hypothesized that dreams help people to cope with recent emotional experiences by organizing them and relating them to knowledge of similar, past situations. There is little doubt that, over time, peoples' improved dream emotionality may reflect improved coping with their waking life situation. However, it would be hard to prove that dreaming helps people to cope with their waking life situation. Though it might sometimes happen, there is little evidence that dreams help people to discover specific solutions to their personal problems. Most commonly, dreams reflect problems, rather than solve them.

Recent Waking Experiences

Since dreams are constructed from memories, dreams are often influenced by recent waking experiences that are particularly prominent in memory. *Recent waking experiences* refers to recent specific, identifiable events in people's waking lives, in contrast to their more general ongoing and anticipated events. Admittedly, the distinction between recent experiences and current concerns is not always clear, since people's recent experiences are often related to their ongoing personal concerns.

Types of effects.   Waking experiences can have any of four different types of effects on dream contents. The same categories can be applied to current concerns and stimuli (such as sounds) that occur during sleep. After describing the types of effects I will give some dream examples to help make them clear.

(1) *Direct incorporation* is the appearance in a dream, in an essentially unmodified form, of any person, object, location or event from a recent waking experience. Day residues, in the narrowest sense, are direct incorporations of recent waking experiences into the manifest dream content—for example, if someone with whom you spoke during the day were to appear in your dream that night. The fact that it was an incorporation from a daytime experience would be especially clear if the person were someone whom you rarely saw or thought about. In general, dream contents—people, objects, locations, and events—may be more clearly classified as incorporations (either direct or associative) from recent daytime experiences if they are not common, everyday occurrences. Otherwise, it is not clear whether their appearance in the dream is due to recent experiences or to memories of older experiences. Direct incorporations are less common than associative or symbolic incorporations.

(2) *Associative or symbolic incorporation.* Two words, objects, or events are *associated* with each other if thinking of one tends to make you think of the other (as in salt-pepper). Associative connections can vary in strength or degree. Associative connections between two things might arise because of sim-

ilarity of appearance, sound, function, family relationship, category membership, location, or temporal contiguity (as in classical conditioning). Dreams may include contents—such as people, objects, places, or events— that are associated with those of recent waking experiences. For example, if during the day you are examined by a doctor, and that night you dream about some interaction with a different doctor, or different type of medical specialist, it could be an associative dream incorporation.

A *symbol* is something (such as a pattern or object) that is chosen to represent a particular idea, person, object, or event. Advertising logos and religious symbols (cross, star) are familiar examples. According to psychoanalytic theories of dream interpretation, objects in dreams may symbolize something quite different from their surface appearances. For example, in Freudian dream interpretation, a cigar might symbolize a penis, and a purse might symbolize a vagina. Freud (1900) thought that dream symbols function mainly to represent repressed wishes or desires, but the modern view is that people, objects, or events from waking experiences may be symbolically represented in dreams. On some occasions, the overall pattern of a dream story may be a symbolic metaphor of a waking experience, even though specific objects in the dream do not all necessarily symbolize specific objects from waking experience (Antrobus 1977).

In principle, symbolic and associative incorporations are distinguished from each other by the idea that symbols are created by intentional thought, or through some sort of dynamic, purposive unconscious process (such as "dreamwork" in Freudian theory). Associations, on the other hand, are relatively simple connections that may be formed through automatic, unintentional processes.

In practice, however, it is virtually impossible to distinguish between associative and symbolic dream incorporations. As in waking thought, a dream-symbolization process might represent an object or event by selecting one that is associatively related to it (such as by family or category membership). To knowledgeable people analyzing their own dreams, it is often obvious that objects and events in their dreams are associatively related to their recent waking experiences. But there is no way of knowing whether dream contents are related to daytime events through a relatively simple, automatic association process, or through a more complex, purposive symbolization process. Furthermore, the idea of dream symbolization is controversial, because different dream interpretation theories (such as Freudian or Jungian) have different ideas about what dream symbols mean, and there is no way to prove which interpretation is correct.

You do not have to embrace any particular theory of dream interpretation to recognize associative relationships between dream contents and objects/events from your recent waking experience. If dream symbolization does occur, I suggest that it is a shallow symbolism, transparent to knowledgeable persons analyzing their own dreams. The best way to know whether a symbolic or associative connection between dream content and waking experience is true or accurate is whether it "rings true" to you—whether it seems intuitively to be accurate. If a psychoanalyst (whether amateur or professional) suggests some far-fetched symbolic interpretation of one of your dreams, and it sounds to you like a lot of baloney, you are probably right!

(3) The *emotional tone* of dreams may be affected by waking emotional experiences, either with or without any identifiable content incorporations (such as persons) from the waking event. The emotional tone of a dream is often related to a general story theme that parallels a waking experience, even though the specific details are different. For example, a waking experience of frustration over your inability to contact your parents by telephone might be followed by a dream involving frustration over your inability to drive across a bridge to visit a friend. Emotional tone is perhaps the most common type of effect of waking experience on dreams.

(4) *Nonspecific effects* are scorable dream characteristics other than content incorporations and emotional tone. Nonspecific effects include dream characteristics such as vividness, length, coherence, and bizarreness.

Retrospective analysis of home dreams.   Here is an example of one of my own dreams that shows several types of influence by a daytime event:

> I was a foot soldier in an ancient army, dressed in leather armor and carrying a sword and shield. It was nighttime, and we were sneaking up a hill, getting ready to attack the castle on top of the hill. As I approached closer to the castle suddenly I heard a loud scream and I turned to see a large Viking warrior, sword drawn, jumping down onto me from a ledge. The warrior had a shaggy reddish-brown beard and a frightening grin. When he raised his sword to strike me, I woke up (GWF dream, March 1982).

After I woke up I thought about the dream, and it was easy to connect it with a daytime event. That evening I had participated in a chess tournament. At one point in the game I thought that I could get a checkmate in three more moves, and I was excited about the prospect of winning against my higher-rated opponent. I made my first move, and my opponent did not make the obvious recapture but instead launched a surprise counterattack in which I myself was defeated in three moves! I was upset with myself for losing, enough so that that night I lay awake thinking about the game for awhile before falling asleep. To a chess player the associations (symbols?) are obvious: chess has ancient origins, and all of the pieces originally represented military figures. The dream theme of being a soldier on the attack and then being defeated in a surprise counterattack obviously parallels the events of the chess game. To top it off, the Viking warrior had a reddish-brown beard like that of my chess opponent! This dream shows associative incorporations of objects (the dream castle represents the castled king in chess) and events (attack and counterattack), as well as a direct incorporation (the beard), and, quite clearly, an effect on emotional tone (unpleasant surprise). The dream seems to be a metaphoric representation of the daytime event (Antrobus 1977).

This next dream of mine is less dramatic, but it shows a direct incorporation of a name from a recent waking event, and it includes people associated with that name in my past experiences:

> I dreamed that I went to a library reading room to meet B. F. Skinner, the leading behaviorist, for a discussion of theoretical issues in psychology. I waited

alone for a while, sitting at one of the wooden tables in a large room with a high ceiling, tall windows, and walls lined with tall bookshelves. Then three other experimental psychologists—Phil Dunham, Barry Dworkin, and Tom Zentall—arrived. We waited together, but Skinner never showed up. Finally we left the library (GWF, August 1990).

The previous morning I had read in the newspaper that B. F. Skinner had died recently. The other psychologists are people I knew in the early years of my career, who shared my interests in operant conditioning and learning theory. Dunham and Dworkin were graduate students with me at the University of Missouri, where Dworkin and I participated in a televised interview with Skinner in May 1968; I met Zentall at a convention shortly after graduate school, and corresponded with him about our mutual interests. I have not seen any of them for ten to twenty years, and I do not recall any of them ever before appearing in my dreams. This dream does not have any profound symbolism. It simply expresses the thought that, if I wanted to talk with Skinner again, it is too late. The large, high-ceilinged library room may be associated with the idea that Skinner was a prominent intellectual figure.

What kinds of waking events are most likely to affect dream contents? Ullman (1969) suggested that the qualities of novelty, intrusiveness, and unpreparedness are important. *Novel events* are outside of our range of past experience. *Intrusive events* are related to important unresolved personal issues. In either case we may be *unprepared* to deal with the event at the time that it occurs. Dreaming may represent an attempt to cope with the event. Tolaas (1980) suggested that dreams are concerned more with our affective reaction to intrusive waking events than with our cognitive reaction. He gave an example of one of his own dreams:

Once when I was trying to avoid a young woman who used to ask me uncomfortably difficult questions about a university extension course, I jumped into our little green car and asked my wife to drive off. In the following night we had a dream-confrontation at a skiing center. I was driving a strange, motorized mini-bobsleigh made of green plastic. All of a sudden, the young woman in question came driving towards me at great speed in a kind of red mini-snowmobile and I was hard put to get away. She has a small red car and her husband drives the snowmobile of the Red Cross corps stationed there (p. 189).

Again, the dream seems to be a metaphoric depiction of waking experience. The waking experience is identifiable in terms of both the emotional reaction, and person and object incorporations—either direct, associative, or symbolic. There is no deep symbolism or hidden meaning. If the dream is symbolic, it is a shallow symbolism of meaning that is obvious to the dreamer when he or she is familiar with the ideas of association, symbolism, and metaphor. Waking events probably influence dreams more than we usually realize, though their influence may not always be as obvious as in these examples.

Laboratory studies.   One problem with using home-dream reports to study the influence of waking events on dreams is that the waking events are uncontrolled. Laboratory studies have the advantage of deliberate manipulation of presleep events, plus the fact that subjects can be awakened from REM sleep for periodic dream reports.

Several laboratory studies have used films as presleep stimuli. For example, Goodenough et al. (1975) collected REM dream reports from twenty-eight male subjects. Following a laboratory adaptation night, on four later nights the subjects viewed one of four different films, in a counterbalanced sequence. Two of the films were intended to be emotionally stressful (for example, the "subincision" film, showing an initiation ceremony in an Australian aborigine tribe during which adolescent boys' penises were slashed with a stone knife), whereas two films were nonstressful (for example, a travelogue about springtime in Paris). Compared to the neutral films, the stressful films produced greater delay of sleep onset. (Other research has shown that spontaneous awakenings during REM periods occur more frequently following stressful than nonstressful films; Baekeland et al. 1968.) There was little evidence for direct incorporation of film elements into the dreams. However, stressful films produced greater anxiety in dreams (as rated by the subjects), and greater respiratory irregularity during REM periods. Respiratory irregularity is an indicator of anxiety, and it is noteworthy that subjects who had shown the greatest respiratory irregularity while watching the stressful films subsequently showed the greatest respiratory irregularity during sleep. This study makes the point that a particular event can have different effects on sleep and dreams for different people, depending upon how they personally interpret and react to the event. (A conclusion similar to that from Cartwright's [1984] study of divorced women's dreams.)

Other studies have not consistently replicated Goodenough et al.'s results regarding anxiety reactions to stressful films. All studies agree, however, that direct or obvious symbolic incorporation of film events into dreams is relatively rare (no more than 5 percent of dreams), and is not consistently more common for stressful than for nonstressful films (see review by Arkin & Antrobus 1978). Cartwright et al. (1969) found no direct incorporation of pornographic film contents into the dreams of heterosexual male medical students, though there were some possibly symbolic incorporations. One cannot be sure whether the subjects did not have sexy dreams, or whether they failed to report dreams that they had had (Cartwright & Kaszniak 1978). One limitation of laboratory studies of presleep events is that it is not possible, for ethical reasons, to expose subjects to authentic, strongly stressful or pleasurable events.

An unintentional but informative laboratory finding is that it is common for dream reports to include some direct or associative reference to the laboratory situation itself, particularly on the first night in the laboratory (the "first-night effect") (see Cohen 1979a; Cartwright and Kaszniak 1978; Dement, Kahn, and Roffwarg 1965). This probably occurs because sleeping in the laboratory is a novel and somewhat stressful event. For example, in Cartwright's (1984) study of divorcées, 28 percent of the married control subjects' dreams had laboratory references. The fact that only 12 percent of the recently divorced subjects' dreams had laboratory content shows that the laboratory effect can be overridden by other emotionally significant concerns.

Stimuli During Sleep

Specific, identifiable sensory stimuli, either external or internal, can affect dream contents. In the next chapter I will discuss Hobson and McCarley's (1977) theory that dreams are influenced by sensory-system events that form part of the unique physiological response pattern of REM sleep. Here the concern is with external stimuli, and internal stimuli that are not specific to REM sleep. In principle, a stimulus during sleep might have any of the four types of effects on dreams that were discussed above in regard to recent waking experiences.

Organic stimuli.   Among internal stimuli that can affect dreams, one of the most potent is pressure from a full bladder. You have probably had dreams in which you felt the need to urinate, and dreamed that you were actually urinating or getting ready to do so, upon which you awakened to the sensations of a full bladder. Or a full bladder might induce dreams with associated contents, such as running water. A female student suffering from bronchitis reported: "I dreamed I was suffocating under something wet and heavy like a pile of wet, warm blankets . . . I was unable to move or breathe" (RM, December 1988).

Freud reported that if he ate anchovies or any other highly salted food in the evening before going to bed: "I dream I am swallowing down water in great gulps, and it has the delicious taste that nothing can equal but a cool drink when one is parched with thirst. Then I wake up and have to have a real drink" (1900/1965, p. 156). Thirst as an internal stimulus was examined in a laboratory study by Dement and Wolpert (1958), who asked subjects to avoid drinking anything for twenty-four hours. There were no cases of REM dreams involving actual feelings of thirst or drinking something. However, five of fifteen reports contained images associated with the thirst drive. For example: "While watching TV I saw a commercial. Two kids were asked what they wanted to drink and one kid started yelling, 'Coca-Cola, orange, Pepsi,' and everything" (p. 549). Using more liberal scoring criteria, Bokert (1968) found actual thirst themes in a minority of his thirsty subjects' dream reports.

External stimuli.   Figure 11.1 shows a plausible example of how an external stimulus, a baby's cry, might be incorporated into a dream. "The French Nurse's Dream" was reproduced by Freud from a Hungarian comic paper. According to Freud, the dream was a response to the sleeping nurse's unconscious recognition of the child's cry and its significance. "The ingenious artist had in this way cleverly depicted the struggle between an obstinate craving for sleep and an inexhaustible stimulus towards waking" (Freud 1900/1965, p. 403).

Several studies have examined the effects of external stimuli on dreams. One of the first was a self-experiment by Maury (1861), in which he arranged for someone to bring a hot iron close to his face while he was asleep. He dreamed that robbers "had made their way into the house and were forcing its inhabitants to give up their money by sticking their feet into braziers of hot coal" (cited in Freud 1900/1965, p. 59).

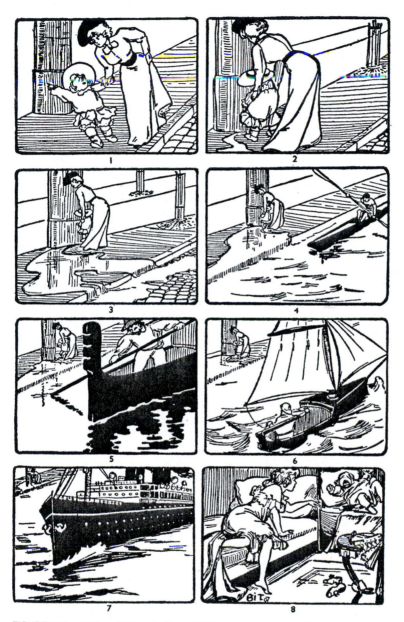

FIGURE 11.1. "A French Nurse's Dream." This cartoon was used by Freud to illustrate the fact that dream contents can be affected by stimuli occurring during sleep. [From Freud, S. (1900/1953). *The Interpretation of Dreams*. Translated from the German and edited by James Strachey. In *The Standard Edition of the Complete Works of Sigmund Freud* (Vols. 4 and 5). Published in the United States by Basic Books, Inc. by arrangement with George Allen & Unwin and The Hogarth Press Ltd. Reprinted by permission of Basic Books (a division of HarperCollins Publishers) and The Hogarth Press Ltd.]

The first modern laboratory study of the effects of external stimuli was done by Dement and Wolpert (1958), who tested twelve subjects for several nights each. In different REM periods the subjects were stimulated with either a 1000 Hz tone, a bright flashing light, or a fine spray of cold water, and a minute later they were awakened by a loud doorbell. The water spray was clearly the most effective stimulus. It awakened the subjects on 39 percent of the trials, but when it did not awaken them it was incorporated into dreams 42 percent of the time, either directly or indirectly (as in images of sudden rainfalls, leaking roofs, and being squirted by someone). The light flashes were incorporated into dreams on 23 percent of the trials (through such images as a fire, a flash of lightning, and the experimenter shining a flashlight into the subject's eyes). The tone was incorporated on 9 percent of the trials, and the waking doorbell was incorporated on 10 percent of trials (as a telephone or a doorbell, for example). The latter effect is similar to what sometimes happens when you use an alarm clock, and you incorporate the alarm sound into your dream (perhaps as a ringing telephone) and go on dreaming for a few seconds before you awaken.

The influence of verbal stimuli—names of people known to the sleeper—on dreams was studied in sixteen subjects by Kramer, Kinney, and Scharf (1983b). The names were tape recorded by the subject himself, and included twenty names of high personal emotional significance, and twenty names of low significance. Each name was played to the subject in a different REM period, and the subject was awakened for a report two to ten minutes later. Stimulus incorporations occurred more often for names of high emotional significance (about 50 percent) than for those of low significance (about 8 percent). The most common type of incorporation was representation, in which the named person appeared in the dream. Other effects included direct incorporations of the spoken name itself, and associations—such as rhyming names and phrases, and other associated contents. For example, after a man's girlfriend's name was spoken to him while he was asleep, he subsequently reported a dream about sailing, with no mention of the girlfriend in the dream report. In the morning, while reviewing the dream report, he commented that he had recently been talking with his girlfriend about their plans to go sailing over summer vacation. (Other studies with verbal stimuli have obtained less frequent incorporations than Kramer et al.; Kramer et al.'s use of significant names spoken by the subject himself may have been critical [see review by Arkin & Antrobus 1978].)

While there is clear evidence that stimuli applied during sleep can affect dream contents, this ordinarily occurs on only a minority of trials. To be effective, a stimulus must be strong enough to be detected during sleep while sensory thresholds are increased, yet not strong enough to awaken the sleeper. Some stimuli affect dreams more than others do, particularly personally meaningful stimuli such as emotionally significant names. A baby's cry may awaken parents when other equally loud stimuli would not. The few studies that tested stimuli during NREM sleep found less effect on NREM dreams than on REM dreams. Sleep stimuli do not cause dreaming *per se*, though they may be incorporated into ongoing dreams.

Conclusion

The influences of recent experiences and so forth on dream contents are not always readily apparent, but they can often be discovered by people who analyze their own dreams and who are familiar with the processes of association and symbolism. Such influences can sometimes be discovered by other people (such as therapists and researchers) who have sufficient knowledge of both the dream and the dreamer and his or her recent experiences.

Though dreams are constructed from knowledge in the individual's memory, they are not mere repetitions of stored knowledge and experiences. Rather, dreaming is a creative process, and the exact contents and narrative sequences of dreams cannot be reliably predicted or experimentally controlled. In the next chapter I will discuss three major theories of dream production, and I will raise the question whether dreaming serves any important psychological function.

SUMMARY

Sleep mentation refers to any conscious mental event that occurs during sleep. A *dream* is a subjective experience, occurring during sleep, that involves complex, organized mental images that show temporal progression or change—in other words, dreams tell stories.

Snyder's (1970) normative study of REM dreams in young adults led to the conclusion that most REM dreams are a "remarkably faithful replica of waking life," insofar as they depict realistic-looking people, objects, and scenes. Most dream events are credible though fictional creations of the dreamer's mind. Most dreams tell coherent stories. The self is the central character in almost all dreams, and verbal communication occurs in most dreams. Contrary to common assumptions about typical dreams, only a small percent of REM dreams are very dramatic, emotional, or bizarre. Misconceptions about "typical" dreams probably arise because of selective recall of more dramatic, emotional, and bizarre dreams under home conditions, compared to laboratory conditions under which more representative dream samples can be collected.

Contrary to beliefs in the early days of laboratory dream research, we now know that dreaming occurs in at least a large minority of NREM sleep periods; other NREM periods may have imageless sleep thoughts. Differences between REM and NREM mentation are relative rather than absolute, and they are greater for deep sleepers than for light sleepers. Compared to REM, NREM mentation tends to be less visually vivid, have less emotion, dramaticity, physical activity, and thematic continuity, more contemporary content, and be more poorly recalled.

The *hypnagogic state* is the drowsy transition period between waking and sleeping, and consists of an alpha SEM phase (alpha EEG with slow eye movements) followed by descending NREM Stage 1. In the hypnagogic state, vivid visual images (hypnagogic hallucinations) occur, which are often relatively static as contrasted with the movie-like temporal progression shown in typical REM dreams. Hypnagogic images are forgotten very rapidly upon awakening. In other respects, hypnagogic images are much like REM dreams.

Five classes of variables that affect dream contents were discussed. (1) Demographic and cultural groups may differ statistically in the frequency of different types of dream contents. Such groups are heterogeneous, and average differences between groups are likely to reflect differences in the current concerns and waking experiences of their members. (2) Different personality and psychopathological types may differ in typical dream characteristics. Chronic nightmare sufferers often show psychotic-like personality characteristics, with oddities of perception and thinking, and report having been sensitive and introspective as children. (3) Current personal concerns, such as anticipated events and unsolved problems, often affect dream contents, particularly when they are related to strong mood states. Cartwright studied dreams of recently divorced women, and found that the most common dream motives of depressed subjects were belongingness and safety, whereas nondepressed subjects' dreams reflected self-esteem and control themes. (4) Recent waking events often affect dream contents, in any of several ways, including (a) direct incorporation, (b) associative or symbolic incorporation, (c) emotional tone, and (d) nonspecific effects (vividness, length, and so forth). Novel and intrusive waking events are most likely to produce day residues in dreams. (5) Stimuli during sleep can affect dreams in the same ways as presleep events. Personally meaningful stimuli, such as names of emotionally significant people, are more likely to affect dreams than are meaningless stimuli. In general, the evidence strongly supports the continuity hypothesis, which says that dreams reflect the individual's waking personality, personal concerns, and recent experiences.

ENDNOTES

[1] A computer search of a Bible (King James Version) database revealed that the word "dream" or "dreams" is used in at least seventy-eight verses (in twenty-seven different chapters) in the Old Testament, and in seven verses (in four chapters) in the New Testament. Dreams are mentioned most often in books Genesis and Daniel. The word "vision" or "visions" is used in at least seventy-eight verses (in forty-eight chapters) in the Old Testament, and in seventeen verses (in thirteen chapters) in the New Testament. Visions are mentioned most often in books Ezekiel, Daniel, and Acts. Some uses of "vision" clearly refer to dreams, and some of the other visions may have been dreams. (Thanks to Jerry Metz and Pat Carol for doing the computer search.) For an interesting example of a biblical dream, read about King Nebuchadnezzar's dream, and Daniel's interpretation of it, in Daniel 4:4–37 in the Old Testament or the Torah.

[2] In discussions of NREM mentation, data from NREM Stages 2, 3, and 4 have usually been lumped together since reliable differences in mentation between those stages generally have not been reported. However, descending Stage-1 NREM, at sleep onset, is a different matter. Stage 1, which is part of the *hypnagogic state*, may differ from other NREM stages, particularly in having more perceptually vivid images. The hypnagogic state is discussed in more detail in a later section.

[3] Though I believe that nowadays most laboratory dream researchers would agree with the picture of NREM sleep mentation that I have presented here, the issue of NREM dreaming is not yet dead. Allan Hobson—whose activation-synthesis theory (Hobson & McCarley 1977; discussed in the next chapter) stipulates that vivid, dramatic, bizarre dreaming is produced by physiological processes specific to REM sleep—has argued recently that reports of dreaming after

NREM awakenings may be a result of experimental demand characteristics. Hobson (1988) said that subjects awakened from NREM Stages 2, 3, and 4 are increasingly disoriented and have difficulty in reaching full arousal and in recalling previous mental activity. Particularly after arousal from Stage 4, subjects appear to be very disoriented, and their EEG may still be in Stage 4. "Following many arousals from Stage 4, subjects often seem to be actively confabulating. . . . This experimental sleep talking, with its completely disorganized brain activity, puts in grave doubt the validity of any reports obtained from Stage 4 awakenings; and subtracting such confabulatory reports may further reduce the amount of dreaming that is actually occurring in the non-REM phase of sleep. . . . Subjects who perceive that the experimenter wants a dream report may be encouraged to confabulate [make up] such a report so that they will be allowed to go back to sleep." (p. 145). Of course, subjects could confabulate dream reports after REM awakenings, too. Most researchers do not seem to feel that confabulation is a serious problem.

[4]The drowsy period of transition from sleep to wakefulness is termed the *hypnopompic state.* There has been little research on the hypnopompic state. Sometimes it is rather arbitrary whether a particular episode is termed hypnopompic or hypnagogic, for example, the drowsy interval after briefly awakening, before falling asleep again.

[5]The difficulty of doing home studies of hypnagogic imagery is that people usually fall asleep before they can recall and record their hypnagogic experiences. In order to wake yourself up just before you fall asleep, Tart (1972c) suggested balancing your forearm vertically (as you lie on your back), such that when you lose muscle tone as you fall asleep, your arm will drop, thus awakening you. Tying a bell to your hand might help. Bertini, Lewis, and Witkin (1964) described a technique for producing and sustaining a drowsy state by using constant, homogeneous sensory stimulation.

[6]Other researchers have found that relatively slow, high-amplitude theta waves (4–7 Hz) in descending NREM Stage 1 are a distinctive feature of the hypnagogic state (Dement & Kleitman 1957; Stoyva 1973), and that the onset of the hypnagogic state is indicated by relaxation of the forehead muscles (reduced frontalis EMG; Stoyva 1973).

[7]Some personal observations lead me to believe that it would be worthwhile to examine the relationship between hypnagogic images, external stimuli, and muscle movements. While falling asleep people sometimes make reflexive muscle jerks that awaken them. Sometimes these jerks are accompanied by hypnagogic images. For example, on one occasion my reflexive leg twitch was accompanied by a hypnagogic image of slipping and falling on a wet, slick floor. Also, recall my thumb-twitch, horn-honking image (described in the section on time experience in dreams). Though in such cases it might seem subjectively that the dream image causes the muscle movement, Hobson and McCarley's (1977) theory says that physiological events (including muscle twitches) can elicit dream images. (More on Hobson and McCarley's theory in the next chapter.)

[8]*DSM-III*, the diagnostic manual of the American Psychiatric Association (APA 1980) lists several personality disorders that involve longstanding, maladaptive traits, but that are not considered to be major clinical syndromes. The *schizotypical* person is eccentric and experiences oddities of thought and perception (such as magical thinking and derealization), and odd behaviors such as speaking digressively and with overelaborations, and is usually socially isolated. The *borderline* person is impulsive and unpredictable, and has an uncertain self-image, intense and unstable social relationships, and extreme mood swings. Both types may appear psychotic under stress (Davison & Neale 1986).

[9]Besides emotionally significant personal concerns, dreams can be affected by people's personal interests or hobbies that occupy their daytime thoughts. An avid birdwatcher in Maine told me that besides keeping lists of birds seen on field trips he also keeps a list of birds seen in his dreams. Over a five-year period he has seen 189 different bird species in his dreams, including some that are not shown in any bird identification books! (For example, the "blue-breasted woodpecker.")

chapter 12 ••••••••••••••••••••••••••••••

Dreaming II: Theories and Research

Theories of dreaming attempt to explain the process by which the manifest dream content is produced. In doing so they need to account for the common characteristics of dreams, such as their visual vividness, their story-like nature, and the incorporation of day residues. Ideally they should also account for other features, such as emotionality and bizarreness, that make some dreams especially salient and memorable, even though they are not present in all dreams. Finally, theories of dreaming should explain why most dreams are so easily forgotten.

Dream theory and research can be divided into four historical stages (Haskell 1986). The *ancient stage* was the prescientific stage, and it included notions of dreams as divine communications, with dreams being interpreted in terms of fixed symbols, as well as the alternative view that the dream world is a separate reality. The major event of the *psychoanalytic stage* was the publication of Sigmund Freud's monumental book *The Interpretation of Dreams* in 1900. Freud saw dreams as a naturalistic phenomenon, rather than a divine or supernatural event, and he attempted to explain how dreams are psychologically motivated and formed by unconscious mental processes within the individual. The *psychophysiological stage* was initiated by Aserinsky and Kleitman's (1953) discovery of REM sleep and its association with dreaming. Hobson and McCarley's (1977) activation-synthesis theory of dreaming is an attempt to explain dreaming in purely physiological terms, an attitude directly opposed to Freud's approach. The *cognitive stage* is the newest, and David Foulkes's (1985) cognitive theory of dreaming is its first major theory.

The cognitive approach attempts to explain dreaming in terms compatible with modern cognitive psychological theory, and also to modify and expand cognitive theory on the basis of dream research. The last three stages, and particularly the last two stages, are overlapping in time and represent shifts in theoretical and methodological approaches to the study of dreaming.

In this chapter I will discuss the theories of dreaming of Freud, Hobson and McCarley, and Foulkes, representing the psychoanalytic, psychophysiological, and cognitive stages of dream theory, respectively. We will see that different theorists have had different ideas as to the most important features of dreams needing explanation, as well as different ideas about dream-production processes and the most important topics for dream research. Freud studied dreams in the course of psychoanalyzing himself and his neurotic patients, whereas Hobson and McCarley studied the brain during sleep and emphasized correlations between neurophysiological events and dream events. Foulkes studied dreaming in children and drew comparisons between the development of dreaming and the development of waking thought. Finally, we will examine the question of what psychological functions dreaming might serve.

SIGMUND FREUD'S PSYCHOANALYTIC THEORY OF DREAMING

Freud's book *The Interpretation of Dreams* (1900/1965) had a profound impact on dream research and theories, extending through to the modern era of laboratory studies. Freud's dominant interest was the practical one of developing a systematic method of dream interpretation, since he believed that dreams are "the royal road to the unconscious" and that neurotic symptoms could be cured by uncovering their unconscious sources. However, he also wanted to develop a psychological theory of dreaming that would explain how manifest dream contents are produced. Freud's theory of dreaming has close ties with other aspects of his psychoanalytic theory, including his ideas about the structure of the psyche in terms of conscious, preconscious, and unconscious levels (see Chapter 1).

Freud distinguished between the *manifest* or surface content of the dream and its *latent* or hidden content. The objects and events in the manifest dream are *symbols* that represent the latent dream thoughts. For example, the manifest content of a dream might include images of riding a train through a tunnel. But, in Freud's view, the true meaning of the dream lies in its hidden content. Thus, the train might be a symbol for a penis, the tunnel might represent a vagina, and riding the train through the tunnel might represent the dreamer's desire for sexual intercourse. Freud's theory of dreaming was intended to explain how the latent content is converted into the manifest content—the dream as it is directly experienced by the dreamer.

In Freud's psychoanalytic theory, the unconscious part of the psyche (the "id") has certain instinctive wishes or desires, primarily of a sexual or aggressive nature. We usually cannot directly fulfill our instinctive wishes because of the constraints of reality. If we were to recklessly pursue our unconscious desires we would be punished by society, and even if our exploits went undetected we would still feel guilt and anxiety (due to the "superego" or conscience). Yet unconscious desires, under the pressure of psychic energy, must find some outlet. Neurotic symptoms are one outlet, but dreams are the main outlet.

Characteristics of Dreams

Every theory of dreaming is influenced by the theorist's ideas about which characteristics of dreams need to be explained. Freud listed several surface characteristics of dreams: (1) The dream thought "is transformed into visual images and speech." (2) The thought "is represented as an immediate situation with the 'perhaps' omitted" (1900/1965, p. 573)—in other words, the dream world is accepted as reality by the dreamer. This is the *hallucinatory* quality of dreams. (3) Dreams are, for the most part, intelligible to the dreamer, though they may contain bizarre elements or distortions of reality. (4) Elements from the waking life—people, objects, and events, as well as desires and conflicts—commonly appear in dreams. These elements are the *day residues*.

How Dreams Are Produced

Dreams are produced in two stages. First, the unconscious wish motivates the production of *latent dream thoughts*. Second, the latent dream thoughts are transformed into the manifest content by the *dreamwork*, a preconscious process. Freud was not concerned with explaining how latent dream thoughts are produced—he took them for granted. His concern was to explain why and how latent thoughts are transformed into the manifest dream.

According to Freud, we do not dream directly—in the manifest content—about our unconscious wishes because to do so would cause us to feel guilt and anxiety, since unconscious wishes are mostly of a sexual or aggressive nature. (Freud wrote at a time when sexual desires were more a cause for guilt feelings than they are today.) The *psychic censor* (part of the preconscious) resists admitting the forbidden wishes to consciousness. Yet the wishes, driven by the psychic energy of the unconscious, are persistent. The dreamwork process translates the latent dream thoughts or forbidden wishes into symbols that form the surface content of the dream. When expressed in the form of a dream, the hidden desires can get past the psychic censor and be admitted to consciousness, since in their disguised form they do not cause anxiety.

If we were to dream directly about our unconscious desires, the resulting anxiety would cause us to awaken. Thus, in translating unacceptable unconscious desires into acceptable dreams, the dreamwork not only prevents conscious anxiety but also serves a secondary function of preserving sleep. In postulating a sleep-preservation function of dreaming, Freud attributed to dreaming a biological adaptive function consistent with Darwin's theory of evolution (R. M. Jones 1970).

The dreamwork.   According to Freud: "At bottom, dreams are nothing other than a particular *form* of thinking, made possible by the conditions of the state of sleep. It is the *dream-work* which creates that form, and it alone is the essence of dreaming—the explanation of its peculiar nature" (1900/1965, p. 545).

In constructing the dream, two conditions must be met: the dream elements must be able to get past the preconscious censor, and the dream must be intelligible. The mental operations used to meet these conditions account for the characteristics of dreams. Four mental operations carried out by the dreamwork and the censor are particularly important in the dream construction process: displacement, condensation, visual representation, and secondary revision.[1]

(1) *Displacement*. The prominent dream elements are the ones most closely scrutinized by the censor. To deceive the censor about what is really important in the dream, the dreamwork may distort the relationship between the manifest content and the latent content in several ways. *Displacement*—the shifting of psychic energy (or affect—emotional feeling) from its original idea or object onto a substitute—is one of the chief means of distortion. With displacement a prominent dream element may appear to be of great emotional significance, whereas the truly important latent thought may be symbolized by a seemingly trivial dream element. A related type of distortion is *reversal*, which occurs when the dream seems to express a wish, or related emotion, that is really the opposite from, or quite different from, the hidden wish or emotion.

Energy displacement and wish distortion are shown in a dream reported to Freud by a young female patient. The patient lived with her sister, who had had two sons, Otto and Karl. But Otto, the patient's favorite, had died several months earlier. The patient reported: "I dreamt that I saw Karl lying before me dead. He was lying in his little coffin with his hands folded and with candles all round—in fact just like little Otto, whose death was such a blow to me" (Freud 1900/1965, p. 186).

The dream does not represent a wish that Karl would die or that he had died instead of Otto. Rather, following further interviews with the patient about her past and recent experiences, and her associations to the dream, Freud discovered the following information: Some time before, the patient had fallen in love with a man, a professor, who was a friend of her sister and often visited her sister's house. After a while the man stopped visiting, but the patient couldn't get over her desire for him, and she often attended his lectures. Over a period of many months she had talked with him only once, when he visited the house for Otto's funeral. But the next day (the day after the dream) she planned to attend a concert where she hoped to catch a glimpse of the professor in the audience. Freud's interpretation of the dream was that the patient strongly desired to see the professor again, so she dreamed of the funeral of a nephew, where she had last seen the professor, and could expect to see him again. The grief attached to her nephew in the dream was a reversal and displacement of her love for the professor. This dream shows how, in Freudian dream interpretation, the meaning of a dream may be far from obvious!

This next dream was told to Freud by a lawyer friend, who was having a love affair with a married woman.

> I dreamt that I came up to my house with a lady on my arm. A closed carriage was standing in front of it and a man came up to me, showed me his credentials as a police officer and requested me to follow him. I asked him to allow me a little time to put my affairs in order (p. 188).

On further questioning, it came out that the dream police had arrested the man for infanticide. The night of the dream, he had spent the night with his mistress. They had had intercourse several times, and he had used the *coitus interruptus* technique of birth control. Freud interpreted the dream to mean two things. The part about taking the woman home was a straightforward expression of the lawyer's wish that he could marry her. The part about being arrested for infanticide reflected his fear that he might have gotten her pregnant. The line of reasoning for the latter interpretation was as follows: The lawyer knew that some religious persons believe that preventing a baby from being conceived is morally equivalent to killing a baby. The dreamwork, Freud concluded, had used reverse symbolism to disguise the lawyer's true anxiety over *failure* to prevent pregnancy as anxiety that he had *succeeded* in preventing pregnancy (symbolized as infanticide). Freud consistently emphasized the point that dreams can be interpreted only in conjunction with knowledge of the dreamer's real-life situation and his or her associations to the dream.

In some dreams the fundamental wish or affect is expressed in its original form, though diminished in intensity, and displaced onto a different person or object from that of the latent thought. Or fears and desires may be reversed. For example, suppose a boy dreamed about the death of his family's dog. Though such an event in reality would cause the boy to feel great distress, during the dream he feels only the slightest sadness over the dog's death. In Freud's view, the latent idea behind the dream might be the boy's wish for the death of his father (the "Oedipus complex"), and the dreamwork selects the dog (a day residue) to represent the father. (The father is the dog's master.) The boy dreams of an event that would make him consciously sad to symbolically represent what he unconsciously desires.

(2) *Condensation.* Freud observed that a written dream analysis is invariably much longer than the written description of the dream itself, and he concluded that the latent dream thoughts are expressed in the dream in a condensed or abbreviated manner. Sometimes two latent ideas will be represented by a single symbol. Speech is also condensed in dreams.

(3) *Visual representation.* Dreams consist mostly of visual mental images; they include some speech, but other auditory images are rare, as are images from other modalities (touch, etc.). Visual images are preferred because they provide the widest range of possibilities for representing ideas in symbols. Visual images are rich in associations, such that one thought can lead to another one due to similarity in appearance, time and place, function, or emotional content. Thus, latent ideas—even abstract ones—can be represented by visual images with which they share some feature. (For example, consider the similarity between the image of a train going through a tunnel and sex-

ual intercourse.) Visual symbols can represent several latent ideas through condensation. Latent ideas have the best chance of getting past the censor when they are symbolized by visual mental images.

(4) *Secondary revision.* The preconscious censor requires that dreams be consciously intelligible. If they operated alone, the three main dreamwork operations—displacement, condensation, and visual representation—would tend to produce dreams that are fragmented and incoherent, with bizarre images. But in fact most dreams seem to tell some coherent sort of story, with recognizable images. The dreamwork selects and constructs symbol-images that are usually realistic or plausible, or at least recognizable. Then the censor does *secondary revision* of the dream, editing it and filling in the gaps to make a comprehendible story. Thus, the dream censor is responsible for the hallucinatory nature of dreams: the fact that the dream world seems to be reality—as long as the dreamer is still asleep.

Day residues.   Why are day residues—memories of people and objects and events of the preceding day—so common in dreams? According to Freud, before an unconscious idea can be symbolized in a conscious dream, the idea must first enter the preconscious, where the dreamwork is done. In order to enter the preconscious, the unconscious idea must first establish some sort of *link* with an idea that is already in the preconscious. Day residues provide that link. The link between a day residue and an unconscious wish can be established in two ways: a wish may transfer its energy to a day residue, or a day residue may stir up an unconscious wish. In either case, an image from the day residue memory comes to serve as a symbolic representation of the unconscious wish.

The connection between day residues and unconscious wishes may not be obvious. Wishes are usually transferred to trivial day residues (displacement), because trivial day residues are less likely to have anxiety-evoking associations. Sometimes the day residue is not easily recognizable, since its appearance may be distorted by the dreamwork.

Forgetting dreams.   Most of our dreams are forgotten. Freud explained this fact in terms of *repression,* an emotional block against retrieval. Presumably there is a danger that if we recall our dreams in the waking state we might see through the dream symbolism and recognize our forbidden unconscious desires, resulting in anxiety and guilt.

Evaluation of Freud's Theory of Dreaming

Freud's *The Interpretation of Dreams* (1900/1965) is one of most influential books of Western intellectual history. It was the seminal work of Freudian psychoanalysis, not only for its exposition of the method of dream interpretation, but for previewing ideas about neurosis that were developed more fully in Freud's later writings. Freud's theory influenced not only psychoanalysis and psychology, but also other disciplines, such as philosophy, literature, art, and anthropology. His ideas were the starting place for several other psychodynamic theories of dreaming and dream interpretation, such as those of Carl Jung and Alfred Adler (R. M. Jones 1970). Most other theorists put less emphasis on sexuality and repressed wishes and more emphasis on current concerns in dreams than Freud. And modern theorists often take the manifest dream content more seriously, putting less emphasis on dream distortion and deep symbolism than Freud. But even when they disagree with Freud, modern dream theorists acknowledge the importance of his ideas and usually take the trouble to compare their ideas with his.

How does Freud's theory of dreaming stand up as a *scientific* theory? The main problem is that it is too vague, and as a consequence, it cannot be rigorously tested. The theory is flexible enough to interpret any dream after the fact, but is not precise enough to make any unique predictions that could be experimentally tested. For example, Freud said that latent wishes are sometimes represented as their opposite, but there is no way of knowing, prior to the dream interpretation, whether a wish will be represented as itself or as its opposite.

The central assumption of Freud's theory of dreaming is that the manifest dream contents are produced through the dreamwork process's purposeful and systematic transformation of latent dream thoughts into symbolic representations. This is a *paradigmatic* assumption: you have to agree with it in order for the rest of the theory to make any sense. And you have to agree with it in order to attempt to test the theory. The only way to test the theory is by interpreting dreams to see whether they could have been constructed by the dreamwork process described by Freud. The problem with using dream interpretation as evidence for dreamwork is that any dream can be interpreted in several ways, and there is no way of knowing which, if any, interpretation is correct. Thus, we cannot assume that interpreting dreams (decoding manifest content into latent content) necessarily reveals the process by which they are generated (encoding latent content into manifest content).

Freud claimed that dreams are symbolic expressions of unconscious desires. To be more specific, he said that "a wish which is represented in a dream must be an *infantile* one"—an instinctive wish with which we are born (1900/1965, p. 592). But in fact, R. M. Jones (1970) found that among the dozens of dreams analyzed by Freud (1900/1965), not a single one was traced to a repressed infantile wish. Every dream discussed by Freud represented either a conscious wish or a suppressed wish of postinfantile origin. Many dreams are blatant expressions of conscious wishes and desires, such as love, sex, social acceptance, prosperity, achievement, or prestige. For example, in the woman's dream of her nephew's death described above, Freud went through a roundabout interpretation to reveal that the dream was about a desire of which the woman was consciously aware, namely, her desire to be with and be loved by the professor.

In attempting to test Freud's theory, researchers have generally been lenient and accepted any evidence of wish fulfillment in dreams as positive evidence for the theory, regardless of whether the wish was adult or infantile, conscious or repressed. Indeed, Freud had an escape clause that encouraged this attitude: "a conscious wish can only become a dream instigator if it succeeds in awakening an unconscious wish with the same tenor and in obtaining reinforcement from it" (1900/1965, p. 591). Thus, Freud allowed that conscious wishes can be expressed in dreams, though he thought that dream interpretation would reveal a repressed wish, too.

Freud's theory can easily be discredited by the evidence, if you are skeptical about the theory in the first place and you cannot see that a particular dream is really a symbolic representation of a wish. Ideally, a good scientific theory should be able to convince a reasonable, fair-minded skeptic that it is plausible, based on the evidence. As we will see, some modern theorists are not willing to grant Freud's assumption that dreams are psychologically motivated, symbolically disguised representations of repressed thoughts or desires.

HOBSON AND McCARLEY'S NEUROPHYSIOLOGICAL THEORY OF DREAMING

Allan Hobson and Robert McCarley (1977) devised the *activation-synthesis hypothesis* to explain dreaming in REM sleep. (They called it "D" sleep, the "D" referring to both desynchronized brain waves and dreaming.) Hobson subsequently elaborated on the hypothesis in his book *The Dreaming Brain* (1988). The activation synthesis hypothesis was developed from a neurobiological viewpoint, rather than a psychological viewpoint, and thus it is different in many ways from Freud's theory. Hobson and McCarley do not grant Freud his main assumptions, that dreams are psychologically motivated, and that the manifest content is a symbolic representation of latent dream thoughts. Rather, the activation-synthesis hypothesis says that dreams are a byproduct of neurophysiological events during REM sleep.

The essence of the activation-synthesis hypothesis is that dreams occur as a result of the forebrain (particularly, the neocortex)[2] constructing images to correspond *isomorphically* to the fluctuating pattern of internally generated stimuli that occurs during REM sleep. Isomorphism means, literally, having the same shape or form. Here, isomorphic correspondence means that the dream images fit or match up in a one-to-one manner with the physiological responses. For example, when the sleeper's eyes move to the right, a fitting dream image is constructed, such as an automobile moving from left to right.

The activation-synthesis hypothesis is designed specifically to account for hallucinoid dreaming during REM sleep. It is not concerned with less vivid or nonperceptual (thought-like) forms of mental activity during sleep, nor is it concerned with dream-like experiences that occur in states other than REM.

Hobson and McCarley's Definition of Dream

Hobson and McCarley's definition of *dream* is important, because it points out what they are trying to explain in the activation-synthesis hypothesis. Their definition of dream has five points, of which the first three are most critical:

A dream may be defined as a mental experience, occurring in sleep, which is characterized by (1) *hallucinoid imagery*, predominantly visual and often vivid; by (2) *bizarre elements* due to such spatiotemporal distortions as condensation, discontinuity, and acceleration; and by (3) a *delusional acceptance* of these phenomena as "real" at the time that they occur. (4) *Strong emotion* may or may not be associated with these distinctive formal properties of the dream, and (5) *subsequent recall* of these mental events is almost invariably poor unless an immediate arousal from sleep occurs (1977, p. 1336, numerals and italics added).

Two Sides of the Activation-Synthesis Hypothesis

Activation.   There are two sides to the activation-synthesis hypothesis: the activation side and the synthesis side. The activation side involves explanations of the cyclic occurrence of REM sleep and of the particular physiological responses that occur during REM. Hobson and McCarley (1977; Hobson 1988) presented evidence showing that the REM sleep cycle is controlled by a neurobiological clock located in the pontine (of the pons) reticular formation of the brain stem (see Figure 5.1). The evidence comes mainly from animal studies involving small brain lesions and/or measurement of brain waves from single neurons in various parts of the brain stem and cortex. For example, bursts of phasic eye movements are strongly correlated with *PGO waves* spreading from the pontine system to the cortex.[3] (PGO stands for pons, lateral geniculate [of the thalamus], and occipital cortex.) Both phasic eye movements and PGO waves are preceded by firings of "giant cells" of the pons, which are an integral part of the biological clock that controls the REM cycle.

Several physiological responses of REM are caused directly or indirectly by the periodic activation of the pontine reticular formation. These responses (see Table 10.1) include: (1) tonic activation of the cortex (shown by desynchronized brain waves [EEG]); (2) tonic inhibition of spinal motoneurons (reduction of muscle tension [EMG] and motor paralysis); (3) phasic rapid eye movements (EOG); (4) blockade of exteroceptive input; and (5) phasic activation of the vestibular system (sense of body position and balance). Also, (6) autonomic responses (heart rate, breathing) become more irregular during REM sleep.

Synthesis.   The synthesis side of the activation-synthesis hypothesis is about the actual production of dreams during REM sleep. The *primary stimuli* for dreams are internally generated stimuli produced by the fluctuating pattern of physiological responses during REM. Primary types of sensory activity include: (1) feedback from eye movements and (2) corollary discharge from the motor system, where the brain commands certain movements and at the same time sends information to sensory systems to allow the brain to anticipate the consequences of those movements. Other stimulation comes from (3) vestibular system activity and (4) feedback from the autonomic nervous system (indicating increased heart rate, and so on). Also important as part of the overall sensory pattern are the *absence* of (or reduced sensitivity to) exteroceptive stimulation (vision, hearing) and the absence of kinesthetic feedback from actual movements (since the major muscles are effectively paralyzed due to motoneuron inhibition during REM sleep).

The dream itself is produced by the brain's attempt to synthesize a series of images to match the changing pattern of internally generated sensory activity. Presumably, the brain selects images—involving activity by the dreamer or events that he or she observes—to correspond isomorphically to the pattern of eye movements and body-movement commands during REM sleep. The synthesized (constructed) images are based on information in memory. Day residues commonly occur in dreams because memories of recent waking experiences are likely to be readily available for selection by the synthesis process.

Hobson and McCarley did not attempt to explain *why* the cortex synthesizes images to fit the sensory frames. Synthesis was assumed to be an automatic cortical process. This is not too far-fetched an assumption. It is related to the fact that the waking brain interprets the varying pattern of sensory input to produce coherent, conscious perceptions of objects and events.

Recently, Hobson (1988) added a third component to the activation-synthesis hypothesis—the concept of *mode switching*, which accounts for the way the activated forebrain synthesizes information in dreaming (compared with waking). Mode switching involves changes in perception, thinking, and memory processes during REM sleep. As a result, unusual or bizarre combinations of objects, scenes, and events may be produced in dreams. Critical judgment and reflective thought are disrupted, such that bizarre dream images may be accepted as reality by dreamers (while they are still asleep). Also, mode switching entails the disruption of information processing for storing new memories.

The activation-synthesis hypothesis attempts to explain only the formal or abstract qualities of dreams, such as variations in the intensity of activity, the direction of movement, scene shifts, bizarre elements such as fragmentation and condensation, and their visual nature. The activation-synthesis hypothesis does not attempt to explain specific dream-image contents (particular persons, places, events). The only requirement of the synthesized images is that they have an isomorphic correspondence with the spatiotemporally specific but fluctuating frames provided by the primary stimuli. The conceptual content of the images is arbitrary, and hence often bizarre: "The forebrain may be making the best of a bad job in producing even partially coherent dream imagery from the relatively noisy signals sent up to it from the brain stem" (Hobson & McCarley 1977, p. 1347).

Examples.   According to the activation-synthesis hypothesis, *flying dreams* could result from irregular activity in the vestibular system, which produces sensations of changes in body position and movement. The forebrain synthesizes an image to fit the proprioceptive information—such as an image of flying, floating, or swimming. A Freudian interpretation in terms of sexual symbolism is unnecessary. *Chase dreams*, where the dreamer has trouble fleeing from a pursuer, could result from the activated motor cortex "commanding" running movements, while at the same time the absence of kinesthetic feedback tells the forebrain that the legs are not moving: hence the dream of trying to run, but not being able to do so. Feelings of *anxiety* in dreams could be the forebrain's interpretation of momentary changes in autonomic arousal (increased heartbeat, breathing) during REM. (This notion is consistent with the Schachter-Singer [1962] cognition-arousal theory of emotion.) Dreams with a lot of rapid movement could result from bursts of eye movements during REM sleep, whereas relatively quiet dream intervals would correspond to periods with relatively little eye movement.

Comparison to Freud.   The activation-synthesis hypothesis differs profoundly from Freud's theory on a number of key issues. (1) The motivating force behind dreams is not wishes or conflicts. Dreams are not psychologically motivated at all. The motivating force is nothing more than the physiological drive for REM sleep. Dreams are a byproduct of physiological responses and brain processes that occur in REM sleep. (2) There is no distinction between manifest dreams and a latent dream contents. Dreams are not symbolic, disguised representations of hidden thoughts. Rather, they are images synthesized to match a fluctuating pattern of physiological responses. (3) Thus, there is no need to assume that there is either a psychic censor or a dreamwork process. (4) The forgetting of dreams is not a result of repression. Rather, in keeping with the neurobiological orientation of the activation-synthesis hypothesis, the usual poor recall of dreams is attributed to a "state-dependent amnesia" having to do with decreases in neuronal activity in memory-encoding circuits during REM sleep (Hobson 1988).

The activation-synthesis hypothesis claims only to account for the formal properties of dreams. It does not attempt to predict or explain the specific meaningful content of dreams. The hypothesis does not deny that dreams may reflect aspects of the dreamer's personality or current concerns. After all, dream images are synthesized from material in the individual's memory.

Research Relevant to the Activation-Synthesis Hypothesis

A major strength of the activation-synthesis hypothesis is that, unlike Freud's theory, it is, in principle, capable of being tested and potentially refuted by research evidence.

Regarding the process of activation of REM sleep, Hobson and McCarley's (1977) original hypothesis that it depends on a biological clock located in a localized group of cells in the pons of the brain stem has been challenged in light of more recent animal research. Vogel (1978) summarized evidence that the REM cycle depends on an interaction between the brain stem and the forebrain. Hobson, Lydic, and Baghdoyan (1986) presented a new neural model that is less localized than the original. The details of the REM cycle-activation process continue to be controversial. However, for our purposes the synthesis side of the hypothesis is more important.

Let us consider evidence about the *synthesis* side of the activation-synthesis hypothesis. The hypothesis makes three major predictions. (1) Dreaming occurs only during REM sleep. (2) Typical REM dreams will have bizarre elements, due to the cortex's difficulty in consistently synthesizing meaningful and coherent images to fit the relatively haphazard and more or less randomly fluctuating pattern of internally generated stimuli. (3) The formal characteristics of REM dreams (such as direction of movement, scene shifts) will show an isomorphic correspondence to the fluctuating pattern of physiological responses during REM sleep.

Limitation of dreaming to REM sleep.

In Chapter 11 I discussed evidence that dreaming with visual imagery does, in fact, occur during NREM sleep, and also during sleep onset (hypnagogic state), when the pattern of physiological responses is quite different from REM sleep. Thus, Hobson and McCarley are incorrect to assume that dreaming occurs only as a response to the physiological events of REM sleep (Vogel 1978).[4] However, insofar as there are some differences between REM and NREM mentation, it is worthwhile to pursue the activation-synthesis hypothesis further to see whether it can account for the characteristics of REM dreams. REM dreams are more readily recalled, and they are more likely to be visually vivid, dramatic, emotional, and bizarre, compared to NREM dreams.

Bizarreness.

On the question of whether typical REM dreams are bizarre, recall the discussion in the preceding chapter of Snyder's (1970) normative study, in which he concluded that most REM dreams are visual and story-like, but not particularly dramatic or bizarre. Snyder defined bizarreness as events that are "outside the conceivable expectations of waking life; to put it bluntly: the craziness of the dream" (p. 146). For example, a dream of Daddy riding a broom to work is bizarre; Daddy riding an airplane is moderately credible but it is not bizarre. In his sample, Snyder found only 13 percent of REM dreams to be moderately or highly bizarre, whereas 28 percent were slightly bizarre. Most laboratory studies have supported Snyder's conclusion that most REM dreams are realistic rather than bizarre (Vogel 1978).

McCarley and Hoffman (1981) presented further evidence on the question of bizarreness, based on a sample of 104 REM dreams collected from fourteen subjects in a sleep laboratory. They defined bizarreness in terms of events that would be impossible or highly improbable or inappropriate in waking life, and they scored bizarre events in three categories: (1) animate characters (such as distorted bodies, monsters, impossible actions); (2) inanimate environment (such as violation of physical laws, fantastic environments); and (3) dream transformations (such as sudden scene shifts "where the entire environment is altered without the character having moved from one scene to another," p. 912). By these criteria some 67 percent of the dreams had at least one bizarre element.

The most common type of bizarreness involved sudden scene shifts (37 percent of dreams), which the activation-synthesis hypothesis attributes to major shifts in the pattern of physiological responses. About 55 percent of the dreams had one or more bizarre elements other than a scene shift. The most common other types of bizarreness were impossible actions (23 percent, for example, humans flying, animals talking) and fantastic environments (15 percent). I would argue that sudden scene shifts should not be classified as bizarre. After all, daydreams often have sudden shifts of topic or scene without creating an impression of bizarreness. (Wollman and Antrobus [1986] found that topic shifts actually occur more often in waking thought than in REM mentation.) Nor do sudden scene shifts in movies create an impression of bizarreness.

Overall, the evidence on bizarreness in REM dreams is mixed. The McCarley and Hoffman (1981) and Snyder (1970) data cannot be directly compared, since they used somewhat different criteria for classifying bizarreness. Snyder rated the degree of bizarreness, whereas McCarley and Hoffman did not rate degrees of bizarreness but went into more detail on types of bizarreness. It seems safe to say that at least a large minority of REM dreams have some degree of bizarreness, though only a small minority of dreams are highly bizarre. If this conclusion is accurate, then the evidence provides only weak support for the activation- synthesis hypothesis, which seems to predict that most REM dreams should be highly bizarre.

Isomorphism.   The isomorphism principle suggests that there will be a correspondence between the form of dream events and the form of physiological events occurring at the same time. According to the activation-synthesis hypothesis, the correspondence should be such that the dream images might plausibly have been generated to match the pattern of physiological responses. One can look for isomorphic correspondence at two levels: (1) *specific isomorphic correspondence*, where specific physiological events can be readily identified with specific dream events (for example, the direction of dream-image movements corresponding to the direction of the sleeper's actual eye movements); and (2) *nonspecific parallelism*, where the overall amount of some type of dream activity is related to the amount of activity in a corresponding physiological subsystem (for example, the amount of observed movement in the dream being greater, the greater the frequency of eye movements). Bear in mind the fact that an observed temporal correlation between dream events and physiological events would not prove the direction of causality between the events; conceivably, the correlation could be caused by some third factor that has not been measured.

Possible correspondence between dream-image movements and the dreamer's eye movements during REM sleep was first investigated by Dement and Kleitman (1957). Earlier REM-dream researchers were interested in testing the *scanning hypothesis*, which suggested that eye movements occur during REM sleep because the dreamer is scanning the visual dream images. Thus, conspicuous movements in dream images (such as somebody jumping) should correspond to actual eye movements as the dreamer "watches" the action. (Note that the direction of causality between dream movements and eye movements assumed by the scanning hypothesis was the opposite of that assumed by the activation-synthesis hypothesis.) In support of the isomorphism principle, in one dream report the dream character walked up a flight of five stairs, and the polygraph chart showed that a series of five upward eye movements had occurred at the same time as the dream (Dement 1976; Roffwarg et al. 1962). Although this case has been widely cited, in fact it is highly unusual. Most studies have found no correspondence between the direction of dream action and the direction of eye movements, and earlier studies that found a correspondence have been criticized on methodological grounds (reviews by Rechtschaffen 1973; Pivik 1978; Schwartz, Weinstein, & Arkin 1978).

In a more recent study, Herman et al. (1984) found that a blind judge could postdict (predict after-the-fact) at a better-than-chance level both the directional axis (vertical or horizontal) and the relative frequency (high, medium, or low) of eye movements based on dream reports. But the researchers searched in vain for evidence of a more detailed correspondence between eye movements and dream images: "In no case did the timing, direction, and amplitude of recorded eye movements exhibit continuous isomorphism with the dream narrative" (p. 59).

Bearing in mind that eye movements are not continuous in REM sleep and may show considerable variability from one REM segment to another, several studies have found a positive correlation between the amount of eye movements and the amount of action in the dream (Dement & Wolpert 1958; Molinari & Foulkes 1969). Foulkes et al. (1972) found a correlation between the amount of eye movement and the amount of visual activity by the self character in the dream report. These studies support the notion of a nonspecific parallelism for eye movements between dream events and physiological events.

Several studies have looked for correspondences between dream events and other physiological events besides eye movements, including measures such as heart rate, vasoconstriction, respiratory rate, and skin potential. Such studies have found mixed, largely negative results. For example, an elaborate study by Hauri and Van de Castle (1973) examined some 120 different correlations between various aspects of dreams and several physiological measures. A few correlations were significant, but their pattern seemed to be random. The only finding that made much sense was a positive correlation between the amount of heart rate variability and the amount of emotionality shown in the dream report, and this finding has not been consistently replicated in other studies.

An isomorphism principle would seem to predict a correlation between the occurrence of penile erections during sleep and sexual activity in dream reports. Fisher (1966) found a relationship between these measures: In seventeen REM periods with little or no erection there were no instances of overt sexual content in the dream, whereas in thirty cases with moderate-to-full erections there were eight dream reports with overt sexual content. (Among the latter group, there was sexual content in dreams in five of six cases with particularly rapid tumescence.) In other words, while erections often occur without sexual dream content, sexual dreams are unlikely to occur in men without an accompanying erection.[5] However, while the activation-synthesis hypothesis would predict a high degree of correspondence between sleep erections and sexual dreams, this high correspondence does not occur.

In conclusion, the evidence on isomorphic correspondence between dream events and physiological events is mixed and largely negative. There are formidable methodological difficulties in testing such a correspondence, for example, getting a sufficiently accurate and detailed dream report and knowing how best to score the dream variables and which physiological measures to correlate with them (Cohen 1979a; Rechtschaffen 1973). Although the evidence on isomorphism is mostly negative, and hence fails to support the activation-synthesis hypothesis, it is conceivable that more positive evidence will be found in the future as a result of improvements in dream-research technology and methodology. Following their review of the literature, Schwartz et al. (1978) were optimistic: "The hypothesis of a relationship between REM activity and dream activity is not dead; we are dealing with a subtle, unimposing but nevertheless real finding" (p. 192).

Summary and Conclusion

The activation-synthesis hypothesis explains, in a general way, the five general features of dreams that Hobson and McCarley (1977) specified in their definition of dream. (1) Visual and motor hallucination result from the brain's attempt to match dream images to patterns of visual and motor system activation in REM sleep. (2) Spatial and temporal distortions occur because the spatiotemporal patterns of internally generated stimuli during REM sleep are unusual, so unusual images may be generated to match them. (3) Dreams are delusional because of the disruption of judgment and reflective thought, and because of the absence of external cues to provide a consistent frame of reference. (4) Intensified emotion occurs because of feedback from activated limbic system emotion centers and the autonomic nervous system (for example, faster or irregular heartbeat), which is synthesized into dream images. (5) Dream amnesia (forgetting of dreams) occurs because of changes in the information-processing mode in REM sleep, as if a "remember this" instruction had been omitted (evidence suggests a reduction of activity in certain aminergic memory-encoding circuit neurons during REM sleep [Hobson 1988]).

Attempts to test the activation-synthesis hypothesis more precisely have met with mixed results. Whereas the activation-synthesis hypothesis predicts that REM dreams will be bizarre and emotional, most sleep laboratory studies have found that most REM dreams are relatively plausible and mundane. Dreams spontaneously recalled at home are more likely to be dramatic and bizarre than are systematically sampled REM dreams, but home dreams are a biased sample of dreams based on selective recall of more salient, attention-grabbing dreams. Furthermore, dreams are not limited to REM sleep; they also occur at sleep onset (hypnagogic state) and in various NREM stages, although NREM dreams are less vivid and memorable than REM dreams. The evidence for the activation-synthesis hypothesis's strongest prediction—that of specific isomorphism between dream events and physiological events, such as between the direction of "dream eye" movements and actual eye movements—is largely negative.

It could be argued that the Hobson and McCarley's activation-synthesis hypothesis is more an explanation of popular dream stereotypes than an explanation of systematically sampled dream data (Foulkes 1990). But on the positive side, the activation-synthesis hypothesis can account for some of the bizarreness that does occur in dreams. And as for isomorphism, at a more general level of correlation between the relative amounts of dream activity and phasic physiological events, the evidence is largely positive (Antrobus 1990). It is to the activation-synthesis hypothesis's credit that it makes some predictions that are specific enough that they can be tested by research.

From an identity-theory viewpoint on the mind-body problem, there is every reason to expect that specific types of conscious events are correlated with specific patterns of brain events at some level. But for both the sleep state and the waking state, the current evidence indicates only a rough correspondence. Perhaps the evidence for specific correspondences will improve in the future, with the help of technological advances in neurophysiological measurement techniques. But insofar as there continues to be a poor correspondence between dream events and internal sensory events in REM sleep, the implication is that the activation-synthesis hypothesis is incorrect in specifying that dreams are just a matter of synthesizing images to fit patterns of internally generated stimulation. Dreams may be synthesized from memory elements, more than from internal stimulus patterns. Or, insofar as dreaming is a thought process occurring during sleep, it may be an active, self-guided process that generates images to suit its own themes, largely (though not entirely) independently of current internal and external stimuli.

Even if it is not correct in all of its details, the activation-synthesis hypothesis probably is at least partly right: internally generated stimulation from physiological events during sleep do influence the dream generation process. Consider, for example, the common experience of dream themes associated with urination being followed by awakening and feeling the need to urinate. Undoubtedly other factors besides internal stimulation are also important. The next section describes Foulkes's cognitive theory, which is similar to the activation-synthesis hypothesis in proposing that dreaming is a process of interpretation and synthesis, but differs in emphasizing activated memory events, not internal sensory events, as the critical information to be synthesized in the dream-production process.

DAVID FOULKES'S COGNITIVE THEORY OF DREAMING

In his book *Dreaming: A Cognitive-Psychological Analysis*, David Foulkes (1985) considered over thirty years of modern laboratory dream research, including his own work on children's dreams, and interpreted it in light of modern cognitive psychology research and theory to provide a new interpretation of the psychological processes involved in dream production.

The Characteristics of Dreams

As with the other theories, I will begin with the theorist's ideas about the fundamental characteristics of dreams. Foulkes's (1985) list of dream characteristics was influenced by his cognitive viewpoint, and it shows what needs to be explained.

"Dreams are involuntary symbolic acts."   By symbolic acts, Foulkes means simply that dreaming is a kind of thinking, and not some sort of faulty perception. In particular, dreaming involves thinking in visual mental images, though speech also occurs in many dreams. In saying that dreams are symbolic acts, Foulkes does not mean the deep symbolism stressed by Freud, where the surface dream contents are assumed to symbolize hidden dream thoughts. Rather, Foulkes sees dreams as symbolic in the more general sense, where a symbol is something that stands for something else and, in particular, a symbol is a mental event that represents some real or imagined external reality. To say that dreams are involuntary means simply that we do not consciously will them to happen.

"The sources of dreams lie in what we know."   Ultimately, all dream images are based on knowledge that we have accumulated throughout our lives, including personal experiences and relatively impersonal, conceptual knowledge. Even our most fantastic and distorted dream images are constructions and transformations based on what we know.

An implication of this characteristic of dreams is that the dreams of young children, who have relatively little conceptual knowledge or life experience, would be simpler than those of adults. Foulkes's research (1982a) shows this to be the case. For example, when my son Michael was a toddler (two years, two months old), as I was getting him up one morning he said "I saw a bus in the air." Upon questioning he revealed that it was a big yellow bus, but there was no elaboration, no story, and no personal involvement revealed in his report. It would be rare for an adult to have such an impoverished dream.

"Dreams draw on dissociated elements of memory and knowledge." Though dreaming is memory-based, it is not mere remembering in the sense of recall of past experiences. Dreaming is creative. We may have dreams with combinations of people, objects, settings, and events that have never occurred together in reality. Individual images can also be novel combinations of elements; for example, *physiognomic fusions* are faces that are a combination of facial features of two or more people, such as the eyes and eyebrows of one person and the mouth, beard, and hair of another. Here, dissociated elements are elements that normally occur together (such as all of the facial features of a person), but which become disconnected and appear separately or in novel combinations in dreams.

"Dreams are organized mental acts."   Even though they are constructed of dissociated elements of knowledge, typical dreams are comprehensible and plausible. The sequence of dream events hangs together to form a narrative or story, rather than being random. Though sudden, dramatic scene shifts sometimes occur in dreams, typical dreams involve a continuity of characters and setting from one scene to the next (Foulkes & Schmidt 1983).

"Dreams are credible world analogs."   Dreams are world analogs in the sense that phenomenologically they represent the shapes of people and objects and their spatial relationships in a manner similar to the way they appear in the real world of waking experience. Most REM dreams are so lifelike that we accept them as real at the time.[6] Truly bizarre dreams are relatively rare, though when they occur they are so striking that we remember them better than we remember the more typical mundane dreams. (The bizarre Hieronymus Bosch paintings sometimes used to illustrate magazine articles on dreaming are not at all like typical dreams.)

"Dreams are self-revelations." Different people have different dreams because they have different knowledge bases, including personal autobiographical knowledge, to draw upon during the dream construction process. Furthermore, the "self" character appears in about 95 percent of REM dreams (Snyder 1970). However, the dream self may differ from the real self as knowledge about different persons (real or fictional) becomes dissociated and recombined in novel ways during the dreaming process.

Summary. To summarize Foulkes's characterization, dreaming is a thinking process, occurring during sleep, that operates "on our memories and knowledge to construct symbolic world-analogues in which events transpire in a narrative sequence" (Foulkes 1983, p. 355).

A Cognitive Theory of Dreaming

Basic assumptions. The two main principles of Foulkes's theory may be summarized before going into more detail. (1) Dreaming is instigated by *diffuse mnemonic activation.* That is, a variety of different memory elements are activated in a random or semi-random manner. The memory units may be either semantic (conceptual) or episodic (personal). (2) A *dream-production system* organizes the activated mnemonic elements into a comprehensible, conscious dream experience. The dream-production system uses our knowledge of narratives or scripts (common or plausible sequences of events) and the world (how things look, how they move, their spatial relationships, etc.) to produce dreams that are comprehensible, and usually plausible, both in terms of the momentary spatial organization of dream scenes and the sequential organization of dream events. Visuospatial thought processes are employed in the construction of organized, recognizable, kinematic (movie-like) conscious mental images.

Foulkes's theory can be clarified by contrasting Foulkes with Freud. Consider the following (hypothetical) dream report by a male subject: "I was driving down the highway in a red sports car. My mother was sitting beside me. I was driving pretty fast. Then a bear ran out in front of the car. I couldn't stop the car in time. I hit the bear and killed it." From a Freudian viewpoint, this dream could be interpreted in terms of the Oedipus complex: The dreamer has a hidden desire for sexual intercourse with his mother (symbolized by driving fast, with his mother beside him) and a desire to kill his father (the bear). The hidden desires motivated the dream, and the dreamwork process selected suitable mnemonic elements to serve as symbols to represent the hidden desires and wove the symbols into a comprehensible story. But in Foulkes's view, the mnemonic elements (mother, bear, sports car) were directly activated in a haphazard manner, without any prior wish or motive. The dream-production system then wove the elements together into a plausible, narrative sequence. Though based on the dreamer's knowledge, the dream is not psychologically motivated, nor does it necessarily symbolize any hidden desires.

Mnemonic activation.   How does mnemonic activation occur? When we are awake, mnemonic activation occurs in three ways: (1) sensory elicitation, by either external stimuli (people and events) or internal stimuli (such as pains, tummy rumbles); (2) associative elicitation by other memory elements that have already been activated (spreading activation leads to the activation of semantically or episodically related concepts and events); and (3) directed retrieval, as when we willfully retrieve information that is relevant to the problem at hand.

When we are asleep, mnemonic activation operates much more haphazardly than when we are awake, for several reasons: (1) when we are asleep mnemonic activation occurs primarily as a result of spontaneous brain activity; (2) sensory elicitation is reduced during sleep, due to reduction of exteroceptive and interoceptive sensitivity; (3) associative elicitation is much freer during sleep, and more likely to follow unusual channels; and (4) directed retrieval is absent during sleep, since there is no voluntary, problem-solving–oriented thinking going on. Thus, mnemonic activation is a more passive process during sleep than when we are awake.

Mnemonic organization: The dream-production system.   Interpreting one's experience seems to be a natural functional characteristic of the human mind/brain system. When we are awake we interpret our sensory experience though processes that select and organize the sensory inputs. In sleep, with external stimuli at a minimum, the interpretive system is bombarded with semi-randomly activated mnemonic units. It interprets this purely mnemonic experience by selecting and organizing it to produce a dream that we can consciously comprehend.

The dream-production process draws on thinking skills and knowledge that are essentially the same as those used in waking thought. Visuospatial thinking skills are used in generating recognizable mental images. Narrative thinking, whether awake or asleep, requires the ability to construct a linear sequence of events in time, which implies a capacity for advance planning. It draws on *script knowledge*—knowledge about typical sequences of events in particular situations (such as eating at a restaurant, going to a store, taking a bath).

It is instructive to compare dreaming with speech. Speech has semantics (meaning) and syntax (rules of correct sequence [grammar]). Ordinarily, when we speak we have a particular meaning that we intend to convey. We select the appropriate words and organize them according to rules of syntax to convey the intended meaning. But in dreaming there is no intent to convey anything in particular. Mnemonic elements are activated haphazardly. But they are organized according to syntactic rules to make them meaningful.

Neuropsychological studies of brain-injured patients suggest that image generation and narrative-sequencing processes in dreaming may occur primarily in the right and left hemispheres, respectively. Damage to the left hemisphere causes more disruption of dreaming than does damage to the right hemisphere (review by Antrobus 1987). Patients with injury to the left cerebral cortex—specifically, the left posterior temporal lobe—may experience both aphasia (loss or disruption of speech) and loss of dream recall. Right-hemisphere damage may lead to dreaming without visual images, though meaningful dream-like thought with narrative form and nonvisual spatial imagery still occurs. (This is also true of subjects blind since birth [Kerr, Foulkes, & Schmidt 1982].) These findings are noteworthy because Foulkes's theory implies that left-hemisphere verbal production processes—including verbal concepts and narrative knowledge—are critical for dream construction. Antrobus (1987) hypothesized that the left hemisphere constructs the dream and gives it its narrative form, and that bizarre events occur in dreams because the right hemisphere sometimes generates an image that does not fit the left hemisphere's narrative.

One dream process. Foulkes (1985) argued that there is one dream-production system that operates in all sleep stages. Differences in dreams or mentation between the different stages mainly reflect differences in the continuity with which the dream-production process operates. Enhanced cerebral excitation during REM sleep presumably produces abundant mnemonic activation. Thus the most fully formed dreams occur in undisturbed REM sleep. In NREM sleep, cortical excitation and hence mnemonic activation are reduced. Though NREM mentation has sometimes been called "thoughtlike," Foulkes said that it more commonly is like a dream fragment, with visual imagery, but with less narrative development than REM dreams. Supporting this point, Foulkes and Schmidt (1983) found that REM dream reports have more persistence of characters from one unit to the next, and more action units, than NREM and sleep-onset reports.

Amnesia for dreams. Foulkes (1985) explained the forgetting of dreams in terms of the type of information processing that occurs during dreaming. He suggested that the reason recall of dreams is poor is that the process of dreaming—involving memory retrieval and synthesis—is incompatible with the encoding process for storing new memories. The dreaming process is comparable to episodic memory recall, which involves construction of memories from retrieval and inference. Thus, trying to recall dreams is not so much like trying to recall actual life events as it is like trying to recall prior episodic memory recall experiences (that is, recalling the experience of recalling something). And recall of prior memory experiences is usually very poor. You may recall what you did last summer, but you probably don't recall yesterday's daydreams about it.

Foulkes suggested that dreams are only likely to be recalled when we wake up during a dream, while it is still fresh in short-term memory. If we can recall a dream from STM and do mnemonic processing on it (such as rehearsal and forming associations), then we can store it in long-term memory for later retrieval.

Meaning in dreams. According to Foulkes (1985), dreams do not have any deep meaning. Dreams are not expressions of unconscious desires or conflicts. Nor are dreams symbolic expressions of anything other than what they appear to be on the surface. Thus, there is no point in trying to interpret dreams to discover their hidden meaning, because they do not have any hidden meaning.

However, dreams are not entirely without meaning, according to Foulkes. They have *indicative meaning*. That is, they indicate something about the mind of the dreamer—his or her conceptual and personal knowledge—which in turn reflects the individual's personality. Thus, it is not surprising that dream analysis studies have found some degree of correspondence between dream contents and peoples' personalities and life situations. But the indicative meaning of dreams does not imply that they were purposefully constructed to reveal a particular meaning. Rather, the dream contents are a result of random mnemonic activation during sleep, and the dream structure is produced by the cognitive dream-construction process.

Do dreams have any psychological adaptive function at all? (This question must be kept separate from the question of whether REM sleep has any function.) Foulkes argued that there is no proof that dreaming serves any adaptive function, or that the dream-production system evolved for the purpose of producing dreams. Rather, the dream-production system is actually the operation of the normal memory and thought processes, operating under the conditions of sleep. Foulkes suggested that rather than trying to interpret dreams to reveal individual personalities and hidden meanings, it would be more profitable for dream researchers to study dreams to increase our understanding of how the human mind/brain system works.

Children's Dreams

A major implication of Foulkes's theory is that children's dreams will differ from adult dreams, since dreaming depends upon knowledge and thought processes that develop with age and experience. To be more specific, he hypothesized that the childhood stages of dream development will correspond to stages of cognitive development in the waking state.

Foulkes himself conducted the most extensive laboratory study of children's dreams (1982a, 1982b, 1983). The subjects were boys and girls in two different age groups at the start of the experiment: younger children, three or four years old (n = 14), and older children, nine or ten years old (n = 16). Each child spent nine nights per year in the sleep laboratory for five years. Thus, the study collected longitudinal data across the range of three to fifteen years of age. A typical test night involved two REM awakenings and one NREM awakening. After each report the experimenter asked a few questions to try to get more details about the dream. Also, each year each child was tested with several personality and cognitive performance scales.

Table 12.1 summarizes some of Foulkes's REM dream data for children at four different age levels. I will concentrate on the results for the younger group, which was followed from ages three/four to eight/nine. This age range is particularly critical, as it corresponds to Piaget's preoperational, transitional, and concrete operational stages.

Ages three to five (between third birthday and fifth birthday).   This is the youngest age range at which it is possible to collect meaningful dream data. (In pilot studies Foulkes found dream reports to be extremely rare in children younger than three years old.) In the three- to five-year age group, the

TABLE 12.1 REM Dream Characteristics in Children at Four Age Levels*

	PRE-OPERATIONAL (AGES 3–5)	TRAN-SITIONAL (AGES 5–7)	CONCRETE OPERATIONAL (AGES 7–9)	FORMAL OPERATIONAL (AGES 13–15)
Frequency of dream reports	15% (median)	31%	43%	73%
Report length (median words)	14	38	59	86
% of reports longer than 100 words	0%	5%	25%	43%
Story form	isolated event	several events in series	complex narrative	complex narrative
Imagery form	static	kinematic	kinematic	kinematic
Common themes	animals, body state	social interaction	social interaction	social interaction
Animal characters:	39%	33%	22%	9%
Self-representation (any activity by subject as dream character):	12%	38%	47%	62%
Social interaction (two or more persons):				
prosocial	6%	38%	40%	40%
antisocial	3%	27%	25%	24%
Activity type (either self or other character):				
verbal	2%	19%	28%	43%
locomotor	26%	63%	69%	62%
Dreamer body state:				
hunger	2%	0%	9%	9%
fatigue	24%	8%	9%	7%
Dreamer feelings (one or more of fear, anger, happy, sad, excited):	8%	29%	34%	32%

*Dream content percentages are the percent of dreams showing that content (mean of medians for males and females). Data for the first three age groups are longitudinal data on the same set of subjects; data for ages 13–15 are from a different set of subjects.

Based on data in Foulkes, D. (1982). *Children's Dreams: Longitudinal Studies.* New York: Wiley. (By permission of the author.)

typical child reported dreams on only 15 percent of REM awakenings. The reports were quite brief, only one or two sentences. They depicted an isolated scene or event, with no story development. The content of the dream reports was quite different from that of adult reports. There was typically no active self character, and in fact most dreams showed no activity by any character. Social interactions were minimal. Strangers (constructed human characters) were quite rare (only 2 percent), while family and known persons appeared more often (about 17 percent). On the positive side, the younger children's dreams had a remarkably high frequency of animal characters, which were typically common farm animals or unaggressive wild animals (like frogs, birds, deer). (Foulkes [1985] speculated that young children might represent themselves by animal characters.) Fatigue was a more common theme at this age than later, for example, in dreams that the child is sleeping somewhere other than where he or she is. Notably absent were dreams with unpleasant emotions.

Here is an example of a dream from the youngest group (Dean, age four years, eight months):

> I was asleep and in the bathtub. [E: Was this in your bathtub at home?] Yes. [Was there anyone else in the dream beside you?] No. [Could you see yourself there?] Uhhh, no. [I mean, did you have like a picture of the bathtub and you could see your body inside the tub?] No. [How did you feel?] Happy. (Foulkes 1982a, p. 66).

Developmental trends. As the children got older the frequency of REM dream reports increased, as did the median report length. By age seven to nine years, the reports were complex story narratives, rather than relatively isolated, static images. Action by the self character, and activity in general, increased. Emotional content became more common, though emotional expression still occurred in only a small minority of reports. Animal characters became less common, whereas strangers became increasingly common. At all ages, the children's dreams represented fictional events that most often were mundane and more-or-less realistic. Though many of their dreams were unlikely, at least they were not terribly bizarre, in most cases.

As an example of changes in dreaming styles in children as they mature, compare my son Michael's simple, static dream at age two years, two months ("I saw a bus in the air") with this dream report made at five and a half years, which shows good narrative development and action by the self character:

> Mom was going somewhere and I couldn't decide if I wanted to go. She started up the car and drove away. Then I decided I wanted to go, so I ran after her. And I got lost. But a policeman found me and took me home. I told him I live on Norfolk street.

Credibility. There is little problem in accepting the dream reports of children five to seven years old or older pretty much at face value, as we do the reports of adults. By that age their language development has advanced to the point that they should be able to describe their dreams with reasonable accuracy. But what about the youngest age group, three to five years: Is it possible that they really had longer, more complex dreams, but were unable to describe them accurately? Foulkes (1983) found this interpretation to be unlikely, based on results from waking measures of the children's mental abilities. For example, in the youngest group, there was no relationship between the frequency of dream reports and waking measures of the ability to describe and remember pictures.

Among the older children (ages five to seven years and older), Foulkes (1982a) found that dream reporting was strongly correlated with certain waking measures of visuospatial performance (for example, the Block Design Test, where subjects construct a visual pattern from colored blocks). This result (replicated in Foulkes et al. 1990) suggests that some of the same skills used in performance of waking visuospatial tasks are also employed by dream construction processes. Waking visuospatial skills were also related to certain aspects of dream reports in the youngest (three to five years) group (such as active self, use of animal characters [Foulkes 1983]). The correlational data on visuospatial performance suggests that differences in dream reporting between different children's age groups represent not differences in the ability to *describe* dreams, but rather, differences in the ability to *have* complex visuospatial dreams.

Implications.   The basis of dreaming is in what the child *knows* and how well he or she can *think*, not what he or she can see or do. Dreaming is not like a videotape playback of what the child has seen. Rather, it is a novel kinematic image sequence constructed from elements of the child's knowledge about the world, including people, animals, and objects—how they look, what they can do, how they interact, and so on. The construction of complex narrative dreams depends upon two factors developed through the child's learning experiences: (1) organized conceptual world knowledge—the raw material from which dreams are constructed—and (2) thought processes involved in dream construction, including visuospatial abilities to construct organized visual mental images, and script knowledge to provide the basis for meaningful sequences of dream events.

Foulkes argued that it is only when children reach Piaget's stage of concrete operations (seven to nine years) that they have the knowledge and thinking abilities to produce nearly adult-like dreams. This is not the place to argue whether it is more realistic to speak of cognitive development as a continuum or as a series of discrete stages. The important point is that dreaming is a cognitive, constructive process, not a perceptual process, and the development of dreaming parallels the development of waking cognitive abilities and knowledge.

Evaluation of Foulkes's Theory

One complaint against Foulkes is that, according to his theory, dreams are not psychologically motivated and do not have any deep meaning. Many people feel that dreams are so dramatic that they surely must have some sort of hidden meaning. But Foulkes (1985) replied that there is no way to prove objectively the validity of any interpretive scheme for revealing deep symbolic meanings in dreams. Acceptance of dream interpretation depends upon one's prior belief system.

I am sympathetic with Foulkes's cognitive approach to dreaming, but I would criticize his theory for not taking more account of the common occurrence of day residues in dreams. Mnemonic activation in sleep does not appear to be entirely random. People's daytime experiences and current concerns affect dream contents more than one would expect from the purely random mnemonic activation. It would not require any major changes in his theory to postulate that some "hot topics" in memory (current concerns, intrusive waking experiences) are more likely to be activated than others. Also, there are many cases where dreams show a "shallow symbolism" in which day residues and current concerns are represented indirectly in ways that are fairly obvious. (Pertinent examples were presented in the previous chapter.) These indirect representations might occur due to highly probable mnemonic associations, rather than due to a process of motivated symbolic disguise, and thus could be incorporated into Foulkes's theory without any major changes.

Haskell (1986) criticized Foulkes for minimizing the dreamer's personal motivational concerns: "If dreaming is the symbolic representation of physical objects and events, as Foulkes suggests, then one is left wondering why feelings, wishes, hopes, fears, and problems are not likewise represented, and fit into syntactic units as they are in the waking expression of a spoken sentence" (p. 150). Implicit in Haskell's comment is a suggestion of how motivational concerns might be incorporated into Foulkes's theory, as mnemonic structures that can be activated and provide a framework for organizing units selected from among randomly activated memories. The motivational units probably would not be randomly activated; rather, they would carry over from waking thoughts into sleep.

Antrobus (1986) took a similar position on incorporating goals into a cognitive theory of dreaming. He agreed with Foulkes that the dream-production system is the same cognitive system that is responsible for producing waking verbal and imaginal narratives. During sleep, where there is ordinarily no variety of external sensory input to produce varied thought associations, the dream narrative may continue on the same topic longer than ordinary thought does, then suddenly shift to a new topic that is, however, in some way related to the prior dream content via connections in individual's memory structure.

Like most theories of dreaming, Foulkes' theory is not an elaborated, step-by-step description of the dream-production process. Rather, it is more a characterization of the nature of the process. What is different and important about Foulkes's theory is that it attempts to explain dreaming in terms consistent with current knowledge about cognitive processes in adults and children. Foulkes's (1985) theory may be regarded as a valuable first approximation to a fully developed cognitive theory of dreaming. It is limited partly by our limited understanding of waking processes of narrative production and imagination.

THE FUNCTIONS OF DREAMING

Although both Hobson and McCarley (1977) and Foulkes (1985) argued that dreaming is merely a byproduct of brain-cognitive processes operating during sleep and serves no practical function, many writers have argued that dreaming is such a common and conspicuous characteristic of humans that it must have some sort of practical function. Conceivably, dreaming was originally a byproduct of brain processes operating during sleep, but later acquired some practical function. But what function? (Bear in mind that the question of the function of dreaming is separate from the question of the function of REM sleep, discussed in Chapter 10.)

As we have seen, Freud (1900/1965) thought that dreaming helps to discharge pressing unconscious desires through symbolic wish fulfillment. By providing symbolic wish fulfillment, dreaming reduces the chances that unconscious desires will produce neurotic symptoms. Also, symbolic dreaming preserves sleep, since direct awareness of our repressed desires would produce anxiety that would awaken us, in Freud's view.

Carl Jung (1933) argued that dreaming serves a compensatory function that helps maintain the individual's psychic balance. "The psyche is a self-regulating system that maintains itself in equilibrium as the body does. Every process that goes too far immediately and inevitably calls for a compensatory activity" (p. 17). In Jung's view, dreaming is a process by which the unconscious seeks to correct unbalanced or inadequate conscious experience. Thus, for example, a shy person might dream of being socially outgoing and popular. Or a sorrowful daytime experience might be followed by dreams with a happy mood. In addition, Jung argued that dreams may symbolically express "archetypes of the collective unconscious" having to do with universal themes of human existence of which Jung believed we have innate, unconscious knowledge (for example the theme of the child's dependence upon the mother, and the necessity of becoming independent of her).

Alfred Adler (1927) believed that dreams serve a personal problem-solving function. Dreams occur in response to significant personal problems, and in dreams people seek solutions that are consistent with their life styles and habitual choices. The problem and its solution may be presented symbolically. For example, a student who is a quitter and who wants to postpone an examination might dream of trying to climb a mountain but falling off the mountain, whereas a more motivated student might dream of struggling hard to overcome the obstacles and successfully reaching the top of the mountain. Problem solutions in dreams may be simplistic or unrealistic. (See Ryckman 1989 for discussions of the role of dreams in several major personality theories.)

Several theorists have hypothesized that dreaming serves a problem-solving function (reviews in Cohen 1979a; R. M. Jones 1970). Some scientists, writers, and artists have reported that creative problem solutions have occurred to them in dreams. Perhaps the most famous report is that of the Austrian chemist Friedrich August von Kekule, who in 1865 was trying to determine the structure of the benzine molecule. He dozed by the fire and had a dream in which he saw a snake seize its own tail, thus forming a ring. Kekule awoke with the inspiration that the form of the benzine molecule is a ring.

His idea proved to be correct: the basic structure of benzine is a ring formed of six carbon atoms linked together. However, Weisberg (1986) has pointed out the flimsiness of the anecdotal evidence for creative problem solving in dreams. It has not been proven experimentally that dreaming *per se* produces useful solutions to practical problems.

Breger (1969) suggested that dreaming serves an emotional information-processing function by helping the individual to organize and assimilate emotionally significant new experiences into thinking and memory schemas that have been effective in handling such experiences in the past. An implication of this hypothesis is that emotionally significant current concerns or recent experiences will be represented in dreams (at least symbolically), and that this will be true to a greater degree, the greater the emotional impact of the experience and the less the individual has been successful so far in resolving the problems associated with it. Over a period of time dreams should reflect solving of emotional problems.

Most theories of dreaming support the *continuity hypothesis*, which says that dreams reflect the individual's personality, current concerns, and emotionally significant daytime experiences. As we saw in the last chapter, the evidence is largely consistent with the continuity process. However, the available evidence does not prove that dreaming has any particular adaptive function. But perhaps researchers have taken too narrow a view of dream function, as Hunt (1986) suggested:

> A self-referential, self-transforming system like the human mind will evolve its uses as creatively and unpredictably as it evolves its structures. Indeed there do seem to be distinct types of dreaming: . . . a lucid-control line, a Freud-type pressure-discharge line, a Jung-type archetypal-mythological line, and perhaps a problem solving line and a Robert Louis Stevenson-type creative story line. It may be *because* dreaming (and human life) has no fixed function that it is open to so many different *uses* (p. 226).

Perhaps Hunt is right in suggesting that dreaming may serve many practical functions. But regardless of whether dreaming *per se* serves any practical functions, many people have found that keeping a dream diary, and trying to interpret their dreams in relation to personal concerns and recent experiences, has been a valuable project for increasing their self-understanding.

Theories of dreaming are only as good as the data on which they are based. In the next chapter I will discuss theories of dream recall and forgetting, and also lucid dreaming—recalling that you are dreaming while you are asleep and dreaming. Finally I will make some concluding comments about dreaming and its implications for consciousness.

SUMMARY

In his psychoanalytic theory of dreaming, Freud said that dreams are psychologically motivated to allow indirect expression of unconscious desires. Manifest dreams are symbolic representations of latent dream thoughts. Symbolic transformations are produced by the dreamwork process in order to prevent anxiety and protect sleep. Freud's theory is hard to test because one has to assume that the theory is correct in order to interpret dream symbols for evidence of repressed desires.

A neurophysiological theory, Hobson and McCarley's activation-synthesis hypothesis, says that dreams serve no purpose, but are merely a byproduct of brain activity during REM sleep. REM sleep, with its unique pattern of physiological responses, is activated periodically by a biological clock in the brain stem. The cortex synthesizes images to fit the semi-random pattern of internally generated sensory events during REM sleep (isomorphism principle). The theory predicts REM dream bizarreness; but laboratory data show that perhaps half or less of REM dreams are bizarre, depending upon one's criterion for bizarreness. The search for specific isomorphic relations between dream events and physiological events has produced largely negative results; for example, eye movements and dream-action movements are usually not correlated.

Foulkes's cognitive theory postulates semi-random activation of memory units in the cortex, which are selected and woven into narrative form by the same cognitive structures that produce narratives in the waking state. Dreams are not psychologically motivated or deeply symbolic, but their content reveals some aspects of the individual insofar as dreams are constructed from material in the individual's memory. Foulkes's research on children's dreams indicates that their characteristics, such as narrative form, develop in parallel with development of waking thought processes.

Several different ideas about the psychological functions of dreaming have been proposed, ranging from wish fulfillment to creative thinking. It is hard to prove that dreaming has any particular psychological function. But most theories support the *continuity hypothesis*, which says that dreams reflect the individual's personality, current concerns, and emotionally significant daytime experiences.

ENDNOTES

[1]Freud said that dreaming is characterized by *regression*, that is, a change to a more primitive or immature form of thinking. Regressive thinking is more visual and less rational than conscious thinking. Freud also characterized dreaming (as well as vivid, wish-fulfilling daydreaming) as *primary process* thinking. Primary process thinking operates under the control of the Id to serve the *pleasure principle*. It is contrasted with *secondary process* thinking, which is rational thinking, mostly verbal, done by the Ego to serve the *reality principle*.

[2]The forebrain includes the cerebral hemispheres, basal ganglia, thalamus, amygdala, hippocampus, and septum. Though Hobson and McCarley consistently refer to the forebrain, we may assume that the image-synthesizing process occurs mainly in the cerebral cortex, so I will usually refer to the cortex.

[3]Phasic events are brief, discrete events, like individual eye movements. Tonic events are relatively long lasting (at least a few minutes), like REM sleep periods.

[4]See Chapter 11, endnote 3, on Hobson's attitude toward the evidence on dreaming in NREM sleep.

[5]In a related study, Karacan et al. (1966) found that REM erections were unlikely to occur during dreams characterized by high anxiety. Perhaps anxiety interferes with REM erections, just as it interferes with erections in the waking state.

[6]Lucid dreams, where we are aware that we are dreaming while we are dreaming, are the exception rather than the rule. In fact, lucidity during dreaming is most likely to occur when dreams are bizarre (LaBerge 1985) (see Chapter 13).

chapter 13 ··································

Dreaming III:
Dream Recall
and Lucid Dreaming

Everything that we know about dreaming depends upon people's abilities to accurately recall and report their dreams when they awaken. Unfortunately, the usual problems of introspective reporting are magnified in research on dreaming. In many cases dreams are recalled only vaguely, or not at all. Theories of dreaming are only as good as the dream report data on which they are based. In this chapter I will discuss the problem of dream recall and forgetting in some detail, because it is central to all research on dreaming.

Perhaps you have had the experience of knowing that you are dreaming, while you are asleep and dreaming. This experience is called *lucid dreaming*. Lucid dreaming is the newest topic of systematic dream research. Most theories of dreaming have said nothing about lucid dreaming, in fact, lucid dreaming is contrary to most dreaming theories. But as we will see, not only can people learn to increase their frequency of lucid dreaming, but some people can learn to control the dream events, and some lucid dreamers have been able to make overt signals to researchers when certain dream events occur. Finally, at the end of the chapter I will make some general concluding comments on dreaming and its implications for consciousness.

DREAM RECALL AND FORGETTING

The question of how to define *dream recall failure* is a problem for research on dream recall (Goodenough 1978). When research subjects say that they do not recall any dream, does it mean that they did not have a dream, or does it mean that they had a dream but forgot it? In practice, the usual assumption is that the mind is continuously active during sleep. Failure to report some sort of sleep mentation—dream or thought—is assumed to represent a failure of recall rather than a failure of occurrence. This practical assumption is made so we can get on with research on dream recall failure. Nonetheless, it is an unproven—and unprovable—assumption.

The major questions about dream recall are: Why are dreams harder to recall than waking experiences? Why are some dreams easier to recall than others? Why do some people recall dreams more frequently than other people do?

On the assumption that some sort of mental activity occurs almost continuously during sleep, four hypotheses have been suggested to explain forgetting of dreams and other sleep mentation: (1) interference with memory encoding; (2) low salience; (3) repression; and (4) physiological state change.

The Interference Hypothesis

David Cohen (1979a, 1979b) argued that the concept of interference can explain most instances of dream-recall failure. Interference occurs when two mental processes or events cannot occur at the same time, either because they are fundamentally incompatible with each other, or because together they would exceed the mind/brain system's limited information processing capacity. The effect of interference on waking memory has been thoroughly documented (see Ashcraft 1989; Klatzky 1980). Interference with dream storage and recall might occur at any of several stages (Cohen 1979a): (1) during dreaming, when incompatible processes can interfere with storing dreams in memory; (2) immediately after awakening, when events can interfere with maintaining dreams in short-term memory; (3) shortly after awakening, when events can interfere with mnemonic processes in STM for storing dreams in long-term memory; (4) at the time of attempted recall from LTM (due to absent or inappropriate retrieval cues); and (5) at the time of dream reporting, when language limitations or social factors might interfere with dream reporting, even though dream recall is adequate.

Foulkes (1985) supported the interference hypothesis of dream forgetting in his cognitive psychological theory of dreaming. He put the emphasis on interference with mnemonic processing during dreaming itself. Dream production is a process of activation and synthesis of memories, and it is incompatible with mnemonic process for storing new memories. Storing dreams in LTM requires a shift in information-processing mode, from synthesis to mnemonic processing, which occurs only after awakening.

The importance of interfering events after awakening was emphasized by Koulack and Goodenough (1976), who argued that the STM trace of a dream is very brief, and most dream recall involves retrieval from LTM. In order for a dream to be retrievable from LTM, it must be subjected to elaborative mnemonic processing (rehearsal, organization, chunking, recoding, association) in STM. Mnemonic processing is poor during sleep. Dream recall is best when people awaken during or immediately after a dream, while the dream is still in STM. The increased arousal level upon awakening enables improved mnemonic processing in STM, thus improving subsequent retrieval of the dream from LTM. However, mnemonic processing of the dream upon awakening is not automatic—it requires thinking. And mnemonic processing is very sensitive to interference by distracting external or internal stimuli.[1]

Experimental test of the interference hypothesis.

The interference hypothesis predicts that dream recall will be reduced when external stimuli or activities occur immediately after awakening and interfere with recall of the dream in STM and mnemonic processing in STM for storage in LTM. Cohen and Wolfe (1973) tested the hypothesis by asking college students to fill out a dream report form the next morning upon awakening. Half of the subjects (distraction group) were instructed that, immediately upon awakening, they should dial the weather-report telephone number and find out the temperature and write it at the top of the page, *before* completing the dream report. The control group was instructed to lie quietly in bed for about ninety seconds (the average amount of time taken by the distraction group to get the temperature) before completing the dream report. Thus, control subjects had an opportunity to think about their dreams for awhile before reporting them. The result was that dream or sleep mentation contents were reported by 63 percent of the control group subjects, compared to only 33 percent of the distraction group subjects.

The implication is that if you want to recall your dreams, it is critically important that you avoid distracting stimuli, thoughts, or activities upon awakening. Dream recall is facilitated by lying still in a quiet room and concentrating on recalling your dreams for a few minutes before starting to write in your dream diary. Individual differences in dream recall frequency could be explained at least partly in terms of differences in interference at the time of awakening.

Interference with dream reporting.

Dream reports are a type of introspective verbal report, and they have the same limitations as other introspective reports (see Chapter 3). One limitation is the possibility of censorship by the subject.

Dream reporting is an interpersonal process, and it can be affected by the social relationships of the dreamer and the audience. This point was demonstrated in a study involving two subjects who were participating in a laboratory dream experiment during the same weeks in which they were undergoing psychotherapy (Whitman, Kramer, & Baldridge 1963). Sometimes the dreams reported to the laboratory technician at night were different from those reported to the therapist in the morning. The male subject reported dreams to the technician but withheld them from the therapist when the dreams reflected the patient's homosexual fears (for example, dreams of closeness to a man or being examined and penetrated by a man). But dreams reflecting the patient's heterosexual adequacy (such as helping a woman or dating women other than his wife) were reported to the therapist. The female subject reported to the technician, but not to the therapist, dreams reflecting her sexual concerns and doubts about the therapist's adequacy. Dreams criticizing the technician were reported to the therapist but not to the technician. It appears that the subjects edited or suppressed their dream reports, depending upon the nature of the social relationship between themselves and the dream audience. In view of the potentially profound effects of social interactions on the accuracy of dream reports, this factor should receive more attention from experimenters than it has in the past.

The Salience Hypothesis

Salience refers to the degree to which objects or events "stand out" perceptually. Highly salient events attract and hold our attention, so we are more likely to remember them. Cohen (1979a) argued that salience also affects the recall of dreams:

> The salience hypothesis suggests that more intense, emotionally exciting, consciously vivid dreams will tend to be more readily recalled, that individuals with good waking imagery will tend to be better dream recallers, and that conditions that increase dream intensity (e.g. presleep distress, REM as opposed to NREM physiology) will more likely be associated with dream recall (p. 256).

The salience hypothesis is not incompatible with the interference hypothesis. Rather, salience explains why some dreams are recalled better than others. In a sense, more salient dreams are more resistant to interference, because they are more likely to attract and hold our attention, so we are more likely to think about them and give them the mnemonic processing that is necessary for LTM storage and retrieval.

Several laboratory experiments have tested the salience hypothesis, at least indirectly, by asking subjects in the morning to *re-recall* all of the dreams that they had reported during the night after REM awakenings. Although reporting dreams after REM awakenings undoubtedly tended to increase their subsequent recallability, subjects did not recall all of their night dream reports in the morning. The dreams that were best re-recalled were those that were highest in salience factors (such as vividness, emotionality, bizarreness, length) in the original reports (review by Goodenough 1978).

The salience hypothesis is also supported by experiments that influenced dream salience by manipulating presleep experiences or instructions. Cohen and Cox (1975) assigned subjects to either a negative (stressful) or a control presleep condition. The negative presleep condition, which was expected to enhance the salience of dreams, included ego-threatening events such as "failure" on a difficult IQ test, social isolation, and perfunctory, impersonal treatment by the experimenters. As predicted by the salience hypothesis, the frequency of morning dream recall (or re-recall) was greater in the negative treatment group (61 percent) than in the control group (38 percent). Both groups re-recalled a higher percentage of REM dreams than NREM dreams, a result that fits with the fact that REM dreams are usually more salient than NREM dreams.

Cohen (1979a) suggested that individual differences in dream-recall frequency may be related factors such as personality, psychopathology, and current life stresses that affect dream salience. Alternatively, these factors might affect the frequency of nighttime awakenings, thus affecting the number of awakenings directly from REM sleep when dream recall is best.

The Repression Hypothesis

Freud developed the repression concept as part of his psychoanalytic theory of personality and psychotherapy. *Repression* is a process that actively interferes with retrieval of objectionable material from long-term memory as a defense against the anxiety that would result if the material were to be retrieved into consciousness. Repressed material includes unacceptable unconscious wishes (sexual, aggressive) and traumatic memories. Freud (1900/1965) extended the repression concept to explain dream-recall failure. In his view, dream memories are normally repressed in order to prevent the anxiety that would occur if we were to recall them and see through their symbolism to comprehend their true meaning. Thus, dream-recall failure is normal, and successful dream recall represents a failure of the repression process, in Freud's view.

Psychoanalysts have claimed support for the repression hypothesis from their clinical case studies, which suggest that "dreams are often recalled at the moment when resistance to the dream content is lifted during the course of analysis" (Goodenough 1978). However, acceptance of this type of evidence depends upon prior acceptance psychoanalytic theory.

The repression hypothesis implies that dreams with the most anxiety-evoking content should be most repressed, and hence least recalled. Thus, the repression hypothesis makes a prediction directly opposed to that of the salience hypothesis. The evidence appears to be strongly against the repression hypothesis, insofar as highly salient dreams (such as highly emotional and bizarre dreams) are re-recalled better than more mundane dreams. Of course, we have no way of knowing the anxiety potential of never-recalled dreams. Furthermore, psychoanalysts argue that the anxiety potential of a dream's latent (hidden) content is more important than that of its manifest (surface) content. Thus, the controversial repression hypothesis is entangled with the controversial dream symbolism hypothesis, making an objective direct test of the repression hypothesis impossible.

Most attempts to test the repression hypothesis have been derived from the idea that repression is an ego defense mechanism that is used more by some people ("repressors") than others ("nonrepressors"). The prediction is that repressors will recall dreams less often than nonrepressors. The greatest difficulty in testing this prediction is in measuring the repressor personality trait. There is some evidence to support the prediction, but other evidence is inconsistent or has alternative interpretations (reviews by Cohen 1979a, 1979b; Goodenough 1978).

Another prediction derived from the repression hypothesis is more susceptible to experimental testing: that following a stressful presleep experience—one that might tend to produce unpleasant dreams—dream recall will be reduced compared to a nonstressful control treatment. Several studies have tested this prediction, with inconsistent, largely negative results. The contents of stressful films viewed before sleep are more likely than those of nonstressful films to be incorporated into dreams, a result that supports the salience hypothesis but not the repression hypothesis.

All in all, there is little experimental evidence for the repression hypothesis. Most of the results can be more parsimoniously explained in terms of the salience or interference hypotheses. The main contribution of the repression hypothesis is to have pointed out a personality dimension (repressor vs. nonrepressor) that may be related to individual differences in dream recall.

The Physiological-State Hypothesis

The physiological state hypothesis is concerned with the question of why dreams are harder to recall than waking experiences. Of course, we should not exaggerate our ability to recall waking experiences. We forget most of our waking experiences, especially those that are relatively trivial, including most of our daydreams. Nonetheless, it is a common experience to awaken with the feeling that you have been dreaming, though you cannot recall what the dream was about, or you recall less of it than you would expect to recall of a waking experience that had occurred only a minute or so earlier.

There are two types of physiological-state hypotheses, in regard to dream-recall failures: (1) The *state dependent memory hypothesis* emphasizes the fact that neurophysiological brain states are different in sleep, when dreaming occurs, than in waking, when recall is attempted. (2) The *encoding-deficiency hypothesis* says that memory-storage processes are inherently deficient during sleep.

State-dependent memory is said to occur when information learned in one physiological state cannot subsequently be retrieved when the organism is in a different physiological state, though the information can be retrieved again when the organism returns to the original physiological state (Overton 1973). State-dependent memory was originally discovered in animal research on transfer of learning between drugged states and normal states. One interpretation of the state-dependency effect is that memory organization is different in different neurophysiological brain states, such that retrieval cues that are effective in the original state are not available or are not as effective in a different state. The state-dependency hypothesis easily explains the fact that REM dreams are better recalled than NREM mentation, since REM is physiologically more similar than NREM to the waking state.

The state-dependent memory hypothesis says that poor dream recall is a case of retrieval failure, not storage failure. Dreams may be stored in LTM during sleep, though they cannot be retrieved (or can be only partially retrieved) in the waking state. An implication of the state-dependency hypothesis is that prior REM dreams will be better recalled during subsequent REM sleep than in the waking state. Repetitive dreams sometimes occur, and one explanation is that repetitive dreams are recollections of earlier dreams. But repetitive dreams can be explained alternatively in terms of continuing personal concerns and waking experiences that affect dream contents.[2]

The *encoding-deficiency hypothesis* says that memory-storage processes are inherently deficient during sleep, so that dreams that are not recalled upon awakening are unlikely to ever be recalled because they have not been stored in LTM. The encoding deficiency hypothesis is consistent with repeated failures of attempted verbal learning during EEG-confirmed sleep to transfer to the waking state (Aarons 1976; Overton 1973). Hobson (1988) supported the encoding deficiency hypothesis of dream forgetting, as part of the activation-synthesis theory of dreaming. He suggested that during REM sleep the brain's information-processing centers concentrate on dream synthesis and do not initiate memory storage processes. He cited evidence that activity in the brain's aminergic neurotransmitter circuits decreases in REM sleep, resulting in a reduction in memory-encoding processes during REM sleep. (In Hobson's view, poor dream recall from NREM stages reflects a lack of NREM dreaming rather than a NREM dream recall problem.) Like Hobson, Foulkes (1985) suggested that mnemonic encoding is deficient during sleep, but Foulkes emphasized the incompatibility of different information-processing modes, rather than changes in neurophysiological states.

Conclusion

I have gone into some detail on the problem of dream recall because the accuracy of dream recall is the limiting factor in the accuracy of all dream research and theory. None of the four hypotheses explains all of the facts about dream forgetting and recall. Memory encoding deficiency during sleep is probably the major reason why recall of dreams is poorer than recall of waking events. The salience and interference hypotheses can explain why we recall some dreams better than others.

LUCID DREAMING

Up to this point I have been discussing research and theory on ordinary dreams, that is, hallucinatory dreams where the dream world seems to be real and you are unaware that you are dreaming. But perhaps you have had the experience of realizing that you were dreaming while you were asleep. Dreams where people know that they are dreaming are called *lucid dreams*. Lucid dreaming is the newest topic for scientific dream research, although lucid dreaming has been known at least since Aristotle and discussed by many writers since then (LaBerge 1988a). Frederik Van Eeden coined the term "lucid dream" in 1913 and described several of his own lucid dreams. The following example from Van Eeden illustrates an important feature of lucid dreams, in which the dreamer can sometimes control the dream action:

> On Sept. 9, 1904 I dreamt that I stood at a table before a window. On the table were different objects. I was perfectly well aware that I was dreaming and I considered what sorts of experiments I could make. I began by trying to break glass, by beating it with a stone. I put a small tablet of glass on two stones and struck it with another stone. Yet it would not break. Then I took a fine claret-glass from the table and struck it with my fist, with all my might, at the same time reflecting how dangerous it would be to do this in waking life; yet the glass remained whole. But lo! when I looked at it again after some time, it was broken.
>
> It broke all right, but a little too late, like an actor who misses his cue. This gave me a very curious impression of being in a *fake-world*, cleverly imitated, but with small failures. I took the broken glass and threw it out of the window, in order to observe whether I could hear the *tinkling*. I heard the noise all right

and I even saw two dogs run away from it quite naturally. I thought what a good imitation this comedy-world was. Then I saw a decanter with claret and tasted it, and noted with perfect clearness of mind: "Well, we can also have voluntary impressions of taste in this dream-world; this has quite the taste of wine" (Van Eeden 1913, reprinted in Tart 1972a, p. 154).

Lucid dreaming involves reflective self-consciousness during sleep. In contrast, ordinary nonlucid dreaming mainly involves primary consciousness. Rechtschaffen (1978) characterized ordinary dreaming as "single-minded," in that there is typically a single stream of thought and action going on at one time, without the alternation of primary and reflective consciousness that often characterizes waking thought. Snyder (1970) showed that people sometimes think reflectively during ordinary dreams, in the sense of having thoughts about their dream experiences (such as "Why did she say that?"), but ordinary dreaming does not involve full reflective self-consciousness with awareness that one's current experience is a dream.

Although lucid dreaming, with its possibility of self-control during dreaming, is inherently fascinating, it has been neglected by scientific dream researchers until recently. There are two reasons for this neglect. First, lucid dreaming is contrary to preconceived notions about what the human mind can do during sleep. For example, it is contrary to the Freudian theory that dreaming is a product of a nonrational, instinct-driven unconscious mind, and to Hobson and McCarley's idea that dreaming is just a byproduct of physiological processes during REM sleep. Second, lucid dreams are relatively rare, and they hardly ever occur in the sleep laboratory. (Only one of 104 REM dream reports collected by McCarley and Hoffman [1981] and none among over 600 dream reports collected by Snyder [1970] were classified as lucid dreams.) In the past, when lucid dreams were reported in the laboratory, they were usually discounted as an artifact of brief awakenings during sleep. However, in recent years scientists have started to take lucid dreaming more seriously, thanks to pioneering research by Stephen LaBerge (1985) and others (Gackenbach & LaBerge 1988) who have demonstrated that lucid dreams occur in a physiologically-verified sleep state, and that it is possible to use special training techniques to increase the frequency of lucid dreams.

Becoming Aware That You Are Dreaming

Lucid dreaming involves a concordance of two events: dreaming and reflective awareness. Thus, lucid dreaming might develop in two ways, according to LaBerge (1981, 1985): (1) people might develop reflective awareness—specifically, awareness of dreaming—after they have already fallen asleep and started to dream, or (2) people might maintain reflective awareness while they are falling asleep, and maintain it until they start dreaming. The first method is the most natural and most common, while the second method requires deliberate effort and practice.

When, while asleep, you ask yourself whether you are dreaming, then you are in a *prelucid* stage of dreaming. Sometimes you reach the wrong conclusion and decide that you are really awake. Then you continue in nonlucid (or prelucid) dreaming. (For example, if, while dreaming, you were to test your state by pinching your dream body, and you felt the pinch, then you might conclude that you are really awake! In such a case, your reality testing was insufficient.) At other times the prelucid question "Am I dreaming?" leads to a "yes" answer, and you are then—by definition—having a lucid dream.

People's spontaneous awareness that they are dreaming usually occurs as a result of some incongruous, bizarre, or anxiety-evoking event that prompts them to ask themselves, "Is this real?" (LaBerge 1985; Price & Cohen 1988). For example, if you notice that you are flying, or breathing under water, you might realize that you are dreaming. If you suspect that you might be dreaming, you can do a "reality test" by trying to control the dream events or trying to do something that you could not do in reality. One of the most commonly used reality tests is attempting to fly. These points are illustrated by a dream that I had some years ago, before I was aware of the research literature on lucid dreaming:

> One summer day I backpacked into a wilderness campsite deep in the Maine woods. On the trail on the way in I met two other backpackers, who were headed out. They said that they had seen a big black bear near the campsite the previous night. That night at the campsite the bear was on my mind. To make matters worse, I was alone, and I had to sleep in a lean-to, without even a tent wall to shield me from the bear if it should come around while I was asleep. I had a hard time falling asleep, due to my anxiety about the bear. Every sound in the woods grabbed my attention. Finally I fell asleep. At some point during the night I heard a scratching noise and the sound of heavy breathing. I sat up and looked, and I saw a huge bear silhouetted in the moonlight. The bear was sniffing around at the open side of the lean-to, a few feet away from me. I quickly crawled out of my sleeping bag and stepped out of the lean-to. Then the bear turned and looked at me. I could see its teeth gleaming in the moonlight. At that point I asked myself, "Is this really happening, or am I dreaming?" I thought that if it was a dream, then I should be able to fly away. So I spread my arms out and flapped them like wings. Then I flew up into the air, and only at that point did I know for sure that I was dreaming. From fifty feet above the ground I looked down on the bear. I could see the bear and the campsite and the surrounding area in vivid detail. I flew out over the nearby pond, and saw the moonlight dancing on the water (August, 1976).

LaBerge's (1985) favorite reality test involves trying to read something. He usually has difficulty reading during dreams because the print keeps changing. Even when he manages to read a few words, if he looks away from the page and then looks back, the words have changed. He concluded that the difference between dreams and waking perceptions is more a matter of stability than vividness. But specific tests of dreaming are not always necessary. Often the mere recognition of bizarreness or anomaly is enough to produce lucidity. Furthermore, if anything prompts you to ask whether you are dreaming, then you probably are. After all, you never have to ask whether you are dreaming when you are awake!

Methods of Increasing Lucid-Dream Frequency

Oneironauts (explorers of the inner world of dreams—a term coined from Greek roots by LaBerge [1985]) have developed several methods of deliberately increasing the likelihood of having a lucid dream. The methods can be classified into two broad categories: intention and suggestion techniques, and external cue techniques (Price & Cohen 1988).

Intention and suggestion techniques. Intention and suggestion techniques involve thought processes that occur in the waking state. The distinction between intention and suggestion is somewhat arbitrary here, but in general intention techniques involve a willful resolve to achieve lucidity, whereas suggestion techniques rely on a more passive, permissive, hypnotic-like attitude (Tholey 1983). The success of these techniques depends on a high level of motivation, so that you will be willing to continue practicing even if initial attempts fail. Also, it helps if you have a high frequency of dream recall. Dream recall—lucid or nonlucid—can be improved by paying attention to your dreams and keeping a dream diary.

Garfield (1974) used autosuggestions (self-suggestions) to increase lucid dreaming. She simply repeated to herself, while falling asleep, "I will have a lucid dream. I will have a lucid dream."

LaBerge (1985) developed the *MILD (Mnemonic Induction of Lucid Dreams) technique*. The underlying principle is to establish cues to remind you to notice—or test—whether you are dreaming the next time you dream. The MILD technique involves three steps: (1) When you wake up from a dream, during the night or early morning, recall the dream in as much detail as possible and replay it several times in your mind to familiarize yourself with it. (2) Then, while you are lying in bed, give yourself the autosuggestion, "The next time I dream I will recognize that I am dreaming." (3) Replay your most recent dream, this time visualizing yourself recognizing that you are dreaming, while you are in that dream. Recycle steps 2 and 3 several times while you are drifting back into sleep. With practice, you will sometimes have a lucid dream after you fall back asleep, though the next dream will not necessarily resemble the one that you rehearsed previously.

A helpful autosuggestion technique is to suggest to yourself before sleep that a particular event, when it occurs during a dream, will trigger lucidity or prompt you to ask whether it is a dream. Additionally, you can use an *action-specific intention*, where you suggest to yourself that you will perform a particular action and that that action, such as flying, will trigger lucidity (Garfield 1974; Price & Cohen 1988; Tholey 1983). Carlos Casteneda's sorcerer, Don Juan, triggered lucidity by finding his hands and lifting them to the level of his eyes in his dreams (Casteneda 1974).

Purcell et al. (1986) compared several different training methods for lucid dreaming—including posthypnotic suggestion, enhanced awareness of dreaming, and a mnemonic technique—against a control group. Dream reports were scored on a nine-point scale of self-reflectiveness. The mnemonic technique produced the highest self-reflectiveness scores. In the mnemonic condition the subjects wore a leather bracelet that reminded them several times each day to intend to dream lucidly and to rehearse a set of possible dream events that would prompt lucidity, including personal dream themes, oddities, and distorted perceptions.

Tholey (1983) described techniques based on the idea of maintaining reflective consciousness while falling asleep. His methods incorporated the idea of enhancing reflective consciousness during the waking state by asking frequently "Am I dreaming?" and attending to relevant cues. He recommended a combination of procedures, including methods of enhancing dream recall, enhancing reflective self-awareness, autosuggestion for self-awareness during dreaming, and resolving to carry out a particular action while dreaming.

If you want to try self-training techniques for lucid dreaming, bear in mind these two points. First, it is common for lucid dreaming beginners to awaken spontaneously when they become aware that they are dreaming. These spontaneous awakenings decrease with practice. Second, false awakenings are fairly common in lucid dreaming, where people believe that they have awakened, but in fact are still asleep (LaBerge 1985; Price & Cohen 1988).

External cueing techniques.   External cueing techniques are limited to the sleep laboratory. It is suggested to the subject that when he or she perceives a particular stimulus it will prompt lucidity. Then the experimenter presents the stimulus while the subject is in REM sleep. Several stimuli have been tried with some success, including a spray of water on the face, a bright light, and a tape-recorded message ("this is a dream") in the subject's own voice (review in Price & Cohen 1978).

Laboratory Studies of Lucid Dreaming

Signaling during sleep.   Does lucid dreaming occur during sleep or during brief periods of wakefulness? LaBerge et al. (1981) set out to answer this question, using five oneironauts trained with the MILD technique. In addition, they sought to find out whether lucid dreamers could perform an overt voluntary act to signal when they became aware that they were dreaming. The voluntary signals included extreme eye movements, fist clinches (detected by wrist EMG), or a combination of both. The subjects spent a total of thirty-four nights in the sleep laboratory, with the usual electrophysiological (polygraph) measures (EEG, EOG, chin EMG) being taken. On thirty-five occasions subjects spontaneously awakened themselves from sleep and reported a lucid dream.

The overwhelming majority (thirty-two; 91 percent) of lucid dreams occurred during REM sleep, and there was no evidence that they were an artifact of brief awakenings during sleep. In thirty cases the subjects reported having signaled during the dream, and in twenty-four (80 percent) of these cases an independent blind judge verified this by matching the dream report with the correct temporal segment of the polygraph record.[3]

The most reliable signal was a series of extreme horizontal eye movements (left, right, left, right). However, the most dramatic record involved a combination of eye movements and fist clinches, shown in Figure 13.1. Similar results were obtained in a subsequent study (LaBerge 1988b; LaBerge,

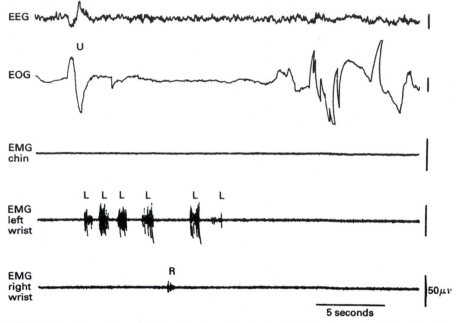

FIGURE 13.1. Polygraph record of a sleeping subject's signal that he knows he is dreaming. The signal was made as planned before sleep: an extreme upward eye movement (marked "u" in the EOG tracing), followed by a sequence of fist clinches shown in the EMG records (LLL LRLL, which signals the dreamer's initials, "S. L.," in Morse code). The sleeper awoke about twenty seconds later and reported that he had been dreaming and had made the prearranged signal. (The upward blip in the EEG record [above the "u"] is an EEG artifact caused by the extreme eye movement.) [Reproduced with permission of the authors and publisher from LaBerge, S., Nagel, L. E., Dement, W. C., & Zarcone, V. P., Jr. (1981). Lucid dreaming verified by volitional communication during REM sleep. *Perceptual and Motor Skills, 52,* 727–32.]

Levitan, & Dement 1986), in which it was shown that lucid dreaming becomes increasingly likely across successive REM periods of the same night. One implication of this research is the development of a methodology for learning more about the correlation between dream events and physiological events, by having subjects signal during sleep when particular dream events occur (LaBerge 1988b; Schatzman, Worsley, & Fenwick 1988).

Physiological correlates.   Are there any differences in physiological responses for lucid versus nonlucid dream periods during REM sleep? LaBerge et al. (1986) did a detailed analysis of polygraph records of some seventy-six lucid dreams (from thirteen subjects) in which the dreamer had used extreme eye movements to signal the onset of lucid dreaming. The records showed increases in eye-movement frequency, respiration rate, heart rate, and skin electrical potential starting thirty seconds before the lucidity signal and continuing for one to five minutes after the signal. These physiological responses indicate that lucidity is associated with increased central nervous system and autonomic arousal. LaBerge (1988b) speculated that lucidity might require increased brain arousal, which would increase the dreamer's thinking capacity.

Sexual activity in lucid dreams.   Patricia Garfield, in *Pathway to Ecstasy* (1979), reported that she could voluntarily initiate sexual activity in her lucid dreams, and that such experiences led to orgasms of "profound" intensity. Having heard similar reports from some of his female oneironauts, LaBerge (1985) attempted to catch such a dream in the sleep laboratory. A female volunteer, Miranda, was fitted with the usual EEG, EOG, and chin-EMG measuring devices, plus others to measure respiration, heart rate, vaginal EMG, and vaginal pulse amplitude. In her fifth REM period of the night, Miranda signaled—using eye movements—that she was having a lucid dream. Two minutes later she signaled that she was beginning dream sexual activity, and about fifteen seconds later she signaled that she was having a dream orgasm. Shortly thereafter she allowed herself to wake up, whereupon she described her dream, and reported that she had felt a mild, but real, orgasm while dreaming. The polygraph recordings showed that between Miranda's second and third signals—during sexual activity leading up to orgasm—her respiration and vaginal blood flow and vaginal muscle activity reached their highest levels of the night, while her heart rate showed a moderate increase. Comparable results were obtained with a male subject.

Characteristics of Lucid Dreams and Lucid Dreamers

Jayne Gackenbach (1988) reviewed evidence on differences between lucid and nonlucid dreams. The main difference, by definition, is that only lucid dreams involve reflective self-consciousness with awareness of dreaming. Compared to nonlucid dreams, lucid dreams tend to have more auditory imagery, more cognitive activity, more obstacles, and fewer characters. Subjects with frequent lucid dreams report kinesthetic (limb movement) sensations and the ability to control dream events in lucid dreams. About 15 percent of lucid dreams are initiated during nightmares. But for a wide variety of characteristics and specific contents, the main conclusion is that lucid and nonlucid dreams are more similar than different.

How often does lucid dreaming occur? Snyder and Gackenbach (1988) found that about 60 percent of adults reported having had at least one lucid dream in their life, with about one third of them claiming to have lucid dreams as often as one or more per month. In a group of people sufficiently interested in dreams to keep a dream diary, about 13 percent of the dreams reported in diaries appeared to be lucid dreams.

Snyder and Gackenbach (1988) reviewed studies on the characteristics of people who frequently have lucid dreams and concluded that they "tend to rely primarily on the self in psychological functioning rather than on external referents" (p. 254). They are more self-oriented than socially oriented; they are open to internal risks but not to external risks; and they have a relatively high arousal level. Also, they are especially sensitive to tactile/kinesthetic and vestibular cues and are "field independent" in that they can maintain body balance and distinguish the vertical orientation without reference to visual cues. Gackenbach et al. (1986) found that compared to nonlucid dreamers, frequent lucid dreamers (untrained subjects) had greater sensitivity in the vestibular system—the structure, located in the inner ear, that is responsible for the sense of balance and body acceleration. Vestibular sensitivity was shown by visual nystagmus (elicited eye movements) and vertigo (dizzy or spinning sensations) in response to irrigation of an ear canal with warm water. These results are noteworthy, in that lucid dreaming often is associated with dreams of flying or spinning, and suggest that natural lucid dreamers have either greater-than-normal vestibular system activation during REM sleep or greater-than-normal sensitivity to such stimulation. The implications of this finding for lucidity training have not yet been investigated.

Applications and Conclusions

LaBerge (1985) suggested several potential practical uses of lucid dreaming. (1) Scientific research on the nature of dreaming: for example, hypotheses about psychophysiological parallelism (mind/brain isomorphism) during dreaming could be tested with the help of voluntary signals. Foulkes (1985) pointed out, however, that lucid dreaming is not the same state as ordinary, hallucinoid dreaming; thus, it is uncertain whether conclusions derived from lucid dreaming will be generalizable to ordinary dreaming. (2) Creative problem solving, rehearsal, and decision making while dreaming. (3) Wish fulfillment and recreation: for example, sexual activity for people without opportunities for real sexual activity. (4) Healing and personal growth: for example, learning to face one's fears and develop competence. Attempts to use lucid dreaming for practical purposes are not new, but progress is likely to accelerate with the development of new methods for training lucid dreaming and identifying it in the laboratory. (See Gackenbach & LaBerge 1988 for more on clinical applications of lucid dreaming.)

Lucid dreaming shows that volition and rational thought and reflective self-consciousness can occur during sleep. However, many examples and speculations about lucid dreaming are still based on home dream reports, where the person's sleep state was not verified. Systematic laboratory research on lucid dreaming is very new. So far, the tentative conclusions about lucid dreaming are based on a relatively small number of subjects, and a relatively small number of dream reports, compared to the large volume of research on ordinary REM dreaming. Many questions remain. How does lucid dreaming occur, and why doesn't it occur more commonly? Can everyone learn to dream lucidly with the right training? How much self-awareness and recall of one's waking intentions and experiences can occur during lucid dreaming? Is lucid dreaming a variety of REM dreaming, or is it a unique state of consciousness, separate from ordinary hallucinatory REM dreaming? Hunt and Ogilvie (1988) discussed lucid dreaming in relation to other altered-consciousness experiences and related it closely to out-of-body experiences (OBE) and meditative states. Lucid dreaming has been largely ignored in most theories of dreaming, but theoretical explanations of lucid dreaming are likely to develop in the wake of increased knowledge from systematic research. The topic of lucid dreaming promises exciting research and theoretical and practical developments in the future.

CONCLUDING COMMENT ON DREAMING

Although people have long been interested in dreams because of their differences from waking thought and perception, researchers are increasingly realizing the importance of the *similarities* between dreaming and waking consciousness (Foulkes 1985, 1990). The study of dreaming reveals that fundamental characteristics of consciousness—the interpretation of experience and the construction of a world model—continue during sleep.

To a degree, dreaming can be compared with waking perception. Perception has been characterized as an interpretive, constructive process, guided by sensory data but influenced by our prior knowledge, needs, and expectancies (Best 1989; Neisser 1976). But it is more accurate to compare dreaming with daydreaming, particularly, daydreaming with visuospatial imagery. In both cases, we use stored knowledge about people, objects, events, spatial relationships, narrative structures, and cause and effect to construct a relatively stable, coherent model of the world and to imagine ourselves undertaking action in that world. In both cases, our thoughts and images are influenced by our current concerns and recent waking experiences—though perhaps more so in daydreaming than in sleep dreaming.

Many writers have discussed the interpretive, constructive nature of waking consciousness (Johnson-Laird 1983; Ornstein 1977). For example, recall Gazzaniga's (1985) ideas about the left-hemisphere interpreter, following from his research on split-brain patients (Chapter 5), and the discussion of interpretive processes that occur when we attempt to introspect the causes of our own behavior (Chapter 7). Research on dreaming indicates that the interpretive, constructive role of consciousness continues while we sleep. As Foulkes's (1985) theory suggests, in dreaming we construct a world model and create narrative stories from images and knowledge stored in memory. Of course dream stories are fictional and sometimes odd or bizarre. There are several reasons for dream oddities: (1) we have no perceptual data from the external world to guide and limit our creations; (2) processes of association and narrative construction operate somewhat differently during sleep; (3) phasic physiological events may disrupt or redirect the construction process; and (4) reflective self-conscious thought is reduced or absent during dreaming, such that dreaming is not consistently checked against and guided by our remembered waking reality, life history, and self concept.

The drastic reduction or absence of reflective self-conscious thinking and volitional control during dreaming is a particularly important difference between sleeping and waking thought. Typical daydreaming involves a great deal of reflective thought—we comment on our experiences, and we think about our own thoughts, feelings, and actions, in order to interpret or evaluate them. Further, there is a strong self-awareness, where we relate our thoughts and experiences to our continuing self- concept and place them in the stories of our lives. In contrast, reflective thought is absent, or minimal, during typical hallucinoid dreaming. There may be some commentary on events—for example, a dream where I walked into a bar and saw adults sitting in oversized baby highchairs, and commented to myself that it seemed odd—but higher levels of reflective thought are absent in ordinary dreaming. There is no relating of events to our self-concept and continuing life story. The process of interpreting events is severely flawed, so that we do not realize that our vivid visual experience is imaginary—hence the delusional quality of dreams. And despite the fact that our dreams are our own creations, we have no feeling of control over them. Thus, typical dreaming and daydreaming are similar in that they both involve construction of world models and imagining our own actions, but they differ in that insight into what is really going on is absent in dreaming, where reflective thought and the feeling of control are absent. (This explains why you are more likely to tell people your dreams than to tell them your daydream fantasies, since you feel that you have less control over your dreams, and hence less personal responsibility for them.)[4]

Of course, there are atypical daydreams and sleep dreams. Reflective thought and the feeling of control are largely absent in the relaxed, vivid reverie type of daydreaming. And lucid dreaming involves a higher than ordinary degree of reflective thought, to the point that we realize that we are dreaming, and we may be able to control the dream action to a degree. Thus, waking reverie is similar to typical hallucinoid dreaming, whereas lucid dreaming is similar to typical daydreaming, as far as reflective thought and feeling of control are concerned. On the other hand, it is noteworthy that waking actions sometimes occur automatically, without reflective self-consciousness or a feeling of voluntary control—as in hallucinoid dreaming. (Further research on lucid dreaming may help us to understand the relationship between primary and reflective consciousness.)

Like waking conscious perception and daydreaming, dreaming is an active process of interpreting and constructing experience. The similarities between waking consciousness and sleeping consciousness are as important as their differences for helping us understand the nature of consciousness. Contrary to Freud's claim that dreams are "the royal road to the unconscious," it now seems that "dreaming reveals not the unconscious, but consciousness" (Foulkes, 1990).

SUMMARY

Our knowledge of dreams is limited by problems of accurate dream recall and reporting. Four factors have been proposed to explain dream recall failures: (1) interference with dream memory-encoding processes, either during dreaming or shortly after awakening; (2) low salience, which reduces attention and memory encoding of dreams (conversely, highly salient dreams are more likely to be recalled); (3) repression, Freud's idea of an emotional block against retrieval from LTM; and (4) physiological state change, where memory-encoding processes for dreams are deficient during sleep and/or dreams are encoded differently than normal so they cannot be retrieved during the waking state.

In lucid dreaming, people are aware that they are dreaming, while they are asleep and dreaming. Spontaneous awareness of dreaming usually occurs as a result of incongruous, bizarre, or anxiety-evoking incidents, which prompt the dreamer to ask "Am I dreaming?" Lucid dreaming occurs during REM sleep. Some lucid dreamers can voluntarily control the dream action, and some can signal lucidity during sleep by means of extreme eye movements and fist clinches. Several methods have been developed to increase lucid dream frequency, enabling it to be studied in the laboratory, and promising practical applications in dream research, psychotherapy, and personal growth.

In conclusion, it was suggested that dreaming has important similarities to waking consciousness, particularly to daydreaming. In both cases, we construct a world model and imagine ourselves acting in that world. Both dreaming and waking consciousness are active constructive processes. Dreaming is different in that it typically occurs with no volitional control or reflective self-consciousness, though this sometimes happens in waking consciousness, too.

ENDNOTES

[1]Laboratory research indicates that dreams are recalled better after rapid arousal from sleep than after gradual arousal (Goodenough et al. 1965). Apparently, rapid arousal allows dreams to be recalled from STM and thought about before they are forgotten.

[2]Consistent with the state-dependency hypothesis is the idea that some *déjà vu* experiences occur when a waking experience seems familiar because it is similar to a prior dream experience, but we do not realize that the prior experience was a dream because we cannot recall the dream. I am not suggesting that dreams predict the future. Rather, I am suggesting that since we spend about 550 to 700 hours per year in REM-state dreaming, and dreams are fictions based on our personal knowledge and episodic memories, some of our dream experiences will by coincidence be similar to our subsequent waking experiences. This is my pet hypothesis about *déjà vu* experiences, but it would be difficult or impossible to test it.

[3]Tyson, Ogilvie, and Hunt (1984) found that lucid dreaming was associated with the occurrence of alpha EEG during REM sleep. This finding is controversial. Some alpha EEG normally occurs during REM sleep, and LaBerge (1988b) found no more alpha waves during lucid dreaming than during nonlucid dreaming.

[4]Foulkes (1990) pointed out a paradox, that the development of adult-style narrative dreaming in children is correlated with the development of reflective self-awareness and controlled daydreaming, yet adult-style dreams typically occur without volitional control and with little or no reflective thought.

chapter 14 ••••••••••••••••••••••••••••

Hypnosis I:
Basic Phenomena,
Hypnotic Susceptibility,
and Applications

The history of hypnosis is longer than the history of psychology. Modern hypnosis methods trace their descent from the work of Franz Anton Mesmer, who practiced "animal magnetism" in Paris in the 1770s (Sheehan & Perry 1976). Mesmer thought that his influence over subjects was due to the transmission of some sort of magnetic force between himself and them. The theory of animal magnetism was discredited quite early by the French Commission of 1784, under the direction of the American ambassador, Benjamin Franklin. As a result, *mesmerism* was ridiculed by the medical and scientific community. Yet, the fact remained that Mesmer's procedures produced some dramatic effects and were sometimes successful in curing or alleviating a variety of physical problems such as rheumatism, pain, skin disease, and convulsive asthma. Because of its demonstrated practical benefits, mesmerism continued to be of interest to a small minority of physicians through the nineteenth century. In 1843 the English physician James Braid coined the term hypnosis (from the Greek *hypnos*, to sleep).

A major theoretical issue was raised in the Nancy-Salpêtrière controversy of the 1880s over whether hypnosis was a neurophysiological phenomenon or a psychological one (Sheehan & Perry 1976). Jean-Martin Charcot, a neurologist at the Salpêtrière Hospital in Paris, claimed that hypnosis is a neurophysiological condition, and that deep hypnosis (then termed "artificial somnambulism") is found only in hysterics (patients with conditions such as functional paralysis or deafness, where there is nothing physically wrong with the organs in question). Charcot believed that there were several stages of increasingly deeper hypnosis, each of which required physical induction techniques such as eye fixation, forcing open the patient's closed eyelids, or pressure to the patient's scalp. In contrast, Hippolyte Bernheim, a medical professor at the University of Nancy (France), argued that hypnosis is a purely psychological condition, where hypnotic induction depends on natural responsiveness to suggestions, and the hypnotic state is one of enhanced suggestibility. Ultimately, Bernheim won the argument by showing that hypnosis can be induced by verbal suggestions alone without physical manipulations and that the "somnambulistic" state is not limited to hysteric patients, but can occur in a substantial minority of the normal population (about 15 to 18 percent of his cases). Also, it was found that the "hypnotic" behavior of Charcot's demonstration cases had been influenced by prior coaching by his assistants. Bernheim's influence continues to the present day, where there is a continuing emphasis on psychological suggestion and related concepts of imagination and the feeling of involuntariness in hypnotic responsiveness. (For more on the fascinating history of hypnosis see Ellenberger 1970; Laurence & Perry 1988; and Sheehan & Perry 1976. Also see Edmonston 1986, on hypnotic methods from past to present.)

There were numerous demonstrations of practical applications of hypnosis during the nineteenth century. For example, James Esdaile, an English surgeon working in India from 1845 to 1851, used hypnosis extensively to control pain and bleeding in both minor and major surgery, including normally traumatic operations such as the removal of large tumors of the scrotum (Bowers 1976). However, most physicians continued to be skeptical that the mere words of hypnotic suggestions could work such wonders, and indeed, there were enough failures to support their skepticism. Surgeons wanted a technique that would work with everybody. The discovery of chemical general anesthesias, ether and chloroform, in the mid-1800s was sufficient to cause most surgeons to lose interest in hypnosis. A few doctors continued to use hypnosis for treatment of psychiatric cases. Sigmund Freud, the father of psychoanalysis, used hypnosis for several years in Vienna in the late 1880s to treat hysteric and neurotic symptoms, but he eventually abandoned it in favor of his psychoanalytic techniques such as free-association and dream analysis.

From Mesmer's time to the present day, hypnosis has continued to fascinate the general public, particularly as a result of stage-show demonstrations and fictional treatments—two sources of misinformation as well as information. Hypnosis has gone through several cycles of interest and disinterest in the medical community, but it has never been practiced widely among physicians. Besides their preference for physical interventions (such as drugs and surgery) and skepticism about psychological methods, another reason for skepticism among physicians is the association of hypnosis with stage shows and occult practices, such as seances and spiritualism, and sometimes with fraud. Hypnosis has been condemned both because it doesn't always work and because it sometimes keeps bad company. And while the general public still finds it fascinating, some religious fundamentalists think that hypnosis is the work of the devil.

From the mid-1900s to the present there has been a revival of interest in hypnosis and an increase in its respectability among doctors, psychiatrists, and psychologists. The American Medical Association and the American Psychological Association recognize clinical hypnosis as a valid type of professional training. The increased respectability of hypnosis is due mainly to modern experimental research on hypnosis, as well as to modern demonstrations of its practical applications, for example, in psychotherapy and in control of pain in cancer patients. Also, the shift in psychology from a behaviorist orientation to a cognitive orientation, with a renewed interest in mental phenomena, provides an intellectual climate for increased interest in and acceptance of hypnosis. There is little doubt that hypnotic methods are effective for treating some types of physical and psychological problems, at least in a minority of patients. But theoretical controversy continues over what is going on in hypnosis.

In this chapter I will consider the basics of hypnosis, including the problem of definition, hypnotic induction, typical hypnotic phenomena, subjective aspects of hypnosis, and how hypnotic responsiveness is measured. I will also discuss research on the personality correlates of individual differences in hypnotizability, and whether hypnotizability can be increased by special training methods. Then I will describe some clinical applications of hypnosis, and finally I will discuss whether hypnosis is dangerous. We will see that hypnosis research has been heavily influenced by theoretical controversies, moreso than any other topic in altered states of consciousness.

The traditional theoretical view is that hypnosis is an altered state of consciousness characterized by both alterations of subjective experience and alterations of mental processes of perception, thinking, memory, and control of behavior (Bowers 1976; Orne 1977; Sheehan & Perry 1976; Shor 1962). The term "hypnotic trance" reflects the traditional altered-state view of hypnosis. Hilgard's (1977) neodissociation theory—which explains hypnosis in terms of dissociations or disconnections between an executive control system, conscious monitoring, and cognitive subsystems—is related to the altered-state view of hypnosis. Spanos (1986a) called the altered-state and dissociation views of hypnosis the *special-process view*, since they assume that people's mental processes operate somehow differently during hypnosis than in the normal waking state.

An alternate view, the *social-psychological view* (or social-cognitive view), is supported by many contemporary researchers (Barber 1969; Coe & Sarbin 1977; Lynn, Rhue, & Weekes 1990; Sarbin & Coe 1972; Spanos 1986a; Spanos & Chaves 1989; Wagstaff 1981, 1986). The social-psychological view says that hypnosis is not an altered state of consciousness, but rather it involves normal thinking and behavior processes operating in a somewhat unusual manner in a special social situation. In this view, subjects in a hypnosis situation enter into a special social role (hypnotic subject) and play that role to the best of their ability using various cognitive and behavioral strategies. Good hypnotic subjects try to convince both the hypnotist and themselves that they are good hypnotic subjects, according to their understanding of the subjective and behavioral characteristics of good hypnotic subjects.

Hypnotic phenomena may be described differently, depending on whether a writer subscribes to an altered-state (or special-process) view or a social-psychological view of hypnosis. This presents a problem for a writer who would like to take an unbiased position. In this chapter I will mostly use the familiar language of the traditional altered-state view of hypnosis. I will also consider the social-psychological view on a number of topics discussed here. In Chapter 15, I will go into more detail on theoretical controversies and research on two particularly important hypnotic phenomena: hypnotic analgesia (pain control) and posthypnotic amnesia. In Chapter 16, I will discuss research on hypnotic age regression and hypnotic hypermnesia (memory enhancement).

THE DEFINITION OF HYPNOSIS

What is hypnosis? It would be nice to have a simple, objective definition of hypnosis in order to know it when we see it or when we experience it. But defining hypnosis is not easy. There is no simple behavioral criterion for identifying hypnosis, nor do hypnotic inductions reliably produce a hypnotic "state." To make matters worse, all attempts to objectively define hypnosis seem to be contaminated by a theoretical view on the nature of hypnosis.

In view of the problems in getting hypnosis researchers to agree on a definition of hypnosis, Hilgard (1973) suggested that we can at least agree on the "domain" of hypnosis. That is, there is a certain set of phenomena that tends to be of interest to hypnosis researchers, regardless of their theoretical viewpoints. Phenomena in the domain of hypnosis tend to be correlated with each other, that is, they tend to occur together in some individuals, but not others. They include responses to various types of hypnotic suggestions (such as temporary paralyses, hallucinations, and amnesia), responses to certain types of waking suggestions (given without a prior hypnotic induction), as well as some measures of spontaneous alterations of consciousness and capacity for imaginative involvement outside of hypnosis. On the other hand, people who are responsive to suggestions in the domain of hypnosis (sometimes termed "primary suggestions") will not necessarily be responsive to other types of social suggestions, such as those involved in conformity and gullibility (termed "secondary suggestions").

A Working Definition of Hypnosis

Regardless of earlier definition problems, it will be useful for our purposes to give a working definition of hypnosis: *hypnosis* is a psychological state or condition, induced by a ritualistic procedure, in which the subject experiences changes in perception, thinking, memory and behavior in response to suggestions by the hypnotist (after Orne 1977).

The purpose of this definition is to narrow the domain of hypnosis to those aspects that will be emphasized in this book and which have, in fact, been the focus of most hypnosis research. Several comments on the definition are in order. (1) By "psychological state or condition" I mean that to hypnotized subjects, hypnosis seems to be subjectively different from their normal waking state or condition. I am not taking a strong stand here on the issue of whether hypnosis is an altered state in the sense of altered brain functioning or altered mental processes. (2) The "ritualistic procedure" refers to the *hypnotic induction*. While a variety of specific techniques (to be described later) can be used, they have in common the fact that they identify the situation to the subject as an attempt at hypnosis. Thus, spontaneous alterations of consciousness are excluded from the definition of hypnosis, though they may be in the larger domain of hypnosis. When I refer to "hypnotized" subjects, I mean subjects who have experienced a hypnotic induction followed by subjective and behavioral responses to suggestions. (3) The "changes in perception, thinking, memory and behavior" refer loosely to several types of hypnotic experiences that are characteristic of hypnosis, such as hallucinations, suggested amnesia, and so forth (to be described later in more detail). (4) The phrase "the subject experiences changes . . ." emphasizes the point that the critical aspect of hypnosis is subjects' conscious experiences, rather than their overt behavior. (5) That the experiences occur "in response to suggestions by the hypnotist" emphasizes two points: First, the characteristic changes in perception, thinking, and so forth occur in response to specific relevant suggestions by the hypnotist, rather than as spontaneous responses to the hypnotic induction alone. Second, I am concerned here with *heterohypnosis*, which involves a social-psychological relationship between the hypnotic subject and another person, the hypnotist, who gives the induction and the suggestions. In contrast, *self-hypnosis* is a situation where the subject provides his or her own induction and suggestions. Self-hypnosis is in the domain of hypnosis, but it is a continuing question as to how similar it really is to heterohypnosis (Fromm et al. 1981; Johnson 1981). (6) This is a quasi-operational definition, in that it implies that the situation involves hypnosis *if* a hypnotic induction is used and *if* the subject experiences the characteristic effects following the hypnotist's suggestions. The induction alone is not sufficient to define the situation as hypnosis. Cases where subjects respond to suggestions without a prior hypnotic induction are certainly within the domain of hypnosis as defined by Hilgard (1973), but they are not, strictly speaking, cases of hypnosis according to the present definition.

Suggestion

Up to this point I have been using the term "suggestion" without defining it. Weitzenhoffer (1957) defined *suggestion* as "any communication, verbal or nonverbal, simple or complex, from the suggestor [hypnotist] to the suggestee [subject], aimed at bringing about some experience and behavior at variance with the suggestee's environment or the behavior he would have otherwise exhibited" (p. 25).

Suggestions can be distinguished from commands or instructions. A command or instruction tells the subject exactly what to do. A suggestion influences the subject's behavior indirectly, by implication. It induces a response, rather than forcing it. In practice, hypnotic suggestions may begin with instructions or commands to set up the suggestion. And suggestions may employ imagination instructions, with the implication that a certain response may follow. For example, the "hands moving together" suggestion begins with these instructions: "Hold your hands straight out in front, at arms length, about a foot apart, with the palms facing each other." Then the hypnotist says, "Now imagine a force between your hands, like a magnet, pulling your hands together." Subjects are not commanded to move their hands together, but it is implied that if they vividly imagine the force, then their hands will move together. Furthermore, Weitzenhoffer (1957, 1978) emphasized the point that in the *classic suggestion effect,* subjects experience their responses (such as hands moving together) as *involuntary* (nonvoluntary) in the sense that they do not involve any conscious volitional command. The response seems to happen by itself, automatically.

Some suggestions sound like commands, for example, response inhibition or "challenge" suggestions ("you will not be able to bend your arm") and posthypnotic amnesia ("you will not be able to remember anything that happened during hypnosis"). Such cases are nonetheless classed as suggestions because they lead to behavior that is contrary to what the subject would ordinarily do, without directly forcing compliance (that is, ordinarily, without the suggestion, the subject would be able to bend the arm or recall what happened during hypnosis).

A demonstration.   Let's try a demonstration, so you can get a better idea what I mean by suggestion. I often do this in my classes as a demonstration of waking suggestion without a prior hypnotic induction. Perhaps you can do it as a waking autosuggestion (self-suggestion). This is best done while sitting on a straight chair, sitting up straight with both feet on the floor. (If you do this with someone else, read the suggestion slowly, allowing time for the subject to use his or her imagination and respond.)

> Hold both hands straight out in front of your body, palms up, both arms straight, elbows straight, at shoulder height. Both hands feel the same. It is easy to hold them up. But soon this will change. Now imagine a heavy object in your left hand. Imagine a brick in your left hand. It weighs five pounds. Feel the weight of the brick. It's hard to hold it up. Your left hand will get very tired, trying to hold up the brick. The brick will tend to push your hand down. Your left hand is getting more and more tired. But your right hand is not tired at all. It just floats there in the air without any effort, as if it were a big helium-filled balloon. It's easy to hold your right hand up. But your left hand is feeling more and more tired and heavy. Feel the weight of the brick as it pushes your left hand down, more and more down . . . .

This is the "differential hand heaviness" suggestion. We can distinguish between objective responses and subjective responses to the suggestion. The *objective response* is your overt, objective response. If somebody else had been watching you, would they have seen that your left hand dropped lower than your right hand? The *subjective response* is your conscious experience during the suggestion. Did it feel like your left hand was heavier or more tired than the right hand (regardless of whether the left dropped lower than the right)? Both objective and subjective responses can vary in degree. As an arbitrary criterion, if your left hand dropped at least two inches below the right, then you objectively passed the item. The objective and subjective responses are highly correlated. Most people who make the objective response also experience the subjective response. But a minority have a subjective response—the left hand feels heavier—without the objective response;

perhaps they made an extra effort to hold up their tired left hand. Also, a minority may make the objective response without feeling the subjective response; perhaps they are faking it by deliberately lowering their left hand. (By the way, it doesn't make any difference whether you imagine the brick in your left hand or your right hand.) You might also try giving yourself a waking autosuggestion for a force pulling your hands toward each other, as in the "hands moving together" item (see Table 14.1).

HYPNOTIC INDUCTION

There are dozens of different techniques for inducing hypnosis (Edmonston 1986; Weitzenhoffer 1957). In a clinical setting hypnotists can be creative and employ whatever technique they believe will be most effective for a particular subject/client. Experienced subjects may enter hypnosis almost immediately in response to a simple cue. However, slower methods are typically used for the first hypnosis experience. Subjects are usually asked to focus their attention on some object, such as a spot on the ceiling or a swinging medallion or metronome, and to listen only to the hypnotist's voice. Then suggestions for progressively greater relaxation are given, and sometimes hypnosis is characterized in terms of a sleep metaphor ("you are falling asleep").

The fact that hypnosis can be induced by such a wide variety of techniques implies that there is nothing magical about the induction itself. *Hypnotic susceptibility*—the subject's ability to respond to hypnotic suggestions—is more important than either the hypnotist's skill or the nature of the specific induction technique. However, it seems to be important to use some sort of induction ritual, since it identifies the situation as hypnosis, distinguishes between the roles of subject and hypnotist, and generates in the subject certain expectancies about the types of experiences that he or she is likely to have.

For experimental research it is important to use a standardized hypnotic induction. The induction is a controlled variable, in that it is the same for all subjects. Also, it is useful for different experimenters, in different laboratories, to use the same standardized induction in order that their results can be compared.

The induction from the Stanford Hypnotic Susceptibility Scale, Form C (SHSS:C) (Weitzenhoffer & Hilgard 1962) is widely used in hypnosis research. It takes about ten minutes to administer. Subjects begin with their eyes open. The hypnotist asks them to focus their eyes on a "target" (a shiny thumbtack placed high on the wall or on the ceiling). The induction begins with some preliminary banter about the importance of concentrating and wanting to be hypnotized and not resisting, and about there being nothing supernatural or frightening about hypnosis. Then suggestions for relaxing various parts of the body are given, as well as suggestions for feeling heavy and becoming sleepy. Suggestions about feeling sleepy and having heavy eyelids are repeated several times. Hypnotizable subjects usually close their eyes spontaneously within a few minutes, but after a while, if a subject has not already done so, the hypnotist instructs him to go ahead and close his eyes. Finally a "deepening" suggestion is given, where subjects are told that they will feel more and more deeply "asleep" as the hypnotist counts slowly from one to twenty.

By itself, hypnotic induction does not seem to do anything very interesting. Subjects simply look and feel very relaxed. The most characteristic hypnotic phenomena involve subjects' responses to specific suggestions that the hypnotist gives following the induction.

THE MEASUREMENT OF HYPNOTIC SUSCEPTIBILITY

One of the most important facts about hypnosis is that people vary widely in *hypnotic susceptibility* (hypnotic responsiveness or hypnotizability), the ability to respond to hypnotic suggestions. Individual differences in hypnotizability is a major topic of hypnosis research. Researchers have studied possible correlates of hypnotic susceptibility, such as personality and cognitive traits, childhood experiences, interests, and attitudes that relate to hypnotizability. And researchers have asked whether an individual's level of hypnotizability is a relatively permanent personality trait or a skill that can be improved by special training.

A major boost to modern hypnosis research was the development of reliable and valid standardized techniques for quantitatively measuring hypnotic susceptibility. Particularly important were the Stanford Hypnotic Susceptibility Scales (SHSS forms A, B, and C), developed by Andre Weitzenhoffer and Ernest Hilgard (1959, 1962). In these scales, subjects are first given a standard hypnotic induction, such as the one described above for SHSS:C. Then they are given a series of different suggestion items, with each suggestion being given with the same wording and at the same pace for every subject. Subjects are given a hypnotic susceptibility score according to how many suggestion items they pass. Passing an item means making an overt movement or verbal report of subjective experience that fits the intention of the suggestion and meets standard scoring criteria. The reliability and validity of the Stanford scales have been thoroughly assessed, and norms have been established so that individuals may be classified as high, medium, or low in hypnotic susceptibility (Hilgard 1965).

The major types of suggestions may be classified into three categories: ideomotor actions, response inhibitions (challenge items), and cognitive distortions (such as hallucinations, amnesia). Posthypnotic suggestions form a fourth category that cuts across the other categories in that posthypnotic suggestions may involve either motor or cognitive responses to a prearranged cue. (The types of hypnotic suggestions are discussed in more detail in the next section.)

Table 14.1 lists the items on the Harvard Group Scale of Hypnotic Susceptibility (HGSHS) (Shor & E. Orne 1962). The HGSHS (based on SHSS:A) was designed to be conveniently administered to moderately large groups of people (about twenty to fifty at a time), including people who have not previously experienced hypnosis. Thousands of research subjects, mostly college students, have been tested with HGSHS. The induction and test suggestions are read aloud to the group, or they may be presented by a tape

TABLE 14.1   Test Items from the Harvard Group Scale of Hypnotic Susceptibility: Form A

1.	Head falling	A waking suggestion item given before the hypnotic induction.
2.	Eye closure	In response to suggestions of eyelid heaviness given during the induction.
3.	Hand lowering (left hand)	In response to suggestion of hand heaviness, with the image of a weight pulling the hand down.
4.	Arm immobilization (right arm)	Inability to lift the arm, in response to suggestion that the arm is very heavy and impossible to lift.
5.	Finger lock	Inability to separate the hands, in response to suggestion that the fingers are tightly interlocked.
6.	Arm rigidity (left arm)	Inability to bend the arm, in response to suggestion that the arm is stiff like a bar of iron, and cannot be bent.
7.	Hands moving together	Outstretched hands moving together, in response to suggestion to imagine a force pulling them toward each other.
8.	Communication inhibition	Inability to shake head "no," in response to suggestion that subject cannot do it.
9.	Fly hallucination	Movement indicating annoyance at hallucinated fly, in response to suggestion flies are buzzing around the subject's head.
10.	Eye catalepsy	Inability to open eyes, in response to suggestion that eyelids are glued shut.
11.	Posthypnotic suggestion	Touching left ankle in response to cue given after arousal from hypnosis, following suggestion that subject will do so but will forget that he was told to do so.
12.	Posthypnotic amnesia	Inability to recall more than three of the suggestions given since eye closure, in response to suggestion that subject will not be able to remember anything that happened during hypnosis until explicitly told "Now you can remember everything."

recording. Subjects score their own responses from memory after the procedure has been completed. Research has shown that the self-scoring procedure has acceptable accuracy, in comparison with scoring by objective observers.

The most commonly used advanced testing procedure is the Stanford Hypnotic Susceptibility Scale: Form C (SHSS:C) (Weitzenhoffer & Hilgard 1962). It is ordinarily administered to subjects individually, though it has been adapted for use in small groups. Table 14.2 shows the SHSS:C items. Compared to HGSHS, SHSS:C employs more cognitive items (age regression, hypnotic dream, negative hallucination), and thus is a more valid mea-

TABLE 14.2   Test Items from the Stanford Hypnotic Susceptibility Scale: Form C

1.	Hand lowering (right hand)	In response to suggestion of hand heaviness, with the image of a weight pulling the hand down.
2.	Moving hands apart	Moving outstretched hands apart, in response to suggestion to imagine a force pushing the hands apart.
3.	Mosquito hallucination	Movement indicating annoyance at hallucinated mosquito, in response to suggestion that a mosquito is buzzing around and landing on right hand.
4.	Taste hallucination	Overt movement, such as lip movement or grimacing, or verbal report of strong taste, in response to either suggested sweet taste or sour taste.
5.	Arm rigidity (right arm)	Inability to bend arm in response to suggestion that it is stiff, as if tightly splinted, and cannot be bent.
6.	Dream	Report of dream-like experience in response to suggestion to sleep and dream about hypnosis. [Should include vivid visual imagery and spontaneous action.]
7.	Age regression	Following suggestion that the subject is growing younger and smaller, and is back in a second-grade classroom, the subject is asked to write his name and shows a clear change in handwriting compared to a sample taken before the regression suggestion.
8.	Arm immobilization (left arm)	Inability to lift the arm, in response to suggestion that the arm is very heavy and impossible to lift.
9.	Anosmia to ammonia	In response to suggestion that subject will be unable to smell odors, he shows no overt reaction to a small bottle of ammonia held under his nose and does not report smelling ammonia.
10.	Hallucinated voice	Overt verbal response to hallucinated questions, in response to suggestion that he will be asked questions over an intercom.
11.	Negative visual hallucination	Subject reports seeing only two small boxes on table, in response to suggestion that he will see only two boxes, though there are actually three boxes.
12.	Posthypnotic amnesia	Inability to recall more than three of the suggestions given since eye closure, in response to suggestion that subject will not be able to remember anything that happened during hypnosis until explicitly told "Now you can remember everything."

sure of hypnotizability. One reason that HGSHS does not include more cognitive items is that, by their nature, they require more personal communication between the subject and the hypnotist. Also, some cognitive items (especially age regression) occasionally elicit an emotional reaction, and such reactions can be handled more easily in an individual test session than in a group session. On both HGSHS and SHSS:C, a score of 0 to 4 is considered low, 5 to 9 is medium, and 10 to 12 is high. On both scales, scores are distributed approximately normally; that is, most people score in the middle range, with only a minority being classified as high, or low, in hypnotizability.

Several other standard scales have been developed. The Stanford Profile Scales of Hypnotic Susceptibility (SPSHS) (Weitzenhoffer & Hilgard 1967) emphasize more difficult cognitive items; they can distinguish highly hypnotizable versus *very* highly hypnotizable subjects better than the shorter and easier scales such as SHSS, Form A or Form C (Hilgard 1978/1979). The Stanford Hypnotic Clinical Scale for Adults (SHCS: ADULT) (Hilgard & J. Hilgard 1983; Morgan & J. Hilgard 1978/1979a) is designed for a relatively quick hypnotic assessment of clinical patients who may have limited mobility. The Stanford Hypnotic Clinical Scale for Children (SHCS: CHILD) (Morgan & J. Hilgard 1978/1979b) has an induction and test items designed especially for children ages six to sixteen years (with an alternate form for children four to eight years old). The Carleton University Responsiveness to Suggestion Scale (CURSS) (Spanos, Radtke, et al. 1983a) is a group scale that may be administered either with or without a prior hypnotic induction; it includes questions about subjective as well as objective responses to suggestions. (These scales [except CURSS] and others are described in detail in Edmonston 1986.)

TYPES OF HYPNOTIC SUGGESTIONS

The major types of hypnotic suggestions also serve to define the major hypnotic phenomena.

Ideomotor Suggestions

In ideomotor suggestions the hypnotist asks subjects to imagine some state of affairs that, if it were true, would cause them to make a particular movement. Subjects pass the item if they make the movement implied by the suggestion. The "hands moving together" item described previously is an example of an ideomotor suggestion.

Ideomotor suggestions are the easiest types of hypnosis items, in that a higher percentage of subjects pass them than other types of items. For example, the four ideomotor items on the HGSHS were passed by an average of 84 percent of the subjects in a sample of 272 students from the University of Maine (Farthing, Brown, and Venturino 1983a). In fact, many people can pass ideomotor items without a prior hypnotic induction.

Response-Inhibition (Challenge) Suggestions

In response-inhibition ("challenge") items the hypnotist first suggests that the subject cannot move some part of his or her body, then the hypnotist challenges the subject to try to move that part. Subjects pass the item if they *do not* move that part of their body. For example, in the arm rigidity item, the hypnotist suggests that the subject's outstretched arm is "stiff, like a bar of iron, and you cannot bend it." Then the hypnotist says, "Now, try to bend the arm. Just try." The subject passes the item if he or she *fails* to bend the arm. Deeply hypnotizable subjects feel that they *cannot* bend the arm, even though they are trying to do so. Challenge items are more difficult than ideomotor items. Five challenge items on the HGSHS were passed by an average of 57 percent of the subjects (Farthing et al. 1983a).

Cognitive Suggestions

Cognitive suggestions, including changes in perception, thinking, and memory, are particularly important for several reasons. Subjectively they are the most dramatic hypnotic experiences. The most important practical applications of hypnosis involve responses to suggestions for cognitive changes—for example, negative hallucination of pain (hypnotic analgesia). And theoretically, cognitive changes define the essence of hypnosis (Orne 1977). Cognitive items vary widely in difficulty, but most of them are more difficult (lower pass percentage) than challenge items. The major cognitive suggestions will be briefly described here, and research on four of the most important cognitive phenomena (hypnotic analgesia, posthypnotic amnesia, age regression, and hypermnesia) will be discussed in more detail in the next two chapters.

Positive hallucinations.   In a positive hallucination the subject believes that he or she perceives something when objectively it is not really there. For example, the hypnotist might suggest to the subject that music will be played on a portable cassette player. Then the hypnotist runs a blank tape. The hallucinating subject will "hear" music and be able to name the tune or sing or hum along with it. Or the hypnotist might tell the subject that when he opens his eyes he will see a puppy sitting on the floor. Subsequently, the subject will "see" the puppy and react to it in a friendly or avoidant manner, depending on how he feels about dogs. Although hallucinations are subjective experiences, the hypnotist/experimenter must observe some sort of overt response in order to judge whether the subject experienced a suggested hallucination. For example, on the HGSHS fly hallucination item, subjects are judged to have passed the item if they make some movement of the hand or face (such as a grimace or twitch) that seems to indicate annoyance at a fly buzzing around their head. On the HGSHS, having a vivid, realistic subjective experience of a fly buzzing nearby is strongly correlated with both objectively passing the item by making an overt annoyance response and experiencing that response as automatic rather than voluntary (Farthing et al. 1983a).

Note that there are two aspects to hypnotic hallucinations: (1) a mental image (a quasi-perceptual visual or auditory experience); and (2) the belief that the mental image is a genuine sensory perception. Some evidence suggests that hypnosis can enhance mental imagery vividness in highly hypnotizable subjects. Also, hypnosis may enhance belief in the reality of the hallucinated object (Naish 1986). A more skeptical view is that during hypnosis some subjects behave *as if* they are hallucinating, although they know that the imagined object is not real (Wagstaff 1981).

Negative hallucinations.   In a negative hallucination the subject fails to perceive something that really is there and that he or she would ordinarily perceive. For example, in hypnotic deafness the hypnotist suggests "you are going deaf," and subjects subsequently fail to react to sounds, such as odd noises, taunts, and jokes. When aroused from hypnosis, they deny that they heard anything while they were "deaf." Yet, electrophysiological recordings of muscle-potential responses to noises show that subjects are not really deaf during hypnotic deafness (Malmo, Boag, & Raginsky 1954). Also, subjects show the usual disruptions of speech fluency during delayed auditory feedback (Barber 1969; Barber & Calverley 1964). What is going on here? One interpretation is that following the deafness suggestion, the hypnotized subjects' attention is turned profoundly inward, so they do not notice external sounds. An alternative, skeptical view is that they hear the sounds, but *behave as if* they do not hear (Wagstaff 1981).

In a suggestion for selective blindness, the negative chair hallucination, the hypnotist suggests that a particular chair has been removed from the room—although it has not really been removed. The subject subsequently fails to mention the chair when describing the contents of the room and denies that the chair is present. It appears that the subject does not see the chair. The skeptical view is that the subject really sees the chair, but behaves as if he does not see it. Paradoxically, while walking across the room the subject may walk around the chair to avoid bumping into it. What is going on here? According to Martin Orne (1959), avoiding the chair is an example of *trance logic,* where good hypnotic subjects may accept two contradictory beliefs without the usual feeling of cognitive conflict. (Trance logic will be discussed in Chapter 16.)

One of the most important practical applications of hypnosis is for pain reduction. Hypnotic analgesia is a type of negative hallucination, in that a normally painful stimulus is not felt to be painful or is perceived as less painful than normal. Because of its importance, I will discuss hypnotic analgesia in detail in the next chapter.

Age regression.   Age regression is often the most dramatic hypnotic experience for the hypnotic subject, as well as for the audience at public demonstrations of hypnosis. In an age-regression suggestion, the hypnotist tells the subject that he or she is becoming younger and smaller and going back to some earlier time in life, such as first grade. Good hypnotic subjects have a subjective experience of feeling much younger and smaller. They may have vivid mental images of past experiences, such as sitting in the classroom and seeing where each of the other children was sitting, or seeing children playing on the playground. Subjects' overt behavior may also change. Their voices may sound different. When asked to write their names they may spontaneously switch to printing in a childlike way. In good age regressions, subjects are more likely to speak in the present tense than in the past tense. For example, a subject might say "I *am* on the playground playing marbles with Jimmy and Johnny," rather than "I *was* on the playground. . . ."

What is going on here? Are age-regressed subjects really mentally younger in the sense of having the knowledge and mental abilities of a child? Are they emotionally younger? Are their vivid images really accurate recollections of scenes from childhood? One interpretation is that age regression is a vivid hallucination of being young again, in another time and place (Orne 1951). Alternatively, apparent age regression may be a strategic role enactment. (In Chapter 16 I will discuss age regression, along with the related issue of hypermnesia—whether hypnotized subjects really have a greater-than-normal ability to recall personal past experiences.)

Hypnotic dreams.   In hypnotic dream suggestions the hypnotist usually suggests that subjects dream about a particular topic. For example, the hypnotist might say, "Now you are going to go to sleep and dream about what being hypnotized means to you." Then subjects are allowed a few minutes of peace and quiet during which to dream. Finally, the hypnotist asks them to describe their dream in as much detail as possible. Subjects are judged to have had a hypnotic dream if they report a mental experience characterized by vivid mental imagery with spontaneous action (that is, the dream events occur spontaneously, without deliberate control by the subject).

Hypnotic dreams are not the same as sleep dreams. Brain-wave recordings show that subjects are not in a sleep state during hypnotic dreaming. Furthermore, hypnotizable subjects usually report that their hypnotic dreams are not as vivid as their sleep dreams, although their hypnotic dreams are more vivid than their typical daydreams.

Surprisingly, the contents of hypnotic dreams often have no obvious relationship to the suggested dream topic. From a psychoanalytic perspective, the manifest or surface content of a hypnotic dream may be only a symbolic expression of latent content (Fisher 1953). On the other hand, Tart (1964) found that, following hypnotic suggestions to have sleep dreams on a particular topic, subsequent sleep dreams often had contents that were obviously related to the suggested topic. Barrett (1979) found that when no specific dream topic was suggested, hypnotizable subjects had hypnotic dreams that were more similar to their night dreams than to their daydreams in aspects such as length, emotional theme, and amount of distortion.

Posthypnotic amnesia.   There are two types of posthypnotic amnesia: *suggested* amnesia, which is common among highly hypnotizable subjects, and *spontaneous* amnesia, which is rare. "Posthypnotic amnesia" always refers to suggested amnesia, unless specified otherwise.

In the posthypnotic amnesia suggestion, prior to arousing subjects from hypnosis the hypnotist says, "You will not be able to recall anything that happened during hypnosis. You won't remember anything until I say to you 'Now you can remember everything.' " When subsequently asked to report everything that happened during hypnosis, highly hypnotizable subjects report little or nothing about the suggestions or what they did during hypnosis. Low hypnotizables, on the other hand, report most of the suggestions and their responses. The degree of apparent amnesia varies among subjects. In some cases, subjects may report "I did something with my hands," but they cannot recall the details.

One of the most important facts about suggested amnesia is its *reversibility* (Kihlstrom & Evans 1976). After the hypnotist gives the *reversal cue* by saying "Now you can remember everything," most high hypnotizables report some additional items not previously reported. Reversibility is important because it shows that the previous recall failure was due to a temporary inability to retrieve information stored in memory, rather than to failure to store it in memory (Kihlstrom & Register 1984).

Spontaneous amnesia, which is rare, occurs when the subject cannot recall what happened during hypnosis even though the hypnotist had not given a suggestion for posthypnotic amnesia. Hilgard (1965) argued that spontaneous amnesia is the result of a self-suggestion for amnesia, due to the subject's prior belief that he or she would be unable to recall what happened during hypnosis.

Suggested posthypnotic amnesia has great theoretical importance, because its occurrence is one of the best ways of distinguishing between highly hypnotizable and less hypnotizable subjects, and because the process by which it occurs may underlie a number of other hypnotic phenomena. For that reason, I will discuss suggested amnesia in more detail in the next chapter. We will see that there is a controversy over whether apparent amnesia is due to an *inability* to retrieve hypnotic experiences or an *unwillingness* to retrieve or report them.

Posthypnotic Suggestions

In posthypnotic suggestions the hypnotist suggests to subjects that after they have been aroused from hypnosis they will perform certain acts, or have certain subjective experiences, in response to specified cues. Further, the hypnotist suggests amnesia for the posthypnotic suggestion and that responses to the cue will occur automatically. For example, the hypnotist might suggest that upon hearing a tapping noise the subject will feel an irrepressible need to cough or clear his throat or that upon hearing the word "experiment" the subject will rub his nose (Hilgard 1965).

Posthypnotic suggestions are particularly important for practical applications of hypnosis, since they enable responsive subjects to modify their experience or behavior without having to be "hypnotized" all day. For example, posthypnotic suggestions can be used to reduce chronic pain or to aid in controlling maladaptive habits such as smoking or overeating. Subjects may perform self-hypnosis in the morning and give themselves posthypnotic suggestions to help deal with their problems during the day (Sacerdote 1981).

The question most often asked about posthypnotic suggestions is how long they last. They may last for several minutes or hours (rarely for several days). How long they are effective depends on several factors, including: (1) the hypnotizability of the subject (the higher the better); (2) the complexity of the response (the simpler the better); (3) the setting in which the response occurs (better in the original clinical or experimental setting); and (4) the subject's awareness that there is something incongruous or unusual about making the response in the current setting (the less awareness the better) (Hilgard 1965). Spanos, Menary, et al. (1987b) found that posthypnotic responses occurred much less often when given by the hypnotist outside of the original experimental context than in the original context, and that responses never occurred when the cue was given by someone other than the hypnotist.

THE SUBJECTIVE EXPERIENCE OF HYPNOSIS

Following hypnosis, subjects may be asked to make introspective verbal reports about their subjective experiences during hypnosis. Low-to-medium hypnotizables usually say simply that they felt relaxed or sleepy. Reports by high hypnotizables vary widely. The variety of descriptions reflects not only subjects' different subjective experiences, but also their selection of different aspects of their experiences for emphasis, and their use of different metaphors to describe their experiences. Here are examples of subjective reports from some of Hilgard's (1965, p. 13) highly hypnotizable subjects:

> "Hypnosis is just *one thing* going on, like a thread . . . focusing on a single thread of one's existence. . . ."
>
> "My thoughts were an echo of what you were saying. . . ."
>
> "Your voice came in my ear and *filled* my head."
>
> "When I felt deepest, I was down in the bottom of a dark hole. I turned over and over on the way down. Now and then I would float up toward the top of the hole. . . ."
>
> "I felt like my eyes were turned around and I could see inside myself . . . as though my eyes and head were not part of my body but suspended on the ceiling. I was completely unaware of any other part of my body."
>
> "I felt as though I were 'inside' myself; none of my body was touching anything. . . ."
>
> "I was very much aware of the split in my consciousness. One part of me was analytic and listening to you. The other part was feeling the things that the analytic part decided I should have." [The feeling of split consciousness is fairly common, and I will return to it and its implications later.]

It is difficult to draw any firm conclusions about typical hypnotic experiences from such varied descriptions. However, they can provide the basis for developing questionnaires with which to find out the relative frequencies of different types of subjective experiences during hypnosis. Table 14.3 shows the percent of subjects who responded affirmatively to various items on a questionnaire on subjective experiences. In general, the higher the level of hypnotic susceptibility, the more subjects who reported having had these types of experience. However, none of the experiences was universal, even among highly hypnotizable subjects. Thus, there is no single subjective criterion identifying the hypnotic state, just as there is no single objective behavioral criterion.

TABLE 14.3 Subjective Reports by Subjects Varying in Measured Hypnotic Susceptibility Based on an Inquiry Following Attempted Hypnosis

INQURY	AFFIRMATIVE REPLIES TO INQUIRY (BY PERCENTAGE)			
	HIGH (N = 48)	MEDIUM (N = 49)	LOW (N = 45)	NONSUSCEPTIBLE (N = 17)
Were you able to tell when you were hypnotized?	65	60	47	31
Disinclination to speak?	89	79	68	31
Disinclination to move?	87	77	64	50
Disinclination to think?	55	48	32	12
Feeling of compulsion?	48	52	20	6
Changes in size or appearance of parts of your body?	46	40	26	0
Feeling of floating?	43	42	25	12
Feeling of blacking out?	28	19	7	6
Feeling of dizziness?	19	31	14	0
Feeling of spinning?	7	17	0	6
One or more of prior four feelings?	60	60	39	25
Any similarity to sleep?	80	77	68	50

From Hilgard, E. R. (1965). *Hypnotic Susceptibility*. New York: Harcourt. By permission of the author.

The disinclination of hypnotized subjects to speak, move, or think for themselves indicates a general feeling of passivity. Although subjects usually report that their responses to suggestions were nonvoluntary or automatic, Hilgard's data showed no consistent feeling of compulsion or coercion to respond. As one of Hilgard's subjects put it: "I didn't feel that I had to, but I felt I might as well do it" (Hilgard 1965, p. 12). The reports of changes in perceived body size or appearance, floating, and so on, can be interpreted as aspects of a trance state involving a loss of "general reality orientation" (Shor 1959).

Some 65 percent of high hypnotizables reported that they were able to tell when they were hypnotized. Perhaps a higher percentage felt that their state of consciousness was somehow different from normal but could not tell with certainty whether they were hypnotized because they didn't know exactly what it feels like to be in a hypnotic trance. In fact, studies indicate that being in a trance is not an all-or-nothing matter; rather, it is a matter of degree.

Trance Depth

It is important to distinguish between the concepts of *hypnotic susceptibility* and *hypnotic depth*. Hypnotic susceptibility is a measure of a person's overall degree of responsiveness to hypnotic suggestions under standardized conditions. Hypnotic depth, on the other hand, has to do with the degree of "profundity" of the subjective hypnotic experience, which can vary from moment to moment within a hypnosis session (Tart 1970).

Tart (1979) developed scales to quantitatively measure hypnotic depth. Such scales are based on the assumptions that "[1] there are dimensions of depth or profundity of the hypnotic state, [2] that a given subject may move along such dimensions from time to time, and [3] that there are experiential correlates of position on each dimension that the subject can consciously perceive or unconsciously react to and report" (Tart 1970, p. 120).

These assumptions seem to be justified by Tart's research showing that subjects can reliably rate their hypnotic depth on a numeric scale, and that these ratings relate meaningfully to other measures of hypnotic behavior and experience. In one study (Tart 1970) subjects were instructed to call out a number from zero to ten whenever they heard the hypnotist say "state?". They were told that "zero" means wide awake, "one" means a borderline state, "two" means lightly hypnotized, "five" means deeply hypnotized, and "ten" means very deeply hypnotized. Subjects were asked for depth (state) reports several times during an administration of SHSS:C, once before each of the test suggestions. There was a high correlation ($+0.74$) between mean state ratings and hypnotic susceptibility scores. Though depth ratings varied from time to time within the session for individual subjects, the average depth ratings were higher, the higher the subject's hypnotic susceptibility. (Mean depth ratings were 5.0, 2.5, and 1.2 for subjects scoring high, medium, or low, respectively, on SHSS:C.)

Conceivably, the high correlation between mean depth ratings and susceptibility scores was a result of subjects' momentary depth ratings being influenced by their overt responses to the immediately preceding suggestions. That is, perhaps they rated their state as deeper if they had responded to the preceding suggestion (such as arm rigidity, hallucination) than if they had not responded. A more valid measure of the *prediction* of hypnotic susceptibility from depth ratings is the correlation between the *first* depth report— the one obtained immediately after the induction—and the susceptibility score obtained from subsequent suggestions. Tart (1970) found this correlation to be moderately high ($+0.56$), which indicates that while hypnotic depth and behavioral hypnotic responsiveness (susceptibility) are related, they are not simply alternative measures of the same thing. Hypnotic susceptibility is a relatively enduring characteristic of the individual, whereas hypnotic depth (state) is a momentary subjective feeling.

What sorts of subjective experiences do subjects use to judge their hypnotic depth? Tart's (1970) subjects reported using the following criteria: "(a) intensity of reaction to previous suggestibility test item, 21 percent [of the cases] (b) feelings of drowsiness, 20 percent; (c) fading of the environment, 14 percent; (d) changes in body image or perceived body position, 12 percent; (e) relaxation, 11 percent; and (f) feelings of compulsiveness of responses, 11 percent. If categories (d) and (e) are combined with several other infrequent categories under the general category of bodily changes, 32 percent of the reports are accounted for" (p. 115).

Tart's results suggest that there is some validity to the idea of hypnotic depth, though it is still a poorly understood concept. Subjects apparently find it meaningful to quantitatively rate their hypnotic depth. The fact that hypnotic depth and hypnotic suggestibility (that is, behavioral responsiveness) are only moderately correlated indicates that on some occasions one could feel deeply hypnotized but be unresponsive to suggestions, or vice versa.

Some researchers have argued, however, that the concept of trance depth as a single, linear dimension is an oversimplification of the complexity of subjective hypnotic experiences (Laurence & Nadon 1986). For example, Ronald Shor (1959, 1962, 1979) argued that there are three dimensions of hypnotic depth: (1) trance depth, concerning shifts of attention and loss of "reality orientation"; (2) depth of hypnotic role taking, where responses are experienced as nonvoluntary; and (3) depth of "archaic involvement," concerning subjects' perceptions of the interpersonal relationship between themselves and the hypnotist (as in the transference effect in psychotherapy).

An alternative view is that the whole idea of hypnotic depth ratings is misleading. According to a social-psychological interpretation, hypnotic depth ratings are not simply ratings of directly felt subjective experiences. Rather, they result from an attribution process, where subjects try to infer their "depth" according to the context, their overt responses to suggestions, and the nature of the questions asked about their subjective experiences (Radtke & Spanos 1981). The importance of context was shown in a study in which subjects rated themselves as more deeply hypnotized following instructions identified as a hypnotic induction than following identical instructions not identified as a hypnotic induction (Spanos, Radtke-Bodorik, & Stam 1980).

The importance of wording of questions was shown in a study in which, following a standard hypnotic susceptibility test (CURSS), different groups were given different types of questionnaires over their experiences. When given the choice between describing themselves as hypnotized versus alternative descriptions (such as "absorbed but not hypnotized"), fewer subjects described themselves as hypnotized, compared to a questionnaire where they could describe themselves only on a single dimension of hypnotic depth; the difference was greatest for medium-hypnotizable subjects (Radtke & Spanos, 1982). On the other hand, another study found that most highly hypnotizable subjects chose to describe themselves as moderately-to-deeply hypnotized even when given the opportunity to describe their experience in other ways (Laurence & Nadon 1986). Thus, it appears that most highly hypnotizable subjects can identify a subjective hypnotic state.

Involuntariness of Responses

Traditionally it has been assumed that true hypnotic responses are experienced by subjects as involuntary, in the sense of occurring without a feeling of volitional command (Weitzenhoffer 1978). If subjects vividly imagine the state of affairs suggested by the hypnotist, then the implied overt response should seem to happen by itself, automatically. For example, consider the "hands moving together" suggestion (see Table 14.1). In a true hypnotic response, you would feel a force between your hands, your hands would gradually move together, and it would feel as if your hands moved because of the imagined force. Alternatively, if you deliberately moved your hands together, then you would be making the correct objective response but without the implied feeling of involuntariness; in that case you would be faking it. Similarly, in a posthypnotic amnesia suggestion, a true hypnotic response would involve not only failing to report the test items, but also a feeling that you are unable to recall them.

Weitzenhoffer (1978) criticized the commonly used hypnotic susceptibility scales because they fail to ask subjects whether they experienced their responses as involuntary (automatic) or as voluntary. Although Weitzenhoffer's complaint may be valid from a theoretical viewpoint, research shows that as a practical matter it is usually not very important to formally assess the involuntariness of responses. In a large majority of cases, correct objective responses are in fact accompanied by a feeling of involuntariness (K. Bowers 1981; P. Bowers, Laurence, & Hart 1988.) For example, Farthing et al. (1983a) found that in a large sample (n = 272) tested on HGSHS, when subjects objectively passed ideomotor and challenge items, they experienced their responses as mostly or fully automatic in 77 percent of the cases, and in only 9 percent did they experience their responses as fully deliberate or voluntary.

When subjects experience their overt responses to suggestions as deliberate or voluntary, it seems that they are faking their responses. Most hypnotic responses could be faked if subjects wanted to do so, but it appears that faking is rare. Nonetheless, as we will see, the fact that faking can occur has important implications for hypnosis theories. One of the problems of hypnosis research is to determine the validity of both overt responses and subjective reports.

The feeling of involuntariness of hypnotic responses is consistent with theories that view hypnosis as an altered state of consciousness. At a minimum, subjective experience is different from normal, if subjects feel that their responses are involuntary when they are the same type of responses that normally are experienced as voluntary. A stronger position is Hilgard's (1977) neodissociation theory. Hilgard said that "one of the most striking features of hypnosis is the loss of control over actions normally voluntary" (p. 115). He interpreted the feeling of involuntariness as an actual loss of control and explained it in terms of a temporary dissociation or disconnection of response subsystems from the conscious executive control system.

Theorists taking the social-psychological viewpoint have questioned the validity of the concept of involuntariness of hypnotic responses. Lynn, Rhue, and Weekes (1990) pointed out some senses in which hypnotic responses are not involuntary or automatic. (1) Hypnotic responses do not happen against the subject's will. Rather, subjects allow them to happen and use cognitive strategies to actively encourage them. Subjects can resist responding to hypnotic suggestions. (2) Hypnotic responses have the volitional response characteristic of purposiveness. Hypnotizable subjects use cognitive strategies—such as goal-directed fantasies and redirection of attention—to make the responses happen. When overt responses to suggestions occur while cognitive strategies are being used, subjects tend to interpret the responses as involuntary (Spanos, Rivers, & Ross 1977). (3) Hypnotic responses do not occur automatically in the sense of occurring without mental effort or the use of limited attentional capacity. Many subjects put consider-able mental effort into using cognitive strategies to make the responses hap-pen. (4) Hypnotic responses are not automatic in the sense of occurring non-consciously; subjects ordinarily are consciously aware of their overt responses.

In essence, the social-psychological approach says that good hypnotic subjects desire to convince both the hypnotist and themselves that they are good hypnotic subjects (Spanos 1982, 1986a). They may delude themselves into thinking that their hypnotic responses are involuntary, when in fact their responses have many of the characteristics of voluntary responses. A minority of subjects may deliberately fake overt responses to suggestions, but more commonly subjects use cognitive strategies that encourage the re-sponses to occur, and they subsequently experience or interpret their re-sponses as involuntary. In conclusion, there is only one sense in which many hypnotic responses are involuntary, namely, that subjects do not feel that they have directly willed or commanded the responses to occur. (The term "involuntary" has unfortunate, inappropriate connotations; "nonvoluntary" would be a better term.) We will pursue the controversy between dissociation theory and the social psychological approach further in the next chapter. For now, I want to mention the fact that among highly hypnotizable subjects, different subjects operate with different cognitive styles, some being more active and some being more passive (Sheehan & McConkey 1982). The social-psychological interpretation of hypnotic responses may apply to many hyp-notizable subjects, but not necessarily to all of them.

CORRELATES OF HYPNOTIC SUSCEPTIBILITY

As I mentioned earlier, one of the most important facts about hypnosis is that there are wide individual differences in hypnotic susceptibility. Further-more, hypnotic susceptibility scores tend to be remarkably stable over time. In a longitudinal study, fifty former Stanford University students were re-tested on SHSS:A at ten years, and again at twenty-five years, after their orig-inal susceptibility tests; moderately high correlations were found between the later scores and the original score (+0.64 and 0.71, respectively) (Mor-gan, Johnson, & Hilgard 1974; Piccione, Hilgard, & Zimbardo 1989). These results suggest that hypnotic susceptibility is a relatively stable personality trait. In a later section, I will discuss the alternative viewpoint that hypnotic responsiveness is a skill that can be learned through special training. For now, however, let us assume that hypnotizability is a relatively stable person-ality trait and ask about its correlates. That is, are there nonhypnotic person-ality and cognitive characteristics that distinguish between people of high, medium, or low hypnotizability? This question is important both for under-standing why some people are more hypnotizable than others and for under-standing the basic nature of hypnosis.

Three different methods have been used in research on the correlates of hypnotic susceptibility: (1) administering paper-and-pencil tests of per-sonality and cognitive traits to relatively large groups of unselected subjects;

(2) intensive interviews of selected subjects about their attitudes, beliefs, interests and experiences; and (3) testing groups of high, medium, and low hypnotizables on laboratory measures of cognitive performance.

In the early 1960s, during the first few years following the publication of the Stanford scales, there were several studies that attempted to find relationships between hypnotic susceptibility and measures of major personality trait variables such as introversion-extraversion and stability-neuroticism, as well as others such as hysteria and perceived locus-of-control (that is, internal versus external control) (Bowers 1976; Hilgard 1965). The results of these studies were disappointing. The correlations were usually insignificant, and occasional moderately high correlations could not be replicated from one study to the next. In addition, hypnotic susceptibility is unrelated to measures of social responsiveness, such as social acquiescence, conformity, or gullibility (Bowers 1976). Thus, traditional personality-trait measures appear to be unrelated to hypnotizability. However, in more recent research some personality traits have been discovered that correlate fairly consistently with hypnotizability.

J. Hilgard's Interview Studies of Personality and Hypnotizability

Josephine Hilgard (1970) discovered personality correlates of hypnotizability by conducting extensive clinical interviews with subjects. She interviewed subjects *before* measuring their hypnotic susceptibility in order to avoid having the interviews being influenced by expectations—either the interviewer's or the subject's—arising from knowing the subject's hypnotizability level. The interview data were used to rate the subjects on a number of scales concerned with activities, imaginative involvements, attitudes, family interactions, and childhood experiences that might conceivably be related to their hypnotizability level.

J. Hilgard found that highly hypnotizable subjects almost always had at least one "pathway" to hypnotizability involving a high degree of imaginative involvement, usually one that had developed during childhood and been continued through to adulthood. The various pathways included high degrees of involvement in: (1) fictional reading (to the point of identifying with the characters and responding emotionally to their experiences); (2) the dramatic arts (identifying with the characters, either as an actor or a viewer); (3) religion (as a true believer, not just a churchgoer); (4) affective arousal through sensory stimulation (either through music or through aesthetic appreciation of nature); (5) adventuresomeness (including mental and physical space traveling); and (6) artistic creativity (such as painting, poetry, or music). Also, (7) having had imaginary companions in childhood was related to hypnotizability. People low in hypnotizability were less likely than high hypnotizables to have these pathways. Surprisingly, people with two or more pathways were no more likely to be highly hypnotizable than were those with only one pathway. Two interests, participation in competitive team sports and majoring in the natural sciences, were negatively related to hypnotizability. J. Hilgard concluded:

The statistical data and the case reports have given consistent support to the relationship between imaginative involvement and hypnotic susceptibility. While the correlations are low, indicating that more is involved, the spontaneous assertions of the subjects leave little doubt that hypnosis capitalizes on features of past experience that have permitted the free play of imagination, the setting aside of reality, and the immersion in an experience that to the subject is absorbing and satisfying (1970, p. 169).

The earlier results were confirmed in a later study (J. Hilgard 1974a), in which subjects preselected for high hypnotizability were found to be more likely than lows to have a high degree of involvement in one or more imaginative activities (see Table 14.4). However, some of the lows were highly involved in imaginative activities. Why were these people not highly hypnotizable? Based on interview data, Hilgard (1974a) suggested three factors that might prevent imaginatively involved persons from becoming hypnotized: (1) apprehensiveness over new and different experiences; (2) unwillingness to accept the hypnotist-subject relationship; and (3) attentional distractibility, which may be compatible with some of the imaginative involvements but which interferes with hypnosis.

Absorption and Mental Imagery Vividness

J. Hilgard's conclusions relating imaginative involvement to hypnotic susceptibility are important, but her clinical interview method takes too much time to use in studies with large numbers of subjects. Tellegen and Atkinson (1974) developed an easily administered questionnaire, the Absorption Scale, using items designed to reflect J. Hilgard's findings on imaginative involvement, as well as those of other researchers concerning hyp-

TABLE 14.4   Areas of High Involvement in Samples of High- and Low-Hypnotizable Subjects

INVOLVEMENT AREAS	PERCENT OF SUBJECTS WITH HIGH INVOLVEMENT*	
	HIGH HYPNOTIZABLE (N = 42)	LOW HYPNOTIZABLE (N = 15)
Savoring of sensory experiences	93	20
Drama	79	20
Reading	76	13
Daydreams—child	74	13
Daydreams—adult	36	7
Mental space travelers	45	0
Physical space travelers	33	0
Creativity	26	13
Religion	19	13

*High involvement was defined as a rating of 6 or 7 on a 7-point scale.

From Hilgard, J. R. (1974a). Imaginative involvement: Some characteristics of the highly hypnotizable and the non-hypnotizable. *International Journal of Clinical and Experimental Hypnosis, 22,* 138–56. Copyright 1974 by the Society for Clinical and Experimental Hypnosis.

notic-like experiences occurring in daily life (Ås 1963; Shor 1960). Table 14.5 shows some representative items from the Absorption Scale.

Tellegen and Atkinson found significant positive correlations between the Absorption Scale and hypnotic susceptibility in two large samples of subjects. This correlation has been replicated in numerous studies.[1] The correlations are typically modest, about +0.3 to 0.4, but it is noteworthy that of all of the personality scales that have been tried, the Absorption Scale is the one that relates most consistently to hypnotizability in study after study (for example, Farthing, Venturino, & Brown 1983b; Spanos & McPeake 1975). The Absorption Scale apparently taps an aspect of personality that is uniquely related to hypnotic susceptibility and is independent of a number of other personality dimensions (O'Grady 1980).

What is *absorption*? Tellegen and Atkinson (1974) interpreted it as a "cognitive-motivational trait" involving the capacity for total attentional involvement:

> Absorption is interpreted as a disposition for having episodes of "total" attention that fully engage one's representational (i.e. perceptual, enactive, imaginative, and ideational) resources ... to a unified representation of the attentional object. ... This kind of attentional functioning is believed to result in a heightened sense of the reality of the attentional object, imperviousness to distracting events, and an altered sense of reality in general, including an empathically altered sense of self (pp. 268, 274).

In view of J. Hilgard's (1970) emphasis on the importance of imaginative involvements, you might expect that the vividness or lifelikeness of one's mental images would be related to hypnotic susceptibility. Such a result has been found in several studies (Sheehan 1979). In such studies, subjects are asked to imagine a number of different scenes as vividly as possible. For example, "Picture a landscape with a lake, trees, and a mountain." After a few

---

TABLE 14.5   Representative Items from the Absorption Scale

"While acting in a play, I have sometimes really felt the emotions of the character and have 'become' him (her) for the time being, forgetting, as it were, both myself and the audience."

"I can sometimes recollect certain past experiences in my life with such clarity and vividness that it is like living them over again, or almost so."

"If I wish, I can imagine (or daydream) some things so vividly that they hold my attention in the way a good movie or story does."

"I am sometimes able to forget about my present self and get absorbed in a fantasy that I am someone else."

"If I wish, I can imagine that my body is so heavy that I could not move it if I wanted to."

"I enjoy—or would enjoy—getting beyond the world of logic and reason to experience something new and different."

From Tellegen, A., & Atkinson, G. (1974). Openness to absorbing and self-altering experiences ("absorption"), a trait related to hypnotic susceptibility. *Journal of Abnormal Psychology, 83,* 268–77.

seconds, the experimenter says "Rate!," and subjects then rate the vividness of their mental image (on a 1 to 7 scale).

Sutcliffe, Perry, and Sheehan (1970) found a positive correlation between hypnotic susceptibility and vividness scores on a questionnaire that included items for several sensory modes (vision, hearing, touch). But most studies have used only visual imagery items, as in the Vividness of Visual Imagery Questionnaire (VVIQ) (Marks 1973). Several studies have found significant modest correlations (+0.3 to 0.4) between hypnotic suggestibility and VVIQ vividness scores (P. Bowers 1978; Crawford 1982a). However, some studies found no significant correlation. It seems that, though vividness and absorption scores are correlated with each other (Crawford 1982a), absorption is more reliable than imagery vividness as a predictor of hypnotizability.

Why are correlations between absorption and imagery vividness scores and hypnotic susceptibility scores only modest, at best? Why aren't the correlations higher? There are several reasons: (1) Hypnotizability depends on a number of other factors besides the absorption and imagery vividness traits. (2) Absorption and vividness questionnaires may not accurately measure what they are supposed to measure. For example, when rating their image vividness on a 1 to 7 scale, different subjects may use different subjective criteria for ratings of 2, 5, and so on. (3) The relationship between hypnotizability and a second variable (such as vividness) may depend on a third variable, called a *moderator variable* (Bowers 1976). For example, in order for high-vividness subjects to be highly hypnotizable, it may also be necessary for them to have a positive attitude about hypnosis and/or a belief that they are capable of experiencing hypnosis. (4) The correlates of hypnotic responsiveness may be different for different types of hypnotic test items. Farthing et al. (1983b) found that a multiple correlation combining absorption and visual imagery vividness scores predicted scores on HGSHS cognitive items better than it predicted scores on ideomotor or challenge items. This result makes sense if cognitive items represent the essence of hypnosis better than ideomotor or challenge items (Orne 1977). (5) The correlates of hypnotizability may be different for subjects with different cognitive styles (such as active or passive) during hypnosis (Sheehan & McConkey 1982).

Other Correlates of Hypnotizability

A variety of other measures of personality, cognitive performance, and experience have been found to correlate significantly with hypnotic susceptibility (Bowers 1976; Crawford 1982b). I can list only a few examples here. Note that, as with absorption and mental imagery vividness measures, the correlates refer to measures taken in the waking state, not during hypnosis.

Several studies have found positive correlations between hypnotizability and measures of creativity (review in P. Bowers & K. Bowers 1979). Patricia Bowers (1978, 1979) suggested that this relationship is mediated by a capacity for nonvolitional or "effortless experiencing" in a variety of imagination tasks, including creative writing, creative problem solving, and hypnosis. She devised a measure of effortless experiencing and demonstrated its correlation with creativity and hypnotizability measures. Helen Crawford (1982a) found hypnotizability to be correlated with daydreaming styles, with high hypnotizables having more vividness, positive affect, and absorption in daydreams. Wilson and Barber (1978) devised the *Creative Imagination Scale* (CIS) and showed its correlations with hypnotizability and other measures of imagination and creativity. Wilson and Barber (1983) also identified a "fantasy prone personality," which includes a small proportion (perhaps 4 percent) of people who are not only highly hypnotizable, but are also characterized by having rich daydreaming fantasy lives, ability to hallucinate (for example, having sexual fantasies leading to orgasm, without physical stimulation), deep absorption in media fantasy (such as TV) along with physiological emotional reactions, occasional out-of-body experiences, and occasional inability to distinguish fantasy from reality. In a large-scale study, Lynn and Rhue (1988) confirmed that highly fantasy-prone individuals tend to be high in hypnotizability and waking suggestibility, though there were some exceptions.

Hypnotizability is related to some measures of perception. Crawford (1981) found that high hypnotizables did better than lows on Gestalt closure tasks, where subjects attempted to identify objects whose outlines have been partly obliterated. Wallace, Knight, and Garrett (1976) found that high hypnotizables were more likely than lows to experience visual illusions and frequent reversals in ambiguous figures (such as the Necker cube). In a visual signal detection task, Farthing, Brown, and Venturino (1982) found a greater positive response bias in highs than lows; that is, highs were more likely to say "yes" when they were uncertain whether they saw the signal. An alternative interpretation is that highs sometimes hallucinated the signal. In contrast to self-report measures of attention (such as the Absorption Scale), it has been hard to find differences between highs and lows on objective measures of selective attention performance (Stava & Jaffa 1988). For example, Venturino (1983) found no differences between highs and lows in the accuracy of performance on a shadowing task, where different strings of unrelated words were presented dichotically (one in each ear) and subjects had to repeat one string word for word.

Crawford (1989) suggested that highly hypnotizable subjects have greater cognitive flexibility than low hypnotizables. "*Cognitive flexibility* is the degree to which an individual has and uses one of several available types of information processing strategies or styles during different tasks, as well as different states of awareness" (p. 155). People with superior ability to adaptively shift cognitive style outside of hypnosis might be able to use this ability for hypnotic experiencing. For example, Crawford and Allen (1983) used a task involving short-term visual memory for complex drawings and found that hypnosis improved memory performance and increased the use of holistic rather than analytic strategies in high but not low hypnotizables. Several cognitive-style characteristics of hypnosis (such as enhanced imagination and imagery ability, holistic perception) have been associated with the talents of the brain's right cerebral hemisphere, in contrast with the more analytic, verbal left hemisphere.

Crawford (1989) hypothesized that greater cognitive flexibility is correlated with greater *physiological flexibility*, which she defined as "the degree to which an individual shows different patterns of cerebral activation when performing different types of tasks or when applying different types of strategies to the same task" (p. 155). This hypothesis is supported by evidence for greater EEG "hemispheric specificity" in high than in low hypnotizables. In the waking state, when performing various cognitive tasks thought to require mainly either right, or left, hemisphere processing (such as spatial versus verbal tasks, respectively), highs show a greater degree of appropriate left-right shifting in cerebral activity according to brain-wave measures. For example, during a visuospatial task the left hemisphere shows more alpha EEG, whereas the right hemisphere shows more beta EEG, indicating that the right hemisphere is more active (MacLeod-Morgan & Lack 1982; see also De-Pascalis, Silveri, & Palumbo 1988).

For many years researchers have searched in vain for reliable physiological correlates of hypnosis. But some recent research shows promising results. MacLeod-Morgan (1982) found increased relative right-hemisphere activity (compared to the left hemisphere) during hypnosis in high hypnotizables, but not in lows. Crawford (1989) studied the effects of hypnosis on regional cerebral blood flow. Subjects inhaled a small amount of radioactive xenon–133. Blood-flow changes were estimated by special sensing devices that detected the xenon–133 levels in various cortical regions. Overall cerebral blood flow increased during hypnosis in high hypnotizables, but not in lows. Highs and lows also differed in patterns of blood-flow changes between and within cerebral hemispheres, but these changes are too complex to describe here, and their functional significance has not been determined. It remains to be seen whether the recent findings of physiological correlates of hypnosis can be replicated. But regardless of the physiological results, the hypothesis of greater cognitive flexibility among high hypnotizables is a promising one.

The findings described here support the idea that hypnotizability is a relatively permanent personality trait that is correlated with other cognitive and personality traits. However, the social-psychological approach says that hypnotizability is not a personality trait, but rather, it is a learnable cognitive skill. In this view, correlates of hypnotizability are probably related to the learning of cognitive skills relevant to hypnotic performance, or they may be procedural artifacts (Council, Kirsch, & Hafner 1986). In the next section I will discuss evidence on the question whether hypnotic responsiveness is a learnable skill.

CAN HYPNOTIC SUSCEPTIBILITY BE MODIFIED?

Can a person's level of hypnotic susceptibility be increased through some sort of special experience or training procedure? This question is important for two reasons. First, if it were possible to train unhypnotizable people to be hypnotizable, then they could take advantage of clinical applications of hypnosis, such as pain reduction or habit control. Second, a critical theoretical issue is at stake: Is hypnotic susceptibility a relatively permanent personality *trait*, or is it a learnable *skill*? The trait theory (Hilgard 1965) allows that hypnotic susceptibility may be strongly affected by childhood experiences

(J. Hilgard 1979). But the trait theory would not expect any special training procedure to be successful in producing large, permanent changes in the hypnotic susceptibility of adults. The skill theory (Diamond 1977; Spanos 1986b) says that hypnotic susceptibility depends upon certain attitudes, beliefs, and cognitive skills (such as how to think, imagine, and interpret one's experience) that can be improved by special training methods. The trait theory has been held by theorists who view hypnosis as an altered state of consciousness or cognitive control systems (Bowers 1976; Hilgard 1977), whereas the skill theory has been held by those who take a social-learning approach to hypnosis (Spanos 1986b). Thus, the outcome of attempts to increase hypnotic responsiveness by special training has great relevance to basic theories of hypnosis.

Early attempts.

In earlier attempts to modify hypnotic susceptibility, most studies used relatively simple training programs. Several studies showed significant increases in hypnotizability scores between pretreatment and posttreatment sessions. For example, increases were found following sensory deprivation (Sanders & Reyher 1969; more recently Barabasz & Barabasz 1989), alpha biofeedback training (London, Cooper, & Engstrom 1974), muscle relaxation biofeedback training (Wickramesekera 1973), and encounter-group experience (Shapiro and Diamond 1972). However, several attempts to modify hypnotic susceptibility have failed; for example, meditation training and practice was ineffective (Spanos, Gottlieb, & Rivers 1980), and some successful studies could not be replicated (review in Spanos 1986b).

Campbell Perry (1977) pointed out several problems with the apparently successful early attempts to modify hypnotic responsiveness: (1) The gains were typically rather small, and there was no proof that the gains were maintained over a relatively long period of time. The special training methods might have produced short-term improvements in hypnotic *performance*—perhaps by changing motivation or compliance—without necessarily producing permanent changes in hypnotic susceptibility.

(2) The pretest to posttest change score might be inflated by using an inappropriate pretest baseline. Anxiety, negative attitudes, or self-consciousness may cause some individuals to score below their capability on their first test of hypnotizability, but they do better on a second test after they overcome the initial problems. Perry argued that, to establish a suitable pretest baseline, researchers should measure *plateau hypnotizability* by giving several tests until there is no further improvement.

(3) Results of modification studies may be biased by *compliance effects*. It is usually obvious to subjects that the experimenter expects the training procedure to increase their hypnotic responsiveness. Subjects might "cooperate" and show increased hypnotic responsiveness through either direct behavioral compliance or self-deception.

Perry (1977) concluded that despite the fact that several studies have shown modest increases in test scores between pretest and posttest, the small size of the gains and the methodological problems of the studies are such that one cannot conclude that long-term hypnotic susceptibility is modifiable by special training. Thus, the trait theory of hypnotic susceptibility appeared to be supported, according to Perry's evaluation, by the earlier research.

The Carleton studies.   In recent years, however, evidence has accumulated in support of the social-psychological viewpoint that hypnotic responsiveness is a learnable skill. Building on earlier work by Diamond (1977) and others, Nicholas Spanos (1986b) and his Carleton University colleagues developed the Carleton Skills Training Program (CSTP). CSTP was designed to modify hypnotic susceptibility by employing three relatively distinct components that earlier research had indicated to be important aspects of hypnotic responsiveness:

1. *Disinhibitory information*. CSTP provides information aimed at rectifying misinformation about hypnosis, reducing anxiety, and producing positive attitudes, expectations, and motivations toward experiencing hypnosis.
2. *General facilitatory information*. CSTP emphasizes the importance of generating and becoming absorbed in imaginary situations consistent with the intent of the suggestion. For example, if it is suggested that an arm is becoming light and starting to float up, then subjects should concentrate on imagining their arm being like a large helium-filled balloon.
3. *Detailed information on how to interpret specific types of suggestions*. Hypnotic suggestions are often ambiguous. They often convey the impression that an implied response should happen by itself, and some subjects wait passively for the response to occur. In fact, research by Spanos (1986a, 1986b) and his colleagues shows that high hypnotizables engage actively in cognitive strategies to make the suggested responses occur. CSTP gives examples of several types of suggestions, explains how to interpret the intent of the suggestion, and instructs subjects how to direct attention and generate images consistent with the suggestion's intent, while avoiding mere behavioral compliance. The specific information is presented in two ways. First, the experimenter gives specific information and practice suggestions with feedback. Second, subjects see a videotaped model who responds to several suggestions while she describes appropriate goal-directed imagery strategies.

Spanos et al. (1986) showed that training with CSTP can produce large increases in hypnotic responsiveness in many subjects. They used groups of originally low-hypnotizable subjects (mean score 1 on the 7-point Carleton suggestibility scale, CURSS) and compared their pretreatment hypnotizability scores with posttreatment scores. The *full CSTP group* got the complete three-part training procedure, while the *partial CSTP group* got only the first two components, without the detailed information and suggestion demonstrations. A *no-treatment control group* was simply retested at a later date, without any intervening training or special instructions, to control for the possibility of changes occurring merely as a result of retesting hypnotic susceptibility. The second hypnotizability test was done by a new experimenter, so subjects would not feel that they had to respond in order to please the experimenter who trained them.

Subjects showed marked increases in hypnotic responsiveness on the second test in the full-CSTP group (mean score 5.5 of 7), but not in the partial-CSTP group (mean 1.7) or the control group (mean 0.8). In fact, 73 percent of the full-CSTP group scored in the high-hypnotizability range on retesting (5 or better on the 7-point CURSS), whereas none of the partial-CSTP or controls showed such an increase. Nor were the changes limited to overt behavioral responses to suggestions. Full-CSTP subjects showed marked increases in subjective responses to suggestions, and they reported that most of their behavioral responses occurred nonvoluntarily. Finally, full-CSTP subjects' gains were not limited to suggestions on which they had had previous training. They also responded more than the partial-CSTP or control subjects on new items on CURSS and on SHSS:C. Thus, subjects could apply their training on interpreting suggestions and developing cognitive strategies to entirely new suggestions. Some 53 percent of full-CSTP subjects scored in the high-hypnotizable range on a second posttest, with SHSS:C. Another finding was that attitudes toward hypnosis improved as much in the partial-CSTP group as in the full-CSTP group. Thus, the improved attitudes of the partial-CSTP group were not sufficient to produce marked increases in hypnotic responsiveness.

A critical question in all attempts to increase hypnotizability is whether apparent gains are merely a matter of behavioral compliance by subjects who want to be cooperative. CSTP subjects are explicitly told that the training procedures are intended to increase their hypnotic responsiveness, and it is conceivable that they faked their responses. To evaluate this possibility, Spanos et al. (1986) included a fourth group of low hypnotizables, the *simulator group*, who were not given any special training but who were instructed to fake responding like a highly hypnotizable subject on the second test of hypnotic susceptibility. The pattern of results for the simulator group was quite different from that of the full-CSTP group. The simulators over-faked, which suggests that the full-CSTP group was not merely faking, because they could have faked better.

Regarding Perry's (1977) argument for measuring plateau hypnotizability, Spanos (1986b) replied that: (1) in fact, hypnotic susceptibility is remarkably stable over short-term test-retest intervals; and (2) a single pretest score is satisfactory in experimental designs that include a no-treatment, test-retest control group.

The dramatic increases in hypnotic responsiveness following training with the full Carleton Skills Training Program have been replicated in several studies. "Created highs" (full CSTP-trained subjects) and untrained "natural highs" have been found to have equivalent levels of subjective responding and feelings of nonvolition on a variety of different hypnotic suggestions (Gfeller, Lynn, & Pribble 1987; Gorassini & Spanos 1986; Spanos, Lush, & Gwynn 1989).

In Spanos's studies, typically about 50 percent of initially low-susceptibles improved to the high hypnotic susceptibility level following training on the full CSTP. The question arises, if hypnotizability can be trained, why can't everybody learn it? Or to turn the question around, who can benefit from hypnotic skills training? Spanos et al. (1987a) found that full-CSTP training was effective only for subjects who scored high on a test of mental imagery vividness. Among untrained subjects, those who are low in imagery vividness are rarely hypnotizable, but those who are high in imagery vividness may be either high or low in hypnotizability. Spanos et al.'s results suggest that subjects must have an underlying capacity for vivid mental imagery in order to use effectively the imagination strategies described in CSTP.

Spanos's results with the Carleton Skills Training Program are impressive. They suggest that hypnotic responsiveness is a learnable skill, and that earlier attempts to increase responsiveness were largely unsuccessful because they took the wrong approach. In some of the earlier studies, researchers assumed that hypnosis is an altered state of consciousness, and that altered-state training (such as through sensory deprivation, biofeedback, or meditation) was necessary. Other early studies were on the right track in trying to improve attitudes and/or general instructions for using imagination, but they did not include training and modeling of how to interpret specific suggestions and develop appropriate cognitive strategies, which is a critical component of the CSTP.

The issue whether hypnotic responsiveness is a learnable skill is not entirely settled, however. More research is needed to compare CSTP-"created highs" with "natural highs" in a variety of situations. One important question concerns the long-term stability of hypnotic responsiveness in CSTP-created highs. Spanos has found stability over one month. But Bates et al. (1988) found that responsiveness gains following CSTP training were not maintained when subjects were tested again four months later (though their subjects' initial increases were not as large as in Spanos's studies). This result contrasts with findings of stability of hypnotic responsiveness over ten- and twenty-five-year periods in untrained subjects. More research on this point is needed. Also, if hypnotic responsiveness is related to the degree of symptom improvement in clinical hypnosis applications, then it seems important to find out whether created highs respond as well as natural highs in clinical hypnosis applications. Spanos (personal communication, 1989) replied that this is not a critical test of created highs, since it assumes a correlation between hypnotizability and clinical outcomes with hypnosis. Spanos (1990) reviewed research on hypnotherapy and concluded that it does not convincingly show that clinical outcomes with hypnotherapy are related to patients' hypnotic susceptibility levels. I will discuss some of the research on hypnotherapy effectiveness and its relation to hypnotizability in the next section.

CLINICAL APPLICATIONS OF HYPNOSIS

Hypnosis has been used to treat a wide variety of medical and psychological disorders over the last 200 years (Crasilneck & Hall 1985; DePiano & Salzberg 1986). Its popularity among practitioners has gone through several cycles, but in recent years it has been used with increasing frequency in behavior therapy (such as habit and anxiety treatment) (Spinhoven 1987), hypnoanalysis (a variety of psychoanalysis) (Fromm 1987), and behavioral medicine (especially for pain and psychosomatic disorders) (Frankel 1987). Thousands of individual case studies have been published over the years (see Dowd & Healy 1986 for recent examples). However, only in the last twenty-five years have researchers begun to do controlled studies to critically examine *hypnotherapy*, the application of hypnotic methods as either a primary means of therapy or as a adjunct to other methods. We are beginning to obtain answers to questions such as: For what types of disorders does hypno-therapy work? For whom does it work? How does it work?

Two different approaches to defining hypnosis in hypnotherapy have been used: hypnosis as an antecedent variable or as a subject variable (Orne 1977; Wadden & Anderton 1982).

Hypnosis as an antecedent variable.

In this operational approach, a therapeutic intervention is said to involve hypnosis (*hypnotherapy*) if: (1) the therapist labels the situation as hypnosis; (2) the patient understands that the situation involves hypnosis; and (3) some sort of hypnotic induction ritual is used. Following induction a variety of different techniques may be used, ranging from imagery suggestions to direct suggestions for behavioral change. It is critical to note, however, that use of a hypnotic induction does not guarantee that a patient will enter a hypnotic state. Therapists taking this approach typically do not assess their patients' hypnotic susceptibility, and in fact they sometimes insist that high hypnotizability is unimportant for therapeutic gain. The benefits of hypnotic induction for a particular prob-lem can be evaluated by comparing groups of patients who do or do not receive hypnotic inductions, where other therapeutic procedures are identi-cal for the two groups. However, in the absence of systematic assessments of hypnotic susceptibility, any apparent benefits of hypnotic induction cannot necessarily be attributed to hypnosis *per se*. Conceivably, just labeling a situa-tion as hypnosis may have indirect benefits—such as relaxation or increased expectancies for therapeutic gain—for all patients, regardless of hypno-tizability level (Wadden & Anderton 1982).

Hypnosis as a subject variable.

In this approach, patients' hypnotic susceptibility levels are systematically measured and therapeutic outcome is evaluated in relation to hypnotic susceptibility. Only when hypnotic meth-ods are used and the benefit is greater for more highly hypnotizable patients can it be concluded that hypnosis *per se* is important for the therapeutic gain. It has been argued that in high hypnotizables, hypnosis can enhance thera-peutic interventions by augmenting process variables, such as relaxation, mental imagery vividness, or suggestibility, though evidence on each of these points is equivocal (Wadden & Anderton 1982). Alternatively, individual dif-ferences related to hypnotizability—such as absorption and imagery vivid-ness—might sometimes affect therapeutic outcome even when hypnosis is not used.

In a review of research on hypnotherapy outcomes, Wadden and An-derton (1982) distinguished between two classes of disorders: voluntary and involuntary. *Voluntary disorders* are maladaptive habits that arise from the patient's voluntary, self-initiated behavior. Among voluntary disorders, hyp-notherapy has been used most often in attempting to modify behaviors of smoking, overeating, and alcoholism. *Involuntary disorders* are undesirable ex-periences or symptoms that occur against the patient's will. Important exam-ples include anxiety, nausea, pain, skin disorders, and asthma. Asthma, some types of pain (such as migraine headache), and some skin disorders (such as warts), are *psychosomatic disorders*—disorders either caused by or exacerbated by psychological factors (DePiano & Salzberg 1979).

From the studies that they reviewed, Wadden and Anderton (1982) concluded that: (1) hypnotherapy is more effective for involuntary disorders than for voluntary disorders; and (2) hypnotic susceptibility is more often related to therapeutic gains for involuntary than for voluntary disorders; but (3) even when hypnotherapy works, it is not necessarily more effective than nonhypnotic methods. Which therapeutic method will be more effective depends on the type of disorder and the patient's characteristics. I will discuss behavioral medicine applications of hypnosis to three involuntary disorders (pain, warts, and asthma), followed by discussion of behavior modification applications of hypnosis to two voluntary disorders (smoking and overeating).

Involuntary Disorders: Pain, Warts, and Asthma

Hypnosis with analgesia suggestions has been used to reduce a wide variety of clinical pains, such as pain of childbirth, major and minor surgery, dentistry, burns, headaches, and chronic pain such as arthritis and cancer (Crasilneck & Hall 1985; Hilgard & Hilgard 1983). Hypnotic analgesia has also been studied extensively in laboratory experiments using pain-stimulation methods designed to hurt subjects without doing any damage (see Chapter 15). There is compelling evidence that hypnotic analgesia suggestions are more effective, the greater the subject's hypnotic susceptibility (Wadden & Anderton 1982; Frankel 1987). For example, migraine headaches are thought to result from an initial vasoconstriction (constricting of blood vessels in the head, resulting in reduced blood flow), followed shortly by an overcompensating vasodilation that produces blurred vision, dizziness, nausea, and pain. In treating migraines, hypnosis has been used to promote relaxation and reduce vasodilation. The degree of therapeutic gain is positively related to individual differences in hypnotizability (Cedercreutz 1978).

J. Hilgard & LeBaron (1982) used hypnosis with children with leukemia who had to undergo repeated bone marrow aspirations, a procedure that is normally quite painful and anxiety provoking. To reduce pain during bone marrow aspirations, the children were given a hypnotic induction followed by suggestions of local analgesia (numbness) and guidance in pleasurable fantasies for distraction from pain. Of some nineteen highly hypnotizable patients, 79 percent showed reduced pain and anxiety according to both self-ratings and ratings by observers (observer ratings based on overt behavior, such as crying). In several cases the hypnotic treatment was so successful that the aspiration procedure was reduced from an unbearable experience to a merely annoying one. Of five low-hypnotizable subjects, none showed benefit from hypnotic methods.

Several types of skin disorders have been treated with the help of hypnosis, including warts, psoriasis (reddish and silvery scales), and others (reviews in DePiano & Salzberg 1979; Wadden & Anderton 1982). Though skin conditions may be caused initially by an irritant (such as poison ivy) or virus (as in warts), psychological factors may influence the severity and duration of symptoms. Some hypnotherapy studies that used no control group have been flawed by failing to consider the spontaneous remission rate. For example, warts tend to disappear spontaneously in about 2.3 years, on the average. However, several cases have been reported where skin conditions that had been resistant to medical treatment for many years showed rapid and dramatic improvement when hypnotherapy was used. Also, several studies have shown better improvement in hypnotherapy groups than in control groups. Hypnotherapy does not work in all cases, and it is more likely to work for highly hypnotizable subjects. In treating warts, the most common method involves suggested images, such as tingling sensations in the affected area, intended to increase the blood supply to that area. In some cases hypnoanalysis revealed that skin symptoms served the function of providing an excuse for the patient to avoid social or sexual encounters that evoked anxiety. Skin symptoms cleared up following psychotherapy to help the patients gain insight into the situation (DePiano & Salzberg 1979).

Asthma symptoms include labored breathing accompanied by wheezing and a sense of constriction in the chest. The etiology (causes) of asthma is not fully understood, but it appears to involve an interaction of allergic, infective, and psychological factors. The symptoms fluctuate in intensity. Asthma attacks may be triggered by anxiety or stress in some patients. In hypnotherapy for asthma, the emphasis is usually on suggestions for tension reduction and increased self-confidence, rather than direct suggestions for symptom removal. Several studies have shown that hypnotherapy can reduce asthma symptoms according to subjects' self-reports, though results with physiological measurements of symptoms have been more equivocal (DePiano & Salzberg 1979). Though most studies did not measure hypnotizability, at least one study showed that treatment gains are positively related to hypnotizability (Collison 1975).

Voluntary Disorders: Smoking and Overeating

Hypnosis has been widely used in attempts to modify maladaptive behaviors, including smoking, alcoholism, and overeating (Wadden & Anderton 1982), and treatment of phobias (McKeegan 1986; Spinhoven 1987). Though some impressive case studies have been reported, controlled research shows equivocal results, at best. Even when hypnotherapy works, it is not necessarily better than other therapy methods, nor is it clear that its benefits depend on hypnosis *per se*.

The health hazards of cigarette smoking are well known. Unfortunately, nicotinism is one of the most difficult addictions to overcome. Smoking is a habit maintained both by positive reinforcement—the pleasures of smoking—and by negative reinforcement—avoidance of the discomforts of nicotine withdrawal. When addicts try to quit smoking, either on their own or with the help of psychotherapy, most of them return to smoking within a few weeks or months. The total abstinence rate after one year is only about 20 percent, regardless of treatment method.

Hypnotherapy for smoking cessation has employed a variety of techniques, including: (1) aversive conditioning that emphasizes the harmful effects of smoking and suggestions that cigarettes taste bad, (2) visualization of the benefits of smoking abstinence, (3) desensitization of aversive feelings during smoking abstinence, (4) increasing confidence in the ability to quit, and (5) mental rehearsal of coping skills for dealing with problem situations where smoking is especially tempting (Sandford 1986). Treatment duration ranges from a single session to several sessions. Success claims range from 4 to 80 percent of patients still abstaining after three to six months. About 30 to 40 percent abstinence is common, which may be contrasted with an estimated 20 percent success rate for placebo treatment (merely being in therapy and expecting benefits). Success rates are highest with treatment packages that combine several methods, though it is impossible to isolate the contribution of hypnosis in treatment packages. Even when hypnotherapy is successful, treatment outcome is usually uncorrelated with hypnotic susceptibility (Perry, Gelfand, & Marcovitch 1979), though there is at least one exception (Barabasz et al. 1986). Perry et al. (1979) found that the best predictor of treatment outcome was the client's motivation to quit smoking, rather than hypnotic susceptibility.

One of the most common uses of hypnosis is for weight reduction. I once received a letter from a man who said "I want you to hypnotize me out of being fat." Unfortunately, it is not that simple. Hypnosis does not have any magical, automatic effects. Changing maladaptive behaviors requires considerable willpower by subjects. Any diet program, with or without hypnosis, requires careful attention to nutritional needs, and benefits are likely to be greatest if physical exercise is part of the program.

Hypnotherapy for weight loss has employed several techniques, including: (1) suggestions for decreased appetite, (2) increased confidence in one's ability to stick to a diet, (3) positive imagery for the social and health benefits of weight loss, (4) covert modeling of effective coping behavior, and (5) suggestions that favorite foods will become nauseating to the individual. Also, (6) hypnoanalysis has been used to uncover deep-seated emotional conflicts that underlie excessive eating behavior. However, most controlled studies have found that hypnotic inductions do not enhance the effectiveness of the treatment program, and treatment effectiveness is not related to hypnotic susceptibility (Wadden & Anderton 1982).

Voluntary maladaptive behaviors are hard to change. While hypnotherapy has been associated with some strikingly successful cases, most controlled studies have found that hypnotherapy is no better than the best nonhypnotic methods. The fact that treatment success is usually uncorrelated with hypnotic susceptibility indicates that hypnosis *per se* (that is, a hypnotic state) is not a factor in treatment effectiveness. Thus, whenever hypnotic induction appears to enhance the treatment, it is probably due to nonspecific factors such as increased expectation of benefit, which may help subjects to gain more self-control.

Concluding Comments on Hypnotherapy

It is impossible to draw firm conclusions about the effectiveness of hypnotherapy. The term "hypnotherapy" has been applied to virtually any clinical application of hypnosis. A wide variety of different techniques has been applied to a wide variety of different disorders. As in other psychotherapy research, the studies have varied widely in quality. Some have used appropriate control groups; some have not. Some have used objective, quantitative assessments of therapeutic gains; some have not. Some have assessed hypnotizability with standardized scales; some have not. Some have controlled for nonhypnotic variables, whereas others have confounded hypnotic procedures with other variables, such as specific suggestions and instructions that were not given to nonhypnotic subjects.

Spanos (1990) reviewed hypnotherapy research for three voluntary disorders—phobic avoidance, smoking, obesity—and three involuntary disorders—asthma, warts, and pain—and drew conclusions from the better-controlled (though often imperfect) studies. His conclusions did not entirely agree with those of Wadden and Anderton (1982).

Spanos agreed with Wadden and Anderton that when hypnotherapy works, it usually does not work any better than nonhypnotic treatments. Furthermore, Spanos suggested that hypnotherapy might work better than nonhypnotic methods for certain individuals, but when that happens it is because of the *mystique* of hypnosis, which may benefit some subjects by increasing their expectations of therapeutic gains. But the opposite result may occur in some individuals, if they fear hypnosis.

Spanos agreed with Wadden and Anderton that with hypnotherapy, hypnotic susceptibility is more likely to be related to therapeutic gains for involuntary disorders (15 of 30 studies) than for voluntary disorders (5 of 17 studies). Even so, only half of the studies with involuntary disorders found a relationship between hypnotizability and therapeutic gain, and the proportion was even lower for studies using standardized measurements of hypnotizability (6 of 18 studies).

Spanos (1990) concluded that hypnotherapy research does not support the traditional interpretation that therapeutic gains occur because of an altered state of consciousness or hypnotic trance, or that hypnotherapy works best for hypnotizable subjects who can enter a hypnotic trance. When hypnotherapy is successful it is because of patients' motivations and expectations and aspects of the therapeutic procedure (such as instructions, suggestions) that also promote positive outcomes for nonhypnotic therapy methods. Spanos hypothesized that in studies where positive relationships between hypnotizability and therapeutic gains are found, the correlation occurs because subjects' perceived success or failure during initial hypnotizability testing engenders expectations of success or failure for hypnotherapy, which in turn affect therapeutic gains. This idea might be tested by manipulating subjects' perceptions of their hypnotic responsiveness and the relationship between hypnotic responsiveness and therapeutic outcome.

Questions about hypnotherapy—which methods work best for particular disorders and why, and the relationship between hypnotizability and therapeutic gains—are far from settled. Additional carefully controlled research is needed (Wadden & Anderton 1982).

IS HYPNOSIS DANGEROUS?

When I invite introductory psychology students to participate in my hypnosis research, most of them are happy to volunteer. Most students are eager to try such an interesting new experience. But some choose not to volunteer. Some people are afraid to be hypnotized. The fear of hypnosis seems to be based largely on fictional treatments of hypnosis, where the ability of hypnotists to control people is exaggerated and evil hypnotists coerce unwilling victims to do evil or immoral things. Some people fear that being hypnotized will make them weak-willed or that they might enter a trance and not be able to come out of it. Is hypnosis really dangerous?

First, it can be said without reservation that hypnosis is safe provided that it is done by a properly trained professional who uses it in an ethical manner. Second, the issue of whether an unethical hypnotist could coerce an unwilling subject into carrying out some immoral, harmful, or illegal act is still controversial.

Let us consider several of the alleged dangers of hypnosis. I will begin with a brief overview of the worries that people might have about hypnosis when it is used in a competent and ethical manner. Then I will discuss the question of loss of control and the unethical use of hypnosis.

(1) Will hypnosis make me weak-willed, so that I will be more easily controlled by other people after the hypnosis session? No. There is no evidence that this happens.

(2) What if the hypnotist should abandon me, or die, while I am hypnotized? Will I stay hypnotized forever? No. The evidence indicates that you will spontaneously come out of hypnosis after about twenty minutes or so (Evans & Orne 1971). You might fall asleep, and when you awaken you will no longer be hypnotized.

(3) Can hypnosis precipitate a psychotic breakdown? There is no convincing evidence that this is the case. Hilgard (1965) reported that there have been a small number of cases where hypnotherapy patients got worse instead of better, but in all of those cases the patients had severe mental problems and got worse despite the use of hypnosis, rather than because of it.

(4) Can hypnosis elicit unanticipated emotional reactions? Yes, this occasionally happens. In particular, during age regression subjects may cry if they are regressed back to an unhappy time of their life. (In my experience, this has happened only once among about 200 subjects tested on SHSS:C.) Crying reactions may be embarrassing to the subject, but they are not a serious problem. Standard hypnotic susceptibility testing procedures are designed to minimize the likelihood of unpleasant emotional reactions. Crying sometimes occurs during some types of hypnotherapy, but crying also occurs in psychotherapy without hypnosis. Experienced psychotherapists know how to deal with patients' emotional reactions. Such emotional reactions are more likely to create an awkward situation when hypnosis is done by amateurs.

(5) Will there be any unpleasant *sequelae* (aftereffects) of hypnosis? A large majority of subjects report that they feel relaxed or rested after hypnosis. However, hypnosis subjects occasionally report some sort of unpleasant feeling following hypnosis, such as feeling drowsy, confused, dizzy or lightheaded, a mild headache, upset stomach, stiff neck, anxiety, or unhappiness (J. Hilgard 1974b). Such symptoms usually last less than an hour, and they do not pose any risk to subjects (Crawford, Hilgard, & Macdonald 1982). The important question is whether hypnosis *per se* is really to blame for such symptoms. Coe and Ryken (1979) put the problem in perspective by comparing the frequency of unpleasant experiences following hypnosis with their

frequencies following other experiences among college students, including attending a college class, taking an exam, participating in a psychology experiment on verbal learning, or college life in general. The results indicated that unpleasant aftereffects were no more common for hypnosis than for the other activities. On the other hand, the subjects rated hypnosis as significantly more pleasant than the other activities.

The Question of Coercion Through Hypnosis

Probably the major source of anxiety over hypnosis is people's fear that they will lose their normal self control and be controlled by the hypnotist. Such fears are based largely on fictional treatments and stage demonstrations of hypnosis. For example, a stage hypnotist may suggest to subjects that they are famous rock or opera singers, and subsequently they will sing in an uninhibited manner, even though they ordinarily would be too timid to sing in front of an audience. It is important to realize that in such cases the subjects have not been coerced into doing anything dangerous or immoral. Hypnosis may reduce people's inhibitions against doing things that they would ordinarily be too timid to do. Even unhypnotizable people may go along with suggestions in a hypnotic setting, since the hypnotic setting provides an excuse for doing unusual things.

But what about the possibility that a hypnotist might coerce a subject into doing something harmful or immoral? Most clinical and research hypnotists with whom I have talked believe that subjects can resist suggestions if they want to do so. Some hypnotists speak of a division of consciousness during hypnosis, where one part, the "censor," is aware of what is going on and can arouse the subject if anything objectionable is suggested.

The point that hypnotized subjects can resist suggestions to do something against their moral standards is illustrated by two incidents described by Hilgard (1971):

> An early demonstration by Pierre Janet . . . was often cited and occasionally repeated. A young woman was being used to demonstrate hypnosis, and under hypnosis she was asked to take off her clothes before an audience of medical students. According to the anecdote, she became spontaneously aroused from hypnosis. The late Professor Dorcus, of the University of California at Los Angeles, told me about his confident undertaking to repeat the demonstration, but his young woman subject began unbuttoning so rapidly that he had to call a halt. It turned out that she was accustomed to "stripping" in a night club, so this was not contradictory evidence after all! It does make the point, however, that something that happens within hypnosis need not happen *because* of hypnosis, and there will always be areas of ambiguity (p. 576).

There have been several reports of people who claimed to have been coerced by a hypnotist to perform objectionable acts. In these cases the subjects voluntarily submitted to hypnosis, and the hypnotist made unethical suggestions after the induction. Most of the cases involved sexual seduction, though there have been a few cases where hypnotists suggested that subjects commit crimes or violent acts.

Perry (1979) reviewed the evidence and testimony of a court case in

Australia, where a lay hypnotist (that is, one without professional credentials) was accused of seducing two female clients under hypnosis. The clients had come to the hypnotist for help in losing weight. The defense called experts who claimed that subjects can resist objectionable suggestions, while the prosecution called experts who claimed that some people may be unable to resist suggestions.

Watkins (1972) made two relevant points. First, he argued that hypnosis is a unique interpersonal relationship, and a person's behavior may be strongly influenced by interpersonal relationships (such as psychotherapy) even without hypnosis. If hypnotic procedures are powerful enough to do patients good, then it is reasonable to suppose they could be misused to do patients harm. Second, he pointed out that hypnosis might be used to distort the perception of reality, and thus trick subjects into committing antisocial acts. For example, Watkins (1947) described the case of an American soldier during World War II who was hypnotized and told that when he opened his eyes he would see "a dirty Jap soldier" who was going to kill him. When he opened his eyes the soldier violently attacked the other man, who in reality was an American officer.

Yet, in the case reviewed by Perry (1979), neither distorted perceptions nor intense interpersonal relationships seem to have been involved. The proper interpretation of the facts is far from certain. It could be argued that in this and similar cases there was "motivated helplessness" on the part of the subjects during the original act, but they later felt guilty about their actions and blamed the hypnotist. However, the most interesting interpretation of such cases concerns subjects' beliefs rather than their underlying motives. According to Perry:

> It is possible that a percentage of people believe that all initiative and self-determination in hypnosis is surrendered to the hypnotist. In hypnosis it may be possible to coerce such people, in the sense that the belief of inability to resist is sufficient to create a *self-fulfilling prophecy* (1979, p. 213, italics added).

In order to test the self-fulfilling prophecy hypothesis, it would be desirable to have some controlled research on the topic. Yet, doing controlled research on the commission of antisocial acts under hypnosis is surprisingly complicated. In one such attempt, Orne and Evans (1965) showed hypnotized subjects a beaker of nitric acid, and demonstrated that is was strong enough to dissolve a penny. When the hypnotist told the subjects to throw the acid into a research assistant's face, five out of six of them did so! When questioned later they said that they trusted the hypnotist/experimenter not to do anything unethical. In fact, the hypnotist had surreptitiously substituted a beaker of an identical-looking but harmless liquid for the acid just before he had made the suggestion.

Coe (1977) discussed problems in doing research on the coercion of antisocial behavior in hypnosis. A satisfactory experiment would have to have an elaborate procedure to deceive subjects into believing that the suggested behavior could really do harm to themselves or to another person or their property. To be convincing, it would have to be carried out in a naturalistic setting, rather than a psychology laboratory. Also, to prove that hypnosis *per se* was responsible for the antisocial acts, it would be necessary to compare a hypnosis group with a control group given the same suggestions without hypnosis. One risk is that subjects would feel guilty if they believed that they had really committed an antisocial act. Though such an experiment would be extremely valuable for understanding the limits of hypnotic coercion, the ethical problems of such research are such that it is unlikely that it would be approved by university committees responsible for evaluating the potential risks of research with human subjects.

Among hypnotists, the belief that hypnosis can be used to coerce subjects to perform antisocial acts is held mainly by clinicians who view hypnosis as an altered state in which subjects respond to suggestions automatically. In the social-psychological view, antisocial acts can be coerced during hypnosis, but antisocial acts can also be coerced in a wide variety of social situations that do not involve hypnosis. Interpersonal relationships that can influence antisocial acts outside of hypnosis can also do so during hypnosis, but no special hypnotic state is responsible during hypnosis (Spanos 1989, personal communication). Both social-psychological hypnosis theorists and most altered-state theorists agree that ordinarily, objectionable suggestions can be resisted. As a practical matter, it is important that you know and believe that you can resist objectionable hypnotic suggestions, even if you are deeply hypnotized. This belief should serve as an "inoculation" against the unethical or improper use of hypnosis, and help you to enter hypnosis in a relaxed and confident manner. Of course, most clinicians use hypnosis in an ethical manner, so there is little need to worry about objectionable suggestions. (See Laurence and Perry [1988] for more information about experimental, clinical, and field studies on coercion with hypnosis.)

SUMMARY

Hypnosis was defined as a psychological state or condition, induced by a ritualistic procedure, in which subjects experience changes in perception, thinking, memory, and behavior in response to suggestions by the hypnotist. A suggestion is a communication intended to induce some experience or behavior that is different from what the subject would normally perceive or do, without actually commanding it. Two major theoretical approaches to hypnosis may be distinguished: (1) The special-process view, which sees hypnosis as an altered state of consciousness, or a dissociative state, in which mental processes function differently than normal; (2) The social-psychological view, which says that hypnosis involves normal thinking and behavior processes operating in an unusual social situation.

People vary widely in *hypnotic susceptibility*, the ability to respond to hypnotic suggestions. Hypnotic susceptibility can be measured by several standardized scales, such as the Stanford scales, which involve a standard induction followed by several standardized suggestions. There are three main types of suggestions: (1) ideomotor suggestions, where the hypnotist asks subjects to imagine some situation which, if it were true, would cause them to make a particular movement; (2) response-inhibition (challenge) suggestions, where the hypnotist suggests that subjects cannot move some part of their body, then challenges them to try to move that part; and (3) cognitive suggestions, which involve changes in perception, thinking, and memory, such as positive hallucinations, negative hallucinations, age regression, hypnotic dreams, and suggested posthypnotic amnesia. According to traditional views, true hypnotic responses are experienced as involuntary, though the social psychological view says that the experience of involuntariness is a delusion promoted by prior expectations.

Hypnotic susceptibility scores are not reliably correlated with standard measures of personality traits, such as introversion-extraversion or stability-neuroticism. However, hypnotizability correlates fairly consistently though modestly with measures of imagery vividness and absorption (a disposition for having episodes of total attention, particularly in regard to aesthetic and imaginary experiences).

Pointing to evidence for the long-term stability of hypnotic susceptibility, trait theory argues that hypnotic responsiveness is a stable personality trait. Skill theory says that hypnotic responsiveness is a learnable skill. Recent research suggests that hypnotic responsiveness can be increased by special training on interpreting hypnotic suggestions and using appropriate cognitive strategies of attention and imagination.

In clinical applications, hypnotherapy has been more successful with involuntary disorders—pain and psychosomatic symptoms (skin disorders, migraine headaches, and asthma)—than with voluntary disorders—maladaptive habits (smoking, overeating, alcoholism) and phobic avoidance. Treatment outcome is correlated with hypnotic susceptibility more often for involuntary disorders than for voluntary disorders. But in general, when hypnotherapy is effective it is no more effective than nonhypnotic therapy methods.

Fears that hypnosis is dangerous stem largely from the fictional treatment of hypnosis. Hypnosis is safe provided that it is done by a properly trained professional who behaves in an ethical manner. The question whether an unethical hypnotist might coerce subjects into doing something illegal, immoral, or harmful is still controversial. It appears that subjects can resist objectionable suggestions if they believe that they can do so.

ENDNOTE

[1]For readers who are unfamiliar with correlation coefficients: see Chapter 7, endnote 1.

chapter 15 ··

Hypnosis II:
Theories and Research on Hypnotic Analgesia and Posthypnotic Amnesia

In this chapter I will go into more detail on the two most influential contemporary hypnosis theories—Hilgard's neodissociation theory and Spanos's social-psychological theory—and I will discuss key research on the two topics that have played the greatest role in theoretical debates: hypnotic analgesia (pain reduction) and posthypnotic amnesia. The theories make more sense if you know about some of the research that supports them, and the research makes more sense if you know about the theory that motivated it and the rationale behind the research design. Therefore, I will interweave the topics of hypnosis theory, research design, and research on specific hypnosis topics, so that you can better appreciate their interrelationships.

HYPNOSIS THEORIES: OVERVIEW

Numerous characterizations and explanations of hypnosis have been offered over the last 200 years, including the ideas of animal magnetism (Mesmer, 1770s), artificial somnambulism (Puysegur, 1780s), lucid sleep (Faria, 1810s), nervous sleep (Braid, 1840s), nervous-system pathology (Charcot, 1880s), heightened suggestibility and imagination (Bernheim, 1880s), and dissociation (Janet, 1890s) or trance state (James, 1890). A major theme of the earlier period of hypnosis theory was the shift from physical explanations (such as magnetism and brain pathology) to psychological explanations emphasizing suggestibility and imagination (Sheehan & Perry 1976). In the modern era of controlled research major ideas have included suggestibility (Hull 1933); altered state of consciousness (Orne 1972; Shor 1962); social role taking (Sarbin and Coe 1972); behavior change influenced by motivation, attitudes, and beliefs (Barber 1969); dissociation (Hilgard 1977); and strategic social enactment aided by cognitive strategies (Spanos 1986a). The importance of profound imaginative involvement is a potential unifying theme that runs through several contemporary approaches to hypnosis (Spanos & Barber 1974).

It is beyond the scope of this book to discuss the various historical theories of hypnosis in any detail (see Ellenberger 1970; Sheehan & Perry 1977). Instead I will briefly discuss the general issue of whether hypnosis is an altered state of consciousness, then concentrate on the two most influential contemporary approaches to hypnosis—the social-psychological viewpoint (as exemplified by Spanos 1982, 1986a) and the special-process viewpoint (as exemplified by Hilgard's neodissociation theory 1977).

Is Hypnosis an Altered State of Consciousness?

During the 1960s and 1970s there was a controversy among hypnosis researchers as to whether hypnosis is really an altered state of consciousness (ASC). Of course the answer depends partly on how ASC is defined and what criterion is used to identify hypnosis as an ASC. In Chapter 9 I defined ASC in terms of a dramatically altered pattern of subjective experience. There can be little doubt that some subjects experience hypnosis as an ASC in that sense. But in the earlier controversy it was assumed by state theorists such as Ernest Hilgard, Martin Orne, and Ronald Shor that hypnotic trance involves an altered state of psychological functioning, such that there are changes in processes of perception, memory, and thinking that are unique to hypnosis (Hilgard 1969).

Nonstate theorists such as T. X. Barber (1969) argued that the state viewpoint is circular. The unusual experiences and behaviors of hypnosis were used as *evidence* for an altered state, and then they were *explained* as being caused by a altered state. A circular argument does not lead to scientific progress. Furthermore, there was no evidence for a changed pattern of neurophysiological responses (such as brain waves) that could provide independent evidence for an altered brain state that presumably underlies the hypnotic state. Barber (1969) argued for a behavioral approach to hypnosis, where hypnotic behaviors—including verbal reports—were explained in terms of various situational and subject variables (motives, attitudes, and beliefs) without reference to altered states or mental processes.

In more recent years there has been some move toward rapprochement between state and nonstate views of hypnosis (Hilgard 1973; Kihlstrom 1985a; Spanos & Barber 1974). Nonstate theorists have acknowledged that important alterations in subjective experience—such as changes in imaginative experience—can occur during hypnosis (Barber, Spanos, & Chaves 1974). State theorists have acknowledged that the state concept does not explain anything, and they acknowledge the importance of the social-psychological variables (such as attitudes and expectancies) that have been stressed by nonstate theorists. The term "hypnotic state," if it is used at all nowadays, refers loosely to the altered subjective experiences that occur during hypnotic procedures (Hilgard 1969, 1973).

Though the old state-versus-nonstate controversy has largely been abandoned as unproductive, a complete rapprochement between the opposing camps is not in sight (Kihlstrom 1985a). Researchers friendly to the old state viewpoint (such as Hilgard, Orne, Kihlstrom) continue to argue that hypnotic procedures produce special effects—different from the normal waking state—in some individuals. From this viewpoint, the unusual phenomena of hypnosis (such as posthypnotic amnesia) result from altered cognitive processes in hypnosis—thus, Spanos (1986a) called this the "special process viewpoint." However, modern special-process theorists do not claim that the altered cognitive processes that occur in hypnosis are necessarily unique to hypnosis. They may also occur in nonhypnotic contexts, particularly among highly hypnotizable people. On the other hand, researchers who take the nonstate, social-psychological approach (such as Spanos, Coe, Lynn, Wagstaff) argue that the behaviors and experiences characteristic of hypnosis do not represent any sort of changed cognitive processes. Rather, they reflect the operation of normal cognitive processes in a special social situation defined as hypnosis.

Are Hypnotic Responses Real?

The hallmark of the hypnotic phenomenon is not the willingness of the subject to do what he is requested to . . . nor that the subject's behavior appears trancelike to the observer. Rather it is the nature and quality of the concomitant subjective events (Orne 1972, p. 421).

Much of the controversy in hypnosis theory boils down to the question of whether hypnotic responses are real. But what does the question mean? From the altered-state or special-process viewpoint, the essence of hypnosis is the alteration of conscious experience in response to suggestions, including altered perceptions, thinking, memory, and feelings of control of one's actions. Hypnotist/experimenters cannot directly observe subjects' conscious experiences. They can know only subjects' overt behaviors, including their verbal reports on subjective experiences. The question of the reality of hypnotic responses is the question of whether subjects' behaviors and verbal reports that seem to indicate altered conscious experiences do, in fact, represent authentic altered conscious experiences.

The difficulty of discovering whether hypnotic responses are real is that overt behaviors that are supposed to indicate subjective responses might be misleading. If they are motivated to do so, subjects can deliberately fake their overt responses to suggestions. For example, in 1850 when he was fifteen years old, Mark Twain volunteered to be the subject for a stage demonstration of mesmerism (hypnosis). Years later he wrote about how he had deliberately faked his way through a demonstration of what we now call hypnotic analgesia:

The professor made passes over [me] and said "his whole body is without sensation now—come forward and test him, ladies and gentlemen" . . . Those were dear good people but they must have carried simplicity and credulity to the limit. They would stick a pin in my arm and bear on it until they drove it a third of its length in, and then be lost in wonder that by a mere exercise of will power the professor could turn my arm to iron and make it insensible to pain. Whereas it was not insensible at all; I was suffering agonies of pain ... I didn't wince; I only suffered and shed tears on the inside. The miseries that a conceited boy will endure to keep up his "reputation"! (adapted from DeVoto 1940, pp. 118–29; reprinted in Sarbin & Coe 1972, pp. 11–15).

In general, faking hypnotic responses involves falsely representing one's subjective experiences in response to suggestions. Overt responses (such as ideomotor actions) might be made deliberately rather than with a feeling of involuntariness, felt pain might be denied, or recalled words might go unreported in a test of amnesia. In principle, any overt hypnotic response—either muscle movement or verbal report—*could* be faked. It is usually obvious from the wording of the hypnotic suggestion what sort of response the hypnotist expects. Hypnosis does not give people any extraordinary abilities, such as superior strength, that they would not have if they were sufficiently motivated without hypnosis (see Chapter 7 in Sheehan and Perry 1976).

The possibility that hypnotic responses are not what they appear to be on the surface is a major theme of the social-psychological approach to hypnosis. Rather than being genuine, spontaneous, involuntary responses to suggestions, hypnotic responses are thought to be either deliberately faked or, more often, produced by voluntary cognitive strategies that allow subjects to delude themselves, and the hypnotist, into thinking that the responses are spontaneous and automatic.

State or special-process theorists have several arguments against claims that hypnotic responses are faked. (1) Some hypnotic responses are unlikely to be faked, in particular, hypnotic analgesia during major surgery that involves making large incisions in the skin (such as Caesarean sections). Though Mark Twain could fake insensitivity to pinpricks, it is unlikely that surgical patients could fake insensitivity to pain caused by a surgeon's incision—nor is there any reason why they would want to fake it under such circumstances (Bowers 1976). (2) Following hypnosis, some subjects have reported dramatic alterations of subjective experience (for example, in response to age regression suggestions). When such reports are made outside of the original test situation, to people other than the hypnotist or experimenter, it seems plausible that they are authentic, honest reports of altered subjective experience during hypnosis. (3) Though many hypnotic responses can be faked, it is beyond belief that over the last 200 years tens of thousands of medical and psychotherapy patients and research subjects have been motivated to fake hypnosis and fool their doctors, therapists, and experimenters.

Nonetheless, a small minority of subjects admit to faking some of their responses—that is, making voluntary responses—to suggestions during hypnotic susceptibility testing (Farthing, Brown, & Venturino 1983a). The fact that some subjects might fake their responses has made it necessary for researchers to develop special methodologies to discover whether hypnotic responses are genuine, that is, whether they represent authentic altered subjective experiences in response to hypnotic procedures *per se*, rather than being behaviors produced by other, nonhypnotic factors.

HYPNOTIC ANALGESIA AND HYPNOSIS RESEARCH METHODOLOGIES

In this section we will consider two experimental designs that have been widely used in hypnosis research: the high-low design and the real-simulator design. Both are intended to help researchers distinguish "true" hypnotic responses—that is, overt responses that depend upon authentic subjective experiences occurring in response to hypnotic suggestions—from responses that can be attributed to nonhypnotic psychological processes. The examples will be drawn from research on *hypnotic analgesia*: the use of hypnotic suggestions to control pain. Besides describing the experimental designs and their rationale, this section will describe procedures for studying pain in the laboratory, and it will provide essential background for understanding Hilgard's research on the "hidden observer" effect, to be discussed in the following section. (See Sheehan & Perry 1976, for more details on hypnosis research methodologies.)

The High-Low Method

The high-low experimental design involves comparing two groups of subjects: high hypnotizables and low hypnotizables. This method has been used extensively by Hilgard and his followers. For them the issue is not whether there is a special hypnotic state of consciousness, but rather, assuming that there is a hypnotic state, what are its subjective and behavioral characteristics. The logic of the high-low method is as follows: if you want to find out about authentic hypnotic responses, compare subjects who have been treated identically in all respects except that some are in the hypnotic state and some are not. This can be accomplished by giving hypnotic inductions to both high and low hypnotizable subjects. Presumably, subjects who have previously been classified as highly hypnotizable ("highs") on a standard hypnosis scale (such as SHSS:C) will reliably enter a hypnotic state following the induction, whereas those low in measured hypnotic susceptibility ("lows") will not. Sometimes "mediums" are also included, in order to compare subjects of average hypnotizability with those who are highly hypnotizable.

Hypnotic analgesia in highs and lows.   Hilgard (1967, 1969) studied pain responses in the *cold pressor test*, where the subject's hand and forearm are immersed in circulating ice water (about 1°C). During the immersion the experimenter periodically says "Report!" and the subjects respond with a number that rates their pain on a scale that can range from zero to ten or more, where "ten" is defined as severe pain. The advantage of the cold pressor test for laboratory research is that it can produce intense pain in a short

period of time without doing any actual damage to the subjects' tissues. (People with blood circulation problems or hypertension are not used as subjects in this sort of research.)

In Hilgard's experiment high- and low-hypnotizable subjects (preselected on SHSS:C) were tested under each of three conditions: (1) *waking control condition* (baseline measure), with no hypnotic induction and no analgesia suggestion; (2) *hypnosis alone*, where prior to hand immersion they heard a hypnotic induction but no analgesia suggestion (the purpose of this condition was to determine whether relaxation during hypnosis could, by itself, reduce pain); and (3) *hypnotic analgesia*, where subjects heard a hypnotic induction followed by an analgesia suggestion. The analgesia suggestion involved telling the subject that his or her hand and arm were numb and insensitive, as if they were made of rubber. Each of the three test immersions lasted for forty seconds, with pain reports being made every five seconds. For all subjects the waking condition was given on the first day, and the hypnosis-alone and hypnotic-analgesia conditions were counterbalanced between the second and third days. (That is, half of the subjects had hypnosis-alone on the second day with hypnotic analgesia on the third day, and half had the reverse sequence.)

Figure 15.1 shows the mean pain ratings under the three test conditions. Two results are important here: (1) Pain in the hypnosis-alone condition was essentially identical to pain in the waking condition. Thus, relaxation during hypnosis is not sufficient to reduce pain by itself. (2) In the group of highly hypnotizable subjects, hypnotic analgesia reduced pain ratings dramatically, compared to both the waking and hypnosis-alone conditions. But hypnotic analgesia had a negligible effect on the low-hypnotizable subjects' pain ratings. These results show that hypnotic analgesia suggestions can reduce pain only among highly hypnotizable subjects—presumably because only "highs" are in a hypnotic state following the hypnotic induction.

Another laboratory procedure for producing pain is the *muscle ischemia test*, in which blood circulation to one arm is cut off by a tourniquet around the upper arm and the subject rhythmically squeezes a rubber bulb to remove oxygen from the blood remaining in the arm. Pain builds more slowly with the ischemia procedure than with the cold pressor procedure, but after a few minutes ischemic pain reaches very high levels. One advantage of ischemia pain is that it resembles clinical pain more than cold pressor pain does, and ischemic pain is sensitive to morphine (Hilgard & Hilgard 1983). Knox, Morgan, and Hilgard (1974) had subjects rate *sensory pain* and *suffering* separately during an ischemia test, and found that both were reduced by hypnotic analgesia suggestions among highly hypnotizable subjects.

The ischemia procedure has also been used to study factors that affect the *pain threshold* (the time until pain is felt) and *pain tolerance* (the time until the subject can no longer endure it and wants to quit). McGlashan, Evans, and Orne (1969) found that hypnotic analgesia suggestions increased both the pain threshold and pain tolerance more in highs than in lows. Also, among highs (but not lows) the analgesia suggestion was more effective than a placebo drug in reducing pain, which suggests that the response to the analgesia suggestion was not merely a placebo effect.

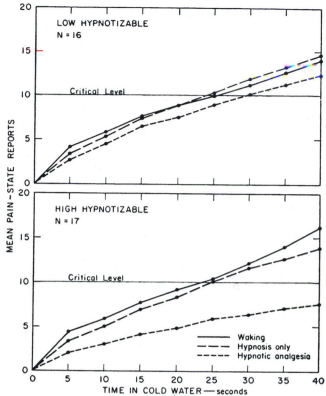

FIGURE 15.1. Pain reports in the cold pressor test as a function of time with hand immersed in ice water (0–1°C). All subjects were tested in the baseline (no hypnosis) condition, with hypnosis only (no suggestion), and with hypnotic analgesia (hypnotic induction followed by analgesia suggestion). [From Hilgard, E. R. (1969). Pain as a puzzle for psychology and physiology. *American Psychologist, 24,* 103–13. Copyright 1969 by the American Psychological Association. Reprinted by permission.]

The Real-Simulator Method

Martin Orne (1959) pointed out that in many types of psychological research there is a danger that misleading results will be obtained because subjects are motivated to try to be helpful and give the experimenter the results that they believe the experimenter expects. The *demand characteristics* of experiments are the situational cues that communicate to subjects—either intentionally or unintentionally—the experimenter's hypothesis or expected results. Demand characteristics may be a particularly serious problem in hypnosis research, insofar as hypnosis may increase subjects' motivation to conform to the perceived wishes of the experimenter. Orne discussed the problem of separating *artifact* from *essence* in hypnosis research. The essence of hypnosis is altered subjective experiences and responses that follow naturally (automatically) from hypnotic inductions and suggestions. Major artifacts include demand characteristics and subjects' motives to respond like good hypnotic subjects.

In order to control for demand characteristics and motivation, Orne (1959, 1972) developed the *real-simulator design*. In this experimental design the hypnotic behavior of real hypnotic subjects is compared with the behavior of unhypnotized subjects who have been instructed to simulate hypnosis, that is, to act as if they are really hypnotized. The rationale is that if simulators behave exactly like "reals" during hypnosis, then the responses of the reals *might* be due to artifacts of demand characteristics, rather than representing the essence of hypnosis. On the other hand, if reals and simulators behave differently, then the difference presumably reveals something of the essence of hypnosis, rather than artifacts of demand characteristics or motivation.

To carry it out properly, the real-simulator method requires at least two experimenters, and several steps must be carefully followed: (1) The first experimenter pretests the volunteers to select groups of high- and low-hypnotizable subjects. Subsequently the highs are the "real" hypnosis subjects, while lows are used as simulators so that the simulators will not accidentally become hypnotized during the main experiment. (2) Just before the main experiment, the first experimenter instructs the simulators on several points: (a) They are to resist becoming hypnotized, but (b) they are to pretend that they are hypnotized, and do or say whatever they believe a truly hypnotized person would do or say in that situation, using their prior knowledge of hypnosis and the hypnotist's cues to figure out how a truly hypnotized person would respond. Also, (c) if the hypnotist detects the fact they are faking, then he or she will immediately stop the experiment. (In fact, hypnotists can rarely distinguish between reals and simulators under ordinary hypnosis test conditions.) Reals are simply told that they will be hypnotized again and that they should respond naturally. (3) The subjects are then turned over to the second experimenter, who does not know which subjects are reals and which are simulators. The second experimenter treats all subjects the same way, giving a standard hypnotic induction followed by whatever special suggestions are appropriate to the problem being studied in that particular experiment (such as hypnotic analgesia, amnesia, hallucination, or posthypnotic suggestions). (4) The main experiment should be followed by a *postexperimental inquiry*, where the subjects return to the *first* experimenter, who tells them that the experiment is over and then asks them to give an honest, accurate description of their subjective experiences during the main experiment. The postexperimental inquiry is important because even if the reals and simulators make identical overt responses to suggestions, their subsequent verbal reports on their subjective responses to the suggestions could reveal a genuine difference between real hypnosis and simulated hypnosis. After all, subjective responses are the essence of hypnosis, according to Orne.

Hypnotic analgesia and the real-simulator design.   Hilgard et al. (1978b) studied pain reduction with hypnotic analgesia suggestions, using

the procedure for the real-simulator design, as described above. Each group was first given a baseline (waking) cold pressor pain test, followed by hypnotic induction, an analgesia suggestion, and a second pain test.

Two aspects of the results are of interest: (1) Comparing reports in hypnotic analgesia to baseline reports, average pain ratings were reduced 90 percent among simulators, compared to a 77 percent reduction by reals. Thus, situational cues were sufficient to tell the simulators that reduced pain ratings were expected; in fact, some of them overfaked. But can we necessarily conclude that the reduced pain reports of the *real* hypnotic subjects were merely faked in response to the demand characteristics of the experiment? No, because (2) in the postexperimental inquiry the reals confirmed that their previous pain reports were accurate (77 percent reduction from baseline), whereas the simulators reported that they had really felt much more pain than they had previously reported (only 18 percent reduction).

Hilgard et al. interpreted the postexperimental inquiry reports as indicating that pain was truly reduced during hypnotic analgesia in the real hypnotic subjects, but not in the simulators. A skeptical interpretation is that only the simulators had been told to fake reduced pain, so they could later admit faking without losing face; reals might have faked pain reduction, but since they had not been instructed to fake, they continued to fake during the postexperimental inquiry in order to avoid losing face (Spanos 1989, personal communication).

Physiological responses as pain indicators. At this point you might ask, "Why go to all of the trouble of the real-simulator method to find out if hypnotic analgesia works? Why not use a physiological measure (such as heart rate or blood pressure) to find out what subjects are *really* feeling during the pain tests?" If a valid physiological measure of pain was available, then it would be unnecessary to trust subjects' verbal pain reports during hypnosis or in a postexperimental inquiry. But the conclusion from several experiments on this issue is that there is, in fact, no known physiological response that is a valid and reliable measure of subjective pain. Some measures, such as heart rate and blood pressure, tend to increase along with verbal pain reports under normal waking test conditions. But physiological measures do not necessarily decrease when drugs or hypnotic suggestions reduce subjective pain reports. Whether physiological measures and pain reports correlate reliably depends on the particular combination of pain-producing method and physiological measure used (Bowers 1976). After doing several experiments on this problem, Hilgard (1969) concluded that verbal pain ratings (or their equivalent) are, in fact, the most reliable and valid measure of felt pain.

With some of the basics of hypnosis research methods behind us, we are now ready to consider contemporary hypnosis theories in more detail.

HILGARD'S NEODISSOCIATION THEORY

As explained in Chapter 1, Ernest Hilgard (1977) drew parallels between hypnosis and certain other psychological conditions. The other conditions—including multiple personality, fugue, and functional amnesia, along with functional paralysis, blindness, and anesthesia (numbness)—were classified as *hysterical syndromes* by the nineteenth-century French psychologist Pierre Janet (1907). The functional disorders mimic neurological disorders, though there is nothing neurologically wrong with the patients. Janet introduced the concepts of *dissociation* and *subconscious* to help account for hysterical syndromes. He hypothesized that in hysterical cases, ideas, memories, or mental functions that are normally associated or connected with each other have become disconnected or dissociated. Thus, the multiple-personality patient has two sets of memories, and the main personality cannot retrieve the alternate personality's memories; and the "glove anesthesia" patient cannot consciously feel anything with her right hand, though there is nothing neurologically wrong with it. The *subconscious* refers to the set of memories and psychological functions that operate outside of consciousness in these syndromes, though under some conditions subconscious knowledge can become conscious.

Janet's ideas did not attain the prominence that they might have because they were overshadowed by Freud's psychoanalytic theory, which appeared at about the same time. Freud's theory was richer, it seemed to have more relevance to ordinary people, and his concept of the repressed unconscious received more recognition than Janet's concept of the dissociated subconscious. Also, Janet's theory was interpreted as predicting that subconscious processes can carry out mental operations (such as mental arithmetic) without interfering with conscious processes. When this prediction was not supported by research, Janet's theory was discredited (Hilgard 1977). Freud's theory, on the other hand, was not precise enough to make any research predictions, so it could not be discredited by research!

Hilgard (1977) noted the similarities between hypnosis—particularly phenomena such as hypnotic amnesia and analgesia—and the hysterical syndromes, and he argued that the concept of dissociation is useful in accounting for hypnotic phenomena. It is noteworthy that hysterical patients typically are highly hypnotizable, and that hypnotic procedures are often effective in treating them (Frankel 1976). Hilgard called his theory *neodissociation theory* to emphasize the point that he was abandoning the claim that subconscious processes would not interfere with conscious processes and to acknowledge that his theory was designed under the influence of modern cognitive psychology theories, rather than the older association theories of learning.

Hilgard argued that the human mind can be characterized as a set of semi-independent specialized cognitive structures or subsystems that operate under the influence of a central regulating system. The central regulating system, which can be identified with consciousness, has two aspects: (1) the *executive function*, which sets short-term and long-term goals, determines their relative priorities, and plans and initiates actions suitable for reaching those goals; and (2) the *monitoring function*, characterized by selective attention, which scans the environment for information pertinent to the goals, as well as being vigilant for unexpected signals from the environment or body that are pertinent to the individual's safety. The executive system can activate various specialized subsystems that control psychological activities such as memory, belief systems, habits, skills, and social roles suitable for particular occasions. The subsystems can regulate their own inputs and outputs (responses) to a large degree. In the case of well-learned habits or skills the subsystems may, once activated, operate in a largely automatic manner with little or no conscious awareness of their activities by the executive system.

Hilgard (1977) suggested that hypnosis involves temporary dissociations or disconnections between various parts of the mind system that are normally well integrated. Depending upon the type of suggestions, there may be dissociations between the executive and the monitoring functions, or specialized subsystems may act independently of the executive function, or the executive or monitoring functions themselves may be divided into two parts that can operate independently of each other. For example, hypnotic analgesia may occur because of a dissociation between pain perception systems and the conscious monitor, whereas hypnotic amnesia is a dissociation between the memory system and the executive system. Hypnotic hallucinations may be due to a dissociation between conscious image-generating mechanisms and reality-oriented judgment processes.

In neodissociation theory the emphasis is on modification of controls over thought and action, rather than on alterations of the quality of conscious experience. Hilgard (1979) suggested that an altered state in the sense of altered quality of conscious experience may be characteristic only of very deeply hypnotized subjects. At the more moderate depths of hypnosis with which researchers and clinicians normally deal, alterations of control may occur without there necessarily being any profound alteration of subjective experience.

The Hidden Observer

The discovery. A serendipitous discovery made during a class demonstration of hypnosis influenced Hilgard's development of the neodissociation theory (Hilgard 1977). While hypnotic deafness was being demonstrated with a highly hypnotizable subject, a student asked whether there might be some part of the subject's mind that could hear. Hilgard tested the idea by suggesting to the subject that there might be some part of him that was aware of what was going on, and if there was, then he (Hilgard) would be able to talk to it when he put his hand on the subject's arm. Subsequently, with Hilgard's hand on his arm, the subject was able to identify sounds and report what people said, but with the hand removed he was unable to do so. (This is an "automatic-talking" procedure, analogous to the "automatic-writing" procedure sometimes used to study unconscious processes.)

Hilgard coined the metaphor *the hidden observer* to describe the subsystem that has knowledge not available to the hypnotized subject's consciousness, but which can be accessed through special methods such as automatic writing and automatic talking. In terms of neodissociation theory, Hilgard suggested that the monitoring system is divided, such that one part feeds information to the hypnotized subject's consciousness, whereas another part registers and retains certain information that is not made available to consciousness. The dissociated part (the "hidden observer") of the monitoring system becomes a separate subsystem that can control responses such as writing and talking. Thus, in the "hand-on-the-arm" method with the hypnotically deaf subject, Hilgard was talking with the subject's hidden observer. It is important to note that the hidden observer is not an alternate personality, nor is it an enduring part of the person. Rather, the hidden observer seems to appear in response to certain kinds of suggestions, such as hypnotic deafness, analgesia, and amnesia. Its function is limited to dealing with the information excluded from consciousness by the suggestion. Some writers use the term *subconscious mind* for the dissociated information system; information in that system is subconscious information (Kihlstrom 1984). Hilgard regards the barrier between consciousness and the hidden observer (or subconscious) as an amnesia barrier, which can be reversed, in contrast to the relatively impermeable repression barrier that separates the conscious and unconscious mind in Freud's psychoanalytic theory.

The hidden observer in hypnotic analgesia.

The hidden-observer effect in hypnotic deafness has been confirmed in a systematic study (Crawford, Macdonald, & Hilgard 1979; Hilgard 1977). It has also been demonstrated in hypnotic analgesia in several experiments by Hilgard and his colleagues. Hilgard, Morgan, and Macdonald (1975) tested twenty highly hypnotizable subjects with cold pressor pain. An automatic key-pressing method (analogous to automatic writing) was used to signal hidden-observer pain reports. Following a waking baseline pain test without hypnosis, subjects were hypnotized and given an analgesia suggestion before the second pain test. In addition it was suggested that while they were making their verbal pain reports, a hidden part of their mind would be able to report the true state of affairs by pressing telegraph keys with the opposite hand. (The left key signaled tens while the right key signaled single digits.) Then an amnesia suggestion for the key-pressing instruction was given, so that the subjects would make the key-pressing responses outside of conscious awareness.

Of twenty subjects, eight showed the *hidden-observer effect*, with "covert" pain reports (hidden reports, made by key pressing) being substantially higher than "overt" pain reports (open reports, made verbally). The mean pain ratings for these eight subjects are shown in Figure 15.2. Here the overt report is the report of the hypnotized conscious mind, as in typical hypnotic analgesia situations. Note that the covert reports were somewhat lower than the waking pain reports, but markedly higher than the overt reports. Knox, Morgan, and Hilgard (1974) obtained similar hidden-observer results using the muscle ischemia pain procedure and the automatic-talking ("hand-on-the-shoulder") method of obtaining covert pain reports.

Hilgard (1977) argued that hidden-observer pain reports indicate that pain is perceived at a subconscious level during hypnotic analgesia, and an amnesia-like barrier prevents the conscious hypnotized mind from being aware of the pain. The subconscious pain can be reported only through a special procedure—the hidden-observer suggestion.

Simulator test of the hidden observer.

Taking a critical view, you might ask whether hidden-observer reports occur merely in response to the demand characteristics of the test situation. Perhaps subjects figure out what responses the experimenter expects and respond accordingly. The question

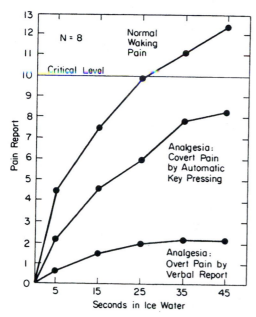

FIGURE 15.2. The "hidden observer" effect in cold pressor pain testing. In the baseline test (normal waking pain), reports were made verbally. Subsequently, subjects made two types of pain reports during hypnotic analgesia: "overt" reports, made verbally (standard procedure); and "covert" reports, made by key pressing (hidden-observer report). Overt and covert reports were made concurrently. The hidden-observer effect refers to the finding that overt pain ratings are higher than covert ratings. [From Hilgard, E. R., Morgan, A. H., & Macdonald, H. (1975). Pain and dissociation in the cold pressor test: A study of hypnotic analgesia with "hidden reports" through automatic key pressing and automatic talking. *Journal of Abnormal Psychology, 84,* 280–89. Copyright 1975 by the American Psychological Association. Reprinted by permission.]

of experimental demands was tested directly in an experiment using Orne's real-simulator experimental design (Hilgard et al. 1978a). First, subjects made pain ratings during a baseline cold pressor test without hypnosis. Second, they made overt verbal pain ratings during cold pressor testing under hypnotic analgesia. Immediately afterward the hidden-observer suggestion was given, and subjects were asked for covert (hidden-observer) reports of the highest level of pain that they had felt during the second test. Finally, in another room, a different experimenter interrogated the subjects and asked them to honestly report the highest levels of pain that they had felt overtly (consciously) and covertly during the second test.

The results of this experiment are shown in Table 15.1. Here the real and simulator groups are divided into two subgroups: those that showed a hidden observer (HO) effect (covert pain exceeds overt pain) and those that did not. Several aspects of the data are important: (1) All of the simulators successfully faked hypnotic analgesia (overt reports prior to honesty interrogation). Not only were their pain ratings low; they also maintained a stoic expression, without grimacing or fidgeting. (2) Nine simulators successfully faked the hidden observer effect (covert pain higher than overt pain, prior to honesty). (3) During the postexperimental honesty interrogation, none of the reals changed their pain reports; that is, they maintained that their prior overt and covert reports were true reports of what they had felt. (4) During honesty interrogation all simulators reported that their overt pain had really been much higher than previously reported. (5) During honesty interrogation, for those subjects who had previously shown a hidden-observer effect, simulators no longer claimed that their overt pain had been lower than their covert pain, whereas reals continued to maintain that this had been the case. In other words, during honesty interrogation the simulators denied that the hidden-observer effect was authentic, while reals maintained that it was authentic. Hilgard et al. (1978a) interpreted the data as indicating that the hidden-observer effect can be faked by simulators, but the six real hypnotized subjects had in fact experienced the hidden-observer effect and had not faked it.

TABLE 15.1   Overt and Covert Pain in Hypnotic Analgesia in Hypnotic (Reals) and Simulator Subjects

| | | MEAN MAXIMUM PAIN AS A PERCENT OF WAKING BASELINE PAIN | | | |
| | | PRIOR TO HONESTY INTERROGATION | | DURING HONESTY INTERROGATION | |
	N	OVERT	COVERT	OVERT	COVERT
Reals					
H.O. effect	6	18	81	18	81
No H.O.	6	15	15	15	15
Simulators					
H.O. effect	9	6	70	70	75
No H.O.	3	21	21	102	102

From Hilgard, E. R., Hilgard, J. R., Macdonald, H., Morgan, A. H., & Johnson, L. S. (1978). Covert pain in hypnotic analgesia: Its reality as tested by the real-simulator design. *Journal of Abnormal Psychology, 87,* 655–63. Copyright 1978 by the American Psychological Association. Adapted by permission.

Subjective experience of the hidden observer.

Here are some introspective verbal reports on the hidden-observer experience, made by several subjects after hypnosis was terminated.

- The hidden part doesn't deal with pain. It looks at what is, and doesn't judge it. It is not a hypnotized part of the self. It knows all the parts.
- The hidden observer seemed like my real self when I'm out of hypnosis, only more objective. When I'm in hypnosis, I'm imagining, letting myself pretend, but somewhere the hidden observer knows what's really going on. I think this is part of the same process as the tendency in hypnosis to stand back and say: "Look what's happening to you. You're slowly going under hypnosis."
- The hidden observer was an extra, all-knowing part of me. I was not at all aware of it when I blotted out the hearing. It was not there until it was told to be there. [From an experiment on hypnotic deafness.] (Hilgard 1977, pp. 207–8)
- I can separate my mind and my head from the rest of my body. The hidden part—reporting on the keys—was controlling my body. My mind was not counting key pressing. My mind was reporting what it felt, verbally. I've always been aware of the difference between the mind and the body when I've been hypnotized.
- It's as though two things were happening simultaneously; I have two separate memories, as if the two things could have happened to different people. The memory of the hidden part is more intellectual, but I can't really comprehend or assimilate the two. (Hilgard et al. 1975, p. 286; Hilgard et al. 1978a)

The point that comes through in many of the descriptions is that the hidden observer is relatively objective and analytical. This was revealed also in subjects' straightforward, unemotional, matter-of-fact ways of speaking during hidden-observer reports. Postexperimental reports also showed that experiencing the hidden observer (reals) did not depend upon subjects' prior beliefs that the hidden observer was plausible. Three of eight subjects who experienced the hidden observer had not thought that it was a plausible idea. And some subjects who had thought that the hidden observer was plausible did not subsequently experience it (Hilgard et al. 1978a).

Comment.

If taken at face value, the hidden-observer effect supports Hilgard's neodissociation theory of hypnosis. It appears that hypnotic analgesia or deafness suggestions can produce functional dissociations between perceptual monitoring processes and consciousness. It is noteworthy that Hilgard (1977) does not claim that dissociation effects are unique to hypnosis. They may also occur in nonhypnotic situations, such as narrowly focused attention with deep imaginative involvement, particularly in hypnotizable subjects. But Hilgard says that dissociation effects are characteristic of deep hypnosis, and hypnosis is an ideal procedure for studying them. One puzzle for neodissociation theory is why only about half of the highly hypnotizable subjects have experienced the hidden-observer effect when tested for it.

On the negative side, neodissociation theory can be criticized for not providing clear criteria for identifying dissociative processes in normal and abnormal states. The theory is not stated precisely enough to make it possible to derive specific hypotheses that can be experimentally tested (Farthing 1980). Rather, tests of the theory have often had to be based on plausible interpretations of the theory and extrapolations from it, where it was not sufficiently detailed. One plausible interpretation, for example, is that high hypnotic responsiveness should be correlated with superior abilities on laboratory tests of divided attention, though this prediction has not fared well in experimental tests (Stava & Jaffa 1988). Furthermore, the dissociation theory interpretation of the hidden-observer effect is controversial. An alternative interpretation has been proposed from the social-psychological viewpoint, as we will see in the next section.

THE SOCIAL-PSYCHOLOGICAL APPROACH TO HYPNOSIS

Psychologists who take the social-psychological (or social-cognitive) approach to hypnosis argue that hypnosis is not an altered state of consciousness or cognition, nor does it involve dissociation of mental subsystems. Rather, it involves normal thinking and behavior processes occurring in a special social situation identified as hypnosis (Barber 1969, 1972; Sarbin & Coe 1972; Wagstaff 1981, 1986). The social-psychological approach is sometimes called the "contextualist" approach, referring to the idea that subjects' behaviors are influence by the current social context, where they play a social role (hypnotized subject) according to their knowledge, beliefs, and expectations and the implicit and explicit demands of the situation (Coe & Sarbin 1977; Coe 1978; Coe & Sluis 1989).

Nicholas Spanos is currently the most prolific hypnosis researcher in the social-psychological camp. I will be emphasizing the work of Spanos and his colleagues because it presents a coherent body of research and theory on a wide variety of hypnotic phenomena. Spanos (1986a) pointed out that contemporary hypnosis research is organized around two broadly defined viewpoints: the state or special-process view and the nonstate or social-psychological view. According to Spanos, the special-process view is based on the (often implicit) assumption that genuine hypnotic responses are automatic or involuntary, rather than voluntary, responses. Thus, theorists in that camp have postulated special processes, such as dissociation, to explain how normally voluntary responses occur involuntarily during hypnosis. In contrast, the social-psychological approach argues that hypnotic phenomena are similar to other forms of social behavior, and they can be explained without postulating special processes such as trance or dissociation. Spanos explained:

> According to [the social-psychological] view, hypnotic behavior is purposeful, goal-directed action that can be understood in terms of how the subjects interpret their situation and how they attempt to present themselves through their actions. This view acknowledges that "good" hypnotic subjects frequently behave *as if* they have lost control over their behavior. However, these aspects of behavior are interpreted as voluntary rather than automatic. Responsive hypnotic subjects behave as involuntary because their preconceptions about hyp-

nosis and the persuasive communications they receive in the hypnotic test situation define acting that way as central to the role of being hypnotized (Spanos 1986a, p. 449).

Spanos explained hypnotic behaviors in terms of two factors: (1) subjects are motivated to present themselves to the hypnotist as good hypnotic subjects; and (2) they use cognitive strategies to meet the requirements of the suggestions while enabling themselves to view themselves as good hypnotic subjects. Cognitive strategies can enable subjects to respond appropriately while interpreting their responses as involuntary, thus maintaining their subjective impressions that they are good hypnotic subjects. Thus hypnotic responses are voluntary *strategic enactments* to meet the social demands of the situation. The social-psychological view sees hypnotic responsiveness as a learnable cognitive skill, rather than a stable personality trait. (Hypnotic skill training was discussed in the last chapter.) Spanos now calls his theory the *social-cognitive theory*, to emphasize the idea that both the social context and cognitive strategies are important factors in hypnotic responding.

The Social-Cognitive View of Hypnotic Analgesia

In the social-cognitive view, hypnotic analgesia is a strategic social enactment where subjects use cognitive strategies such as diversion of attention away from pain stimuli.

Is hypnotic induction necessary for hypnotic analgesia?   One implication of the social-cognitive viewpoint is that if a hypnotic induction does not really produce an altered state of consciousness or special process (such as dissociation), then it should not be necessary to have a prior hypnotic induction in order for an analgesia suggestion to be effective in reducing pain.

Spanos, Radtke-Bodorik, et al. (1979a) tried to separate the effects of the hypnotic induction and the analgesia suggestion by using a between-subjects experimental design, where separate groups of high and low hypnotizables were given the cold pressor pain test under each of four conditions following the baseline immersion: (1) *hypnotic analgesia*: hypnotic induction followed by analgesia suggestion; (2) *hypnosis alone*; (3) *analgesia suggestion alone* ("waking analgesia"); and (4) *control*: no hypnosis, no suggestion. The results indicated significant pain reduction only among highs who were given an analgesia suggestion (conditions 1 and 3); the reduction was no greater with than without a prior hypnotic induction. This is a rather surprising result: Hypnotic susceptibility makes a difference, but hypnotic induction does not.[1] The implication is that individual differences in response to hypnotic suggestions involve something other than an ability to enter a special trance or dissociative state following a hypnotic induction.

Suggestion and distraction.   How does an analgesia suggestion work? Hilgard (1977) argued that two processes are involved: (1) a nonhypnotic component that involves attention diversion, relaxation, and reduced anxiety—this component can be effective for both lows and highs, and does not

require a prior hypnotic induction—and (2) a hypnotic component that involves a dissociation or amnesia-like process and is possible only for highs who are in a hypnotic state. According to Hilgard, the nonhypnotic component alone can reduce pain by about 20 percent, but major reductions in pain are available only to those who can use the hypnotic component.

The social-cognitive view is that suggested analgesia is produced by cognitive strategies, particularly by subjects diverting their attention away from the painful stimulus, aided by belief in the efficacy of the attention-diversion strategy. Perhaps high hypnotizables can use analgesia suggestions (both hypnotic and waking) more effectively than lows because highs are better at focusing attention on the suggested images (such as "your hand will become numb and insensitive, like a piece of rubber"), thus making the suggestion an effective distractor.

An implication of the attentional distraction hypothesis is that other sorts of distractors besides suggestions should be effective in reducing pain, at least among highly hypnotizable subjects. Several studies have found other distractors besides suggestions to be effective. Spanos et al. (1984c) tested independent groups of high and low hypnotizables in the cold pressor situation under three conditions (without hypnosis) following the baseline immersion: (1) waking analgesia suggestion; (2) external distraction by a shadowing task (a list of words was read at a rapid rate, and subjects had to pay attention and repeat back each word immediately); and (3) control (no treatment). The result was that for highs the analgesia suggestion and external distraction were equally effective in reducing pain ratings, whereas for lows only the external distraction was effective. Farthing, Venturino, and Brown (1984) obtained similar results, where the external distraction task involved listening to a list of words and trying to memorize them for a subsequent recall test.[2]

The difference between highs and lows in these studies suggests that highs may be better than lows at using imagination strategies (such as suggestions) to distract themselves from pain, whereas lows are as good as highs at reducing pain by attending to external distractors. This interpretation is consistent with interpretations of hypnotic susceptibility in terms of imagination ability. An alternative interpretation is that highs—but not lows—know how to interpret passively worded suggestions to use them effectively as distractors, whereas both highs and lows can use external distractors because they require no special interpretation (Spanos & Katsanis 1989; Spanos, Kennedy, & Gwinn 1984b).

The distraction hypothesis is consistent with Spanos's (1986a) general approach to hypnosis as a social-cognitive phenomenon, in which subjects use whatever cognitive strategies are available to them to meet the requirements of the testing situation. When given permission to do so, subjects will devise their own pain-coping strategies, when they are not given explicit suggestions or distraction tasks (Spanos et al. 1984a). Several experiments have demonstrated the effectiveness of nonhypnotic pain-coping strategies (reviews in Spanos 1986a; Turk, Meichenbaum, & Genest 1983).

In reply to Spanos's explanation of hypnotic analgesia as a distraction effect, critics have pointed out that, like Barber (1969) before him, Spanos is using the logic of equivalence, claiming that where different methods produce the same degree of pain reduction, both methods must be using the same underlying cognitive process. That argument is not necessarily valid (Sheehan & Perry 1976). The question whether hypnotic analgesia suggestions invoke some special process, at least in some highly hypnotizable subjects, is still a matter of controversy.

The Hidden Observer Examined

In view of Spanos's skepticism about other claims by special-process theorists, it comes as no surprise that he disputes Hilgard's interpretation of the hidden-observer effect in terms of a dissociation process. In contrast, Spanos (1986a) argued that hidden-observer reports are—like other hypnotic responses—behaviors made by people who are trying to be good hypnotic subjects and behave according to their interpretations of the hypnotist's instructions and suggestions. In support of his argument, Spanos offered two experiments that showed that "covert" (hidden observer) pain reports could be either higher or lower than "overt" (standard procedure) pain reports, depending on the nature of the hidden-observer suggestion.

Spanos and Hewitt (1980) compared the effects of "more aware" and "less aware" hidden-observer suggestions on covert pain reports in the cold pressor test. As in Hilgard et al.'s (1975) procedure, subjects received hypnotic analgesia and hidden-observer suggestions, then made periodic overt verbal pain ratings, followed shortly by covert ratings made by key-pressing responses. Following Hilgard's procedure, it was suggested to the "more aware" subjects that there was a "hidden part" of themselves that knew that "things are going on in your body, things unknown to the part of you to which I am now talking" (Knox, Morgan, & Hilgard 1974, p. 842). Subjects in the "less aware" group received the suggestion that the hidden part would "know even less about things going on in your body than the hypnotized part of you to which I am now talking" (Spanos & Hewitt 1980, p. 1206).

The result was that the "more aware" group showed the typical hidden observer effect, with covert (key press) pain reports being markedly higher than overt (verbal) pain reports. Conversely, the "less aware" group made covert pain reports that were significantly lower than their overt pain reports, and markedly lower than the covert reports made by the more aware group. Spanos and Hewitt argued that their results showed that the hidden observer is not so much a discovery as an experimental creation: subjects made "covert" responses that were consistent with the behaviors implied by the hidden-observer suggestions. Furthermore, their responses were not necessarily just a matter of voluntarily faking. In Spanos's view, subjects want not only to be good hypnotic subjects in their overt responses; they also want to be good subjects by having the subjective experiences implied by the suggestions, and they devise cognitive strategies in order to have those experiences. Thus, they might shift their attention toward or away from the pain stimuli, in order to feel more or less pain in accordance with the demand characteristics of the experimental suggestions.

Spanos and Hewitt's (1980) conclusions were criticized on several grounds by Laurence, Perry, and Kihlstrom (1983; reply in Spanos 1983). Laurence et al. argued, in effect, that a "genuine" or "more aware" hidden observer is a natural occurrence during hypnotic analgesia, representing a dissociation process. But the "less aware" hidden observer found in Spanos and Hewitt's less aware group was a response to specific suggestions for a hidden part that would be less aware of the pain than was the hypnotized part.

Spanos, Gwynn, and Stam (1983a) replied to the above argument with an experiment in which the hidden observer was tested in a neutral way, without indicating to subjects whether the hidden observer would be more aware or less aware of pain than the conscious hypnotized part. The result was that covert pain reports did not differ from overt reports. This finding is contrary to the neodissociation theory prediction of higher covert than overt pain reports.

In conclusion, research by Spanos and his colleagues raises serious questions about the proper interpretation of the hidden-observer effect. Spanos's results cannot be readily accounted for by the neodissociation theory (see also Spanos al. 1985). It may be the case that Hilgard's hidden observer effect is a response to a particular hypnotic suggestion given in a particular context. The ball is now in the neodissociation theory's court, so to speak. The neodissociation theory needs to be stated in more precise terms that enable it to be tested, and theorists need to specify the boundary conditions (such as the subject's prior beliefs and expectancies, and the experimental demands) that affect its predictions. Spanos and others have shown convincingly that social-psychological factors have a strong impact on hypnotic behavior. Nonetheless, the alterations in subjective experience in deep hypnosis suggest that something special is going on, perhaps some special process that goes beyond hypnotic role playing.

POSTHYPNOTIC AMNESIA

The procedure for posthypnotic amnesia suggestions and amnesia testing was explained in the last chapter. While not as dramatic as age regression or as practical as hypnotic analgesia, posthypnotic amnesia is perhaps the most theoretically important hypnotic phenomenon, for several reasons (Kihlstrom 1977, 1985b). On hypnotic susceptibility tests, the amnesia item is the one that correlates most consistently with other items, suggesting that something about the cognitive process in hypnotic amnesia is involved also in other types of hypnotic performance. Hilgard (1977) sees amnesia as the prototype case of dissociation in hypnosis. Also, the retrieval problems in posthypnotic amnesia may be related to both clinical functional amnesias and retrieval problems in normal, everyday forgetting. Thus, an understanding of posthypnotic amnesia is critical for understanding hypnosis, and it may have implications that reach beyond the domain of hypnosis.

Explanations of Posthypnotic Amnesia

What is going on during posthypnotic amnesia? Is the information really forgotten? One thing we know for sure is that the information has not been permanently lost from memory. The fact of amnesia reversibility proves that point.

If the information is still in memory, then why don't subjects report it? There are two alternatives (Table 15.2): subjects do not *retrieve* the information from memory (left column); or subjects retrieve the information but do not *report* it (right column). In the latter case, if subjects retrieved the information, why wouldn't they report it? Either they are *unable* to report it (cell B), or they are *unwilling* to do so (cell D). The same possibilities apply also to retrieval failure: either subjects are unable to retrieve the information (cell A), or they are unwilling to do so (cell C) (Kihlstrom 1977).

In Table 15.2, the only situation that we would call *true amnesia* is if subjects are actually unable to retrieve the required information from memory (cell A). Other situations would be *pseudoamnesia*—they look like amnesia on the surface, but the reason for nonreporting is something other than inability to retrieve the information. When subjects retrieve the information but are unwilling to report it, it is a case of faked amnesia or "keeping secrets" (cell D) (Kihlstrom 1977).

The cells in Table 15.2 are only the first step in explaining posthypnotic amnesia. Theorists need to explain *why* subjects are unable (or unwilling) to retrieve (or report) the required information.

According to Hilgard's (1977) neodissociation theory, amnesia suggestions establish (in highly hypnotizable subjects) a temporary dissociation or disconnection between consciousness and the part of the memory-storage system where the amnesic (to be forgotten) items reside. Thus, conscious control processes for memory retrieval are unable to gain access to the amnesic items. The inability to retrieve is involuntary; subjects may honestly try to retrieve the information, but they cannot do it.

According to Spanos's social-cognitive theory, posthypnotic amnesia does not involve an inability to retrieve the information. Instead, amnesia is accomplished through voluntary response strategies aimed at meeting the demands of the test situation. There are two response strategies: voluntary nonreporting—faking amnesia (cell D in Table 15.2), and voluntary nonretrieval (cell C). Retrieval can be avoided by not trying to retrieve the information and by deliberately shifting one's attention to something else. Spanos (1986a; also Coe 1978) argued that voluntary nonretrieval is the most

---

TABLE 15.2   Explanations of Posthypnotic Amnesia

		REASON FOR NONREPORTING OF INFORMATION	
		RETRIEVAL FAILURE	REPORT FAILURE*
Reason for retrieval or report failure	Unable (involuntary)	(A) True Amnesia	(B) Response Inhibition
	Unwilling (voluntary)	(C) Retrieval Avoidance	(D) Faked Amnesia

*"Report failure" means that the subject successfully retrieved the required information but did not report it.

common strategy. By voluntarily avoiding retrieval, subjects comply with the suggestion and appear to the hypnotist/experimenter to be good hypnotic subjects, while at the same time maintaining the self-delusion that they are good subjects. Now let us consider some research relevant to the theories of posthypnotic amnesia.

Breaching Posthypnotic Amnesia

Kihlstrom et al. (1980) argued that if amnesia is voluntary, it should be possible to breach (reverse) amnesia by some means besides giving the prearranged reversal cue. They gave subjects a hypnotic susceptibility test with a standard amnesia suggestion to forget the test items, followed by arousal from hypnosis and the first recall attempt. Then, to try to breach amnesia, three experimental groups were given different instructions ("report honestly," "try harder," or "try to recall the sequence of events"), followed by the second recall attempt. A control group was told simply to "try again" before the second recall attempt. Finally, the prearranged reversal cue was given ("Now you can remember everything . . ."), followed by the third recall attempt. Two results were important: all four groups showed small and equal gains on the second (prereversal) recall attempt; and all four groups showed additional and equal gains on the third (postreversal) recall attempt. Kihlstrom et al. concluded that there was no evidence of breaching, insofar as none of the experimental groups recalled more items than the control group on the second attempt. Gains on the second recall attempt were apparently just a result of being given a second recall opportunity. The additional gains on the third recall attempt show that amnesia had not been completely overcome during the second attempt.

Several other experiments have tried to get subjects to breach amnesia without the reversal cue, some successfully. For example, some subjects breached amnesia when tested after they had viewed a videotaped playback of their hypnosis session (Sheehan & McConkey 1982). Howard and Coe (1980) found that subjects who experienced an earlier amnesia response as voluntary would breach amnesia on a second test if they thought that they were being monitored by a "lie-detector" machine.

Special-process theorists have pointed out that in all of the breaching experiments, some of the high hypnotizables have not breached amnesia, so for them amnesia must be an involuntary response. Spanos (1986a) argued that even the nonbreachers do not experience a truly involuntary amnesia. Rather, the nonbreachers interpret the situation as calling for continued amnesia, so they continue to avoid retrieving or reporting the items in order to present themselves as good subjects. Some subjects need more compelling instructions than others to convince them that the hypnotist/experimenter truly desires that they report the items, prior to the prearranged reversal cue. Coe and Sluis (1989) were able to get nineteen of twenty subjects—both voluntary and involuntary amnesics—to breach amnesia with sufficient pressure, which included a combination of honesty instructions, lie-detector test, and videotaped playback of the hypnosis session.

Spanos, Radtke, and Bertrand (1985) arranged a convincing scenario for breaching amnesia, using a variation of the hidden-observer procedure.

The subjects were eight high hypnotizables who had been very amnesic on a previous test and had said that their amnesia was involuntary. They were told that during hypnosis "hidden parts" of their mind know things that their conscious mind cannot remember. Then during hypnosis they learned a list of words that included both concrete nouns (names of objects) and abstract nouns. Half of the subjects were told that abstract nouns are stored in the left cerebral hemisphere, and concrete nouns in the right hemisphere; half were told the opposite. Next, all subjects were given an amnesia suggestion, followed by a recall test. All subjects showed a strong amnesia effect, reporting few or none of the words. Then, without giving the amnesia reversal cue, the hypnotist contacted each subject's left and right "hidden parts" by touching the left or right shoulder. Subjects who had been told that the left side stores abstract nouns and the right side concrete nouns reported abstract nouns when the left hidden part was contacted, and concrete nouns when the right hidden part was contacted (and vice versa for subjects told that the left side stores concrete nouns). According to Spanos, these results indicate clearly that hypnotic amnesia is a strategic enactment. Good hypnotic subjects maintain the appearance of being good subjects by maintaining voluntary control of memory and behaving as if voluntary control had been lost, in order to meet the demand requirements of the hypnotic test situation. In this experiment, subjects inferred that breaching hypnosis (via the "hidden part") was consistent with being a good hypnotic subject.[3]

Lazar (1989) found that amnesia could be breached by a paraphrase of the reversal cue or by a polite request to report what had happened during hypnosis, regardless of whether the paraphrase or request was given by the hypnotist in the original experimental context or by someone else in a different room after the experiment was over. Lazar concluded that subjects will reverse hypnosis whenever they believe that they have permission to do so.

In conclusion, breaching experiments provide more support for the social-psychological view than for the special-process view. Depending on which breaching method is used, either a minority or a majority of subjects will reverse amnesia without the prearranged reversal cue. It appears that, *for subjects who breach*, amnesia is voluntary. However, it is still uncertain what is going on with those who do not breach. Either they are truly unable to retrieve the critical information, as special-process theorists assert, or they are simply not yet willing to retrieve or report the information, in the social-psychological view. Different subjects may interpret the amnesia suggestion and breaching instructions in different ways. Conceivably, some subjects who are truly amnesic interpret the breaching instruction as the reversal cue. If this is the case, then for those subjects breaching is not critical evidence against the special-process view.

Disorganized Retrieval in Posthypnotic Amnesia

Tests of posthypnotic amnesia use a *free recall* procedure, in which subjects may report items in any order they choose. Several studies have found that when amnesic subjects recall a few items, the organization of items during free recall is disrupted, compared to nonamnesic subjects. Disrupted organization of recall has been found for temporal sequencing of hypnotizability test items (Evans & Kihlstrom 1973), category clustering of semantically related words (Radtke-Bodorik, Planas, & Spanos 1980), and subjective organization of items originally presented in random sequences (Tkachyk, Spanos, & Bertrand 1985), though there have been some exceptions (Spanos 1986a; Wilson & Kihlstrom 1986).

Kihlstrom (1977, 1985b) argued that amnesia suggestions make hypnotizable subjects unable to recall specified information by disrupting the retrieval processes for episodic memory. Disrupted retrieval is shown by reduced temporal organization, category clustering, and subjective organization. Kihlstrom suggested that posthypnotic amnesia appears to represent a "temporary dissociation of episodic features from memory traces, so that the subject has difficulty in reconstructing the context in which the target events occurred" (1980, p. 227).

Spanos (1986a) disagreed. He argued that recall failure and disorganization during amnesia result from subjects deliberately diverting attention away from the recall task. To test the plausibility of this explanation, Spanos and D'Eon (1980) compared category clustering during posthypnotic amnesia with clustering during a distraction task, in which subjects were required to count backwards by threes (in writing) at the same time that they tried to recall words memorized during hypnosis. Semantic organization was disrupted as much by the attentional distraction task as it was by the amnesia suggestion. Similar results were obtained for subjective organization (Tkachyk et al. 1985). Thus, since deliberate distraction can disrupt the organization of items during retrieval without amnesia, it is plausible that disrupted organization during posthypnotic amnesia is due to subjects deliberately distracting themselves during the recall test, as a cognitive strategy to appear amnesic and meet the experimental demands.

Conclusions Regarding Posthypnotic Amnesia

How do the experimental results relate to Table 15.2 on explanations of hypnosis? First, we can reject the response inhibition interpretation of amnesia (cell B). Tests of semantic memory during posthypnotic amnesia (Kihlstrom 1980; Williamsen, Johnson, & Eriksen 1965) show that subjects are able to say or write the critical words in tests—such as word associations or completion of partial-words—similar to the methods used to test implicit memory in brain-damaged amnesic patients (see Chapter 6). Second, the breaching studies make it clear that some subjects fake amnesia by deliberately failing to report retrieved items (cell D); for example, Howard and Coe's (1980) finding that reporting was increased when subjects thought that they were being monitored by a lie-detector apparatus. However, it appears that only a small minority of subjects fake amnesia in this way (Kihlstrom 1985b). Thus, the main controversy is between the true amnesia (cell A) versus the retrieval avoidance (cell C) interpretations of amnesia responses.

In most breaching studies there are some subjects who do not breach amnesia. What is going on with those subjects? Kihlstrom (1977, 1985b) argued that they are experiencing true amnesia—they are *unable* to retrieve the critical items. Spanos (1986a) disagreed and argued that amnesia is voluntary nonretrieval, and whether subjects breach or not depends upon their interpretation of what is expected of good hypnotic subjects in the context of the particular test situation. The critical question is whether the subjects *could have* recalled the items. Was their failure to recall voluntary or involuntary? When apparently amnesic subjects are subsequently asked whether their amnesia was voluntary or involuntary, most of them reply that it was involuntary. Spanos (1986a) argued that claiming involuntary amnesia is part of the whole process of voluntarily presenting oneself as a good hypnotic subject. It would be inconsistent to fail to report the critical items, then admit "Yes, I could have recalled them but I didn't try." The issue of voluntary versus involuntary retrieval failure in hypnotic amnesia still has not been settled. The critical difficulty is deciding whether to take subjects' introspective reports of involuntariness at face value.

Up to this point it is clear that the social-psychological (social-cognitive) approach presents a serious challenge to special-process theories of hypnosis, though the issues are not yet settled. In the next chapter I will continue the theoretical debate with research on age regression and trance logic. Then I will discuss the question of hypnotic hypermnesia—whether memory can really be enhanced through hypnosis, and the related question of whether pseudomemories can be implanted during hypnosis. These questions have theoretical implications, as well as practical implications in the domains of psychotherapy and criminal interrogation. Finally, I will make some general concluding remarks about hypnosis and hypnosis theories.

SUMMARY

The question of whether hypnotic responses are real is the question of whether they represent authentic changes in subjective experience or merely compliant behavior to meet the social demands of the situation. Two research designs have been used to try to discover the characteristics of authentic hypnotic responses: (1) the high-low method, where highly hypnotizable subjects are compared with low hypnotizables under identical conditions; and (2) the real-simulator method, where hypnotized subjects are compared with low hypnotizables who have been instructed to fake being hypnotized.

According to special-process theories, hypnosis involves an altered state of consciousness or cognitive processing. It is assumed that true hypnotic responses occur with a feeling of involuntariness, and that they reflect changes in underlying cognitive processes that are characteristic of hypnosis (though not necessarily unique to hypnosis). Hilgard's neodissociation theory states that hypnotic responses such as analgesia (pain reduction) and posthypnotic amnesia involve temporary dissociations or disconnections between cognitive subsystems, such that stimuli and responses that normally occur with awareness and control can occur without conscious awareness and control. The "hidden-observer" effect, involving reports of hidden pain during hypnotic analgesia, was offered in support of the neodissociation theory.

In contrast, the social-psychological approach says that hypnosis involves ordinary thinking and behavior processes operating in a special social situation identified as hypnosis. In this approach, subjects' verbal reports of subjective experiences are treated as a type of behavior to be explained. Spanos's social-cognitive theory explains hypnotic behaviors in terms of two factors: (1) subjects are motivated to present themselves to the hypnotist as good hypnotic subjects; and (2) they use cognitive strategies to meet the requirements of the suggestions while enabling themselves to view themselves as good hypnotic subjects. Thus hypnotic responses are voluntary strategic enactments to meet the social demands of the situation. Spanos argued that hypnotic analgesia involves an attention-diversion strategy and that the hidden-observer effect is a strategic social enactment under voluntary control, rather than a spontaneous dissociation in response to hypnotic suggestions.

Posthypnotic amnesia is seen by special-process theorists such as Kihlstrom as a case of disrupted retrieval from episodic memory, whereas semantic-memory retrieval is not normally affected. Spanos explained amnesia in terms of strategic enactment and attention diversion, such that amnesic subjects do not really try to retrieve the critical information. In both analgesia and amnesia, cognitive strategies may enable subjects to interpret their responses an involuntary, thus maintaining the subjective impression that they are good hypnotic subjects.

ENDNOTES

[1]In an earlier experiment Hilgard et al. (1978b) had found hypnotic analgesia to be more effective than waking analgesia. The different conclusions from the Hilgard et al. and Spanos et al. (1979a) studies appear to be due to the use of within-subject (repeated measures on the same subjects) versus between-subjects (independent groups) designs, respectively. Stam and Spanos (1980) confirmed this interpretation by showing that in a within-subjects design they could make waking analgesia (suggestion-alone) more effective, less effective, or equally as effective as hypnotic analgesia, depending upon different expectations induced by different treatment sequences used for different groups of subjects.

[2]Note that the subjects were not hypnotized in these studies, so the question of whether hypnosis might change the relative effectiveness of suggestion versus external distraction for highs, or make external distraction more effective for highs than for lows, remains open.

[3]To be consistent with the hidden-observer procedure, Spanos et al. (1984d) tested amnesia within hypnosis, rather than posthypnotically. It is assumed that their results are relevant to the explanation of posthypnotic amnesia, though so far there has been little research to compare hypnotic versus posthypnotic amnesia.

chapter 16 ··········

Hypnosis III:
Hypnotic Age Regression and Hypermnesia

Hypnotic age regression is the most dramatic subjective hypnotic experience, according to many subjects. This chapter begins with a discussion of research on age regression and asks what, if anything, is regressed following age regression suggestions. Some regressed subjects report a duality or divided consciousness experience, where they report that one part is a child and another part is an adult. This is one of several types of incongruent responses in hypnosis, which Orne (1959) interpreted as *trance logic*—the acceptance of contradictory beliefs. This chapter asks whether trance logic is a common characteristic of hypnotized subjects.

Next I will discuss *hypnotic hypermnesia*, the enhanced recall of personal experiences during hypnosis. Hypermnesia seems to occur during age regression, where subjects report unusually vivid memories of childhood experiences. It may also occur when hypnosis is used to interrogate victims or witnesses to crimes. Because of the practical as well as theoretical implications of hypermnesia, it is important to ask whether it is valid. I will discuss research on hypnotic hypermnesia and a related issue with forensic implications—whether hypnosis increases susceptibility to false leading questions during interrogation, and whether it enhances the creation of pseudo-memories that persist after hypnosis. Finally, I will make some concluding comments about hypnosis theories and about the implications of hypnosis for understanding consciousness.

AGE REGRESSION

In the age regression item of SHSS:C (Weitzenhoffer & Hilgard 1962), the hypnotist suggests that the subject is gradually becoming younger and smaller, going back in time, until finally he or she is back in the second grade, sitting in the classroom on a nice day, writing or drawing. The usual criterion for "passing" age regression is that, when asked to write his or her name, the subject prints the name in a childlike manner (whereas the signature before regression is cursive). About 40 percent of college student subjects pass by this criterion. However, handwriting change is too lax a criterion for age regression. The most important aspect of age regression is changes in subjective experience, in which subjects feel as if they are younger and reliving a childhood event. By this criterion the proportion of subjects experiencing age regression is probably much smaller than the 40 percent figure (Perry et al. 1988).

While answering questions during regression ("Where are you?" "What are you doing?") some subjects speak in a childlike voice. They may describe the classroom scene in vivid detail and tell where various students sat in the room. If it is suggested that they go outside for recess, they describe a typical school recess scene, and they describe what they are doing—joining in the play (tag, hopscotch, jump rope) or in some cases just standing and watching. The most convincing subjects describe the scene in the present tense, saying, for example, "I *am* playing hopscotch with Ruth and Susie" rather than "I *was* playing hopscotch. . . ." Many subjects list age regression as their most vivid and interesting hypnotic experience. Infrequently, subjects spontaneously recall sad or traumatic events from childhood and show emotional reactions that may include crying, accelerated breathing, and so on. In one case, a subject age-regressed to infancy wet his pants when he was frightened unexpectedly (Laurence et al. 1985; Perry et al. 1988).

What is going on during age regression? The credulous view is that regressed subjects are genuinely like children mentally and emotionally and, furthermore, that the scenes they describe are accurate memories of actual childhood experiences. When recall of childhood experiences appears to be more accurate during hypnosis than in the normal waking state, hypnotic hypermnesia (memory enhancement) is said to occur. Credulous psychotherapists have sometimes used hypnotic age regression to induce clients to recall repressed childhood events, with the assumption that their recollections are accurate. We will see, however, that the credulous view is not valid.

Research on Age Regression

Michael Nash (1987) reviewed some eighty studies of age regression conducted over a period of sixty years. The specific question he asked was, "Does hypnotic age regression enable subjects to exhibit developmentally previous modes of mental functioning?" The studies were directed at four different regression topics: (1) reinstatement of childlike physiological responses (EEG and reflexes); (2) cognitive regression, including (a) reinstatement of childlike cognitive processes (childlike performance on IQ tests and Piagetian cognitive tasks, such as conservation of volume), and (b) recall of childhood events; (3) reinstatement of childlike perceptual processes (illusions and eidetic [photographic] memory); and (4) reinstatement of childlike personality processes, including emotional attachments and projective test performance.

In order to demonstrate genuine hypnotic age regression, two criteria must be met, according to Nash: (1) the responses of adults regressed to a particular age must be similar to those of typical children of that age, and (2) the childlike responses must not be successfully duplicated by adults following waking suggestions or instructions to simulate hypnosis. The latter criterion is necessary to ensure that apparent age regression in hypnosis is not mere acting or role playing based on the subjects' knowledge of children's behavior.

In all four of the regression categories Nash found the same pattern of experimental results: Where studies were properly controlled (by the criteria described above) and had more than one subject, the results were predominantly (84 percent) *against* genuine age regression. For example, O'Connell, Shor, and Orne (1970) found that following hypnotic age regression suggestions, highly hypnotizable subjects did not behave in an age-appropriate manner on Piagetian cognitive tasks, nor was their behavior any more age-appropriate than that of simulator controls. Nash found the evidence supporting genuine age regression to be weak; it comes mostly from older studies (pre-1954) that had only one subject and no controls. In controlled studies the hypnotically "regressed" subjects either failed to respond like children, or if they did, waking or simulator controls also did so, suggesting that the hypnotic subjects could have been using their accurate knowledge of child behavior to act like children without experiencing regressive changes in their own mental states.

Nash (1987) found *no* well-controlled studies showing evidence of reinstatement of childlike physiological or cognitive states or convincing hypermnesic retrieval of childhood memories. Only for the topics of perceptual changes and personality or affective changes were there a few studies that suggested that something like age regression might have occurred. Nash's own study of affective (emotional) regression is especially interesting; I will describe it next.

Age Regression and Reinstatement of a Childhood Affective State

Some of the most compelling evidence for a regression-like process in response to hypnotic age-regression suggestions comes from the work of Nash and colleagues (Nash, Johnson, & Tipton 1979). Nash et al. noted that, in spite of the failures of laboratory studies to find convincing evidence of age regression, a number of clinical cases have shown dramatic revivifications (reliving) of childhood affective experiences, almost always frightening and unpleasant, and with significant therapeutic implications (O'Connell et al. 1970).

Nash et al. devised an experimental procedure to test the possibility that a childlike affective state might be induced by suitable suggestions. They noted that most children pass through a stage, between ages one to six years, when they are strongly attached to some inanimate object (a doll, stuffed animal, or blanket) that they want to hold in times of stress or insecurity, such as when their mother is absent. Such objects are termed *transitional objects*, and—according to psychodynamic theory—they symbolically represent the love and security of the mother while children are making the transition from more imaginary to more reality-oriented modes of thought and learning to adapt to frustration. Research shows that about 60 percent of children have transitional objects, and that those who have them adopt them by the end of the second year in about 89 percent of the cases, and that the attachment typically lasts for about three years (Rudhe & Ekecrantz 1974).

Nash et al.'s plan was to first give age regression suggestions, then give additional suggestions to try to induce an affective state of stress or insecurity and see whether the subjects then desired a transitional object. They compared real hypnotic subjects with control subjects who were instructed to simulate hypnosis. Presumably, if subjects experience a childlike stressful state, they should desire the transitional object. And if age regression is more than mere role playing, then desire for transitional objects should be greater in hypnotized subjects than in simulators.

Nash et al. gave subjects suggestions to regress to the age of three years. Then they suggested that subjects were experiencing a series of stressful situations: being alone in a dark bedroom, waking up alone in a living room, or seeing mother arrange some toys and then leave. These suggestions were accompanied by suggestions for feelings of isolation, loneliness, fear, and a desire to "touch something." In each of the stressful situations the experimenters asked a series of questions intended to discover whether the subjects were thinking about transitional objects: "What's happening?"; "What are you touching?"; "Do you want something else?"

Nash et al. used three dimensions—derived from earlier research with children—to score subjects' transitional object relating: (1) *spontaneity*, a spontaneous desire for the object in stressful situations, scored positive if the subject mentioned the same object in two of the three stress test situations; (2) *specificity*, where only one specific object is desired, scored positive if the subject said "no" when asked whether he or she wanted anything else; and (3) *affective intensity*, where the object is affectionately cuddled and excitedly loved and mutilated; the hypnotist-experimenter judged the intensity of the subject's responses and assigned a numerical rating from zero to twenty.

Table 16.1 shows the results for Nash et al.'s real hypnotized and simulator control adult subjects, as well as data for actual children one to six years of age (based on interviews with the children's mothers; Rudhe & Ekecrantz 1974). Two aspects of the results are noteworthy: (1) on all three behavioral measures of transitional object relating the real hypnotic subjects scored significantly higher than the simulators, and (2) nearly identical percentages of hypnotic reals and children showed the spontaneity and specificity responses to transitional objects, whereas on both measures both of those groups responded significantly more often than simulator subjects. These results were replicated in a follow-up study, which also showed that, among hypnotically age regressed subjects, spontaneous desire for transitional objects was significantly greater with the mother absent (69 percent) than with the (imagined) mother present (38 percent) (Nash et al. 1985).

TABLE 16.1   Responses to Transitional Objects in Hypnotic Real and Simulating Adults and Actual Children Ages 1 to 6 Years

Subject group	n	BEHAVIORAL MEASURE		
		SPONTANEITY*	SPECIFICITY*	INTENSITY**
Reals	16	69%	75%	13.5
Simulators	15	27%	40%	7.5
Children	77	60%	78%	—

n = Number of subjects in group.

* Percent of subjects showing positive response.

** Numerical rating on 0 to 20 scale.

From Nash, M. R., Johnson, L. S., & Tipton, R. (1979). Hypnotic age regression and the occurrence of transitional object relationships. *Journal of Abnormal Psychology, 88,* 547-55. Copyright 1979 by the American Psychological Association. Reprinted by permission.

Nash et al. (1979, 1985) concluded that through age regression suggestions a childlike affective state relating to stress and insecurity was produced, which was similar to that experienced by actual children, as evidenced by the desire for transitional objects. Furthermore, the hypnotic responses were not mere faking in response to the demands of the experimental situation, as is shown by the markedly lesser responding by the simulator subjects. However, further research showed that regressed highs were not very accurate at recalling the transitional objects that they had actually had as children (about 21 percent accuracy, according to interviews with their mothers), nor were they any more accurate than low-hypnotizable simulator subjects (Nash et al. 1986). Thus, there was no evidence for hypermnesic recall of transitional objects in regressed highs.[1]

Explanations of Apparent Age Regression

If hypnotized subjects do not really age regress in the sense of either reinstatement of childhood cognitive stages or hypermnesia of childhood events, then what is going on? Why is "age regression" such a dramatic and convincing experience for hypnotized subjects?

According to skeptics, motivated hypnotic subjects use their knowledge of children and their imaginations to behave *as if* age regressed; age regression is more of an act than a true feeling of being younger (Barber 1969). Though such shamming may be possible, the skeptical view is implausible as an explanation of the dramatic age regressions that sometimes occur during hypnotherapy, where clients have strong emotional reactions with anxiety and crying and report afterward that they actually felt younger and smaller, and as if they were reliving childhood experiences. It seems that regression is more than just acting: it is a dramatic subjective experience that needs to be explained.

Orne (1951) argued that, for deeply hypnotized subjects, age regression is a compelling hallucination of being a child again. Orne suggested that apparent age regression is "role taking on a primarily emotional basis," which is not the same thing as shamming or simulating. In response to regression suggestions, subjects try to imagine being younger, and they reconstruct childhood scenes using a combination of recalled personal experiences, knowledge of children and typical childhood experiences, and imagination. When this reconstruction process occurs in hypnosis, where imagination is particularly vivid and reality testing is reduced, the result is *believed-in imagination*—in other words, a hallucination of being a child again. Hallucinations of age regression can be so vivid that they can produce authentic emotional reactions, even though the hallucinated scenes may be more products of imagination than of memory.

Spanos's social-cognitive view of regression (1989, personal communication) is similar to Orne's in some respects. Spanos sees regression as a case of strategic role enactment to meet the demands of the situation, where subjects vividly imagine childhood scenes. Some subjects may become so absorbed in the role of being a child that they may temporarily feel as if they are children. However, in Spanos's view the regression experience does not require or involve a special hypnotic state.

Hilgard (1977) acknowledged that the evidence is largely against cognitive regression and hypermnesia in age regression and that the behavior of regressed highs usually does not differ from that of simulators. However, Hilgard suggested that regression may have a dissociation component, indicated by the fact that some subjects describe a double consciousness experience, where one part feels regressed while an "observer" part maintains a realistic view of the situation. I will discuss research on this "duality experience" in the section on trance logic, after a brief comment on hypnotic reincarnation.

Age regression and hypnotic reincarnation. A number of years ago public interest was stirred by a report that a Colorado housewife had regressed in hypnosis back to a prior life as a woman named Bridey Murphy in nineteenth-century Ireland (Bernstein 1956). Several similar reports have appeared since then (Venn 1986). To those who want to believe it, such reports appear to provide evidence for reincarnation of souls. However, reincarnation reports can be explained in scientific terms. In most cases of "hypnotic reincarnation," there is no evidence that the prior-life person ever existed. In the few cases that have been thoroughly investigated, where a plausible prior-life identity was reported along with a suitable historical context, it was found that the hypnotic subject had previously learned about that time and place through normal sources, such as reading, conversations, and movies. Some cases apparently involved *source amnesia*, where subjects recalled the historical information but did not recall where they had learned it (Perry et al. 1988; Venn 1986). Thus *pseudomemories* were created, where hypnotized subjects reported as their own memories experiences that were, in fact, constructed from secondary sources. With suggestions that suitably stimulate the imagination and the will to comply, it is not hard to get reports of prior lives from hypnotized subjects (Baker 1982; Spanos 1987–88). The basis of the prior-lives reports is essentially the same as that for ordinary age regression: a mixture of knowledge and imagination and hypnotic role-taking. The same principles have been applied to produce hypnotic age "progressions," reports of experiences that have not yet occurred (Hilgard 1977).

RESPONSE INCONGRUITIES AND TRANCE LOGIC

In his search for studies showing authentic cognitive age regression, Nash (1987) rejected studies where regressed adults failed to behave like real children. Yet some of the incongruous (out of place) and inconsistent responses of hypnotized subjects are interesting in their own right.

Orne (1951) observed several logical incongruities of responses in age-regressed subjects. In one case, a twenty-six-year-old man regressed to age six was asked questions about his birthday. He understood the questions asked in English and replied in English. Yet, when he was six years old he was living in a German-speaking household and had not yet learned English. When he was reminded that his mother had spoken to him in German, he shifted to speaking German. Thereafter, during regression, he replied to English questions in German, and when asked if he understood English he repeatedly replied "nein!" When he was asked the time, he looked at his wristwatch—which he surely did not wear at age six.

Another adult regressed to age six was asked to write the sentence "I am conducting an experiment which will assess my psychological capacities." He spelled all of the words correctly, though a normal six-year-old would not be able to do so. He also understood and defined the word "hypochondriac." (Orne 1951, p. 219).

These response incongruities have two implications (Orne, 1951): (1) they argue against the old *ablation* hypothesis, which claimed that age-regressed subjects cannot retrieve knowledge acquired since the age to which they are regressed; and (2) they represent a form of hypnotic behavior that is counterintuitive and hence unlikely to be faked to please the hypnotist. Such incongruent behaviors are instances of *trance logic*, in which hypnotized subjects readily accept logical incongruities in their responses, more so than one would expect of a nonhypnotized subject.

Orne (1959) argued that trance logic is characteristic of deeply hypnotized subjects. Response incongruities, or trance logic, also occurs in other hypnotic situations besides age regression. Other examples include: *transparent hallucinations*, where hypnotized subjects say that they can really see a hallucinated person, yet they also acknowledge that they can see through the person; and *double hallucinations*, where subjects say that they can see a hallucinated individual (who is not in the room), and when that individual walks into the room the subjects say they see two of that individual. More recent research has asked whether trance logic is an authentic hypnotic response, or merely a matter of responding to experimental demands and trying to please the hypnotist.

Duality in age regression and the hidden observer.   In a postexperimental inquiry following hypnosis, about half of Perry and Walsh's (1978) highly hypnotizable subjects reported that during age regression their conscious experience had alternated between being a five-year-old child and

being an adult. This shifting of awareness in age regression is called the *duality experience*. Here is an example of a duality report:

> I became small again; small, small. Physically . . . I saw myself again with my curls at school. . . . I felt 5, and I felt 23 also. . . . I knew I was 5 years old at school, but I knew I was 23 years old, also, that I was an adult. . . . I really felt 5 years old. I would not be able to say that I was solely 23 years old (Laurence & Perry 1981, p. 338).

The duality experience during age regression seems similar to the hidden observer effect during hypnotic analgesia. Laurence and Perry (1981) examined the relationship between the two experiences in some twenty-three highly hypnotizable subjects. About half of the subjects reported hidden observer experiences during hypnotic analgesia, and these same subjects were highly likely to also report duality experiences in age regression. In contrast, the other subjects did not report hidden observer experiences during hypnotic analgesia or duality experiences during age regression. Also, the hidden-observer subjects were more likely than the others to spell big words correctly when asked to write complex sentences during age regression.

All of the responses measured by Laurence and Perry (1980) can be conceptualized as cases of incongruous responding or trance logic, and all were highly correlated with each other. In a subsequent study, Nogrady et al. (1983) replicated the earlier results, and also showed that simulator subjects behaved like no-observer hypnotic reals: they did not report either hidden observer or duality experiences.[2] Nogrady et al. interpreted their results as a convincing demonstration that neither duality nor hidden observer reports are merely the result of experimental demands. The results are consistent with a dissociation theory interpretation of the hidden observer and duality experiences. However, it remains a mystery why only about half of the highly hypnotizable subjects reported hidden observer and duality experiences in experiments by Hilgard et al. (1975, 1978a), Laurence and Perry (1981), and Nogrady et al. (1983).

Trance logic and the hidden observer as incomplete responding.   Spanos (1986a) proposed two principles to account for the results of trance logic experiments. First, incongruous responses—supposedly indicators of trance logic—really represent *incomplete responding* to hypnotic suggestions. Hypnotized subjects, under constraints to report their experiences honestly, admit failing to fully experience the suggestions. Hence, they admit to "transparent" positive hallucinations, they admit to alternating old/young awareness (duality experience) during age regression, and they spell big words correctly during age regression. Hidden observer reports are also cases of incongruous, incomplete responses during hypnosis, in Spanos's view.

Second, the fact that simulators make fewer incongruous responses than hypnotic reals is due to *differential demands* on real and simulator subjects. Real hypnotic subjects are motivated to try to experience the suggestions and be *good* hypnotic subjects. Simulators, on the other hand, are instructed to behave like *excellent* hypnotic subjects. The demands for compliance are stronger for simulators than for reals. Thus, simulators behave consistently in ways that make them appear to be excellent hypnotic subjects: they report solid rather than transparent hallucinations, they report unified age-regression experiences, and they report no hidden observer or hidden pain greater than overt pain.[3]

Spanos's argument was supported in a study by Spanos, de Groot, and Gwynn (1987b). They found more incongruous responses in hypnotic reals than in simulators. In their interpretation, simulators overfaked by behaving consistently. For example, simulators denied transparent hallucinations and duality experiences, and reported more details in their hallucinations, compared to hypnotized subjects. Within the hypnosis group, incongruous responses were *negatively* correlated with ratings of strength of subjective experience of the suggestions; for example, subjects reporting stronger subjective age-regression experiences were *less* likely to report duality experiences. This negative correlation is clearly contrary to Orne's (1959) characterization of strong subjective experiences and trance logic both being characteristics of hypnosis. Also, studies have found that various trance logic items (double hallucination and so on) are not reliably correlated among hypnotizable subjects (Obstoj & Sheehan 1977; Spanos et al. 1987b).

In conclusion, research by Spanos and others has cast serious doubt on the notion that trance logic is a general and common characteristic of hypnotized subjects. Others have argued, however, that individual instances of trance logic may be spontaneous and authentic hypnotic responses (McConkey & Sheehan 1980).

HYPNOTIC HYPERMNESIA

Hypnotic hypermnesia refers to enhanced retrieval of memories during hypnosis, compared to non-hypnotic retrieval. Here I will discuss the question of whether hypnotic hypermnesia is real.

One source of belief in hypnotic hypermnesia comes from hypnotic age regression. Regressed subjects may seem to be reliving actual experiences from childhood, complete with emotional reactions and recall of details that had presumably been forgotten. In psychotherapy, age regression may produce reports of memories, such as traumatic childhood experiences, that have important therapeutic implications (Frankel 1988).

Another source of belief in hypnotic hypermnesia comes from its use by police for the investigation of crimes (Block 1976). It often happens that crime victims or eyewitnesses cannot recall details that the police need to identify and track down the criminal and make an arrest. This is a problem particularly in violent or frightening crimes, such as physical assault, rape, or armed robbery. Memory difficulties are compounded by fear at the time of the crime, lack of attention to important details, and the passage of time between the crime and the interrogation. In numerous cases, when victims or eyewitnesses were regressed through suggestions back to the time and place of the crime they have reported additional information relevant to the case. In some, but not all, cases this information has helped lead to the arrest of the alleged criminal. In view of the apparent potential of hypnotic hypermnesia for practical use and abuse, it is important to ask whether memory recall under hypnosis is, in fact, better than recall without hypnosis.

How hypnosis might aid memory recall. Belief in the marvelous possibilities of hypnotic recollection is often predicated on a belief in the "videotape" theory of memory. According to the videotape theory, everything that you experience is stored permanently in memory in vivid detail, and any event of your life can be "played back" in consciousness in vivid detail if you are sufficiently motivated and you have the right retrieval cues. In fact, the videotape theory of memory has been thoroughly discredited by modern research. Episodic long-term memories are certainly not stored in vivid detail, nor is there convincing evidence that all memories are stored permanently (Loftus & Loftus 1980). Nonetheless, the possibility remains that hypnosis might be helpful in retrieving whatever pertinent information happens to be stored in memory.

There are several mechanisms through which hypnosis might conceivably aid memory recall (Orne et al. 1988). (1) Imagery-mediated recall might be enhanced, if hypnosis increases the vividness of mental images. (2) Reinstatement of the original scene through suggested images might serve as a retrieval cue to help witnesses recall additional details. (3) Reinstatement of the original mood through suggested images might serve as a retrieval cue. (4) Relaxation during hypnosis might reduce anxiety produced by recall of the critical memories, thus helping overcome repression of traumatic memories. (5) Repeated recall attempts can lead to retrieval of additional items— an effect not limited to hypnosis (Erdelyi 1988). In order to show that hypnosis *per se* produces hypermnesia, it is necessary to show that improved recall is not due merely to repeated recall attempts.

Research on Hypnotic Hypermnesia

It is difficult to evaluate claims of hypermnesia in hypnotic age regression because it is usually impossible to check on the accuracy of subjects' reports. Age-regressed hypnotherapy clients and research subjects often report vivid childhood memories that they accept as accurate, often with strong conviction. But subjects' beliefs in the accuracy of their recollections is not proof that they are accurate. If we disregard clinical case studies that made no attempt to verify the accuracy of patient's recollections, there is really very little evidence for hypnotic hypermnesia in age regression. The few studies that have attempted to verify such reports (for example, by checking school records or talking with parents) have found that the reports contained many errors (Nash et al. 1986; O'Connell et al. 1970). The situation is somewhat better for verifying claims of hypnotic hypermnesia in eyewitnesses, since police can sometimes verify their reports, although in most cases eyewitness reports cannot be verified.

We are interested in knowing the accuracy of memory reports collected through hypnotic methods, but more important, we need to ask whether such reports are any more accurate than reports obtained without hypnosis—other things being equal. In other words, is hypnotic hypermnesia real?

Experimental studies with verifiable facts.   The best way to test hypnotic hypermnesia is through controlled experiments where the experimenter knows the facts, so the accuracy of subjects' recollections can be verified. The usual procedure involves three stages: (1) exposing subjects to material to be learned (such as a film or series of pictures); (2) giving the first recall test, without hypnosis; and (3) before the second recall test, hypnotizing half of the subjects and suggesting that they will be able to recall the learned material; a control group is not hypnotized, but simply asked to try again (and try harder). If the amount of improvement in recall (additional correct items) is greater for the hypnosis group than for the control group, the difference might be interpreted as evidence for hypnotic hypermnesia, though, as we will see, other interpretations are possible.

Orne et al. (1988) reviewed a large number of experimental studies on hypnotic hypermnesia and summarized several conclusions based on the evidence available so far. Most experimental tests have failed to find evidence for hypnotic hypermnesia. Where apparent successes have occurred, they have involved meaningful materials (such as pictures, stories, films, and live dramatic enactments) rather than meaningless materials (such as lists of unrelated words). Enhanced recall is more likely for visual than for verbal material, and for material that has been deeply processed, rather than superficially processed (Shields and Knox 1986). Apparent hypermnesia occurs only with recall tests of memory, and not with recognition tests. For example, hypnosis failed to improve recognition of faces in a lineup of suspects (Wagstaff 1982). Unfortunately, there is no convincing evidence that hypnosis can aid recall of the impersonal, semantic types of information that college students usually encounter on exams.

Memory enhancement versus response criterion shift in hypnotic recall.
According to the *generate-and-recognize model* of recall, recall of target items (names, events, etc.) involves three stages: (1) using whatever retrieval cues are available, people retrieve from memory a list of candidate items (the list might include both correct and incorrect items); (2) they subjectively rate each candidate item according to how confident they are that it is correct; and (3) they report only the items for which subjective confidence is greater than a criterion level (the *response criterion*).

The generate-and-recognize model, in conjunction with signal detection theory, says that increases in the number of correct reported items might occur for either of two reasons: increased *memory sensitivity*, where new correct candidate items are retrieved; or *response criterion shift*, where the response criterion is lowered, such that people now report previously retrieved items for which their subjective confidence is low. If the response criterion is lowered, subjects will also report *incorrect* low-confidence items, along with correct ones.[4]

For older studies where only correct responses were recorded, it is impossible to tell whether an increase in correct reports was due to increased memory sensitivity or to a lowered response criterion. Jane Dywan and Kenneth Bowers (1983) initiated a new generation of hypnotic hypermnesia studies by using an improved procedure in which subjects reported all candidate items, then indicated which ones they thought were correct memory recollections.

Dywan and Bowers' procedure involved four stages: (1) Preselected high- and low-hypnotizable subjects viewed a series of sixty slides of drawings of common objects. (2) Then they did a *forced recall* memory test in which they were required to make sixty different responses, each response being the name of an object that might have been among the target pictures. For each response, subjects indicated whether it was a memory or just a guess. Presumably they only labeled responses as memories if they were fairly confident; and presumably, only these items would have been reported on an ordinary free-recall test in which subjects were not forced to report guesses. (The purpose of the forced recall procedure was to provide data to test the criterion shift hypothesis, as I will explain momentarily.) (3) Then, in order to be sure that subjects recalled everything they could before the hypnosis test, they were required to do another forced recall test (without hypnosis) every day for a week. As expected, there was some improvement during the week simply as a result of repeated recall efforts: the mean number of correct responses increased from 30 in the first test to 38 in the last test before hypnosis. (4) Finally, the subjects were randomly assigned to two treatments: half of the highs and lows were given a hypnotic induction and suggestions for enhanced recall, while the others (control condition) were given task-motivational instructions ("you can do better if you try harder") without hypnosis; then all subjects did their final recall test.

Figure 16.1 shows the number of *new items reported as memories* on the final recall test, for each group. (New memory items include both items previously reported as guesses but now reported as memories, and completely new items reported as memories.) Three aspects of the results are important: (1) For all four groups, a large majority of the new items reported as memories were, in fact, incorrect. (2) The total number of new memory items was much greater for hypnotized subjects (highs in the hypnosis condition) than for any of the other groups. Hypnotized highs reported both more correct new items, and more incorrect new items, than other groups. (3) The percent of new memory items that were correct (about 20 percent) was not significantly greater for hypnotized subjects than for other groups.

Dywan and Bowers' study provides no convincing evidence for hypermnesia. Though the number of new correct items increased during hypnosis, the increased number of incorrect items was much greater. This result can be explained in terms of the criterion shift hypothesis: hypnotized subjects lowered their response criterion and reported as memories items for which their confidence was low. In the final test, many of the newly reported "memories" were items that had previously been reported as guesses, and most of these items were incorrect. Some completely new memory items were reported during hypnosis, and most of them were incorrect, too. A practical implication of Dywan and Bowers' results is that in criminal investigations any new information reported during hypnosis would be likely to include many errors along with, perhaps, a few correct reports.

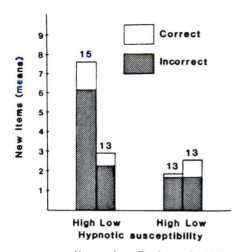

FIGURE 16.1. New items reported as memories after hypnotic or task-motivating (control) suggestions to enhance recall (includes both items previously reported as guesses and completely new items). Under all conditions, most new items reported as memories were, in fact, incorrect. [From Dywan, J., & Bowers, K. (1983). The use of hypnosis to enhance recall. *Science, 222,* 184–85. Copyright © 1983 by the AAAS.]

Dywan and Bowers' (1983) conclusions have been confirmed in other studies (Sheehan 1988). Whitehouse et al. (1988) used forced-recall tests for the contents of a film, and found that subjects' confidence in the accuracy of responses that were, in fact, incorrect was increased by hypnosis. The implication is clear: increased confidence in recall during hypnosis cannot be taken as an indicator that the reported "memories" are necessarily correct.

Implanting Pseudomemories During Hypnosis

We can distinguish between lying and confabulation in memory reporting. *Lying* involves telling a falsehood that you know is false. *Confabulation* involves confusing fantasies with memories and unknowingly reporting as true memories events that are really fantasies (Bowers & Hilgard 1988). Confabulation seems to be a common occurrence during hypnotic age regression, and perhaps also during hypnotic eyewitness interrogation (Perry et al. 1988).

Besides confabulation, another source of error in hypnotic recall is *pseudomemories:* memories that the individual believes to be based on personal experience of an event, but which are in fact based on information learned after the event. Pseudomemories can be created when witnesses to crimes are asked leading questions during interrogation (Loftus 1979). For example, after a bank robbery, a witness might be asked by police "Did you see a blue Volkswagen bus parked outside the bank?" Later, the witness might report in court that he remembered seeing a blue Volkswagen bus outside of the bank (though in fact he never saw it). Pseudomemories can be created by leading questions in interrogations without hypnosis. But there is a particular concern that hypnosis might increase the risk of creating pseudomemories and further, that such pseudomemories would subsequently be believed by the witness with great confidence and be resistant to disconfirmation through cross-examination (Orne 1979). Creation of pseudomemories might be increased during hypnosis because hypnotized subjects tend to be particularly attentive and responsive to hypnotists' communications. Also, hypnotized subjects might vividly imagine events suggested in leading questions and subsequently fail to distinguish between imagined and remembered experiences.

Some studies have found that hypnotized subjects are more likely than waking controls to reply affirmatively to false leading questions about filmed incidents. For example, hypnotized subjects were more likely to reply "yes" to the question, "Did you see the stop sign at the intersection?" when in fact there was no stop sign (Putnam 1979; Zelig & Beidleman 1981). Also, some studies have found that hypnosis increases the likelihood of pseudomemories being implanted through leading questions containing misleading information (Laurence & Perry 1983; Sheehan, Grigg, & McCann 1984). However, some evidence is inconsistent with these conclusions.

In an elaborate experiment by Spanos et al. (1989a), high- and low-hypnotizable subjects watched videotape of a (simulated) bank robbery and shooting, and later they were exposed to misleading information about the robber in a videotaped newscast. Subsequently, different groups were interrogated with misleading questions about the robber ("Visualize the man's upper left arm. Do you see a tattoo?") either with or without hypnosis; a control group was asked nonleading questions ("Describe the man."). Subsequently, subjects tried to identify the robber in a set of mug shots (photographs). Finally, they were cross-examined by a different experimenter, who tried to break down (get them to deny) their earlier incorrect responses to interrogation questions and choices of mug shots.

Two aspects of the results were especially important: (1) Most subjects exposed to misleading questions during interrogation agreed to some of them (for example, seeing a tattoo when in fact the robber had no tattoo), but hypnotized subjects (highs in the hypnosis condition) were no more likely to do so than other subjects. (2) During cross-examination, most subjects broke down on some of their earlier answers, but previously hypnotized highs were no more, or less, likely to do so than subjects not previously hypnotized. Thus, hypnotically implanted pseudomemories are no more resistant to cross-examination than those implanted without hypnosis.

Spanos et al. (1989a) concluded that during interrogation subjects responded to social pressures to answer affirmatively to leading questions. But under cross-examination a new set of social pressures was introduced, with demands for accuracy, and subjects complied by reversing some of their earlier responses. Assuming that subjects want to be both accurate and consistent, during cross-examination they may feel conflict over reversing their prior responses, so they don't reverse all of them. In other words, subjects might fail to reverse some of their responses in order to save face—they don't want to appear inconsistent by admitting that all of their prior responses were wrong. Social-contextual influences on memory reports can occur either with or without hypnosis (see also Spanos & McLean 1986).

Implications of Hypermnesia Research for Forensics and Psychotherapy

Research on hypnotic hypermnesia has some clear implications for the forensic use of hypnosis: (1) Witnesses' reports during hypnotic interrogation should not be taken at face value. They will likely contain many errors or confabulations. For example, in one case a hypnotized witness claimed to describe a face seen at the time of a crime, though in fact the distance and lighting conditions at the time of the crime would have made it impossible for him to see the face in question (Orne 1979).

(2) Reports during hypnosis may include some accurate information. Thus, hypnotic reports may sometimes be useful as a source of *leads* for the police to independently verify. However, both laboratory experiments and a study of witnesses to actual crimes (Sloane 1981) indicate that hypnosis is no better than the waking state in producing useful leads. Recall tends to improve with repeated attempts, to some degree, even without hypnosis.

(3) The fact that hypnotized subjects often have a high degree of confidence in their recollections cannot be taken as proof of the accuracy of their reports. Independent verification of reports is needed.

(4) Both hypnotized and unhypnotized subjects often reply affirmatively to false leading questions during interrogation. Research evidence is not entirely clear on whether hypnotized subjects are more susceptible to leading questions than unhypnotized subjects. In any case, it is clear that there is no hypermnesia effect in hypnosis to counteract the tendency to comply with leading questions.

(5) Leading questions—either with or without hypnosis—can create pseudomemories that persist after hypnosis. Pseudomemories created during hypnosis are not necessarily more resistant to cross examination than those created without hypnosis. In any case, interrogation sessions should be videotaped so it can be determined whether leading questions were asked.

There is a special risk in allowing the use of "hypnotically refreshed" testimony in court. Because of popular myths about hypnosis, jurors may give hypnotic testimony more credibility than it deserves, particularly when hypnotized witnesses show strong confidence in their reports. Thus, claims based on hypnotic interrogations alone should not be allowed.

In concluding that research evidence is largely against the validity of hypnotic hypermnesia, certain limitations of the laboratory experiments must be acknowledged. Some laboratory studies have used memory testing materials, such as word lists and photographs, that are far different from the type of information that is important in forensic or psychotherapy situations. Other studies have achieved a degree of ecological validity by using dramatic films or live simulated crimes (Wagstaff, Traverse, & Milner 1982). But for obvious ethical reasons, laboratory studies cannot duplicate the emotional upheaval that often accompanies violent crimes and other traumatic personal events. Conceivably, hypnosis might be particularly helpful for enhancing retrieval of memories in such cases, though there is no proof that this is the case. Even if hypnosis was helpful in such cases, the reports would likely include many errors and confabulations. (See Laurence and Perry [1988] for more information on forensic applications of hypnosis, including discussion of case studies.)

The reservations that apply to hypnotic recall in criminal investigations do not necessarily apply to psychotherapy. In psychotherapy the actual facts of earlier experiences may be less important than patients' *beliefs* about what happened. In some cases therapists have deliberately implanted benign pseudomemories to counteract the effects of anxiety-evoking memories or beliefs (Frankel 1988; Orne et al. 1988; Perry et al. 1988).

CONCLUDING COMMENTS ON HYPNOSIS

Hypnosis is interesting because it can produce unusual, sometimes dramatic subjective experiences, and it has important clinical applications. However, the theoretical conflict between the special-process and social-psychological approaches is sometimes confusing to students. These different approaches represent radically different *paradigms*, that is, different views of the basic nature of hypnosis that affect the questions that are asked, the way research is designed, and how the results are interpreted (Sheehan & Perry 1976).

The traditional view, dating back over 200 years to Mesmer, is that hypnosis involves some sort of special process, though ideas about the nature of the special process have changed over the years. Nowadays the special processes are framed in terms such as altered subjective states (Orne 1977), altered cognitive processes (Kihlstrom 1984, 1985b), or dissociations of cognitive subsystems (Hilgard 1977). A major criticism of special process theories is that they have never been developed in much detail, so it is hard to derive unique predictions that can be tested by research. The main research emphasis has been on demonstrating special effects of hypnosis, that is, showing that hypnotized subjects (hypnotized highs) respond differently than non-hypnotized subjects (lows, simulators, waking controls), and trying to discover the nature of the special underlying processes that are assumed to be responsible for the responses of hypnotized subjects.

The social-psychological approach argues that hypnosis does not involve any special processes, but rather involves ordinary processes of thinking, motivation, and behavior control operating in a special social situation identified as hypnosis (Barber 1969; Sarbin & Coe 1972; Spanos 1982, 1986a; Wagstaff 1981, 1986). The main research emphasis for social-psychological theorists has been to show that the behaviors of hypnotized subjects can be duplicated by nonhypnotized subjects that are given appropriate instructions for motivation, attitudes, beliefs, and effective cognitive strategies. Spanos has been concerned to show that social and cognitive variables affect subjective experiences and subjective reports, as well as overt responses to suggestions.

Spanos and others in the social-psychological camp have produced an impressive body of research in support of their view. However, criticisms of social-psychological interpretations of this research have been made. For example, Barber (1969) and Spanos (1986a) argued that, since the behavior (including subjective reports) of hypnotized subjects can often be duplicated by nonhypnotized subjects with appropriate motivation, cognitive strategies, and so forth, the underlying processes are identical. But this logic of equivalence is not necessarily valid (Sheehan & Perry 1976): while identical response is consistent with identical process, it does not prove identical process. Spanos, in attempting to explain everything in terms of his theory (strategic social enactment using voluntary strategies) is unprepared to allow for alternative explanations. Another criticism of Spanos is that he is not consistent in his treatment of subjects' introspective reports. Sometimes they are treated as behaviors influenced by the social context, whereby subjects try to present themselves as good hypnotic subjects; at other times they are deemed to be authentic reports of subjective experience (such as in Spanos's interpretation of trance logic as incomplete responses to suggestions)— whichever interpretation seems to best suit Spanos's theoretical viewpoint.

When researchers in different laboratories obtain different results in similar experiments (such as tests of the hidden observer effect), one possible explanation is that there are different demand characteristics in different laboratories. Experimenter beliefs, perhaps subtly and unintentionally communicated to subjects, can affect the way subjects respond, including their subjective reports (Perry et al. 1988).

Kihlstrom (1985a, 1985b) suggested that the special-process and social-psychological approaches have some important points of agreement, and that a rapprochement between them is possible, in principle. Special-process theorists do not deny that hypnotic responsiveness is influenced by social-behavioral processes such as motivation, attitudes, expectancies, and the desire to be a good hypnotic subject. "True, many of us do not typically manipulate social-psychological variables in our experiments. But this is not because we deny the importance of such variables. It is because we take their effects for granted and wish to determine what other processes may also be involved" (Kihlstrom 1986, p. 475). These special processes are assumed to be different from common everyday occurrences, though not necessarily unique to hypnosis. Yet hypnosis is a particularly good situation for engaging and studying these special processes.

Special-process theorists have sometimes suggested that the social-psychological approach can explain hypnotic responsiveness in low and moderately hypnotizable subjects and in those who fake their responses, but that some sort of special process is involved for hypnotic virtuosos—very highly hypnotizable subjects who respond strongly to the full range of hypnotic suggestions and experience their responses as nonvoluntary. But insofar as the social-psychological approach does not claim that hypnosis involves any special processes, it is the more conservative viewpoint. The burden of proof is on special-process theorists to demonstrate convincingly that hypnosis involves some sort of special processes of cognition, dissociation, or whatever.

An alternative approach to theoretical reconciliation is to analyze the different cognitive styles of different highly responsive subjects. For example, some subjects seem to react in a relatively passive way and experience their responses as nonvoluntary, whereas others use more active strategies to experience the suggestions. Future progress in understanding hypnosis is likely to depend on a more intensive examination of individual subjects, in order to understand how individuals with particular traits and skills respond to particular types of suggestions in particular social contexts (Sheehan & McConkey 1982).

Implications of hypnosis for consciousness.

The implications for understanding consciousness that one might draw from hypnosis research depends largely on one's theoretical interpretation of hypnosis. Hilgard's (1977) neodissociation theory and the hidden-observer effect are loosely consistent with modern cognitive psychological and neuropsychological theories that see the mind/brain system as made up of a number of specialized cognitive subsystems that are coordinated by an executive control system. In Hilgard's view, consciousness includes both control and monitoring processes. Hypnosis involves dissociations between specialized subsystems (perception, memory) and the executive control system, or between the control system and the monitoring system. Thus, hypnotic subjects can sometimes respond to stimuli without awareness, or with a feeling of nonvolition, as sometimes occurs in neuropsychological conditions with brain-damaged patients. Just as we have learned much about the normal mind/brain by studying its abnormal operations in psychopathology and brain-damaged patients, we can learn more about the mind/brain system by studying temporary alterations in hypnotized subjects in dissociative states. It should be pointed out, however, that while hidden-observer effects can be interpreted in terms of dissociations in a mind/brain system, the hidden-observer effect is not predicted by other systems theories, and alternative interpretations of the hidden observer effect would not discredit mind/brain system theories based on neuropsychological or other data.

From the social-cognitive viewpoint, hypnosis is a special case of the general rule that behavior and subjective experience are strongly affected by social contexts. Hypnotic inductions and suggestions are relatively benign manipulations: they do not change subjects' physical or cognitive abilities. Rather, they encourage and guide subjects to use the natural abilities of their own minds. Hypnotic inductions and suggestions can alter subjective experience (such as pain) by encouraging the use of cognitive strategies, such as imagination, redirection of attention, and reinterpretation of experiences. With appropriate procedures, these same abilities can be engaged to produce the same effects in nonhypnotic contexts, within the limits of individuals' capacities for imagination and attentional absorption.

In the hypnosis social context, suggestions can create response expectancies that in turn affect subjective experiences, such as the feeling of nonvolition of responses (Kirsch 1985). Feelings of nonvolition are encouraged by the passive wording of suggestions and the use of imagery strategies to bring about the suggested effects (Spanos, Rivers, & Ross 1977; Spanos & Katsanis 1989). What is changed in hypnosis is not so much the functioning of cognitive and behavioral control processes as subjective interpretations of control processes. In hypnosis, as in ordinary waking consciousness and dreaming, consciousness is—or results from—an interpretive process that attempts to bring coherence and consistency to our subjective experiences, including our behavior and social contexts as they relate to each other.

SUMMARY

Controlled research on age regression indicates that cognitive regression does not occur, though emotional regression may occur. Age regression seems to involve either a hallucination of being younger or a strategic social enactment. Incongruous behaviors during hypnosis were interpreted by Orne as evidence for trance logic—the acceptance of contradictory beliefs—which he believed to be characteristic of hypnotized subjects. Incongruous responses in age regression include incongruous writing (spelling big words correctly) and the duality experience (feeling that one is simultaneously a child and an adult), both responses being correlated with the hidden observer effect. Spanos argued that trance logic—including the duality and hidden observer effects—involves incomplete responses to suggestions. Simulator subjects are less likely than hypnotized subjects to show trance logic because simulators often overfake, since they are under strong pressure to appear to be excellent hypnotic subjects.

Claims of hypnotic hypermnesia (enhanced memory) have practical implications where hypnosis is used for eyewitness interrogation and psychotherapy. Experiments on hypermnesia have usually involved slide sequences or films of crimes, where subjects first recalled the events without hypnosis, then were tested again either with or without hypnosis. Controlled research indicates that hypnotic hypermnesia is not authentic, in the sense of enhanced accuracy of memory retrieval in hypnotized subjects compared to controls. Rather, hypnosis can increase the frequency of memory reports, but the reports will include many incorrect responses as well as, perhaps, a few correct ones. These findings can be explained in terms of signal detection theory: hypnosis lowers the response criterion, such that subjects are willing to report items that were previously withheld because of low confidence in their accuracy (or alternatively, hypnosis may increase subjects' confidence in the accuracy of their memories, without increasing actual accuracy).

Hypnosis may increase subjects' tendencies to agree to false leading questions during interrogation. Either with or without hypnosis, leading questions may create pseudomemories that persist afterward, where subjects cannot reliably distinguish between their memories of the original event and information suggested later during interrogation. Hypnotic testimony should not be taken at face value, because it is full of errors. However, some hypnotic recollections may be accurate, so hypnotic testimony may be a useful source of leads that police can check for verification.

ENDNOTES

[1]One question that was not addressed in Nash's research is whether high hypnotizables might be better than lows at play-acting childlike behavior, even without hypnosis or age regression suggestions. There is independent evidence that this might be the case (Troffer 1965, cited in Hilgard 1977, p. 57), though it has not been tested with Nash's procedure.

[2]In Nogrady et al.'s (1983) study, the absence of hidden-observer reports among the simulators is noteworthy, considering that Hilgard et al. (1978a) earlier had reported successful faking of the hidden observer effect by simulators. The different results of the two experiments is probably due to Nogrady et al. using a nonleading hidden observer suggestion that did not imply that the hidden part would feel more pain than the hypnotized part of consciousness.

[3]Note that Spanos (1986a) is making an important reinterpretation of the simulator control condition. The traditional interpretation has been that simulators and hypnotic reals have equivalent experimental demands, so any differences between reals' and simulators' responses cannot be explained in terms of compliance with experimental demands; differences might be due to altered cognitive processes in the reals (Orne 1959; Sheehan & Perry 1976). But in Spanos's view, simulators and hypnotic reals have *different* experimental demands, so differences in the responses of simulators and reals might, in fact, be due to differences in the experimental demands for the two groups. Another problem with the standard simulator control procedure is that the reals are high hypnotizables whereas the simulators are low hypnotizables. Thus, in some test situations (such as where vivid imagination is important) response differences between the two groups might be due to preexisting subject differences.

[4]Alternatively, rather than lowering the response criterion hypnosis might raise subjective confidence for all candidate items. The practical result would be the same: subjects would now report items (both correct and incorrect) previously unreported because of low confidence.

chapter 17 ••••••••••••••••••••••••••••••

Meditation

Meditation is a ritualistic procedure intended to change one's state of consciousness by means of maintained, voluntary shifts in attention. There are dozens of meditation techniques, but they all employ some means of shifting attention away from habitual modes of perception and thinking to enable people to perceive themselves and the world in a different way.

Meditation has been developed and practiced most extensively in connection with religious traditions, but these days in the Western world it is often practiced secularly. Meditation is done to achieve some benefit for the individual. But while applied hypnosis (another nondrug, ritualistic procedure) involves relatively specific, short-term goals for changes in behavior, thinking, and memory, the goals of meditation are of a more general and long-term nature, such as increased self-understanding and spiritual growth.

In this chapter you will learn how to meditate. I will discuss the aims of meditation and claims about its benefits, and research on its short-term and long-term effects. I will also discuss mystical states of consciousness, which some people have reached through meditation. Finally, I will consider the question whether a meditation-like state (the "alpha" state) can be achieved through biofeedback procedures.

AIMS OF MEDITATION

Why do people meditate? The goals of meditation mostly fall into two categories: religious and secular. The religious meditation tradition is at least

2500 years old, and it has included most religions, including Hinduism, Buddhism, early Judaism and Christianity, and Islam, as well as many minor or more localized religions (Goleman 1977; Ornstein 1977; West 1987a). The goals of religious meditation are defined somewhat differently for different religions, but in each case they relate to a central feature of the religion. In Christianity, for example, the anonymous author of a fourteenth-century work titled *The Cloud of Unknowing* wrote that the way to attain union with God is to strike down everyday thoughts by continuously repeating a simple word such as "God" or "love" (West 1987a). Prayer, an attempt to talk to God, may or may not be similar to meditation, depending upon whether it involves a "meditative mood" or a mere mechanical repetition in order to fulfill religious obligations (Carrington 1986).

Meditation is a central practice in Buddhism, as important as prayer in Christianity (Claxton 1987). One of the fundamental Buddhist ideas is that the world as we know it is an illusion, created by our habitual ways of separating and classifying and labeling our perceptual experiences. In Buddhist belief, much human unhappiness (such as embarrassment, guilt, anxiety, depression, jealousy, and self-doubt) stems from our way of perceiving reality through the filter of language and habitual modes of thought. Thus, Buddhists recommend meditation as a way of learning to break through habitual ways of perceiving by suppressing the tendency to categorize and label our experiences in our inner speech or thinking.[1] Meditators may ultimately reach a mystical state of "oneness" or "unity," where their sense of self as a separate entity is overcome and they are absorbed into God. The Buddhist meditation tradition has been characterized as Buddhist psychology, with meditation being both a means of achieving inner peace and a means of discovering how the mind works (Claxton 1987; West 1987a).

The secular meditation tradition, which is relatively new, includes the use of meditation to improve one's sense of well-being, for example, by gaining personal insight, increasing creativity, or coping with the stress of life's daily hassles and major transitions. Secular meditation may be a form of self-therapy, or part of a directed psychotherapy program (Carrington 1987; Shapiro 1980). Noncultish varieties of meditation have been devised for psychotherapy use, for example Clinically Standardized Meditation (CSM) (Carrington 1987).

The most widely used form of meditation in the Western world is Transcendental Meditation (TM), which was derived from Hindu yoga practices and first introduced in the United States in the 1960s by Maharishi Mahesh Yogi (1966; Goleman 1977). TM is based on the Maharishi's theory called the Science of Creative Intelligence. It is taught by the Maharishi's disciples for a fee. TM teachers have made wide-ranging, and sometimes excessive, claims for the benefits of TM, ranging from relaxation to increased mental efficiency and creativity to the attainment of mystical states. TM is, in a sense, in between the religious and the secular traditions, in that, though rather cultish, it is not tied to any established religious tradition and it can be practiced with either secular or spiritual goals in mind.

Several writers have emphasized the point that meditation is a path to knowledge of a personal nature (Goleman 1977; Ornstein 1977).

It seems that at the heart of each tradition, underneath all the various, and even conflicting, formulations, there is a remarkable consensus. Behind the mundane benefits that meditation can bring lies, if a person is willing to undertake it, a deep and very personal journey of enquiry—a 'journey beyond belief' as one meditator (Walsh 1983) has called it—into such profound and perennial questions as 'What is life?', 'What does it mean to be happy?', and, right at the bottom, 'Who—or what—am I?' (Claxton 1987, p. 24)

The meditation path to knowledge is empirical in the sense that it involves direct experience, and subjective in that the meditative state can be directly known only by the experiencer and it may be difficult or impossible to fully describe it in words (ineffable). Meditation stands in contrast to two other major modes of acquiring knowledge: scientific inquiry and reception from authority. Scientific inquiry is empirical and objective, in that its observations are in principle available to and verifiable by other individuals. Knowledge received from authority is nonempirical for the receiver; it is accepted on faith. The most deeply felt and influential knowledge is that gained from direct personal experience, and on some personal and spiritual issues the experience is necessarily of a subjective nature. Thus, meditation may be a path to some types of personal knowledge not available by other means.

TYPES OF MEDITATION TECHNIQUES

There are dozens of specific meditation techniques. Two broad categories of meditation techniques have been distinguished: concentration techniques, and "opening up" or mindfulness techniques (Goleman 1978; Ornstein 1977). The techniques differ in the way attention is deployed. Concentrative techniques restrict attention to a single image or object; mindfulness involves attending to everything in a fresh, nonhabitual way.

Concentrative Meditation

In all forms of concentrative meditation the immediate goal is to restrict attention to a single, unchanging stimulus or thought, in order to achieve what many traditions call "one-pointedness of mind" (Ornstein 1977). An immediate effect of successful concentration is the cessation of inner speech and narratization, the ongoing commentary on experience, memories, and personal concerns in which we often engage when our attention is not fully concentrated on some task at hand. As one TM teacher put it, "Meditation is a way to get that incessant 'roof-brain chatter' to shut up for awhile and give you some peace of mind." Deep meditation is a form of *trance*. The term trance has been used in a variety of ways, but its essence is a restricting of attention to one thing, so that the individual's response to distracting thoughts and stimuli is reduced or absent.

A variety of different objects or thoughts have been employed for concentrative meditation (Goleman 1977; Ornstein 1977). In Zen Buddhist meditation, a beginner's technique involves concentrating on breathing and counting the breaths, one to ten, and repeating. *Mantra* meditation uses special sounds or words that are repeated over and over, either aloud or silently as an auditory mental image. Mantra meditation is used in a number of traditions including Hindu yoga, Buddhism, and Judaism, and is the basis of the TM practice. Another yoga method is concentrating on a visual object, such as a candle flame, vase, waterfall, or *mandala* (a circular design, either simple or complex, often with symbolic significance). Visual mental images of such objects may also be used. *Mudra* meditation involves cyclic repetition of physical movements of arms, legs, or fingers. The mudra may be coordinated with a mantra. For example, touching of the thumb to each of the other four fingers, in turn, can be synchronized with each of the four words of the ancient mantra, "Om mani padme hum" (Ornstein 1977). Among the "whirling" dervishes of the Sufi sect of Islam, chanting is coordinated with whirling dancing movements of the body.[2] In Rinzai Zen the student may be asked to concentrate on a *koan*, a riddle or paradox that cannot be solved by logical thinking ("What is the sound of one hand clapping?" "What did your face look like before you were born?"). Continued concentration on the koan leads to frustration and finally the cessation of logical thinking and liberation from the forms imposed by language (Goleman 1977).

Concentrative meditation is usually practiced for a limited period of time on a regular schedule, once or twice a day. It is hard to concentrate perfectly, though concentration improves with practice. Paradoxically, some of the most important benefits of meditation occur during brief failures of concentration. *Thought intrusions* during meditation may offer profound insights into matters such as self-understanding, philosophical or religious beliefs, or creative solutions to problems in domains such as interpersonal relations, art, and science. However, such valuable thought intrusions cannot be forced. You do not start out deliberately "meditating on a problem." Insights may come once in a while, if you are mentally prepared. You must be patient. The immediate goal is merely to concentrate. According to a variety of traditions that use concentration, with practice people eventually reach an altered state characterized by a loss of sensory awareness, one-pointed attention to the meditation object to the exclusion of all other thoughts, and sublime blissful feelings. Several stages or levels of concentrative meditation states have been described in Buddhist literature (Brown 1977; Goleman 1977, 1978).

Mindfulness Meditation

In "opening-up" or mindfulness types of meditation, the method is virtually the opposite of that in concentrative meditation. Rather than limiting attention to one object or thought, the meditator tries to maintain full awareness of all conscious thoughts, actions, and perceptions. Full awareness is not natural. Normally we go through the day largely on "automatic pilot." We perform many routine actions through habit, without giving them much conscious thought, if any. For example, each weekday morning I get up and wash and shave, fix and eat breakfast, and drive to work on autopilot, with thoughts on other matters such as the things I need to do at work. We also don't give much attention to our routine thoughts and perceptions. For example, you might drive a certain road to school or work dozens of times without being able to recall many of the details of things that you see or the exact sequence in which they are encountered.

Opening-up types of meditation are particularly characteristic of advanced Zen Buddhist practices. (In the Zen Buddhist tradition, meditation is called "zazen.") In Soto Zen, in the *shikan-taza* ("just sitting") method, the individual just sits, not thinking of a mandala or breathing, but maintaining alertness and a passive receptivity, being fully aware of every thought and stimulus that enters consciousness, but without making any comment or emotional reaction. Shikan-taza is often practiced with the eyes open, facing a blank wall. It is a form of introspection, believed by Zen practitioners to be a way to notice the difference between mental contents and mental processes and so to discover how the mind works (Claxton 1987). Another Zen practice, "right-mindedness," makes meditation a continuous aspect of daily life. It requires that one maintain full awareness of one's actions, rather than performing them habitually and mindlessly. For example, one should be fully aware of one's movements and perceptions in activities such as washing, eating, and routine tasks at work.[3]

In mindfulness types of meditation the goal is to break through our habits of automatic perception, thought, and action, to "deautomatize" our experience so we can be more fully aware of it (Ornstein 1977). One takes a *receptive* attitude to experience, rather than a *reactive* attitude. If we can deautomatize our perceptions, perceiving each thing as if for the first time, then presumably we should be able to learn to break through the tendency to react to things (people, self, problems) according to habitual categories and assumptions (Ornstein 1977). Eventually, through mindfulness practice the meditator learns to distinguish between mind and the mind's objects and observe the workings of the mind itself, according to Buddhist psychology (Goleman 1978). According to Buddhist tradition, through mindfulness practice the meditator can journey through several stages of *insight*, including increasingly finer perception of the mind's workings, detachment from the mind and its objects, and a focus on the present moment. Ultimately a mystical state of *nirvana* may be reached, in which consciousness is empty with no awareness of sensations or thoughts (Goleman 1978).[4]

The differences in the techniques of concentrative versus mindfulness meditation are great enough that one would expect different subjective effects from each type of practice. Such differences have been noted by individuals who are highly practiced in each type, and they have been described in Buddhist literature (Goleman 1977). However, there has been little comparative research from a scientific approach. Most of the research has been concerned with concentrative meditation, for two reasons: first, concentrative meditation is a simpler, more uniform practice than mindfulness meditation, so less variability of results would be expected, along with easier theoretical interpretation; and second, when researchers need experienced meditators for subjects, people experienced with concentrative meditation (especially TM) are easier to find than mindfulness meditators in the United States. In the discussion of meditation effects it may be assumed that I am talking about concentrative meditation, unless explicitly stated otherwise.

HOW TO MEDITATE

Based on my experience and that of other meditators from whom I have learned by talking or reading, I offer the following practical advice on concentrative meditation technique for beginners (see also Goleman 1977; Shapiro 1980; West 1987a).

(1) *Body position.* The position or posture of your body is important, because you need to be relaxed, but not so much that you fall asleep. Try sitting on a firm, straight-backed chair; sit near the front of the seat (don't lean against the backrest). Keep your back straight (don't slouch) and rest both feet on the floor (don't cross your legs); rest your hands on your thighs. Alternatively, try sitting on the floor cross-legged, in the lotus position, if you find it comfortable. Breathe in a normal, relaxed way; don't force yourself to breathe in an abnormally deep or shallow manner. Close your eyes.

(2) *Concentration object.* The two most widely used methods are mantra meditation and breath-counting. I suggest that you try each method initially, then choose the one that you like best and stick with it until you become highly practiced with it.

Mantra meditation: Choose a simple word or sound that you like. The best mantras are sonorous, flowing words that can be repeated easily, for example, "Om." The exact sound or meaning of the mantra is probably not very important. In the East, one of the most commonly used mantras is "Om Mane Padme Um" (a translation: "The jewel in the center of the Lotus"). Repeat the mantra over and over throughout the meditation period. Say it slowly enough that you clearly pronounce each syllable. Mantra meditation is usually done silently, but if you can find a private place you might try saying it out loud.

Breath-counting: While you are breathing in a normal, relaxed manner, pay attention to the feeling of movement of the air as it goes in and out. With each exhalation count to yourself "one," then "two," and so on until you reach ten, then start over. Do not try to count the total number of exhalations in the session; that isn't the point. Just concentrate on your breathing, and count exhalations in cycles of ten. That's all.

(3) *Duration and frequency.* According to TM teachers, you should meditate for two twenty-minute sessions each day. I suggest that you begin with ten-minute sessions and gradually work up to fifteen or twenty minutes. Try to be very consistent about meditating every day, at least once, preferably twice.

(4) *Time and place.* Though physically relaxed, you want to be awake and mentally alert during meditation. TM teachers recommend meditating before breakfast and before supper. It is best not to meditate just after a meal, since you may get sleepy at that time. (Alcohol will make the sleepiness problem even worse.) Choose a quiet, private place where you won't be interrupted. To maintain alertness, avoid a room that is too warm. For a new experience, experiment with meditating in a natural place such as a forest, mountaintop, or the seashore.

(5) *Starting and finishing.* It may be hard to suddenly shift gears from an active, externally oriented mode to a more relaxed, internally oriented mode. So begin each session by taking a minute or two to sit quietly and relax

before you close your eyes and begin to actually meditate. At the end of the session, open your eyes and look around, but stay relaxed for a while before you get up. Your chances of maintaining a meditative mood for a while after the session will be increased if you make a gradual transition to normal activity. (Some people sometimes feel dizzy if they abruptly stand up and walk away after meditating.)

(6) *Motivation and attitude.* Using a meditation technique does not guarantee that you will enter a meditative state of consciousness. Meditation takes practice, and some people do it more easily than others. Many beginning meditators quit after a few sessions because they have difficulty concentrating and nothing dramatic happens. It is important to approach meditation with an attitude of patience, thinking of it as a skill that develops with practice. The benefits of meditation are usually subtle, not dramatic. And as with most activities of life, there will be good days and there will be bad days. I ask my students to try meditation for at least thirty days, since many people find that it takes a couple of weeks or more before they begin to feel comfortable meditating and notice some interesting effects.

Your attitude toward failures of concentration is especially important. Beginners are often highly concerned with following the prescribed technique, and they may become frustrated over failures of concentration (thought intrusions). Don't berate yourself for lapses of concentration. When a thought "bubble" floats up into consciousness, don't grasp at it, but just let it float on through, out of consciousness, and go back to concentrating on your meditation object. With practice the thought intrusions will become less frequent, though they will never stop altogether, except perhaps for a minute or so at a time. And bear in mind that the thought intrusions will sometimes contain worthwhile personal insights.

EFFECTS OF MEDITATION: A CASE STUDY

A wide variety of beneficial effects of meditation have been claimed by TM teachers and others. The list includes reduction of anxiety and stress and stress-related illnesses, increased alertness and ability to control attention, improvement in sleep, control of drug and alcohol abuse, greater self-understanding and self-acceptance, more inner independence, positive mood changes, improved interpersonal relationships, and transcendent or mystical experiences. In a later section I will discuss scientific research that tested some of these claims. For now it is worth noting that most of the claimed effects of meditation had their origin in individuals' reports on their meditation experiences.

One limitation of individual case studies is that different people may report different meditation experiences, depending on the particular technique that they used, the amount of practice, and their unique set of personal characteristics (such as personality and cognitive traits, attitudes, beliefs, and expectations). To the extent that an individual is atypical, his or her results may not predict the effects of meditation for typical people, or for you. Nonetheless, case studies are valuable for showing *possible* effects of meditation practice.

Tart's report.　The following is a summary of a report by Charles Tart (1972d) following a year of daily practice of TM. I like his report because Tart is an experimental psychologist who was skeptical at first about the possibility of TM having any beneficial effects. Tart is only slightly hypnotizable, and does not slide easily into hypnosis or spontaneous altered states. Thus, the effects reported by Tart are probably rather conservative claims for TM effects, in contrast to the exaggerated claims sometimes made by TM teachers.

(1) *No "bliss consciousness."* Tart's TM teacher had claimed that diligent TM practice would lead to transcendental or "bliss consciousness," an ecstatic state in which one loses all sense of self and experiences a joyful, oceanic feeling. Tart never reached bliss consciousness, though he did feel rather joyful at times.

(2) *"Psychic lubricant."* A second claim by the TM teacher was a sort of "psychic lubricant" effect (Tart's term). This refers to a tendency to have thoughts during meditation about personally meaningful events that were not sufficiently processed at the time of the original event. For example, a friend's subtle remark in a conversation might have gone unnoticed at the time, but during meditation you might become aware of the remark and its implications. Tart reported that he experienced such psychic lubricant effects to a considerable degree. During the first few months of meditation the recalled events were typically days, months, or even years old. But over time he worked through most of the old material so that the thoughts were more about events of the last day. Tart noted that the recalled events were not truly repressed; they were simply events that he hadn't thought about enough to realize their significant implications. Note that such thoughts during meditation are *intrusive thoughts*, in that they represent a failure of concentration on the mantra, but nonetheless they are a potential benefit of meditation.

(3) *Loss of desire for alcohol.* Tart had been in the habit of having a glass or two of wine each evening after work. But he found that he could not meditate effectively for a period of two or three hours after drinking alcohol. "As soon as I turned my attention inward to meditate, it was clear that my intellect was *very* dull, that my mind was wandering from subject to subject, like a man terribly drunk lurching down the street and hardly being aware of his environment" (p. 138). Meditation made him more aware of the negative effects of alcohol, reducing both his enjoyment of alcohol and his pleasure in meditation. Consequently he stopped his daily alcohol habit.

(4) *Mental quiet.* As a result of meditation practice, Tart learned to reach a state of mental quiet, where he could stop thinking for fifteen to twenty seconds at a time, while still being alert to incoming stimuli.

(5) *Reduced tension.* Tart felt that as a result of meditation practice he became a calmer, more relaxed person. "I feel more sensitive to my inner processes, and generally do not get as wound up in my daily activities" (p. 139).

(6) *Need to meditate.* Meditation became a habit with Tart, such that if something prevented him from meditating he felt "slightly jangled and excited" and anxious to sit down and meditate to relax and "let any partially processed material come out."

(7) *Concern with technique.* Initially, like most beginners, Tart was very

concerned with meditating correctly. But after a while he learned to accept the fact that he could not concentrate perfectly, and would always be subject to distractions. Thus he became less obsessed with correct technique: when he realized that he was distracted, he simply returned to the mantra.

(8) *Resistance to cold.* Tart meditated in a room that frequently got very cool (50–60°F). He noted that he didn't feel chilly while meditating, though he started feeling chilly soon afterward. He speculated that the cold-resistance effect might have something to do with a physiological effect of meditation; alternatively, it might be a result of inward attentional focus during meditation.

Tart's report is noteworthy because he found meditation to be worthwhile and enjoyable, even though he could not concentrate perfectly on the mantra, and even though he never reached the mystical state of bliss consciousness. (For other individual case reports see Shapiro [1980], who discussed his own experiences and those of other individuals, including clinical case studies.)

Limitations of case studies.

As valuable as they may be for revealing possible meditation effects, individual case studies have several limitations: (1) Meditation experiences vary widely, and the individual making the report may be atypical. (2) In case studies the effects of meditation are usually assessed in an unsystematic manner, such as a personal diary, so the data cannot be readily compared with other cases or group studies, and some important questions may have been overlooked. (3) In case studies it is impossible to distinguish between the effects of meditation practice *per se* and effects due to uncontrolled variables, such as the individual's expectations about meditation's effects, and life-style changes that may accompany long-term meditation practice, such as more time spent relaxing. Thus, while case studies can reveal possible meditation effects and serve as sources of research hypotheses, it is important to do group studies under controlled conditions in order to get firmer evidence on the effects of meditation.

EFFECTS OF MEDITATION: SYSTEMATIC RESEARCH

Some of the claimed effects of meditation were supported by the results of early research on meditation, and the Transcendental Meditation organization, which teaches TM for a fee, has cited that research in its advertising publications (for example, Maharishi International University 1974). However, much of the research on meditation has flaws in design and procedure, such that conclusions drawn from it are questionable. Meditation, by its nature, presents some special research difficulties. I will discuss several of the claims about meditation effects, including phenomenological (subjective experience) effects, and effects on brain waves, physiological arousal, and anxiety. In asking about the effects of meditation, we must also consider problems of doing good meditation research to find out its effects. The answers are only as good as the research methods.

Researchers have asked about the effects of meditation in several time frames: (1) immediate *state effects,* that is, what happens during meditation *per se*; (2) *short-term aftereffects* of meditation that may last for a few minutes or hours after the meditation session; and (3) *trait effects*, that is, long-term changes in the individual's personality or cognitive traits, attitudes or behavior, as a result of meditation practice.

One of the problems of meditation research is to establish suitable control conditions for comparison. Another problem is that it may take a lot of practice for some subjects to learn to enter a meditative state of consciousness. Solutions to the problems of control and practice may differ, depending on the particular effects being studied and the time frame that is of interest.

Phenomenological Effects of Meditation

In asking about the phenomenological effects of meditation, we are concerned with subjective experiences during meditation practice. A variety of claims have been made by experienced meditators, such as mental calmness, physical relaxation, altered time sense, altered visual and auditory perception, feelings of floating, altered body sensations, insights into interpersonal relationships, creative ideas, and mystical experiences (Carrington 1986; West 1980b). But what does the systematic research show?

Pekala (1987) reviewed a number of studies of the phenomenology of meditation, including single case studies, studies involving meditation groups only, and studies comparing meditation groups with nonmeditation control groups or groups using alternative procedures. In the group studies some sort of subjective experience questionnaire was used in order to get a quantitative estimate of meditation effects.

Pekala evaluated the studies in terms of the adequacy of the subjective experience assessment and the adequacy of the experimental design. Good subjective experience questionnaires should be comprehensive (measure all effects that might occur), have demonstrated reliability (test-retest stability), and have demonstrated validity (be able to distinguish between alternate states of consciousness). Regarding experimental designs, ideally there should be comparisons between meditating experienced meditators and a nonmeditation condition, though it is somewhat controversial whether the best comparison condition is resting nonmeditators or experienced meditators who are resting but not meditating. Ideally there should be controls both for subjects' prior beliefs and expectations about meditation's effects and for experimental demands (situational cues that reveal the researcher's expectations to the subjects).

All of the studies reviewed by Pekala had one or more flaws in assessment or controls. In addition, some of the studies with the best experimental controls had the flaw of using subjects with little or no meditation experience. Under these conditions it is impossible to draw firm conclusions about the phenomenological effects of meditation. The only fairly consistent finding across studies was increased relaxation during meditation. *Variability* of effects is the rule. Different subjects show different responses to meditation. For example, in a questionnaire study of experienced TM meditators, West (1980b) found more than a dozen types of subjective experiences, but none of them were reported by a majority of subjects. The subjective effects reported by experienced meditators show the *possibilities* for meditation effects. But the particular effects experienced by an individual will vary depending on such factors as his or her personality and cognitive traits (such as ability to focus attention), prior attitudes, beliefs, and expectations about meditation's effects, duration of practice, and the particular meditation technique that is used.

Attention control during meditation.   Good concentration during meditation means focusing your attention steadily on the mantra and avoiding distracting thought intrusions. Van Nuys (1973) devised an event-recording method of measuring thought intrusions during meditation by having subjects hold an electronic push-button device in their lap while meditating. Subjects were instructed that whenever they became aware of an intruding thought, they should push the button, then return to concentrating on the mantra. He found that better attention during meditation (fewer button-pushes) was reliably correlated with hypnotic susceptibility scores: more highly hypnotizable subjects concentrated better during meditation and had fewer thought intrusions than less hypnotizable subjects.

Kubose (1976) used the push-button method to measure intrusions in beginning meditators over their first ten fifteen-minute meditation sessions. He found that, within sessions, the mean number of intrusions increased from the first to the second to the third five-minute interval. This confirms the informal observations of many beginners that it gets harder and harder to maintain concentration as the session continues. Also, Kubose found that the number of intrusions decreased as training continued. Thus, concentration improved during the first ten sessions of meditation practice. (The practice effect was greatest for the last five-minute interval.) In other studies with the push-button method, thought intrusions occurred less often in experienced meditators (six months or more of practice) than in non-meditators (Spanos et al. 1979b) and less often in more highly motivated beginner meditators than in less motivated beginners (Spanos et al. 1980c).

The event-recording (push-button) method is a quasi-objective way to measure concentration during meditation. However, Spanos et al. (1980c) found no correlation between this measure and self-ratings of "nonanalytic attending" during meditation, and it is uncertain which measure is more valid. Nor is it clear how much the button-push method interferes with meditating, or how much its results are influenced by demand characteristics of the situation. Nonetheless, since no single method of assessing consciousness is perfect, it is worthwhile to try different methods to see whether they yield useful data.

Effects on Physiological Arousal

In the early years of scientific research on meditation, considerable interest was generated by demonstrations of brain wave changes and reductions in physiological arousal during meditation (Wallace 1970, 1977; Wallace & Benson 1972). These findings were important for two reasons. First, they suggested that meditation could be useful as a therapeutic technique for reducing physiological stress reactions. Second, they gave meditation a new scientific respectability. Scientists, including experimental psychologists, have long been skeptical of introspective reports, including reports of altered states of consciousness during meditation. But physiological responses provide objective evidence that something happens during meditation.

Robert K. Wallace and Herbert Benson (1972) used experienced TM meditators and measured physiological responses while subjects were sitting quietly during three twenty-minute periods: before, during, and after meditation. Thus, each subject served as his or her own control in the before and after periods. The results indicated that during meditation there were significant physiological changes, including reduced respiration rate and volume of air breathed, reduced oxygen consumption and carbon dioxide elimination, and reduced blood lactate. All of these changes suggest that meditation is a hypometabolic state, with reduced energy metabolism. In addition, heart rate and the skin's electrical conductance decreased, suggesting reduced autonomic nervous system arousal, and alpha brain waves increased, suggesting reduced cortical arousal. The physiological changes were greater during meditation than during hypnosis.

The physiological data show clearly that meditation reduces physiological arousal, compared to a premeditation resting period. These results were widely publicized by the Transcendental Meditation organization in their advertising. And in his book *The Relaxation Response*, Benson (1975) recommended a meditation procedure to reduce physiological stress reactions.

However, David Holmes (Holmes et al. 1983) asked whether physiological arousal is reduced more by meditation than by just resting. This question is important for two reasons: It has theoretical implications, since it has been claimed that the meditation practice (mantra concentration) *per se* has physiological effects, and practical implications, since there would be no point in making the effort of meditating if equivalent effects could be produced by the easier method of simply resting. Holmes et al. used a between-groups design to compare meditation with resting.[5] The meditators were highly practiced at TM (mean seven years), while the control subjects had never learned meditation. Physiological measures were taken during three time intervals: (1) relaxed pretest interval, where subjects merely sat quietly; (2) treatment interval, where the meditation group practiced TM and the control group sat quietly and attempted to rest as much as possible; and (3) relaxed recovery interval. The result was that, from the pretest interval to the treatment interval, meditators showed decreased physiological arousal in their heart rate and breathing and also increased subjective relaxation. However, the comparison between groups showed that physiological and subjective changes were no greater for TM than for just resting. This result suggests that reduced arousal during meditation is due to its rest-relaxation aspects and does not depend on the specific meditation practice (such as mantra concentration) *per se*.

Holmes (1987) reviewed numerous studies on this issue and concluded that while meditation can reduce physiological arousal and increase subjective relaxation while meditation is in progress, it is not superior to other relaxation techniques, such as simply resting, in this regard. He also reviewed studies on the question of whether meditation practice could reduce physiological responses to stressful activities, such as public speaking and viewing horrifying films of industrial accidents, carried out after meditating. He concluded that controlled experiments provide no convincing evidence that meditation reduces physiological reactions to stressful activities.

Brain-Wave Changes

Increased alpha waves. No meditation research has aroused as much excitement as the discovery of brain-wave changes during meditation (reviewed by Fenwick 1987; Pagano & Warrenburg 1983; West 1980a). Bagchi and Wenger (1957) and Anand, Chhina, and Singh (1961) measured EEG in highly experienced yoga meditators before and during *samadhi* (concentrative meditation) practice. They found that alpha EEG (8–13 Hz) increased during meditation. Kasamatsu and Hirai (1966) studied EEG responses in Japanese priests who were highly experienced in mindfulness meditation. Four levels of EEG response during meditation were distinguished: (1) alpha with eyes open (comparable to the usual alpha during relaxation with eyes closed); (2) increased alpha amplitude; (3) decreased alpha frequency (in Hz); and (4) occasional runs of theta waves (6–7 Hz). Subjects tended to reach higher levels of EEG response as the meditation session progressed, but some subjects reached higher levels than others. The level of EEG response reached was correlated with the amount of meditation practice (from one to more than twenty years) and even better correlated with the degree of progress on the Zen pathway, as rated by the subjects' Zen master teacher. Several more recent studies, using experienced TM meditators, have found increased alpha EEG (increased percent time alpha and/or increased alpha amplitude) during meditation, and some have found theta waves during meditation (review in Fenwick 1987). These EEG findings indicate that cortical arousal is decreased in the meditative state, this decrease presumably being associated with decreased cognitive processing.

Alpha blocking. When novel or unexpected stimuli are presented to relaxed subjects, they normally show an *orienting response* (OR). The OR has several physiological correlates, including *alpha blocking* (blocking of EEG alpha waves for a few seconds) and increased skin conductance (as in emotional reactions). The OR normally *habituates* (decreases) with repeated presentations of a meaningless novel stimulus. Early studies showed an interesting contrast in alpha blocking responses between highly practiced yoga (concentrative) and Zen (mindfulness) meditators. When stimuli such as loud noises and flashing lights were presented during meditation, yoga meditators showed little or no alpha blocking, though they showed the normal alpha-blocking response while just resting without meditating (Anand et al. 1961; Bagchi & Wenger 1957). This result supports the claim that concentrative attention reduces attention to external stimuli. In contrast, when click noises were presented to Zen monks during meditation, they showed the normal alpha blocking response, but surprisingly, alpha blocking did not habituate with repeated stimulation (Kasamatsu & Hirai 1966). This result supports the claim that during mindfulness meditation attention to all stimuli is maintained, as if each event was being perceived for the first time.

Unfortunately, the early findings on alpha blocking during meditation have not been successfully replicated. Becker and Shapiro (1981) compared alpha blocking responses in five groups of subjects: highly experienced meditators in the Zen, yoga, and TM traditions, as well as control subjects told to either attend to or ignore the stimuli. The stimuli were auditory clicks, which were presented periodically through headphones while the subjects were meditating or resting. All subjects showed alpha blocking to the initial click presentations, including those highly practiced in concentrative meditation (yoga and TM subjects with five to seven years of practice); there were no differences between the five groups. All subjects also showed habituation of the alpha-blocking response (with the response being eliminated by the twenty-fifth trial), including subjects practicing Zen Shikan Taza (mindfulness) meditation; there were no differences between the groups. The same results were found for skin conductance: the conductance-increase response was elicited by early clicks, and the response habituated with repeated click presentations. The authors concluded that earlier conceptualizations of meditation in terms of voluntary attention shifting do not apply to the orienting response to novel stimuli. Apparently, voluntarily turning attention inward during concentrative meditation does not prevent the orienting response from being automatically elicited by a novel external stimulus, nor does mindfulness meditation prevent habituation of the orienting response to a novel stimulus. Before accepting this conclusion as the final word, however, it would be worthwhile to repeat this research using different types of external stimuli. Clicks presented through headphones would seem to be highly intrusive and unnatural, and perhaps more common or natural sounds (voices, music, bird songs, household sounds) would yield different results. Furthermore, there has been no systematic study of subjective reactions to external stimuli during meditation and how they relate to physiological reactions.

Meditation and sleep.   The question has been raised whether deep meditation is simply a sleep onset (hypnagogic) state, in view of the theta waves that occur both in deep meditation and in Stage 1 sleep (Fenwick 1987; Pagano & Warrenburg 1983; West 1980a). Several studies have shown that meditators spend an average of about 20 percent of their meditation time in NREM sleep Stage 1 and about 20 percent in Stage 2. Thus, people sometimes become drowsy and fall asleep during meditation, particularly if they were tired at the start of the meditation session (Pagano & Warrenburg 1983). However, experienced meditators can maintain a relaxed wakefulness most of the time while meditating. Compared to control subjects who are just resting, meditators are often better able to resist falling asleep.

In one study (Fenwick et al. 1977), meditators whose EEG showed them to be in the hypnagogic (Stage 1) or sleep (Stage 2) state subsequently insisted that they had been awake and meditating. Were they really asleep? Different investigators have different opinions about whether the EEG data or the subjective reports should be taken more seriously. Conceivably, the subjective experience correlates of EEG patterns are different for meditation and the hypnagogic or sleep states. For example, hypnagogic hallucinations do not typically occur in the meditative state.

Pagano and Warrenburg (1983) compared EEG responses to a brief tone stimulus during meditation and napping. When the tone was presented during Stage 2 EEG, the response (a K-complex) was identical during meditation and napping. However, in Stage 1 the response (a shift from fast EEG to slower alpha waves) was greater during napping than during meditation. This result suggests that EEG Stage 1 is not psychologically equivalent for meditation and napping.

Furthermore, a detailed comparison of the overall EEG frequency profiles (relative amounts of different EEG wave frequencies) during meditation and napping shows that while the meditation EEG is on a continuum between waking and drowsiness, it is quite different from sleep Stages 1 and 2 (Fenwick 1987; Fenwick et al. 1977; Stigsby, Rodenberg, & Moth 1981). Thus, though people sometimes fall asleep while meditating, the meditation state is not the same as a light sleep state.

Hemispheric shifts.   Ornstein (1977) suggested that meditation involves a shift from left-hemisphere dominance to right-hemisphere dominance, since it involves a decrease of verbal-analytic thinking and an increase in intuition and holistic perception (functions associated with the left and right cerebral hemispheres, respectively, in his view). The implication is that the EEG spectrum should show a bilateral shift during meditation, with a decrease in left-hemisphere activity (increased alpha waves) and an increase in right-hemisphere activity (decreased alpha). Several studies on this issue do not provide clear support for this hypothesis. In the early stages of meditation, shifts in EEG hemispheric symmetry sometimes occur; they can be attributed to shifts in the direction of attention with certain meditation techniques, for example, with decreased verbal thinking and increased mental imagery. However, in advanced stages of meditation there is a general decrease in cortical activation (increased alpha and theta waves) without, however, a shift in EEG hemispheric symmetry (review by Earle 1984).

Conclusion.   The clearest finding of the EEG research is an increase in the production of alpha waves, and sometimes theta waves, during meditation compared to premeditation baseline measurements. An increase in alpha waves also occurs during relaxation with the eyes closed, though with eyes open alpha is greater during meditation than resting. Increased alpha EEG indicates decreased cortical arousal, reflecting decreased cortical information processing during meditation. The TM organization has cited the EEG results in its advertising, suggesting that the EEG data prove the effectiveness of meditation. It should be pointed out that there is no known benefit of EEG alpha waves *per se*, though under some conditions they are a correlate of beneficial relaxation responses (Benson 1975). (In a later section I will discuss the possibility that alpha-wave biofeedback training can produce a meditative subjective state.)

The studies comparing EEG in meditation and napping should remind us that an altered state of consciousness cannot be defined simply in terms of its induction method. In other words, people who sit down to meditate might enter a meditative state, they might enter the hypnagogic state or fall asleep, or they might remain wide awake and restless. Nor can one necessarily infer backward from the objective EEG pattern to identify the subjective state of consciousness, at least as far as typical waking, relaxed, and Stage 1 EEG profiles are concerned. This is not to doubt that subjective state differences correspond to underlying neurophysiological state differences, but the EEG is a rather crude measure of brain activity. In order to do research on altered states of consciousness, we must rely on introspective reports. Physiological measures are useful, but they are not sufficient.

LONG-TERM (TRAIT) EFFECTS OF MEDITATION

Many people have reported that meditation has had beneficial long-term effects for them. That is, it has had long-term effects on their personality or abilities that continued outside of meditation practice sessions (trait effects). For example, reduced anxiety and stress reactions, reduced depression, and improved intellectual performance have been claimed. If these claims are valid, there are important implications for the use of meditation in psychotherapy. Unfortunately, much of the research on long-term effects is flawed, and the better controlled research has often failed to support the claims.

Meditation Research Designs and Their Problems

Jonathan C. Smith (1975, 1976) reviewed the methods and problems of research on trait effects of meditation, particularly in regard to anxiety reduction. One problem concerns the necessity of using experienced, well-practiced meditators, since any long-term (trait change) effects of meditation would be expected to depend on extended meditation practice. Another problem is choosing an appropriate control condition against which to assess possible effects of meditation.

In some studies questionnaires about effects of meditation were given to experienced, self-selected meditators (that is, people who decided on their own to meditate, such as people who paid to learn TM and subsequently practiced if for several months or years). The questionnaire method has several flaws: (1) *Inaccurate memory.* It requires subjects to recall the traits (anxiety symptoms and so forth) that they had before they started meditation (perhaps a year or more in the past), and compare them with their current traits. Such recall from long-term memory may be inaccurate even under the best conditions. (2) *Expectancy or placebo effects.* People who choose to meditate expect it to have certain effects, and their expectations could have effects of their own, independent of any effects of meditation practice *per se.* (3) *Cognitive dissonance effects.* Cognitive dissonance is a feeling of subjective discomfort that people feel when they realize that their behavior and their beliefs are incompatible. As a result of dissonance, people may change their beliefs. For example, you would probably feel dissonance if you had practiced meditation for many months and you had obtained no benefits whatsoever. The result might be that you would believe and report that you had achieved some sort of benefit, however imaginary it might be. Thus, though questionnaire studies support the claim that meditation reduces anxiety, the questionnaire method is inadequate to prove this effect.

Some studies have compared self-selected meditators with a control group of nonmeditators. For example, Davidson et al. (1976) compared groups of nonmeditators, beginning meditators (less than one month of practice), short-term meditators (one to twenty-four months practice), and long-term meditators (over two years practice). They found that increased meditation practice was correlated with decreased anxiety trait scores and increased scores on the Absorption Scale (a measure of the tendency to become attentionally absorbed in imaginative and aesthetic experiences). However, correlational research cannot prove cause-and-effect relationships. Differences between meditators and nonmeditators, or between short-term and long-term meditators, might be due to preexisting differences between the groups, rather than to meditation practice *per se*. For example, in Davidson et al.'s study, higher absorption scores in longer-term meditators might indicate a preexisting trait that enabled them to derive more enjoyment from meditating, thus increasing the likelihood that they would continue meditating. Self-selection studies can be improved by comparing pretest scores on traits of interest (anxiety and so forth) with posttest scores collected after several months of meditation practice. But the lack of random assignment of subjects to conditions still makes interpretation difficult. Also, expectancy and cognitive dissonance effects for meditators can confound this sort of research.

In order to draw convincing conclusions about long-term effects of meditation, it is best to do a true experiment where subjects are randomly assigned to meditation and control conditions. The procedure involves several steps: (1) using only subjects previously inexperienced at meditation, pretest all subjects on the critical measure (such as anxiety); (2) randomly assign subjects to meditation and control groups; (3) train the meditation group subjects to meditate, and ask them to meditate regularly for several months; (4) call back all subjects, both meditation and control, for a posttest on the critical measure; and (5) compare *change scores* between the two groups, to see whether the meditation group changed more than the control group on the critical measure.

The dropout problem. Though a random-assignment experimental design is good in principle, there is a problem with dropouts in the meditation group. Perhaps due to frustration stemming from difficulties in meditating correctly, or boredom from failure to experience any dramatic effects, many beginning meditators quit meditating within a few days or weeks. Thus, there is a serious problem: meditation effects such as anxiety reduction would be expected to be greater, the longer meditation is practiced, but the longer it is practiced, the more dropouts there will be. For example, in an experiment with a six-month TM practice period, some 59 percent of the meditation group subjects dropped out, compared to only 13 percent of the control (no-treatment) subjects (Smith 1976). Unfortunately, the preexisting characteristics of the dropouts may be different from those of subjects who continue meditating. For example, Smith (1978) found that TM dropouts were more psychologically disturbed and less self-critical than those who continued meditating. West (1980b) found a 43 percent dropout rate among people who had paid to learn TM; reported neurotic symptoms were higher among the dropouts than among those who continued meditating. Thus, the dropout problem works against the random assignment of subjects to meditation and control groups, making it hard to draw firm conclusions about the effects of meditation practice.

Expectancy effects and anxiety reduction.

Smith (1976) pointed out another limitation of experimental designs with a no-treatment control group. Such designs do not control for possible expectancy effects in the meditation condition, nor do they control for possible effects of periodic daily relaxation. Thus, it is uncertain whether anxiety reductions in the meditation group are really due to the effects of meditation practice *per se*. In an improved study, Smith recruited volunteers for free anxiety-reduction treatments, gave them pretests on anxiety (questionnaires on mental and physical symptoms of anxiety), and randomly assigned subjects to a TM training group, a no-treatment control group, and a special control group called PSI (Periodic Somatic Inactivity). The TM subjects were taught standard TM techniques by two certified TM teachers, who gave the usual lectures on TM theory and supporting research. PSI was a placebo control treatment intended to produce *expectancy* of anxiety reduction. The PSI subjects heard lectures that included a believable but phony theoretical rationale for PSI practice, which consisted simply of sitting still with the eyes closed; PSI had no mantra or other attention control method. The PSI deception went so far as to use PSI teachers who themselves had been deceived about PSI and believed that it was a tried-and-proven treatment. (This was done because psychotherapy research suggests that psychotherapy works best if therapists believe in the methods that they are using.) The TM and PSI subjects were asked to practice their techniques twice daily for six months, whereas the no-treatment control subjects simply waited. Finally, all subjects were recalled for posttesting on the anxiety measures.

The result was that pretest-to-posttest decreases in anxiety test scores were reliably greater in the TM group than in the no-treatment control group. But anxiety reductions were equally as great in the PSI control group as in the TM group. This result suggests that, at least for anxiety reduction, believing in TM's benefit and/or periodically sitting still are more important than the specific practice of mantra concentration. This conclusion was further supported by Smith's (1976) second experiment, where different groups were taught different practices termed Cortically Mediated Stabilization (CMS). CMS1 was a TM-like meditation practice, whereas CMS2 was virtually an antimeditation technique, where subjects sat still and tried to think a series of "positive thoughts," such as pleasurable fantasies, during each session. The two groups showed equal anxiety symptom reductions. Smith drew two conclusions from his (1976) research: (1) meditation is effective in reducing self-reported anxiety symptoms; but (2) "the crucial therapeutic component of TM is not the TM exercise" *per se* (p. 630). Belief in the effectiveness of meditation is an essential ingredient.

Personality and Cognitive Effects of Meditation

Delmonte (1987; also Pagano & Warrenburg 1983) reviewed a number of studies on personality effects of meditation. Considering both the quality of experimental designs and procedures and the data, he found no convincing evidence for changes in self-concept, psychosomatic symptomatology, perceived locus of control (internal versus external), or introversion-extraversion. There is evidence suggesting meditation effects of decreased anxiety, decreased depression, and increased psychological well-being or self-actualization.

Delmonte cautioned that some of the apparent differences between meditators and nonmeditators could be due to self-selection effects, either in initially deciding to meditate or in deciding to continue or discontinue meditating. Meditation is less likely to be effective with subjects suffering from long-term anxiety neuroses. Meditation benefits are more likely, the greater the amount of meditation practice. And expectation of benefits is especially important in producing benefits of meditation, as with other psychotherapeutic practices.

Claims of meditation effects on cognitive functioning, supported by early studies comparing self-selected meditators with nonmeditators, have not been supported by newer studies involving appropriate control groups and random assignment of subjects to groups. For example, Yuille and Sereda (1980) compared two types of meditation (three months' practice) with expectancy and no-treatment control groups, and found no effects of meditation practice on short-term or long-term memory, perceptual speed, reading efficiency, or general intelligence.

Implications for psychotherapy.   Although its effects are not unique, research suggests that meditation can produce, in some people, relaxation, reduced physiological arousal, and reduced anxiety. Some psychotherapists teach their patients meditation as a means of self-control of anxiety and stress (Carrington 1987; Smith 1987). Meditation may be helpful for treating hypertension and insomnia. Regarding the psychotherapeutic use of meditation, Delmonte (1987) concluded:

> Although [meditation] practice has been found to be associated with personality changes in the direction of psychological well-being, it may be incorrect to conclude that meditation techniques 'produce' these changes independently of the practitioner's wishes and desires. Meditation is a self-directed and active process in which a technique is used *by* a person (not *on* a person) in the context of particular subjective expectations and objectives. For this reason meditation may not be readily dispensed, like medication, to anxious or depressed patients if they show little motivation to practice. The value of meditation may be greater for those who wish to be involved in directing their own development than for those wanting to be 'cured' passively (p. 132).

Smith (1987) stressed the importance of giving subjects a good rationale for meditation to generate positive expectancies and teaching meditation behavior as a type of skill that can be improved with practice and shaped with suitable guidance. He also pointed out the need for research designed to predict who (what personality and cognitive traits) can benefit from what particular type of meditation practice or alternative therapy methods.

THE MEDITATION PARADOX

Much of the evidence reviewed here is negative in the sense that it shows either no effects of meditation or that the effects of meditation (relaxation, anxiety reduction) can also be achieved by other methods and are not necessarily produced by the meditation technique *per se*. In view of the largely negative evidence on meditation, it does not seem worthwhile to spend much time discussing alternative theories intended to explain meditation's effects.[6] In fact, most meditation research has been atheoretical (not guided by a theory of meditation).

Michael West (1987b) was puzzled by the paradox inherent in the fact that he and other long-term meditators have found great personal benefits from meditation, and yet the evidence from controlled research on meditation's benefits is largely negative. Why the discrepancy? It may be due partly to practical problems in meditation research, such as the need to get motivated but randomly assigned subjects to continue meditating for many months without quitting. Also, as with hypnosis, only a minority may be able to achieve a deep meditative state in which distinctive alterations of consciousness occur, with possible long-term aftereffects. Yet West saw an even deeper basis for the meditation paradox: in his view, the truly important aspects of meditation have not been explored in systematic meditation research. You may have noticed that there was little connection between the aims of meditation—such as personal knowledge and mystical experience—discussed in the introduction to this chapter and the psychological research discussed in later sections. West made the point:

> The questions I asked about my meditation were very different from the questions research psychologists asked about meditation. I meditated and examined such things as the nature of shifts in awareness, profound experiences [during meditation], and subtle shifts in the quality of my moment to moment experiencing outside meditation. These are very different questions from those researchers have asked and it is not surprising therefore that we arrived at different answers.
>
> Conducting research on meditation involves conducting research on a method of research, since meditation is the methodology of Eastern psychology. Recognizing this involves 'breaking set' away from seeing meditation as simply a therapeutic tool and viewing it as a vehicle for the exploration of consciousness. Change resulting from meditation according to this view is likely to be subtle, demanding sensitivity of measures beyond personality tests and electrodes (West 1987b, p. 209).

As a means of exploring consciousness, meditation is a form of introspection, subject to all of the limitations of introspection. Rather than viewing it as a means of studying consciousness in general, it is best viewed as a means for individuals to explore their own consciousness and its varieties. West (1982, 1987b) argued that one of meditation's greatest values is to increase the individual's self-awareness and self-understanding. Thus, another paradox of meditation lies in the observation that, while the immediate goal of concentrative practice meditation is to concentrate on the mantra and exclude other thoughts, the intrusive thoughts that occur can offer valuable insights about the self, values, and interpersonal relationships, as well as creative ideas on other topics of interest to the meditator. These insights cannot be forced. Their unpredictability and their variety of content and type of impact make them hard to study scientifically. Yet to the individual, these insights may be extremely valuable.

Is meditation worthwhile? This question is too vague. The better question is: What benefits can occur from meditation, for what persons, under what conditions? Scientific psychology can attempt to find objective answers based on systematic research. But for the individual searching for benefits such as increased self-understanding, stress reduction, or a means of producing and exploring alterations of consciousness, the question becomes: Is meditation worthwhile for me? The only way to find out is to try it. Approach it with a positive, receptive attitude, and give it a fair trial.

MYSTICAL EXPERIENCES

For many centuries meditation has been a part of religious traditions where it has been used as a means for achieving profound religious or mystical experiences (Deikman 1966; Goleman 1977; Ornstein 1977; West 1982). Mystical experiences are not limited to meditation, however. They can occur spontaneously in some individuals, and the probability of their occurrence can be increased (though not guaranteed) by the use of psychedelic drugs. William James quoted several reports of mystical experience in *Varieties of Religious Experience* (1902/1961), his book on the psychology of religion. Though some mystical experiences are paranoid and frightening, the large majority are pleasant and of a religious nature. The following example came from a Canadian psychiatrist, Dr. R. M. Bucke, in whom the mystical experience arose from a state of reverie.

> I had spent the evening in a great city, with two friends, reading and discussing poetry and philosophy. We parted at midnight. I had a long drive in a hansom [a horse-drawn carriage] to my lodging. My mind, deeply under the influence of the ideas, images, and emotions called up by the reading and talk, was calm and peaceful. I was in a state of quiet, almost passive enjoyment, not actually thinking, but letting ideas, images, and emotions flow of themselves, as it were, through my mind. All at once, without warning of any kind, I found myself wrapped in a flame-colored cloud. For an instant I thought of fire, an immense conflagration somewhere close by in that great city; the next, I knew that the fire was within myself. Directly afterward there came upon me a sense of exultation, of immense joyousness accompanied or immediately followed by an intellectual illumination impossible to describe. Among other things, I did not merely come to believe, but I saw that the universe is not composed of dead matter, but is, on the contrary, a living Presence; I became conscious in myself of eternal life. It was not a conviction that I would have eternal life, but a consciousness that I possessed eternal life then; I saw that all men are immortal; that the cosmic order is such that without any peradventure all things work together for the good of each and all; that the foundation principle of the world, of all the worlds, is what we call love, and that the happiness of each and all is in the long run absolutely certain. The vision lasted a few seconds and was

gone; but the memory of it and the sense of the reality of what it taught has remained during the quarter of a century which has since elapsed. I knew that what the vision showed was true. I had attained to a point of view from which I saw that it must be true. That view, that conviction, I may say that consciousness, has never, even during periods of the deepest depression, been lost (Bucke 1901, quoted in James 1902/1961, pp. 313–14).

James (1902/1961) argued that mystical experiences are the origin and foundation of all religions, though in institutionalized religions they have come to be deemphasized in favor of church doctrine. In some religions, such as Zen Buddhism, Hindu yoga, and the Sufi sect of Islam, mystical experiences are sought as a standard part of religious practice, with meditation and *renunciation* of worldly goods and pleasures forming the path to mystical experiences (Deikman 1966). Transcendental meditation is a Westernized form of Hindu practice, offered as a path to possible mystical experiences (a path where renunciation is not required) (Goleman 1977). In fact, mystical or spiritual experiences occur in only a small minority of TM practitioners (West 1980b). It is well to bear in mind that meditation can have other benefits (such as increased self-understanding) even if a mystical state never occurs.

Features of mystical experiences.   Mystical experiences or states exhibit wide variety in their details and specific contents, but they share some similarities in their abstract features. Six features may be listed. The first four features were discussed by James (1902/1961); Deikman (1966) added two more to the list. James emphasized the first two—ineffability and noetic quality—as the essential features of mystical experiences. (1) *Ineffability.* Mystical experiences cannot be adequately described in words. Like the experience of being in love, mystical experiences must be directly experienced to be fully understood. (2) *Noetic quality.* At the same time that they are states of feeling, mystical states are also *states of knowledge.* "They are states of insight into depths of truth unplumbed by the discursive intellect. They are illuminations, revelations, full of significance and importance, all inarticulate though they remain; and as a rule they carry with them a curious sense of authority for aftertime" (James 1902/1961, p. 300). The most pervasive theme of mystical insight is a profound experience of unity or oneness, where the self melts into unity with all of nature, or with God. But words cannot adequately describe this experience or its impact on the individual. (3) *Transiency.* Mystical experiences do not last very long, usually just a few seconds or minutes, and rarely as long as an hour. Mystical experiences can be but imperfectly recalled after they fade away, though they can be recognized if they occur again. (4) *Passivity.* Although you can facilitate mystical experiences by practices such as meditation, you cannot force their occurrence. When they happen, they happen spontaneously to people who are in a passive, receptive frame of mind. In many cases they take the person entirely by surprise; perhaps the surprise element increases their impact. (5) *Realness.* Mystical insights are experienced as intensely real, just as you would feel about the reality of something you perceived with your senses. (6) *Unusual percepts.* Mystical experiences are sometimes accompanied by altered perceptions (such as fire, bright light, or a halo around people or objects), visions, or "sensory translation," where changing thoughts are translated into changing sensory images. The unusual percepts are experienced as real.

The scientific approach to mystical experiences.   From the viewpoint of scientific psychology, mystical experiences are natural states, in the sense that they are a product of natural—though unusual—psychological and physiological conditions, and not a result of some sort of divine intervention or revelation. James saw mystical experiences as being in a series with related natural experiences, such as *déjà vu*, moments of insight into the meaning or significance of experiences, experiences of awe and wonderment, as well as intoxication and depersonalization. All of these experiences involve a decrease in normal distinctions and category boundaries and increased perception of similarities and connections, as in moments of creative inspiration.

A scientific approach seeks to discover the conditions that are conducive to the occurrence of mystical experiences, though this is difficult because of the rarity and variety of such experiences and the fact that they cannot be reliably produced under controlled conditions. The available evidence and pertinent theories (Deikman 1966; Tart 1975) suggest the following hypotheses about the origin of mystical experiences: (1) Mystical experiences are most likely to occur in people who are capable of spontaneous alterations of consciousness, including absorption and dissociation experiences. (2) The likelihood of mystical experiences can be increased by practices that disrupt and *deautomatize* normal perception and thinking processes, including meditation, sensory isolation, and taking of psychedelic drugs (Deikman 1966). (3) Whether the reorganized consciousness that follows from deautomatization is a mystical experience, and if so, the particular nature and content of the mystical experience, will be influenced by the individual's prior knowledge, attitudes, beliefs, and expectations, as well as the mode of induction of the state (such as drugs or meditation) (Tart 1975).

Some individuals experience alterations of consciousness that are conducive to mystical experiences, but they are not experienced as such due to the absence of a suitable set of beliefs. For example, one summer afternoon I was meditating at my cabin in northern Maine, after over a year of regular concentrative meditation practice. I had an experience in which thinking seemed to stop for several seconds (I'm not sure how long). The experience was "like floating in a green void," with no verbal thoughts or structured mental images. After a few seconds I became aware that I had stopped thinking, and I observed my empty consciousness in a detached manner. Thoughts occurred to the observing part of consciousness, but the empty part continued. I also became aware that my breathing was exceptionally shallow. Afterward, I thought my "empty consciousness" experience (perhaps the same as TM's "transcendental consciousness"[7]) was interesting and clearly different from my normal conscious experience and other meditation experiences, but I did not attach any great significance to it. Perhaps this is because I am a relatively skeptical person, and I had not been seeking a mystical experience. Other things being the same, a different person, with different beliefs and expectations, might have interpreted such an event as a mystical experience. For example, the observing consciousness might have interpreted the "green void" experience as the disappearance of the self and absorption into God. Mystical experiences are more likely to happen in the prepared mind.

The truth or validity of mystical insights.   It is important to separate the question of the causes of mystical states of consciousness from the question of the truth or validity of the insights that occur to people in such states. Science cannot judge the truth of mystical insights except insofar as they make claims about topics that can be studied by scientific methods, which is rarely the case. Mystical insights are more likely to be in the realm of faith than in the realm of science. Whether someone's mystical insights are valued by others, or interpreted as signs of insanity, depends upon the particular culture and subculture in which they occur.

James (1902/1961) closed his discussion of mysticism with three points that are worth repeating: (1) Mystical states, when well developed, are usually *authoritative* over those who have them. The mystic's values, behavior, and life course may be changed by a mystical revelation. Mystical experiences are intensely real to those who have them, and there is no point in trying to argue with them from a logical standpoint. "The mystic is, in short, *invulnerable*, and must be left, whether we relish it or not, in undisturbed enjoyment of his creed. Faith, says Tolstoy, is that by which men live. And faith-state and mystic state are practically convertible terms" (p. 332). (2) Nonmystics have no obligation to accept uncritically the revelations described by mystics, nor should mystics expect them to do so, no matter how compelling is the truth of their revelations to the mystics themselves. (3) "The existence of mystical states absolutely overthrows the pretension of non-mystical states to be the sole and ultimate dictators of what we may believe" (p. 335). As a general rule, mystical insights do not contradict the facts known from sensory perception. But mystical states may enable people to see new connections, to make new interpretations of ordinary experiences, and to add new dimensions of emotionality, value, and morality to their lives. Mystical insights need not be accepted uncritically, but they can offer *hypotheses* worth serious consideration.

BIOFEEDBACK AND THE "ALPHA" STATE: ELECTRONIC MEDITATION

Since meditation can produce both a relaxed, meditative state of consciousness and increased production of alpha brain waves, it is tempting to assume that there is some intrinsic relationship between alpha EEG and the subjective meditative state. Conceivably, any procedure that increases alpha waves might also induce a subjective meditative state.

In a report that stirred considerable interest among researchers concerned with consciousness and mind-body relationships, Joe Kamiya (1968,

1972) said that people could learn to either increase or decrease alpha brain waves with biofeedback training, in which a soft tone was sounded whenever the subjects were producing alpha waves. His subjects reported that alpha-enhancement training was associated with a pleasant, relaxed state of consciousness. The subjective state during alpha-enhancement training—termed the "alpha state" or "alpha experience"—has been characterized as a quasi-meditational state. It is a pleasant, serene state of alert relaxation in which thinking is slowed and deliberate and critical thought, thoughts about the self, awareness of the body and the passage of time, and emotionality are decreased (Plotkin 1979).

At first it appeared that alpha-enhancement biofeedback training might be a shortcut to meditative states of consciousness—perhaps even to mystical states. Reports in the popular press led to public interest, and an alpha-feedback industry developed that sold electronic alpha-feedback devices for people to use at home.

However, subsequent research by William Plotkin (1977, 1978, 1980) and others, using careful control procedures, has cast doubts on the earlier conclusions. It has been found that: (1) alpha-biofeedback training does not reliably increase alpha abundance above the level of a baseline control condition; (2) the so-called "alpha state" of consciousness is not a consistent result of alpha-feedback training; (3) the degree of alpha experience is not correlated with the amount of alpha wave production; and (4) factors other than alpha biofeedback *per se* are responsible for producing the alpha state during alpha-biofeedback training. These nonfeedback factors include: sensory deprivation, introspective sensitization (Hunt & Chefurka 1976), perceived success (rather than actual success) at the feedback task, suggestion and expectation for particular subjective effects, and belief in the effectiveness of feedback training for altering subjective experience (reviews in Plotkin 1978, 1979). Plotkin (1980) suggested that, when properly used, biofeedback training may be an "ultimate placebo" technique for inducing alterations of consciousness.

These findings are important because they show how a number of subtle factors can combine to influence a person's state of consciousness—factors that may be different from the ones that he or she, or the experimenter, originally thought were important. Also, these findings cast doubt on oversimplified assumptions about mind-body relationships by showing that particular subjective states cannot be produced simply by inducing physiological changes that usually coincide with them. But rather than viewing alpha-biofeedback research as a failure, it can be viewed as a success for revealing people's abilities to control their own states of consciousness. Plotkin put it this way:

> The chain of research on alpha feedback, from Kamiya's first paper to the present, has been valuable in showing us that, although we once thought that a box of amplifiers and filters had made it possible to induce a desirable state of consciousness more rapidly and effectively than ever before, in fact we were really always doing it "on our own." We simply discovered once again that often people only need a certain degree of faith in their natural powers and abilities,

along with an appropriate setting and simple instructions, in order to accomplish what they feel is normally beyond their potential. . . . The power to enter altered states of consciousness is a *natural* ability that we all can potentially tap; learning how to do this without *external* devices such as electronics and drugs will serve to expand our behavior potential in the widest range of circumstances (1976, p. 97).

SUMMARY

"Meditation" is a ritualistic procedure (or set of procedures) intended to change one's state of consciousness by means of maintained, voluntary shifts in attention. Most meditation techniques fall into one of two categories: concentration techniques (such as Transcendental Meditation), where one tries to maintain focus on one thing (such as a mantra [sound], or breathing), and avoid intrusive thoughts; and mindfulness techniques, where one tries to perceive all thoughts and events freshly, and avoid automatic habits of perception and response.

Meditation research has been most concerned with two temporal time frames of meditation effects: state effects—what happens during meditation—and trait effects—long-term changes in the individual's personality or cognitive traits resulting from meditation practice. Case studies and reports by experienced meditators have revealed a variety of possible meditation effects, but controlled research is needed for firmer evidence. Meditation research is plagued by a variety of problems. Comparisons of self-selected meditators with nonmeditators are hard to interpret because of the possibility of preexisting differences between the groups. But experimental studies with random assignment of subjects to groups suffer from a high rate of dropouts from meditation groups, where dropouts may have preexisting differences from those who continue meditating.

Studies of the phenomenological (subjective experience) effects of meditation are characterized by wide variability of results; relaxation is the most common effect. Several studies have shown reductions in physiological arousal (reduced heart rate, breathing, skin conductance) and reduced cortical arousal (increased alpha waves) during meditation, compared to nonmeditation periods. However, other relaxation methods may have equally large effects. As a trait effect, self-reported anxiety symptoms are reduced by meditation practice. However, J. Smith's placebo control group showed just as much anxiety reduction, indicating that the expectation of benefit is more important than the actual meditation practice (such as mantra concentration) in reducing anxiety. West commented on the meditation paradox—the discrepancy between controlled research results and the benefits experienced by many individual meditators—and suggested that researchers have been asking the wrong questions; meditation's main benefit may be in increased self-understanding.

At one time it was thought that biofeedback training to enhance alpha brain wave production could induce a quasi-meditational state, the so-called "alpha state." Subsequent research showed, however, that the alpha state was

really produced by nonfeedback factors such as sensory deprivation, introspective sensitization, suggestion, and expectations.

Meditation has long been a part of religious practices aimed at producing mystical experiences. James emphasized two main features of mystical
experiences: ineffability, and its noetic (knowledge) quality. Other features
include transiency, passivity, realness, and unusual percepts. Mystical experiences occur in only a small minority of meditators. The likelihood of mystical experiences appears to be influenced by three factors: a personality
trait involving the ability to experience spontaneous altered states of consciousness; procedures that deautomatize thinking and perception; and the
individual's prior knowledge, beliefs, and expectations.

ENDNOTES

[1]Deikman (1966) translated Buddhist theory into modern psychological terms, referring to
the *deautomatization* of experience during meditation, leading to a mystical state.

[2]Some people have noted similarities in the states of consciousness engendered by meditation and by long distance running (Glasser 1976; Spino 1976). Glasser (1976) recommended
both meditation and running as types of "positive addiction" to regain self-control and self-
esteem.

[3]Goleman (1977) said of shikan-taza: "In this type of Zen meditation, the student marshals a
heightened state of concentrated awareness with no primary object. He just sits, keenly aware of
whatever goes on in and around him. He sits alert and mindful, free from points of view or
discriminating thoughts, merely watching" (p. 93). Different descriptions of Zen theory are
somewhat contradictory (Claxton 1987), and it is not entirely clear whether mindfulness involves a decrease of reflective awareness and sustaining of primary awareness of events or, alternatively, an increase in reflective awareness of our experience. One interpretation is that mindfulness involves an attempt to sustain primary awareness without reflection, but that it can lead
to insightful breakthroughs of reflective thought.

[4]The idea of empty consciousness (termed "transcendental" or "pure" consciousness by TM
teachers) might seem like a contradiction of terms, insofar as I defined consciousness as a subjective state of awareness of something. The solution to this seeming paradox is that in the state
of pure consciousness, the meditator's consciousness is not entirely empty. Rather, the flow of
thoughts has slowed severely, until at last the meditator is aware only of the absence of structured thoughts and images.

Michael West commented: "It is very difficult I think to get descriptions about mystical states
which satisfy both the naive reader and those familiar with Eastern writings. I think some people
would argue strongly with a notion of 'no awareness of sensations or thoughts.' . . . In some
traditions people talk about awareness of emptiness; in others they talk of awareness of awareness; and in some Tibetan Buddhist schools they talk of awareness of the cloudless sky where
clouds represent thoughts" (1989, personal communication).

[5]An advantage of a between-group comparison (with an independent relaxation-only control group) over a within-subjects comparison (where each subject is tested under both relaxation and meditation conditions) is that it avoids the possibility that in a within-subject comparison experienced meditators might "hold back" their maximum relaxation in the relaxation
control period, in order to allow for greater relaxation during the meditation period. Also, experienced meditators report that when they try to rest, they tend to "slip into" meditation, so for
them a within-subjects comparison of meditation versus resting would not be appropriate
(Holmes 1989, personal communication).

[6]For discussions of Western psychological theories of meditation, see Carrington 1986 and
Delmonte 1987. For Eastern traditional interpretations, see Goleman 1977, Claxton 1987, Naranjo 1971, and Brown 1977.

[7]Farrow (1977) reported that episodes of "transcendental consciousness" are associated with
reduction of breath flow to near zero. His subject, an advanced TM meditator, was asked to

meditate and to push a button whenever she emerged from periods of transcendental consciousness—subjective experiences of unusual mental calmness and clarity without thoughts. Such periods occurred once every fifty-two seconds, and lasted eighteen seconds, on the average. They were associated with: (1) breathing reduced to near zero, with no compensatory hyperventilation afterward; (2) increased theta EEG coherence between different recording sites; (3) decreased heart rate; and (4) reduced phasic skin responses (GSR). The results indicate extreme mental and physical relaxation.

chapter 18 ··································

Psychedelic Drugs I: Marijuana

Aside from REM sleep, the most dramatic altered states of consciousness are those produced by psychoactive drugs. Psychedelic drugs, in particular, have been used to produce altered states that will—the user hopes—enhance self-understanding, interpersonal communication, creativity, or mystical experience. Failing more profound achievements, they may provide entertainment—with certain risks attached. Psychologists, too, are interested in the effects of psychoactive drugs, not only for their therapeutic benefits, but also for their implications for understanding the workings of the human mind and consciousness.

A *drug* is a chemical, other than food, that is administered to or taken by an individual in order to affect the functioning of the brain or other body organs. Drugs used primarily for their psychological effects, such as effects on mood, thinking, perception, or behavior, are termed *psychoactive drugs*. Of course, some drugs used primarily for other purposes, such as reduction of blood pressure, may have unintended psychological side effects. Table 18.1 shows a classification scheme for psychoactive drugs.[1]

Psychoactive drugs affect consciousness and behavior by modifying the process of *synaptic transmission* in the brain. Excitatory and inhibitory connections between neurons are carried out by transfer of special biochemicals, termed *neurotransmitters*, across the tiny synaptic gap between neurons. Drugs can affect synaptic transmission in a variety of ways, such as blocking the production or reception of a neurotransmitter or mimicking (imitating) a neurotransmitter, thus effectively increasing its activity level. Different

TABLE 18.1   Six Classes of Psychoactive Drugs*

1. CNS Stimulants
    Amphetamines (*Benzedrine, Dexedrine, Methedrine*)
    Cocaine ("coke," "crack")
    Caffeine (coffee, tea, cola drinks, chocolate)
    Nicotine (tobacco)

2. CNS Depressants
    Alcohol (ethanol: whiskey, wine, beer)
    Sedative-hypnotics (sleep-inducing substances) and antianxiety agents
       (minor tranquilizers)
           Barbiturates: pentobarbital (*Nembutal*); secobarbital (*Seconal*)
           Benzodiazepines: clordiazepoxide (*Librium*); diazepam (*Valium*)
           Others: methaqualone (*Quaalude*); meprobamate (*Miltown, Equanil*)
    Anesthetic gasses and solvents (ether, chloroform, etc.)

3. Narcotic Analgesics
    Opiates: opium (active ingredients: morphine; codeine);
       heroin (semi-synthetic derivative of morphine)
    Synthetic opiates: meperidine (*Demerol*); methadone (*Dolophine*)

4. Antipsychotic Agents (Major Tranquilizers)
    Antipsychotic tranquilizers: chlorpromazine (*Thorazine*)
    Antimanic agent: Lithium carbonate (*Eskalith*)

5. Clinical Antidepressants
    Monamine oxidase (MAO) inhibitors (*Nardin, Parnate*)
    Tricyclic compounds (*Tofranil, Elavil*)

6. Psychedelics
    Major psychedelics (hallucinogens)
       Psilocybin mushrooms (active ingredient: psilocybin)
       Peyote (active ingredient: mescaline)
       LSD (lysergic acid diethylamide)
    Minor psychedelics
       Cannabis (marijuana, hashish; main active ingredient: delta-9-THC)

*Examples in each category are representative, not comprehensive. Representative brand names are shown in italics. The major categories of drugs are based on their most characteristic effects or uses. However, most drugs have multiple effects, and their effects vary depending on dosage, time since administration, and personal and situational factors. For more information about these and other psychoactive drugs see McKim 1986, Ray and Ksir 1987, or Julien 1985.

neurotransmitters are present in different parts or circuits of the brain, and the type of psychological effects that a drug has will depend upon which particular neurotransmitter it affects and how it affects it (McKim 1986).

As Tart (1975) explained, however, the psychological effects of drugs depend on more than just their neurophysiological effects. Drug effects are produced by an *interaction* between pharmacological drug factors (type, dose) and several nondrug factors, including: (1) long-term personal factors (personality, culture, attitudes, knowledge, beliefs, learned drug skills); (2) immediate personal factors (mood, expectations, desires); and (3) situational or experimental factors (physical and social setting, formal instructions, implicit demands). The emphasis in the *interaction model* is on factors of *set* (expectations—what the person believes can and will happen as a result of tak-ing the drug) and *setting* (especially the social context in which the drug is taken).

The topic of psychoactive drugs is a large one, and it gets larger each year as new drugs are invented and marketed, either legally or illegally, and the volume of research literature grows at an overwhelming pace. Several books have dealt comprehensively with the physiological and psychological effects of a wide range of psychoactive drugs—from tobacco and alcohol to cocaine and heroin—and the personal and social problems resulting from drug abuse (for example, Julien 1985; McKim 1986; Ray & Ksir 1987). In the limited space available here, it is not possible to thoroughly review the full range of psychoactive drugs. Rather than superficially reviewing the full range of drugs, I will go into some detail on certain drugs that are particu-larly important for the study of consciousness and altered states, namely, the psychedelic drugs.

Psychedelic drugs are a heterogeneous group whose most striking subjec-tive effects include changes in perception and imagination. "Psychedelic" literally means "mind manifesting" or "mind expanding": the implication is that these drugs may reveal inherent but normally hidden aspects of the individual's mind and/or expand consciousness in the sense of enabling the individual to have sensory perceptions or mystic revelations that would not normally occur. Tart (1972a) distinguished between minor psychedelics and major psychedelics. For minor psychedelics "the effects are felt to be under a fair amount of volitional control by most individuals who use the drugs" (p. 327). Marijuana is the most important minor psychedelic. The major psyche-delics are the *hallucinogens*: drugs such as LSD, psilocybin, and mescaline, which produce hallucinations at normal "social" doses. Marijuana does not produce true hallucinations at normal doses, though it may do so at high doses. Indeed, many drugs not usually classed as hallucinogens will produce hallucinations at high or toxic doses.

This chapter will go into some detail on marijuana for two reasons. First, there has been more systematic research on the psychological effects of marijuana than of any other psychedelic drug. Thus, marijuana is a good example to illustrate drug effects on a variety of psychological processes, and also to illustrate psychopharmacology research methods. Second, of the psy-chedelic drugs, marijuana is the one most widely used by college students, and I suspect that many readers of this book will have some first-hand famil-iarity with it. If you have used marijuana yourself, you will be interested in comparing your personal experiences with the research findings on marijuana's effects. If you have not used marijuana, this chapter will help you to weigh the potential novel experiences against the potential risks. In the next chapter I will consider the major hallucinogens—LSD, psilocybin, and mescaline—with an emphasis on the hallucination experience.

A BRIEF HISTORY OF MARIJUANA USE

The hemp plant, *Cannabis sativa*, is one of the most important plants in human history (see Figure 18.1). Its fibers have been used to make rope, sails,

SEPALS

PISTILS

MALE

FEMALE

STAMENS

BRACT

FIGURE 18.1.   *Cannabis sativa* (marijuana, or hemp) "is classified as a dioecious plant, that is, the male reproductive parts are on one individual (left) and the female parts are on another (right). Details of the two types of flower are shown at bottom. The active substances in the drug are contained in a sticky yellow resin that covers the flower clusters and top leaves of the female plant when it is ripe." [From Grinspoon, L. (1969, June). Marihuana. *Scientific American, 221,* 17–25. Copyright © 1969 by Scientific American, Inc. All rights reserved.]

and fine cloth. Its leaves and flowers (marijuana) and resin (hashish) have served as both medicine and euphorant, imbibed through smoking or as a drink or cooked in food.

The main active ingredient of cannabis is *delta-9-tetrahydro-cannabinol* (abbreviated as delta-9-THC or simply THC). However, there are over 80 *cannabinoids* (chemicals found exclusively in cannabis), many of which can contribute to the behavioral effects of cannabis, depending on its method of preparation and administration. For example, when marijuana is taken orally, *cannabidiol* (CBD) is ineffective, but when it is smoked the heat converts CBD to delta-9-THC. Other cannabinoids may be converted to more active forms during digestion and metabolism. THC concentration is greatest in the resin found on the flowers, seeds, and upper leaves of the female plant. The resin is a yellowish sap extruded by the flowers. *Hashish* is the resin scraped from the leaves and dried, whereupon it turns dark, almost black. It is usually smoked in a small pipe. THC is not water soluble, but it is soluble in alcohol and fat. Thus, marijuana drinks are usually made with alcohol, whereas marijuana food recipes (such as cookies or brownies) are made with butter (McKim 1986).

Today marijuana is the second most popular recreational drug in America (alcohol is the first). Like alcohol, marijuana has been used for several millennia in many cultures, and its use has been controversial. There is evidence of early use of marijuana throughout much of Asia, India, the Middle East, and Africa. The ancient Greeks used alcohol as an intoxicant, rather than marijuana; however, they traded with marijuana-using peoples, the Scythians. In the twentieth century, laborers from cultures as diverse as India, South Africa, Greece, South America, and Jamaica have used marijuana while they work, in the belief that it helps them to work more energetically, with less fatigue, and with more enjoyment. The Jamestown settlers brought hemp to Virginia in 1611 to cultivate it for its fiber. George Washington grew hemp at Mount Vernon in 1765 for its fiber and perhaps also for medicinal use (Brecher 1972). We do not know whether George ever got stoned just for fun.

During the nineteenth century, marijuana was often prescribed as a medicinal drug, usually administered as an alcohol extract. It was listed in the official *United States Pharmacopeia* (a catalog of accepted medical drugs) from 1850 to 1942. In 1851 its use was recommended for calming nerves, inducing sleep, stimulating appetite, and for ailments and discomforts including neuralgia, gout, rheumatism, tetanus, hydrophobia, epidemic cholera, convulsions, chorea, hysteria, mental depression, delirium tremens, insanity, and uterine hemorrhage and cramps. In 1898 migraine headache was added to the list (Brecher 1972). Today better treatments are available for these problems. However, in recent years marijuana has been used to reduce the unpleasant side effects of chemotherapy for cancer and to reduce intraocular pressure that can lead to blindness from glaucoma (Cohen & Stillman 1976).

In addition to its medicinal use, marijuana has had a long history of recreational use in Europe and the United States. The French writer Théophile Gautier described his experiences in "The Club des Hachichins" in 1846 (Gautier 1846/1966). He was introduced to the club by Dr. J. J. Moreau, who warned him that his time intoxicated with hashish "will be subtracted from your share in Paradise." In the 1860s, following the suppression of opium dens by the police, hashish houses were opened in New York City; many of their customers were upper-class people.

Marijuana for smoking was introduced into the United States in the early twentieth century by Mexican laborers, and its use slowly spread, especially among racial minorities and jazz musicians. In 1926 two New Orleans newspapers published sensational exposés of the "menace" of marijuana. Marijuana was accused of causing violence, insanity, and moral degeneration, although there was no scientific evidence to support such claims. This was the beginning of a national campaign to suppress the sale and use of marijuana. Congress passed the Marijuana Tax Act of 1937, which effectively outlawed marijuana by imposing exorbitant taxes ($100 per ounce) for nonmedicinal use. The Controlled Substances Act of 1970 denied the medicinal use of marijuana and treated it legally as if it were a narcotic, though pharmacologically it is not a narcotic (McKim 1986). (Narcotics include opium and its derivatives, morphine and heroin. See Table 18.1.)

Of course, making marijuana illegal did not eliminate its use any more than alcohol use was eliminated by the prohibition amendment in the 1920s. The major surge in marijuana use began with the youth counterculture of the 1960s, and its use soon spread from "hippies" to more socially respectable middle-class, even middle-age, citizens. In 1982, according to a survey by the National Institute on Drug Abuse, some 64 percent of young adults in the eighteen- to twenty-five-year age group reported that they had used marijuana at least once, and 27 percent were current users (defined as having used marijuana within the last 30 days). In this age group the frequency of marijuana use was about the same for college students and nonstudents. The number of people using marijuana is remarkably high, considering that users are taking the risk of being arrested and paying fines and/or serving jail sentences, and possibly damaging their careers, as well as their health. Why is marijuana so popular? What are the psychological and physical effects of marijuana?

I will discuss research on the effects of marijuana on conscious experience and behavior, emphasizing the *acute* effects of marijuana, that is, the immediate effects of being stoned (intoxicated) on marijuana. The *chronic* health effects of long-term marijuana use will be discussed briefly in a later section. (For more details on the history, pharmacological aspects, and health aspects of marijuana, see McKim 1986 or Ray & Ksir 1987.)

SUBJECTIVE EFFECTS OF MARIJUANA

Many writers, both literary and scientific, have attempted to describe the subjective effects of marijuana (examples in Solomon 1966). Literary descriptions usually consist of an author describing his or her own experiences—experiences that may or may not be typical. Descriptions from a scientific viewpoint, on the other hand, usually are composites based on the subjective reports of several people. Composite descriptions may give the false impression that everyone has the same subjective experiences during marijuana intoxication. In fact there are few, if any, subjective effects that occur in every person every time they get stoned on marijuana. The best that can be done is to list a variety of *potential* effects, and then try to discover the particular combination of personal, situational, and drug factors that produces each of these effects when they occur.

Charles Tart (1971) did a systematic survey of the potential effects of marijuana and their relative frequencies. He believed that researchers doing controlled laboratory studies would be unable to discover the full variety of marijuana's effects as they occur in more natural physical and social settings. In order to avoid the artificialities of the laboratory, he obtained his data by the public survey method. He had college students in California circulate a 220-item questionnaire addressed "to anyone who has smoked marijuana more than a dozen times." The questionnaires were filled out and returned anonymously. (The questions were based on preliminary research in which marijuana users had been asked to describe the full range of subjective experiences that they had had while stoned.) For each item, respondents indicated on a five-point scale the relative frequency with which they had experienced that particular effect: never, rarely, sometimes, very often, or usually. (Each point was defined: for example, "very often" meant that the experience had occurred on more than 40 percent of the smoking occasions.) Tart's final data were based on 150 completed questionnaires; most respondents were in the nineteen- to thirty-year age range. Table 18.2 summarizes Tart's results, showing the characteristic and common subjective responses to marijuana.

Changes in sensory perception are particularly characteristic of marijuana intoxication, and they are probably the main reason that many people find the experience to be so enjoyable. In addition to the characteristic and common subjective effects listed in Table 18.2, Tart (1971) noted some other effects that are relatively rare but interesting. These include apparent "paranormal" experiences, such as telepathy and out-of-body experiences, and also religious experiences. Unpleasant experiences were relatively rare, though 80 percent of the respondents reported that they had felt paranoid on at least one smoking occasion. If unpleasant experiences were more common or more severe, then marijuana smoking would not be so popular.

Another interesting subjective effect of marijuana—doubling of consciousness—was not included in Tart's questionnaire, though it has been mentioned by other writers (Robinson 1946/1966; Grinspoon 1969). According to Grinspoon:

> There is often a splitting of consciousness, so that the smoker, while experiencing the high, is at the same time an objective observer of his own intoxication. He may, for example, be afflicted with paranoid thoughts yet at the same time be reasonably objective about them and even laugh or scoff at them and in a sense enjoy them (p. 19).

Robinson's subject, Mr. C., reported:

> Throughout the experiment I experienced a peculiar double consciousness. I was perfectly aware that my laughter, etc., was the result of having taken the

TABLE 18.2 Characteristic* and Common Subjective Responses to Marijuana

Sensory perception. 1. *I can see patterns, forms, figures, meaningful designs in visual material that does not have any particular form when I'm straight.
2. *Pictures acquire an element of visual depth.
3. The edges and contours of things stand out more sharply.
4. *I can hear more subtle changes in sounds . . . [for example, the notes and rhythm of music].
5. Touch*, taste*, and smell sensations take on new qualities.
6. *I enjoy eating very much and eat a lot.
7. *My sense of touch is more exciting, more sensual.
8. *Orgasm has new, pleasurable qualities.

Mental imagery. 9. Mental imagery seems more vivid than usual in the modalities of vision*, audition, taste, and touch.
10. Sounds have visual images or colors associated with them, synchronized with them [synesthesia].

Time perception. 11. *Time passes very slowly.
12. Certain experiences seem outside of time, are timeless.

Body image. 13. My body feels very light or as if it is floating.

Sense of identity. 14. I lose all sense of self, of being a separate ego, and feel at one with the world.

Memory. 15. I experience unusually rapid forgetting of conversations that I am involved in*, tasks I have started*, what I have read, and my own train of thought.
16. *I find it difficult to read.

Thinking. 17. *I can understand the words of songs which are not clear when I'm straight.
18. *I have meaningful insights about myself, my personality.
19. My ideas are more original than usual.
20. *I am more willing to accept contradictions between two ideas.
21. I get so wound up in thoughts or fantasies that I won't notice what's going on around me.
22. *I give little or no thought to the future; I am completely in the here and now.

Judgment of meaning or significance. 23.*I appreciate very subtle humor in what my companions say, and say quite subtly funny things myself.
24. Commonplace sayings or conversations seem to have new meanings, more significance.
25. *I feel more childlike, more open to experiences of all kinds, more filled with wonder and awe at the nature of things.

Emotions. 26. *I almost invariably feel good when I turn on, regardless of whether I felt bad before turning on.
27. I feel emotions much more strongly, so they affect me more.

Self-control. 28. *I can 'come down' at will if I need to be straight for a minute to deal with some complicated reality problem.
29. *I get physically relaxed and don't want to get up or move around.
30. *I find it easy to accept whatever happens.
31. I giggle a lot.
32. My inhibitions are lowered so that I do things I'm normally too inhibited to do.
33. *I find it very easy to go to sleep at my usual bedtime.

TABLE 18.2   Continued

Interpersonal relations.   34.   *I have feelings of deep insights into other people (regardless of whether they actually check out later).
35.   *I empathize tremendously with others.
36   When making love I feel I'm in much closer mental contact with my partner; it's much more a union of souls as well as bodies.
37.   I become more sociable.
38.   I become less sociable.

Characteristic effects (marked with asterisks*) were defined as those that occurred "very often"(over 40 percent of occasions) in at least half of the respondents; common effects occurred at least "sometimes" (10 to 40 percent of occasions) in at least half of the respondents. (In fact, most of the characteristic effects occurred at least sometimes in 80 to 95 percent of respondents; most of the common effects occurred sometimes in 60 to 80 percent of respondents.) In the questionnaire, each statement included the phrase, "the effect is more pronounced during marijuana intoxication than normal."

[Selected from data in Tart, C. T. (1971). On Being Stoned: *A Psychological Study of Marijuana Intoxication.* Palo Alto, CA: Science and Behavior Books. By permission of the author.]

drug, yet I was powerless to stop it. . . . In the same way the extension of the sense of time induced by the drug was in itself indubitable . . . yet I remained able to convince myself at any moment by reflection that my sense of time was fallacious (p. 258).

The double consciousness experience is particularly interesting in relation to the concept of dissociation discussed in Chapter 15 on hypnosis. Crawford (1974) found that responding to hypnotic-type suggestions was increased as much by marijuana as by hypnotic induction.

Several subjective effects of marijuana are especially noteworthy because of their frequency and the fact that they have been evaluated by objective research (to be discussed shortly). These subjective effects include: (1) sensory-perceptual effects, particularly the impression of increased sensitivity; (2) disruption of memory; (3) changed time experience; (4) increased creativity; (5) enhancement of interpersonal perception and communication; and (6) ability to "come down" at will.

First-time effect.   The subjective effects described above are based on reports of experienced users. It is noteworthy that many people do not feel "high" or "stoned" the first time they smoke marijuana, even though physiological measures show clear physiological changes (such as increased heartbeat rate) in first-time users.[2] This finding suggests that feeling stoned depends on more than just the drug itself. It also depends on learning, attitudes, and experience. For example, novice marijuana smokers may not know what to expect initially. But novices may be taught by friends how to perceive the rather subtle effects of marijuana and interpret them positively while ignoring any discomforting effects. On future occasions, the novices will be prepared to easily detect marijuana's effects and to label their experiences as a pleasant marijuana high (Becker 1963; Carlin et al. 1974).

EXPERIMENTAL RESEARCH ON MARIJUANA

Experimental Procedures

Although Tart (1971) may be right in suspecting that the subjective effects of marijuana differ between laboratory and home settings, it is nonetheless important to assess the effects of marijuana under controlled experimental conditions in order to better analyze cause-and-effect relationships. Here I will describe some general procedural considerations that apply to most marijuana experiments.

Subjects.   Most marijuana experiments with humans have employed male subjects, eighteen to thirty years old, who are experienced but casual marijuana smokers, not heavy users.

Dose and administration method.   Ideally, pharmacological research should obtain dose-effect curves, where the effects of several different dose levels are measured. However, for practical reasons having to do with research costs and research subject availability, most human marijuana experiments have employed a single dose level. Most experiments with smoked marijuana have used a *nominal* dose in the 8 to 14 mg THC range. This dose range has been used because it is the so-called "social dose" level—the amount that experienced marijuana users consume in order to produce a "nice high" in informal social situations. With smoked marijuana the *actual* dose of THC is always somewhat lower than the nominal dose, and it varies depending on the efficiency of people's smoking techniques.

Some experiments have used THC capsules or drinks in order to precisely control the dose and ensure that all subjects get the same actual THC dose level. On the other hand, research using smoked marijuana is more likely to produce effects like those experienced by marijuana users in more natural (nonlaboratory) settings. Smoking produces a "high" faster than oral ingestion, and the subjective nature of the high may be different with smoking, perhaps partly due to a different mix of cannabinoids in smoked marijuana (R. T. Jones 1971). Therefore, in discussing the research literature I will give preference, where possible, to studies that used smoked marijuana.

Placebo controls.   One of the main complications of drug research with human subjects is that the apparent effects of the drug may be heavily influenced by subjects' expectations about the effects that will occur. In order to distinguish between the actual pharmacological effects and expectancy effects, it is customary to employ a placebo control condition. A *placebo* is a capsule, drink, or "joint" (marijuana cigarette) that looks, tastes, and smells like the one containing the drug, but which does not contain any of the active drug ingredient. (A marijuana placebo may be prepared by using ethyl alcohol to extract the THC and other cannabinoids from marijuana.) In a *single-blind* experimental design, subjects do not know whether they are taking the actual drug or a placebo. They are led to believe that they are taking the actual drug in both cases, so their expectancies are the same in both cases. Most experiments use a *double-blind* procedure, where neither the experimenter who administers the drugs nor the subjects know which subjects are getting the real drug and which are getting the placebo. (This is accomplished by having a second experimenter prepare the joints or capsules.) The purpose of the double-blind procedure is to avoid having the experimenter unintentionally influence the subjects' expectations by behaving differently toward them in the drug and placebo conditions. Thus, with the double-blind procedure, any difference in response between the drug and placebo conditions can be attributed to the pharmacological effects of the drug.

A *placebo effect*—a response to the placebo similar to the response to the real drug—was demonstrated in a double-blind study by R. T. Jones (1971). Frequent marijuana users (who smoked marijuana seven or more times per week) rated themselves as equally "high" on marijuana and placebo joints (52 and 48, respectively, on a 0 to 100 scale). Infrequent users (less than twice a week) responded much less to the placebo than to the real drug ("high" ratings of 67 and 22, respectively, for marijuana and placebo). Apparently, with the placebo, expectations associated with the familiar smell, taste, and ritual of marijuana smoking produced a marked subjective "high" in the frequent users but not in the infrequent users. On the other hand, there was little or no placebo effect on heart rate; heart rate changes were markedly greater for drug than placebo in both groups.

Physiological Effects of Marijuana

The acute physiological effects (short-term effects—while stoned) of marijuana are relatively mild and not particularly distinctive, at least with normal "social" doses. The most reliable physiological effect is an increase in heartbeat rate (pulse rate). When marijuana is smoked, the heart rate reaches its maximum in about 15 minutes and then declines. (When THC is taken orally, the heart rate change is slower than with smoked marijuana. See Figure 18.2, top panel.) The heart rate increase is greater, the greater the dose of THC (up to about 30 bpm increase at 15 mg THC) (Klonoff & Low 1974). R. T. Jones (1971) found a greater heart rate increase in infrequent users (31 bpm) than in frequent (17 bpm) users, indicating a *tolerance effect* in the frequent users. The heart rate increase is reliable enough that some researchers have used it to determine whether their subjects have smoked marijuana effectively enough to get the chemicals into their bloodstream. Conjunctival injection (reddening of the eyes due to dilation of the capillaries on the eyeball surface) is commonly observed after high doses, though it is less marked or absent with low doses (Weil, Zinberg, & Nelsen 1968).

Smoked marijuana at social doses does not produce any dramatic changes in brain wave (EEG) recordings from the cortex surface. Some rather small, not particularly reliable effects (reduced power and slowing of frequency in the alpha band) have been found at social doses. These effects are stronger with very high THC doses (R. T. Jones 1978; Tassinari et al. 1974).

It now seems likely that the most important neurophysiological effects of marijuana are on subcortical structures of the brain, rather than the cerebral cortex. Heath (1976) took EEG recordings through miniature electrodes implanted in the limbic systems of monkeys. Marijuana produced increased high-voltage, slow waves, and some unusual spikes in the EEG records. Similar observations were made on a human subject, and it was noted that the EEG spikes were associated with subjective feelings of euphoria (Heath 1972). There is evidence that marijuana disrupts cholinergic synaptic transmission in the limbic system, particularly in the septal-hyppocampal circuit, which is important for memory processes (Miller & Branconnier 1983).

Marijuana often makes people feel sleepy, particularly if they smoke alone where they do not have social stimulation to keep them awake. Marijuana tends to increase total sleep time, but it decreases the time spent in the REM sleep stage. When marijuana use is discontinued after a period of prolonged use of high doses, there is a REM rebound effect (Feinberg et al. 1976).

Cognitive Effects of Marijuana

Sensory-perceptual effects.   Changes in subjective sensory-perceptual experiences for vision, hearing, taste, and touch are commonly reported by marijuana users. For example, users report that marijuana enables them to hear things in music that they hadn't heard before. In a questionnaire about reasons for using marijuana, users indicated pleasurable sensory-perceptual changes more often than any other reason (Roth, Tinklenberg, & Kopell 1976). However, it is noteworthy that studies with objective measures have failed to find evidence of enhanced sensory-perceptual abilities during marijuana intoxication; in fact, the opposite is often the case.

Moskowitz and McGlothlin (1974) examined the effects of marijuana on performance on an auditory signal detection task. On some trials the signal (a brief, soft, 1000 Hz tone) was presented superimposed on a "white" background noise (like "ssshhh . . ."). On other trials, randomly mixed, the noise was presented alone. The subject's task was to report, on each trial, whether he detected a tone. Signal detection sensitivity (d') decreased with increasing marijuana dose, compared to a placebo control condition. With increasing doses the frequency of hits (correct "yes" responses) decreased slightly, whereas the frequency of false alarms (incorrect "yes" responses) increased more dramatically. Thus, there is no proof that marijuana affects the sensitivity of the auditory system *per se*. Rather, it appears that marijuana interferes with auditory signal detection by increasing the frequency of lapses of attention to external stimuli, due to a shift of attention inward to thoughts and mental images. Also, marijuana changes subjects' response biases, such that they are more likely to say "yes" when they are uncertain, thus making more false alarms. (Alternatively, false alarms might indicate that subjects sometimes hallucinate signals when they are tested during marijuana intoxication.)

There is really no conflict between subjective reports of increased music appreciation and objective findings of reduced auditory signal-detection sensitivity during marijuana intoxication. What is at issue is not the ability to hear, but the ability to listen, and what one listens to. Marijuana may actually decrease the efficiency and frequency of automatic attention switching, resulting in a tendency to stay focused or "locked in" on a particular internal image or external stimulus for a greater than usual amount of time before switching attention to something else. Thus, when stoned, one might attend to music to an abnormal degree and notice subtle musical events that had not been noticed previously. Many marijuana users have reported that their appreciation of classical music increased during marijuana intoxication; perhaps they noticed and appreciated the music's complexities more with marijuana.

Other research indicates that, contrary to subjective reports, marijuana reduces visual signal detection sensitivity and visual acuity (Moskowitz, Sharma, & Shapero 1972) and color discrimination ability (Adams et al. 1976), and it has no effects on depth perception (Clark & Nakashima 1968). Marijuana increases the autokinetic effect, in which a small stationary light is perceived to be moving when it is viewed in a dark room (Moskowitz et al. 1972). On the positive side, marijuana improved performance on a visual completion task in which subjects had to identify objects from drawings that had large parts of their outlines missing (Harshman, Crawford, & Hecht 1976).

Contrary to subjective reports of increased touch sensitivity with marijuana, a controlled experiment found no effect of marijuana on any of four different measures of cutaneous or tactile sensitivity (Milstein et al. 1974). Studies of effects of marijuana on pain sensitivity and pain tolerance have produced inconsistent results (Milstein et al. 1975). In the past marijuana was prescribed to reduce pain, though its benefits may have resulted more from attentional distraction than from reduced pain sensitivity *per se*.

In conclusion, the striking thing about laboratory studies of sensory-perceptual effects of marijuana is their rather consistent failure to confirm the subjective reports of marijuana users. In retrospect this inconsistency is not very surprising. The subjective reports were not obtained in controlled conditions that would allow users to systematically compare their experiences with and without marijuana. Subjective reports are particularly susceptible to effects of the subjects' attitudes, beliefs, and expectancies. However, this is not to say that the subjective reports are erroneous. Rather, they seem to indicate something different from what is measured by objective means. In one sense, there is nothing more private and at the same time nothing more real than subjective perceptual experiences. Even a perceptual illusion is very real to the person who experiences it. Thus, in future research the important question will not be whether marijuana affects objective sensory sensitivity, but rather how and why does it affect subjective perceptual experience.

Sensory-motor performance.

Sensory-motor performance.   Sharma and Moskowitz (1974) tested the effect of marijuana on the ability to maintain continuous attention to a task. In a *vigilance* task, subjects responded to visual signals that occurred unpredictably, at irregular intervals over the course of an hour. Marijuana caused increasingly greater disruptions of performance, compared to placebo, as the amount of time-on-task increased. Also, performance was disrupted as much on a focused-attention task (one stimulus source) as it was on a divided-attention task, where subjects had to attend to two stimulus sources at the same time (Moskowitz & McGlothlin 1974; Moskowitz et al. 1972). These results suggest that marijuana's effects are due to subjects having periodic lapses of attention to the task, rather than to a decreased ability to perform when they are concentrating on the task.

The same conclusion comes from research on reaction time (RT). Marijuana increases the mean reaction time on both simple reaction-time tasks (one stimulus, one response) and complex reaction-time tasks (several different stimuli and responses) (Borg, Gershon, & Alpert 1975). However, a detailed examination of the results shows that marijuana also increases the variability of reaction times. Most responses are as fast with marijuana as with placebo, but marijuana increases the frequency of unusually long reaction times (Clark, Hughes, & Nakashima 1970). The long RTs reflect lapses of attention to the task.

Automobile driving.   Marijuana users often claim that when they are stoned, they can "come down" at will in order to drive safely. Controlled experiments have cast serious doubt on this claim. In a driving simulator apparatus, both THC and alcohol disrupted attempts to maintain a 40 km/hr speed, as well as disrupting distance estimation and slowing braking reaction times (Rafaelsen, Bech, & Rafaelsen 1973). The most dramatic result was one subject on THC who completely failed to respond to eight of ten red lights! Obviously, his attention had drifted away from the driving task.

Klonoff (1974) studied the effects of marijuana on actual driving performance in a restricted test area and on city streets. In the special test area the subjects drove a complex course of sharp turns and narrow "tunnels" marked by cones; they knocked over more cones after smoking marijuana than after smoking a placebo. The test on city streets involved taking a driver's license driving performance test under normal traffic conditions. The testing officer did not know whether the subjects had smoked marijuana or placebo. The mean test score (a composite score based on general driving skills and related cognitive factors such as judgment and concentration) was significantly reduced by marijuana compared to placebo.

These results indicate that marijuana might significantly increase your risk of having a traffic accident, particularly under difficult driving conditions. In a double-blind study, Rafaelsen et al. (1973) found that marijuana slowed automobile braking reaction times by 0.2 seconds, on the average, compared to placebo (0.4 seconds slowing for alcohol, under the doses used). I suggest that you compute how many extra feet your car would travel in 0.2 seconds at, say, 55 miles an hour, and see whether you think the extra distance might be enough to cause a collision if you had to stop quickly to avoid hitting another car or a pedestrian.

Memory.   One of the most characteristic subjective effects of marijuana is disruption of memory for recent events. Conversations may be disrupted when you forget what your friend has just said, or you forget what you yourself have just said, perhaps right in the middle of a sentence! Reading can become pointless if a sentence doesn't make any sense because you cannot remember the meaning of earlier sentences. Objective research has confirmed that marijuana disrupts both reading comprehension (Clark et al. 1970) and the production of coherent, meaningful speech (Weil & Zinberg

1969). Both of these effects result from memory disruptions. The memory-disruption effects of marijuana have been systematically studied in several experiments. In fact, memory disruption is probably the most reliable objective behavioral effect of marijuana.

Short-term memory (STM) for letter strings was disrupted by marijuana when subjects had to retain the information for several seconds and rehearsal was prevented by requiring them to do mental arithmetic during the retention interval (the Brown-Peterson procedure) (Dornbush, Fink, & Freedman 1971). However, marijuana does not affect performance on memory span tasks where subjects can report a string of letters or digits immediately (Miller 1976). Nor does marijuana slow the speed of serial search through STM to determine whether a target item is present (the Sternberg task) (Darley et al. 1973a). Thus, marijuana affects short-term memory operations only when reporting is delayed, allowing time for a shift of attention to occur, resulting in interference with STM. It appears that marijuana decreases STM's functional capacity by increasing its susceptibility to interference. Short-term memory (working memory) is critical for complex thinking tasks, where several items of information must be maintained, compared, and manipulated. Performance on logical syllogism and inference problems is disrupted by marijuana, probably due to the disruption of working memory operations (Harshman et al. 1976).

Many marijuana users have noticed that reading or studying while stoned on marijuana is not very effective, since their later recall of the material is poor. Darley et al. (1973b) asked whether marijuana's disruption of recall from long-term memory (LTM) is due to (1) disruption of the learning process, that is, the process of transferring new information from STM to LTM, or (2) disruption of the process of retrieving stored information from LTM, or (3) both. Their experiment involved two parts. The first part was intended to find out whether marijuana (actually, THC capsules in this study) affects retrieval of previously learned material. Subjects learned a series of ten word lists while straight (before taking any drugs). Then, in a double-blind procedure, half of the subjects took a THC capsule, while the others took a placebo capsule. An hour later they tried to recall all of the words learned earlier, and the THC group did as well as the placebo group. Thus, THC did not interfere with retrieval from LTM of material learned earlier while straight.

The second part of the experiment was intended to find out whether THC affects learning, that is, the transfer of new information from STM to LTM. After taking either THC or placebo pills, the subjects learned ten new word lists, and an hour later they tried to recall all of the words. The THC group did significantly worse than the placebo group during both initial learning (fewer words recalled after a single exposure to each list) and during delayed recall testing of all of the words from all ten lists. Thus, THC interfered with learning of new material when subjects tried to learn while stoned. In terms of the multistore theory of memory (Atkinson & Shiffrin 1968), THC interfered with transfer of new information from STM to LTM.[3]

Darley et al.'s (1973b) conclusions are not limited to word lists. Other studies have shown that when marijuana is smoked before initial learning, later recall is disrupted for meaningful prose passages, pictures, and complex visual stimuli (Miller et al. 1977a, 1977b). On the other hand, marijuana does not interfere with retrieval of miscellaneous items of general information (arts, science, current events) learned previously in a nondrugged state (Darley et al. 1977).

Before you conclude that it is all right to take tests while stoned, as long as you do the initial studying straight, you should be aware that some research has shown effects of marijuana on retrieval from LTM. Miller et al. (1977a) had subjects read prose passages under placebo conditions, then tested their recall the next day under either marijuana or placebo conditions. Recall was worse with marijuana. Miller and Branconnier (1983) argued that marijuana does, in fact, interfere with LTM retrieval. They cited evidence that on recall tests, besides decreasing correct responses, marijuana sometimes increases the number of *intrusions* (errors in which subjects report words that were not on the list of to-be-remembered items). Other evidence comes from some studies where marijuana decreased performance on recall tests, but not on recognition tests of memory. Miller and Branconnier argued that by providing retrieval cues to make retrieval easier, recognition tests provide a better measure of what is stored in LTM than do recall tests. Thus, they argued, lack of effect of marijuana on recognition performance shows that it does not affect the storage of material in LTM once it has been learned, but marijuana's disruption of recall performance shows that it interferes with retrieval of stored information. Overall, however, the bulk of the evidence indicates that marijuana disrupts initial learning (transfer from STM to LTM storage) more than it disrupts retrieval from LTM.

What is the process by which marijuana affects memory? The limbic system in the brain, particularly the hippocampus, is known to be critical for memory storage and retrieval. Miller and Branconnier (1983) described several types of evidence that, taken together, suggest that marijuana affects transmission at cholinergic synapses in the limbic system, particularly in the septal-hippocampal pathway: (1) Drugs that disrupt limbic cholinergic transmission have effects on memory and attention similar to marijuana's effects. (2) THC decreases the turnover rate of acetylcholine (a neurotransmitter) in the hippocampus. (3) Electrophysiological recordings show effects of marijuana on limbic system activity (Heath 1972). (4) There are similarities between marijuana effects and certain neurological syndromes (including herpes simplex encephalitis, Korsakoff's syndrome, and Alzheimer's disease) where memory deficits have been linked to disruption of neurotransmission in the limbic system. Thus, the evidence suggests that the effects of marijuana on memory are due to its effects on the limbic system, particularly the hippocampus.

Time estimation.   One of the most characteristic subjective effects of marijuana is that time seems to pass more slowly. For example, if you are stoned and your friend goes into the kitchen to get some snacks, it may seem like he has been gone for fifteen minutes when he has really been gone for only five minutes. Several experiments have confirmed that marijuana slows temporal duration experience.

Two different methods have been used to measure temporal duration experience. In the *time-estimation* method the experimenter presents a signal

of a certain duration (such as a 30-second tone) and the subject tries to estimate its duration in seconds. (Of course, wristwatches are not allowed in the
laboratory.) In the *time-production* method the subject is required to produce
an interval of a specified duration (such as by pushing a button to maintain
a tone for 30 seconds). With these methods a slowing of subjective time is
indicated by overestimation or by underproduction. (For example, if you
were asked to produce a 30-second interval, you might hold the button down
for 10 seconds, if 10 seconds [subjective time] seemed like 30 seconds to you.)

It is important to understand that when external time seems (subjectively) to be going slower, it is because your "internal clock" is beating faster.
For the sake of argument, imagine that you have an internal clock that beats
at a rate of one beat per second of external clock time. You can estimate the
duration of a time interval from the number of beats of your internal clock
during that interval, so long as the beating of your internal clock matches (or
is highly correlated with) that of the external clock ("real" time). But if your
internal clock speeds up and you don't realize that it has speeded up, then
you would estimate a time interval to be longer than it really is. For example,
if your internal clock speeds up from one to three beats per second, then you
would estimate a 10-second interval to be 30 seconds. (In fact, there is no
clear evidence that time estimation is based on an actual internal clock or
pacemaker, though "internal clock" is a convenient name for the internal
process involved in time estimation, whatever that process might be.)

Tinklenberg, Roth, and Kopell (1976) studied the effects of THC, alcohol (ethanol), and placebo drinks on time production. Each subject was
tested under each drug condition on different days in a counterbalanced sequence. One half hour before taking the drink, and periodically thereafter,
subjects were asked to produce a 120-second interval. They were instructed
to count internally and report when they thought the interval had elapsed.
Also, their heart rates were monitored, and they were asked periodically to
rate their degree of subjective intoxication on a zero to 100 scale.

Figure 18.2 shows the results on all three measures. In the third panel,
time production scores have been converted to internal clock rate, r, which
is defined as the number of objective seconds per subjective second. THC
produced underproduction (equivalent to overestimation) of time intervals,
whereas alcohol produced overproduction (equivalent to underestimation).
In other words, the internal clock rate is faster with THC, and slower with
alcohol, compared to placebo.[4]

There have been two major approaches to explaining temporal duration experience (Ornstein 1969). According to the biological clock theory,
subjective time experience is based on an internal physiological clock or
pacemaker. Thus, the slowing of subjective duration estimates with THC
might be related to the speeding up of an internal pacemaker, such as heart
rate. However, Figure 18.2 shows that changes in internal clock rate were not
closely correlated with changes in heart rate across the 4.5-hour test session
for either THC or alcohol conditions. In fact, no physiological pacemaker
that consistently correlates with subjective duration experience has been discovered.

According to the cognitive theory, the subjective duration of an interval increases with the frequency of conscious mental events during the inter-

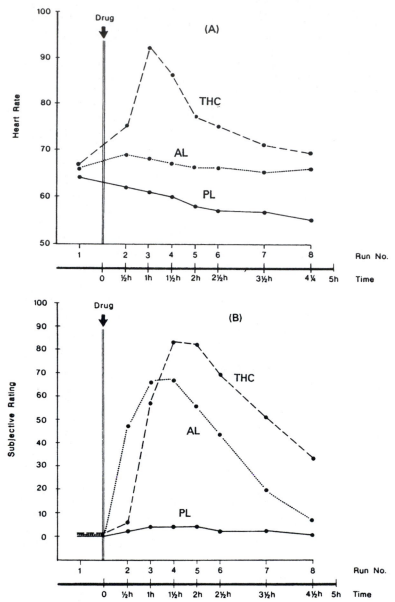

FIGURE 18.2. Heart rates (panel A), subjective intoxication ratings (panel B), and internal clock rates (panel C) during three different drug treatments as a function of time since drug ingestion. Drugs: THC; alcohol (AL); placebo (PL). The internal clock rate, *r*, is the mean number of objective seconds per subjective second. For example, with THC, r = 0.65 means that subjects produced an interval 65% as long as the target interval; with alcohol, r = 1.35 means subjects produced an interval 135% as long as the target interval. [From Tinklenberg, J. R., Roth, W. T., & Kopell, B. S. (1976). Marijuana and ethanol: Differential effects on time perception, heart rate, and subjective response. *Psychopharmacology, 49*, 275–79. Reprinted by permission of Springer-Verlag, Heidelberg.]

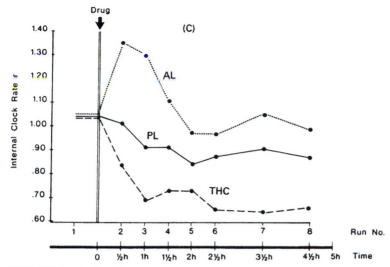

FIGURE 18.2   Continued

val. Thus, the overestimation (or underproduction) of time intervals during marijuana intoxication can be explained by the fact that many users report an increased rate of flow and change of ideas during marijuana intoxication. For example, one of Tinklenberg et al.'s (1972) subjects reported: "My mind shifts rapidly from one new thought to another, each very different . . . I feel hopped up and want to really groove with an experience, but the subject keeps changing." Conversely, the fact that alcohol makes many users feel mentally sluggish is consistent with the underestimation (and overproduction) of time intervals during alcohol intoxication, according to the cognitive theory of time perception. A further prediction of the cognitive theory is that, after a marijuana intoxication period has ended, a retrospective estimate of its duration would be reduced, compared to a placebo condition, since fewer events would be recalled from the marijuana intoxication period. This prediction agrees with some subjective reports, though it has not been experimentally tested.

The motivation problem.   In evaluating the disruptive effects of marijuana on cognitive task performance, it is important to determine whether the effects are due to decreased *ability* to perform or decreased *motivation* to perform. Some marijuana users claim to be able to "come down" at will, suggesting that marijuana effects are at least partly motivational. This notion has been tested in several studies, where subjects were given incentives to perform to the best of their ability.

Cappell and Pliner (1973) gave subjects either marijuana or a placebo and then gave half of the subjects in each group special motivating instructions urging them to use whatever means they could to try to overcome the drug's effects and perform to the best of their ability. (Bear in mind that placebo subjects believe that they are smoking real marijuana.) The motivating instructions reduced the disruptive effects of marijuana on time estimation, but not on a memory test. Casswell (1975) used a monetary incentive to motivate subjects to perform as well as possible. The incentive did not reduce marijuana's disruptive effects on either a complex reaction time task or a speeded cognitive task requiring decoding a set of arbitrary symbols. However, the incentive reduced marijuana's disruptive effects on a mental arithmetic task, but only for those subjects with the highest mental arithmetic ability. In conclusion, the evidence indicates that increased effort can reduce the disruptive effects of marijuana on some tasks, but not others. The ability to "come down" is not a general one. It seems to depend upon both the nature of the task and upon the subject's prior skill at the task. Prior practice doing the task while stoned may also be important. Klonoff (1974) found that only a minority of subjects could drive as safely with marijuana as with placebo. Where your safety or important academic or professional goals are at stake, it would be wise not to count on being able to "come down" and perform well when you are stoned.

Creativity.   Many marijuana users have reported that when they are stoned they have a lively imagination and sometimes have creative inspirations. These inspirations may involve a variety of topics, such as art, music, humor, scientific theory, or the solution of personal or practical problems. People sometimes write down their "profound" and "creative" thoughts while they are stoned, but afterward their thoughts usually seem quite mundane or even incomprehensible. Yet, even if only a minority of the marijuana-induced inspirations are truly creative and useful, it is a phenomenon worth studying.

In discussing the question of whether marijuana enhances creativity, it is important to keep in mind that true creativity involves more than mere novelty of responses. MacKinnon (1962) pointed out that true creativity also implies that an idea is adaptive in the sense of serving to accomplish some recognizable goal, and that the idea is fully developed, elaborated, and evaluated. Of course, having a creative idea during marijuana intoxication does not prove that marijuana increases creativity; it is necessary to compare marijuana with a placebo control condition to see whether creativity is greater with marijuana than with placebo. Also, it is important to use blind testing and scoring procedures, where judges who score the creativity of productions do not know whether they came from the marijuana or the placebo condition. Unfortunately, no suitably controlled experiments have been done to evaluate the effects of marijuana on creativity in solving "real-world" types of problems.

The best available evidence on possible effects of marijuana on creativity involves studies using so-called creativity tests. For example, Guilford (1967) argued that tests of divergent thinking are related to creative ability. *Divergent thinking* involves producing several potential solutions to a problem, whereas *convergent thinking* (which is emphasized on most intelligence tests) is involved in solving problems where there is only one correct solution. An example of a divergent thinking test is the Alternate Uses Test, where subjects are given one minute to think of as many uses as possible for a common object, such as a brick or paper clip. Tests of divergent thinking can be scored on several dimensions: fluency (number of responses), flexibility (number of conceptually different types of responses), originality (rarity of responses), and elaboration (embellishment or figural detail).

Tinklenberg et al. (1978) found no effect of marijuana on divergent thinking tests. Carlin et al. (1972) found that marijuana lowered scores on two divergent thinking tests (alternate uses and verbal associations). Weckowicz et al. (1975) used a battery of fourteen different tests of convergent and divergent thinking. Marijuana lowered scores on most tests and increased scores on only one test that might be related to creativity (originality in predicting possible consequences of a specified situation).

Roth et al. (1975) found that oral THC increased the novelty of stories produced in response to pictures on the Thematic Aperception Test (TAT) cards, though it did not lead to production of polished literary creations. According to the authors, "Under marijuana the stories had a timeless, nonnarrative quality, with greater discontinuity in thought sequence and more frequent inclusion of contradictory ideas" (p. 261). Similar conclusions were reached by Weil and Zinberg (1969) in a study of the effects of smoked marijuana on spontaneous oral narrations. While Roth et al. found that marijuana changed the stories, making them unusual in several ways, their results did not demonstrate an enhancement of creativity in the socially relevant manner described by MacKinnon (1962), where adaptiveness and development are important in addition to novelty.

In conclusion, there is no convincing evidence that marijuana enhances the creativity of people while they are stoned. It may sometimes increase the fluency or unusualness of ideas, without increasing creativity in the fullest sense involving novelty combined with adaptiveness and full development of ideas. This is not to say, of course, that worthwhile creative ideas never occur to people while they are stoned. Creative artists, for example, have sometimes had creative inspirations while stoned, but these people were creative before they smoked marijuana; marijuana cannot turn a noncreative person into a creative one (Krippner 1977). In any case, people's subjective impressions that their ideas are very witty and creative is undoubtedly one of the enjoyable aspects of marijuana that provides an incentive for its use.

Social and Personality Effects of Marijuana

Social cognition.   One of the common subjective effects of marijuana is the feeling of having deep insights into other people and enhanced interpersonal communication. If this is true then one would expect that people under the influence of marijuana would be particularly good at perceiving the emotional reactions of others. Experimental research shows that this is not necessarily the case. Clopton et al. (1979) had subjects view filmed social encounters and found that marijuana reduced the accuracy of emotion perception, compared to a presmoking score, whereas a placebo caused no such decline. The detrimental effect of marijuana on emotion perception might be due to changes in complex social perception processes, or it might be due to changes in more elementary processes of attention and memory.

Janowsky et al. (1979) evaluated interpersonal skills in live social encounters, in which each male subject conversed with a female stranger about her personal problems. Each subject was tested twice, once with marijuana and once with placebo. The conversations were filmed, and the subjects' interpersonal skills were scored on several dimensions: regard (warmth), empathy, unconditionality (acceptance), congruence (genuineness), and a composite total score. The authors concluded:

> Overall, it seems that intoxication with marijuana leads to a decrease in interpersonal skills. . . . In our view, those subjects evidencing the most severe decrements in interpersonal skills became confused easily and had obvious difficulty following conversations. They also became withdrawn and seemed to be more interested in their own thoughts and behavior and less interested in their partners. In a few subjects, the deterioration was so severe that the experimental subjects became afunctional as interviewers. [The minority of] subjects who improved in their interpersonal skills after the administration of active marijuana were observed to become more communicative, more outgoing, and less defensive during the active-marijuana interview (p. 784).

Janowsky et al. also assessed subjects' moods and found that the degree of congruence (similarity) between the moods of the male subjects and their female partners was reduced by marijuana, compared to placebo. This finding is contrary to users' reports of an increased emotional resonance with their friends during marijuana intoxication. However, the decreased emotional resonance under marijuana in Janowsky et al.'s study might be related to the fact that only the subjects were stoned, and not their partners, and/or the fact that the subjects and partners were strangers. The experimental setting was quite different from the usual marijuana-smoking situation where people get high with their friends. Rossi, Kuehnle, and Mendelson (1978) found increased mood congruence during marijuana smoking in a group of subjects who lived together in a hospital and had unlimited access to marijuana for three weeks.

Mood.   Regular marijuana users report marijuana smoking to be a pleasurable experience most of the time. Anxiety, depression, and paranoia sometimes occur, but more common is frequent laughter when people smoke in a group, or pleasurable daydreaming when they smoke alone. When a variety of moods have been measured systematically in experimental studies, no consistent effects of marijuana have been found, other than the fact that marijuana is typically rated as more pleasurable than placebo. Insofar as people's moods tend to be strongly affected by their companions' moods, we would expect that people's moods during marijuana smoking would be affected more by the social situation than by marijuana *per se*.

Psychiatric symptoms.   In normal people using normal social doses, acute marijuana intoxication does not cause psychiatric symptoms. Marijuana does not typically increase anxiety, hostility, or depression, compared to placebo (Janowsky et al. 1979). Contrary to old myths about marijuana, there is no evidence that marijuana increases violence or aggression. However, anxiety and paranoid reactions sometimes occur. Negative reactions to marijuana have been linked to personal fears about losing self-control and an altered sense of personal identity. It is suspected that marijuana can precipitate full-blown psychosis in people with psychotic tendencies, and it can intensify schizophrenic and paranoid symptoms that already exist (McKim 1986; Tunving 1985).

INTERPRETATIONS OF MARIJUANA'S EFFECTS

Regardless of the results of objective experiments on marijuana's perceptual, cognitive, and interpersonal effects, there is no doubt that marijuana alters subjective experience. Going beyond the analysis of specific symptoms of marijuana intoxication, Andrew Weil (1972) characterized marijuana intoxication as a shift in the style of thought from "straight thinking" to "stoned thinking." Our normal, reality-oriented straight thinking is analytic and intellectual, whereas stoned thinking is holistic and intuitive. Also, stoned thinking involves "acceptance of the ambivalent nature of things" and the "experience of infinity in its positive aspect." The characteristics of stoned thinking are similar to those of the mystic experience (Deikman 1966) and what Ornstein (1977) described as the right-hemisphere mode of consciousness.

In a related proposal, Harshman, Crawford, and Hecht (1976) suggested that the process of becoming high on marijuana consists, in part, of shifting into a new cognitive style or mode that involves "less reliance on analytic, sequential, verbal processing, and more reliance on synthetic, holistic, imagistic processing." Several types of evidence support this characterization. Marijuana disrupts the smooth and coherent flow of conversational speech (Weil & Zinberg 1969) and decreases reading comprehension (Clark et al. 1970). Also it decreases performance on logical syllogism and inference problems (Harshman et al. 1976). Conversely, marijuana produces subjective effects of enhanced spatial and figural perception, music appreciation, flow of imagination, and novelty or creativity of ideas. It increases performance on a measure of holistic perception, where subjects try to recognize objects in drawings that have large parts of their outlines missing (Harshman et al. 1976). Also, marijuana increases primary suggestibility, the performance of hypnotic-type suggestions, which is believed to be related to an increase in imagination and a decrease in reality orientation (Crawford 1974; Kelly, Fisher, & Kelly 1978).

It has been suggested that the shift in cognitive style during marijuana intoxication involves a decrease in left-cerebral-hemisphere activity, and an increase in right-hemisphere activity (Harshman et al. 1976; Ornstein 1976). However, there is no direct evidence (such as EEG studies) supporting this hypothesis. As we saw earlier (Chapter 5), the linking of alternative modes of consciousness or cognitive styles with the two hemispheres appears to be an oversimplification, since many complex thought processes involve both hemispheres.

Although marijuana's effects can be described as a shift in cognitive style, this is not an explanation of its effects. No theory, either psychological or neuropharmacological, has been developed that adequately explains all of marijuana's subjective, cognitive, and behavioral effects. One approach to a cognitive psychological theory would be to try to explain effects on more complex or higher-level processes in terms of effects on simpler, more basic processes. For example, it is clear that marijuana makes short-term memory (working memory) more susceptible to interference. Working memory is critical for many cognitive operations, such as judgment of new inputs against information retrieved from LTM, speech comprehension and production, imagery processes, and elaborative rehearsal for storing new information in LTM in an organized, retrievable manner.

IS MARIJUANA HARMFUL?

Marijuana has always been controversial. In the early years of marijuana use in the United States, straight society disapproved of marijuana because of its association with racial and ethnic minorities. Also, since violent criminals sometimes smoked marijuana, it was claimed that marijuana causes violence and moral degeneracy. In the 1960s, marijuana was associated with hippies and their political liberalism and contempt for middle-class values. More recently marijuana has been condemned as a "stepping-stone" drug that leads to the use of more dangerous drugs, such as cocaine. Opposition to marijuana was based more on guilt by association and myths about its harmful effects than on research evidence on its actual harmful effects. What is the evidence on harmful effects of marijuana? I have already discussed the effects of acute marijuana intoxication. Here the emphasis will be on the effects of chronic (frequent, long-term) use on health and mental functioning.

Cognitive effects. At extremely high doses, marijuana can cause delirium, toxic psychosis, and loss of consciousness; this is true of most other drugs, too (McKim 1986). Long-term (daily for six months) high-dose THC administration produced learning deficits in rats, from which they did not recover after THC was discontinued (Feher et al. 1976). The implication is that maintained very high doses of marijuana may cause brain damage, as occurs also with alcohol. However, studies of chronic marijuana users (daily use at fairly high doses over several years) have failed to find any evidence that marijuana causes permanent deficits in cognitive functioning or psychopathology (Grinspoon 1977; Schaeffer, Andrysiak, & Ungerleider 1981).

The absence of clear proof of harmful cognitive or behavioral effects of chronic marijuana use should not, however, be interpreted as proof that marijuana is safe. While work adaptation has been found to be adequate in chronic marijuana users, the subjects have been employed at jobs that do not have heavy intellectual demands, such as agricultural work and physical labor. Also, while chronic users have usually been found to be average or above in performance on intelligence tests and other cognitive measures, it is possible that their scores would have been even higher if they had not been habitual marijuana users. Due to practical problems of such research, studies of chronic marijuana use have been correlational, rather than experimental. They have not taken psychological measures before chronic use to compare with measures taken after long-term use, nor have they had suitable control groups. Despite the absence of clear evidence of permanent cognitive impairment being caused by chronic marijuana use, people whose careers depend on being mentally sharp should ask themselves whether the pleasure of marijuana (as well as alcohol and other drugs) is worth the risk.

Amotivational syndrome.   Habitual marijuana use, particularly among adolescents, has been associated with changes in behavior termed the *amotivational syndrome*. Its symptoms include:

> apathy, loss of effectiveness, and diminished capacity or willingness to carry out complex, long-term plans, endure frustration, concentrate for long periods, follow routines, or successfully master new material. Verbal facility is often impaired both in speaking and writing. Some individuals exhibit greater introversion, become totally involved with the present at the expense of future goals, and demonstrate a strong tendency toward regressive, childlike, magical thinking (McGlothlin & West 1968, p. 372).

Some studies have found lower grade averages and higher dropout rates among marijuana users than among nonusers, though this is not always the case, as some marijuana users continue to function at high levels of motivation for academic or career advancement. Recent studies continue to suggest an amotivational syndrome correlated with marijuana use in adolescents, involving not only achievement orientation but also deviant behavior and poor interpersonal relations with peers and parents (Brook et al. 1989).

Though the amotivational syndrome is correlated with frequency of marijuana use, there is no proof that marijuana causes the amotivational syndrome. A plausible alternative interpretation is that the personality and social factors that produce the amotivational syndrome also lead to frequent marijuana use. People who are not motivated to study or work are likely to spend more time on idle recreation, including marijuana smoking. Nonetheless, the possibility remains that some individuals would find the pleasures of marijuana to be so reinforcing that marijuana-smoking behavior would increase to the point that it would interfere with other behavior, such as studying and work, associated with less pleasurable or longer-delayed reinforcers. Also, even for those who maintain their motivation for studying, marijuana can interfere with attention, learning, and memory, thus producing the same effects as loss of motivation (McKim 1986).

"Stepping stone" to other drugs.   Most people who use stronger, more dangerous drugs, such as heroin or cocaine, used marijuana first. It has been claimed that marijuana was somehow responsible for the progression to "harder" drugs. Yet, as with the amotivational syndrome, the evidence is entirely correlational, and there is no proof that marijuana *causes* progression to other drugs. Marijuana use does not produce any physiological need or craving for stronger drugs. Most marijuana users do not progress to harder drugs. But for those who do make the progression, the explanation is psychological and sociological, not pharmacological. The personality traits of curiosity and risk taking that lead some people to use marijuana will lead some of them to try harder drugs. And where people have the opportunity to buy

marijuana, harder drugs may also be available (McKim 1986). Many false or exaggerated claims have been made about harmful effects of marijuana, so that people who have tried marijuana without any apparent bad effects may subsequently disbelieve claims about harmful effects of harder drugs, and thus be willing to try the harder drugs. The stepping-stone hypothesis is, at best, an oversimplification of the facts.

Physiological effects.   Heavy marijuana use can lead to physiological *tolerance*, in the sense that physiological responses (such as heart rate) to a given dose are reduced. However, this tolerance effect does not lead to a craving for higher doses, as it does with some drugs such as heroin and cocaine. Physical dependence (or physiological addiction) was found in a study where very high doses of THC were taken every four hours for ten to twenty days. When THC use was stopped, subjects had withdrawal symptoms—such as irritability, nausea, and sleep disturbances—that peaked after eight hours and declined over the next three days (Jones & Benowitz 1976). However, physical dependence and withdrawal symptoms do not occur with ordinary chronic use and normal doses (Ray & Ksir 1987).

Are there any harmful physiological effects of chronic marijuana use? Yes. Marijuana reduces the activity of the body's immune system, which fights against invading microorganisms to prevent disease. Like tobacco smoke, marijuana decreases the activity of macrophages in the lungs, which attack bacteria and foreign substances. Also, like tobacco smoke, marijuana smoke is an irritant to lung tissue. However, though it is highly plausible that heavy marijuana use can cause an increased frequency of lung infections, and possibly lung cancer, there is no clear proof that this is the case. A major problem complicating research on effects of chronic marijuana use is that heavy marijuana users usually use other drugs—such as tobacco and alcohol—so it is virtually impossible to distinguish the effects of marijuana from the effects of other drugs (McKim 1986).

Some studies have found that marijuana use lowers levels of the male hormone testosterone. It is not clear whether this has any functional significance in adult males, since testosterone levels vary widely between different men and from time to time within individuals. More important is the role of testosterone in biological development. Testosterone is important for the growth spurt and physiological changes that take place at puberty in males, including secondary sex characters such as beard growth and lowered voice pitch. Heavy marijuana use at puberty might interfere with these changes. Also, in the unborn fetus, at eight to ten weeks after conception the male fetus starts secreting testosterone, which plays a critical role in differentiation of the brain and the urogenital system, including the male sex organs. Thus, normal physical development of the male fetus could be disrupted if the mother uses marijuana. Again, there is no clear evidence that this happens, because mothers who are heavy marijuana users usually use other drugs, too.

Conclusion.   It is clear that marijuana is not a "killer weed," nor does casual marijuana use make people violent, crazy, or stupid. Most of the possibly harmful effects of chronic marijuana use are suggestive, rather than proven. It has been impossible to get clear proof of harmful effects of chronic marijuana use in humans because of the limitations of correlational studies and the fact that most heavy marijuana users also use other drugs, such as tobacco and alcohol.

Without exaggerating the dangers of marijuana, three cautions about its use are in order: (1) Acute marijuana intoxication has been shown to interfere with safe automobile driving by slowing reaction times, increasing attentional distraction, and interfering with judgment. The claim that stoned people can "come down" to drive safely is a myth. For the safety of yourself and your friends, as well as innocent strangers, don't drive stoned. (2) Acute marijuana intoxication increases susceptibility to attentional distraction, disrupts thought processes, and interferes with learning. If you want to do your best work as a student, you should study and go to classes straight, not stoned. The same point applies if you have a job that requires flexible, intelligent thought. (3) Though the proof is not as clear for marijuana as it is for some other drugs, such as tobacco and alcohol, there is reason to suspect that marijuana can interfere with the development of the unborn fetus. If you are pregnant, or think that you might be pregnant, avoid using marijuana and other drugs, except those prescribed by your doctor. You might be willing to take risks for yourself, but it would be wrong to take risks for your unborn child.

THE MARIJUANA PARADOX

The marijuana paradox is that so often the strongly felt subjective effects of marijuana turn out to be illusions when they are tested by objective methods. For example, subjective impressions of increased sensory sensitivity conflict with the results of psychophysical tests, which typically show no change or a decrease in sensitivity. Intuitive social perceptions often turn out to be false, and apparently creative insights often turn out to be mundane in the light of sober judgment. Even the "reverse tolerance" effect (the belief that experienced users become more sensitive to marijuana) has turned out to be an illusion by objective criteria (R. T. Jones 1971).

Believers in the reality of "alternative realities" that appear during altered states of consciousness will protest that the claim that the subjective experiences are illusions is incorrect or even arrogant, since it assumes that the experimenter's "objective reality" is more real or true than the marijuana smoker's subjective reality. I prefer not to get sidetracked by philosophical arguments about how to decide whether one reality is more valid than another. However, it is important to stress the point that, regardless of their correspondence with objective measurements, the altered subjective experiences during marijuana intoxication are often intensely real to the user and are an important psychological phenomenon in their own right. We need to know more about the reasons why people who are stoned on marijuana have such unusual but intense subjective experiences, such as feelings of increased sensitivity, insights into oneself and others, changed judgments of the humorous and the profound, and feelings of creativity, regardless of whether any of these beliefs correspond to the results of objective measurements. I predict that part of the explanation of marijuana's subjective effects will come from a further understanding of its neurophysiological effects, but that a complete answer will also have to consider the social psychology of attribution, expectation, and belief.

SUMMARY

Psychedelic ("mind manifesting") drugs are a heterogeneous group whose most striking subjective effects include changes in perception and imagination. They include marijuana and the hallucinogens. As Tart explained, reactions to psychoactive drugs depend on an *interaction* of drug factors (type, dose) with long-term personal factors (personality, attitudes, knowledge, beliefs), immediate personal factors (mood, expectations), and situational or experimental factors (physical and social setting, instructions, implicit demands).

Marijuana (active ingredient, THC) can produce a variety of subjective effects, which vary from one individual or occasion to another. The *marijuana paradox* refers to the fact that some strongly felt subjective effects are not supported by objective evidence. Important subjective effects and objective results during marijuana intoxication include the following: (1) Subjective reports of increased sensory sensitivity are contradicted by results of signal-detection experiments; in fact, sensitivity is decreased, mainly due to attention shifts during testing. (2) Subjective reports of memory disruption are supported by laboratory experiments. Marijuana disrupts short-term memory by increasing its susceptibility to interference. It also interferes with learning (transfer of new information from STM to LTM). (3) Subjective reports of changed time experience are confirmed by quantitative studies showing overestimation of time intervals. (4) Subjective feelings of increased creativity are not supported by objective measures, such as tests of divergent thinking. (5) Subjective impressions of enhanced interpersonal perception and communication are contradicted by experimental results; in fact, the opposite usually occurs. (6) The subjective impression of ability to "come down" at will is contradicted by evidence that marijuana slows automobile braking time and increases driving errors. The subjective and cognitive effects of marijuana have been interpreted as a shift in cognitive style, but no theory adequately explains all of marijuana's effects.

Marijuana has been blamed for the "amotivational syndrome" in adolescents and accused as a "stepping stone" to stronger drugs, but the evidence has alternative interpretations. Claimed harmful effects of marijuana have often been exaggerated or unfounded, but caution was advised especially in regard to three situations: automobile driving; school or work requiring peak intellectual performance and learning; and pregnancy.

ENDNOTES

[1]William McKim advised me that it is impossible to devise an entirely satisfactory classification of psychoactive drugs based on their psychological or behavioral effects, since they have

such a wide variety of effects and clinical uses. But I wanted a concise table, and I thank him for his suggestions on Table 18.1. For more information on the drugs in Table 18.1, see McKim 1986.

[2]In surveys conducted in General Psychology classes at the University of Maine, students were asked whether they had ever smoked marijuana, and if so, did they get "stoned" the first time they smoked (a lot, a little, or not at all). Between 1976 (n = 157), 1983 (n = 151), and 1989 (n = 160), the percent who had ever smoked marijuana decreased from 72 to 60 to 46 percent. But of those who had smoked, the percent who felt stoned the first time increased from 36 to 43 to 59 percent. It is uncertain whether the changes in percent who felt stoned are due to changes in the smoking population, changes in the quality of marijuana, or some other variable (G. W. Farthing, unpublished data).

[3]In the study described here, Darley et al. (1973b) used a free-recall procedure and examined effects of THC on the primacy and recency effects in the serial position curve. Briefly, THC affected the primacy effect (recall of words early in the list, which depends on recall from LTM), but not the recency effect (recall of the last few words on the list, which involves recall from STM). The serial position curve and its significance is described in most cognitive psychology textbooks (for example, Best 1989; Klatzky 1980). Readers interested in more details on the effects of THC on the serial position curve should consult Darley et al. (1973b).

[4]Computationally, r = produced interval divided by target interval. For example, under THC, when asked to *produce* a 120-second target interval, a subject might sound the tone for only 80 seconds (underproduction), since 80 (objective) seconds seems to him (subjectively) like 120 seconds. This would compute to 80/120 = 0.67 objective seconds per subjective second. In other words, his internal clock has speeded up. It "ticks" once every 0.67 seconds, or three ticks in two seconds. But he assumes it is still ticking once per second. Thus, if asked to estimate the duration of a tone, this subject would *estimate* a 120-second tone to be 180 seconds long (overestimation), since his inner clock would beat 180 times in 120 seconds. Underproduction is equivalent to overestimation of time intervals.

chapter 19 ·······························

Psychedelic Drugs II: The Major Hallucinogens

Hallucinogens are a chemically heterogeneous group of drugs that are capable of inducing hallucinations at normal dose levels. A *hallucination* is a percept-like experience that the individual interprets as real, although it has no objective counterpart (for example, if you believe you see someone standing in front of you, but in fact nobody is there, or if you believe you see a tunnel of light, but the "light" is really inside your head, and not "out there"). People in different cultures around the world have used hallucinogenic drugs for many centuries. But in the older cultural traditions people did not use hallucinogens just to produce entertaining psychedelic light shows in their heads. Rather, in most cases they used hallucinogens as a route to mystical or religious experiences. And they didn't think of it as "using drugs." Rather, they used plants as a religious sacrament and believed that God was in the plant or that God communicated through the plant (Schultes & Hofmann 1979).

First I will discuss the major hallucinogens used in the Americas—psilocybin mushrooms, peyote, and LSD—with an emphasis on their cultural context and reports of subjective experiences. Then I will go into more detail on hallucinations *per se*.

PSILOCYBIN MUSHROOMS

The hallucinogen *psilocybin* is found in several species of mushrooms—popularly known as "magic mushrooms"—found in North America. Most of them grow only in Mexico and southern United States, though some are found in northern forests. Psilocybin mushrooms include *Psilocybe mexicana* and several others (Figure 19.1). These mushrooms have been considered sacred in Mexico and Central America for thousands of years, according to archaeological records. When the Spaniards conquered the Aztecs in Mexico in the early 1500s they found an important religious cult that used mushrooms as a sacrament. The Aztecs called the mushrooms *teonanacatl*, which means "God's flesh" (McKim 1986). The Spaniards suppressed the mushroom cult.

In the 1930s it was discovered that magic mushrooms were still being used by natives in southern Mexico. In 1952 Gordon Wasson, a retired banker turned ethnobotanist, established rapport with the Indian natives in Mexico and ate twelve of the mushrooms as part of a religious ceremony. Wasson described his experience as follows:

> It permits you to travel backwards and forward in time, to enter other planes of existence, even (as the Indians say), to know God. . . .
>
> What is happening to you seems freighted with significance, beside which the humdrum events of every day are trivial. All these things you see with an immediacy of vision that leads you to say to yourself, 'Now I am seeing for the first time, seeing direct, without the intervention of mortal eyes'.
>
> Your body lies in the darkness, heavy as lead, but your spirit seems to soar and leave the hut, and with the speed of thought, to travel where it listeth, in time and space, accompanied by the shaman's singing . . . at last you know what the ineffable is, and what ecstasy means. Ecstasy! The mind harks back to the origin of that word. For the Greeks *ekstasis* meant the flight of the soul from the body. Can you find a better word to describe this state? (Crahan 1969, cited in Ray 1978, pp. 371–72).

Wasson's description shows that hallucinogens can produce not only hallucinations, but also emotional reactions and the feeling that one's thoughts and images are profoundly important, though the experience in its details is ineffable and it can be described only in vague generalizations.

When Harvard University psychologist Timothy Leary used magic mushrooms in Mexico in 1960, his experiences led him to become a proselytizer of psychedelic drug use as a route to mystical experiences. From his observations of other people he estimated that psilocybin, when taken in a supportive setting, could induce "intense and life-changing religious experiences" in 40 to 75 percent of subjects (Leary 1967–68). Leary became a guru of the hippie generation of the 1960s, though he lost his position at Harvard because of the controversy over his drug advocacy and questions about the quality of his research (Ray 1978). Leary and his followers used primarily LSD because it was stronger and easier to obtain and to use than magic mushrooms. In recent years, however, many hallucinogenic drug devotees have returned to natural hallucinogens such as psilocybin mushrooms, since it is impossible to be confident that street LSD is really pure LSD (and not PCP or some other drug). Lest you be tempted to search the woods for magic mushrooms, you should be warned that there are many similar-looking mushrooms, and some of them are poisonous. To be "safe" you have to find

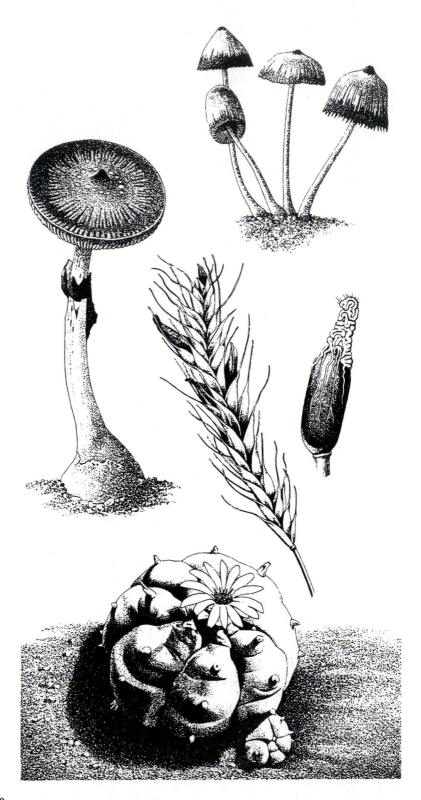

exactly the right species and take it in the right dose. The wrong species of mushroom, or too high a dose, could have disastrous effects.

PEYOTE

Peyote (peyotyl) is another natural hallucinogen from Mexico. Peyote is a small, spineless cactus (*Lophophora williamsii*) that grows in the desert (see Figure 19.1). Most of it grows below ground, like a carrot; only the grayish-green pincushion-like top shows above ground. Archaeological evidence indicates that peyote has been used for thousands of years, and like psilocybe mushrooms and morning glory seeds, it was a sacred plant of the Aztecs. They used it as a medicine and to promote visions of the future, and for divination. The Spaniards thought that peyote visions were "satanic trickery" and tried to suppress it. But as with the mushrooms, peyote traditions survived among the Mexican Indians and later spread north to the Plains Indians. Several of the peyote cults combined to form the Native American Church, which was first chartered in Oklahoma in 1918. Efforts were made immediately in Congress to pass laws against peyote use, but the Secretary of the Interior forbade the Indian Bureau from interfering with the religious practices of the Native American Church. In 1970 a formal act of the U.S. Congress recognized the right of the church members to use peyote as a sacrament (McKim 1986; Ray 1978).[1]

To use peyote, the top part of the cactus is cut into slices called "mescal buttons," which are set in the sun to dry. (Mescal buttons should not be confused with the hallucinogenic mescal bean, which is a different plant and is highly toxic [Ray 1978].) The mescal buttons are soaked in the mouth until soft, then chewed and swallowed. They have a bitter, disagreeable taste. Several buttons may be swallowed in a peyote ceremony. Within a few minutes the individual experiences several disagreeable symptoms, including nausea, vomiting, tremor, and incoordination. These symptoms eventually pass, and after an hour or so psychedelic and hallucinatory experiences begin; the subjective effects may last several hours (McKim 1986).

One of the first non-Indian investigators of peyote was Dr. Weir Mitchell, who used a peyote extract. He tried to describe his hallucinatory experience:

> The display which for an enchanted two hours followed was such as I find it hopeless to describe in language which shall convey to others the beauty and splendor of what I saw. Stars, delicate floating films of color, then an abrupt rush of countless points of white light swept across the field of view, as if the

---

FIGURE 19.1. Natural sources of the main hallucinogens. Psilocybin comes from the mushrooms *Stropharia cubensis* (top left) and *Psilocybe mexicana* (top right). LSD was originally synthesized from an alkaloid in ergot (*Claviceps purpurea*), a fungus that grows on cereal grains; an ergot-infested rye seed head is shown (center) together with a larger-scale drawing of the ergot fungus. Mescaline is from the peyote cactus *Lophophora williamsii* (bottom). [From Barron, F., Jarvik, M. E., & Bunnell, S. (1964, April). The hallucinogenic drugs. *Scientific American*. Copyright © 1964 by Scientific American, Inc. All rights reserved.]

unseen millions of the Milky Way were to flow in a sparkling river before my eyes . . . zigzag lines of very bright colors . . . the wonderful loveliness of swelling clouds of more vivid colors gone before I could name them (1896, cited in DeRopp 1957, p. 34).

Then, Mitchell reported, "A white spear of grey stone grew up to huge height, and became a tall, richly furnished Gothic Tower of very elaborate and definite design, with many rather worn statues standing in the doorways" and decorated by huge precious stones, "like masses of transparent fruit," of green, purple, red, and orange. Later, he looked over the edge of a huge cliff "that seemed to project over a gulf of unseen depth." A huge bird claw of stone perched on the edge. From the bird leg, folds of half-transparent purple stone floated out for miles. "Now and then soft golden clouds floated from these folds . . . and things like green birds fell from it, fluttering down into the gulf below." Finally, he saw the beach of Newport with huge rolling waves "of wonderfully pure green, or red or deep purple" breaking on the beach.

Peyote contains some thirty different psychoactive chemicals, of which *mescaline* has been isolated and identified as the one mainly responsible for the vivid colors and other visual hallucination effects. Mescaline is chemically similar to the neurotransmitter norepinephrine. Aldous Huxley described his mescaline experiences in *The Doors of Perception* (1954/1970), where he concluded:

> To be shaken out of the ruts of ordinary perception, to be shown for a few timeless hours the outer and the inner world, not as they appear to an animal obsessed with survival or to a human being obsessed with words and notions, but as they are apprehended, directly and unconditionally, by Mind at Large— this is an experience of inestimable value to everyone and especially to the intellectual (p. 73).

If only there was a way for healthy, prepared people to legally have such an educational experience without opening up the possibility of drug overuse and abuse. But Huxley also warned of the possibility of bad trips on mescaline. For any psychedelic drug, the possibility of bad trips—characterized by depression, anxiety, and possibly panic—is greater for people who are emotionally unstable, depressed, or undergoing great stress in their lives.

LSD

Though traditional cultures used plants to produce hallucinations, the most popular hallucinogenic during the hippie era was a synthetic drug, LSD (lysergic acid diethylamide). Like psilocybin, the chemical structure of LSD is similar to the neurotransmitter serotonin. LSD was more popular than mescaline or psilocybin because it is more potent and easier to synthesize, and hence less expensive per dose. The effective hallucinogenic dose for LSD is only about 0.05 mg; for psilocybin it is about 6 mg; mescaline, about 200 mg. (These doses are ED_{50}s, which means that they are effective for 50 percent of adult users [McKim 1986].) LSD is taken orally. LSD's effects begin within about 30 to 90 minutes and last for a few hours, more or less, depending on the dose. *Tolerance* develops very quickly, so that with repeated daily doses the dose has to be increased to have the same effect; tolerance subsides after a few days of abstenance. *Cross-tolerance* occurs between LSD, psilocybin, and mescaline, such that a dose of one drug will reduce the effectiveness of a dose of one of the other drugs taken several hours later. Cross-tolerance is greater between LSD and psilocybin, because of their greater chemical similarity; they seem to produce identical psychological effects at functionally equivalent doses. LSD, psilocybin, and mescaline produce similar physiological symptoms, including pupil dilation, increased pulse rate and blood pressure, and elevated body temperature. Headache, nausea, and vomiting sometimes occur. None of these drugs are physiologically addictive (McKim 1986; Ray & Ksir 1987).

LSD was first synthesized in 1938 by Albert Hofmann, working at the Sandoz Laboratories in Basel, Switzerland. It was synthesized from ergot alkaloids (taken from a highly toxic mold that sometimes grows on rye grain [Figure 19.1]) in the course of a search for useful drugs, because of its chemical similarity to other known psychoactive drugs. It was not until 1943 that LSD's hallucinogenic effects were discovered by Dr. Hofmann, after he accidentally ingested some. Apparently he absorbed it through his fingers while working in the laboratory. His report is especially interesting in view of the fact that he did not know that he had taken a drug, and thus had no prior expectations about what would happen:

Last Friday, April 16, 1943, I was forced to stop my work in the laboratory in the middle of the afternoon and to go home, as I was seized by a peculiar restlessness associated with a sensation of mild dizziness. Having reached home, I lay down and sank in a kind of drunkenness which was not unpleasant and which was characterized by extreme activity of imagination. As I lay in a dazed condition with my eyes closed (I experienced daylight as disagreeably bright) there surged upon me an uninterrupted stream of fantastic images of extraordinary plasticity and vividness and accompanied by an intense, kaleidoscope-like play of colors. This condition gradually passed off after about two hours (Hofmann 1968, pp. 184–85; cited in Ray & Ksir 1987, p. 276).

A few days later Hofmann took a high dose of LSD (0.25 mg) deliberately. For the first few hours he experienced some unpleasant symptoms including dizziness, delirium, visual disturbances, coldness and loss of feeling in the hands, choking sensations, and fear that he might be losing his mind. Sometimes he felt as if he was out of his body (tripping). After six hours he felt better and reported experiencing "an unending series of colorful, very realistic and fantastic images." He also experienced *synesthesia*, where sensations in one modality are translated into images in a different modality: ". . . all acoustic perceptions (e.g., the noise of a passing car) were transformed into optical effects, every sound causing a corresponding colored hallucination constantly changing in shape and color like a kaleidoscope."

Subsequent to Hofmann's early reports, a number of studies of LSD's psychological effects and potential applications were carried out, mostly in the early 1960s. It was initially thought that LSD produced psychotic-like symptoms (hence the term, *psychotomimetic* drug) and that LSD might be useful for producing experimental psychosis for the purpose of understanding natural psychoses. However, investigators later came to realize that there are a number of differences between LSD effects and psychosis. For example, whereas LSD produces primarily visual hallucinations, schizophrenic hallucinations are primarily auditory, consisting of "hearing voices," often accompanied by paranoid reactions. Other studies suggested that LSD might be useful for psychotherapy, for alcoholism treatment, and for reducing pain and depression of patients with terminal cancer. However, these studies were controversial, and government agencies soon stopped funding this type of research.

In the 1960s LSD became a common street drug, popular with hippies. Some users, such as Leary, advocated LSD as a route to self-understanding and spiritual discovery. Most, however, probably used LSD just to produce a pleasant high with an entertaining hallucinatory movie show. LSD was unpopular with the establishment because of its association with hippies and their liberal, antimaterialist, anti–Vietnam War values. LSD users (who were also marijuana users) tended to spend a lot of time sitting around in apparently useless contemplation or listening to rock music. LSD effects were not always pleasant. Some users had bad trips with panic reactions. Although personality and stress factors are undoubtedly important in producing bad trips, another contributing factor was "bad acid," that is, LSD that was contaminated with other substances or, in some cases, was not really LSD but another drug entirely, such as PCP ("angel dust"). Another negative effect of LSD is *flashbacks*, where LSD-like experiences, usually unpleasant ones, are experienced several days or months after LSD was used. Flashbacks do not occur in everyone. They are hard to predict, though they seem to be most likely at times of stress. Some researchers suspect that LSD causes lasting brain changes that can produce flashbacks, but this has not been clearly proven (Ray & Ksir 1987).

Research on effects of LSD in humans pretty much ground to a halt in 1974, when the U.S. National Institute of Mental Health (NIMH) stopped funding university-sponsored research on that topic. The National Cancer Institute and the National Institute on Alcohol Abuse and Alcoholism stopped supporting LSD research in 1975. The reason given for dropping LSD research was that it was "unproductive," though it could be argued that it was stopped prematurely and that valuable new discoveries might have been made in new research using better methods and building on what had been learned earlier. Undoubtedly social and political pressures also influenced the decision to stop funding LSD research. Popular tastes changed, too. LSD use apparently reached its peak around the time of the Woodstock music festival in 1969. LSD use declined when the aging hippie generation got tired of it and the next generation of young people turned back toward materialism and had less interest in inner exploration. For dealers in illegal drugs, LSD is unattractive because it is not addictive and virtually nobody uses it on a daily basis. Today's drug dealers find cocaine to be more profitable than LSD.

The LSD trip.   Every LSD trip is different in its details, depending on the interaction of drug factors (dose, time), personal factors (personality, mood, expectations, etc.), and situational factors (physical and social setting). Drawing on descriptions by Houston (1969) and others, Ray (1978) synthesized a description of "typical" reactions to LSD as a function of dose level and time since the drug was taken. (Presumably this description applies also to psilocybin, since LSD and psilocybin appear to have the same subjective effects at functionally equivalent doses.) In Ray's description, the user goes through a series of five temporal stages or levels in which different effects (autonomic, sensory, etc.) are most prominent. The higher the dose, the higher the level that can potentially be reached. However, personal factors are also important: successively higher levels are reached by fewer and fewer people. Also, at successively higher levels the potential for meaningful experiences, either good or bad, increases.

Ray's five levels of LSD response are as follows: (1) *Autonomic* level: Autonomic reactions (increased heart rate, etc.) develop gradually over the first 20 minutes, when the individual may feel dizzy or hot and cold or have a dry mouth. (2) *Sensory* level: Sensory effects develop over the next 20 to 50 minutes, including altered body sensations, altered color and space and time perception, sensory synesthesias, and visual hallucinations. Cognitive changes also occur in this stage, where things, people, and experiences may be categorized differently because new similarities and relationships are noticed; these new ways of categorizing things may be carried over into the nondrug state. LSD is best known for its sensory effects; most trips don't go beyond this level. (3) *Recollective-analytical* level: The individual's own personality and life history are the center of focus, and aspects of the self may be recategorized and reevaluated. The result may be increased self-understanding and a positive attitude or anxiety and panic. (4) *Symbolic* level: ". . . there is an appreciation of our oneness with the universal concepts expressed in myths and in the archetypes of Jungian psychology" (Ray 1978, p. 360). (5) *Integral* level: Mystical experiences occur, and the individual has a feeling of unity with God or the universe. For some people, mystical experiences can have profound effects on their values and life course. One would expect wide differences in reactions at the two highest levels, depending on individual differences in knowledge of universal concepts and prior religious beliefs. At the higher levels, particularly, LSD users have the feeling that their thoughts are profound and valuable. Sometimes negative reactions occur. For example, the feeling of loss of self and unity with the universe may be a mystical religious experience for some but a frightening depersonalization experience for others.

Since visual hallucinations are a dramatic and commonly experienced subjective effect of LSD and other hallucinogens, I will go into some detail on hallucinations in the next section.

HALLUCINATIONS

Slade and Bentall (1988) defined a true hallucination as: "Any percept-like experience which (a) occurs in the absence of an appropriate stimulus, (b) has the full force or impact of the corresponding actual (real) perception, and (c) is not amenable to direct and voluntary control by the experiencer" (p. 23). An example would be a schizophrenic who believes he hears a voice—perhaps the voice of God—speaking to him, when in fact nobody is speaking. The most critical feature of true hallucinations is their apparent reality. The hallucinated voice or object seems to be "out there," rather than inside the subject or patient's head. Hallucinations have been compared with vivid mental images, but hallucinations are not necessarily vivid.

A *pseudohallucination* is a perceptual experience that the individual knows not to be real, though it may be just as vivid and spontaneous as a true hallucination (Siegel & Jarvik 1975; Slade & Bentall 1988). In many cases people who have taken hallucinogenic drugs are aware that their perceptual experiences are caused by the drug, and hence pseudohallucinatory by definition. Much confusion has been caused by the practice of some writers of lumping together true hallucinations with pseudohallucinations, such as vivid mental images.

Hallucinations should also be distinguished from *illusions*, which are misperceptions or misinterpretations of objective reality. Illusions occur as a result of the normal functioning of the sensory-perceptual system in an unusual situation, such that reality is misperceived (for example, the Ames distorted room [pictured in many general psychology textbooks], where a room without right angles or rectangular walls is perceived as an ordinary room when viewed with one eye from a certain position). Illusions occur as a result of knowledge and assumptions leading to certain expectations, which automatically influence our sensory perceptions. Illusions involve the misperception of objects (or sounds, etc.) that are really there, whereas the prototype hallucination occurs in the complete absence of real objects that could be misperceived.

There are some transition cases between hallucinations and illusions, which we may term *semi-hallucinations*, where there is a genuine sensory event but its misperception is so drastic as to be clearly based more on imagination than on ordinary perceptual processes (for example, when the wind is making noises in the trees and the camper, lying in his tent, believes that he hears voices, though there are no voices [the "voices in the wind" effect]). Perhaps many or most hallucinations are really semi-hallucinations in this sense, though the relevant sensory event has not been identified. Slade and Bentall's (1988) definition of hallucination encompasses semi-hallucinations, by specifying that the percept-like experiences occur in the absence of an *appropriate* stimulus; thus, hallucinations do not have to occur in the absence of *any* stimulus.

Systematic Analysis of Drug-Induced Visual Hallucinations

Starting in 1926, Heinrich Klüver (1966) began investigating visual hallucinations produced by mescaline. Comparing the reports of a variety of subjects, he noted that most of the hallucination patterns or designs fell into four categories, which he termed *form constants*. The four types were: (1) lattice (also called grating, fretwork, filigree, honeycomb, or chessboard); (2)

cobweb-like; (3) tunnel (also called funnel, alley, cone, or vessel); and (4) spiral. The form constants had varied and saturated colors, intense brightness, and symmetrical configuration. They could occur with the eyes closed, but with the eyes open they seemed to be projected in space at about reading distance. They varied greatly in apparent size and generally could not be voluntarily controlled. Klüver noted that the same form constants appear in a variety of other situations, including the hypnagogic (drowsy presleep) state, in insulin hypoglycemia, and occasionally in fever deliriums. Other investigators have noted form constants occurring in other situations, including epileptic seizures, schizophrenia, advanced syphilis, migraine headache, sensory deprivation, constant invariant photostimulation, crystal gazing, electrical stimulation, and a variety of hallucinogenic and toxic drugs (Siegel 1977). The fact that similar hallucinatory form constants occur in such a wide variety of situations suggests that the same underlying mechanisms are involved in the different situations.

Klüver's *simple form constants* are characteristic of only the first of three stages of hallucinogen-induced imagery. *Complex images*—images that include meaningful symbols and forms (such as animals, faces, familiar objects, and landscapes)—occur in the second and third stages. In the second stage (*complex combined images*), meaningful forms (images of animals, objects, faces, etc.) are combined with form constants (such as spirals and lattices) by superimposing meaningful forms on, or incorporating them into, form constants (see Figure 19.4, upper right panel). In the third stage (*complex memory images*) the form constants disappear and meaningful dream-like scenes appear, with people, landscapes, and so on (Balestrieri 1964; Siegel 1977).

Siegel's study.   Ronald K. Siegel (1977; Siegel & Jarvik 1975) did a systematic analysis and comparison of visual hallucinations produced by a variety of psychoactive drugs. He was interested in several dimensions of the visual images, including: (1) form (simple form constant patterns as well as complex image meaningful forms); (2) colors; (3) movement (such as linear, explosive, rotational, pulsating); and (4) action patterns (applying only to complex images, such as actions by objects, image combinations, scene changes). A major problem in research on hallucinations is that it depends upon the subjects' introspective verbal reports, and different subjects may use different vocabularies to describe similar-looking images, thus making it hard to compare their experiences. Siegel overcame this problem by training the subjects to use an image classification system prior to the drug sessions. For example, they were taught to classify and name the forms in a set of slides with several examples each of webs, lattices, spirals, tunnels, and so forth (see Figure 19.2). Other slides were used to train the subjects to correctly name various colors and movement patterns. After sufficient training the subjects were able to correctly name the form, color, and movement pattern for each pattern in a series of rapidly presented slides, including new ones. The purpose of the speeded image-naming sessions was to prepare subjects for the drug test sessions, where it was expected that hallucinogenic drugs would produce rapidly changing images.

In the test sessions, subjects lay on their backs, alone, in a completely dark, soundproof chamber, with their eyes open. They were instructed to

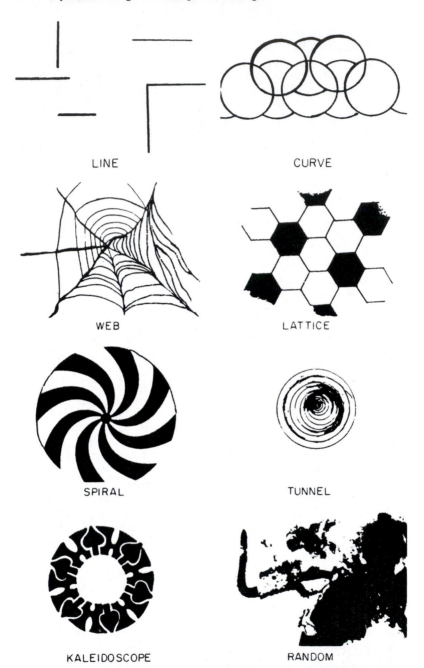

LINE

CURVE

WEB

LATTICE

SPIRAL

TUNNEL

KALEIDOSCOPE

RANDOM

FIGURE 19.2.   Examples of slides used to train subjects to classify and name various types of forms in Siegel's hallucination study. [From Siegel, R. K., & Jarvik, M. E. (1975). Drug-induced hallucinations in animals and man. In R. K. Siegel & L. J. West (Eds.), *Hallucinations: Behavior, experience, and theory* (pp. 81–161). New York: Wiley. Copyright © 1975 by John Wiley & Sons, Inc. Reprinted by permission of John Wiley & Sons, Inc.]

report continuously on their visual images, using the previously trained categories except when they described complex (meaningful) images. Each subject was tested in several sessions, a week apart, with a different drug in each session. The drugs included mescaline, LSD, psilocybin, THC, d-amphetamine (a stimulant), phenobarbital (a barbiturate sedative), and BOL (a drug that, like LSD, blocks serotonin neurotransmission, but is not known to produce hallucinations). There were also placebo sessions and baseline sessions (no drug or placebo). Each session lasted about six hours.

Data for the simple image reports are presented in Figure 19.3, with the percentage distributions in various form, color, and movement categories shown in the top, middle, and bottom graphs, respectively. Some 67 percent of the reports were simple forms (like Klüver's form constants); the other reports involved complex images. Reports from baseline and placebo could be characterized largely as black and white images of random forms moving about aimlessly.

In general, simple image reports for amphetamine, phenobarbital, and BOL sessions did not differ significantly from placebo or baseline sessions. However, reports for the major hallucinogens (mescaline, LSD, psilocybin) and THC sessions were largely similar to each other, and different from placebo and baseline sessions. (1) Forms: About 90 to 120 minutes after ingestion of hallucinogens or THC, subjects started perceiving mostly lattice and tunnel forms. In some cases a bright central spot produced a tunnel-like effect. The lattice and tunnel forms were often combined in the same image, such as a tunnel with lattice-patterned walls (Figure 19.4, upper right). (2) Colors: The hallucinogens (mescaline, LSD, psilocybin) induced predominantly red, orange, and yellow patterns. THC produced a higher proportion of blue reports than did the other drugs. (The major hallucinations often produced blue images early in the session, but longer wavelengths predominated in the middle and later part of the session.) (3) Movement patterns: The hallucinogens and THC induced mostly explosive (outward from center) and rotational motion patterns. Subjects noted that all images tended to pulsate or flicker, no matter what other motion they showed.[2]

Complex images, with meaningful forms, did not appear until well after the shift to lattice-tunnel forms in the hallucinogen sessions. Once started, complex images tended to be the most common type (43 to 75 percent of reports). In *complex combined images*, meaningful forms often overlaid lattice and tunnel form constants (Figure 19.4, upper right panel). In other complex combined images, meaningful forms were duplicated and repeated, often in symmetrical geometric arrays.[3]

In later stages of complex imagery, most of the images lost their geometric quality, and meaningful forms occurred in *complex memory images*. Complex memory images are meaningful scenes constructed from meaningful forms (landscapes, people, animals, objects) stored in the individual's long-term memory. Some of the memory images were scenes from childhood or from occasions when the subject had undergone strong emotional experiences. Others were elaborate and fantastic novel scenes. The scenes often had unusual perspectives (Figure 19.4). During the memory image stage, a shift from pseudohallucination to true hallucination occurred:

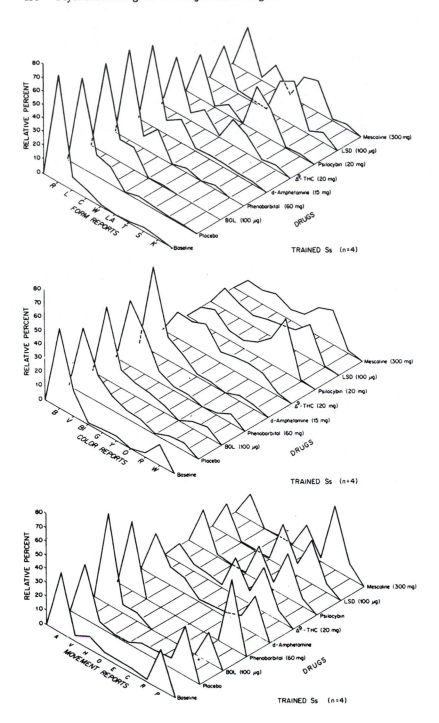

Initially subjects reported that form imagery was like a slide show or movie located about two feet in front of their eyes. As the high-dosage hallucinogen sessions progressed, subjects frequently claimed that they became part of the imagery itself. . . . It was at these times that subjects stopped using similes ["like," "as if"] in their imagery reports and started reporting that images were, in point of fact, really what they appeared to be (Siegel & Jarvik 1975, p. 128).

At the true hallucination stage subjects frequently reported feeling dissociated from their bodies.

Though the complex images changed rapidly—sometimes several changes per second—the changes were not random. Successive scenes usually included some visual features from the preceding scene, and novel features could have associative connections to features of the previous scene. In the middle of the sessions the subjects were taken outdoors for fifteen minutes, where they wore blindfold goggles and lay on the grass. During the outdoors intervals memory imagery decreased, and there was an "increase in reports of birds, planes, trees, and other objects, often triggered by auditory and tactile cues in the outdoor garden setting" (Siegel & Jarvik 1975, p. 130).[4]

How Hallucinations Are Produced

According to Siegel and Jarvik (1975), the similarity of the visual hallucinations produced by a variety of hallucinogens suggests that the same mechanisms are involved for the different drugs. The same mechanisms may also operate when people have visual hallucinations in other situations (like the hypnagogic state, migraine headaches, etc.) to the extent that the hallucinations are similar to the drug hallucinations. It is important to note, however, that the mechanisms are likely to be different for the first hallucination stage—characterized by form constants—than for later stages characterized by meaningful forms and, sometimes, by complex and fantastic scenes.

Some authors have suggested that the first-stage form constants are produced by *entoptic* (within the eye) structures and events, such as the pattern of retinal blood capillaries or "floater" blood cells within the capillaries. Perhaps hallucinogens somehow increase perception of entoptic events that normally go unnoticed. Siegel and Jarvik argued against the entoptic explanation for two reasons. First, a detailed analysis of entoptic events such as capillary patterns shows that they are not really as similar to hallucinogenic form constants as was originally assumed; hallucinogenic form constants are more symmetrical and organized. Second, perception of such entoptic

---

FIGURE 19.3.   Mean percent distribution of form (top), color (middle), and movement (bottom) reports for trained subjects in each six-hour high-dose drug condition. Form reports: R = random, L = line, C = curve, W = web, LA = lattice, T = tunnel, S = spiral, K = kaleidoscope. Color reports: B = black, V = violet, Bl = blue, G = green, Y = yellow, O = orange, R = red, W = white. Movement reports: A = aimless, V = vertical, H = horizontal, O = oblique, E = explosive, C = concentric, R = rotational, P = pulsing. [From Siegel, R. K., & Jarvik, M. E. (1975). Drug-induced hallucinations in animals and man. In R. K. Siegel & L. J. West (Eds.), *Hallucinations: Behavior, experience, and theory* (pp. 81–161). New York: Wiley. Copyright © 1975 by John Wiley & Sons, Inc. Reprinted by permission of John Wiley & Sons, Inc.]

FIGURE 19.4. Examples of complex images—images with meaningful forms—from the later stages of hallucinogen intoxication. The upper right panel shows a complex combined image with meaningful forms incorporated into a simple form constant (spiral). The other panels show complex memory images involving meaningful scenes constructed from information in the individual's long-term memory. Memory-image scenes often seem to be viewed from unusual perspectives. "Characteristic perspectives include a distant scene (with abundant detail) often recognized as an event that was experienced in childhood (upper left), a scene viewed as if the subject were under water, looking up toward and through the surface (lower left), and an aerial perspective (lower right), which may be accompanied by sensations of floating and flying." [From Siegel, R. K. (1977, April). Hallucinations. *Scientific American, 237,* 132–40. Copyright © by Scientific American, Inc. All rights reserved.]

events requires light, whereas the form constants occurred in Siegel's subjects even when they were tested in complete darkness.

However, one type of entoptic event, *phosphenes*, does not require light. Phosphenes are sensations of light that occur in total darkness, particularly as the eye becomes more dark adapted and the individual adopts a relaxed, receptive attitude. Phosphenes appear as rapidly changing patches of pastel colors, sometimes with more elaborate patterns such as lattices and spirals. The patterns can be intensified and altered by gentle pressure on the eyeball, produced by closing the eyelids very tightly or by gentle pressure with a finger on the closed eyelid (Oster 1970). Phosphenes are associated with neuronal discharges in the retina, lateral geniculate, and visual cortex. Oster pointed out their similarity to first-stage visual images produced by hallucinogenic drugs.

Another type of internally produced visual experience is the *fortification illusions*—patterns, usually white or monocolored, composed of angular lines or dots—experienced just prior to and during migraine headaches (Richards 1971). The migraine visual patterns are associated with neural activity in the visual cortex.[5] Also, images of moving or stationary colored lights, simple lines, and more complex patterns can be produced by electrical stimulation of neurons at various places in the visual cortex and adjacent areas.

Siegel and Jarvik (1975) suggested that the form, color, and movement constants produced by hallucinogens are a result of drug-induced increases in activity in the visual pathway of the central nervous system, particularly in the visual cortex. The visual nervous system is identical for people in different cultures, and it is noteworthy that drug-induced form-constant hallucination patterns are similar for people of different cultures (Siegel & Jarvik 1975). This observation supports the idea that visual hallucination patterns are affected more by visual nervous system excitation patterns than by prior belief systems.

More complex images, with meaningful forms and scenes, are constructed from information stored in the individual's memory. However, such images are not mere replays of scenes from memory. Like night dreams, they are original, dynamic, organized constructions that incorporate elements from memory. Siegel and Jarvik suggested that increased arousal produced by hallucinogenic drugs may activate memory-storage systems. At the same time, external sensory input and attention to external tasks are reduced, resulting in attention being shifted to internal images. At very high levels of arousal the images appear to be projected externally, and at that point true (believed-in) hallucinations occur.[6] (The first stage of complex imagery, where meaningful images are combined with form constants, may be regarded as an intermediate stage between the simple form constant stage and the complex memory image stage.)

Thus, like the color-form constants, meaningful memory-based images in drug hallucinations are a result of nervous-system excitation. However, while color-form constants are closely similar across cultures, memory-image contents differ between different individuals and cultures, depending on differences in memory contents. Also, one would expect an individual's *interpretation* of a hallucination's meaning—for example, as a religious revelation or as an uncovering of personal unconscious contents—to be affected by his or her prior belief systems, which would in turn be affected by the culture.

Slade and Bentall (1988; Bentall 1990) argued that the critical factor in true hallucinations is the subject's or patient's failure of "reality discrimination," where imagination becomes confused with reality. Siegel and Jarvik's theory of drug hallucinations explains how vivid memory images come to be produced, but it does not explain why these images are confused with reality. Indeed, in most cases hallucinogen users are aware that their vivid visual images are imaginary, though a bad trip could occur if the images are believed to be real. When true hallucinations do occur, one factor may be a disruption of logical analysis and automatic reality-checking functions of the brain. Another factor may be expectancy, perhaps related to cultural or religious beliefs, which would predispose some people to interpret unusual images as real (Slade & Bentall 1988).

CONCLUDING COMMENTS ON PSYCHEDELIC DRUGS

The altered states of consciousness induced by psychedelic drugs are interesting in their own right, and they also have implications for understanding consciousness and mind/brain relationships. Support for a materialist view on the mind-body problem is provided by the fact that both conscious experience and cognitive performance can be altered by psychedelic drugs, as well as other psychoactive drugs. Whereas brain damage can cause permanent changes in consciousness and cognitive performance, drugs can cause temporary changes by altering neurotransmission in the otherwise normal brain. Even though neuroscientists have a long way to go to explain *how* the brain produces the variety of conscious experience and controls cognitive performance, the effects of drugs and brain damage leave no doubt that conscious experience and cognitive performance are functions of the material brain, and not of some immaterial mind stuff.

Whenever subjective or behavioral effects of a drug are very similar in different individuals, the implication is that the effects are due to alterations in particular brain circuits or subsystems. For example, simple form constant hallucinations, produced by hallucinogenic drugs, are similar for different individuals and for people in different cultures. Apparently, they are caused by effects of the drugs on the brain's visual system. Also, effects of marijuana on memory can be explained in terms of drug effects on neurotransmission in parts of the brain's memory system (such as the hippocampus).

On the other hand, some psychedelic drug experiences are quite variable from one individual to another. For example, Tart (1971) found that subjective responses to marijuana vary widely, and some subjective effects occur only rarely (for example, paranormal experiences). With hallucinogenic drugs, some people experience their vivid images as especially vivid daydream fantasies, whereas others experience them as real perceptions— true hallucinations. Some people have mystical or religious experiences with hallucinogenic drugs, while most people have merely entertaining experiences.

When a drug induces effects that vary widely between different individuals—and within the same individual at different times and settings—the implication is that the effect is not produced simply by neurotransmission changes in a particular brain subsystem. Rather, it suggests that a mind/brain system that interprets lower-level inputs to produce (construct) conscious experience is producing different interpretations for different individuals. Different interpretations result from individual differences in expectancies, beliefs, knowledge, and personal past experiences stored in memory. In some cases, a relatively unchanged interpreter may be interpreting altered inputs from altered subsystems (such as vision, proprioception, memory, emotion). In other cases, the functioning of the interpreter system itself may be altered by the drug, either independently or along with changes in lower-level subsystems. For example, hallucinogens can induce experiences of vivid, complex, meaningful images that vary between individuals. In the true hallucination experience—where people believe that their mental images are real—it is clear that the functioning of the interpreter system itself has been altered, since it cannot distinguish between vivid images and reality. In cases where people have vivid fantasy images but know that they are imaginary (pseudohallucinations), it appears that the interpreter system is still functioning normally but altered lower-level visual and memory systems are producing altered inputs to the interpreter.[7]

Drug research and the study of consciousness.

Obviously, we cannot do experimental brain surgery on humans to study the relationships between altered mind/brain subsystems, cognitive performance, and conscious experience. Natural accidents provide opportunities to study such relationships (see Chapter 6), but such injuries occur under uncontrolled conditions, and almost every case is different from the others. Controlled research with psychedelics and other psychoactive drugs could potentially provide valuable insights about the functional relationships between various specialized mind/brain subsystems and a (hypothesized) conscious interpreter system and/or executive control system. We need to learn more about the interaction of various factors (drug, personal, situational) in producing subjective and behavioral effects.

Most of the research on subjective and behavioral effects of psychedelic drugs has been atheoretical. That is, it has not been guided by theories of mind/brain functioning. Rather, it has been designed simply to discover some of the psychological/behavioral effects of the drugs, and has often used rather arbitrary procedures and measurements that have little relationship to those used in basic theory-related research in mainstream psychology. Basic research on subjective, cognitive, and behavioral effects of psychedelic and other psychoactive drugs could make valuable contributions for developing and testing theories of mind/brain functioning. Such research should be guided by current theories drawn from cognitive psychology, social-personality psychology, and neuropsychology, as well as other branches of neuroscience. In principle, such research could be done safely by careful selection of drugs, doses, procedures, and volunteer subjects. However, it is virtually impossible to do such basic research, because of federal laws and policies restricting drug research. Even marijuana—nonaddictive, relatively mild in its effects, and apparently harmless when administered occasionally under controlled conditions—is treated essentially the same as dangerous narcotics as far as drug research policies are concerned.

In closing, I want to reiterate what I said earlier in conjunction with discussion of the marijuana paradox: subjective experiences produced by drugs may not correspond to the results of objective behavioral measures. We should keep in mind that conscious experience is the essence of human existence. It is an important and legitimate topic of study in its own right. In order to increase our understanding of conscious experience and factors that affect it, it would be worthwhile to have more controlled research on the effects of psychedelics and other psychoactive drugs, in interaction with other factors, on conscious experience.

SUMMARY

Hallucinogens are drugs that can produce hallucinations at normal dose levels. The major hallucinogens used in the Americas include psilocybin mushrooms ("magic mushrooms"; active ingredient, psilocybin); peyote (active ingredient, mescaline); and the synthetic drug LSD. Although altered perceptions or hallucinations are the most common effects of hallucinogens, some people experience profound self-revelatory and/or mystical experiences. LSD was initially thought to be a "psychotomimetic" drug that could produce psychotic symptoms, but now it is realized this is not the case. However, some users have experienced bad trips with panic reactions and, later, flashbacks. None of these hallucinogens leads to physical dependency.

A true hallucination is a percept-like experience that the individual believes to be real, though it has no objective counterpart. A pseudohallucination is a perceptual experience that the individual knows is not real, though it may be just as vivid and spontaneous as a true hallucination. The frequency of hallucinations during hallucinogen use has been exaggerated, since many reports have classified pseudohallucinations as true hallucinations.

Siegel used trained observers to obtain introspective reports of perceptual experiences during intoxication by psilocybin, mescaline, LSD, and THC (high dose) and found similarities in responses to those drugs. Visual-hallucinatory experiences go through three temporal stages: (1) simple form-constant images, of which the lattice-tunnel type is most common; (2) complex combined images, with meaningful images (such as animals, objects, faces) superimposed on or incorporated into form-constant figures; and (3) complex memory images, with meaningful scenes. Simple form-constant images depend on the drug's effect on the visual pathway in the brain and show striking similarities across individuals and cultures, whereas complex meaningful images are constructed from information stored in memory and can vary markedly between individuals. Slade and Bentall argued that the critical factor in true hallucinations is not their visual-perceptual quality, but rather, a failure of reality discrimination, where imagination is confused with reality. Failures of reality discrimination can be attributed to altered functioning of a conscious interpreter system.

ENDNOTES

[1]On April 17, 1990, the U. S. Supreme Court ruled that there is no constitutional right to take illegal drugs, such as peyote, for religious reasons. According to an Associated Press item, dissenting justices said the 6–3 ruling permits religious oppression of American Indians and perhaps others with unorthodox views. The ruling allows Oregon officials to deny unemployment benefits to two fired drug counselors who took small amounts of peyote in an Indian religious ceremony. However, the court also said that states may allow religious use of illegal drugs. I am not sure where this leaves the rights of Native American Church members to use peyote.

[2]Marijuana is not usually classed as a hallucinogen, since hallucinations rarely occur at the THC levels consumed in typical social marijuana-smoking situations. Thus, it is noteworthy that in Siegel's study a relatively high dose of THC produced hallucination reports similar to those produced by the hallucinogens (mescaline, LSD, and psilocybin). Siegel also obtained reports of vivid images with lattice-tunnel forms, usually blue, in subjects who had smoked marijuana. Perhaps marijuana-induced images were noticed more readily in Siegel's restricted-sensory-input test condition (dark, soundproof room) than they are in normal social marijuana-smoking situations.

[3]See Siegel & Jarvik 1975 for illustrations of visual hallucinations, including full-color reproductions of paintings by artists who depicted their psychedelic hallucinations and examples of Huichol (Mexican Indian) yarn paintings inspired by peyote hallucinations. Other illustrations are in Siegel 1977. See John Lilly's popular book *The Center of the Cyclone* (1972) for a description of complex hallucinations that he experienced when he took LSD under sensory deprivation conditions.

[4]To what extent were Siegel's trained subjects' image reports influenced by their prior image-naming training? Siegel tested some untrained subjects and found that they reported images less often (about five per minute) than did trained subjects (about twenty per minute). At high doses of hallucinogens the untrained subjects sometimes had long pauses between reports, especially when they were lost in their hallucinations. The distribution of form constant reports was similar for untrained and trained subjects, allowing for some differences in their choice of words to describe the images. Thus, it appears that prior training affected the rate of image reporting and the consistency of image naming, but probably had little or no effect on image experiences *per se.*

[5]For illustrations of phosphenes and migraine visual patterns, see Oster 1970 and Richards 1971, respectively.

[6]Siegel and Jarvik's 1975 explanation of meaningful drug hallucination images as constructions from memory and sensory elements is similar to Foulkes's 1985 explanation of dream production.

[7]See Gazzaniga's book *Mind Matters* (1988b) for a discussion of how the interpreter system produces conscious experiences, such as anxiety and depression, in response to natural biochemical reactions in the brain.

References

AARONS, L. (1976). Sleep-assisted instruction. *Psychological Bulletin, 83*, 1–40.

ACH, N. (1905). *Ueber die Willenstätigkeit und das Denken.* Göttingen, Germany: Vanderhoeck & Ruprecht.

ADAMS, A. J., BROWN, B., HAGERSTROM-PORTNORY, G., FLOM, M. C., & JONES, R. T. (1976). Evidence for acute effects of alcohol and marijuana on color discrimination. *Perception and Psychophysics, 20*, 119–24.

ADLER, A. (1927). *The practice and theory of individual psychology.* New York: Harcourt.

ALLISON, T., & CICCHETTI, D. V. (1976). Sleep in mammals: Ecological and constitutional correlates. *Science, 194*, 732–34.

American Psychiatric Association. (1980). *Diagnostic and statistical manual of mental disorders* (3rd ed.). Washington, DC: American Psychiatric Association. [Commonly known as *DSM-III*. The latest edition is *DSM-III-R*, 1987.]

ANAND, B., CHHINA, G., & SINGH, B. (1961). Some aspects of electroencephalographic studies in Yogis. *Electroencephalography and Clinical Neurophysiology, 13*, 452–56. [Reprinted in Tart, 1972a.]

ANCH, A. M., BROWMAN, C. P., MITLER, M. M., & WALSH, J. K. (1988). *Sleep: A scientific perspective.* Englewood Cliffs, NJ: Prentice Hall.

ANDERS, T. F., CARSKADON, M. A., & DEMENT, W. C. (1980). Sleep and sleepiness in children and adolescents. *Pediatric Clinics of North America, 27*, 29–43.

ANDERSON, J. R. (1983). *The architecture of cognition.* Cambridge, MA: Harvard University Press.

ANTROBUS, J. S. (1968). Information theory and stimulus-independent thought. *British Journal of Psychology, 59*, 423–30.

ANTROBUS, J. S. (1977). The dream as metaphor: An information-processing and learning model. *Journal of Mental Imagery, 2*, 327–38.

ANTROBUS, J. S. (1986). Dreaming: Cortical activation and perceptual thresholds. *Journal of Mind and Behavior, 7*, 193–212.

ANTROBUS, J. S. (1987). Cortical hemisphere asymmetry and sleep mentation. *Psychological Review, 94*, 359–68.

ANTROBUS, J. S. (1990). Neurocognition of sleep mentation: Phasic and tonic REM sleep. In R. R. Bootzin, J. F. Kihlstrom, & D. L. Schacter (Eds.), *Sleep and cognition*. Washington, DC: American Psychological Association.

ANTROBUS, J. S., ANTROBUS, J. S., & SINGER, J. L. (1964). Eye movements accompanying daydreaming, visual imagery, and thought suppression. *Journal of Abnormal and Social Psychology, 69,* 244–52.

ANTROBUS, J. S., COLEMAN, R., & SINGER, J. L. (1967). Signal detection performance by subjects differing in predisposition to daydreaming. *Journal of Consulting Psychology, 31,* 487–91.

ANTROBUS, J. S., SINGER, J. L., GOLDSTEIN, S., & FORTGANG, M. (1970). Mindwandering and cognitive structure. *Transactions of the New York Academy of Sciences, 32,* 242–52.

ANTROBUS, J. S., SINGER, J. L., & GREENBERG, S. (1966). Studies in the stream of consciousness: Experimental enhancement and suppression of spontaneous cognitive processes. *Perceptual and Motor Skills, 23,* 399–417.

ARKIN, A. M. (1978). Sleeptalking. In A. M. Arkin, J. S. Antrobus, & S. J. Ellman (Eds.), *The mind in sleep: Psychology and psychophysiology* (pp. 513–32). Hillsdale, NJ: Erlbaum.

ARKIN, A. M., & ANTROBUS, J. S. (1978). The effects of external stimuli applied prior to and during sleep on sleep experience. In A. M. Arkin, J. S. Antrobus, & S. J. Ellman (Eds.), *The mind in sleep: Psychology and psychophysiology* (pp. 351–91). Hillsdale, NJ: Erlbaum.

ARKIN, A. M., ANTROBUS, J. S., ELLMAN, S. J., & FARBER, J. (1978). Sleep mentation as affected by REMP deprivation. In A. M. Arkin, J. S. Antrobus, & S. J. Ellman (Eds.), *The mind in sleep: Psychology and psychophysiology* (pp. 459–84). Hillsdale, NJ: Erlbaum.

ARMSTRONG, D. M. (1968). *A materialist theory of the mind.* London: Routledge & Kegan Paul.

ÅS, A. (1963). Hypnotizability as a function of nonhypnotic experiences. *Journal of Abnormal and Social Psychology, 66,* 142–50.

ASERINSKY, E., & KLEITMAN, N. (1953). Regularly occurring periods of eye motility and concomitant phenomena during sleep. *Science, 118,* 273–74.

ASHCRAFT, M. H. (1989). *Human memory and cognition.* Glenview, IL: Scott, Foresman.

Association of Sleep Disorders Centers. (1979). *Diagnostic classification of sleep and arousal disorders* (1st ed.), prepared by Sleep Disorders Classification Committee, H. P. Roffwarg, Chairman. *Sleep, 2,* 1–137.

ATKINSON, R. C., & SHIFFRIN, R. M. (1968). Human memory: A proposed system and its control processes. In W. K. Spence & J. T. Spence (Eds.), *The psychology of learning and motivation: Advances in research and theory* (Vol. 2; pp. 89–195). New York: Academic Press.

ATKINSON, R. L., ATKINSON, R. C., SMITH, E. E., & HILGARD, E. R. (1987). *Introduction to psychology* (9th ed.). New York: Harcourt.

BAARS, B. J. (1983). Conscious contents provide the nervous system with coherent, global information. In R. J. Davidson, G. E. Schwartz & D. Shapiro (Eds.), *Consciousness and self-regulation* (Vol. 3; pp. 41–79). New York: Plenum.

BAEKELAND, F., KOULACK, D., & LASKY, R. (1968). Effects of a stressful presleep experience on electroencephalograph-recorded sleep. *Psychophysiology, 4,* 436–43.

BAGCHI, B., & WENGER, M. A. (1957). Electrophysiological correlates of some Yogi exercises. *Electroencephalography and Clinical Neurophysiology,* Supplement No. 7, 132–49.

BAKER, R. A. (1982). The effect of suggestion on past-lives regression. *American Journal of Clinical Hypnosis, 25,* 71–76.

BALESTRIERI, A. (1964). Hallucinatory mechanisms and the content of drug-induced hallucinations. In P. B. Bradley, F. Flugel, & P. H. Hoch (Eds.), *Neuro-psychopharmacology* (Vol. 3). New York: Elsevier.

BANDURA, A. (1986). *Social foundations of thought and action: A social cognitive theory.* Englewood Cliffs, NJ: Prentice Hall.

BARABASZ, A. F. (1982). Restricted environmental stimulation and the enhancement of hypnotizability: Pain, EEG alpha, skin conductance and temperature responses. *International Journal of Clinical and Experimental Hypnosis, 30,* 147–66.

BARABASZ, A. F., BAER, L., SHEEHAN, D. V., & BARABASZ, M. (1986). A three-year follow-up of hypnosis and restricted environmental stimulation therapy for smoking. *International Journal of Clinical and Experimental Hypnosis, 34,* 169–81.

BARABASZ, A. F., & BARABASZ, M. (1989). Effects of restricted environmental stimulation: Enhancement of hypnotizability for experimental and chronic pain control. *International Journal of Clinical and Experimental Hypnosis, 37,* 217–31.

BARBER, T. X. (1969). *Hypnosis: A scientific approach.* New York: Van Nostrand Reinhold.

BARBER, T. X. (1972). Suggested ("hypnotic") behavior: The trance paradigm versus an alternative paradigm. In E. Fromm & R. E. Shor (Eds.), *Hypnosis: Research developments and perspectives* (pp. 115–82). Chicago: Aldine.

BARBER, T. X., & CALVERLEY, D. S. (1964). Experimental studies in "hypnotic" behavior: Suggested deafness evaluated by delayed auditory feedback. *British Journal of Psychology, 55*, 439–46.

BARBER, T. X., SPANOS, N. P., & CHAVES, J. F. (1974). *Hypnosis, imagination, and human potentialities.* New York: Pergamon.

BARRETT, D. (1979). The hypnotic dream: Its relation to nocturnal dreams and waking fantasies. *Journal of Abnormal Psychology, 88*, 584–91.

BARRON, F., JARVIK, M. E., & BUNNELL, S. (April 1964). The hallucinogenic drugs. *Scientific American, 210*, 29–37.

BATES, B. L., MILLER, R. J., CROSS, H. J., & BRIGHAM, T. A. (1988). Modifying hypnotic suggestibility with the Carleton Skills Training Program. *Journal of Personality and Social Psychology, 55*, 120–27.

BAUER, R. M. (1984). Autonomic recognition of names and faces in prosopagnosia: A neuropsychological application of the guilty knowledge test. *Neuropsychologia, 22*, 457–69.

BEAUMONT, J. G. (1981). Split brain studies and the duality of consciousness. In G. Underwood & R. Stevens (Eds.), *Aspects of consciousness, Volume 2: Structural issues* (pp. 189–213). London: Academic Press.

BECHTEL, W. (1988). *Philosophy of mind: An overview for cognitive science.* Hillsdale, NJ: Erlbaum.

BECHTEL, W., & ABRAHAMSEN, A. (1991). *Connectionism and the mind: An introduction to parallel processing in networks.* Cambridge, MA: Basil Blackwell.

BECKER, D. E., & SHAPIRO, D. (1981). Physiological responses to clicks during Zen, Yoga, and TM meditation. *Psychophysiology, 18*, 694–99.

BECKER, H. S. (1963). Marihuana: A sociological overview. In *Outsiders.* Glencoe, IL: Free Press. [Reprinted in D. Solomon, 1966.]

BELENKEY, M. F., CLINCHY, B. M., GOLDBERGER, N. R., & TARULE, J. M. (1986). *Women's ways of knowing: The development of self, voice, and mind.* New York: Basic Books.

BENSON, H. (1975). *The relaxation response.* New York: Morrow.

BENTALL, R. P. (1990). The illusion of reality: A review and integration of psychological research on hallucinations. *Psychological Bulletin, 107*, 82–95.

BERLYNE, D. E. (1965). *Structure and direction in thinking.* New York: Wiley.

BERNSTEIN, M. (1956). *The search for Bridey Murphy.* Garden City, NY: Doubleday.

BERTINI, M., LEWIS, H. B., & WITKIN, H. A. (1964). Some preliminary observations with an experimental procedure for the study of hypnagogic and related phenomena. *Archivio di Psicologia Neurologia e Psichiatria, 6*, 493–534. [Reprinted in Tart, 1972a.]

BEST, J. B. (1989). *Cognitive psychology* (2nd ed.). St. Paul, MN: West.

BINDRA, D. (1970). The problem of subjective experience: Puzzlement on reading R. W. Sperry's "A modified concept of consciousness." *Psychological Review, 77*, 581–84.

BLOCK, E. B. (1976). *Hypnosis: A new tool in crime detection.* New York: David MacKay.

BOGEN, J. E. (1969). The other side of the brain: An appositional mind. *Bulletin of the Los Angeles Neurological Societies, 34*, 135–62. [Reprinted in Ornstein, 1973.]

BOKERT, E. (1968). The effects of thirst and a related verbal stimulus on dream reports. *Dissertation Abstracts, 28*, 4753B.

BORG, J., GERSHON, S., & ALPERT, M. (1975). Dose effects of smoked marihuana on human cognitive and motor functions. *Psychopharmacologia* (Berlin), *42*, 221–28.

BORING, E. G. (1953). A history of introspection. *Psychological Bulletin, 50*, 169–89.

BORRIE, R. A., & SUEDFELD, P. (1980). Restricted environmental stimulation therapy in a weight-reduction program. *Journal of Behavioral Medicine, 3*, 147–61.

BOWERS, K. S. (1976). *Hypnosis for the seriously curious.* New York: Norton.

BOWERS, K. S. (1981). Do the Stanford scales tap the "classic suggestion effect"? *International Journal of Clinical and Experimental Hypnosis, 29*, 42–53.

BOWERS, K. S. (1984). On being unconsciously influenced and informed. In K. S. Bowers & D. Meichenbaum (Eds.), *The unconscious reconsidered* (pp. 227–72). New York: Wiley.

BOWERS, P. (1978). Hypnotizability, creativity and the role of effortless experiencing. *International Journal of Clinical and Experimental Hypnosis, 26*, 184–202.

BOWERS, P. (1979). Hypnosis and creativity: The search for the missing link. *Journal of Abnormal Psychology, 88*, 564–72.

BOWERS, P., LAURENCE, J.-R., & HART, D. (1988). The experience of hypnotic suggestions. *International Journal of Clinical and Experimental Hypnosis, 36*, 336–49.

BOWERS, P., & BOWERS, K. S. (1979). Hypnosis and creativity: A theoretical and empirical rapprochement. In E. Fromm & R. E. Shor (Eds.), *Hypnosis: Developments in research and new perspectives* (2nd ed.) (pp. 351–79). New York: Aldine.

BRECHER, E. M. (1972). *Licit and illicit drugs.* Boston: Little, Brown.

BREGER, L. (1969). Dream function: An information processing model. In L. Breger (Ed.), *Clinical cognitive psychology* (pp. 182–227). Englewood Cliffs, NJ: Prentice Hall.

BREGER, L., HUNTER, J., & LANE, R. (1971). The effect of stress on dreams. *Psychological Issues, 7,* Monograph 27.

BROOK, J. S., GORDON, S., BROOK, A., & BROOK, D. W. (1989). The consequences of marijuana use on intrapersonal and interpersonal functioning in black and white adolescents. *Genetic, Social, and General Psychology Monographs, 115,* 351–69.

BROUGHTON, R. J. (1966). Sleep disorders: Disorders of arousal? *Science, 159,* 1070–78.

BROWN, D. P. (1977). A model for the levels of concentrative meditation. *International Journal of Clinical and Experimental Hypnosis, 25,* 236–73.

BRUNER, J. (1957). On perceptual readiness. *Psychological Review, 64,* 123–52.

BURGHARDT, G. M. (1985). Animal awareness: Current perceptions and historical perspective. *American Psychologist, 40,* 905–19.

CAMPION, J., LATTO, R., & SMITH, Y. M. (1983). Is blindsight an effect of scattered light, spared cortex, and near-threshold vision? *The Behavioral and Brain Sciences, 6,* 423–86.

CANN, D. R., & DONDERI, D. C. (1986). Jungian personality typology and the recall of everyday and archetypal dreams. *Journal of Personality and Social Psychology, 50,* 1021–30.

CAPPELL, H. D., & PLINER, P. I. (1973). Volitional control of marijuana intoxication: A study of the ability to "come down" on command. *Journal of Abnormal Psychology, 82,* 428–34.

CARLIN, A. S., BAKKER, C. B., HALPERN, L., & POST, R. D. (1972). Social facilitation of marijuana intoxication: Impact of social set and pharmacological activity. *Journal of Abnormal Psychology, 80,* 132–40.

CARLIN, A. S., POST, R. D., BAKKER, C. B., & HALPERN, L. M. (1974). The role of modeling and previous experience in the facilitation of marijuana intoxication. *Journal of Nervous and Mental Disease, 159,* 275–81.

CARLSON, N. R. (1986). *Physiology of behavior* (3rd ed.). Boston: Allyn & Bacon.

CARRINGTON, P. (1986). Meditation as an access to altered states of consciousness. In B. B. Wolman & M. Ullman (Eds.), *Handbook of states of consciousness* (pp. 487–523). New York: Van Nostrand Reinhold.

CARRINGTON, P. (1987). Managing meditation in clinical practice. In M. A. West (Ed.), *The psychology of meditation* (pp. 150–72). Oxford, England: Oxford University Press.

CARTWRIGHT, R. (1986). Affect and dream work from an information processing point of view. *Journal of Mind and Behavior, 7,* 411–28. [Special issue, *Cognition and dream research,* R. E. Haskell (Ed.).]

CARTWRIGHT, R., BERNICK, N., BOROWITZ, G., & KLING, A. (1969). Effect of an erotic movie on the sleep and dreams of young men. *Archives of General Psychiatry, 20,* 262–71.

CARTWRIGHT, R., & KASZNIAK, A. (1978). The social psychology of dream reporting. In A. M. Arkin, J. S. Antrobus, & S. J. Ellman (Eds.), *The mind in sleep: Psychology and psychophysiology* (pp. 277–91). Hillsdale, NJ: Erlbaum.

CARTWRIGHT, R., LLOYD, S., KNIGHT, S., & TRENHOLME, I. (1984). Broken dreams: A study of the effects of divorce and depression on dream content. *Psychiatry, 47,* 251–59.

CASSWELL, S. (1975). Cannabis intoxication: Effects of monetary incentive on performance: A controlled investigation of behavioral tolerance in moderate users of cannabis. *Perceptual and Motor Skills, 41,* 423–34.

CASTANEDA, C. (1971). *A separate reality: Further conversations with Don Juan.* New York: Simon & Schuster.

CASTENEDA, C. (1974). *Tales of power.* New York: Simon & Schuster.

CEDERCREUTZ, C. (1978). Hypnotic treatment of 100 cases of migraine. In F. H. Frankel & H. S. Zamansky (Eds.), *Hypnosis at its bicentennial.* New York: Plenum.

CHEESMAN, J., & MERIKLE, P. M. (1984). Priming with and without awareness. *Perception & Psychophysics, 36,* 387–95.

CHEESMAN, J., & MERIKLE, P. M. (1986). Distinguishing conscious from unconscious perceptual processes. *Canadian Journal of Psychology, 40,* 343–67.

CHURCHLAND, P. M. (1988). *Matter and consciousness: A contemporary introduction to the philosophy of mind* (rev. ed.). Cambridge, MA: MIT Press.

CHURCHLAND, P. S. (1986). *Neurophilosophy: Toward a unified science of the mind-brain.* Cambridge, MA: MIT Press.

CLARK, L. D., HUGHES, R., & NAKASHIMA, E. N. (1970). Behavioral effects of marihuana. *Archives of General Psychiatry, 23,* 193–98.

CLARK, L. D., & NAKASHIMA, E. N. (1968). Experimental studies of marihuana. *American Journal of Psychiatry, 125,* 379–84.

CLAXTON, G. (1987). Meditation in Buddhist psychology. In M. A. West (Ed.), *The psychology of meditation* (pp. 23–38). Oxford, England: Oxford University Press.

CLOPTON, P. L., JANOWSKY, D. S., CLOPTON, J. M., JUDD, L. L., & HUEY, L. (1979). Marijuana and the perception of affect. *Psychopharmacology, 61,* 203–06.

COE, W. C. (1977). The problem of relevance versus ethics in researching hypnosis and antisocial conduct. *Annals of the New York Academy of Sciences, 296,* 90–104.

COE, W. C. (1978). The credibility of posthypnotic amnesia: A contextualist's view. *International Journal of Clinical and Experimental Hypnosis, 26,* 218–45.

COE, W. C., & RYKEN, K. (1979). Hypnosis and risks to human subjects. *American Psychologist, 34,* 673–81.

COE, W. C., & SARBIN, T. R. (1977). Hypnosis from the standpoint of a contextualist. *Annals of the New York Academy of Sciences, 296,* 2–13.

COE, W. C., & SLUIS, A. S. E. (1989). Increasing contextual pressures to breach posthypnotic amnesia. *Journal of Personality and Social Psychology, 57,* 885–94.

COHEN, D. B. (1979a). *Sleep and dreaming: Origins, nature and functions.* New York: Pergamon.

COHEN, D. B. (1979b). Remembering and forgetting dreaming. In J. F. Kihlstrom & F. J. Evans (Eds), *Functional disorders of memory* (pp. 239–74). Hillsdale, NJ: Erlbaum.

COHEN, D. B., & COX, C. (1975). Neuroticism in the sleep laboratory: Implications for representational and adaptive properties of dreaming. *Journal of Abnormal Psychology, 84,* 91–108.

COHEN, D. B., & WOLFE, G. (1973). Dream recall and repression: Evidence for an alternative hypothesis. *Journal of Consulting and Clinical Psychology, 41,* 349–55.

COHEN, S., & STILLMAN, R. C. (Eds.). (1976). *The therapeutic potential of marihuana.* New York: Plenum.

COLEMAN, R. M. (1986). *Wide awake at 3:00 a.m..* New York: Freeman.

COLLISON, D. R. (1975). Which asthmatic patients should be treated by hypnotherapy? *Medical Journal of Australia, 1,* 776–81.

COMTE, A. (1830). *Cours de philosophie positive* (Vol. 1). Paris: Bachelier.

CORBALLIS, M. C. (1980). Laterality and myth. *American Psychologist, 35,* 284–95.

CORTEEN, R. S., & WOOD, B. (1972). Autonomic responses to shock-associated words in an unattended channel. *Journal of Experimental Psychology, 94,* 308–13.

COUNCIL, J. R., KIRSCH, I., & HAFNER, L. (1986). Expectancy versus absorption in the prediction of hypnotic responding. *Journal of Personality and Social Psychology, 50,* 182–89.

CRAHAN, M. E. (1969). God's flesh and other pre-Columbian phantastica. *Bulletin of the Los Angeles County Medical Association, 99,* 17.

CRAIK, F. I. M., & LOCKHART, R. S. (1972). Levels of processing: A framework for memory research. *Journal of Verbal Learning and Verbal Behavior, 11,* 671–84.

CRASILNECK, H. B., & HALL, J. A. (1985). *Clinical hypnosis: Principles and applications* (2nd ed.). Orlando, FL: Grune & Stratton.

CRAWFORD, H. J. (1974). The effects of marijuana on primary suggestibility. (Doctoral dissertation, University of California, Davis, 1974.) *Dissertation Abstracts International, 35.* (University Microfilms 74–29, 298.)

CRAWFORD, H. J. (1981). Hypnotic susceptibility as related to gestalt closure tasks. *Journal of Personality and Social Psychology, 40,* 376–83.

CRAWFORD, H. J. (1982a). Hypnotizability, daydreaming styles, imagery vividness, and absorption: A multidimensional study. *Journal of Personality and Social Psychology, 42,* 915–26.

CRAWFORD, H. J. (1982b). Cognitive processing during hypnosis: Much unfinished business. *Research Communications in Psychology, Psychiatry and Behavior, 7,* 169–79.

CRAWFORD, H. J. (1989). Cognitive and physiological flexibility: Multiple pathways to hypnotic responsiveness. In V. A. Gheorghiu, P. Netter, H. J. Eysenck, & R. Rosenthal (Eds.), *Suggestion and suggestibility: Theory and research* (pp. 155–67). New York: Springer-Verlag.

CRAWFORD, H. J., & ALLEN, S. N. (1983). Enhanced visual memory during hypnosis as mediated by hypnotic responsiveness and cognitive strategies. *Journal of Experimental Psychology: General, 112,* 662–85.

CRAWFORD, H. J., HILGARD, J. R., & MACDONALD, H. (1982). Transient experiences following hypnotic testing and special termination procedures. *International Journal of Clinical and Experimental Hypnosis, 30,* 117–26.

CRAWFORD, H. J., MACDONALD, H., & HILGARD, E. R. (1979). Hypnotic deafness: A psychophysical study of responses to tone intensity modified by hypnosis. *American Journal of Psychology, 92*, 193–214.

CRICK, F., & MITCHISON, G. (1983). The function of dream sleep. *Nature, 304*, 111–14.

CRICK, F., & MITCHISON, G. (1986). REM sleep and neural nets. *Journal of Mind and Behavior, 7*, 229–50. [Special issue, *Cognition and dream research*, R. E. Haskell (Ed.).]

DANZIGER, K. (1980). The history of introspection reconsidered. *Journal of the History of the Behavioral Sciences, 16*, 241–62.

DARLEY, C. F., TINKLENBERG, J. R., HOLLISTER, L. E., & ATKINSON, R. C. (1973a). Marihuana and retrieval from short-term memory. *Psychopharmacologia, 29*, 231–38.

DARLEY, C. F., TINKLENBERG, J. R., ROTH, W. T., HOLLISTER, L. E., & ATKINSON, R. C. (1973b). Influence of marihuana on storage and retrieval processes in memory. *Memory and Cognition, 1*, 196–200.

DARLEY, C. F., TINKLENBERG, J. R., ROTH, W. T., VERNON, S., & KOPELL, B. S. (1977). Marijuana effects on long-term memory assessment and retrieval. *Psychopharmacology, 52*, 239–41.

DARLEY, J. M., GLUCKSBERG, S., & KINCHLA, R. A. (1991). *Psychology* (5th ed.). Englewood Cliffs, NJ: Prentice Hall.

DAVIDSON, R. J., GOLEMAN, D. J., & SCHWARTZ, G. E. (1976). Attentional and affective concomitants of meditation: A cross-sectional study. *Journal of Abnormal Psychology, 85*, 235–38.

DAVISON, G. C., & NEALE, J. M. (1986). *Abnormal psychology* (4th ed.). New York: Wiley.

DEIKMAN, A. J. (1966). Deautomatization and the mystic experience. *Psychiatry, 29*, 324–38. [Reprinted in Ornstein 1973, and in Tart 1972a.]

DELMONTE, M. M. (1987a). Personality and meditation. In M. A. West (Ed.), *The psychology of meditation* (pp. 118–32). Oxford, England: Oxford University Press.

DELMONTE, M. M. (1987b). Meditation: Contemporary theoretical approaches. In M. A. West (Ed.), *The psychology of meditation* (pp. 39–53). Oxford, England: Oxford University Press.

DEMENT, W. C. (1955). Dream recall and eye movement during sleep in schizophrenics and normals. *Journal of Nervous and Mental Disease, 122*, 263–69.

DEMENT, W. C. (1960). The effect of dream deprivation. *Science, 131*, 1705–7.

DEMENT, W. C. (1976). *Some must watch while some must sleep*. New York: Norton.

DEMENT, W. C., KAHN, E., & ROFFWARG, H. P. (1965). The influence of the laboratory situation on the dreams of the experimental subject. *Journal of Nervous and Mental Disease, 140*, 119–31.

DEMENT, W. C., & KLEITMAN, N. (1957). Cyclic variations in EEG during sleep and their relation to eye movements, bodily motility and dreaming. *Electroencephalography and Clinical Neurophysiology, 9*, 673–90.

DEMENT, W. C., & WOLPERT, E. (1958). The relation of eye movements, body motility, and external stimuli to dream content. *Journal of Experimental Psychology, 55*, 543–53.

DEPASCALIS, V., SILVERI, A., & PALUMBO, G. (1988). EEG asymmetry during covert mental activity and its relationship with hypnotizability. *International Journal of Clinical and Experimental Hypnosis, 36*, 38–52.

DEPIANO, F. A., & SALZBERG, H. C. (1979). Clinical applications of hypnosis to three psychosomatic disorders. *Psychological Bulletin, 86*, 1223–35.

DEPIANO, F. A., & SALZBERG, H. C. (Eds.). (1986). *Clinical applications of hypnosis*. Norwood, NJ: Ablex.

DE ROPP, R. S. (1957). *Drugs and the mind*. New York: Grove Press.

DE VOTO, B. A. (Ed.). (1940). *Mark Twain in eruption*. New York: Harper.

DIAMOND, M J. (1977). Hypnotizability is modifiable: An alternative approach. *International Journal of Clinical and Experimental Hypnosis, 25*, 147–66.

DIMOND, S. J. (1976). Brain circuits for consciousness. *Brain, Behaviour and Evolution, 13*, 376–95.

DIXON, N. F. (1971). *Subliminal perception: The nature of a controversy*. London: McGraw-Hill.

DIXON, N. F. (1981). *Preconscious processing*. Chichester, England: Wiley.

DOMHOFF, B., & KAMIYA, J. (1964). Problems in dream content study with objective indicators: A comparison of home and laboratory dream reports. *Archives of General Psychiatry, 11*, 519–24.

DORNBUSH, R. L., FINK, M., & FREEDMAN, A. M. (1971). Marihuana, memory and perception. *American Journal of Psychiatry, 128*, 194–97.

DOWD, E. T., & HEALY, J. M. (1986). *Case studies in hypnotherapy*. New York: Guilford.

DYWAN, J., & BOWERS, K. (1983). The use of hypnosis to enhance recall. *Science, 222*, 184–85.

EARLE, J. B. (1984). Cerebral laterality and meditation: A review of the literature. In D. Shapiro & R. Walsh (Eds.), *Meditation: Classic and contemporary perspectives* (pp. 155–73). New York: Aldine.

ECCLES, J. C. (1977). Part II in Karl R. Popper & J. C. Eccles, *The self and its brain.* New York: Springer International.

EDMONSTON, W. E. (1986). *The induction of hypnosis.* New York: Wiley.

EKMAN, P., & FRIESEN, W. V. (1971). Constraints across cultures in the face and emotion. *Journal of Personality and Social Psychology, 17,* 124–29.

EKMAN, P., FRIESEN, W. V., & TOMKINS, S. S. (1971). *Emotions in the human face: Guidelines for research and integration of findings.* New York: Pergamon.

ELLENBERGER, H. F. (1970). *The discovery of the unconscious: The history and evolution of dynamic psychiatry.* New York: Basic Books.

ELLIS, A. W., & YOUNG, A. W. (1988). *Human cognitive neuropsychology.* Hillsdale, NJ: Erlbaum.

ELLMAN, S. J., SPIELMAN, A. J., LUCK, D., STEINER, S. S., & HALPERIN, R. (1978). REM deprivation: A review. In A. M. Arkin, J. S. Antrobus, & S. J. Ellman (Eds.), *The mind in sleep: Psychology and psychophysiology* (pp. 419–57). Hillsdale, NJ: Erlbaum.

ENGLISH, H. B., & ENGLISH, A. C. (1958). *A comprehensive dictionary of psychological and psychoanalytic terms.* New York: David McKay.

ERDELYI, M. H. (1988). Hypermnesia: The effect of hypnosis, fantasy, and concentration. In H. M. Pettinati (Ed.), *Hypnosis and memory* (pp. 64–94). New York: Guilford.

ERICKSON, M. H. (1965). A special inquiry with Aldous Huxley into the nature and character of various states of consciousness. *American Journal of Clinical Hypnosis, 8,* 17–33. [Reprinted in Tart 1972a.]

ERICSSON, K. A., & SIMON, H. A. (1980). Verbal reports as data. *Psychological Review, 87,* 215–51.

ERIKSEN, C. W. (1960). Discrimination and learning without awareness: A methodological survey and evaluation. *Psychological Review, 67,* 279–300.

EVANS, F. J., COOK, M. R., COHEN, H. D., ORNE, E. C., & ORNE, M. T. (1977). Appetitive and replacement naps: EEG and behavior. *Science, 197,* 687–89.

EVANS, F. J., & KIHLSTROM, J. F. (1973). Posthypnotic amnesia as disrupted retrieval. *Journal of Abnormal Psychology, 82,* 317–23.

EVANS, F. J., & ORNE, M. T. (1971). The disappearing hypnotist: The use of simulating subjects to evaluate how subjects perceive experimental procedures. *International Journal of Clinical and Experimental Hypnosis, 19,* 277–96.

EYSENCK, M. W. (1982). *Attention and arousal.* New York: Springer.

FANCHER, R. E. (1990). *Pioneers of psychology* (2nd ed.). New York: Norton.

FARROW, J. T. (1977). Physiological changes associated with transcendental consciousness, the state of least excitation of consciousness. In D. W. Orme-Johnson & J. T. Farrow (Eds.), *Scientific research on the transcendental meditation program: Collected papers* (Vol. 1; pp. 108–33). Maharishi European Research University Press.

FARTHING, G. W. (1980). Review of *Divided consciousness: Multiple controls in human thought and action,* by Ernest R. Hilgard. *Journal of Altered States of Consciousness, 5,* 259–62.

FARTHING, G. W., BROWN, S. W., & VENTURINO, M. (1982). Effects of hypnotizability and mental imagery on signal detection sensitivity and response bias. *International Journal of Clinical and Experimental Hypnosis, 30,* 289–305.

FARTHING, G. W., BROWN, S. W., & VENTURINO, M. (1983a). Involuntariness of response on the Harvard Group Scale of Hypnotic Susceptibility. *International Journal of Clinical and Experimental Hypnosis, 31,* 170–81.

FARTHING, G. W., VENTURINO, M., & BROWN, S. W. (1983b). Relationship between two different types of imagery vividness questionnaire items and three hypnotic susceptibility scale factors. *International Journal of Clinical and Experimental Hypnosis, 31,* 8–13.

FARTHING, G. W., VENTURINO, M., & BROWN, S. W. (1984). Suggestion and distraction in the control of pain: Test of two hypotheses. *Journal of Abnormal Psychology, 93,* 266–76.

FEHER, K. A., KALANT, H., LeBLANC, A. E., & KNOX, G. V. (1976). Permanent learning impairment after chronic heavy exposure to cannabis or ethanol in the rat. In G. G. Nahas (Ed.), *Marihuana: Chemistry, biochemistry and cellular effects* (pp. 495–506). New York: Springer-Verlag.

FEINBERG, I., JONES, R. T., WALKER, J. M., CAVNESS, C., & FLOYD, T. (1976). Marijuana extract and THC: Similarity of effects on EEG sleep patterns in man. *Clinical Pharmacology and Therapeutics, 19,* 782–94.

FENWICK, P. (1987). Meditation and the EEG. In M. A. West (Ed.), *The psychology of meditation* (pp. 104–17). Oxford, England: Oxford University Press.

FENWICK, P., DONALDSON, S., GILLIES, L., BUSHMAN, J., FENTON, G., PERRY, I., TILSLEY, C., & SERAFINOWICS, H. (1977). Metabolic and EEG changes during transcendental meditation. *Biological Psychology, 5,* 101–18.

FINE, T. H., & TURNER, J. W., JR. (1985). The use of restricted environmental stimulation therapy (REST) in the treatment of essential hypertension. In T. H. Fine & J. W. Turner, Jr. (Eds.), *REST and Self-Regulation: Proceedings of the First International Conference* (pp. 136–43). Toledo, OH: IRIS Publications.

FISCHER, R. (1978). Cartography of conscious states: Integration of east and west. In A. A. Sugerman & R. E. Tarter (Eds.), *Expanding dimensions of consciousness* (pp. 24–57). New York: Springer.

FISHER, C. (1953). Studies on the nature of suggestion: I. Experimental induction of dreams by direct suggestion. *Journal of the American Psychoanalysis Association, 1*, 222–55.

FISHER, C. (1966). Dreaming and sexuality. In R. Lowenstein, L. Newman, M. Schur, & A. Solnit (Eds.), *Psychoanalysis: A general psychology.* New York: International Universities Press.

FISHER, C., GROSS, J., & ZUCH, J. (1965). Cycle of penile erections synchronous with dreaming (REM sleep): Preliminary report. *Archives of General Psychiatry, 12*, 29–45.

FISHER, C., KAHN, E., EDWARDS, A., & DAVIS, D. M. (1974). A psychophysiological study of nightmares and night terrors. *Psychoanalysis and Contemporary Science, 3*, 317–98.

FLANAGAN, O. (1985). Consciousness, naturalism, and Nagel. *Journal of Mind and Behavior, 6*, 373–90.

FODOR, J. A. (January, 1981). The mind-body problem. *Scientific American, 244*, 114–23.

FODOR, J. A. (1983). *The modularity of mind.* Cambridge, MA: MIT Press.

FODOR, J. A. (1985). Précis of *The modularity of mind. The Behavioral and Brain Sciences, 8*, 1–42. [Includes peer commentaries.]

FOULKES, D. (1962). Dream reports from different stages of sleep. *Journal of Abnormal and Social Psychology, 65*, 14–25.

FOULKES, D. (1982a). *Children's dreams: Longitudinal studies.* New York: Wiley.

FOULKES, D. (1982b). REM-dream perspectives on the development of affect and cognition. *Psychiatric Journal of the University of Ottawa, 7*, 48–55.

FOULKES, D. (1983). Dream ontogeny and dream psychophysiology. In M. H. Chase & E. D. Weitzman (Eds.), *Sleep disorders: Basic and clinical research* (pp. 347–62). Jamaica, NY: Spectrum.

FOULKES, D. (1985). *Dreaming: A cognitive-psychological analysis.* Hillsdale, NJ: Erlbaum.

FOULKES, D. (1990). Dreaming and consciousness. *European Journal of Cognitive Psychology, 2*, 39–55.

FOULKES, D., HOLLIFIELD, M., SULLIVAN, B., BRADLEY, L., & TERRY, R. (1990). REM dreaming and cognitive skills at ages 5–8: A cross-sectional study. *International Journal of Behavioral Development, 13*, 447–65.

FOULKES, D., & SCHMIDT, M. (1983). Temporal sequence and unit composition in dream reports from different stages of sleep. *Sleep, 6*, 265–80.

FOULKES, D., SHEPHERD, J., LARSON, J. D., BELVEDERE, E., & FROST, S. (1972). Effects of awakenings in phasic vs. tonic stage REM on children's dream reports. *Sleep Research, 1*, 104.

FOULKES, D., SPEAR, P. S., & SYMONDS, J. D. (1966). Individual differences in mental activity at sleep onset. *Journal of Abnormal Psychology, 71*, 280–86.

FOULKES, D., & VOGEL, G. (1965). Mental activity at sleep onset. *Journal of Abnormal Psychology, 70*, 231–43.

FRANKEL, F. H. (1976). *Hypnosis: Trance as a coping mechanism.* New York: Plenum.

FRANKEL, F. H. (1987). Significant developments in medical hypnosis during the past 25 years. *International Journal of Clinical and Experimental Hypnosis, 35*, 231–47.

FRANKEL, F. H. (1988). The clinical use of hypnosis in aiding recall. In H. M. Pettinati (Ed.), *Hypnosis and memory* (pp. 247–64). New York: Guilford.

FREUD, S. (1900/1965). *The interpretation of dreams.* (J. Strachey, Trans. & Ed.) New York: Avon Books. (Original work published 1900). [The Avon paperback is reprinted from *The standard edition of the complete psychological works of Sigmund Freud* (Vols. 4–5). London: Hogarth, 1953.]

FROMM, E. (1987). Significant developments in clinical hypnosis during the past 25 years. *International Journal of Clinical and Experimental Hypnosis, 35*, 215–30.

FROMM, E., BROWN, D. P., HURT, S. W., OBERLANDER, J. Z., BOXER, A. M., & PFEIFER, G. (1981). The phenomena and characteristics of self-hypnosis. *International Journal of Clinical and Experimental Hypnosis, 29*, 189–246.

FUSELLA, V. (1973). Blocking of an external signal through self-projected imagery: The role of inner acceptance, personality style, and categories of imagery. (Doctoral dissertation, City University of New York.) *Dissertation Abstracts International, 33*, 5489B–5490B. (University Microfilms No. 73-11, 352.)

GACKENBACH, J. (1988). Psychological content of lucid versus nonlucid dreams. In J. Gackenbach & S. LaBerge (Eds.), *Conscious mind, sleeping brain: Perspectives on lucid dreaming* (pp. 181–220). New York: Plenum.

GACKENBACH, J., & LABERGE, S. (Eds.). (1988). *Conscious mind, sleeping brain: Perspectives on lucid dreaming.* New York: Plenum.

GACKENBACH, J., SNYDER, T. J., ROKES, L. M., & SACHAU, D. (1986). Lucid dreaming frequency in relation to vestibular sensitivity as measured by caloric stimulation. *Journal of Mind and Behavior, 7,* 277–98.

GALLUP, G. G., JR. (1977). Self-recognition in primates: A comparative approach to the bidirectional properties of consciousness. *American Psychologist, 32,* 329–38.

GARDNER, H. (1985). *Frames of mind: The theory of multiple intelligences.* New York: Basic Books.

GARDNER, R. A., & GARDNER, B. T. (1969). Teaching sign language to a chimpanzee. *Science, 165,* 664–72.

GARFIELD, P. (1974). *Creative dreaming.* New York: Ballantine.

GARFIELD, P. (1979). *Pathway to ecstasy.* New York: Holt, Rinehart & Winston.

GAUTIER, T. (1966). *The hashish club.* English translation reprinted in D. Solomon (Ed.), *The marihuana papers.* New York: Signet. (Originally published 1846.)

GAVANSKI, I., & HOFFMAN, C. (1987). Awareness of influences on one's own judgments: The roles of covariation detection and attention to the judgment process. *Journal of Personality and Social Psychology, 52,* 453–63.

GAZZANIGA, M. S. (August 1967). The split brain in man. *Scientific American, 217,* 24–29.

GAZZANIGA, M. S. (1970). *The bisected brain.* New York: Appleton-Century-Crofts.

GAZZANIGA, M. S. (Narrator). (1977). *The split brain and conscious experience.* [Film.] Written and produced by Concept Films, Inc. Harper Media.

GAZZANIGA, M. S. (1983). Right hemisphere language following brain bisection: A 20-year perspective. *American Psychologist, 38,* 525–37. [Also, see Gazzaniga's reply to comments by Levy and Zaidel, pp. 547–49.]

GAZZANIGA, M. S. (Ed.) (1984). *Handbook of cognitive neuroscience.* New York: Plenum.

GAZZANIGA, M. S. (1985). *The social brain: Discovering the networks of the mind.* New York: Basic Books.

GAZZANIGA, M. S. (1988a). Brain modularity: Toward a philosophy of conscious experience. In A. J. Marcel & E. Bisiach (Eds.), *Consciousness in contemporary science* (pp. 218–38). Oxford, England: Oxford University Press.

GAZZANIGA, M. S. (1988b). *Mind matters: How mind and brain interact to create our conscious lives.* Boston: Houghton Mifflin.

GAZZANIGA, M. S. (1989). Organization of the human brain. *Science, 245,* 947–52.

GAZZANIGA, M. S., & LEDOUX, J. E. (1978). *The integrated mind.* New York: Plenum.

GFELLER, J., LYNN, S., & PRIBBLE, W. (1987). Enhancing hypnotic susceptibility: Interpersonal and rapport factors. *Journal of Personality and Social Psychology, 52,* 586–95.

GIAMBRA, L. M. (1974). Daydreaming across the life span: Late adolescent to senior citizen. *International Journal of Aging and Human Development, 5,* 115–40.

GIBSON, J. J. (1982). The information available in pictures. In E. Reed & R. Jones (Eds.), *Reasons for realism: Selected essays of James J. Gibson* (pp. 269–83). Hillsdale, NJ: Erlbaum. (Originally published 1971).

GLASSER, W. (1976). *Positive addiction.* New York: Harper.

GLOBUS, G. G., MAXWELL, G., & SAVODNIK, I. (Eds.) (1976). *Consciousness and the brain: A scientific and philosophical inquiry.* New York: Plenum.

GOLEMAN, D. (1977). *The varieties of the meditative experience.* New York: Irvington.

GOLEMAN, D. (1978). A taxonomy of meditation-specific altered states. *Journal of Altered States of Consciousness, 4,* 203–13.

GOODENOUGH, D. R. (1978). Dream recall: History and current status of the field. In A. M. Arkin, J. S. Antrobus, & S. J. Ellman (Eds.), *The mind in sleep: Psychology and psychophysiology* (pp. 113–40). Hillsdale, NJ: Erlbaum.

GOODENOUGH, D. R., LEWIS, H. B., SHAPIRO, A., JARET, L., & SLESER, F. (1965). Dream reporting following abrupt and gradual awakenings from different types of sleep. *Journal of Personality and Social Psychology, 2,* 170–79.

GOODENOUGH, D. R., WITKIN, H. A., KOULACK, D., & COHEN, H. (1975). The effects of stress films on dream affect and on respiration and eye-movement during rapid-eye movement sleep. *Psychophysiology, 15,* 313–320.

GOODENOUGH, D. R., WITKIN, H. A., LEWIS, H. B., KOULACK, D., & COHEN, H. (1974). Repression, interference, and field dependence as factors in dream forgetting. *Journal of Abnormal Psychology, 83,* 32–44.

GORASSINI, D. R., & SPANOS, N. P. (1986). A social-cognitive skills approach to the successful modification of hypnotic susceptibility. *Journal of Personality and Social Psychology, 50,* 1004–12.

GRAF, P., SQUIRE, L. R., & MANDLER, G. (1984). The information that amnesic patients do not forget. *Journal of Experimental Psychology: Learning, Memory, and Cognition, 10,* 164–78.

GRIFFIN, D. R. (1978). Prospects for a cognitive ethology. *Behavioral and Brain Sciences, 1,* 527–38. [See also commentary, *1,*555–629 and *3,*615–23.]

GRIFFIN, D. R. (1981). *The question of animal awareness* (2nd ed.). New York: Rockefeller University Press.

GRIFFIN, D. R. (1984). *Animal thinking.* Cambridge, MA: Harvard University Press.

GRINSPOON, L. (December 1969). Marihuana. *Scientific American, 221,* 17–25.

GUILFORD, J. P. (1967). *The nature of human intelligence.* New York: McGraw-Hill.

HALL, C., & VAN DE CASTLE, R. L. (1966). *The content analysis of dreams.* New York: Appleton-Century-Crofts.

HARSHMAN, R. A., CRAWFORD, H., & HECHT, E. (1976). Marihuana, cognitive style, and lateralized hemispheric functions. In S. Cohen & R. C. Stillman (Eds.), *The therapeutic potential of marijuana* (pp. 205–54). New York: Plenum.

HARTMANN, E. (1967). *The biology of dreaming.* Springfield, IL: Charles C Thomas.

HARTMANN, E. (1973). *The functions of sleep.* New Haven, CT: Yale University Press.

HARTMANN, E. (1984). *The nightmare: The psychology and biology of terrifying dreams.* New York: Basic Books.

HARTMANN, E., RUSS, D., OLDFIELD, M., SILVAN, I., & COOPER, S. (1987). Who has nightmares? The personality of the lifelong nightmare sufferer. *Archives of General Psychiatry, 44,* 49–56.

HASKELL, R. E. (1986). Cognitive psychology and dream research: Historical, conceptual, and epistemological considerations. *Journal of Mind and Behavior, 7,* 131–60. [Special issue, *Cognition and Dream Research,* R. E. Haskell (Ed.).]

HATFIELD, G. (1988). Neuro-philosophy meets psychology: Reduction, autonomy, and physiological constraints. A commentary on *Neurophilosophy* by P. S. Churchland. *Cognitive Neuropsychology, 5,* 723–46.

HAURI, P. (1982). *The sleep disorders.* Kalamazoo, MI: Upjohn.

HAURI, P., SAWYER, J., & RECHTSCHAFFEN, A. (1967). Dimensions of dreaming: A factored scale for rating dream reports. *Journal of Abnormal Psychology, 72,* 16–22.

HAURI, P., & VAN DE CASTLE, R. L. (1973). Psychophysiological parallels in dreams. *Psychosomatic Medicine, 35,* 297–308.

HEATH, R. G. (1972). Marihuana: Effects on deep and surface electroencephalograms of man. *Archives of General Psychiatry, 26,* 577–84.

HEATH, R. G. (1976). Marihuana and delta-9-tetrahydrocannabinol: Acute and chronic effects on brain function of monkeys. In M. C. Braude & S. Szara (Eds.), *The pharmacology of marihuana* (Vol. 1; pp. 345–56). New York: Raven.

HEBB, D. O. (1974). What psychology is about. *American Psychologist, 29,* 71–79.

HECKHAUSEN, H., & BECKMANN, J. (1990). Intentional action and action slips. *Psychological Review, 97,* 36–48.

HERMAN, J. H., ELLMAN, S. J., & ROFFWARG, H. P. (1978). The problem of NREM dream recall re-examined. In A. M. Arkin, J. S. Antrobus, & S. J. Ellman (Eds.), *The mind in sleep: Psychology and psychophysiology* (pp. 59–92). Hillsdale, NJ: Erlbaum.

HERMAN, J. H., ERMAN, M., BOYS, R., PEISER, L., TAYLOR, M. E., & ROFFWARG, H. P. (1984). Evidence for a directional correspondence between eye movements and dream imagery in REM sleep. *Sleep, 7,* 52–63.

HERON, W. (January 1957). The pathology of boredom. *Scientific American, 196,* 52–56.

HILGARD, E. R. (1962). Impulsive versus realistic thinking: An examination of the distinction between primary and secondary processes in thought. *Psychological Bulletin, 59,* 477–89.

HILGARD, E. R. (1965). *Hypnotic susceptibility.* New York: Harcourt.

HILGARD, E. R. (1967). A quantitative study of pain and its reduction through hypnotic suggestion. *Proceedings of the National Academy of Sciences, 57,* 1581–86.

HILGARD, E. R. (1969a). Pain as a puzzle for psychology and physiology. *American Psychologist, 24,* 103–13.

HILGARD, E. R. (1969b). Altered states of awareness. *Journal of Nervous and Mental Disease, 149,* 68–79.

HILGARD, E. R. (1971). Hypnotic phenomena: The struggle for scientific acceptance. *American Scientist, 59,* 567–77.

HILGARD, E. R. (1973). The domain of hypnosis. *American Psychologist, 28,* 972–82.

HILGARD, E. R. (1977). *Divided consciousness: Multiple controls in human thought and action.* New York: Wiley. (Expanded edition 1986.)

HILGARD, E. R. (1978/1979). The Stanford Hypnotic Susceptibility Scales as related to other measures of hypnotic responsiveness. *American Journal of Clinical Hypnosis, 21* (2 & 3), 68–82.

HILGARD, E. R. (1979). Consciousness and control: Lessons from hypnosis. *Australian Journal of Clinical and Experimental Hypnosis, 7,* 103–15.

HILGARD, E. R. (1980). Consciousness in American psychology. *Annual Review of Psychology, 31,* 1–26.

HILGARD, E. R., & HILGARD, J. R. (1983). *Hypnosis in the relief of pain* (2nd ed.). Los Altos, CA: William Kaufmann. (First edition 1975.)

HILGARD, E. R., HILGARD, J. R., MACDONALD, H., MORGAN, A. H., & JOHNSON, L. S. (1978a). Covert pain in hypnotic analgesia: Its reality as tested by the real-simulator design. *Journal of Abnormal Psychology, 87,* 655–63.

HILGARD, E. R., MACDONALD, H., MORGAN, A. H., & JOHNSON, L. S. (1978b). The reality of hypnotic analgesia: A comparison of highly hypnotizables with simulators. *Journal of Abnormal Psychology, 87,* 239–46.

HILGARD, E. R., MORGAN, A. H., & MACDONALD, H. (1975). Pain and dissociation in the cold pressor test: A study of hypnotic analgesia with "hidden reports" through automatic key pressing and automatic talking. *Journal of Abnormal Psychology, 84,* 280–89.

HILGARD, J. R. (1970). *Personality and hypnosis: A study of imaginative involvement.* Chicago: University of Chicago Press. (Second edition 1979).

HILGARD, J. R. (1974a). Imaginative involvement: Some characteristics of the highly hypnotizable and the non-hypnotizable. *International Journal of Clinical and Experimental Hypnosis, 22,* 138–56.

HILGARD, J. R. (1974b). Sequelae to hypnosis. *International Journal of Clinical and Experimental Hypnosis, 22,* 281–98.

HILGARD, J. R., & LEBARON, S. (1982). Relief of anxiety and pain in children and adolescents with cancer: Quantitative measures and clinical observations. *International Journal of Clinical and Experimental Hypnosis, 30,* 417–42.

HOBSON, J. A. (1988). *The dreaming brain.* New York: Basic Books.

HOBSON, J. A., LYDIC, R., & BAGHDOYAN, H. A. (1986). Evolving concepts of sleep cycle generation: From brain centers to neuronal populations. *Behavioral and Brain Sciences, 9,* 371–448.

HOBSON, J. A., & MCCARLEY, R. W. (1977). The brain as a dream state generator: An activation-synthesis hypothesis of the dream process. *American Journal of Psychiatry, 134,* 1335–48.

HOFMANN, A. (1968). Psychotomimetic agents. In A. Burger (Ed.), *Drugs affecting the central nervous system* (Vol. 2). New York: Marcel Dekker.

HOLENDER, D. (1986). Semantic activation without conscious identification in dichotic listening, parafoveal vision, and visual masking: A survey and appraisal. *The Behavioral and Brain Sciences, 9,* 1–66. [Includes peer commentaries.]

HOLMES, D. S. (1987). The influence of meditation versus rest on physiological arousal: A second examination. In M. A. West (Ed.), *The psychology of meditation* (pp. 81–103). Oxford, England: Oxford University Press.

HOLMES, D. S., SOLOMON, S., CAPPO, B. M., & GREENBERG, J. L. (1983). Effects of transcendental meditation versus resting on physiological and subjective arousal. *Journal of Personality and Social Psychology, 44,* 1245–52.

HORNE, J. A., & MCGRATH, M. J. (1984). The consolidation hypothesis for REM sleep function: Stress and other confounding factors—A review. *Biological Psychology, 18,* 165–84.

HOUSTON, J. (1969). Phenomenology of the psychedelic experience. In R. E. Hicks & P. J. Fink (Eds.), *Psychedelic drugs.* New York: Grune & Stratton.

HOWARD, M. L., & COE, W. C. (1980). The effects of context and subjects' perceived control in breaching posthypnotic amnesia. *Journal of Personality, 48,* 342–59.

HOYT, M. F., & SINGER, J. L. (1978). Psychological effects of REM ("Dream") deprivation upon waking mentation. In A. M. Arkin, J. S. Antrobus, & S. J. Ellman (Eds.), *The mind in sleep: Psychology and psychophysiology* (pp. 487–510). Hillsdale, NJ: Erlbaum.

HULL, C. L. (1933). *Hypnosis and suggestibility.* New York: Appleton-Century.

HUNT, H. T. (1986). Some relations between the cognitive psychology of dreams and dream phenomenology. *Journal of Mind and Behavior, 7,* 213–28.

HUNT, H. T., & CHEFURKA, C. M. (1976). A test of the psychedelic model of altered states of consciousness: The role of introspective sensitization in eliciting unusual subjective reports. *Archives of General Psychiatry, 33*, 867–76.

HUNT, H. T., & OGILVIE, R. D. (1988). Lucid dreams in their natural series: Phenomenological and psychophysiological findings in relation to meditative states. In J. Gackenbach & S. LaBerge (Eds.), *Conscious mind, sleeping brain: Perspectives on lucid dreaming* (pp. 389–417). New York: Plenum.

HUXLEY, A. (1970). *The doors of perception.* New York: Harper & Row. (Original edition 1954.)

IRWIN, H. J. (1985). *Flight of mind: A psychological study of the out-of-body experience.* Metuchen, NJ: Scarecrow.

IRWIN, H. J. (1989). *An introduction to parapsychology.* Jefferson, NC: McFarland & Co.

ISAACS, D. (1975). Cognitive styles in daydreaming. Unpublished doctoral dissertation, City University of New York.

IZARD, C. E. (1980). The emergence of emotions and the development of consciousness in infancy. In J. M. Davidson & R. J. Davidson (Eds.), *The psychobiology of consciousness* (pp. 193–216). New York: Plenum.

JAMES, W. (1893). *Psychology: Briefer course.* Cambridge, MA: Harvard University Press. (Original work published 1892.)

JAMES, W. (1961). *The varieties of religious experience.* New York: Macmillan. (Original work published 1902.)

JAMES, W. (1983). *The principles of psychology.* Cambridge, MA: Harvard University Press. (Original work published 1890.)

JANET, P. (1889). *Psychological automatisms.* Paris: Alcan.

JANET, P. (1907). *The major symptoms of hysteria.* New York: Macmillan.

JANOWSKY, D. S., CLOPTON, P. L., LEICHNER, P. P., ABRAMS, A. A., LEWIS, L. J., & PECHNICK, R. (1979). Interpersonal effects of marijuana. *Archives of General Psychiatry, 36*, 781–85.

JAYNES, J. (1976). *The origin of consciousness in the breakdown of the bicameral mind.* Boston: Houghton Mifflin.

JAYNES, J. (1986). Consciousness and the voices of the mind. *Canadian Psychology, 27*, 128–82.

JOHNSON, L. S. (1981). Current research in self-hypnotic phenomenology: The Chicago paradigm. *International Journal of Clinical and Experimental Hypnosis, 29*, 247–58.

JOHNSON-LAIRD, P. (1983). *Mental models.* Cambridge, MA: Cambridge University Press.

JOHNSON-LAIRD, P. (1988). A computational analysis of consciousness. In A. J. Marcel & E. Bisiach (Eds.), *Consciousness in contemporary science* (pp. 357–68). New York: Oxford University Press.

JONES, A. (1969). Stimulus-seeking behavior. In J. P. Zubek (Ed.), *Sensory deprivation: Fifteen years of research* (pp. 167–206). New York: Appleton-Century-Crofts.

JONES, R. M. (1970). *The new psychology of dreaming.* New York: Viking.

JONES, R. T. (1971). Tetrahydrocannabinol and the marijuana-induced social "high," or the effects of the mind on marijuana. *Annals of the New York Academy of Sciences, 191*, 155–65.

JONES, R. T. (1978). Marihuana: Human effects. In L. L. Iverson, S. Iverson, & S. H. Snyder (Eds.), *Handbook of psychopharmacology* (Vol. 12; pp. 627–42). New York: Plenum.

JONES, R. T., & BENOWITZ, N. (1976). The 30-day trip—clinical studies of cannabis tolerance and dependence. In M. C. Braude & S. Szara (Eds.), *Pharmacology of marijuana* (Vol. 2; pp. 627–42). New York: Raven.

JULIEN, R. M. (1985). *A primer of drug action* (4th ed.). New York: Freeman.

JUNG, C. (1933). *Modern man in search of a soul.* New York: Harcourt.

KAGAN, J. (1981). *The second year: The emergence of self-awareness.* Cambridge, MA: Harvard University Press.

KAHN, E., FISHER, C., & EDWARDS, A. (1978). Night terrors and anxiety dreams. In A. M. Arkin, J. S. Antrobus, & S. J. Ellman (Eds.), *The mind in sleep: Psychology and psychophysiology* (pp. 533–42). Hillsdale, NJ: Erlbaum.

KAHNEMAN, D. (1973). *Attention and effort.* Englewood Cliffs, NJ: Prentice Hall.

KAHNEMAN, D., & TVERSKY, A. (1973). On the psychology of prediction. *Psychological Review, 80*, 237–51.

KALES, A., & KALES, J. D. (1974). Sleep disorders: Recent findings in the diagnosis and treatment of disturbed sleep. *New England Journal of Medicine, 290*, 487–99.

KALES, A., SOLDATOS, C. R., CALDWELL, A. B., CHARNEY, D. S., KALES, J. D., HUMPHREY, F. J., III, & SCHWEITZER, P. K. (1980). Somnambulism: Clinical characteristics and personality patterns. *Archives of General Psychiatry, 37*, 1406–10.

KALES, J. D., KALES, A., SOLDATOS, C. R., CALDWELL, A. B., CHARNEY, D. S., & MARTIN, E. D. (1980). Night terrors: Clinical characteristics and personality patterns. *Archives of General Psychiatry, 37,* 1413–17.

KAMIYA, J. (1961). Behavioral, subjective, and physiological aspects of drowsiness and sleep. In D. W. Fiske & S. R. Maddi (Eds.), *Functions of varied experience* (pp. 145–74). Homewood, IL: Dorsey.

KAMIYA, J. (1968). Conscious control of brain waves. *Psychology Today, 1,* 56–60.

KAMIYA, J. (1972). Operant control of the EEG alpha rhythm and some of its reported effects on consciousness. In C. T. Tart (Ed.), *Altered states of consciousness* (pp. 519–29). Garden City, NY: Anchor Books.

KARACAN, I., GOODENOUGH, D. R., SHAPIRO, A., & STARKER, S. (1966). Erection cycle during sleep in relation to dream anxiety. *Archives of General Psychiatry, 15,* 183–89.

KASAMATSU, A., & HIRAI, T. (1966). An electroencephalographic study on the Zen meditation (zazen). *Folia Psychiatrica et Neurologica Japonica, 20,* 315–36. [Reprinted in Tart, 1972a.]

KELLY, S. F., FISHER, S., & KELLY, R. J. (1978). Effects of cannabis intoxication on primary suggestibility. *Psychopharmacology, 56,* 217–19.

KERR, N. H., FOULKES, D., & SCHMIDT, M. (1982). The structure of laboratory dream reports in blind and sighted subjects. *Journal of Nervous and Mental Disease, 170,* 286–94.

KIHLSTROM, J. F. (1977). Models of posthypnotic amnesia. *Annals of the New York Academy of Sciences, 296,* 284–301. [Special issue, *Conceptual and investigative approaches to hypnosis and hypnotic phenomena,* W. E. Edmonston (Ed.).]

KIHLSTROM, J. F. (1980). Posthypnotic amnesia for recently learned material: Interactions with "episodic" and "semantic" memory. *Cognitive Psychology, 12,* 227–51.

KIHLSTROM, J. F. (1984). Conscious, subconscious, unconscious: A cognitive perspective. In K. S. Bowers & D. Meichenbaum (Eds.), *The unconscious reconsidered* (pp. 149–211). New York: Wiley.

KIHLSTROM, J. F. (1985a). Hypnosis. *Annual Review of Psychology, 36,* 385–418.

KIHLSTROM, J. F. (1985b). Posthypnotic amnesia and the dissociation of memory. In G. H. Bower (Ed.), *The psychology of learning and motivation: Advances in research and theory* (Vol. 19; pp. 131–78). Orlando, FL: Academic Press.

KIHLSTROM, J. F. (1986). Strong inferences about hypnosis. *Behavioral and Brain Sciences, 9,* 474–75. [Comment on Spanos, 1986a.]

KIHLSTROM, J. F. (1987). The cognitive unconscious. *Science, 237,* 1445–52.

KIHLSTROM, J. F., & EVANS, F. J. (1976). Recovery of memory after posthypnotic amnesia. *Journal of Abnormal Psychology, 85,* 654–59.

KIHLSTROM, J. F., EVANS, F. J., ORNE, E. C., & ORNE, M. T. (1980). Attempting to breach posthypnotic amnesia. *Journal of Abnormal Psychology, 89,* 603–16.

KIHLSTROM, J. F., & REGISTER, P. A. (1984). Optimal scoring of amnesia on the Harvard Group Scale of Hypnotic Susceptibility, Form A. *International Journal of Clinical and Experimental Hypnosis, 32,* 51–57.

KINGET, G. M. (1975). *On being human: A systematic view.* New York: Harcourt.

KIRSCH, I. (1985). Response expectancy as a determinant of experience and behavior. *American Psychologist, 40,* 1189–1202.

KIRSCH, I., & HYLAND, M. E. (1987). How thoughts affect the body: A metatheoretical framework. *Journal of Mind and Behavior, 8,* 417–34.

KLATZKY, R. L. (1980). *Human memory: Structures and processes* (2nd ed.). New York: Freeman.

KLATZKY, R. L. (1984). *Memory and awareness: An information-processing perspective.* New York: Freeman.

KLINGER, E. (1971). *Structure and functions of fantasy.* New York: Wiley.

KLINGER, E. (1975). Consequences of commitment to and disengagement from incentives. *Psychological Review, 82,* 1–25.

KLINGER, E. (1978). Modes of normal conscious flow. In K. S. Pope & J. L. Singer (Eds.), *The stream of consciousness: Scientific investigations into the flow of human experience* (pp. 225–58). New York: Plenum.

KLINGER, E. (1978–79). Dimensions of thought and imagery in normal waking states. *Journal of Altered States of Consciousness, 4,* 97–113.

KLINGER, E. (1987). Current concerns and disengagement from incentives. In F. Halisch & J. Kuhl (Eds.), *Motivation, intention, and volition* (pp. 337–47). New York: Springer.

KLINGER, E., BARTA, S. G., & MAXEINER, M. E. (1980). Motivational correlates of thought content frequency and commitment. *Journal of Personality and Social Psychology, 39,* 1222–37.

KLINGER, E., & COX, W. M. (1987–88). Dimensions of thought flow in everyday life. *Imagination, Cognition and Personality, 7,* 105–28.

KLONOFF, H. (1974). Effects of marijuana on driving in a restricted area and on city streets.: Driving performance and physiological changes. In L. L. Miller (Ed.), *Marijuana: Effects on human behavior* (pp. 359–97). New York: Academic Press.

KLONOFF, H., & LOW, M. D. (1974). Psychological and neurophysiological effects of marijuana in man: An interaction model. In L. L. Miller (Ed.), *Marijuana: Effects on human behavior* (pp. 121–55). New York: Academic Press.

KLÜVER, H. (1966). *Mescal and mechanisms of hallucinations.* Chicago: University of Chicago Press.

KNOX, V. J., MORGAN, A. H., & HILGARD, E. R. (1974). Pain and suffering in ischemia: The paradox of hypnotically suggested anesthesia as contradicted by reports from the "hidden observer." *Archives of General Psychiatry, 30,* 840–47.

KOLB, B., & WHISHAW, I. Q. (1990). *Fundamentals of human neuropsychology* (3rd ed.). New York: Freeman.

KOSSLYN, S. (1980). *Image and mind.* Cambridge, MA: Harvard University Press.

KOULACK, D. (1968). Dream time and real time. *Psychonomic Science, 11,* 202.

KOULACK, D., & GOODENOUGH, D. R. (1976). Dream recall and dream recall failure: An arousal-retrieval model. *Psychological Bulletin, 83,* 975–84.

KRAMER, M., KINNEY, L., & SCHARF, M. (1983a). Dream incorporation and dream function. *Sleep,* 369–71.

KRAMER, M., KINNEY, L., & SCHARF, M. (1983b). Sex differences in dreams. *Psychiatric Journal of the University of Ottawa, 8,* 1–4.

KRAUT, R. E., & LEWIS, S. H. (1982). Person perception and self-awareness: Knowledge of influences on one's own judgments. *Journal of Personality and Social Psychology, 42,* 448–60.

KRIPKE, D. F., & SONNENSCHEIN, D. (1978). A biologic rhythm in waking fantasy. In K. S. Pope & J. L. Singer (Eds.), *The stream of consciousness: Scientific investigations into the flow of human experience* (pp. 321–32). New York: Plenum.

KRIPKE, D. F., MULLANEY, D. J., & FLECK, P. A. (1985). Ultradian rhythms during sustained performance. *Experimental Brain Research,* Supplement 12, 201–16.

KRIPPNER, S. (1977). Research on creativity and psychedelic drugs. *International Journal of Clinical and Experimental Hypnosis, 25,* 274–308.

KUBOSE, S. K. (1976). An experimental investigation of psychological aspects of meditation. *Psychologia, 19,* 1–10.

LABERGE, S. (1981). Lucid dreaming: Directing the act as it happens. *Psychology Today, 15,* 48–57.

LABERGE, S. (1985). *Lucid dreaming.* Los Angeles: Tarcher.

LABERGE, S. (1988a). Lucid dreaming in western literature. In J. Gackenbach & S. LaBerge (Eds.), *Conscious mind, sleeping brain: Perspectives on lucid dreaming* (pp. 11–26). New York: Plenum.

LABERGE, S. (1988b). The psychophysiology of lucid dreaming. In J. Gackenbach & S. LaBerge (Eds.), *Conscious mind, sleeping brain: Perspectives on lucid dreaming* (pp. 135–53). New York: Plenum.

LABERGE, S., LEVITAN, L., & DEMENT, W. C. (1986). Lucid dreaming: Physiological correlates of consciousness during REM sleep. *Journal of Mind and Behavior, 7,* 251–58.

LABERGE, S., NAGEL, L. E., DEMENT, W. C., & ZARCONE, V. P., JR. (1981). Lucid dreaming verified by volitional communication during REM sleep. *Perceptual and Motor Skills, 52,* 727–32.

LANDIS, T., REGARD, M., & SERRANT, A. (1980). Iconic reading in a case of alexia without agraphia caused by a brain tumor: A tachistoscopic study. *Brain and Language, 11,* 45–53.

LATANÉ, B., & DARLEY, J. M. (1970). *The unresponsive bystander: Why doesn't he help?* New York: Appleton-Century-Crofts.

LAURENCE, J.-R., & NADON, R. (1986). Reports of hypnotic depth: Are they more than mere words? *International Journal of Clinical and Experimental Hypnosis, 34,* 215–33.

LAURENCE, J.-R., NADON, R., BOWERS, K., PERRY, C., & REGHER, G. (1985). *Clinical encounters in the experimental context.* Paper presented at the 93rd Annual Convention of the American Psychological Association, Los Angeles.

LAURENCE, J.-R., & PERRY, C. (1981). The "hidden observer" phenomenon in hypnosis: Some additional findings. *Journal of Abnormal Psychology, 90,* 334–44.

LAURENCE, J.-R., & PERRY, C. (1983). Hypnotically created memory among highly hypnotizable subjects. *Science, 222,* 523–24.

LAURENCE, J.-R., & PERRY, C. (1988). *Hypnosis, will, and memory: A psycho-legal history.* New York: Guilford.

LAURENCE, J.-R., PERRY, C., & KIHLSTROM, J. (1983). "Hidden observer" phenomenon in hypnosis: An experimental creation? *Journal of Personality and Social Psychology, 44*, 163–69.

LAZAR, J. D. (1989). The effects of changing demand characteristics and external cues on post-hypnotic amnesia. Doctoral dissertation, University of Maine, Orono.

LEAHEY, T. H. (1987). *A history of psychology: Main currents in psychological thought* (2nd ed.). Englewood Cliffs, NJ: Prentice Hall.

LEARY, T. (1967–68). The religious experience: Its production and interpretation. *Journal of Psychedelic Drugs, 1*, 3–23.

LEDOUX, J. E. (1985). Brain, mind and language. In D. A. Oakley (Ed.), *Brain and mind* (pp. 197–216). London: Methuen.

LEVY, J. (1983). Language, cognition, and the right hemisphere. *American Psychologist, 38*, 538–41.

LEVY, J., & TREVARTHEN, C. (1976). Metacontrol of hemispheric function in human split-brain patients. *Journal of Experimental Psychology: Human Perception and Performance, 2*, 299–312.

LEVY, J., TREVARTHEN, C., & SPERRY, R. W. (1972). Perception of bilateral chimeric figures following hemispheric disconnection. *Brain, 95*, 61–78.

LIEBERMAN, D. A. (1979). Behaviorism and the mind: A (limited) call for a return to introspection. *American Psychologist, 34*, 319–33.

LILLY, J. C. (1972). *The center of the cyclone: An autobiography of inner space.* New York: Julian.

LILLY, J. C. (1977). *The deep self.* New York: Simon & Schuster.

LOFTUS, E. F. (1979). *Eyewitness testimony.* Cambridge, MA: Harvard University Press.

LONDON, P., COOPER, L. M., & ENGSTROM, D. R. (1974). Increasing hypnotic susceptibility by brain wave feedback. *Journal of Abnormal Psychology, 83*, 554–60.

LUDWIG, A. M. (1966). Altered states of consciousness. *Archives of General Psychiatry, 15*, 225–34. [Reprinted in Tart, 1972a.]

LURIA, A. R. (1973). *The working brain.* New York: Basic Books.

LURIA, A. R. (1978). The human brain and conscious activity. In G. E. Schwartz & D. Shapiro (Eds.), *Consciousness and self-regulation: Advances in research and theory* (Vol. 2; pp. 1–35). New York: Plenum.

LURIA, A. R. (1987). *The man with a shattered world: The history of a brain wound.* (Translated from the Russian by L. Solotaroff.) Cambridge, MA: Harvard University Press. (Original work published 1972.)

LYNN, S. J., & RHUE, J. W. (1988). Fantasy proneness: Hypnosis, developmental antecedents, and psychopathology. *American Psychologist, 43*, 35–44.

LYNN, S. J., RHUE, J. W., & WEEKES, J. R. (1990). Hypnotic involuntariness: A social cognitive analysis. *Psychological Review, 97*, 169–84.

LYONS, W. (1986). *The disappearance of introspection.* Cambridge, MA: MIT Press.

MACKAY, D. G. (1973). Aspects of a theory of comprehension, memory and attention. *Quarterly Journal of Experimental Psychology, 25*, 22–40.

MACKINNON, D. W. (1962). The nature and nurture of creative talent. *American Psychologist, 17*, 484–95.

MACLEOD-MORGAN, C. (1982). EEG lateralization in hypnosis: A preliminary report. *Australian Journal of Clinical and Experimental Hypnosis, 10*, 99–102.

MACLEOD-MORGAN, C., & LACK, L. (1982). Hemispheric specificity: A physiological concomitant of hypnotizability. *Psychophysiology, 19*, 687–90.

MAHARISHI INTERNATIONAL UNIVERSITY. (1974). *Fundamentals of progress: Scientific research on transcendental meditation.* MIU Press.

MAHARISHI MAHESH YOGI. (1966). *The science of being and the art of living.* Los Angeles: SRM Publications.

MALMO, R. B., BOAG, T. J., & RAGINSKY, B. B. (1954). Electromyographic study of hypnotic deafness. *International Journal of Clinical and Experimental Hypnosis, 2*, 305–17.

MANDLER, G. (1984). *Mind and body: Psychology of emotion and stress.* New York: Norton.

MARCEL, A. J. (1980). Conscious and preconscious recognition of polysemous words: Locating the selective effect of prior verbal context. In R. S. Nickerson (Ed.), *Attention and Performance* (Vol. 8; pp. 435–57). Hillsdale, NJ: Erlbaum.

MARCEL, A. J. (1983a). Conscious and unconscious perception: Experiments on visual masking and word recognition. *Cognitive Psychology, 15*, 197–237.

MARCEL, A. J. (1983b). Conscious and unconscious perception: An approach to the relations between phenomenal experience and perceptual processes. *Cognitive Psychology, 15*, 238–300.

MARCEL, A. J. (1986). Consciousness and processing: Choosing and testing a null hypothesis. *The Behavioral and Brain Sciences, 9*, 40–41.

MARCEL, A. J. (1988). Conscious experience and functionalism. In A. J. Marcel & E. Bisiach (Eds.), *Consciousness in contemporary science* (pp. 121–58). New York: Oxford University Press.

MARKS, D. F. (1973). Visual imagery differences in the recall of pictures. *British Journal of Psychology, 64,* 17–24.

MARSHALL, J. C., & HALLIGAN, P. W. (1988). Blindsight and insight in visuo-spatial neglect. *Nature, 336,* 766–67.

MARTINDALE, C. (1981). *Cognition and consciousness.* Homewood, IL: Dorsey.

MARTINDALE, C. (1991). *Cognitive psychology. A neural-network approach.* Pacific Grove, CA: Brooks/Cole.

MAURY, L. F. A. (1861). *Le sommeil et les rêves.* Paris.

MAY, R. (1967). *Psychology and the human dilemma.* Princeton, NJ: D. Van Nostrand.

McCARLEY, R. W., & HOFFMAN, E. (1981). REM sleep dreams and the activation-synthesis hypothesis. *American Journal of Psychiatry, 138,* 904–12.

McCONKEY, K. M., & SHEEHAN, P. W. (1980). Inconsistency in hypnotic age regression and cue structure as supplied by the hypnotist. *International Journal of Clinical and Experimental Hypnosis, 28,* 394–408.

McDONALD, D. G., SCHICHT, W. W., FRAZIER, R. E., SHALLENBERGER, H. D., & EDWARDS, D. J. (1975). Studies of information processing in sleep. *Psychophysiology, 12,* 624–29.

McGLASHAN, T. H., EVANS, F. J., & ORNE, M. T. (1969). The nature of hypnotic analgesia and placebo response to experimental pain. *Psychosomatic Medicine, 31,* 227–46.

McGLOTHLIN, W. H., & WEST, L. J. (1968). The marihuana problem: An overview. *American Journal of Psychiatry, 125,* 370–78.

McGRATH, M. J., & COHEN, D. B. (1978). REM sleep facilitation of adaptive waking behavior: A review of the literature. *Psychological Bulletin, 85,* 24–57.

McKEEGAN, G. F. (1986). Hypnosis in the treatment of phobias. In F. A. DePiano & H. C. Salzberg (Eds.), *Clinical approaches to hypnosis* (pp. 104–26). Norwood, NJ: Ablex.

McKIM, W. A. (1986). *Drugs and behavior: An introduction to behavioral psychopharmacology.* Englewood Cliffs, NJ: Prentice Hall.

MERIKLE, P. M., & CHEESMAN, J. (1986). Consciousness is a "subjective" state. *The Behavioral and Brain Sciences, 9,* 42.

MILBERG, W., & BLUMSTEIN, S. E. (1981). Lexical decision and aphasia: Evidence for semantic processing. *Brain and Language, 14,* 371–85.

MILES, H. L. (1983). Apes and language: The search for communicative competence. In J. de Luce & H. T. Wilder (Eds.), *Language in primates: Implications for linguistics, anthropology, psychology, and philosophy.* New York: Springer.

MILLER, L. L. (1976). Marihuana and human cognition: A review of laboratory investigations. In S. Cohen & R. C. Stillman (Eds.), *The therapeutic potential of marijuana* (pp. 271–92). New York: Plenum.

MILLER, L. L., & BRANCONNIER, R. J. (1983). Cannabis: Effects on memory and the cholinergic limbic system. *Psychological Bulletin, 93,* 441–56.

MILLER, L. L., CORNETT, T. L., BRIGHTWELL, D. R., McFARLAND, D. J., DREW, W. G., & WIKLER, A. (1977). Marijuana: Effects on storage and retrieval of prose material. *Psychopharmacology, 51,* 311–16.

MILLER, L. L., McFARLAND, D. J., CORNETT, T. L., BRIGHTWELL, D. R., & WIKLER, A. (1977). Marijuana: Effects on free recall and subjective organization of pictures and words. *Psychopharmacology, 55,* 257–62.

MILNER, B., CORKIN, S., & TEUBER, H. L. (1968). Further analysis of the hippocampal amnesia syndrome: 14-year followup study of H. M. *Neuropsychologia, 6,* 215–34.

MILSTEIN, S. L., MacCANNELL, K. L., KARR, G., & CLARK, S. (1974). Marijuana-produced changes in cutaneous sensitivity and affect: Users and non-users. *Pharmacology, Biochemistry, and Behavior, 2,* 367–74.

MILSTEIN, S. L., MacCANNELL, K., KARR, G., & CLARK, S. (1975). Marijuana-produced changes in pain tolerance: Experienced and non-experienced subjects. *International Pharmacopsychiatry, 10,* 177–82.

MITCHELL, S. W. (1896). The effects of Anhalonium Lewinii (the mescal button). *British Medical Journal, 2,* 1625.

MOLINARI, S., & FOULKES, D. (1969). Tonic and phasic events during sleep: Psychological correlates and implications. *Perceptual and Motor Skills, 29,* 343–68.

MONROE, L. J., RECHTSCHAFFEN, A., FOULKES, D., & JENSEN, J. (1965). Discriminability of REM and NREM reports. *Journal of Personality and Social Psychology, 2,* 456–60.

MOODY, R. A. (1975). *Life after life.* Covington, GA: Mockingbird.

MOOK, D. G. (1987). *Motivation: The organization of behavior.* New York: Norton.

MORGAN, A. H., & HILGARD, J. R. (1978/1979a). The Stanford Hypnotic Clinical Scale for Adults. *American Journal of Clinical Hypnosis, 21* (2 & 3), 134–47.

MORGAN, A. H., & HILGARD, J. R. (1978/1979b). The Stanford Hypnotic Clinical Scale for Children. *American Journal of Clinical Hypnosis, 21* (2 & 3), 148–69.

MORGAN, A. H., JOHNSON, D. L., & HILGARD, E. R. (1974). The stability of hypnotic susceptibility: A longitudinal study. *International Journal of Clinical and Experimental Hypnosis, 22,* 249–57.

MOSKOWITZ, H., & MCGLOTHLIN, W. (1974). Effects of marihuana on auditory signal detection. *Psychopharmacologia* (Berlin), *40,* 137–45.

MOSKOWITZ, H., SHARMA, S., & SHAPERO, M. (1972). A comparison of the effects of marihuana and alcohol on visual functions. In M. F. Lewis (Ed.), *Current research in marihuana* (pp. 129–50). New York: Academic.

MOSS, S., & BUTLER, D. C. (1978). The scientific credibility of ESP. *Perceptual and Motor Skills, 46,* 1063–79.

MYERS, J. J. (1984). Right hemisphere language: Science or fiction? *American Psychologist, 39,* 315–20.

NAGEL, T. (1979). What is it like to be a bat? In T. Nagel, *Mortal questions.* London: Cambridge University Press.

NARANJO, C. (1971). Meditation: Its spirit and techniques. In C. Naranjo & R. E. Ornstein, *On the psychology of meditation.* New York: Viking.

NAISH, P. L. N. (1986). Hypnosis and signal detection: An information-processing account. In P. L. N. Naish (Ed.), *What is hypnosis?* (pp. 121–44). Philadelphia: Open University Press.

NASH, M. R. (1987). What, if anything, is regressed about hypnotic age regression? A review of the empirical literature. *Psychological Bulletin, 102,* 42–52.

NASH, M. R., DRAKE, S. D., WILEY, S., KHALSA, S., & LYNN, S. J. (1986). Accuracy of recall by hypnotically age-regressed subjects. *Journal of Abnormal Psychology, 95,* 298–300.

NASH, M. R., JOHNSON, L. S., & TIPTON, R. (1979). Hypnotic age regression and the occurrence of transitional object relationships. *Journal of Abnormal Psychology, 88,* 547–55.

NASH, M. R., LYNN, S. J., STANLEY, S., FRAUMAN, D. C., & RHUE, J. (1985). Hypnotic age regression and the importance of assessing interpersonally relevant affect. *International Journal of Clinical and Experimental Hypnosis, 33,* 224–35.

NATSOULAS, T. (1978). Consciousness. *American Psychologist, 33,* 906–14.

NATSOULAS, T. (1981). Basic problems of consciousness. *Journal of Personality and Social Psychology, 41,* 132–78.

NATSOULAS, T. (1983). Concepts of consciousness. *Journal of Mind and Behavior, 4,* 13–59.

NATSOULAS, T. (1985). An introduction to the perceptual kind of conception of direct (reflective) consciousness. *Journal of Mind and Behavior, 6,* 333–56.

NATSOULAS, T. (1987). Roger W. Sperry's monist interactionism. *Journal of Mind and Behavior, 8,* 1–22.

NEISSER, U. (1976). *Cognition and reality.* New York: Freeman.

NEMIAH, J. C. (1984). The unconscious and psychopathology. In K. S. Bowers & D. Meichenbaum (Eds.), *The unconscious reconsidered* (pp. 49–87). New York: Wiley.

NEWMAN, L. S., & ULEMAN, J. S. (1989). Spontaneous trait inference. In J. S. Uleman & J. A. Bargh (Eds.), *Unintended thought* (pp. 155–88). New York: Guilford.

NISBETT, R. E., & BELLOWS, N. (1977). Verbal reports about causal influences on social judgments: Private access versus public theories. *Journal of Personality and Social Psychology, 35,* 613–24.

NISBETT, R. E., & ROSS, L. (1980). *Human inference: Strategies and shortcomings of social judgment.* Englewood Cliffs, NJ: Prentice Hall.

NISBETT, R. E., & SCHACTER, S. (1966). Cognitive manipulations of pain. *Journal of Experimental Social Psychology, 2,* 227–36.

NISBETT, R. E., & WILSON, T. D. (1977). Telling more than we can know: Verbal reports on mental processes. *Psychological Review, 84,* 231–59.

NOGRADY, H., MCCONKEY, K. M., LAURENCE, J.-R., & PERRY, C. (1983). Dissociation, duality and demand characteristics in hypnosis. *Journal of Abnormal Psychology, 92,* 223–35.

NORMAN, D. A. (1968). Towards a theory of memory and attention. *Psychological Review, 75,* 522–36.

NORMAN, D. A., & SHALLICE, T. (1986). Attention to action: Willed and automatic control of behavior. In R. J. Davidson, G. E. Schwartz, & D. Shapiro (Eds.), *Consciousness and self-regulation: Advances in research and theory* (Vol. 4; pp. 1–18). New York: Plenum.

OBSTOJ, I., & SHEEHAN, P. W. (1977). Aptitude for trance, task generalizability, and incongruity response in hypnosis. *Journal of Abnormal Psychology, 86,* 543–52.

O'CONNELL, D. N., SHOR, R. E., & ORNE, M. T. (1970). Hypnotic age regression: An empirical and methodological analysis. *Journal of Abnormal Psychology: Monograph, 76* (3, Pt. 2).

O'GRADY, K. E. (1980). The absorption scale: A factor-analytic assessment. *International Journal of Clinical and Experimental Hypnosis, 28,* 281–88.

O'KEEFE, J. (1985). Is consciousness the gateway to the hippocampal cognitive map? A speculative essay on the neural basis of mind. In D. A. Oakley (Ed.), *Brain and mind* (pp. 59–98). London: Methuen.

ORNE, M. T. (1951). The mechanisms of hypnotic age regression: An experimental study. *Journal of Abnormal and Social Psychology, 46,* 213–25.

ORNE, M. T. (1959). The nature of hypnosis: Artifact and essence. *Journal of Abnormal and Social Psychology, 58,* 277–99.

ORNE, M. T. (1962). On the social psychology of the psychological experiment: With particular reference to demand characteristics and their implications. *American Psychologist, 17,* 776–83.

ORNE, M. T. (1972). On the simulating subject as a quasi-control group in hypnosis research: What, why, and how? In E. Fromm & R. E. Shor (Eds.), *Hypnosis: Research developments and perspectives* (pp. 399–443). Chicago: Aldine-Atherton.

ORNE, M. T. (1977). The construct of hypnosis: Implications of the definition for research and practice. *Annals of the New York Academy of Sciences, 296,* 14–33.

ORNE, M. T. (1979). The use and misuse of hypnosis in court. *International Journal of Clinical and Experimental Hypnosis, 27,* 311–41.

ORNE, M. T., & EVANS, F. J. (1965). Social control in the psychological experiment: Antisocial behavior and hypnosis. *Journal of Personality and Social Psychology, 1,* 189–200.

ORNE, M. T., & SCHEIBE, K. E. (1964). The contribution of non-deprivation factors in the production of sensory deprivation effects: The psychology of the panic button. *Journal of Abnormal and Social Psychology, 68,* 3–12.

ORNE, M. T., WHITEHOUSE, W. G., DINGES, D. F., & ORNE, E. C. (1988). Reconstructing memory through hypnosis: Forensic and clinical implications. In H. M. Pettinati (Ed.), *Hypnosis and memory* (pp. 21–63). New York: Guilford.

ORNSTEIN, R. E. (1969). *On the experience of time.* New York: Penguin.

ORNSTEIN, R. E. (Ed.). (1973). *The nature of human consciousness: A book of readings.* New York: Freeman.

ORNSTEIN, R. E. (1977). *The psychology of consciousness* (2nd ed.) New York: Harcourt.

ORNSTEIN, R. E. (1986). *The psychology of consciousness* (rev. ed). New York: Viking Penguin.

ORTONY, A., & TURNER, T. J. (1990). What's basic about basic emotions? *Psychological Review, 97,* 315–31.

OSTER, G. (February 1970). Phosphenes. *Scientific American, 222,* 83–87.

OVERTON, D. A. (1973). State-dependent retention of learned responses produced by drugs: Its relevance to sleep learning and recall. In W. P. Koella & P. Levin (Eds.), *Sleep: Physiology, biochemistry, psychology, pharmacology, clinical implications.* Basel, Switzerland: S. Karger.

PACKARD, V. O. (1957). *The hidden persuaders.* New York: D. McKay.

PAGANO, R. R., & WARRENBURG, S. (1983). Meditation: In search of a unique effect. In R. J. Davidson, G. E. Schwartz, & D. Shapiro (Eds.), *Consciousness and self-regulation: Advances in research and theory* (Vol. 3; pp. 153–210). New York: Plenum.

PAILLARD, J., MICHEL, F., & STELMACH, G. (1983). Localization without content: A tactile analogue of "blind sight." *Archives of Neurology, 40,* 548–51.

PEKALA, R. J. (1987). The phenomenology of meditation. In M. A. West (Ed.), *The psychology of meditation* (pp. 59–80). Oxford, England: Oxford University Press.

PEKALA, R. J., & WENGER, C. F. (1983). Retrospective phenomenological assessment: Mapping consciousness in reference to specific stimulus conditions. *Journal of Mind and Behavior, 4,* 247–74.

PERRY, C. W. (1977). Is hypnotizability modifiable? *International Journal of Clinical and Experimental Hypnosis, 25,* 125–46.

PERRY, C. W. (1979). Hypnotic coercion and compliance to it: A review of evidence presented in a legal case. *International Journal of Clinical and Experimental Hypnosis, 27,* 187–218.

PERRY, C. W., GELFAND, R., & MARCOVITCH, R. (1979). The relevance of hypnotic susceptibility in the clinical context. *Journal of Abnormal Psychology, 88,* 592–603.

PERRY, C. W., & LAURENCE, J.-R. (1984). Mental processing outside of awareness: The contributions of Freud and Janet. In K. S. Bowers & D. Meichenbaum (Eds.), *The unconscious reconsidered* (pp. 9–48). New York: Wiley.

PERRY, C. W., LAURENCE, J.-R., D'EON, J., & TALLANT, B. (1988). Hypnotic age regression techniques in the elicitation of memories: Applied uses and abuses. In H. M. Pettinati (Ed.), *Hypnosis and memory* (pp. 128–54). New York: Guilford.

PERRY, C. W., & WALSH, B. (1978). Inconsistencies and anomalies of response as a defining characteristic of hypnosis. *Journal of Abnormal Psychology, 87,* 574–77.

PHILPOTT, W. H., & KALITA, D. K. (1980). *Brain allergies: The psycho-nutrient connection.* New Canaan, CT: Keats Publishing.

PICCIONE, C., HILGARD, E. R., & ZIMBARDO, P. G. (1989). On the degree of stability of measured hypnotizability over a 25-year period. *Journal of Personality and Social Psychology, 56,* 289–95.

PIVIK, R. T. (1978). Tonic states and phasic events in relation to sleep mentation. In A. M. Arkin, J. S. Antrobus, & S. J. Ellman (Eds.), *The mind in sleep: Psychology and psychophysiology* (pp. 245–71). Hillsdale, NJ: Erlbaum.

PLOTKIN, W. B. (1976). On the self-regulation of the occipital alpha rhythm: Control strategies, states of consciousness, and the role of physiological feedback. *Journal of Experimental Psychology: General, 105,* 66–99.

PLOTKIN, W. B. (1977). On the social psychology of experiential states associated with EEG alpha biofeedback training. In J. Beatty & H. Legewie (Eds.), *Biofeedback and behavior* (pp. 121–34). New York: Plenum.

PLOTKIN, W. B. (1978). Long-term eyes-closed alpha-enhancement training: Effects on alpha amplitudes and on experiential state. *Psychophysiology, 15,* 40–52.

PLOTKIN, W. B. (1979). The alpha experience revisited: Biofeedback in the transformation of psychological state. *Psychological Bulletin, 86,* 1132–48.

PLOTKIN, W. B. (1980). The role of attributions of responsibility in the facilitation of unusual experiential states during alpha training: An analysis of the biofeedback placebo effect. *Journal of Abnormal Psychology, 89,* 67–78.

PLUTCHIK, R. (February 1980). A language for the emotions. *Psychology Today,* pp. 68–78.

POPE, K. S. (1978). How gender, solitude, and posture influence the stream of consciousness. In K. S. Pope & J. L. Singer (Eds.), *The stream of consciousness: Scientific investigations into the flow of human experience* (pp. 259–99). New York: Plenum.

POPE, K. S., & SINGER, J. L. (1978). Some dimensions of the stream of consciousness: Towards a model of ongoing thought. In G. E. Schwartz & D. Shapiro (Eds.), *Consciousness and self-regulation: Advances in research* (Vol. 2; pp. 101–37). New York: Holt.

POPE, K. S., & SINGER, J. L. (1980). The waking stream of consciousness. In J. M. Davidson & R. J. Davidson (Eds.), *The psychobiology of consciousness* (pp. 169–91). New York: Plenum.

PRICE, R. F., & COHEN, D. B. (1988). Lucid dream induction: An empirical evaluation. In J. Gackenbach & S. LaBerge (Eds.), *Conscious mind, sleeping brain: Perspectives on lucid dreaming* (pp. 105–34). New York: Plenum.

PUCCETTI, R. (1981). The case for mental duality: Evidence from split brain data and other considerations. *The Behavioral and Brain Sciences, 4,* 93–123. [Includes peer commentaries.]

PURCELL, S., MULLINGTON, J., MOFFITT, A., HOFFMANN, R., & PIGEAU, R. (1986). Dream self-reflectiveness as a learned cognitive skill. *Sleep, 9,* 423–37.

PUTNAM, W. H. (1979). Hypnosis and distortions in eyewitness memory. *International Journal of Clinical and Experimental Hypnosis, 27,* 437–48.

RADTKE, H. L., & SPANOS, N. P. (1981). Was I hypnotized? A social psychological analysis of hypnotic depth reports. *Psychiatry, 44,* 359–76.

RADTKE, H. L., & SPANOS, N. P. (1982). The effect of rating scale descriptors on hypnotic depth reports. *Journal of Psychology, 111,* 235–45.

RADTKE-BODORIK, H. L., PLANAS, M., & SPANOS, N. P. (1980). Suggested amnesia, verbal inhibition, and disorganized recall for a long word list. *Canadian Journal of Behavioral Science, 12,* 87–97.

RAFAELSEN, O. J., BECH, P., & RAFAELSEN, L. (1973). Simulated car driving influenced by cannabis and alcohol. *Pharmakopsychiatrie, 6,* 71–83.

RANDI, J. (1982). *Flim-flam! Psychics, ESP, unicorns and other delusions.* Buffalo, NY: Prometheus Books.

RAY, O. (1978). *Drugs, society, and human behavior* (2nd ed.). St. Louis, MO: C. V. Mosby.

RAY, O., & KSIR, C. (1987). *Drugs, society, and human behavior* (4th ed.). St Louis, MO: Times Mirror/Mosby.

RECHTSCHAFFEN, A. (1973). The psychophysiology of mental activity during sleep. In F. J. Mc-

Guigan & R. A. Schoonover (Eds.), *The psychophysiology of thinking: Studies of covert processes* (pp. 153–205). New York: Academic Press.

RECHTSCHAFFEN, A. (1978). The single-mindedness and isolation of dreams. *Sleep, 1*, 97–109.

RECHTSCHAFFEN, A., GILLILAND, M. A., BERGMANN, B. M., & WINTER, J. B. (1983). Physiological correlates of prolonged sleep deprivation in rats. *Science, 221,* 182–84.

RECHTSCHAFFEN, A., & KALES, A. (1968). *A manual of standardized terminology, techniques and scoring systems for sleep stages of human subjects.* (National Institute of Health Publication No. 204). Washington, DC: United States Government Printing Office.

RECHTSCHAFFEN, A., VOGEL, G., & SHAIKUN, G. (1963). Interrelatedness of mental activity during sleep. *Archives of General Psychiatry, 9,* 536–47.

RICHARDS, W. (November 1971). The fortification illusions of migraines. *Scientific American, 225,* 89–96.

RICHARDSON, A. (1969). *Mental imagery.* New York: Springer.

RICHARDSON, A. (1977). Verbalizer-visualizer: A cognitive style dimension. *Journal of Mental Imagery, 1,* 109–26.

RICHARDSON, A. (1984). *The experiential dimension of psychology.* St. Lucia, Australia: University of Queensland Press.

RING, K. (1980). *Life at death: A scientific investigation of the near-death experience.* New York: Coward, McCann, & Geoghegan.

RING, K. (1984). *Heading toward Omega: In search of the meaning of the near-death experience.* New York: Morrow.

ROBINSON, V. (1946). Experiments with hashish. *Ciba Symposia, 8.* [Reprinted in D. Solomon 1966.]

ROFFWARG, H., DEMENT, W., MUZIO, J., & FISHER, C. (1962). Dream imagery: Relationship to rapid eye movements of sleep. *Archives of General Psychiatry, 7,* 235–58.

ROFFWARG, H.P, MUZIO, J. N., & DEMENT, W. C. (1966). Ontogenic development of the human sleep-dream cycle. *Science, 152,* 604–19.

ROHRBAUGH, J. W. (1984). The orienting reflex: Performance and central nervous system manifestations. In R. Parasuraman & D. R. Davies (Eds.), *Varieties of attention.* Orlando, FL: Academic Press.

ROITBLAT, H. L. (1987). *Introduction to comparative cognition.* New York: Freeman.

ROSCH, E. (1973). Natural categories. *Cognitive Psychology, 4,* 328–50.

ROSENZWEIG, M. R., & LEIMAN, A. L. (1989). *Physiological psychology* (2nd ed.). New York: Random House.

ROSSI, A. M., KUEHNLE, J. C., & MENDELSON, J. H. (1978). Marihuana and mood in human volunteers. *Pharmacology, Biochemistry & Behavior, 8,* 447–53.

ROTH, W. T., ROSENBLOOM, M. J., DARLEY, C. F., TINKLENBERG, J. R., & KOPELL, B. S. (1975). Marihuana effects on TAT form and content. *Psychopharmacologia, 43,* 261–66.

ROTH, W. T., TINKLENBERG, J., & KOPELL, B. (1976). Subjective benefits and drawbacks of marihuana and alcohol. In S. Cohen & R. C. Stillman (Eds.), *The therapeutic potential of marihuana* (pp. 255–69). New York: Plenum.

RUDHE, L., & EKECRANTZ, L. (1974). Transitional phenomena. *Acta Psychiatrica Scandinavica, 50,* 381–400.

RYAN, E., & SIMONS, J. (1982). Efficacy of mental imagery in enhancing mental rehearsal of motor skills. *Journal of Sport Psychology, 4,* 41–51.

RYCKMAN, R. M. (1989). *Theories of Personality* (4th ed.). Monterey, CA: Brooks/Cole Publishing Co.

SABOM, M. B. (1982). *Recollections of death: A medical investigation.* New York: Harper & Row.

SACERDOTE, P. (1981). Teaching self-hypnosis to adults. *International Journal of Clinical and Experimental Hypnosis, 29,* 282–99.

SACKS, O. (1987). *The man who mistook his wife for a hat.* New York: Harper & Row.

SANDERS, R. S., & REYHER, J. (1969). Sensory deprivation and the enhancement of hypnotic susceptibility. *Journal of Abnormal Psychology, 74,* 375–81.

SANDFORD, J. A. (1986). A review and analysis of hypnotherapeutic approaches for the control of smoking behavior. In F. A. DePiano & H. C. Salzberg (Eds.), *Clinical approaches to hypnosis* (pp. 73–93). Norwood, NJ: Ablex.

SARBIN, T. R., & COE, W. C. (1972). *Hypnosis: A social psychological analysis of influence communication.* New York: Holt.

SCHACHTER, S., & SINGER, J. (1962). Cognitive, social, and physiological determinants of emotional state. *Psychological Review, 65,* 379–99.

SCHACTER, D. L. (1976). The hypnagogic state: A critical review of the literature. *Psychological Bulletin, 83*, 452–81.

SCHACTER, D. L. (1985). Priming of old and new knowledge in amnesic patients and normal subjects. *Annals of the New York Academy of Sciences, 444*, 41–53.

SCHACTER, D. L. (1987). Implicit memory: History and current status. *Journal of Experimental Psychology: Learning, Memory, and Cognition, 13*, 501–18.

SCHACTER, D. L. (1989). On the relation between memory and consciousness: Dissociable interactions and conscious experience. In H. L. Roediger & F. I. M. Craik (Eds.), *Varieties of memory and consciousness* (pp. 355–89). Hillsdale, NJ: Erlbaum.

SCHACTER, D. L. (1990a). Perceptual representation systems and implicit memory: Toward a resolution of the multiple memory systems debate. In A. Diamond (Ed.), *Development and neural bases of higher cognitive functions. Annals of the New York Academy of Sciences, 608*, 543–71.

SCHACTER, D. L. (1990b). Toward a cognitive neuropsychology of awareness: Implicit knowledge and anosognosia. *Journal of Clinical and Experimental Neuropsychology, 12*, 155–78.

SCHACTER, D. L., HARBLUK, J. L., & MCLACHLAN, D. R. (1984). Retrieval without recollection: An experimental analysis of source amnesia. *Journal of Verbal Learning and Verbal Behavior, 23*, 593–611.

SCHACTER, D. L., MCANDREWS, M. P., & MOSCOVITCH, M. (1988). Access to consciousness: Dissociations between implicit and explicit knowledge in neuropsychological syndromes. In L. Weiskrantz (Ed.), *Thought without language* (pp. 242–78). Oxford, England: Oxford University Press.

SCHAEFFER, J., ANDRYSIAK, T., & UNGERLEIDER, J. T. (1981). Cognition and long-term use of ganja (cannabis). *Science, 213*, 465–66.

SCHATZMAN, M., WORSLEY, A., & FENWICK, P. (1988). Correspondence during lucid dreams between dreamed and actual events. In J. Gackenbach & S. LaBerge (Eds.), *Conscious mind, sleeping brain: Perspectives on lucid dreaming* (pp. 155–79). New York: Plenum.

SCHLAADT, R. G., & SHANNON, P. T. (1986). *Drugs of choice: Current perspectives on drug use* (2nd ed.). Englewood Cliffs, NJ: Prentice Hall.

SCHNEIDER, W., DUMAIS, S. T., & SHIFFRIN, R. M. (1984). Automatic and control processing and attention. In R. Parasuraman & D. R. Davies (Eds.), *Varieties of attention* (pp. 1–27). Orlando, FL: Academic Press.

SCHNEIDER, W., & SHIFFRIN, R. M. (1977). Controlled and automatic human information processing: I. Detection, search, and attention. *Psychological Review, 84*, 1–66.

SCHULMAN, C. A., RICHLIN, M., & WEINSTEIN, S. (1967). Hallucinations and disturbances of affect, cognition and physical state as a function of sensory deprivation. *Perceptual and Motor Skills, 25*, 1001–24.

SCHULTES, R. E., & HOFMANN, A. (1979). *Plants of the gods: Origins of hallucinogenic use.* New York: McGraw-Hill.

SCHWARTZ, D. G., WEINSTEIN, L. N., & ARKIN, A. M. (1978). Qualitative aspects of sleep mentation. In A. M. Arkin, J. S. Antrobus, & S. J. Ellman (Eds.), *The mind in sleep: Psychology and psychophysiology* (pp. 143–241). Hillsdale, NJ: Erlbaum.

SCOTT, T., BEXTON, W. H., HERON, W., & DOANE, B. K. (1959). Cognitive effects of perceptual isolation. *Canadian Journal of Psychology, 13*, 200–209.

SEGAL, S. J., & FUSELLA, V. (1970). Influence of imaged pictures and sounds on detection of visual and auditory signals. *Journal of Experimental Psychology, 83*, 458–64.

SHALLICE, T. (1978). The dominant action system: An information-processing approach to consciousness. In K. S. Pope & J. L. Singer (Eds.), *The stream of consciousness: Scientific investigations into the flow of human experience* (pp. 117–57). New York: Plenum.

SHAPIRO, D. (1977). A biofeedback strategy in the study of consciousness. In N. E. Zinberg (Ed.), *Alternate states of consciousness.* New York: Free Press.

SHAPIRO, D. H. (1980). *Meditation: Self-regulation strategy and altered state of consciousness.* Chicago: Aldine.

SHAPIRO, J. L., & DIAMOND, M. J. (1972). Increases in hypnotizability as a function of encounter group training: Some confirming evidence. *Journal of Abnormal Psychology, 79*, 112–15.

SHAVER, P. (1986). Consciousness without the body. *Contemporary Psychology, 31*, 645–47.

SHARMA, S., & MOSKOWITZ, H. (1974). Effects of two levels of attention demand on vigilance performance under marihuana. *Perceptual and Motor Skills, 38*, 967–70.

SHEEHAN, P. W. (1979). Hypnosis and the process of imagination. In E. Fromm & R. E. Shor (Eds.),

Hypnosis: Developments in research and new perspectives (2nd ed.; pp. 381–411). New York: Aldine.

SHEEHAN, P. W. (1988). Memory distortion in hypnosis. *International Journal of Clinical and Experimental Hypnosis, 36*, 296–311.

SHEEHAN, P. W., GRIGG, L., & McCANN, T. (1984). Memory distortion following exposure to false information in hypnosis. *Journal of Abnormal Psychology, 93*, 259–65.

SHEEHAN, P. W., & McCONKEY, K. M. (1982). *Hypnosis and experience.* Hillsdale, NJ: Erlbaum.

SHEEHAN, P. W., & PERRY, C. W. (1976). *Methodologies of hypnosis: A critical appraisal of contemporary paradigms of hypnosis.* Hillsdale, NJ: Erlbaum.

SHIELDS, I. W., & KNOX, V. J. (1986). Level of processing as a determinant of hypnotic hypermnesia. *Journal of Abnormal Psychology, 95*, 358–64.

SHIMAMURA, A. P., & SQUIRE, L. R. (1987). A neuropsychological study of fact learning and source amnesia. *Journal of Experimental Psychology: Learning, Memory, and Cognition, 13*, 464–74.

SHOR, R. E. (1959). Hypnosis and the concept of the generalized reality-orientation. *American Journal of Psychotherapy, 13*, 582–602.

SHOR, R. E. (1960). The frequency of naturally occurring "hypnotic like" experiences in the normal college population. *International Journal of Clinical and Experimental Hypnosis, 8*, 151–63.

SHOR, R. E. (1962). Three dimensions of hypnotic depth. *International Journal of Clinical and Experimental Hypnosis, 10*, 23–38.

SHOR, R. E. (1979). A phenomenological method for the measurement of variables important to an understanding of the nature of hypnosis. In E. Fromm & R. E. Shor (Eds.), *Hypnosis: Developments in research and new perspectives* (2nd rev. ed.; pp. 105–35). New York: Aldine.

SHOR, R. E., & ORNE, E. C. (1962). *Harvard Group Scale of Hypnotic Susceptibility, Form A.* Palo Alto, CA: Consulting Psychologists Press.

SIEGEL, R. K. (April 1977). Hallucinations. *Scientific American, 237*, 132–40.

SIEGEL, R. K. (1980). The psychology of life after death. *American Psychologist, 35*, 911–31.

SIEGEL, R. K., & JARVIK, M. E. (1975). Drug-induced hallucinations in animals and man. In R. K. Siegel & L. J. West (Eds.), *Hallucinations: Behavior, experience, and theory* (pp. 81–161). New York: Wiley.

SINGER, J. L. (1975a). Navigating the stream of consciousness: Research in daydreaming and related inner experience. *American Psychologist, 30*, 727–38.

SINGER, J. L. (1975b). *The inner world of daydreaming.* New York: Harper & Row.

SINGER, J. L. (1978). Experimental studies of daydreaming and the stream of thought. In K. S. Pope & J. L. Singer (Eds.), *The stream of consciousness: Scientific investigations into the flow of human experience* (pp. 187–223). New York: Plenum.

SINGER, J. L. (1984). The private personality. *Personality and Social Psychology Bulletin, 10*, 7–30.

SINGER, J. L., & ANTROBUS, J. S. (1965). Eye movements during fantasies. *Archives of General Psychiatry, 12*, 71–76.

SINGER, J. L., & ANTROBUS, J. S. (1972). Daydreaming, imaginal processes, and personality: A normative study. In P. Sheehan (Ed.), *The function and nature of imagery* (pp. 175–202). New York: Academic Press.

SINGER, J. L., & POPE, K. S. (1978). *The power of human imagination.* New York: Plenum.

SKINNER, B. F. (1953). *Science and human behavior.* New York: Macmillan.

SKINNER, B. F. (1971). *Beyond freedom and dignity.* New York: Knopf.

SKINNER, B. F. (1974). *About behaviorism.* New York: Knopf.

SKINNER, B. F. (1987). Cognitive science and behaviorism. In *Upon further reflection.* Englewood Cliffs, NJ: Prentice Hall.

SLADE, P. D., & BENTALL, R. P. (1988). *Sensory deception: A scientific analysis of hallucination.* Baltimore: Johns Hopkins University Press.

SLOANE, M. C. (1981). A comparison of hypnosis vs. waking state and visual vs. non-visual recall instructions for witness/victim memory retrieval in actual major crimes. Doctoral thesis, Florida State University, Tallahassee. *Dissertation Abstracts International.* University Microfilms No. 8125873.

SMITH, E. R., & MILLER, F. D. (1978). Limits on perception of cognitive processes: A reply to Nisbett and Wilson. *Psychological Review, 85*, 355–62.

SMITH, J. C. (1975). Meditation as psychotherapy: A review of the literature. *Psychological Bulletin, 82*, 558–64.

SMITH, J. C. (1976). Psychotherapeutic effects of transcendental meditation with controls for expectation of relief and daily sitting. *Journal of Consulting and Clinical Psychology, 44*, 630–37.

SMITH, J. C. (1978). Personality correlates of continuation and outcome in meditation and erect sitting control treatments. *Journal of Consulting and Clinical Psychology, 46*, 272-79.

SMITH, J. C. (1987). Meditation as psychotherapy: A new look at the evidence. In M. A. West (Ed.), *The psychology of meditation* (pp. 136-49). Oxford, England: Oxford University Press.

SNYDER, F. (1970). The phenomenology of dreaming. In L. Madow & L. H. Snow (Eds.), *The psychodynamic implications of the physiological studies on dreams* (pp. 124-51). Springfield, IL: Charles C Thomas.

SNYDER, F., HOBSON, J. A., MORRISON, D. F., & GOLDFRANK, F. (1964). Changes in respiration, heart rate, and systolic blood pressure in human sleep. *Journal of Applied Physiology, 19*, 417-22.

SNYDER, T., & GACKENBACH, J. (1988). Individual differences associated with lucid dreaming. In J. Gackenbach & S. LaBerge (Eds.), *Conscious mind, sleeping brain: Perspectives on lucid dreaming* (pp. 221-59). New York: Plenum.

SOLOMON, D. (Ed.). (1966). *The marihuana papers.* New York: Signet.

SOLOMON, P., KUBZANSKY, P. E., LEIDERMAN, P. H., MENDELSON, J., & WEXLER, D. (Eds.) (1961). *Sensory deprivation.* Cambridge, MA: Harvard University Press.

SPANOS, N. P. (1982). A social psychological approach to hypnotic behavior. In G. Weary & H. L. Mirels (Eds.), *Integrations of clinical and social psychology* (pp. 231-71). New York: Oxford University Press.

SPANOS, N. P. (1983). The hidden observer as an experimental creation. *Journal of Personality and Social Psychology, 44*, 170-76.

SPANOS, N. P. (1986a). Hypnotic behavior: A social-psychological interpretation of amnesia, analgesia, and "trance logic." *The Behavioral and Brain Sciences, 9*, 449-502. [Includes peer commentaries.]

SPANOS, N. P. (1986b). Hypnosis and the modification of hypnotic susceptibility: A social psychological perspective. In P. Naish (Ed.), *What is hypnosis?* (pp. 85-120). Philadelphia: Open University Press.

SPANOS, N. P. (1987-88). Past-life hypnotic regression: A critical view. *The Skeptical Inquirer, 12*, 174-80.

SPANOS, N. P. (1990). Hypnosis, hypnotizability and hypnotherapy. In C. R. Snyder & D. Forsyth (Eds.), *Handbook of social and clinical psychology: The health perspective.* New York: Pergamon.

SPANOS, N. P., & BARBER, T. X. (1974). Toward a convergence in hypnosis research. *American Psychologist, 29*, 500-511.

SPANOS, N. P., & CHAVES, J. F. (Eds.) (1989). *Hypnosis: The cognitive-behavioral perspective.* Buffalo, NY: Prometheus.

SPANOS, N. P., CROSS, W. P., MENARY, E. P., BRETT, P. J., & DE GROH, M. (1987a). Attitudinal and imaginal ability predictors of social cognitive-skill training enhancements of hypnotic susceptibility. *Personality and Social Psychology Bulletin, 13*, 379-98.

SPANOS, N. P., & D'EON, J. L. (1980). Hypnotic amnesia, disorganized recall and inattention. *Journal of Abnormal Psychology, 89*, 744-50.

SPANOS, N. P., DE GROOT, H. P., & GWYNN, M. I. (1987b). Trance logic as incomplete responding. *Journal of Personality and Social Psychology, 53*, 911-21.

SPANOS, N. P., GOTTLIEB, J., & RIVERS, S. M. (1980a). The effects of short-term meditation practice on hypnotic responsivity. *Psychological Record, 30*, 343-48.

SPANOS, N. P., GWYNN, M. I., COMER, S. L., BALTRUWEIT, W. J., & DE GROH, M. (1989a). Are hypnotically induced pseudomemories resistant to cross-examination? *Law and Human Behavior, 13*, 271-89.

SPANOS, N. P., GWYNN, M. I., & STAM, H. J. (1983a). Instructional demands and ratings of overt and hidden pain during hypnotic analgesia. *Journal of Abnormal Psychology, 92*, 479-88.

SPANOS, N. P., & HEWITT, E. C. (1980). The hidden observer in hypnotic analgesia: Discovery or experimental creation? *Journal of Personality and Social Psychology, 39*, 1201-14.

SPANOS, N. P., HODGINS, D. C., STAM, H. J., & GWYNN, M. (1984a). Suffering for science: The effects of implicit social demands on response to experimentally induced pain. *Journal of Personality and Social Psychology, 46*, 1162-72.

SPANOS, N. P., & KATSANIS, J. (1989). Effects of instructional set on attributions of nonvolition during hypnotic and nonhypnotic analgesia. *Journal of Personality and Social Psychology, 56*, 182-88.

SPANOS, N. P., KENNEDY, S. K., & GWYNN, M. I. (1984b). The moderating effect of contextual variables on the relationship between hypnotic susceptibility and suggested analgesia. *Journal of Abnormal Psychology, 93*, 282-94.

SPANOS, N. P., LUSH, N. I., & GWYNN, M. I. (1989b). Cognitive skill-training enhancement of hypnotizability: Generalization effects and trance logic responding. *Journal of Personality and Social Psychology, 56,* 795–804.

SPANOS, N. P., & MCLEAN, J. (1986). Hypnotically created pseudomemories: Memory distortions or reporting biases? *British Journal of Experimental and Clinical Hypnosis, 3,* 155–59.

SPANOS, N. P., MCNEIL, C., GWYNN, M. I., & STAM, H. J. (1984c). Effects of suggestion and distraction on reported pain in subjects high and low on hypnotic susceptibility. *Journal of Abnormal Psychology, 93,* 277–84.

SPANOS, N. P., & MCPEAKE, J. D. (1975). Involvement in everyday imaginative activities, attitudes toward hypnosis and hypnotic susceptibility. *Journal of Personality and Social Psychology, 31,* 594–98.

SPANOS, N. P., MENARY, E., BRETT, P. J., CROSS, W., & AHMED, Q. (1987c). Failure of posthypnotic responding to occur outside the experimental setting. *Journal of Abnormal Psychology, 96,* 52–57.

SPANOS, N. P., RADTKE, H. L., & BERTRAND, L. D. (1985). Hypnotic amnesia as a strategic enactment: Breaching amnesia in highly susceptible subjects. *Journal of Personality and Social Psychology, 47,* 1155–69.

SPANOS, N. P., RADTKE, H. L., HODGINS, D. C., BERTRAND, L. D., STAM, H., & DUBREUIL, D. L. (1983b). The Carleton University Responsiveness to Suggestion Scale: Stability, reliability, and relationships with expectancies and hypnotic experiences. *Psychological Reports, 53,* 555–63.

SPANOS, N. P., RADTKE, H. L., HODGINS, D. C., BERTRAND, L. D., & STAM, H. L. (1983c). The Carleton University Responsiveness to Suggestion Scale: Normative data and psychometric properties. *Psychological Reports, 53,* 523–35.

SPANOS, N. P., RADTKE-BODORIK, H. L., FERGUSON, J. D., & JONES, B. (1979a). The effects of hypnotic susceptibility, suggestions for analgesia, and the utilization of cognitive strategies on the reduction of pain. *Journal of Abnormal Psychology, 88,* 282–92.

SPANOS, N. P., RIVERS, S. M., & ROSS, S. (1977). Experienced involuntariness and response to hypnotic suggestions. *Bulletin of the New York Academy of Sciences, 296 ,* 208–21. [Special issue, *Conceptual and investigative approaches to hypnosis and hypnotic phenomena,* W. E. Edmonston, Jr. (Ed.).]

SPANOS, N. P., ROBERTSON, L. A., MENARY, E. P., & BRETT, P. J. (1986). Component analysis of cognitive skill training for the enhancement of hypnotic susceptibility. *Journal of Abnormal Psychology, 95,* 350–57.

SPANOS, N. P., STAM, H. J., RIVERS, S. M., & RADTKE, H. L. (1980b). Meditation, expectation and performance on indices of nonanalytic attending. *International Journal of Clinical and Experimental Hypnosis, 28,* 244–51.

SPANOS, N. P., STEGGLES, S., RADTKE-BODORIK, H. L., & RIVERS, S. M. (1979b). Nonanalytic attending, hypnotic susceptibility, and psychological well-being in trained meditators and nonmeditators. *Journal of Abnormal Psychology, 88,* 85–87.

SPERRY, R. W. (January 1964). The great cerebral commissure. *Scientific American, 210,* 42–52.

SPERRY, R. W. (1966). Brain bisection and mechanisms of consciousness. In J. C. Eccles (Ed.), *Brain and conscious experience* (pp. 298–313). New York: Springer-Verlag.

SPERRY, R. W. (1968). Hemisphere deconnection and unity in conscious awareness. *American Psychologist, 23,* 723–33.

SPERRY, R. W. (1969). A modified concept of consciousness. *Psychological Review, 76,* 532–36.

SPERRY, R. W. (1970). An objective approach to subjective experience: Further explanation of a hypothesis. *Psychological Review, 77,* 585–90.

SPERRY, R. W. (1976). Mental phenomena as causal determinants in brain function. In G. G. Globus, G. Maxwell, & I. Savodnik (Eds.), *Consciousness and the brain: A scientific and philosophical inquiry* (pp. 163–77). New York: Plenum.

SPERRY, R. W. (1980). Mind-brain interaction: Mentalism, yes; dualism, no. *Neurosciences, 5,* 195–206.

SPERRY, R. W. (1987). Structure and significance of the consciousness revolution. *Journal of Mind and Behavior, 8,* 37–66.

SPERRY, R. W., ZAIDEL, E., & ZAIDEL, D. (1979). Self-recognition and social awareness in the disconnected minor hemisphere. *Neuropsychologia, 17,* 153–66.

SPINHOVEN, P. (1987). Hypnosis and behavior therapy: A review. *International Journal of Clinical and Experimental Hypnosis, 35,* 8–31.

SPINO, M. (1976). *Beyond jogging: The innerspaces of running.* Millbrae, CA: Celestial Arts.

SPRINGER, S. P., & DEUTSCH, G. (1985). *Left brain, right brain* (rev. ed.). New York: Freeman.

STAM, H. J., & SPANOS, N. P. (1980). Experimental designs, expectancy effects, and hypnotic analgesia. *Journal of Abnormal Psychology, 89,* 751–62.

STAM, H. J., & SPANOS, N. P. (1987). Hypnotic analgesia, placebo analgesia, and ischemic pain: The effects of contextual variables. *Journal of Abnormal Psychology, 96*, 313–20.

STARKER, S. (1974). Daydreaming styles and nocturnal dreaming. *Journal of Abnormal Psychology, 83*, 52–55.

STARKER, S. (1978). Dreams and waking fantasy. In K. S. Pope & J. L. Singer (Eds.), *The stream of consciousness: Scientific investigations into the flow of human experience* (pp. 301–19). New York: Plenum.

STARKER, S. (1982). *Fantastic thought.* Englewood Cliffs, NJ: Prentice Hall.

STAVA, L. J., & JAFFA, M. (1988). Some operationalizations of the neodissociation concept and their relationship to hypnotic susceptibility. *Journal of Personality and Social Psychology, 54*, 989–96.

STEWART, K. (1972). Dream theory in Malaya. In C. T. Tart (Ed.), *Altered states of consciousness* (pp. 161–70). Garden City, NY: Anchor Books (Doubleday).

STIGSBY, B., RODENBERG, J. C., & MOTH, H. B. (1981). Electroencephalographic findings during mantra meditation (transcendental meditation): A controlled quantitative study of experienced meditators. *Electroencephalography and Clinical Neurophysiology, 51*, 434–42.

STOYVA, J. (1973). Biofeedback techniques and the conditions for hallucinatory activity. In F. J. McGuigan & R. A. Schoonover (Eds.), *The psychophysiology of thinking.* New York: Academic Press.

SUEDFELD, P. (1969). Changes in intellectual performance and in susceptibility to influence. In J. P. Zubek (Ed.), *Sensory deprivation: Fifteen years of research* (pp. 126–66). New York: Appleton-Century-Crofts.

SUEDFELD, P. (1975). The benefits of boredom: Sensory deprivation reconsidered. *American Scientist, 63*, 60–69.

SUEDFELD, P. (1980). *Restricted environmental stimulation: Research and clinical applications.* New York: Wiley.

SUEDFELD, P. (1990). Restricted environmental stimulation and smoking cessation: A fifteen-year progress report. *International Journal of the Addictions, 25*, 861–88.

SUEDFELD, P., BALLARD, E. J., BAKER-BROWN, G., & BORRIE, R. A. (1986). Flow of consciousness in restricted environmental stimulation. *Imagination, Cognition and Personality, 5*, 219–30.

SUEDFELD, P., & COREN, S. (1989). Perceptual isolation, sensory deprivation, and REST: Moving introductory psychology texts out of the 1950s. *Canadian Psychology, 30*, 17–29.

SUEDFELD, P., & IKARD, F. F. (1974). The use of sensory deprivation in facilitating the reduction of cigarette smoking. *Journal of Consulting and Clinical Psychology, 42*, 888–95.

SUEDFELD, P., & KRISTELLER, J. L. (1982). Stimulus reduction as a technique in health psychology. *Health Psychology, 1*, 337–57.

SUEDFELD, P., TURNER, J. W., Jr., & FINE, T. H. (Eds.) (1990). *Restricted environmental stimulation: Theoretical and empirical developments in flotation REST.* New York: Springer-Verlag.

SUTCLIFFE, J. P., PERRY, C. W., & SHEEHAN, P. W. (1970). Relation of some aspects of imagery and fantasy to hypnotic susceptibility. *Journal of Abnormal Psychology, 76*, 279–87.

SUTHERLAND, S. (1989). *The international dictionary of psychology.* NY: Continuum (Macmillan Press).

TART, C. T. (1964). A comparison of suggested dreams occurring in hypnosis and sleep. *International Journal of Clinical and Experimental Hypnosis, 7*, 163–70.

TART, C. T. (1970). Self-report scales of hypnotic depth. *International Journal of Clinical and Experimental Hypnosis, 18*, 105–25.

TART, C. T. (1971). *On being stoned: A psychological study of marijuana intoxication.* Palo Alto, CA: Science and Behavior Books.

TART, C. T. (Ed.) (1972a). *Altered states of consciousness.* Garden City, NY: Anchor Books (Doubleday). (Originally published by Wiley, 1969.)

TART, C. T. (1972b). States of consciousness and state-specific sciences. *Science, 176*, 1203–10.

TART, C. T. (1972c). Introduction to section 3. Between waking and sleeping: The hypnagogic state. In C. T. Tart (Ed.), *Altered states of consciousness* (pp. 75–76). Garden City, NY: Anchor Books (Doubleday).

TART, C. T. (1972d). A psychologist's experience with Transcendental Meditation. *Journal of Transpersonal Psychology, 3*, 135–40.

TART, C. T. (1975). *States of consciousness.* New York: E. P. Dutton.

TART, C. T. (1979). Measuring the depth of an altered state of consciousness, with particular reference to self-report scales of hypnotic depth. In E. Fromm & R. E. Shor (Eds.), *Hypnosis: Developments in research and new perspectives* (2nd ed.; pp. 567– 601). New York: Aldine.

TASSINARI, C. A., PERAITA-ADRADOS, M. R., AMBROSETTO, G., & GASTAUT, H. (1974). Effects of marihuana and delta-9-THC at high doses in man: A polygraphic study. *Electroencephalography and Clinical Neurophysiology, 36*, 94.

TELLEGEN, A., & ATKINSON, G. (1974). Openness to absorbing and self-altering experiences ("absorption"), a trait related to hypnotic susceptibility. *Journal of Abnormal Psychology, 83*, 268–77.

TERRACE, H. S. (1979). *Nim.* New York: Knopf.

TERRACE, H. S., PETITTO, L. A., & BEVER, T. G. (1979). Can an ape create a sentence? *Science, 206*, 891–902.

THAGARD, P. (1986). Parallel computation and the mind-body problem. *Cognitive Science, 10*, 301–18.

THOLEY, P. (1983). Techniques for inducing and manipulating lucid dreams. *Perceptual and Motor Skills, 57*, 79–90.

TINKLENBERG, J. R., DARLEY, C. F., ROTH, W. T., PFEFFERBAUM, A., & KOPELL, B. S. (1978). Marijuana effects on associations to novel stimuli. *Journal of Nervous and Mental Disease, 166*, 362–64.

TINKLENBERG, J. R., KOPELL, B. S., MELGES, F. T., & HOLLISTER, L. E. (1972). Marihuana and alcohol: Time production and memory functions. *Archives of General Psychiatry, 27*, 812–15.

TINKLENBERG, J. R., ROTH, W. T., & KOPELL, B. S. (1976). Marijuana and ethanol: Differential effects on time perception, heart rate, and subjective response. *Psychopharmacology, 49*, 275–79.

TKACHYK, M., SPANOS, N. P., & BERTRAND, L. D. (1985). Variables affecting subjective organization during posthypnotic amnesia. *Journal of Research in Personality, 19*, 95–108.

TOLAAS, J. (1980). Dreams, dreaming, and recent intrusive events. *Journal of Altered States of Consciousness, 6*, 183–210.

TORJUSSEN, T. (1978). Residual function in cortically blind hemifields. *Scandinavian Journal of Psychology, 17*, 320–22.

TULVING, E. (1983). *Elements of episodic memory.* New York: Oxford University Press.

TULVING, E. (1985a). How many memory systems are there? *American Psychologist, 40*, 385–98.

TULVING, E. (1985b). Memory and consciousness. *Canadian Psychology, 26*, 1–12.

TULVING, E. (1989). Memory: Performance, knowledge, and experience. *European Journal of Cognitive Psychology, 1*, 3–26.

TULVING, E., & SCHACTER, D. L. (1990). Priming and human memory systems. *Science, 247*, 301–6.

TUNVING, K. (1985). Psychiatric effects of cannabis use. *Acta Psychiatrica Scandinavia, 72*, 209–17.

TURK, D. C., MEICHENBAUM, D., & GENEST, M. (1983). *Pain and behavioral medicine: A cognitive-behavioral perspective.* New York: Guilford Press.

TURNER, J. W., JR., FINE, T., EWY, G., SERSHON, P., & FREUNDLICH, T. (1989). The presence or absence of light during flotation restricted environmental stimulation: Effects of plasma cortisol, blood pressure and mood. *Biofeedback and Self-Regulation, 14*, 291–300.

TYSON, P. D., OGILVIE, R. D., & HUNT, H. T. (1984). Lucid, prelucid, and nonlucid dreams related to the amount of EEG alpha activity during REM sleep. *Psychophysiology, 21*, 442–51.

ULLMAN, M. (1969). Dreaming as metaphor in motion. *Archives of General Psychiatry, 21*, 696–703.

VAN DE CASTLE, R. (1971). *The psychology of dreaming.* New York: General Learning Press.

VAN DER KOLK, B. A., BLITZ, R., BURR, W., SHERRY, S., & HARTMANN, E. (1984). Nightmares and trauma: A comparison of nightmares after combat with lifelong nightmares in veterans. *American Journal of Psychiatry, 141*, 187–90.

VAN EEDEN, F. (1913). A study of dreams. *Proceedings of the Society for Psychical Research, 26*, 431–61. [Reprinted in Tart 1972a.]

VAN NUYS, D. (1973). Meditation, attention, and hypnotic susceptibility: A correlational study. *International Journal of Clinical and Experimental Hypnosis, 21*, 59–69.

VENN, J. (1986). Hypnosis and the reincarnation hypothesis: A critical review and intensive case study. *Journal of the American Society for Psychical Research, 80*, 409–25.

VENTURINO, M. (1983). Perceptual monitoring and allocation of attention. Doctoral dissertation, University of Maine, Orono. *Dissertation Abstracts International, 1984, 45*, 707B. (University Microfilms No. DA8412527.)

VOGEL, G. W. (1975). Review of REM sleep deprivation. *Archives of General Psychiatry, 32*, 749–61.

VOGEL, G. W. (1978). An alternative view of the neurobiology of dreaming. *American Journal of Psychiatry, 135*, 1531–35.

VOLPE, B. T., LeDOUX, J. E., & GAZZANIGA, M. S. (1979). Information processing of visual stimuli in an 'extinguished' field. *Nature, 282*, 722–24.

VON WRIGHT, J. M., ANDERSON, K., & STENMAN, U. (1975). Generalization of conditioned GSRs in dichotic listening. In P. M. A. Rabbitt & S. Dornic (Eds.), *Attention and performance* (Vol. 5; pp. 194–204). New York: Academic Press.

WADDEN, T. A., & ANDERTON, C. H. (1982). The clinical use of hypnosis. *Psychological Bulletin, 91,* 215–43.

WAGSTAFF, G. F. (1981). *Hypnosis, compliance and belief.* New York: St. Martin's.

WAGSTAFF, G. F. (1982). Hypnosis and recognition of a face. *Perceptual and Motor Skills, 55,* 816–18.

WAGSTAFF, G. F. (1986). Hypnosis as compliance and belief: A socio-cognitive view. In P. L. N. Naish (Ed.), *What is hypnosis?* (pp. 59–84). Philadelphia: Open University Press.

WAGSTAFF, G. F., TRAVERSE, J., & MILNER, S. (1982). Hypnosis and eyewitness memory—two experimental analogues. *IRCE Medical Science: Psychology and Psychiatry, 10,* 894–95.

WALLACE, B., KNIGHT, T. A., & GARRETT, J. B. (1976). Hypnotic susceptibility and frequency reports to illusory stimuli. *Journal of Abnormal Psychology, 85,* 558–63.

WALLACE, R. K. (1970). Physiological effects of transcendental meditation. *Science, 167,* 1751–54.

WALLACE, R. K. (1977). The physiological effects of transcendental meditation: A proposed fourth major state of consciousness. In D. W. Orme-Johnson & J. T. Farrow (Eds.), *Scientific research on the transcendental meditation program: Collected papers* (Vol. 1; pp. 43–78). Maharishi European Research University Press. [Based on the author's doctoral dissertation at the University of California, Los Angeles, 1970.]

WALLACE, R. K., & BENSON, H. (February 1972). The physiology of meditation. *Scientific American, 226,* 84–90.

WARRINGTON, E. K. (1982). The double dissociation of short- and long-term memory deficits. In L. S. Cermak (Ed.), *Human memory and amnesia.* Hillsdale, NJ: Erlbaum.

WARRINGTON, E. K., & WEISKRANTZ, L. (1974). The effect of prior learning on subsequent retention in amnesic patients. *Neuropsychologia, 12,* 419–28.

WATKINS, J. G. (1947). Antisocial compulsions induced under hypnotic trance. *Journal of Abnormal and Social Psychology, 42,* 256–59.

WATKINS, J. G. (1972). Antisocial behavior under hypnosis: Possible or impossible. *International Journal of Clinical and Experimental Hypnosis, 20,* 95–100.

WATSON, J. B. (1924). *Behaviorism.* Chicago: University of Chicago Press.

WEBB, W. B. (1969). Partial and differential sleep deprivation. In A. Kales (Ed.), *Sleep: Physiology and pathology* (pp. 221–31). Philadelphia: Lippincott.

WEBB, W. B. (1975). *Sleep, the gentle tyrant.* Englewood Cliffs, NJ: Prentice Hall.

WEBB, W. B., & AGNEW, H. W. (1974). The effects of a chronic limitation of sleep length. *Psychophysiology, 11,* 265–74.

WECKOWICZ, T. E., FEDORA, O., MASON, J., RADSTAAK, D., BAY, K. S., & YONGE, K. A. (1975). Effect of marijuana on divergent and convergent production cognitive tests. *Journal of Abnormal Psychology, 84,* 386–98.

WEGNER, D. M. (1989). *White bears and other unwanted thoughts.* New York: Viking.

WEGNER, D. M., SCHNEIDER, D. J., CARTER, S. R., & WHITE, T. L. (1987). Paradoxical effects of thought suppression. *Journal of Personality and Social Psychology, 53,* 5–13.

WEIL, A. (1972). *The natural mind.* Boston: Houghton Mifflin.

WEIL, A. T., & ZINBERG, N. E. (1969). Acute effects of marihuana on speech. *Nature, 222,* 434–37.

WEIL, A. T., ZINBERG, N. E., & NELSEN, J. M. (1968). Clinical and psychological effects of marihuana in man. *Science, 162,* 1234–42.

WEIMER, W. B. (1976). Manifestations of mind: Some conceptual and empirical issues. In G. G. Globus, G. Maxwell, & I. Savodnik (Eds.), *Consciousness and the brain: A scientific and philosophical inquiry.* New York: Plenum.

WEISBERG, R. (1986). *Creativity: Genius and other myths.* New York: Freeman.

WEISKRANTZ, L. (1980). Varieties of residual experience. *Quarterly Journal of Experimental Psychology, 32,* 365–86.

WEISKRANTZ, L. (1985). On issues and theories of the human amnesic syndrome. In N. Weinberger, J. McGaugh, & G. Lynch (Eds.), *Memory systems of the brain: Animal and human cognitive processes* (pp. 380–415). New York: Guilford.

WEISKRANTZ, L. (1986). *Blindsight.* New York: Oxford University Press.

WEISKRANTZ, L. (1988a). Some contributions of neuropsychology of vision and memory to the problem of consciousness. In A. J. Marcel & E. Bisiach (Eds.), *Consciousness in contemporary science* (pp. 183–99). Oxford, England: Oxford University Press.

WEISKRANTZ, L. (Ed.). (1988b). *Thought without language.* Oxford, England: Oxford University Press.

WEISKRANTZ, L. (1990). Outlooks for blindsight: Explicit methodologies for implicit processes. *Proceedings of the Royal Society of London, 239,* 247–78.

WEISKRANTZ, L., Warrington, E. K., Sanders, M. D., & Marshall, J. (1974). Visual capacity in the hemianopic field following a restricted occipital ablation. *Brain, 97,* 709–28.

WEISZ, R., & FOULKES, D. (1970). Home and laboratory dreams collected under uniform sampling conditions. *Psychophysiology, 6,* 588–96.

WEITZENHOFFER, A. M. (1957). *General techniques of hypnotism.* New York: Grune & Stratton.

WEITZENHOFFER, A. M. (1978). What did he (Bernheim) say? In F. H. Frankel & H. S. Zamansky (Eds.), *Hypnosis at its bicentennial* (pp. 47–56). New York: Plenum.

WEITZENHOFFER, A. M., & HILGARD, E. R. (1959). *Stanford Hypnotic Susceptibility Scale, Forms A and B.* Palo Alto, CA: Consulting Psychologists Press.

WEITZENHOFFER, A. M., & HILGARD, E. R. (1962). *Stanford Hypnotic Susceptibility Scale, Form C.* Palo Alto, CA: Consulting Psychologists Press.

WEITZENHOFFER, A. M., & HILGARD, E. R. (1967). *Revised Stanford Profile Scales of Hypnotic Susceptibility, Forms I and II.* Palo Alto, CA: Consulting Psychologists Press.

WEST, M. A. (1980a). Meditation and the EEG. *Psychological Medicine, 10,* 369–75.

WEST, M. A. (1980b). Meditation, personality and arousal. *Personality and Individual Differences, 1,* 135–42.

WEST, M. (1982). Meditation and self-awareness: Physiological and phenomenological approaches. In G. Underwood (Ed.), *Aspects of consciousness, Volume 3: Awareness and self-awareness* (pp. 199–234). London: Academic Press.

WEST, M. A. (1987a). Traditional and psychological perspectives on meditation. In M. A. West (Ed.), *The psychology of meditation* (pp. 5–22). Oxford, England: Oxford University Press.

WEST, M. A. (1987b). Meditation: Magic, myth, and mystery. In M. A. West (Ed.), *The psychology of meditation* (pp. 192–210). Oxford, England: Oxford University Press.

WHITE, K., ASHTON, R., & LEWIS, S. (1979). Learning a complex skill: Effects of mental practice, physical practice, and imagery ability. *International Journal of Sport Psychology, 10,* 71–78.

WHITE, K., SHEEHAN, P. W., & ASHTON, R. (1977). Imagery assessment: A survey of self-report measures. *Journal of Mental Imagery, 1,* 145–70.

WHITE, P. (1980). Limitations on verbal reports of internal events: A refutation of Nisbett and Wilson and of Bem. *Psychological Review, 87,* 105–12.

WHITEHOUSE, W. G., DINGES, D. F., ORNE, E. C., & ORNE, M. T. (1988). Hypnotic hypermnesia: Enhanced memory accessibility or report bias? *Journal of Abnormal Psychology, 97,* 289–95.

WHITMAN, R., KRAMER, M., & BALDRIDGE, B. (1963). Which dream does the patient tell? *Archives of General Psychiatry, 8,* 277–82.

WICKRAMASEKERA, I. (1973). The effects of electromyographic feedback on hypnotic susceptibility: More preliminary data. *Journal of Abnormal Psychology, 82,* 74–77.

WILDE-FRENZ, J., & SCHULZ, H. (1983). Rate and distribution of body movements during sleep in humans. *Perception and Motor Skills, 56,* 275–83.

WILLIAMS, G. W. (1963). Highway hypnosis: An hypothesis. *International Journal of Clinical and Experimental Hypnosis, 11,* 143–51.

WILLIAMSEN, J. A., JOHNSON, H. J., & ERIKSEN, C. W. (1965). Some characteristics of posthypnotic amnesia. *Journal of Abnormal Psychology, 70,* 123–31.

WILSON, D. L. (1978). Brain mechanisms, consciousness, and introspection. In A. A. Sugerman & R. E. Tarter (Eds.), *Expanding dimensions of consciousness* (pp. 3–23). New York: Springer.

WILSON, L., & KIHLSTROM, J. F. (1986). Subjective and categorical organization of recall during posthypnotic amnesia. *Journal of Abnormal Psychology, 95,* 264–73.

WILSON, S. C., & BARBER, T. X. (1978). The Creative Imagination Scale as a measure of hypnotic responsiveness: Applications to experimental and clinical hypnosis. *American Journal of Clinical Hypnosis, 20,* 235–49.

WILSON, S. C., & BARBER, T. X. (1983). The fantasy-prone personality: Implications for understanding imagery, hypnosis, and parapsychological phenomena. In A. A. Sheikh (Ed.), *Imagery: Current theory, research, and application* (pp. 340–90). New York: Wiley.

WILSON, T. D. (1985). Strangers to ourselves: The origins and accuracy of beliefs about one's own mental states. In J. H. Harvey & G. Weary (Eds.), *Attribution: Basic issues and applications* (pp. 9–36). Orlando, FL: Academic Press.

WILSON, T. D., DUNN, D. S., KRAFT, D., & LISLE, D. J. (1989). Introspection, attitude change, and attitude-behavior consistency: The disruptive effects of explaining why we feel the way we do. In L. Berkowitz (Ed.), *Advances in experimental social psychology* (Vol. 22; pp. 287–343). Orlando, FL: Academic Press.

WILSON, T. D., LASER, P. S., & STONE, J. I. (1982). Judging the predictors of one's own mood: Accuracy and the use of shared theories. *Journal of Experimental Social Psychology, 18,* 537–56.

WILSON, T. D., & NISBETT, R. E. (1978). The accuracy of verbal reports about the effects of stimuli on evaluations and behavior. *Social Psychology, 41,* 118–31.

WILSON, T. D., & STONE, J. I. (1985). Limitations on self-knowledge: More on telling more than we can know. In P. Shaver (Ed.), *Review of personality and social psychology* (Vol. 6; pp. 167–83). Beverly Hills, CA: Sage.

WINGET, C., KRAMER, M., & WHITMAN, R. (1972). Dreams and demography. *Canadian Psychiatric Association Journal, 17,* 203–8.

WOLLMAN, M. D., & ANTROBUS, J. S. (1986). Sleeping and waking thought: Effects of external stimulation. *Sleep, 9,* 438–48.

WRIGHT, P., & RIP, P. D. (1981). Retrospective reports on the causes of decisions. *Journal of Personality and Social Psychology, 40,* 601–14.

YUILLE, J. C., & SEREDA, L. (1980). Positive effects of meditation: A limited generalization. *Journal of Applied Psychology, 65,* 333–40.

ZAIDEL, E. (1983). A response to Gazzaniga: Language in the right hemisphere, convergent perspectives. *American Psychologist, 38,* 542–46.

ZELIG, M., & BEIDLEMAN, W. B. (1981). The investigative use of hypnosis: A word of caution. *International Journal of Clinical and Experimental Hypnosis, 29,* 401–12.

ZEPELIN, H., & RECHTSCHAFFEN, A. (1974). Mammalian sleep, longevity and energy metabolism. *Brain, Behavior and Evolution, 10,* 425–70.

ZIHL, J., TRETTER, F., & SINGER, W. (1980). Phasic electrodermal responses after visual stimulation in the cortically blind hemifield. *Behavioral and Brain Research, 1,* 197–203.

ZIMMERMAN, W. B. (1970). Sleep mentation and auditory awakening thresholds. *Psychophysiology, 6,* 510–49.

ZUBEK, J. P. (Ed.). (1969). *Sensory deprivation: Fifteen years of research.* New York: Appleton-Century-Crofts.

ZUBEK, J. P. (1973). Behavioral and physiological effects of prolonged sensory and perceptual deprivation: A review. In J. E. Rasmussen (Ed.), *Man in isolation and confinement* (pp. 9–83). Chicago: Aldine.

ZUCKERMAN, M. (1969a). Variables affecting deprivation results. In J. P. Zubek (Ed.), *Sensory deprivation: Fifteen years of research* (pp. 47–84). New York: Appleton-Century-Crofts.

ZUCKERMAN, M. (1969b). Hallucinations, reported sensations, and images. In J. P. Zubek (Ed.), *Sensory deprivation: Fifteen years of research* (pp. 85–125). New York: Appleton-Century-Crofts.

Afterword

Writing this book has been an arduous but interesting and rewarding experience. Looking back over what I have written and trying to anticipate the responses of readers and reviewers, two comments occur to me. First, I have tried to maintain a critical and scientific approach to the various topics and problems of consciousness and altered states. Many "pop" psychology books have been written on topics of consciousness, but this is not one of them. Some readers may be disappointed that I have not actively promoted such "far out" ideas as miraculous cures achieved through hypnosis and guided imagery, life-after-death revealed by out-of-body and near-death experiences, transcendental states reached through meditation or psychedelic drugs, or dream interpretation for personality revelation, problem solving, or prediction of the future. Rather, I have tried to rescue the psychology of consciousness from pop psychology by evaluating such creative, sometimes wild, ideas in light of empirical investigations and current psychological theories. On the other hand, I have not hesitated to offer my own evaluations and speculations where appropriate, while making clear the distinction between my personal comments and the empirical data.

Second, I have tried to provide a broad treatment of topics of consciousness, including both normal consciousness and altered states. Some readers may feel that I have not given enough attention to their favorite topic, and that I have given too much attention to topics of lesser interest to them. Some students, for example, might prefer a book exclusively on altered states of consciousness, with more discussion of topics such as dream interpretation and mystical states, and less on conceptual and philosophical issues and the brain. My own interest in consciousness was originally stimulated by questions about altered states of consciousness. However, these questions led to more fundamental questions about the nature of consciousness and its relationship to the brain. Currently, problems of normal consciousness are being actively debated by psychologists, brain researchers, and philosophers, and I am convinced that these issues should be an important part of a general course on the psychology of consciousness (Marcel & Bisiach, 1988). I hope I have managed to convey the excitement of some of these topics of normal consciousness.

Readers who are mainly interested in topics of normal consciousness may feel that I have not given sufficient attention to some of those topics. For example, I might have said more about theories of consciousness, the development of consciousness in children, the relationship between language and consciousness, and the concept of intentionality ("aboutness") of consciousness. These are worthwhile topics, but I had to make some hard choices based on space limitations, my areas of interest and competence, and my guesses about the interests of the majority of my readers. Some pertinent topics, such as perception, attention, and mental imagery, were given light treatment because they are adequately covered in textbooks of perception and cognitive psychology.

In my opinion, the most important issue that I have not systematically discussed is the question of the function of consciousness. This is a difficult problem and I do not propose to solve it here, but I want to elaborate on it to show why it is important and controversial.

From introspection, it seems obvious that consciousness, or the conscious self, is the executive decision maker that controls our behavior. To be sure, most of our behavior—other than simple reflexes and habitual responses—is accompanied by conscious awareness of what we are doing, and our actions are usually preceded by conscious feelings of intention to act. It seems to be only common sense that if consciousness attends so closely to behavior then consciousness must have something to do with controlling behavior. Furthermore, the folk-psychology belief that human actions are consciously and voluntarily controlled is fundamental to our religious, moral, and legal ideas about people bearing personal responsibility for their actions.

Yet, a number of important lines of psychological theory and research call into question the common-sense view that consciousness controls behavior. For example, as a radical behaviorist, B. F. Skinner denied that conscious thoughts and feelings have any role in causing or explaining behavior. Rather, he argued that the causes of behavior lie in the history of the species, the individual, and the culture. He emphasized operant conditioning, in which the individual's behavior is selected according to its consequences, that is, its history of reinforcement and punishment. Though behavior is accompanied by thoughts and feelings, such subjective experiences are an epiphenomenon and play no role in causing behavior, in Skinner's view. Introspection does not reveal the causes of behavior. Rather, it is more likely that "what we see through introspection are the early stages of our behavior, the stages that occur before the behavior begins to act upon the environment" (Skinner, 1990, p. 1207-8).

Contrary to Skinner's emphasis on environmental control of behavior, cognitive theorists emphasize the role of inner mental processes. However, most cognitive theories make no distinction between conscious and nonconscious processes, and in fact, conscious awareness plays no role in most cognitive-psychological explanations of behavior. Rather, some cognitive theorists have argued that the attempt to explain human behavior in scientific terms necessarily requires that people be approached as automata, that is, as machine-like or computer-like objects.

The theoretical deemphasis or disregard of consciousness is supported by research on introspective access to the causes of behavior. As we saw in Chapters 3, 5, 6, and 7, introspection does not reliably reveal the causes of behavior, contrary to popular beliefs. At best, introspection can give a partially accurate report, under certain conditions. But if consciousness controls behavior, and if introspective reports are reports on consciousness, then we would expect introspective reports to more accurately reveal the causes of behavior.

This brings us back to fundamental questions about the concept of consciousness. In Chapter 1, I defined consciousness as "the subjective state of being currently aware of something." I argued that consciousness as subjective awareness is the most fundamental concept of consciousness. Some cognitive theorists have identified consciousness with working memory or an executive control system, though conscious awareness per se plays little or no role in such theories. Yet, if we did not have the personal experience of conscious awareness, we would not think to ascribe it to human decision-making systems. Artificial intelligence theorists have argued that decision functions can be explained without assuming conscious awareness.

In contrast, Anthony Marcel (1988) argued that conscious awareness per se has causal efficacy. Consciousness may permit or enable certain forms of behavior to occur, without being the direct, efficient cause of the behavior, and perhaps not always being necessary for the behavior to occur. For example, conscious self-monitoring, which enables us to evaluate our performance and current situation in comparison with our past experiences and future goals, seems to be critical for behavioral decision making. Also, I would add, consciousness as the output of a high-level interpreter system could be critical for executive decision making. Joseph Rychlak (1988) defined awareness in terms of knowledge of alternative possible future situations and actions. His "rigorous humanism" approach to explaining human action in terms of final causes—consciously known purposes or goals—implies a functional role for consciousness.[1]

I do not mean to argue that conscious awareness has no role in controlling or influencing human behavior. Rather, I wish to point out, first, that the role of consciousness is not as obvious as it seems from introspection, and second, that the role of consciousness is a fundamental, unresolved issue in psychological theory. The subjective fact of conscious awareness cannot be denied. Our theoretical view of the nature and role of consciousness is basic to our view of the nature of human beings, and to how we treat them and morally and legally judge them. It may be that folk psychology gives too much credit to consciousness and volition, and that cognitive psychology gives too little credit. In future research and theorizing, in order to better understand human experience and behavior, psychology must come to grips with the problem of the functions of consciousness.[2]

ENDNOTES

[1]Recently White (1990) has provided a helpful overview of ideas about the nature of causation in philosophy and psychology, and Sappington (1990) has provided a thoughtful discussion of the issue of free will versus determinism in human behavior.

[2]References for the afterword:

MARCEL, A. J. (1988). Conscious experience and functionalism. In A. J. Marcel & E. Bisiach (Eds.), *Consciousness in contemporary science* (pp. 121–58). New York: Oxford University Press.

MARCEL, A. J., & BISIACH, E. (Eds.). (1988). *Consciousness in contemporary science.* Oxford, England: Oxford University Press.

RYCHLAK, J. F. (1988). *The psychology of rigorous humanism* (2nd ed.). New York: New York University Press.

SAPPINGTON, A. A. (1990). Recent psychological approaches to the free will versus determinism issue. *Psychological Bulletin, 108,* 19–29.

SKINNER, B. F. (1990). Can psychology be a science of mind? *American Psychologist, 45,* 1206–10.

WHITE, P. A. (1990). Ideas about causation in philosophy and psychology. *Psychological Bulletin, 108,* 3–18.

Name Index

Subject Index